Of the Past, for the Future:
Integrating Archaeology
and Conservation

Of the Past, for the Future: Integrating Archaeology and Conservation

Proceedings of the Conservation Theme at the 5th World Archaeological Congress, Washington, D.C., 22–26 June 2003

Edited by Neville Agnew and Janet Bridgland

THE GETTY CONSERVATION INSTITUTE

LOS ANGELES

The Getty Conservation Institute

Timothy P. Whalen, *Director*
Jeanne Marie Teutonico, *Associate Director, Field Projects and Science*

The Getty Conservation Institute works internationally to advance conservation and to enhance and encourage the preservation and understanding of the visual arts in all of their dimensions—objects, collections, architecture, and sites. The Institute serves the conservation community through scientific research; education and training; field projects; and the dissemination of the results of both its work and the work of others in the field. In all its endeavors, the Institute is committed to addressing unanswered questions and promoting the highest possible standards of conservation practice.

Getty Publications
1200 Getty Center Drive, Suite 500
Los Angeles, California 90049-1682
www.getty.edu

Chris Hudson, *Publisher*
Mark Greenberg, *Editor in Chief*
Sheila Berg, *Project Manager and Editor*
Hespenheide Design, *Designer*
Pamela Heath, *Production Coordinator*

Printed in Canada by Friesens

Every effort has been made to contact the copyright holders of the photographs in this book to obtain permission to publish. Any omissions will be corrected in future editions if the publisher is contacted in writing.

Library of Congress Cataloging-in-Publication Data

World Archaeological Congress (5th : 2003 : Washington, D.C.)
    Of the past, for the future : integrating archaeology and conservation, proceedings of the conservation theme at the 5th World Archaeological Congress, Washington, D.C., 22–26 June 2003 / edited by Neville Agnew and Janet Bridgland.
        p. cm. — (Getty Conservation Institute symposium proceedings series)
        ISBN-13: 978-0-89236-826-6 (pbk.)
        ISBN-10: 0-89236-826-8 (pbk.)
1. Antiquities—Collection and preservation—Congresses. 2. Excavations (Archaeology)—Historic sites—Conservation and restoration—Congresses.
I. Agnew, Neville, 1938– II. Bridgland, Janet. III. Title. IV. Series.
    CC135.W67 2006
    363.6′9—dc22   2005019750

Contents

PART FIVE

Issues at World Heritage Sites

PART SIX

Archaeology and Tourism: A Viable Partnership?

Foreword

I am very pleased to write the foreword to this publication of papers from the conservation theme of the Fifth World Archaeological Congress (WAC-5), an international gathering of professional archaeologists, held in Washington, D.C., 21–26 June 2003.

Since its earliest days, the Getty Conservation Institute (GCI) has had as one focus of its work the conservation and management of archaeological heritage. Over the past twenty years, the GCI has established itself as a leader in this area, in particular, through conducting training courses and undertaking projects in different parts of the world. At sites as diverse as the Laetoli hominid trackway in Tanzania, the tomb of Nefertari in the Valley of the Queens in Egypt, the Maya site of Joya de Cerén in El Salvador, and rock art sites in Baja California, Mexico; through conferences such as "Management Planning for Archaeological Sites" (2000) and "Conservation of Archaeological Sites in the Mediterranean Region" (1995) and the publication of the conference proceedings; and in specialist colloquia on site reburial and sheltering, the GCI has worked with partners and colleagues on issues related to the conservation of archaeological sites. Many of these undertakings have extended over many years. Most recently, the GCI has embarked on an initiative, with the New York–based World Monuments Fund, to assist in supporting the management of archaeological sites and capacity building of archaeological and conservation professionals in Iraq.

The Getty Conservation Institute's emphasis on and approach to the conservation and management of archaeological sites corresponds directly with its mission. It is especially appropriate, given the significance of the archaeological record as an archive of the past—a record that increasingly is under threat from looting, war, development, and mass tourism in many parts of the world.

In recognition of these threats to archaeological sites, the World Archaeological Congress, the only representative worldwide body of practicing archaeologists, which includes among its primary aims promoting the conservation of archaeological sites, invited the GCI to organize the conservation theme, "Of the Past, for the Future: Integrating Archaeology and Conservation," for its 2003 meeting. This was the first time that conservation was a major theme and an integral part of the agenda of an international archaeological conference. This publication serves as the permanent record of the presentations and discussions on conservation at the congress. Nine resolutions calling for the integration of archaeological and conservation practice came out of the congress and are now included in the statutes of WAC. This is an important step forward.

The partnering organizations for the program sessions are from around the world, and many of the major institutions in the field of cultural heritage conservation co-organized and participated in the sessions. The GCI is grateful for their important and thoughtful contributions to the success of the undertaking. We are grateful also for the invitation of the WAC-5 organizing committee to the GCI to undertake and organize the conservation theme.

With about twelve hundred delegates from sixty-five countries in attendance at WAC-5, the GCI and its partnering organizations created and sustained a successful collaboration that included bringing to Washington, D.C., many foreign delegates, among them—and for the first time—participants from Afghanistan, Iraq, and China. One result is that there is now a member from China on the WAC council.

This step in strengthening the relationship between the professions of archaeology and conservation will bear fruit now and over the long term and will serve as a landmark in encouraging the two disciplines, not only to work together, but also to integrate their thinking and practice for the survival of the archaeological record into the future.

My particular thanks are extended to the steering committee for WAC-5. This included colleagues from within the The J. Paul Getty Trust: Neville Agnew, GCI, who led the committee and our fruitful collaboration with WAC; Claire Lyons, Getty Research Institute; Jerry Podany, J. Paul Getty Museum; and Jeanne Marie Teutonico, Martha Demas, and Tom Roby, all from the GCI. Janet Bridgland undertook the challenge of coordinating various partner organizations and worked closely with Neville Agnew in the preparation of the manuscript for publication.

Timothy P. Whalen
Director
The Getty Conservation Institute

Introduction

Neville Agnew
The Getty Conservation Institute

The Pulitzer Prize–winning biologist Edward O. Wilson speculates in his book *In Search of Nature* that we are genetically predisposed to think only one or two generations into the future. An intellectual adventurer, Wilson, in a later book, *Consilience,* strives to make a case for the unity of all intellectual disciplines. The essence of these two ideas—overcoming blindness to the needs of the generation to come and applying a holistic approach to how we should meet obligations to the future—increasingly underlies conservation thinking. Conservation is a futuristic activity vested in the belief that we, who have the power today to safeguard or degrade what is of value to society, should strive to be good ancestors for future generations.

It is this philosophy that prompted the Getty Conservation Institute's partnership with organizations from around the world to present integrated conservation approaches at the Fifth World Archaeological Congress (WAC-5) in June 2003 in Washington, D.C.

Preservation of the archaeological heritage has always been the concern of archaeology and practicing archaeologists, but it has not truly been integral to the theory and practice of the discipline. The degree to which this concern has been manifested in preservation efforts has covered the spectrum from conscientious attempts to care for and protect sites and excavated artifacts to abandonment. In the past, no doubt, neglect of conservation resulted from the lack of a defined, acknowledged profession to provide the guidance and expertise necessary to ensure preservation, to which may be added that the primary interest of archaeology is in the research and informational content of sites and their buried objects rather than as cultural heritage in need of protection and preservation. In recent times, however, increasingly a central role in conceptualizing, decision making, and implementation regarding preservation of archaeological materials and sites has been claimed as the domain of conservation. It is clear too that conservation has matured as a truly interdisciplinary profession in response to needs that transcend the traditional role of the conservation technician working on an archaeological site. Indeed, the interface between archaeology and conservation has been growing stronger, particularly as a holistic approach to decision making that includes stakeholder and community involvement has become more the norm in the planning, assessment, management, and conservation of archaeological sites and collections. And more field archaeologists have come to seek the expertise of conservation professionals, both during and after excavation; but much progress has yet to be made.

When the GCI was invited by WAC-5 to organize sessions on conservation throughout the congress, an unparalleled opportunity presented itself. The WAC-5 organizing committee identified conservation as a major theme for the congress, reflecting the trend of archaeological organizations, most of which have highlighted conservation as a core value of their code of ethics, mission statements, and governance.

Here was an invitation to reach out to the archaeology profession and to communicate a message of holistic conservation, stressing the partnership role that conservation, broadly defined, can play in archaeology, particularly if brought into the process from the beginning. The fifth congress is the first to have a major theme running throughout its duration devoted to the conservation of archaeological sites and materials.

In defining the scope and subject matter for the conservation theme at WAC-5, the emphasis of the GCI planning committee, which included staff members from the Getty Research Institute and the J. Paul Getty Museum, has been to address global issues that are crucial to the survival of the archaeological heritage in today's world. Among these positive aspects of the evolution of the discipline are policy based and social issues that now counterbalance the traditional scientific and technical domains of expertise in archaeological conservation. Foremost among the directions in which archaeological conservation has moved are methodological site management planning and implementation and support for the increasing participation of indigenous peoples and communities and other stakeholders in decision making and in interventions on sites together with a say in the disposition of excavated objects.

On the other hand, in many countries war and development increasingly threaten the archaeological record, while mass tourism to archaeological sites, with its many attendant stresses on fabric and authenticity, has been a boom industry of recent decades and shows no sign of abatement. The discipline of conservation, and the expertise it brings, is likely to increase in the future as it takes on more aspects of decision making for the management, use, and sustainable preservation of sites and collections. Here awareness and education, for the professional and, indeed, for the public as well, are increasingly relevant to the acceptance of this role. Thus, a fusion of interests between archaeology and conservation serves both disciplines.

In conceptualizing the conservation theme, it was apparent that the voice of the discipline would be heard with greater emphasis were partner organizations to be involved; therefore, a coalition was formed to authoritatively represent and address components of the theme. The GCI joined with ten international organizations and three U.S.-based institutions to develop subthemes and identify potential speakers. Participating organizations are listed at the end of this introduction. Three plenary addresses and eleven panel sessions were presented in which leaders in their fields, some sixty-three professionals, presented papers to bring forth critical issues and stimulate discussion from the audience.

Designing a thematic program linking archaeology and conservation to fit the time constraints of the congress was challenging. Issues of urgency and threats to the archaeological heritage were the first consideration, but geographic representation—a desire of the congress organizers and consonant with that of the GCI as well—was also important. In the end a mix was decided on: mass tourism to sites, war and the inevitable accompanying looting, community and stakeholder participation in decision making, the curation and uses of archaeological collections, and issues at archaeological World Heritage Sites, among other topics, were balanced by seeking representation from geographic areas that had not been well represented at previous congresses: China, Afghanistan, Iraq, Africa, and Latin America.

The themes of the conservation sessions are intended to address most of the major issues facing the survival of the archaeological heritage today. Among these are the threats to archaeological World Heritage Sites; the increasing (and appropriately so) demands of stakeholders for a voice in decision making about the care and use of sites and artifacts; the challenges facing the conservation of archaeological collections; mass tourism to iconic sites, which in many developing countries are exploited as a springboard for economic growth but are also a source of national pride; technical responses to sites at risk (how one assesses the best types of intervention, from sheltering and interpreting a site to its reburial); innovative approaches to site preservation (both pros and cons), from private acquisition of a site to protect it to privatization of national heritage (a step that has been greeted by some with outrage); meeting the challenges of rapid economic growth in China today; and the management of archaeological sites and rock art in the southern African subcontinent.

Rather than present papers or case studies at WAC-5, the representatives of the partnering organizations and the GCI formed panels of ninety minutes' to two hours' duration—each addressing a particular topic—with five to six well-known professionals presenting the issues and entering into dialogue with the audience. As much as possible, professional archaeologists were sought to present the case for conservation by speaking from their own knowledge and experience. Each topic was introduced by short presentations to define the issues. After the topic was elaborated on by responses from other panelists, the discussion was opened to the audience. This publication is the record of the sessions.

The outbreak of war in Iraq immediately prior to the congress brought into acute focus the issues of heritage destruction and looting (which continues) but regrettably led to the withdrawal from the conservation theme of one partner organization because the congress venue was Washington, D.C. The panel "Preserving the Cultural Heritage of Iraq and Afghanistan" linked the common issues of these two countries, and papers were presented on the basis of firsthand observation.

It is hoped that the conservation theme at WAC-5 and this volume will help to undo the artificial divide between archaeology and conservation—two disciplines that are natural partners. Like many other disciplines, archaeology and conservation have tended to go their own ways, as specialization became the rule. Scholars may claim that understanding causes and rates of deterioration is not within their professional remit, nor is knowledge of how to stop or slow destructive processes. This is true, but when one considers the entire range and scope of heritage, of which archaeology is one part, the fragmentation and pigeonholing of disciplines and responsibilities becomes apparent. If this separation is reversed, meshing of the two can work powerfully to secure the archaeological record for the future while allowing its study and appropriate current use for the benefit of society.

At the close of the congress, nine resolutions were put forward by the organizers of these sessions for consideration by the WAC Executive. After revisions, these were among the resolutions adopted by the executive branch in December 2003, and they now form part of the organization's statutes. These resolutions, given below, will help to foster close working relationships between archaeology and conservation for the benefit of the global archaeological heritage.

Partner Organizations

American Institute for Conservation of Historic
  and Artistic Works
Australia ICOMOS
English Heritage
ICCROM
Council of National Monuments of Chile
South African Heritage Resources Agency
State Administration of Cultural Heritage of China
US/ICOMOS
World Monuments Fund
World Tourism Organization

Two delegates from Afghanistan, one from the National Museum in Kabul and the other from the Afghanistan Institute of Archaeology, participated in collaboration with Wellesley College and New York University to present the enormous problems they face in the aftermath of years of war and destruction.

Resolutions Relating to the Theme

"Of the Past, for the Future"
Adopted by the WAC Executive in December 2003

Addressed to Professionals

Resolution 1: WAC resolves to promote a close working relationship between archaeologists and conservation professionals in order to foster an integrated approach to archaeology that includes research, conservation, management, and the interpretation of archaeological sites and collections.

Resolution 2: It is the responsibility of archaeologists to plan for the conservation of the sites on which they work, the materials they excavate, and the associated records they create over an entire project through the provision of adequate funding and professional expertise, regardless of whether these responsibilities are mandated by law or not.

Resolution 3: Proposed interventions, such as the restoration or reconstruction of sites and artifacts for interpretation and presentation, should be critically assessed beforehand to ensure that authenticity and integrity are not adversely (negatively) impacted.

Resolution 4: It is the responsibility of archaeologists conducting fieldwork to make themselves familiar with, acknowledge, and respect all the cultural values of the sites they are working on, including social and spiritual values, and in turn to share their knowledge about the archaeological significance of the sites with the local communities.

Resolution 5: In cases where the archaeological heritage is impacted by armed conflict, WAC strongly recommends that conservation professionals be included in the initial response teams to assess damage and prepare action plans.

Addressed to National Authorities

Resolution 6: Recognizing that partnerships between the public and private sectors can further the goals of conservation, WAC nevertheless calls upon national authorities not to relinquish their responsibilities for the preservation and stewardship of archaeological heritage places and collections.

Resolution 7: WAC urges that decision makers strive for the inclusion of all stakeholder voices in the use, management, and preservation of archaeological places and collections.

Addressed to International Organizations

Resolution 8: WAC resolves to recommend to UNESCO that an active program to inventory and document archaeological collections in museums and other repositories be undertaken and that duplicate records be safeguarded elsewhere than at the location of the collections.

Resolution 9: WAC notes that many World Heritage Sites have archaeological values which need protecting, but that management planning provisions do not always recognize archaeological values or provide adequately for their protection, and recommends to the World Heritage Centre that it sponsor workshops on the conservation and management of the archaeological resources of World Heritage Sites, and also that it reexamine the management provisions that need to be met for the nomination and inscription of archaeological sites to the World Heritage List.

PART ONE

Plenary Presentations

Looking Forward, Not Backward:
Archaeology and the Future of the Past

Brian Fagan

Scientists have it within them to know what a future-directed society feels like, for science itself, in its human aspect, is just that.

—C. P. Snow, *Science and Government* (1961)

Abstract: *The destruction of archaeological sites is reaching crisis proportions. At the same time, a chasm exists between the disciplines of academic archaeology and archaeological conservation. Archaeological ethics are basically little changed from the early twentieth century, and cultural resource management activity is based on the same premise—that digging is the best conservation. Archaeology places the highest value on original discoveries rather than activities such as conservation, which further compounds the problem. This paper argues for fundamental changes in archaeological value systems, for better training in ethics at the graduate level, and for changes in the ways in which archaeologists are trained, beginning with a sustained dialogue between academic archaeologists and the conservation community, so that what remains of the archives of the past is the first priority. Originally a keynote address, this is a general statement about the current state of archaeology, designed as a basis for discussions and actions that bring together archaeology and conservation into a common discipline.*

I am a rare breed in an archaeological world of increasing specialization—a generalist. This means that I work with a broad canvas and appreciate more than many people what a grim future archaeology faces. There are powerful lessons behind the destruction that surrounds us, but I often despair of bringing them to a wider audience. Thus it was that some months ago I fell into a profound depression about the future of the past, which lingers still. I needed a dispassionate observer who would help to point the way ahead. There was no one, until I thought of Kent Flannery's "Master," an Eastern wise man who resided in Antelope Springs, Oregon—but he was unavailable (Flannery 1986). As Flannery had feared, the local populace had fed him into a belt-driven International Harvester shredder.

So I decided instead to consult that most fashionable of individuals in contemporary rock art circles—a shaman. As it happened, I knew one, a former graduate student with supernatural powers, but had lost touch with him. One summer evening I called on him high in Southern California's Santa Ynez Mountains.

The shaman sat motionless by a smoldering hearth, his countenance wreathed in swirling tobacco smoke. He gestured at a place in the dirt by the fire. I sat down gingerly, brushing aside the detritus of several meals.

"So you've come at last," he remarked. "Depressed are we? Well, I'm not surprised. You archaeologists live in a never-never land."

"You can't say that," I exclaimed. "Look at the spectacular scientific advances since you left graduate school—the Lords of Sipán, the Ice Man, and dozens of other discoveries."

He cut me off with a gesture. "Discoveries, discoveries—that's all you talk about! Nothing's changed since I left graduate school.

"So many archaeologists, and so many of them in pursuit of the trivial, their papers full of pretentious theory, and so specialized. Everyone seems to be wearing intellectual blinkers. And in the academic journals, hardly a word about conservation. Where are your priorities? Have you forgotten what Petrie, Pitt-Rivers, and others said over a century ago?

Who reads Petrie's *Methods and Aims in Archaeology* [1904] today?"

I admitted that I had never read it.

"There you are!" he said. "At least some of your forebears had some ethics behind their study of the past. Do you teach your students ethics today? You certainly didn't in my time."

"Of course we do," I replied defiantly. "They're fundamental to any archaeological course. I've taught them to college freshmen for years."

"Ah, but do you teach graduate seminars on ethics? They're the future professionals."

I had to admit that courses on ethics were virtually unknown in graduate schools and barely mentioned in passing in any seminar.

The shaman pounced at once.

"Discovery, discovery—that's all you people seem to think about! Why? What's going to happen in a generation or two, when there is less and less to discover, to dig up? What about conservation? What does 'conservation' mean to you?"

"Petrie's conservation strategy was straightforward," I responded. "Excavation and yet more excavation, with careful attention to the smallest object, and, above all, prompt and full publication. But he was no paragon of archaeological virtue. He recovered many objects by paying his workers for them, lest precious finds ended up in a dealer's hands."

"True," said the shaman quietly. "But what about today? All this talk about cultural resource management? Isn't that more of the same philosophy?"

I started to explain that cultural resource management was all about legal compliance and management of a finite resource, but he waved aside my words.

*   *   *

The cave was now pitch-black, save for some flickering candles and the smoldering hearth. My host resumed his discourse.

"Mention the word *conservation* to most archaeologists, and they'll regale you with their minor triumphs in the field—such as lifting a delicate infant burial or piecing together a clay pot. In most archaeological circles, conservation means conservation of artifacts, or of buildings, rock art, or other tangible remains.

"I'm amazed how most archaeologists are blissfully unaware that archaeology and conservation are closely intertwined. Conservation encompasses a much broader field of endeavor than only the care of objects!"

"We all know that," I remarked sharply. "It's commonplace. Look at the work done by the Getty, by English Heritage, and by dozens of other organizations."

"Ah yes, but do you academics place conservation at the very center of your research, as an integral part of the project? In most cases, you don't."

I defended my colleagues and myself. "Of course fieldwork and conservation go hand in hand. We all know we are disturbing a finite archive."

"Yes, yes," replied the shaman testily. "But you're just paying lip service. Do you plan conservation as part of your research design on a non-CRM project? Almost invariably, you don't. Look at the number of academic archaeologists who are out there just surveying and digging even today without regard to conservation. Many of them go out summer after summer and just go digging, with no regard to the long-term future. They have a question to answer, important or trivial, have students to train, who also act as their labor, and data for publications to acquire. Often they never publish a final report. People have been doing this with impunity for years."

"We are encouraged, nay begged, to publish," I pointed out. "Haven't you heard of publish-or-perish? Believe me, it's a reality!"

The shaman pounced once more. "What I am talking about is *final* publication that puts a site on permanent record. That's one of the most fundamental aspects of preservation, quite apart from building conservation strategies for now and the future into your research."

I pointed out that antiquities laws in most countries carefully define ownership, protection, and permit requirements for excavation.

"Yes, they do," said the shaman, as he lit still another cigarette. "In many nations, tight regulation surrounds any form of fieldwork, and so it should. In fact, in some countries, the notion that conservation comes first, archaeology second, is commonplace. The United States isn't among them."

I agreed with him.

"But what about people who choose to work overseas because it's easier and they can avoid bureaucratic regulation and conservation requirements?"

The shaman's eyes narrowed. "Such people deserve our utter contempt," he snapped. "When will they realize that conservation is a deadly serious issue that affects all stakeholders in the past—not just archaeologists?"

To that there was no reply.

*   *   *

"You seem to take a long-term view of conservation," I observed.

He agreed. "So many people talk about conservation as if it's instant gratification. You can't just preserve a site and walk away. There are all kinds of issues: the long-term future of the site, the changing roles of stakeholders, the potential impact of tourism, and so on. You should be conserving for eternity."

"That's a very different perspective that looks far beyond a few years," I remarked. "I doubt if many archaeologists think this way."

"No, they don't, because they're obsessed with short-term goals and their careers. They don't think about the long-term future."

"Somewhat like the debates over global warming," I said. "We have great difficulty making decisions that affect our grandchildren rather than ourselves."

"Right. And this is where archaeologists need to change their thinking profoundly. The irony is that they're comfortable dealing with long spans of time in the past—and ignore the implications of their work for the long-term future. All this quite apart from the issue of stakeholders."

"Stakeholders? Why are these important?"

"Who owns the past? You don't! Does the local archaeologist you may or may not work with? Does a landowner, the merchant, or tour operator who runs people to Stonehenge? Do indigenous people? For years, you archaeologists have assumed that you were the only game in town. You talk of linear, scientific accounts of human history, of restoring history to people without writing or history? Well, you're not the only game in town. Stakeholders are an integral part of conservation. They have as much right to be consulted as you do."

"This is too much," I snapped. "So far you have insulted archaeology, implied that we ignore conservation, and accused us of living in a never-never land! Why are you so angry?"

*   *   *

There was a long silence. The shaman drew a blanket around his naked shoulders.

"I'm afraid for the future of the past," he whispered. The fire flared up, casting his face in deep shadow. "Why am I angry? Because your value system is flawed. Your priorities and ethics stink! That's why I'm trying to make you uncomfortable! In the competitive world of museums and research universities, archaeology is a science of discovery: survey, excavation, laboratory work, and peer-reviewed publication. Wrong! It's so much more. Look at the social pyramid of archaeology—academics and discovery at the summit, then CRM, teaching, curating collections, public archaeology, and administrative roles in descending order. Conservation doesn't figure in the hierarchy at all, except as a generally accepted, and ill-defined, basic ethic, which is taught in virtually no graduate programs.

"What you don't realize is just how firmly you're stuck on an endless treadmill of survey and excavation, publication, then more fieldwork and yet more publication. Your life's driven by a constant search for research money, by the guidelines of university promotion committees. Deans urge you to think constantly of national rankings, as if academia were a football game."

"You can't judge archaeology, or its practitioners, by the excesses of the publish-or-perish world," I responded.

"Oh yes you can! Look closely, and you'll see a fundamental reason why conservation is on the margins—the treadmill of the social values of archaeology and academia generally."

The shaman lit another cigarette and inhaled deeply. "I think it's safe to say that most of you would rather excavate and write stimulating preliminary reports than undertake the laborious, time-consuming work of a final report. And few agencies give grants or summer salaries for writing up research."

"Yes, publication is definitely archaeology's dirty little secret. We're really lax about it."

"Just look at biblical archaeology. Look at all those people digging away every summer and ignoring their publication responsibilities. Have they no ethics, no care to leave a permanent record behind them? All they are leaving are devastated sites."

*   *   *

The shaman looked at me shrewdly. "Feeling bad?" he asked.

"Yes, and, like Kent Flannery, deeply depressed. You make me feel a failure."

He smiled maliciously. I sensed we had come to the moment of truth, that my mentor had been clearing the decks. He turned the pages of a battered southwestern journal, the *Kiva,* lying on a nearby boulder.

When I knew you were coming, I reread Bill Lipe's "A Conservation Model for American Archaeology" from back in 1974. A shrewd man, Lipe."

"I know Bill and his work. He's written a whole stream of important papers on conservation. The *Kiva* article is a very perceptive contribution. It's required reading in a lot of graduate programs," I added triumphantly.

A loud snort echoed around the cave.

"Yeah, they just get to read that and then go back to academic theory and culture history—what they call 'the data.' How many graduate programs take conservation, heritage, and CRM really seriously?"

I agreed with him for once. "Last time I looked into it, precious few. I read somewhere that some of the first rate programs said they were 'too busy' and understaffed to teach such things."

"Remember what Lipe said: 'We are now beginning to realize that all sites are rather immediately threatened, if one takes a time frame of more than a few years'" (Lipe 1974:214).

"True," I said. "But he also talked of 'leisurely salvage'—'when we know the date at which the site may be lost.' I think that a lot of academic archaeologists would say they work on such sites."

"But he said something else, remember. 'If our field is to last for more than a few decades, we need to shift to a resource conservation model as primary.' I think history will judge this as one of the more influential papers of late-twentieth-century archaeology—I wager it'll be cited longer than any of Binford's pronouncements."

"Why?" I asked.

"Because Lipe talked about managing the past, about putting conservation right in the center of our world, and not at the side. He stressed that basic research kept the field healthy, but there was another priority as well."

"Conservation?" I said. "So we are good guys after all."

The shaman shook his head. "Lipe's paper was successful in that he drew attention to the basic strategies for managing the past, the Big Book, and advocated it as a priority. It's still not a priority in much of the academic world."

"So he was one of the founders of CRM!" I retorted. "And look how that dominates archaeology in most parts of the world. He certainly made us think about conservation."

The shaman shook his head. "Call CRM a success if you will, but, in the final analysis, it's a highly sophisticated extension of the Flinders Petrie philosophy: dig it up before someone else destroys it. Undeniably there are triumphs where discoveries have been snatched from the jaws of bulldozers,

then published thoroughly. Europeans have done some wonderful work this way. So have the Chinese and Japanese. CRM is often the only strategy to employ as sites vanish. But all too often there's a chasm, and antipathy, between the academy and the CRM world."

I had to admit that there was some truth in what he was saying. Only last week, I heard a graduate student lamenting her summer spent doing CRM.

"Look at the job opportunities in archaeology these days. Almost all of them are in CRM, and more and more of them in private sector companies, who do archaeology for profit. CRM's an attempt to salvage as much information as possible with the time, money, and methods available. In some respects, it indeed represents the successful implementation of part of Lipe's conservation model. Yet many academics denigrate it as a potential career. They forget that if current trends continue, archaeology will soon become a profession focused almost entirely on managing the past."

"Nonsense," I retorted. "Academic archaeology is alive and well. Look at the opportunities compared to even thirty years ago."

"You've missed the point. There'll be academic jobs all right, but will the candidates for them have the conservation-based training that brings CRM activities and basic training together? We can't afford snobbery, or overproduction of academic researchers."

"Your point about overspecialized researchers and too many of them is well taken," said I. "After all, it's easy to train clones of oneself. But it sounds as if you're talking about a new type of academic archaeologists who place conservation at the center of their work and take the ethics of placing the archive on record very seriously."

The shaman nodded. He cast a glance behind him, at his bulging library on crude shelves at the back of the cave.

"You can see one problem there," he remarked. He gestured at rows of what appeared to be mimeographed reports.

"The gray literature?"

"Yes. Reports of limited circulation, or in cyberspace, which, despite efforts to the contrary, are effectively inaccessible to most people."

"Here you go again, generalizing without thinking." I retorted. "Haven't you seen some of the wonderful, intellectually sound monographs that are coming out of CRM? Haven't you heard of the research of [I mentioned a series of names]? They're on the cutting edge."

The shaman shrugged. "Sure, I generalize. But, you know, I'm right. Yes, some CRM folk expiate archaeological sin. But look at all those dreadful limited-circulation reports that are purely descriptive, all too often inadequate, and supervised by bureaucrats who are interested merely in legal compliance."

"The point is this," he added. "CRM is reactive. Integrating academic archaeology and conservation will be proactive. That's the priority, and something that happens only rarely."

*   *   *

I heard the shaman sigh. Then he said, "You people have played while Rome burns. When are you going to wake up?"

"Fine," I said. "Let's assume you are right. What do you suggest we do to make conservation part of the central fabric of archaeology?"

He sat back, clutched his blanket and inflated his chest as if making a pronouncement.

"First, reorient graduate training and exercise serious population control in the number of newly minted academic specialists, many of who end up in the CRM world and hate it. These are the last people who should be salvaging the past. Start some serious training in conservation as a mainstream part of archaeology."

"How do you do this?" I asked, knowing just how hard innovation is in academia.

"Remember all the academic debates about early states, the center and the periphery? You don't have to confront anyone. Work at the periphery."

The suggestions came fast and furious.

"Start a debate between academic archaeologists and conservation folk about curriculum. Is this happening at the moment? Hardly. Stand-alone conservation programs aren't enough. As part of this, integrate conservation into the very fabric of academic research, the powerful notion of stewardship of the past as a fundamental responsibility."

I stopped him in full oratorical flood. "But how do we do all this? It's all very well just talking—"

"My dear sir, shamans are talkers. We use our supernatural perceptions to show the way forward. All I can give you are ideas:

- Foster intensive research into—and development of—nonintrusive archaeological methods to minimize excavation in the future.
- Require that all doctoral dissertation proposals make conservation a centerpiece of the proposed research.

- Stop insisting that every Ph.D. dissertation involve fieldwork. That's nonsense in these days of huge unpublished collections. Encourage grant-giving agencies to insist on conservation plans as part of all funding proposals, as the first priority.
- Decouple archaeology from the publish-or-perish culture, and reward conservation projects with the kudos given basic research.
- And what about a series of highly prestigious prizes or awards that give prominence and prestige to archaeological conservation?"

"Stop!" I cried. "Are you seriously suggesting that we give up basic research altogether?"

He laughed. "Of course not. It's the lifeblood of archaeology. But you need to look far beyond the transitory gratification of a new discovery, or of a peer-reviewed paper published in the pages of *Science*—to the long, long term. We don't need more mindless, overspecialized fieldwork that culls a diminishing inventory of undisturbed sites.

"Nor do we need an archaeology with dozens of desperate, unemployed, overspecialized academics. What about some redirection and some population control in graduate programs? If this doesn't happen, then academic archaeology really will become irrelevant.

"Enough said," he said with finality. "I want you to look at the future without such redirection. Take this." He threw me a fragment of desiccated mushroom, which I eyed with apprehension. His eyes dared me to swallow it.

*   *   *

The bright sparks triggered by the hallucinogen intensified in dazzling showers. I found myself in a nightmare archaeology of the future . . .

High season along the Nile. Egypt's Valley of Kings fenced off as hundreds of tourists press for a glimpse of just a tomb entrance. Inside, the tomb walls are devoid of paintings, eroded by the sweat and humidity of thousands of visitors.

The Petén rainforest in Guatemala—except almost all the forest has gone, swept away in the accelerating global deforestation of the early twenty-first century. Crumbling Maya cities stand out against a landscape of stunted grasslands and rocky outcrops, looters' trenches on every side. They are naked to inexorable forces of destruction. No archaeologists monitored the deforestation.

Then I find myself in a university library back in the United States in late evening. A weary graduate student labors over her dissertation research. She searches in vain for final reports, for detailed accounts of the data recovered from now-destroyed sites. She abruptly leaves the room, looks up at the stars, and screams in helpless frustration. The Big Book is empty, the site gone, the published record merely a few preliminary reports. The archaeologist's stewardship had been found lacking . . .

*   *   *

I shuddered involuntarily as I returned to the real world. The shaman glanced across at me and raised an eyebrow.

"Ah," said he, stirring the fire with a stick. "Enlightenment at last. You've left your comfortable intellectual cocoon."

"I think Flinders Petrie was right," I said eventually. "Because he said, 'Has not the past its rights—as well as the present and the future?' [1904:112]. I think we have forgotten that, which is one reason we are in trouble."

"Petrie said that a century ago—I was forgetting," said the shaman, as he watched the sunrise.

"Well, go and do something about the future of the past . . ."

References

Flannery, K. 1986. *Guilá Naquitz*. Orlando, Fla.: Academic Press.

Lipe, W. D. 1974. "A Conservation Model for American Archaeology." *Kiva* 39(1–2):213–43.

Petrie, F. 1904. *Methods and Aims in Archaeology*. London: Macmillan.

Snow, C. P. 1961. *Science and Government*. Cambridge, Mass.: Harvard University Press.

The Monumental and the Trace: Archaeological Conservation and the Materiality of the Past

Rosemary A. Joyce

Abstract: *Beginning from critiques of universalism in concepts of global cultural heritage, I propose that archaeologists and conservation professionals reconceptualize archaeological materials as traces. A collection of traces, materials of archaeological interpretation and preservation, from decontextualized objects to landscapes, are transcribed into documents. These representations of traces embody specific points of view. The universally valued monument that dominates archaeological heritage places archaeological practitioners in the position of antiquarians or contemporary collectors of antiquities. Forced to participate in authentication of high culture, archaeologists lose opportunities to represent perspectives more accessible to people who do not identify with elite producers of monuments. Reenvisioning their position with respect to material traces of the past, archaeologists may find common ground with conservation professionals increasingly concerned about preserving active life histories of things.*

During my field season in June 2003 in Honduras, working at a site declared a national monument and recently opened for visitation, I was faced every day with contradictions between different forms of archaeological materiality. As our ground-penetrating radar and magnetometer surveys covered the apparently featureless surface around the twenty-meter-high mounds of Los Naranjos, visitors stood at the side of our test excavations and asked me, not about the visible soil color contrasts, all that was left of perishable buildings and past human activities, but about the massive grass-covered mounds rising untouched by us. When, one history teacher asked, would the site be visible in all its splendor?

I struggled to explain to her that earthen construction is incompatible with the restoration of pristine ancient buildings she was imagining, based on her experience of Copan, a World Heritage Site in western Honduras. I sketched out the construction history of the mounds, revealed in the 1960s by archaeologists who trenched them, indicating that there were multiple periods: which should be restored? I talked about the kind of construction materials used and indicated cobble-faced terraces reexposed by recent excavations (unrelated to our project) already eroding from the earthen core of the structure. As I explained the challenges posed by trying to expose, stabilize, and monitor such features, I was struck by the way that the monument, not a target of our project at all, dominated the exchanges I had with visitors at this public site of history, overriding interest in features representing the lives of the ancient inhabitants of the site.

What do we seek to preserve, conserve, interpret, and present when we manage archaeological sites? The same archaeological materials can have distinct importance for different people. William Lipe (1984) identified a range of values, from the aesthetic interests that motivate art collectors to connections with the past identified as heritage, with the values specific to archaeology—the use of materials as evidence of past societies—somewhere in between. More recently, Claire Lyons (2002), in a perceptive discussion of opposing amicus curiae briefs filed in regard to Italian claims to repatriate a gold vessel illegally imported into the United States, highlighted differences between archaeology and museum communities in concepts of authenticity, authority, and the relation of art and artifact. "Holistic scientific knowledge" was the ultimate measure of value for archaeologists, while "the perceived aesthetic qualities of an object" were the universal values championed by museums.

As Lyons (2002:125–26) noted, contemporary archaeo-logical explorations of materiality stress the fluidity, perfor-mativity, and polysemous nature of material things. Rather than see the perspectives sketched out by these and other authors as simply different viewpoints on unchanging materi-als, we need to explore how archaeological materials are trans-formed when different values are invoked. Pursuing this, I identify a tension between monumentality—the material con-dition assumed in cultural heritage management legislation and policy—and the trace—archaeological materiality that is more subtle and contextual, and, in the absence of special attention, much more fleeting.

Considerable attention has been directed to preserva-tion and interpretation of monumental materiality. Less thought and effort is usually expended on heritage manage-ment of traces of past human presence on landscapes. One unfortunate side effect of this imbalance is the perpetuation of an image of archaeology that is not that far from the posi-tion espoused by art collectors. Another undesirable outcome is alienation from people who might potentially be interested in material traces of the past but feel no inherent tie to actors foregrounded by archaeological monumentality. Contempo-rary archaeologists need to reexamine our role in perpetuat-ing an antiquarian perspective that values the monumental over the trace and the negative effects this has had on helping to foster archaeological conservation.

Monumental and Trace Materialities

To define monumentality, we can do no better than begin with criteria for inclusion of cultural properties in the United Nations World Heritage List (UNESCO 2001). These imple-ment Article 1 of the UNESCO Convention on World Her-itage, which defines eligible properties as *monuments, groups of buildings,* or *sites.* To be eligible as World Heritage, proper-ties must to be of "outstanding universal value" as determined by application of certain criteria and a test of authenticity. I return to the issue of "authenticity" later; first, let us consider what criteria determine that some material remains of the past are of outstanding universal value. I give the exact text of these criteria, as enumerated in the Operational Guidelines of the World Heritage Organization, to demonstrate that they embody a particular point of view on what events and people in the past had global significance (see Cleere 1996, 1998).

A World Heritage Site should

   i. represent a masterpiece of human creative genius; or

  ii. exhibit an important interchange of human values, over a span of time or within a cultural area of the world, on developments in architecture or tech-nology, monumental arts, town-planning or landscape design; or

 iii. bear a unique or at least exceptional testimony to a cultural tradition or to a civilization which is living or which has disappeared; or

 iv. be an outstanding example of a type of building or architectural or technological ensemble or land-scape which illustrates (a) significant stage(s) in human history; or

  v. be an outstanding example of a traditional human settlement or land-use which is representative of a culture (or cultures), especially when it has become vulnerable under the impact of irre-versible change; or

 vi. be directly or tangibly associated with events or living traditions, with ideas, or with beliefs, with artistic and literary works of outstanding universal significance (the Committee considers that this criterion should justify inclusion in the List only in exceptional circumstances and in conjunction with other criteria, cultural or natural).

Criteria (i) and (iv) are framed in terms of the idea that cer-tain materials represent masterpieces of creative genius made at certain points in time. By implication, everyday materials that make up the bulk of past materiality—everything I cover here with the term "trace" (following Petzet 1995)—is not worthy of appreciation, protection, preservation, conserva-tion, and interpretation on a global scale.

Criteria (ii) through (vi) specify further some of the conditions under which material remains of the past may merit global appreciation as human heritage: when they exemplify essentialized cultures, categorized as "civilizations" and "traditions," and their settlements, and in particular when they exemplify exchanges of human values. These criteria require material traces of the past to be conceptualized in terms of macroscale groups, ideally groups that can be thought of in terms of narratives of progress over time culmi-nating in civilizations.

Only criterion (vi) opens any space for a less macro-scale past, in the particularity of "events," "ideas," "beliefs," and "works." The reservations expressed in the original guide-lines about this criterion underline the inherent assumption of a macroscale unity of the past that is itself conceptually monumental.

The significant past envisaged in World Heritage criteria is a past of peoples and nations, of cities and landscapes, but not of people and their actions and surely not of people and the actions through which, every day, societies were produced and reproduced. The materiality that these criteria invoke is monumental in scale, both physically and temporally, enduring over time, surviving to act as a sign for future generations. It is monumental in its homogenization of the diverse interests and identities of past actors under individual essentialized icons. It lends itself to nation-building projects while failing to connect to individual actors other than leaders who are assumed to be necessary for such projects to be carried out.

In contrast, the excluded archaeological traces are the stuff of the fleeting everyday world of repeated actions. Traces are often all that remain of living sites of the majority of people. Traces attest to placement of work spaces and thus directly to the labor through which individual actors produced the things that they needed, things that sometimes persisted to be taken up today as evidence for archaeological interpretation. Products of everyday labor rarely survive as complete and unaltered objects; however, large intact objects loom in the popular and scholarly imagination, whose emphasis is on tombs and temples. Rather, products of everyday life survive as discarded material that ceased to have its original purpose and was transformed into refuse. The sense of unexpected survival against the odds that such traces embody stands in sharp contrast to interpretations of monuments as things *intended* to endure intact and without significant decay, conveying set meanings over time.

These two forms of materiality contrast fundamentally in the way they are taken to signify the passage of time. Traces are unintended consequences of action with life histories from production to use, disuse, and reuse; monuments are treated as intentional statements and often as causes of large-scale social and cultural cohesion that inherently deny human scale temporality (Herzfeld 1991). Monumental materiality has a point of view distinct from that of the trace. And it is that uninterrogated point of view that dominates much thinking about cultural heritage, including assessments about what it means to preserve archaeological sites and monuments (Omland 1997).

Material Points of View

Once we acknowledge that concepts of heritage, even those purporting to represent universal values, actually represent particular points of view on time, change, and the role of materiality in social cohesion, then we must consider whose

point of view we inhabit when we favor the monumental over the trace. In comparing contrasting attitudes expressed by museum representatives and archaeologists, Lyons (2002:131) proposed that from the archaeological point of view, "sites . . . are essentially monuments—monuments that go down into the earth rather than rise up from it." This image captures a sensibility peculiar to archaeologists, where traces of past human actions we document as we disassemble sites have a significance equal to, or more important than, the meaning assumed to reside in conventional monumentality. But by adopting the term "monument" as the image to which archaeological sites are equated, we may inadvertently cede the unique position that archaeology occupies with respect to the trace.

I suggest that we think seriously about another, alternative equation: monuments are essentially traces, traces whose materiality is so obtrusive that we are forced to attend to them, traces whose materiality often points us away from their very contingency and active lives. Michael Petzet (1995) argues convincingly that archaeological excavation is a form of transcription in which an original document (the traces that make up a site, including monumental traces) is replaced by a new document (the transcript of the site in archaeological records). The point of view of the trace is the perspective of archaeologists, a position from which a transformed concept of stewardship can be articulated (Joyce 2002a, 2002b). The perspective of the trace could bring together archaeologists, conservation professionals, and other stakeholders unconvinced that the universal values of monumental world heritage speak to their concerns.

Archaeologists no longer control management of the traces we transcribe. The philosopher Alison Wylie (1996, 1999), in analyses of the reinterpretation of "stewardship" in the revision of the ethics statement of the Society for American Archaeology, argues that because contemporary archaeological ethics acknowledge that there are multiple legitimate stakeholders in the past, archaeologists can no longer claim that archaeological stewardship includes rights to the final word in disputes about managing archaeological resources. Archaeologists once made the assumption that the relative contribution to solving problems of general scientific concern could be used as an objective, and hence universal, measure of significance (Raab and Klinger 1977). Wylie's analyses expose the limitations of this approach, which assumed that all interested parties agree that science is objective, universal, and hence a reliable way to judge competing claims. Many archaeologists have accepted that we do not have grounds to enforce decisions on—or over the objections of—descendant groups. Archaeologists also have begun to question our role in assessing authenticity of links proposed between contemporary stakeholders and archaeological materials (Lyons 2002:123–27).

Arguments about authenticity involve judgments about connections among persons, stereotyped identities, and specific places (and the things used at those places) that can be incongruous in light of contemporary perspectives on identity in the social sciences. Arif Dirlik (1996) argues that such postmodern questioning of authenticity of identity is problematic for those in less privileged economic and political positions who are only beginning to consolidate places in the world on the basis of such identities. He advocates a firmer conception of "history as project" in which "the past . . . is constructed at all times, and ties to the past require an ongoing dialogue between present and past constructions" (Dirlik 1996:24). Judgment of authenticity teeters between assuming static, ahistorical, changeless, uniform cultures or choosing as exemplary particular moments in what in reality are ongoing historical trajectories. It is precisely the latter strategy, whose violence to living residents of a Cretan town Herzfeld (1991) exposed, that has been characteristic of archaeological judgments of authenticity.

As archaeologists seek to avoid the questionable moves of invoking authenticity or universality as ultimate grounds for judging claims of different stakeholders, we have to seriously engage with all those who make a claim to a stake in the past. This may include not only descendant communities with a voice in defining objectives of archaeological investigation (e.g., Lilley and Williams 2005) but also other members of descendant groups who view sites as most significant as sources of economic gifts from ancestors (Matsuda 1998) or as the location of agricultural land gained through more recent histories of revolution and republic (Rodriguez 2001). Nor can we arbitrarily ignore such commonly dismissed groups as New Age believers, goddess movement members, and even tourists.

What constitutes a material trace of past human activity is itself subject to incommensurate understandings by different stakeholders. An "unaltered" landscape may be imbued with historical knowledge, as Keith Basso (1996) has poetically shown for the Apache of the U.S. Southwest. The plant communities present on a landscape, perceived as "natural" vegetation, may have resulted from intensive and long-term inhabitation by human populations (Cleere 1998). In many places in the world, locations of past human passages through landscapes, marked or unmarked, served and continue to serve to orient people with spiritual beings.

Moving from landscapes to more durably marked locations of human activity, we can see that even in the communities of archaeology and conservation, what constitutes a significant material trace of past human activity is a very fluid thing. Some sites in North America that would be highly significant for a history of labor, class, and racial and ethnic relations cannot qualify for inclusion on the U.S. National Register because their materiality takes the form of the trace rather than the monumental materiality of the stereotypic cultural heritage site (Ludlow Collective 2001).

Even in the realm of sites that conform to the requirements of definition as national or world heritage monuments, distinct aspects of materiality may be held less important, without debate about their potential to illuminate aspects of the past that might be of significance to certain stakeholders, such as daily life and the experiences of those who created monuments that glorified an elite few. The potential significance of the trace and the potential loss of knowledge entailed in destruction of apparently featureless deposits become more evident as new technical analytic approaches proliferate, like micromorphology, applied to pick up physical signs of such quotidian actions as sweeping a floor.

Archaeological Conservation and the Materiality of the Past

The destabilization of the condition of objects once buried in archaeological sites, curated without thought to their actual fragility and standing as miraculous traces of past human efforts, dramatizes the real impact of excavation, as objects assumed by archaeologists to be durable erode away in curation facilities. An expressed value of preservation has been a constant in archaeological ethics statements since the first examples were set on paper. Lack of concern for and attention to the postexcavation condition of the majority of excavated objects seems to contradict this. This contradiction illustrates points of conjunction and disjunction between archaeologists and conservation professionals, stakeholders whose position with respect to past materiality at first glance seems identical.

Like sites and landscapes, objects are transformed when seen as monuments or traces. As Lyons (2002:131–32) notes, the art perspective on objects views the multiplicity of excavated things of similar classes as redundant examples of interchangeable value until converted to art market commodities, unique monuments to past human genius validated by the aesthetic judgment and economic capital of the collector. Conservation professionals and archaeologists see objects as traces of unique sequences of events, as biographies. For archaeologists, the contextual interrelations of things endow them with historical specificity. Usually thought of as connections between objects and features in sites, context also includes relations among traces preserved in the material of objects themselves.

Conservation professionals and archaeologists diverge in other aspects of their relationship to traces. Debates at a meeting held in 1997 to consider how to manage deteriorating sculpture at Copan exposed significant differences in these perspectives (Joyce 2002c). Archaeologists working at the site represented traces and monuments as data for scientific analysis, resulting in documentation of the historical development of the ancient Maya kingdom. From their perspective, information contained in stone sculpture could be enhanced by abstracting the original, eroded monuments from the site and replacing them with replicas in which details had been filled in by employing specialist knowledge.

Conservation professionals represented a distinct perspective. They emphasized an ideal of minimal intervention and a commitment to gathering data over a long term before taking action. Conservation professionals were more closely engaged with the monument as an object with a material history sketched out in traces of alteration that might be measured over the short term and projected onto the long term.

The preservation of sculptures at Copan, a monument with universal cultural significance, should not have been open to such radically different viewpoints by otherwise similarly situated persons. As a monument, *restoration* of the sculpture to its appearance when newly constructed might seem the self-evident correct action. But the debates did not turn on differences in interpretation of the significance of the site at a *monumental* scale. Instead, they reflected diversity in understanding the site as a set of traces of human and natural action.

Attending to the history of the alteration of the site reinstates a sense of the passage of time, including time at the human scale. Archaeological conservation could not simply be directed to stopping time and turning back the clock. Rather, the interventions of conservation professionals can add to the documentation of traces of the experiences of durability and perishability that all archaeological sites offer (cf. Petzet 1995). Viewed as a set of traces, Copan exposes the reality implicit in many things considered monuments today: they were not created to last forever, unchanged and unambiguous.

Back to Los Naranjos

Reflecting on these experiences, I return to my beginning point: Los Naranjos, an archaeological site whose monumental materiality is fragile and whose anthropological significance is best justified by its status as a place where repeated traces of past human action crossed and recrossed a landscape. The disassembly of parts of the traces of human presence at the site requires adoption of a perspective that values individual action in the past, juxtaposing it to the macroscale monumentality that first strikes a visitor. To interpret and present the site as traces requires a new form of dialogue with the visiting public.

In this trace-centered dialogue, there can be no question of authenticity conceived as a judgment of the consistency and value of cultural wholes at particular points in time. The residents who added a house platform to one of the monumental earthen pyramids in about 400 B.C.E. were not inauthentic in their conversion of use of space. An adequate representation of the site in—as the local teacher quoted earlier called for—"todo su esplendor" (all its splendor) requires a complex history of the life of the material remains both of monuments and of traces. This alternate presentation poses different questions concerning preservation and conservation.

As archaeologists, we seek to *preserve* sites. Conceived as traces, this obligates us to refrain from excavation as much as possible—a mandate that should lead us to champion the presentation of unexcavated, un-"restored" structures as often as or more often than the problematically restored and unstable buildings that proliferate at heritage sites. In common with conservation professionals, we share a commitment to *conserve* archaeological materials. Conceived as traces of life histories, this should entail a shared ethic of minimal intervention and stabilization, again as often as or more often than "restoration." The challenge this presents is to manage archaeological places as historicized spaces in a process of transformation that we intersect at a point in an ongoing history—not as timeless, unalterable, static monuments.

Conclusion

All exposure and use of material traces of past human activity shortens the possible life span of things that were not built with the intention that they survive forever. Each stakeholder who claims a voice in dealing with the materiality of the past inherits with that claim a responsibility for the effects this stake has on the ultimate life span, contextual integrity, and interpretive potential of these astonishing points of contact with the living human past (Omland 1997). Contending claims must be judged at least in part by the damage their exercise would inflict on those who see other significances in the same materialities.

Such conflicts are not easily resolved through the formulation of guidelines and rules, however detailed, since they stem from very different understandings of how material things are significant in the contemporary world and for the future. In debating decisions about preservation, conservation, interpretation, and presentation, archaeologists and conservation professionals can legitimately, and indeed must ethically, each represent the expertise that is unique to their stakeholding positions, without demanding the final word. Their perspectival differences constitute different stakes in the same materialities, stakes that may be incommensurate. These differences must be understood if we are to be able to collaborate on the task of ensuring that future generations will have any opportunity to experience the kind of direct connection to past human action that surviving material makes possible for us today.

References

Basso, K. 1996. *Wisdom Sits in Places.* Albuquerque: University of New Mexico Press.

Cleere, H. 1996. The concept of "outstanding universal value in the World Heritage Convention." *Conservation and Management of Archaeological Sites* 1:227–33.

———. 1998. Uneasy bedfellows: Universality and cultural heritage. Paper presented at the WAC Intercongress on the Destruction and Conservation of Cultural Property, Island of Brac, Croatia, 3–7 May 1998. Consulted online at http://www.wac.uct.ac.za/croatia/.

Dirlik, A. 1996. The past as legacy and project: Postcolonial criticism in the perspective of indigenous historicism. *American Indian Culture and Research Journal* 20:1–31.

Herzfeld, M. 1991. *A Place in History: Social and Monumental Time in a Cretan Town.* Princeton: Princeton University Press.

Joyce, R. A. 2002a. Academic freedom, stewardship, and cultural heritage: Weighing the interests of stakeholders in crafting repatriation approaches. In *The Dead and Their Possessions: Repatriation in Principle, Policy and Practice,* ed. C. Fforde, J. Hubert, and P. Turnbull, 99–107. London: Routledge.

———. 2002b. *The Languages of Archaeology: Dialogue, Narrative, and Writing.* Oxford: Blackwell.

———. 2002c. Solid histories for fragile nations: Archaeology as cultural patrimony. Paper presented at the conference "Beyond Ethics: Anthropological Moralities on the Boundaries of the Public and the Professional," Peter Pels and Lynn M. Meskell, organizers. Wenner Gren Foundation for Anthropological Research Symposium 130. Cabo San Lucas, Baja California, Mexico.

Lilley, I., and M. Williams. 2005. Archaeological and indigenous significance: A view from Australia. In *Heritage of Value, Archaeology of Renown: Reshaping Archaeological Assessment and Significance,* ed. C. Mathers, T. Darvill, and B. Little, 227–47. Gainesville: University Press of Florida.

Lipe, W. D. 1984. Value and meaning in cultural resources. In *Approaches to Archaeological Heritage,* ed. H. Cleere, 1–11. Cambridge: Cambridge University Press.

Ludlow Collective. 2001. Archaeology of the Colorado Coal Field War, 1913–1914. In *Archaeologies of the Contemporary Past,* ed. V. Buchli and G. Lucas, 94–107. London: Routledge.

Lyons, C. 2002. Objects and identities: Claiming and reclaiming the past. In *Claiming the Stones, Naming the Bones: Cultural Property and the Negotiation of National and Ethnic Identity,* ed. E. Barkan and R. Bush, 116–37. Los Angeles: The J. Paul Getty Trust.

Matsuda, D. 1998. The ethics of archaeology, subsistence digging, and artifact looting in Latin America: Point, muted counterpoint. *International Journal of Cultural Property* 7:87–97.

Omland, A. 1997. World heritage and the relationship between the global and the local. M. Phil. thesis, Cambridge University. Published online at http://folk.uio.no./atleom/master/contents.htm.

Petzet, M. 1995. "In the full richness of their authenticity"—The test of authenticity and the new cult of monuments. In *Nara Conference on Authenticity in Relation to the World Heritage Convention,* ed. K. E. Larsen, 85–99. Trondheim, Norway: TAPIR.

Raab, L., and T. Klinger. 1977. A critical appraisal of "significance" in contract archaeology. *American Antiquity* 42:629–34.

Rodriguez, T. 2001. Maya perceptions of ancestral remains: Multiple places in a local space. *Berkeley McNair Research Journal* 9:21–45.

UNESCO. 2001. Criteria for inclusion of cultural properties in the World Heritage List. Webpage at http://whc.unesco.org/nwhc/pages/home/pages/homepage.htm. Reviewed 1 June 2003.

Wylie, A. 1996. Ethical dilemmas in archaeological practice: Looting, repatriation, stewardship, and the (trans)formation of disciplinary identity. *Perspectives on Science* 4:154–94.

———. 1999. Science, conservation, and stewardship: Evolving codes of conduct in archaeology. *Science and Engineering Ethics* 5:319–36.

PART TWO

Innovative Approaches to Policy and Management of Archaeological Sites

Introduction

Douglas C. Comer

Archaeologists and preservationists typically deal with the shell of the nautilus after its vital inhabitant has expired. This is true for nearly all prehistoric archaeological sites and the cities, villages, and settlements of most ancient civilizations. The Temple of Dendur, Angkor Wat, Macchu Pichu, and Petra are well-known examples. Exceptions are in places where the infrastructure and social organization that originally created and supported the site remain somewhat intact, such as marketplaces in the Middle East, wats in Thailand, and Plains Indian medicine wheels in the western United States.

Everywhere, however, the forces of entropy are relentless. Because of the interrelationship of physical order and social order, successful archaeological site preservation depends on bolstering, modifying, or reintroducing the social order necessary to support physical remains. Preservation goes far beyond conducting archaeological research and determining conservation treatments. It goes to site management.

The papers in Part II speak of a range of efforts to establish the social organizations required to maintain sites. In the absence of the feast days and social hierarchies that once focused human attention and labor on the repair of architecture and the prevention of vandalism, efforts must be made to mobilize bureaucracies, universities, nongovernmental organizations (NGOs), indigenous inhabitants, and the private sector to such ends.

The involvement of the private sector is often seen by preservationists and academics as problematic. Clearly, site management guided by an unrestrained profit motive could produce shallow tourist attractions, destroy original site fabric, and lead to exploitation of local communities and indigenous populations. In my paper, the first to follow, I examine the private sector's role in establishing the world's first system of protected areas, the U.S. national park system. That system would not exist today without initial enthusiastic support from a private sector that expected visitation to national parks to produce profits. I also observe that the World Heritage Convention was modeled on the U.S. national park system. Finally, I argue that successful management of protected areas requires obtaining support from the private sector, which must be considered a key stakeholder, along with indigenous groups and international preservation organizations.

Pisit Charoenwongsa, director of the SEAMEO Regional Centre for Archaeology and Fine Arts (SPAFA), located in Bangkok, also advocates a holistic approach, one involving, in Charoenwongsa's words, "various stakeholders, sometimes more than one donor, and possibly more than one implementing organization or agency." This sort of coordination, he argues, can work very effectively at the regional level. He sees the establishment of site management as a development project that can only succeed when formulated and carried out in a culturally sensitive way. Coordination of such projects by a regional cultural center such as SPAFA, which can become deeply familiar with the social conventions and mores of member countries, is both logical and effective.

Cultural sensitivity emerges as a central theme again in the paper by Aysar Akrawi, executive director of the Petra National Trust, a Jordanian NGO. In recounting efforts to establish effective site management at Petra, a World Heritage Site in southern Jordan, she maintains that the patterns have largely been provided by studies conducted by international preservation organizations that did not sufficiently involve local communities. A national NGO, she argues, can provide an essential link between international experience in establishing site management organizations and the cultural environments of the nation and the local communities.

In his paper, Larry Armony, general manager of the Brimstone Hill Fortress National Park Society (BHFNPS), notes that the cultural organization that once sustained the monumental defensive structures of Brimstone Hill and Fort Charles—one that had as a central element the practice of slavery—is now defunct. No one would dispute that this is a quantum improvement in social mores, but what social organization can now maintain these structures? Armony reports that the BHFNPS has evolved into an organization "that recognizes and promotes the fact that structures such as Brimstone Hill Fortress embody the contributions of the colonized and are testimony to the multicultural nature of Caribbean society." He argues that an NGO such as BHFNPS can exercise the finesse necessary to balance the promotion of an emerging national consciousness with the need to educate visitors about the history of the site and to elevate the standard of living for the island by increasing revenues from tourism.

Gaetano Palumbo sets forth the sense of community as an ideal. In response to the recent advent of privatization of heritage sites in many countries, in particular, Italy, he argues that the community, not the private sector, should play the lead role in preserving archaeological sites. He draws a distinction between cultural heritage *exploitation* and cultural heritage *use*. Exploitation occurs when value is placed only on the economic benefits of heritage. The private sector, he maintains, will invest in properties only in ways that will increase financial return and only so long as sites return a profit. Investment by the private sector will likely focus on increasing tourist appeal as opposed to preservation of original fabric, research, and community involvement. This will lead to degradation of the site, an eventual decrease in financial returns, and, finally, abandonment of the site, which then will again become the concern of the state. Better, says Palumbo, to strengthen ties between the site and the community by encouraging community *use,* thereby increasing the likelihood of long-term and sensitive site stewardship.

Interpretation at archaeological sites has often been regarded as a desirable but unessential aspect of site management. Neil Silberman and Dirk Callebaut argue vigorously that interpretation is a central element in that effort. Silberman was instrumental in drafting a charter for interpretation that is now being reviewed and modified by ICOMOS for possible universal acceptance by UNESCO. This has, since its inception, been called the Ename Charter, after an archaeological site in Belgium where innovative technologies were employed. These technologies were effective in telling a story about the site, and preservation professionals involved with the project were pleased. However, they realized that such technologies could be used to tell not only stories based on rigorous research and evaluations of findings that complied with academic standards but also erroneous or biased ones. The charter, which Silberman and Callebaut describe, addresses this concern and related ones.

Each of these papers has been prepared by a preservationist with long experience in the field. The authors are, or have been, academics or employees or heads of NGOs, employees of governmental organizations charged with site preservation, and practicing site managers. The topics addressed reflect this diversity of background. At the same time, despite differences in their points of view, all of the authors recognize, explicitly or implicitly, that their concern must be cultural dynamics: the vital organisms that produced the shells that attract our attention and that sustain them today. Our effort to preserve archaeological sites permits us the hope that one day we will more fully understand the cultural dynamics that gave rise to them. Understanding the cultural dynamics that affect them today allows us to hope that we can preserve them.

Ideology, Economics, and Site Management

Douglas C. Comer

Abstract: *Many approaches to archaeological site policy and management that might be termed innovative, including privatization, have been prompted by the widespread lack of resources necessary to adequately manage archaeological sites, including World Heritage Sites. This paper argues against privatization but also that the current situation stems in large part from the failure of preservationists to recruit the private sector as the principal supporter of government-managed protected areas. It offers an anthropologically based context in which to examine cultural site management as part of an ongoing dialectic among stakeholders, including the private sector. This approach explicitly recognizes that ideology and economics determine the roles played by all stakeholders, including archaeologists and preservationists. The U.S. National Park Service has been the model for many protected area programs, including the World Heritage Convention. An examination of this case reveals that the private sector must be involved in two ways: the protected cultural site must provide economic opportunities to local communities and groups; and international companies that benefit from visitation to protected areas must be brought into the site management dialogue for political support and, in some cases, as contributors of needed resources.*

Francesco Bandarin, head of the World Heritage Centre, remarked at a recent observance of the thirtieth anniversary of the signing of the World Heritage Convention that a list showing how many of the 754 World Heritage Sites were threatened would comprise about 754 entries. Of the 754 World Heritage Sites, 582 are inscribed because of outstanding cultural values, and another 23 are inscribed for reasons of mixed cultural and natural values.

Many World Heritage Sites are located in developing countries that lack the means needed to ensure that development, looting, and poaching will not produce damage to the very qualities that prompted their inscription on the World Heritage List. At the typical World Heritage Site, money and trained personnel are in short supply. Consequently, deficiencies in management organization, facilities, and equipment are common.

Many approaches have been taken to remedy the chronic lack of resources necessary to effectively manage archaeological sites, especially those that are open to public visitation. Among these are privatization, management of sites by nongovernmental organizations (NGOs), management by NGO and government partnerships, and assistance to site management by government-supported regional centers. Enhancements in the way sites are presented as a means of increasing site revenue and improving the visitor's experience may also be used as means to overcome scarcity of resources.

To facilitate and widen the dialogue on innovative approaches to site management, this paper considers the global ideological and economic context in which archaeological site management takes place, that of postmodern culture and hypercapitalist economy. It also makes some recommendations as to how preservationists' efforts should be informed by the structure of this context.

It is important for the dialogue to be widened because typically preservationists do not talk to the right people in the right way. At present, they spend most of their time talking with each other, and occasionally with employees and representatives of the governments of the countries in which the sites they wish to preserve are located. Among themselves, they discuss policy, technique, and frustration. With countries, they promulgate standards, recommend good management practices, and warn against privatization. Unfortunately, they have few useful recommendations for securing the resources necessary to implement good management practices. Preservationists should spend more time talking with the private sector in ways that will motivate it to lobby governments to build effective site management organizations and to contribute the resources necessary to accomplish that goal. There is a model, a history, that preservationists can deploy in that effort—that of the U.S. National Park Service (NPS).

The perspective here is anthropological. Preservation, like all human undertakings, is a cultural one, and preservationists are subject to the same sorts of cultural forces that determine the success or failure of the activities of all human groups. These ideological and economic forces drive the uses to which archaeological sites are put and define the roles played by a variety of stakeholders, including archaeologists and preservationists, as both protectors and exploiters of archaeological sites. Preservationists must direct those forces to the best of their ability while also being subject to them.

To begin the argument, it is essential to state what many scholars have noted before: protected areas exist largely because political and economic leaders at certain times and places believed that they would provide substantial economic benefits to the countries and regions in which they were located. Business interests have actively promoted the establishment of protected areas, to the extent that one might wonder if these areas would exist at all without their intervention.

The close interweaving of the goals of business and preservationists is clearly illustrated by the genesis and growth of the U.S. NPS, which has served as the precedent for the establishment of nationally protected areas worldwide. As Joan Zenzen (1997) has noted, among others (Kinsey 1992; Runte 1979), the railroads were instrumental in the drive to establish a national park system in the United States and in promoting the parks after they were established. Parks gave people a reason to travel to undeveloped areas (fig. 1). Zenzen says:

> For national parks, western railroads were essential to their early survival and development. No other nineteenth-century transportation system could have reliably moved so many people to such isolated areas as Yellowstone and the Grand Canyon. Railroads shaped the national park experience by building rustic luxury hotels, constructing trails and roads, and providing comfortable transportation. . . . The railroads extended the national park myth's

FIGURE 1 Poster encouraging travel by railroad to national parks.

nationalistic message to their own ends of promoting tourism and land sales [and] had established a regular tourism business to the national parks by the second decade of the twentieth century. (1997:274)

Other providers of lodging, food, and any number of products and services to travelers soon joined the railroads in forming a strong and vocal base of support for the national park system in the United States. One notable example was the

Fred Harvey Company. Even more notable is the coalition that formed between the railroads and conservationists. In 1899 the chairman of the board of the Union Pacific Railroad, Edward Harriman, undoubtedly one of the most powerful figures in America at the time, hosted twenty-six of the nation's leading scientists along with authors, poets, artists, and photographers on an expedition to Alaska. For two months, aboard his 250-foot steamer, Harriman exchanged ideas with such conservation luminaries as George Bird Grinnell, himself a former, and extremely successful, businessman; John Muir, the archetypical crusading environmentalist; Edward Curtis, who began his most notable achievement, documenting the lives and culture of Native Americans, on the trip; and C. Hart Merriam, founder of the National Geographic Society. It is certain that Harriman exerted influence pivotal to the establishment of national parks in the United States. In 1905 John Muir asked Harriman to lobby the U.S. Senate for passage of the bill that would establish Yosemite as the first national park. Given that the bill passed by a single vote after energetic lobbying by Harriman, there is little doubt that his support was crucial.

The U.S. system, being the first, has been used as the pattern by which to establish park systems in many other countries. It also set the pattern for preservation of what are now regarded globally as the premier cultural and natural sites, World Heritage Sites. Yet while the private sector has benefited from the establishment of World Heritage Sites, it has not provided support on a par with that which it provided to the U.S. national park system. Prime among the reasons for this is that the type of dialogue that occurred between industrialists and conservationists one hundred years ago has no parallel today.

Before the establishment of park and world heritage systems, archaeological sites in the developing world were considered by archaeologists and conservators as preserves for research, properly opened only to the elite, Western or Westernized, who brought with them the economic and intellectual resources necessary to undertake and appreciate the visit. That elitist past is largely responsible for what archaeological sites, especially those containing architecture, are today: items of value in both ideological and economic systems. The value first attached to these sites in the early nineteenth century, which can be seen in the drawings of David Roberts (fig. 2) and Frederick Catherwood and the writings of "explorers" such as John Lloyd Stevens, Johann Ludwig Burckhardt, and Richard Burton, eventually made it possible to market them to a broader audience within the tourism industry. Readers of,

for example, *Incidents of Travel in Egypt and Petraea* and *Incidents of Travel in the Yucatan* became the first "consumers" of archaeological sites.

The market for archaeological sites increased rapidly following a number of developments over the past half century. Improvements in transportation systems, most notably air travel, have made archaeological and, more generally, cultural sites accessible to large numbers of people. As the bourgeois of the 1960s and 1970s followed in the footsteps of the elite in the nineteenth and early twentieth century, certain sites experienced enormous increases in visitation. One felicitous result of this increased visitation was that it produced a constituency for these sites. That constituency comprised not only site visitors but also members of the various sectors of the economy that enjoyed revenue derived from visitation. This alliance of business interests and private individuals—which depended on the belief that cultural sites somehow conveyed something valuable to all who had a chance to visit them—grew alarmed at the well-publicized damage brought about by natural disasters and infrastructure developments in the 1960s.

Flooding in Venice prompted the formulation by the United Nations Educational, Scientific and Cultural Organization (UNESCO) of the Charter for the Conservation and Restoration of Monuments and Sites in 1964. Out of this, the International Council on Monuments and Sites (ICOMOS), an international NGO dedicated to the conservation of the world's historic monuments and sites, was born. At the UNESCO general conference in Paris in 1972, the Convention Concerning the Protection of the World Cultural and Natural Heritage, or World Heritage Convention, was adopted. This convention noted that "the cultural heritage and the natural heritage are increasingly threatened with destruction not only by the traditional causes of decay, but also by changing social and economic conditions which aggravate the situation with even more formidable phenomena of damage or destruction." The Intergovernmental Committee for the Protection of the Cultural and Natural Heritage of Outstanding Universal Value, called the World Heritage Committee, was formed by the Convention, and this committee was charged with maintaining a World Heritage List. The list was to comprise sites possessing outstanding universal value, "in terms of such criteria as it shall have established."

As Russell Train noted at the ceremony to commemorate the thirtieth anniversary of the World Heritage Convention, it was no coincidence that the convention was signed on 16 November 1972, one hundred years to the day from the

FIGURE 2 Engravings by David Roberts, popularizing exotic archaeological destinations.

date when the U.S. national park system was established. According to Train, a former undersecretary of the Department of the Interior and the first chair of the President's Council on Environmental Quality, the World Heritage Convention was born in the White House. In his Message on the Environment in 1972, President Richard Nixon (who Train declares was anxious to be remembered kindly for his environmental record) said, "It would be fitting by 1972 (that being the centennial anniversary of the establishment of Yellowstone National Park) for the nations of the world to agree to the principle that there are certain areas of such unique worldwide value that they should be treated as part of the heritage of all mankind and accorded special recognition as part of a World Heritage Trust" (Train 1992). Thus the system of World Heritage Sites was very consciously patterned after the U.S. national park system.

There are certainly flaws in the model, but it has worked well in the United States for several reasons. Economically, the U.S. national parks remain an enormous engine for tourism

revenue and tourism-related jobs. Although the park system was first promoted by the railroads, automobile travel brought the parks within the reach of virtually the entire middle class, and airplanes now bring in millions of foreign tourists to "must-sees" like the Grand Canyon, Yellowstone, the monuments in Washington, D.C., and the Statue of Liberty in New York. All of these are managed by the U.S. NPS.

The national parks are almost entirely supported by tax dollars. A vigorous economy makes this possible, as does the dominance of an ideological system that differs in some respects from those in place in many areas of the world. Although there are many divisions in American society, the idea of nationhood is well accepted, and from there it is an easily negotiated leap to the idea that a national institution should be formed with the mission to protect and present tangible portions of the national heritage. The U.S. private sector is well developed, and the legal system is vigorous, to say the least. Our media thrive on exposés that if not always thoughtful, are engaging to most of the populace. This opens up opportunities both to involve the private sector in preservation and to subject that involvement to critical review.

It is important not to underestimate a final factor in this regard, however. The national park system in the United States has succeeded as well as it has in no small part because of the role played by conservationists in mediating between the interests of the business sector and local, usually traditional, communities. The workforce at U.S. national parks is drawn about equally from local people and the well-educated specialists who relocate to the remote areas where most national parks are situated. Willing to forgo the luxuries of more populated areas and to work for little pay, these staff members often come from a background in the sciences. They are typically motivated by what they see as the opportunity to play a role in an important effort to preserve irreplaceable resources. They occupy a middle ground between the interests of traditional groups and those of businesses and bureaucracies and knit these together in a common social network.

Social networks depend on the internalized standards and modes of behavior that make up culture. "Culture" is an enormously popular term today, and it is most frequently used in the sense that anthropologists assigned to it after a century of studying collective human behavior. Culture in the anthropological sense is not the high culture of operas and art museums but the forces that determine patterns of human behavior. Although anthropologists are not in perfect agreement about all aspects of culture, it is probably safe to say that most anthropologists learn in college that culture is influenced mostly by notions of kinship. Kinship defines patterns of appropriate behavior based on each person's position within a web of ancestry. In traditional societies, this web is inevitably seen by societal members as stretching back to the founding ancestors. The founding ancestors are those that made the world and established the standards that all succeeding generations must meet. In traditional societies, one may have disagreements with one's relatives but will band together with them against nonrelatives. To create alliances and avoid conflict, fictive kinship can be established through paying joint homage to a fictive ancestor, usually one among the group regarded as founding ancestors.

As I have argued elsewhere (Comer 1996), we in the West often call groups that define identity through explicit reference to ancestry and homeland "primitive" or "traditional." We ignore the fact that capitalism employs its own ways of establishing fictive kinship. Often, this is through membership in a corporation, but it might also be through membership in a professional or avocational society. We see in such groups the same veneration for founding ancestors and the same concern with emblems of status that are laden with great meaning to those in the group, although not necessarily to those outside it. The structure of culture is the same, every-

where. The difference is really a matter of degree and context, not of kind.

There are in the United States a great number of traditional societies having what academics readily identify as traditional or "folk" cultures. This is something that we frequently celebrate. The largest and most famous U.S. national parks tend to be located in areas where traditional societies are the norm. This in itself is evidence that traditional and modern groups can coexist and even thrive while maintaining their differences, as long as each side maintains an ideological and economic place for the other. That place is usually created by mutual economic benefit. If production of certain items and provision of special services falls comfortably within the ideological system of one side and is valued by the other and if both sides feel that value is gained by the exchange, then peace and a certain level of prosperity often follow. In fact, this is largely the situation that obtains within the U.S. NPS, which is a modern, federal system that employs the services and purchases the products of the more traditional groups that reside in the interior of the country.

This involves establishing a management system at each site that is largely tried and proven and that is standard enough that personnel can function if rotated from site to site. At the same time, the system must be sufficiently flexible to allow for local cultural variability. Most personnel can be trained to function well in such a system. Rising within it, however, usually involves adopting a worldview less grounded in immediate kin and homeland points of reference and more grounded in the fictive kinship of the central authority and the more abstract landscape of the nation.

All of this can work so long as the central authority can bring to the table jobs and the opportunity to market the services and products that the local community feels comfortable providing. A viable income is needed not only for the most obvious reasons—to maintain the site and to provide visitors with protection, interpretation, and other amenities—but also as the means by which to engage the local communities and populations in an exchange that is meaningful and satisfactory to them. To provide the latter benefit, income does not have to go through the government. It can go directly to local providers of goods and services, as long as (1) there is the general understanding that such exchange is attributable to the presence of the archaeological site and (2) the central government is perceived as the steward of the archaeological site.

In the end, effective site management is a matter of establishing good governance. Government must take ultimate responsibility not only for preserving the site but also for seeing to it that the site generates income that accrues fairly to all stakeholders, especially those in the private sector. The exact manner in which that is done must involve local communities and other stakeholders in open and transparent transactions, according to standards and regulations that ensure that resources and communities are not destroyed in the process of generating the income that is necessary to preserve them. In doing so, governments must balance the interests of the international and local private sectors.

Governance, however, involves more than the government. While a legitimate role of government is to regulate and reform the private sector, the private sector can play a strong role in reforming government. The private sector is especially likely to promote policies and programs that encourage social stability and economic growth, conditions that benefit it as well. Among these programs can be those that provide the structure and resources necessary for effective management of archaeological sites. Dialogue with these organizations is also essential to ensure that local economic interests are not overwhelmed by competition with large international companies. In some cases, for example, international companies might be induced to provide support and training to small, local firms.

In conclusion, management of cultural sites should not be turned over to the private sector. Preservationists and, more broadly, conservationists face the difficult but essential task of educating not only the private sector but also local, tra-ditional groups about the value of safeguarding resources. The interests of both groups must be acknowledged as a step in convincing them to add their voices to those of preservationists in declaring the need to effectively manage cultural resources.

References

Comer, D. 1996. *Ritual Ground.* Berkeley: University of California Press.

Goetzmann, W. H., and K. Sloan. 1982. *Looking Far North: The Harriman Expedition to Alaska, 1899.* Princeton: Princeton University Press.

Kinsey, J. L. 1992. *Thomas Moran and the Surveying of the American West.* Washington, D.C.: Smithsonian Institution Press.

Runte, A. 1979. *National Parks: The American Experience.* Lincoln: University of Nebraska Press.

Train, R. 1992. The World Heritage Convention: The first twenty years and beyond. Speech delivered at the International World Heritage Committee Meeting, Santa Fe, New Mexico, 7 December 1992. http://whc.unesco.org/archive/repcom92.htm#inf1.

Zenzen, J. 1997. Promoting national parks: Images of the West in the American imagination, 1864–1972. Ph.D dissertation, University of Maryland, College Park.

NGO and Government Collaboration in Archaeological Site Management: The Case of Petra, Jordan

Aysar Akrawi

Abstract: *The Petra National Trust (PNT) is a nongovernmental and nonprofit organization that was established in 1989. It is one of the organizations responsible for the preservation of the cultural and natural heritage of Petra. PNT does not set policy but works with the policy makers in the government of Jordan and with other nongovernmental organizations to achieve its objectives. This paper addresses the experience of Jordan in site management, using the case of Petra to portray developments in this field. It describes the situation in Petra today and cites some of the management models that the government has adopted. It concludes with a proposal for how Jordan should proceed toward management of its archaeological heritage.*

Petra is located halfway between the Red Sea and the Dead Sea (fig. 1) and has been inhabited for more than two hundred thousand years. Traditionally the tribes were shepherds and farmers. Today people in the area live in modern hillside villages and Bedouin encampments. In recent years, with the arrival of tourists, they have moved closer to the archaeological site and earn a living by working on excavations and guiding tourists. One of the most spectacular sites in the Near East, Petra (fig. 2) has long attracted travelers and explorers, and archaeological investigations have been conducted in the area since the 1930s.

The site of Petra covers a protected area of 264 square kilometers and is surrounded by six main villages (fig. 3) with a total population that has grown from 2,000 in 1960 to 25,000 today. In the absence of zoning and building regulations, came

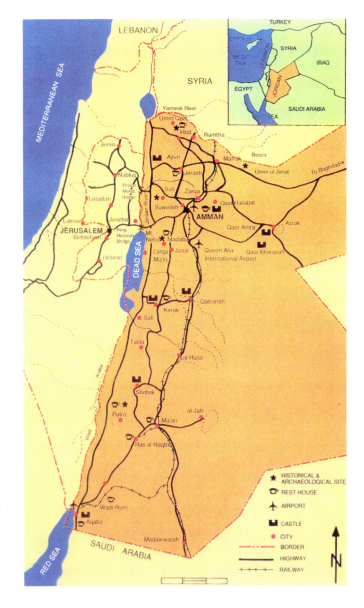

FIGURE 1 Jordan. Courtesy of Petra National Trust

FIGURE 2 al-Deir. Courtesy of Petra National Trust

Stakeholders

A number of stakeholders have an interest in the region as a whole. These are

- local inhabitants
- the government, including the Department of Antiquities, the Ministry of Tourism, the Jordan Tourism Board, the Petra Regional Authority, and other ministries
- Jordanian and international archaeologists
- conservation professionals
- international institutes and aid agencies involved in research and preservation
- tour operators, tourism investors, hotel owners, and souvenir vendors
- tourists
- NGOs

uncontrolled construction to meet the expanding requirements of the communities and to cater to tourists. Statistics issued by the Ministry of Tourism and Antiquities show that the number of tourists more than quadrupled between the years 1989 and 2000. The high concentration of visitors coupled with the lack of circulation plans within the site presented a threat to its integrity (fig. 4).

Site Management

Petra Archaeological Park is managed by the Department of Antiquities, which is part of Jordan's Ministry of Tourism and Antiquities. Numerous other government departments are also involved, and their responsibilities often overlap. Jordan has undertaken a number of measures to resolve the confusion in responsibilities and chain of command, as explained below. The sudden surge in numbers of visitors spurred by the peace agreement with Israel in 1994 abruptly brought to the surface the issue of site management. The Department of Antiquities, whose primary concern had been archaeological research, found itself unprepared to effectively manage Petra or other sites in Jordan.

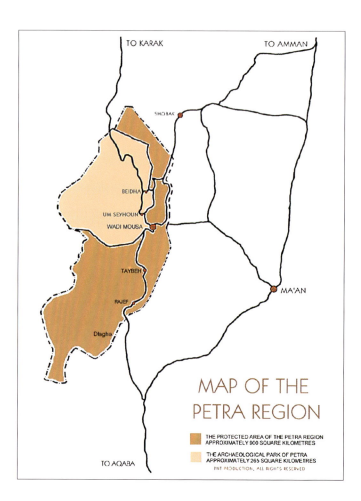

FIGURE 3 Petra region and protected area. Courtesy of Petra National Trust

FIGURE 4 Restaurant. Courtesy of Petra National Trust

The differing and often incompatible interests and roles of these groups need to reviewed and defined to avoid friction between them.

Management Plans

In 1985 Petra was inscribed on the UNESCO list of World Heritage Sites in recognition of its unique cultural and natural heritage. In 1999 Petra was put on the World Monuments Fund's Watch List of 100 Most Endangered Sites, and that designation was renewed in 2002. Well before those dates, the government, in response to the potential impact of increasing tourism and later the increase in visitation numbers, invited international institutions, on four occasions, to prepare management plans for Petra:

- the U.S. National Park Service Master Plan for the Protection and Use of the Petra National Park, in 1968;
- the UNESCO Petra National Park Management Plan, in 1994;
- the US/ICOMOS Management Analysis and Recommendations for the Petra World Heritage Site, in 1996; and
- the U.S. National Park Service Operational Plan, in 2000.

In 1968 the U.S. National Park Service (NPS) was invited to prepare a master plan that was to be used as a guide for the use, development, interpretation, protection, and general administration of what came to be known as the Petra National Park. Many of the issues identified in this plan have now intensified. Whereas the Ministry of Tourism and Antiquities is now independent, in 1968 it was a department within the Ministry of Culture, and there is no institutional recollection of the procedure that was followed by the U.S. NPS in this study. In the ensuing plans, some participation of Jordanian counterparts was included. It is clear, however, that there was no systematic participation of stakeholders in any of the stages of master plan development or thereafter in the formulation and follow-up of the recommendations they presented, and to this date this approach largely continues.

The first two studies analyzed the management structure at a time when the Ministry of Culture and later the Ministry of Tourism and Antiquities managed Petra from their headquarters in Amman. The Ministry of Tourism was responsible for issuing development licenses; the Department of Antiquities was responsible for scientific research and the management of the archaeological resources. With limited staff and poor coordination, the management of the entire area was ineffective. Most of the problems then and now are a result of this circumstance. On the basis of their findings, the U.S. NPS and later UNESCO stressed the need to create a single independent governmental authority that would manage and coordinate all aspects of park management. They differed in their approach as to whom this new body would report to. The outcome was the Petra Regional Planning Council (PRPC), which was established in 1995 (fig. 5). The charter gave the council the mandate to comprehensively manage an area of 1,000 square kilometers, inclusive of the protected area, disregarding the fact that the Law of Antiquities gives the Department of Antiquities (DOA) full authority to manage all aspects of the park. Herein lies one of the fundamental problems affecting the efficient management of the park—that of the appropriate location of this body within the government.

The 1996 study conducted under the auspices of ICOMOS recommended the introduction of a separate authority for the protected area of the park, the Petra National Park Agency (PNPA), which would be dedicated solely to the management of the park. Once again the location of the PNPA within the framework of the government was disputed; its final location was a subject of intense controversy.

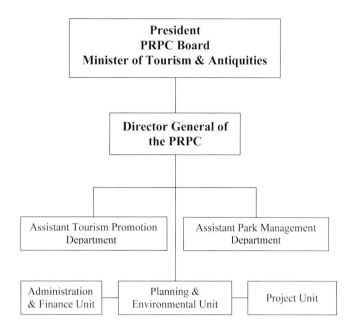

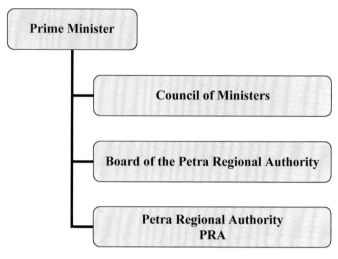

FIGURE 6 PRA organization chart. Courtesy of Petra National Trust

FIGURE 5 PRPC organization chart. Courtesy of Petra National Trust

In 2001 the PRPC was replaced by the Petra Regional Authority, now reporting directly to the Prime Minister's Office rather than the Ministry of Tourism (fig. 6). The new board was composed of government officials and a few members of the local community, but it eliminated the membership of PNT. The undeclared reason was that in its efforts to protect the buffer area from overdevelopment, PNT was seen as an obstruction to progress. The new law gave the Petra Regional Authority control of the entire area; however, more important, the jurisdiction of all aspects of the management of the Petra Archaeological Park finally lay with the Department of Antiquities, thus resolving on paper at least the issue of which governmental department would be responsible for the management of the site.

The government has not officially endorsed any of these plans. Nevertheless, they have served as a reference point in many instances, for example, in the development of the institutional capacity of park staff and tourist-related facilities. The neglect of the recommendations, on the other hand, has had a negative effect on several parameters, social, environmental, economic, and visual.

The final plan that was submitted in July 2000 differs from its predecessors in that it constitutes a major step toward the establishment of comprehensive management policies, detailed operating procedures and standards, a training plan, and the recommended position of Petra Archaeological Park under the purview of the Ministry of Tourism and Antiquities. Regrettably, however, some very important prerequisites such as the financial and human resources essential to making the plan feasible were missing, and the practicability of any plan depends on the government's commitment to providing the necessary resources. Once again, the preparation of this plan did not include any local participation until after its submission to the government. Difficult as it may be to coordinate, local participation of key stakeholders is vital if the plan is to be identified with and implemented. To date, this plan has not been put into practice.

The Role of NGOs in Site Management

Today we discuss archaeological and cultural sites in very specific ways. It should be emphasized that Jordan is only beginning to define how it preserves, conserves, and yet makes available the wonders of its cultural heritage. Both government and nongovernmental organizations are involved in site management and preservation of heritage, and cultural and natural heritage NGOs have existed since 1966. There are three NGOs whose activities are related to this field in Jordan, the earliest being the Royal Society for the Conservation of

Nature (RSCN), which was established in 1966; it owns and manages six natural parks successfully. PNT was established in 1989. In reality it is the only cultural NGO that has been actively involved in the preservation and protection of archaeological sites, although its mandate is restricted to Petra, and as such it is a pioneer. Over the years it has been active in two main roles, advocacy and preservation. As such, it maintains a close relationship with both the UNESCO World Heritage Centre and the World Monuments Fund. For example, it played a pivotal role in supporting the creation of a separate entity within the park to manage the site of Petra independently under the aegis of the Department of Antiquities and consequently resolved the controversy regarding which government body ultimately was to be responsible for the management of archaeological sites. In its role as a preservation organization, it has executed a number of preservation projects in the fields of hydrology (fig. 7), biodiversity (fig. 8), and local community development. In the execution of these projects, PNT partners with the government and conservation specialists in the private sector. Finally, the Friends of Archaeology was established in 1990; its main involvement has been concentrated on public awareness about the field of archaeological heritage.

Site Management Models

Three site management models involving NGOs have been experimented with recently: in Petra, in Wadi Rum, and at the Baptism site. All three sites fall within the boundaries of semi-autonomous regions—the Petra Regional Authority, the Aqaba Special Economic Zone (ASEZA), and the Jordan Valley Authority. These models are described here briefly. In the case of Petra, unlike the other two models, and in compliance with the Law of Antiquities, the site is managed by the Department of Antiquities. The U.S. NPS Operational Plan, submitted in 2000, is yet to be implemented. Its implementation will constitute a major step toward the establishment of a comprehensive policy for safeguarding Petra and the sustainable development of its region, as well as the implementation of much-needed sound management and conservation practices. Whereas PNT has been instrumental in initiating and following up cooperation between the U.S. NPS and the government, its future role in the implementation stage is currently under consideration. Because of lack of experience in site management, the government needs the assistance of an NGO—PNT or a similar body—that can serve as facilitator

FIGURE 7 Water channels. Courtesy of Petra National Trust

and catalyst between the U.S. NPS and the government to ensure adaptation of the plan to local conditions and constraints as well as its long-term continuation.

In the case of Wadi Rum, the Royal Society for the Conservation of Nature was contracted to prepare a master plan

FIGURE 8 *Cercaetus gallicus*. Courtesy of Petra National Trust

for the management of the area and to conduct training. The RSCN was successful on both counts: however, as the RSCN is specialized in the protection of natural parks and not in the preservation of cultural sites, its management plan reflected weakness in archaeological conservation. Despite its good performance, the regional authority under whose jurisdiction Wadi Rum falls preferred to manage the site itself rather than exercise the option of partnering with an NGO. It should be noted here that the initiative to contract an NGO to introduce more effective site management was promoted at the outset by the World Bank and not by the government..

The third model is the Baptism Site Commission, founded in 2002. It was established by royal decree and operates independently of the Ministry of Tourism, the Department of Antiquities, and the Jordan Valley Authority within whose boundaries it falls. While the Department of Antiquities retains responsibility for archaeological conservation, the Site Commission manages other aspects of the site.

The concept of establishing protected areas to manage cultural heritage sites in Jordan is still in its very early stages. The 1996 USAID study addressed important park policy issues by providing recommendations for a protected area policy and an integrated management system. It investigated several options but fell short of recommending a specific organizational structure. This document has not been activated, and to date there is no national policy streamlining the responsibility for the management and protection of the multitude of archaeological sites in Jordan.

Conclusion

Site management has been a concern for at least the past thirty-four years. As the region became more accessible, policy makers understood the importance of Petra and other sites for economic advancement. Hence the number of studies conducted and models adopted. There has been consensus in the government recently for the need to explore innovative approaches to site management and to allow NGOs to participate; however, it has been inconsistent in its approach, which has been prompted more by economic factors than preservation and protection, and it has hesitated to relinquish some

responsibility to NGOs. Instead of developing a unified park policy throughout Jordan, the government selected models that have resulted in overlapping responsibilities, duplication, and the ultimate fragmentation of the role of the Department of Antiquities. There is an urgent need for the parties concerned to come together to consolidate the numerous studies and their recommendations and to reevaluate the role of the Department of Antiquities and its appropriate position within the government, as well as its role vis-à-vis the geographic regions within the country; and to assess the management models adopted and emerge with an integrated nationwide policy for the protection of archaeological sites. The integrated approach being put forward here speaks to a complementary partnership between governmental and nongovernmental organizations in the field of site management, which is the most effective way for Jordan to achieve this objective. NGOs, unlike the government, are in the unique position of being nonprofit and, therefore, not motivated by economic gain; at the same time, they are not overburdened by bureaucracy, which gives them the ability to operate effectively. For this union to succeed, both the Department of Antiquities and related NGOs need to expand their capacity and hence their effectiveness. The department furthermore is required urgently to reinforce its role and to enhance its capacity to manage sites at Petra and elsewhere.

References

UNESCO. 1994. Petra National Park management plan. UNESCO, Paris.

U.S. National Park Service. 1968. Master plan for the protection and use of the Petra National Park. Petra National Trust, Amman, Jordan.

———. 2000. Petra Archaeological Park operating plan. Petra National Trust, Amman, Jordan.

USAID. 1996. Jordan's park policy project. Petra National Trust, Amman, Jordan.

US/ICOMOS. 1996. Study on the management analysis and recommendations for the Petra World Heritage Site. Petra National Trust, Amman, Jordan.

Privatization of State-owned Cultural Heritage: A Critique of Recent Trends in Europe

Gaetano Palumbo

Abstract: *Privatization, the market sale of cultural heritage properties belonging to the state, is a growing trend. Examples from Italy, Britain, and France show that this trend is not likely to stop, putting at risk the concept of the state as steward of public good. The risk for the resource itself is in its loss of authenticity following market-oriented attempts to develop it to enhance its economic value. This paper introduces the concepts of cultural heritage* exploitation *and* use *as two different models of heritage management. It argues that cultural heritage exploitation has only an apparent economic advantage but in reality is nonsustainable over the long term as it requires continuous reinvestment to remain competitive; cultural heritage use can be sustainable as it implies active involvement of the local community in the decision-making process and state–private partnerships in the process of development, conservation, management, and protection of the cultural resource.*

The subject of privatization of cultural heritage is vast, as each country has different legislation under which various forms of privatization or private input in heritage conservation and management may be allowed. Privatization may be limited to the management of services of a heritage place, such as ticketing, restaurants, general maintenance and upkeep, museum shops, security, and, in some cases, even inventory and conservation. In other cases, privatization refers to the sale of a scheduled building or site, for which change of use is allowed (which potentially takes the site out of public use). In still other cases, privatization refers to the selling of a heritage place to a private company so that it can be transformed into a tourist attraction.

In this paper privatization is discussed as one of the elements of *désétatisation,* a French term indicating decentraliza-

tion and the state's attempt to reduce expenditures. As mentioned above, there can be many forms of privatization in the cultural sphere.[1] This critique is limited to the actual sale of cultural heritage sites to private individuals or corporations, either for further development as cultural attractions or for other use.

Recent episodes are used to illustrate changes being introduced in some countries. For example, in Italy a century-long tradition of promoting public over private interests in heritage conservation is being dismantled in favor of an approach that sees privatization as the only cure to the problem of lack of maintenance and management. In Britain, an alarmed English Heritage realized perhaps too late that local history was at risk of being lost following the selling off of local council properties, including those of local and regional importance. These new and different approaches to managing cultural heritage mark a turning point in the traditional approach whereby government bodies are seen as most qualified and responsible for the conservation of cultural heritage sites.

The privatization of cultural heritage has always been considered by the proponents of "lighter" government (where state ownership of immovable property is reduced to an absolute minimum and most services are privatized) as a way to ease the burden of conserving, protecting, and managing so-called lesser heritage. If by "lesser heritage" is normally meant all those historic buildings and monuments that are of local or regional importance and not usually considered worth listing in national registers or being given special protection status, the distinction between major and minor heritage, between important and less important sites, is very dangerous and should be avoided. Altogether these buildings and sites form the character of historic towns and cultural landscapes, and their existence as an integrated system transforms these buildings into "heritage" and gives communities a cultural landscape in which they identify themselves (Settis 2002). It may be argued that it is not the change of ownership that modifies the physical structure of a town; however, if the change of ownership is also associated with radical change of use and the commercialization of public spaces, the effect can be disruptive for the sociocultural and physical structure of the town (Hassler, Algreen-Ussing, and Kohler 2002).

The exploitation of heritage sites by private entities is indeed more dynamic than that by public organizations. It is more market oriented, as income is needed to maintain the property and obtain a financial return. It is more customer oriented, as economic success is the result of strategies aimed at attracting more visitors and rewarding them with an experience that meets or exceeds their expectations. By allowing private individuals or corporations to buy heritage properties with the purpose of obtaining revenues from them (especially if such revenues are tied to the cultural marketing of the property), the central government accepts the principle that it is not able, as private enterprise is, to promote, market, and exploit all heritage sites and monuments under its jurisdiction and that private enterprises have the flexibility required to make a profitable business by "selling" heritage.

Why, then, criticize a model that seems to work? I argue that the privatization of cultural heritage is a risky business that may have some short-term economic advantage for the state and the private sector (which makes it so appealing), but in the long term it may weaken or destroy the trust that citizens have in the state as the steward of public good ("public good" being intended here not as commodity but as a political process) (Throsby 2002).

Noneconomic parameters in what is mainly an economic justification to privatize heritage places have often been ignored, but they should not be. Economists such as David Throsby, Arjo Klamer, and Peter Zuidhof have warned that especially in cultural heritage matters, the long-term economic advantage is not necessarily the one that produces revenue but the one that improves the well-being of the people (Klamer and Zuidhof 1999; Throsby 2002). Improving services with the help of the private sector is one thing; encouraging the private sector to support conservation and maintenance activities is another (Settis 2002). However, the hands-off approach that some governments are taking, where the selling off of sites and buildings of cultural importance is presented

as a revolutionary step rather than the extremely conservative approach that it is, makes the privatization of cultural heritage as a whole a very difficult topic to discuss.

Access by the private sector to the cultural industry is a trend that cannot be stopped; but its consequences must be better understood. More important, this access must be better regulated, especially in terms of controlling the quality of the private intervention and ensuring that the public benefit is enhanced rather than limited by the change in status of the cultural property.

In Italy, the present government's efforts to find financial support for its program of infrastructure development and tax reduction extend to the listing of many properties, including those scheduled for natural or cultural reasons, for possible sale directly or through competitive bidding. The original plan included the creation of a new holding, Patrimonio SpA, which translates as Heritage Inc., to which state properties could be transferred by a decree signed by the minister of finance (and endorsed by the minister of culture and the minister of environment in the case of scheduled properties). The properties on this list could be sold or given in concession to private enterprises. By a simple signature, the minister of finance could also transfer any of these properties to another holding, Infrastrutture SpA (Infrastructures, Inc.). The market value of the properties in this holding was intended to be used to issue bonds and as security for bank loans. The bank would, in effect, then become the new owner of the property until repayment of the loan.

Critics of this approach, which include Salvatore Settis, director of the Scuola Normale Superiore in Pisa and previously director of the Getty Research Institute in Los Angeles, have pointed out several issues:

- There was no need to include scheduled properties in the lists, as the state owns a large quantity of buildings and land having no cultural or environmental value.
- That they were included means that there is a complete lack of understanding of values other than purely economic ones.
- The laws accompanying the creation of these holdings, as well as those authorizing the direct sale of state properties to private companies, explicitly deny the Ministry of Cultural Heritage the right of first refusal. This has recently been put into practice with the sale to the Carlyle Group of the buildings of the state-owned tobacco company, Manifatture Tabacchi,

most of which were scheduled modernist buildings from the 1920s and 1930s, without informing the local authorities. In the case of the Manifatture buildings in Florence and Milan, projects had already been prepared—and paid for—by the city councils to transform them into community and art centers.

- The inclusion of many cultural heritage properties on these lists marks a worrying trend in the identification of these properties as moneymaking opportunities for the state to take advantage of their added cultural heritage value by selling and for the new owner to transform or resell.

- In the case of Italy, no prior assessments were made of the significance of these properties, and many nonscheduled properties put up for sale were actually worthy of scheduling, thus also showing a lack of commitment by the state to its own constitutional principles, according to which the public good takes precedence over economic considerations (Article 9 of the Italian constitution). The example of disused prisons and military barracks is particularly relevant, as not even the State Board of Architectural Heritage, the Soprintendenze, has protested their inclusion in the list of salable properties, and this when the cultural, historic, and social value of these properties is recognized internationally.

- Although a transitory and not a permanent regulation, the present evaluation of the market value of state properties made by the Demanio dello Stato, the authority that administers buildings and land owned by the state, is accompanied by a time limit of 120 days for the Soprintendenze to declare whether a site should not be put on sale because of its heritage value. Although in theory this time frame would allow such an evaluation to be conducted, in practical terms it is absolutely insufficient, given the work overload of every Soprintendenza in Italy. The invitation by the minister of culture to the Soprintendenti to take a site off the list of properties that can be sold, when in doubt, does not relieve critics' concerns about the consequences of this law in the long term, nor does the directive to the Soprintendenti by higher state hierarchies to use this power with discretion.

The Italian example has been followed by France, which has recently announced the sale of a number of buildings and landholdings, mostly belonging to the army or to various ministries (Masse-Stamberger and Richard 2004).

These examples show that there is a clash between different concepts of use of cultural heritage resources: one more market oriented, the other more inclined to accentuate the social value of cultural heritage. This is not limited to Italy; it is a global trend whose effects are visible in many countries.

The market approach may be defined as *cultural heritage exploitation* and the social approach as *cultural heritage use* (table 1). The first seeks economic return; the second looks at the broader role the resource can play in society, without limiting it to an economic one. The first identifies a basic value (frequently an aesthetic or a historic one) and markets it in order to promote the site; the second balances all the values and allows them to define the significance of the site. The first isolates the site from its surroundings, as it sees the resource as a single element; the second sees the site in its wider physical and social context. The first needs continuous reinvestment in terms of new infrastructure, new exhibitions, or restoration to determine success based on visitor numbers and straight economic return; the second creates the means for its own conservation, as it balances social and economic benefits by entering into the cultural sphere of the community. Since this protection is not based on massive restorations and interventions, it is locally apt and sustainable. It creates the opportunity for community involvement, which is not necessarily dedicated solely to tourism services but can also cover aspects of documentation, assessment, conservation, and education.

The local community in a cultural heritage exploitation approach is seen as being at the service of this initiative, by providing a labor force for all the activities generated by the tourism industry. In a cultural heritage use approach, the community "owns" the resource (not necessarily in a legal sense but rather in a social way) and organizes itself around this ownership.

The nonsustainability of the cultural heritage exploitation approach is demonstrated by the fact that rapid exploitation tends to degrade the resource, especially if reinvestments after the initial push, usually encouraged through bank loans or preliminary investments, are not adequate. The sustainability of the cultural heritage use approach is given by the involvement of the community and its understanding of the values of the resources and means to preserve these values without radically altering them.

In short, *exploitation* sees cultural heritage as a product to manipulate, a product that exists on its own and has

Table 1 Cultural Heritage: Exploitation or Use?

	Market Approach: Cultural Heritage "Exploitation"	Social Approach: Cultural Heritage "Use"
Economy	Seeks immediate economic return.	Does not consider economic value as most important.
Values	Marketing of limited sets of values, favoring those that can be easily sold to the public, such as aesthetic value.	All values shape the significance of the site, with high importance given to local interpretations and feelings about this heritage.
Context	Considers the site an isolated entity, a monument that has little relationship with its surroundings.	Considers the site part of a cultural continuum with its surroundings.
Management	Needs continuous reinvestment to maintain competitiveness.	Balances use and conservation.
Main Objective	Tourism	Public good
Local Community	Local community is in service to cultural heritage exploitation.	Local community participates in conservation.
Effects	Exploitation degrades the cultural resource.	Use adds value to the resource.
Sustainability	Nonsustainable	Sustainable

superficial links, if any, to society at large and to the local community in particular. The relationship to the resource is purely aesthetic for the consumer, purely economic for the manager. This is not an overly pessimistic view. Concepts of *edutainment,* theme parks and the like, where interpretations of past and present cultures are naive at best and deceptive at worst, are now seen also at the level of interpretation of cultural resources.

The other consequence of the indiscriminate sale of cultural heritage is the isolation of a few universally recognized monuments, thus severing the cultural relationship they have with their physical and social environment. The disruption of this continuity is what the critics of the indiscriminate sale and state hands-off policy fear the most. This is expressed by English Heritage in its 2002 *State of the Historic Environment,* where a generally good condition of protection and conservation for Grade I listed buildings does not extend to buildings of local value, which are being sold by cash-strapped local councils.

What is at risk with the present trend of privatization of cultural heritage sites is the loss of significance (as a balance and an expression of many values) and the loss of authenticity of the resource. In the longer term, this will translate into decreasing community interest, as the resource does not "belong" to them anymore, and decreasing visitor satisfaction, with dire consequences for a site that the private owner no longer sees as profitable, thus encouraging a process of rapid sale of nonprofitable properties or of their contents, such as furniture or art objects, to raise cash for repairs (English Heritage 2002). This has serious conse-

quences for the ability of state authorities to control the legislation protecting the resource. In the United Kingdom, for example, many manors and villas were destroyed by owners who were not able to maintain them, requiring that specific legislation be introduced to ensure their protection (Settis 2002). (See table 2.)

What is the alternative? How can private enterprise help cultural heritage conservation and not be part of the problem?

First, the hands-off policy of the state does not pay in the long term. Partnerships between state and private bodies should be strengthened, with the understanding that the advantage to the private sector comes especially from tax incentives rather than from theoretical, often illusory economic advantage. The result would be a general improvement in the social and economic condition of the community in which the site is located, because a conservation approach is more balanced than an aggressive strategy for extracting income. Many economists are now looking at cultural heritage sites in a community as an element that contributes to its well-being even in the absence of direct moneymaking opportunities. These sites, if well managed, and the benefits they provide in terms of generating culture, social cohesion, and a sense of ownership are sufficient to start a process of upgrading and economic improvement that can be assessed and properly evaluated.

Given the trends observed in Europe, there is reason for pessimism. If, on one side, there are opportunities for private enterprises to successfully contribute to cultural heritage conservation and to the public good, if states realize the benefit of such partnerships, pessimism still prevails because of the

Table 2 Privatization: Does It Work?

Expectations	Reality
Sale of property frees the state of administrative and financial burden and the property is better taken care of.	Private company reduces expenditures on conservation and protection to maximize revenues.
The new private ownership can make money from the resource.	Conservation costs may be higher than revenues, thus forcing the company to either resell or reduce the exploitation of the site.
State gains from the sale of the property.	State may be forced to pay for the site's conservation if the private company fails to do so. The immediate revenue from the sale may also be absorbed or canceled by expenditures required to provide public services, such as road access or other needed infrastructure.
Site increases in economic and cultural value following its privatization and development.	Site loses authenticity after inappropriate interventions and excessive development and/or change of use.
Investment in cultural heritage calls for more investments.	Scarce revenues do not justify reinvestments.
U.S. model shows that large museums and historic properties can be private and make a profit.	There is no profit without large donor base (difficult to achieve in other countries with more restrictive fiscal legislation concerning donations).

strong temptation of public officers to equate private sector participation in heritage conservation with its privatization.

Public administrators, unfortunately, lack the capacity to think and program long term. Although cultural heritage management curricula now exist in many institutions of higher learning in Europe, it is still difficult for these newly formed programs to have a say in the processes of urban, economic, and cultural heritage planning, especially at the local level. The development of these new professional programs cannot, alone, help to better manage cultural heritage assets if local communities do not realize that their history, memory, and, ultimately, social cohesion are at risk if they fall victim to the sirens of hastily accepted economic models.

Notes

1   John Myerscough (2001) illustrates several aspects of privatization in the cultural sector: *plural funding* (search for funding—and finance—from nonpublic sources); *purchaser provider splits* (separating the purchase of public services from their provision); *outsourcing* (contracting out by government department or public undertaking to independent for-profit or not-for-profit suppliers). He adds that "privatization" is also applied to the "process of giving state institutions more responsibility and freedom of action, by simplifying their financial regulations or reconstituting them as non-departmental public bodies or as non-profit companies or trusts or foundations" (p. 8).

References

English Heritage. 2002. *The State of the Historic Environment Report 2002.* Accessed at http://www.english-heritage.org.uk/sher/report.htm.

Hassler, U., G. Algreen-Ussing, and N. Kohler. 2002. *Cultural Heritage and Sustainable Development in SUIT.* Accessed at http://www.lema.ulg.ac.be/research/suit/Reports/Public/SUIT5.2c_Paper.pdf.

Klamer, A., and P. Zuidhof. 1999. The values of cultural heritage: Merging economic and cultural appraisals. In *Economics and Heritage Conservation,* 23–61. Los Angeles: Getty Conservation Institute.

Masse-Stamberger, B., and T. Richard. 2004. A vendre, cause réforme de l'Etat. L'Express, 15 March 2004. Accessed at http://www.lexpress.fr/info/economie/dossier/etatargent/dossier.asp.

Myerscough, J. 2001. *Transversal Reviews of National Cultural Policies: National Institutions in Transition: Désétatisation and Privatisation. Final Report.* Strasbourg: Council of Europe, Council of Cultural Co-operation. CC-CULT (2001)10, accessed at http://www.coe.int/T/E/Cultural Co-operation/Culture/Resources/Publications/CC-CULT(2001)10_EN.pdf.

Settis, S. 2002. *Italia SpA: L'assalto al patrimonio culturale.* Torino: Einaudi.

Throsby, D. 2002. Cultural capital and sustainability concepts in the economics of cultural heritage. In *Assessing the Values of Cultural Heritage,* M. de la Torre, 101–18. Los Angeles: The Getty Conservation Institute.

Regional Site Management Planning and Training: The SPAFA Example in Southeast Asia

Pisit Charoenwongsa

Abstract: This paper examines the Southeast Asian regional approach adopted for the management of archaeological sites as encapsulated in the training programs of the Regional Centre for Archaeology and Fine Arts (SPAFA) of the Southeast Asian Ministers of Education Organisation. It seeks to show how SPAFA, based in Bangkok, Thailand, has achieved a balanced approach that can satisfy the varying demands of all the stakeholders concerned and overcome constraints often dictated by economic necessities. In particular, attention is paid to promoting the active engagement of local communities in archaeological site management.

With the introduction of training workshops, the Regional Centre for Archaeology and Fine Arts (SPAFA) of the Southeast Asian Ministers of Education Organisation (SEAMO) enables professionals in various disciplines, such as cultural specialists and managers, to undertake sustainable heritage preservation projects throughout Southeast Asia. Providing skilled management techniques is just one facet of this regional center's commitment to a successful ongoing training program.

As an intergovernmental organization, or IGO, SPAFA has extensive experience dealing with governmental and nongovernmental agencies in the public and private sectors alike. This provides a sound understanding of the issues involved in developing training programs that address the challenges that must be met to achieve a balanced approach to site management.

Why Adopt a Holistic Approach?

The policies and management of archaeological sites take place in a complex setting involving various stakeholders, sometimes more than one donor and more than one implementing organization or agency.

The framework of economics, trade, and politics provides a wider backdrop that often makes it difficult to follow a cohesive approach that can achieve a balance among donor and recipient needs. Thus there is a need to consider the management of an archaeological site as a specific development project but in a broader economic and political context. For this reason, all stakeholders need to develop an understanding of one another's perceptions and values, so that potential conflict between different stakeholders can be managed and productive working relationships achieved. This requires "cultural analysis" (involving historical and archaeological research and site evaluation) during planning and implementation. In other words, a holistic approach needs to be adopted in management planning and training. This should be seen as an opportunity to ensure viability and sustainability.

The use of cultural analysis to develop a better understanding of values in a particular community can contribute to the following long-term goals:

- Equitable sharing of natural resources in social and economic development;
- Reduction of poverty through effective and sustainable project implementation;
- Increased sustainability through the fulfillment of community-based action (known as demand-oriented community action), commitment, and ownership; and
- Increased understanding, tolerance, and respect for cultural diversity.

The Need to Innovate

Over the past decade, the objectives of development programs have shifted from direct intervention to capacity building through partnerships, with "recipients" as stakeholders who participate in and own the development process. This is because development can be defined as a transformation that reflects improvement for all sectors of society—a better standard of living and access to health care and education—and thus enables poor people to have better opportunities. All too often, however, advocacy for such participatory processes is only abstract or academic. The need to innovate, to be "inclusive," can foster equitable economic development. This is crucial for a successful outcome.

Quite often, the failure—or limited success—of many management interventions can be attributed to a lack of cultural sensitivity in the planning and implementation processes. This has a negative impact because development policies conducted in a top-down manner do not accommodate local knowledge and experience, and hence overlook communities or individuals as contributors or innovators. This, in turn, has negative consequences for the achievement of sustainability and the future independence of donor-initiated programs or projects because the crucial importance of capacity building is neglected. Only when there is mutual understanding, tolerance, and respect for cultural diversity and people's life contexts—so that the local community is involved in design, planning, and implementation—can development programs and projects truly succeed.

Learning from the Past for a Better Future

SPAFA has been collaborating with governments, international and academic organizations, universities, other not-for-profit organizations, and the private sector for the past eighteen years. Thus it has a wealth of experience to draw on, and even past mistakes can provide valuable lessons.

In November 2002 SPAFA held its first international conference on the theme, "Issues of Culture, Context, and Choice in Development." The conference came about in response to the recognition that there is an urgent need to ensure the successful outcome of "responsible" development policies. Thus its major aim was to provide vital stimulus to the conceptualization and conduct of development projects, including management interventions at archaeological sites.

At its close, I stated my belief that the conference would contribute to inculcating in the implementers of development projects the need to emphasize cultural context as a priority for the benefit of the communities for which these projects are intended. The forthcoming training program is a tangible outcome of the conference and demonstrates that SPAFA was able to set in motion a train of events that place culture on the development map as a central issue.

The conference brought together representatives from the governmental, nongovernmental, and corporate sectors. Discussions focused on the issues raised here: different management models, models of private–public partnership, and local community participation. Corporate or private sector involvement is seen as key to privatizing the alleviation of poverty. By capitalizing on the business skills of the corporate sector, skills that are usually lacking in government agencies and NGOs, a way forward can be provided for income generation through cooperation and mutual benefit, not just donation. Participatory, mutually beneficial projects truly can happen. Moreover, they can be sustainable and self-funding.

At SPAFA, we are now devising the content for a training course in managing the integration of culture in development projects. The course will address the fundamental issues of ownership, governance, consensus-building processes, and rights-based approaches, choice and knowledge, perceptions, honesty, and tolerance. I believe that SPAFA's direction here can be usefully applied in the future, specifically, in providing guidance regarding innovative approaches for the policy and management of archaeological sites.

SPAFA and Training

SPAFA began to conduct ASEAN Foundation–funded training workshops, "Training for Managing the Integration of Culture into Development Programs," in August 2003. The course objectives were to

- increase awareness of the need to include cultural dimensions in development initiatives;
- highlight cultural opportunities to facilitate innovative and participatory programs;
- equip participants to plan and implement programs that are sustainable because they are culturally integrated;
- devise tools for identifying and managing potential situations of conflict;
- facilitate access to resources; and
- strengthen regional networks.

It must be noted that the training program is not designed specifically for archaeologists. As the experts, archaeologists provide key discipline-based knowledge, but in the planning and implementation stages of the management of an archaeological site, many players are involved.

The SPAFA training programs that are being developed are aimed at those people who share an interest in the preservation of cultural heritage. Participants from all ten member countries (Brunei, Cambodia, Indonesia, Laos, Malaysia, Myanmar, Philippines, Singapore, Thailand, and Vietnam) will be invited. The immediate beneficiaries of the workshops will include project managers from donor and implementing agencies and organizations and technical and cultural specialists. The ultimate beneficiaries will be the grassroots stakeholders of development projects. It is these people, working alongside the experts, who also have to be aware of the critical importance of fully integrating culture into any sustainable heritage project.

A total of forty participants per workshop is viable, based on the successful experience of the August 2003 workshop. University faculty and cultural specialists from the ASEAN countries as well as cultural and technical experts from international organizations such as UNESCO and ICCROM will teach the workshops. They will instill knowledge about how to plan and implement sustainable programs that are integrated in the recipient culture. In this respect, more innovative and participatory site management planning will be achieved. Moreover, potential conflicts will be identified, and methods to manage these conflict situations will be devised.

The success of the training program will be evaluated as follows:

- Workshop participants will be asked to write a report on their individual management planning projects. They can comment on how the workshop helped to shape and determine improvements in sustainable outcomes. Based on positive (and any negative) feedback, the training program can be reviewed and reassessed before further training is carried out.
- Previous participants will be invited to facilitate future workshops.
- Final evaluation of the training workshops will be conducted.
- A guidelines handbook will be developed from the outcomes of the training workshops. This handbook will serve as a reference for further discussions and will include practical activities and examples for training purposes.

This type of training is an exciting departure for SPAFA. It represents a new and innovative Southeast Asian response that aims to address the root cause that can undermine the successful outcome of any management practice when it is not culturally conceived.

Interpretation as Preservation: Rationale, Tools, and Challenges

Neil Silberman and Dirk Callebaut

Abstract: This paper surveys some of the new philosophical approaches and technological tools for the public presentation of archaeological sites and historic monuments and landscapes that have been developed in Europe in recent years. It suggests that the interpretation of the significance of historical and archaeological remains is an essential component of physical conservation. In particular, it describes the central concepts of the Ename Charter Initiative, carried out under the sponsorship of ICOMOS, which seeks to establish a set of international professional standards for the interpretation of public heritage resources. The draft charter makes recommendations for the preparation of school enrichment programs, public outreach, university heritage curricula, and professional training in interpretive methodology. This paper highlights the motivations for the proposed charter and some of the most important background considerations. Finally, it discusses the practical advantages of such a set of general international guidelines—and the ideological challenge of avoiding cultural homogenization in their formulation and implementation.

Europe—especially in its rapidly expanding incarnation as the European Union—possesses an extraordinary quantity of recognized, preserved, and heavily visited historical monuments and archaeological sites. These range in magnitude from World Heritage Sites and international cultural attractions to regional landmarks to places of strictly local significance. Likewise, their states of preservation, presentation, and maintenance vary widely, from well equipped, well staffed, and packed with satisfied visitors to crumbling, abandoned, and all too often littered with garbage and scarred by graffiti. As the other papers in this volume clearly demonstrate, the situation is universal, and archaeologists everywhere are playing an increasingly important role in addressing the central challenges of conservation—both in planning and in the physical preservation of significant material remains.

It has become abundantly clear that the activity of *physical* conservation, although the indispensable core and focus of all attempts to preserve the material heritage for future generations, is entangled in a dense web of political, economic, social, and even psychological relationships that—if ignored—can doom even the most sophisticated restoration projects to neglect and eventual destruction (Hall and McArthur 1998). Thus the initial stage of professionalizing and codifying the international standards for physical preservation (exemplified by the 1964 Charter of Venice and the 1992 Malta Convention) has been broadened and strengthened by the formulation of international standards on professional training, heritage tourism, and cultural site management, among others (Petzet and Ziesemer 2000). All have addressed the importance of site interpretation in varying degrees of detail but have rarely examined the relationship among the various types of interpretation that might be subtly connected to the success or ultimate failure of continuing preservation efforts at a heritage site.

As we suggest here, the modern social function of interpretation—its modes, its audiences, and the various public, private, and professional interests that determine its form and meanings—is of paramount concern. The local community's general and personal identification with the site, no less than the sophistication of the formulation and presentation of its significance by (usually) outside scholars, designers, and educators, can determine whether it will be maintained and protected by everyone, from the mayor to the members of the local preservation society to the general public to the neighbors or even to a bored, unemployed seventeen-year-old with a can of spray paint.

*   *   *

In recent years the importance of interpretation has been acknowledged among international heritage professionals, and the range of practical applications and scholarly literature on this subject has expanded enormously (e.g., Jameson 1997; Little 2002; Uzzell and Ballantyne 1999). Traditional didactic, museum-type text displays are now used primarily when budgetary constraints mandate only the cheapest, no-frills presentation—not by choice. More creative and energetic interpretive solutions, such as special-interest or thematic guided tours, costumed or character-based interpreters, special educational activities, and interactive applications and virtual reality experiences, are usually employed when the project budget permits. But they are of widely differing cost, quality, and technical means. And their impact on visitors, on attendance figures, and indeed on the perception of the site as a whole among the local community has only now begun to be studied in great detail.

Among the increasingly popular multimedia solutions —especially virtual reconstructions—a basic problem exists. Scientific standards of evidence and proper archaeological documentation, through which the virtual reconstruction might have a demonstrable connection with reality, are subjects that are widely discussed but not yet resolved (Frischer, Niccolucci, and Ryan 2002). A common scientific solution— to use conspicuously unrealistic schematic models that allow for incompleteness—often fail to capture the attention and imagination of visitors (especially younger visitors, accustomed from infancy to watching television and playing video games). Yet the most elaborate of the virtual presentations, loosed from the bonds of what is perceived as overly aggressive scholarly oversight, are so perfect in their vivid re-creations that they are sometimes more Hollywood than heritage.

The gulf between scholarship and entertainment is itself part of a central philosophical problem in heritage interpretation today. In an era when public culture budgets are shrinking and cultural institutions of all kinds are being forced to be self-sustaining, the viability of a preservation and presentation project is, in the long run, often tied to its success in stimulating economic development—by paid admissions, subsidiary sales of postcards and other museum shop items, employment opportunities, and a steady flow of tourist rev-

enue for hotels, shops, and restaurants in the immediate vicinity (e.g., Leask and Yeoman 1999). Finances and balance sheets are the real tyrants in this age of increasingly self-supporting culture. Everything may look perfect to the invited dignitaries and guests at an elaborately preserved and interpreted site on a festive opening day. But three to five years later, when unrealistic expectations of increased visitation have failed to materialize and the costs of adequate staffing, maintenance, and regular content updating have soared, its physical state and its once-enthusiastic acceptance by its promoters and the general public may have radically changed for the worse.

*   *   *

These are some of the challenges regarding the wider roles of interpretation in the larger preservation effort that led to the idea for the Ename Charter Initiative, "Authenticity, Intellectual Integrity and Sustainable Development in the Public Presentation of Archaeological and Historical Sites and Landscapes." In 2004 three preliminary drafts of the charter text were produced by the staff of the Ename Center under the sponsorship of the Institute of the Archaeological Heritage of the Flemish Community of Belgium and the Province of East-Flanders—both longtime supporters of the public presentation program at the site of Ename. The initial charter drafts have been circulated for continuing review and revision under the auspices of ICOMOS and are available for general review.[1]

A central theme is the importance of integrated planning—in which the interpretation is not seen merely as the attractive or enlightening feature that is meant to fill the silences and empty spaces of a physical site. Interpretation must effectively communicate significance, and it must be the rationale for the preservation project itself. The present charter draft text is divided into four sections: scientific and professional guidelines; planning, funding, and management; tourism aspects; and heritage education. The section on scientific standards stresses the importance of scholarly standards for virtual reconstructions and other computer re-creations and underlines the dangers of interpretive technology that is too elaborate or more concerned with visitor satisfaction than historical accuracy. The section dealing with the integrated planning of site presentation projects offers recommendations for cooperative strategies in which scholars, managers, and community members set quantifiable and achievable goals for heritage projects—especially in regard to educational and social goals for the local population beyond the mere raising of tourist revenues. The section on tourism aspects deals with sustainability and quality-of-life issues, in which realistic projections of site carrying capacity are determined at the outset and the final form of the heritage site's presentation is designed, not as a conspicuous "tourist attraction," but as a natural part of the community's landscape and daily patterns of life. Finally, the section on heritage education stresses the need for programs aimed at four distinct audiences: local school children, adults in the local community, university students, and heritage professionals. The goal is to address the most common problems that time and again have doomed lovingly preserved sites to become deteriorating eyesores in just a few years.

Regarding the physical infrastructure of interpretive programs, the present draft of the Ename Charter makes some general recommendations. The careful consideration of size, scale, intrusiveness, and appropriate technology must be one of the first elements in the planning of a preservation project—and not solely on the basis of educational or informational criteria but also on the kind of infrastructure that a particular site is capable of supporting in a sustainable, long-term way. Budgets available or anticipated in succeeding years for proper staffing, maintenance, and security should become a primary factor in determining the ambitiousness of the presentation at the start.

With regard to the information conveyed in the interpretation, particularly archaeological sites, a basic method of allowing visitors to recognize the difference between authentic remains and conjectured reconstructions—without detracting from the coherence of the presentation—must somehow be made. An even more complex challenge is accommodating sometimes widely differing meanings of the site and possible relationships to it by young, old, local, foreign, male, and female visitors. The primary significance of a castle kitchen, stable, or chapel, for example, is neither single nor unequivocal to various visitors. And this is where the usefulness of interactive installations is particularly evident; permitting visitors to explore a wide range of possible interpretations offers a flexible, personalized approach.

In the larger issue of project planning, continuous, close consultation with the local community is stressed. The charter draft suggests that representatives of the local community be meaningfully involved in the creation of their own historical self-representation and that they be given the opportunity to offer comments and constructive suggestions at every stage of the work. In addition, the physical impact likely to be felt by the residents around an interpreted site must also be considered and carefully balanced with the needs of touristic development and effective integration with the local economy.

Last, it is stressed that raising of visitor attendance figures or increasing visitor attendance alone should not be the only target or criterion of success. The presentation must also serve a range of educational and social objectives for the benefit of the local community. These may include special educational programs, training and employment opportunities in the interpretive programs, and regularly scheduled community activities. The underlying rationale for all of these recommendations is the achievement of a basic and far-reaching transformation—not of an excavated site into a beautifully and entertainingly presented site but rather of an excavated site into an active, dynamic cultural institution within a living community.

*   *   *

We welcome input, suggestions, and reactions to the ICOMOS-Ename Charter as it is expanded and improved through intensive review and revision under the auspices of ICOMOS. But it may be worthwhile to skip ahead briefly to consider the possibility that some day, in some form, an international charter on interpretive standards and techniques may indeed be adopted and widely accepted. Will that solve all our problems? It has long been assumed that increasing the quality or extent of site interpretation will increase public awareness and thus interest in participating in the wider preservation cause itself. But is this always true? Will we pay enough attention to both the art of creating vivid public interpretations and the social significance of the newly established heritage site as an element in the complex landscape of a modern community?

Indeed, the positive impact of interpretation on preservation is not to be taken for granted. Recent studies (e.g., Lowenthal 2002) and our experience in European heritage projects have shown that in the planning stages, if the right balance is not achieved between the contribution of outside professionals and the input from the local community, the preservation project, even if successful, can appear to local residents as an outside imposition—like a shopping mall or a private theme park—with solely or mainly economic significance for the community. If it succeeds, the commercial benefits will make those with a direct economic stake in its success or failure potentially great supporters of preservation. Yet it can also sow resentment among those not immediately benefiting from the gains, and who often suffer from the successful site's side effects—a lack of parking, traffic congestion, and disruption of normal routines. It can thus be dismissed as "someone else's" monument, an alien intrusion not meaningfully integrated into the memories, stories, and attitudes that constitute the entire community's shared identity.

Thus the key linkage between interpretation and preservation lies not only in professional creativity, technology, and rational planning but also in the intensity and honesty of interaction with the local community and in the depth of commitment to creating a valuable local institution—sustainable in the long run not because of how it looks or what information it contains but because of how it functions within the community. Its sustainability is a function of its social relevance and benefit to the local inhabitants. And that modern dimension of heritage must become an integral part of preservation planning.

There is no question that interpretation has great potential for stimulating public interest in preservation. But it can only do so when all of the potential preservers—from scholars to design consultants to heritage administrators to businesspeople to the seventeen-year-old with a can of spray paint—are meaningfully involved in what is perceived as a community effort and have reason to consider the site not only "theirs" but also an important part of their lives. That is an intellectual and social challenge that any true preservationist of the twenty-first century must increasingly be forced to confront.

Notes

1 The initial charter drafts may be accessed at http://www. enamecenter.org/pages/public_progr_charter.html.

References

Frischer, B., F. Niccolucci, and N. Ryan. 2002. From CVR to CVRO: The past, present, and future of cultural virtual reality. *British Archaeological Reports* 834:7–18.

Hall, C. M., and S. McArthur. 1998. *Integrated Heritage Management: Principles and Practice.* London: The Stationery Office.

Jameson, J. H. 1997. *Presenting Archaeology to the Public: Digging for Truths.* Walnut Creek, Calif.: Altamira Press.

Leask, A., and I. Yeoman, eds. 1999. *Heritage Visitor Attractions: An Operations Management Perspective.* London: Cassell.

Little, B., ed. 2002. *Public Benefits of Archaeology.* Gainesville: University Press of Florida.

Lowenthal, D. 2002. The past as a theme park. In *Theme Park Landscapes: Antecedents and Variants,* ed. T. Young and R. Riley, 11–24. Washington, D.C.: Dumbarton Oaks Press.

Petzet, M., and J. Ziesemer, eds. 2000. *International Charters for Conservation and Restoration.* Paris: International Council on Monuments and Sites.

Uzzell, D., and R. Ballantyne, eds. 1999. *Contemporary Issues in Heritage Interpretation: Problems and Prospects.* London: The Stationery Office.

Preservation of Heritage Sites in the Caribbean: The Experience of the Brimstone Hill Fortress National Park of St. Kitts and Nevis

Larry Armony

Abstract: *St. Kitts and Nevis are part of a group of Caribbean islands that were once prosperous sugar colonies. Most of the country's people are of African ancestry—a consequence of the infamous Atlantic slave trade—with some Europeans, Asians (Indians), and Amerindians. The intangible culture is a syncretic blend of these ethnicities, but the built cultural heritage derives mainly from Europe. As the islands moved toward independence, for the most part the inhabitants eschewed physical reminders of the colonial past. This paper discusses a parallel movement to protect the forts, greathouses, and other colonial structures because of their perceived heritage value. It focuses on the Brimstone Hill Fortress National Park Society (BHFNPS), which, from its beginnings in 1965 as an elitist and seemingly Eurocentric clique, has evolved into a more egalitarian organization that recognizes and promotes the fact that structures such as Brimstone Hill Fortress embody the contributions of the colonized and are testimony to the multicultural nature of Caribbean society. The inscription of the fortress on the World Heritage List and the process of application for nomination have taught valuable lessons and provided impetus to the growing recognition by the people of the value of such sites.*

St. Kitts and Nevis are two islands that constitute one independent sovereign state, referred to as the Federation of St. Kitts (or sometimes St. Christopher) and Nevis. Located at the northeastern curve of the arc of Caribbean islands that extend eastward from the tip of Florida and then southward to the South American mainland, this nation-state is just 270 square kilometers in area and has a population of 45,000.

The islands of the eastern Caribbean were once sugar colonies of England, France, and the Netherlands. Today, the Dutch islands are semiautonomous territories; the French islands are departments of France; and some of the British islands, like St. Kitts and Nevis, are independent states, while a few of the smaller ones are still colonies. Some among the former and present British colonies have come together to share judicial, monetary, and economic services as the Organization of Eastern Caribbean States (OECS). The Caribbean Community (CARICOM) is a large trade grouping of former British colonies and now includes Haiti and the former Dutch mainland colony of Surinam.

The people of the OECS are predominantly of African ancestry, descended from those brought in bondage during the appalling Atlantic slave trade of the sixteenth through nineteenth century. There are sprinklings of ethnic Europeans (French and English), Asians (Indians), and native Caribs, with a significant proportion combining in various degrees the major ethnic groups of the world. The culture of the Caribbean, as expressed especially in its intangible forms, comprises a syncretic blend deriving mainly from Africa and Europe but including East Indian and Amerindian elements. Its systems of law and governance are European.

For the people of the young nations that emerged in the 1960s, 1970s, and 1980s, some questions inevitably arose: To what structures and institutions could they justly lay claim? What could they embrace in affirmation of a new and sovereign identity? The built structures, after all, spoke of an era of colonial exploitation and neglect by European powers. How could they identify with the ruins of plantation factories and greathouses abandoned by absentee "aristocrats" after sugar had become unprofitable, and with Brimstone Hill Fortress and the Forts Charleses and Georges replicated throughout the chain of islands and seen as symbols of slavery and oppression?

The purely African material heritage was ephemeral, not readily apprehended. And there was little knowledge of or, where there was, no value attributed to the remains of the indigenous Amerindian societies. As a result, "culture" became confined to and defined by performances in dance, music, storytelling, and festivals where African survivals seemed clear and evident. Yet it is increasingly becoming apparent to those students of Caribbean history and culture who are unfettered by the neocolonialist perspectives perpetuated by regional academia and influenced by a more holistic scholarship expressed by anthropology, archaeology, and sociology that all areas of Caribbean culture, including built structures, are syncretic expressions incorporating elements from Africa, Europe, native America, and, in some cases, Asia.

Culturally, the people are indeed distinctive, formed by environment and history. The more enduring elements of the built cultural heritage, made of stone—the forts, churches, mill houses—are, in a sense, products of Europe and Africa in the Caribbean. And just as (by way of one example repeated throughout history everywhere) the English today proudly present Viking archaeological sites, Roman walls, and Norman castles—the cultural remains of conquerors and plunderers—as aspects of British heritage (which, it must be added, provide also a basis for a booming tourism industry), so it is that the people of the Caribbean, are the *inheritors* of a colonial legacy that can be used for their education and edification and for the creation of revenue and employment.

These are important —indeed, crucial—considerations: for these countries, still afflicted by poverty, facing a challenging future in a globalized world, and increasingly dependent on tourism, are allowing the tremendous resources of their rich and diverse cultural and natural heritage to be eroded, and to be destroyed, day by day. The story of the Brimstone Hill Fortress, however, provides an alternative option. The Brimstone Hill Fortress National Park Society (BHFNPS) is a nonprofit voluntary organization, registered as a company, and empowered by legislation to administer the Brimstone Hill Fortress National Park, which is the property of the state.

The BHFNPS was founded in 1965 on the initiative of the then British colonial administrator and comprised for the most part members of the plantocracy and representatives of the mercantile community—who were essentially the same people or their agents. The founding members also included, however, the chief minister at the time, an erstwhile adversary of British colonialism and advocate of the working-class descendants of African slaves who only thirteen years before had attained the right to vote for limited representative government.

The objective was to acquire management control over the extensive but deteriorating complex of man-made struc- tures on the upper slopes and top of the volcanic cone called Brimstone Hill and to rescue, reinstate, and restore the once-magnificent fortress often referred to as the "Gibraltar of the West Indies." The human, material, and financial resources of the sugar estates, the wealthy merchant houses, and the government were brought to bear on the immense task of clearing, stabilizing, restoring, and—very important—maintaining Brimstone Hill.

In 1987 the National Conservation and Environment Protection Act, "in recognizing its national and international significance as an outstanding cultural and historical resource," declared Brimstone Hill a national park and empowered the BHFNPS "to make and enforce regulations for (its) management and administration." This was a signal acknowledgment of the accomplishments of the BHFNPS under the visionary leadership of D. Lloyd Matheson, president from 1967 to 1989.

Also in 1987, the BHFNPS, encouraged by the interest of the Caribbean Conservation Association, prepared and submitted a nomination dossier to the World Heritage Committee. After nearly two years of back-and-forth letters and telegrams, it was informed that nomination applications were to be submitted only by the state party. Another, more developed nomination dossier was prepared by the BHFNPS and presented in 1990 to the state party (government) through the Ministry of Education for submission to UNESCO. This dossier has never been found, neither in the files of the Ministry of Education nor at the offices of UNESCO or the World Heritage Centre.

In retrospect, this seeming setback proved fortuitous. The work of the BHFNPS had become more complex as successive externally funded projects were executed and the rate of visitation steadily increased. Beginning in 1990, volunteerism (with Peace Corps park managers playing an important role) gave way to a more professional management structure. In that year and in the years following, local people were employed in various newly created positions. There evolved a shift in emphasis in the presentation of the fortress and the interpretation of its history from a mainly Eurocentric and segregationist perspective to an approach that recognized the African and Creole involvement in the construction, maintenance, and defense of the fortress. Archival and archaeological investigations had been undertaken in the pursuit of historical balance. At the same time, the practice, as developed in the earlier period, of procuring professional and technical expertise as the needs arose was continued, and it remains an important element of the modus operandi of management.

Then, in 1996, at a UNESCO-sponsored workshop for the directors of culture for CARICOM member countries held in St. Kitts, the BHFNPS was made aware of the new requirements of the World Heritage Committee: management plans, national legislation, and buffer zones. Thus in 1998 it was better prepared to submit a new nomination proposal, one that was more complete and representative of the history and culture of the country. After preparation and submission to the minister representing the state party, it was, with his permission, dispatched by the society via courier to the World Heritage Centre.

In late 1999 at the twenty-third session of the World Heritage Committee the Brimstone Hill Fortress National Park was inscribed on the World Heritage List of Cultural Properties of "universal cultural value." The inscription reads: "The Brimstone Hill Fortress National Park is an exceptional and well-preserved example of seventeenth- and eighteenth-century military architecture in a Caribbean context. Designed by the British and built by African slave labor, the Brimstone Hill Fortress is testimony to European colonial expansion, the Atlantic slave trade, and the emergence of new societies in the Caribbean."

Meanwhile, the organization entrusted with the management of this national, regional, and universal monument had been keeping pace with the new developments while maintaining its fundamental commitment to the proper management, preservation, and protection of the fortress. There is now, moreover, greater recognition by the people of the country of the value of Brimstone Hill and of their responsibility as custodians of the World Heritage Site. The site is a major tourist attraction, but it is also a popular venue for picnics, family reunions, weddings, and concerts. It is a place where the people can, through its interpretation, learn more about their history.

PART THREE

Conserving Archaeological Sites: New Approaches and Techniques

Introduction

Neville Agnew

The papers in Part III address sitewide, holistic conservation and discuss the challenges of conserving archaeological sites from different but coherently consistent perspectives. Frank Matero's perceptive overview synthesizes advances in thinking, which are exemplified by two pragmatic and yet creative case studies by Giorgio Buccellati and by Martha Demas and Neville Agnew. Their approaches to the conservation and interpretation of fragile sites—one mud-brick, the other a fossil imprint site—could be effectively implemented only as a result of the archaeologist and the conservation professional working in tandem.

The enormous range of responses of various materials to deteriorative influences is certainly widely realized, perhaps more so by conservators than by archaeologists. Yet this realization must be brought explicitly to the fore when undertaking fieldwork. I was reminded of this recently when looking at the sandstone Colossi of Memnon on the floodplain of the Nile. They sit with their feet almost in the river, having endured, though much weathered, more than three millennia, and expecting to go on forever: *sedent aeternumque sedebunt.* Excavated earthen sites of similar antiquity can be expected usually to survive perhaps a few years before disappearing with hardly a trace remaining. Acknowledging this great variability in materials' susceptibility is among the first steps on the path to designing appropriate protection and conservation strategies, and the two case studies do just this before consideration of other ways in which further needs may be met.

Matero states that archaeological sites, like all places of human activity, are constructed and that conservation still begins and ends as an interpretation of the site. The aerial view of Buccellati's site of Tell Mozan shows what Matero means but reminds us that the second "construction" is but liberating the shell of the ancient site. Conservation as interpretation of an excavated past is no less well illustrated by this image. We also see in the image key points in new approaches and techniques to the conservation of archaeological sites: a demonstration of the critical importance of collaboration between archaeology and conservation for in situ preservation during excavation; and an example of the increasing emphasis on preventive conservation through an innovative, reversible shelter that itself interprets the site.

Buccellati calls for a true partnership of archaeology and conservation, each informing the other. His approach achieves protection of the excavated mud-brick walls through a synthesis of protection that is modular and progresses simultaneously with excavation and archaeological interpretation. He insists that conservation is (or should be) intrinsic to excavation for the good reason that "it teaches us about excavation." To achieve this synthesis, he calls for an educational component in the training of both archaeologists and conservators. In northern Syria, where it is possible to see the gamut of approaches to preservation of excavated mud-brick of great antiquity, from wholesale reconstruction to stabilization (itself displaying many techniques), his treatment of the excavated structures at Tell Mozan immediately affords the viewer a reading of the architecture. But Buccellati explores the consequences of this quickly and easily reversible protection further: it provides to the archaeologist a perceptual enrichment of the excavated walls—when the protection is in place "wholly unexpected relationships emerge"—not the least of which is to enhance the understanding and enthusiasm of the local people for the project.

The rigorous analysis for decision making about conservation, further scientific study, and whether the site should be opened to visitation or moved to a museum or buried again, coupled with a technically sophisticated reburial design, itself to be sustained by a straightforward monitoring and maintenance plan, is presented in the paper on Laetoli. Here a case of reexcavation and conservation of a previously excavated and reburied site of the first scientific rank is presented. This remote site within a natural and cultural landscape presents an interesting example of the mutability of values, since following exhaustive scientific study of the hominid trackway, the scientific information perforce diminished but was replaced by a growing awareness of the symbolic importance of the footprints. Because reburial resulted in denial of future access to the site by visitors, the compensation was a robust museum display, designed for international visitors. This project brought together all the key elements to withstand the rigors of a harsh environment, to serve both local people and long-term preservation of the site: clear exposition of values of the footprint trackway; stakeholder involvement; an analy-

sis of how the values would be affected by consideration of alternative options (including radically different ones) for conservation, pointing to an irrefutable decision for reburial after reexcavation; an engineered reburial using technically advanced as well as locally available materials; and a straightforward routine monitoring and maintenance plan.

Matero points out the inherently oppositional nature of archaeology and conservation: excavation is subtractive, destructive, and irreversible; conservation is concerned with safeguarding physical fabric and by so doing preserving authenticity and significance. There may seem to be an irony here when often repeated in the volume is the claim that archaeology and conservation are "natural partners." Both are true, for, so long as excavation is done and the remains exposed for visitors or further study, the onus is on professionals from the two disciplines to integrate their approaches and to plan for coordinated work both of the exposed remains and of the ex situ artifacts.

Making Archaeological Sites: Conservation as Interpretation of an Excavated Past

Frank G. Matero

Abstract: Archaeological sites, like all places of human activity, are constructed. Despite their fragmentation, they are complex places that depend on the legibility and authenticity of their components for visual meaning and appreciation. How legibility and authenticity of such structures and places are realized and ensured must be carefully considered and understood for effective conservation. Among the repertoire of conservation techniques applied to archaeological sites have been structural stabilization, reconstruction, including anastylosis, reburial, protective shelters, and myriad fabric-based conservation methods. Each solution affects the way archaeological information is preserved and how the site is perceived, resulting in a push and pull of competing scientific, associative, and aesthetic values. In an effort to address the economic benefits from tourist development, many archaeological sites have been directly and heavily manipulated to respond to didactic and recreational programs deemed necessary for appreciation by the public. In many cases this has resulted in a loss of place, sometimes accompanied by accelerated physical damage to those sites unprepared for development and visitation. This paper suggests that to balance this growing trend of seeing archaeological sites as predominantly outdoor museums, shaped by current museological attitudes and methods of display, it would be useful to approach them instead as cultural landscapes with phenomenological and ecological concerns. A more balanced combination of approaches could also mediate the often difficult but powerful overlay of subsequent histories visible on archaeological sites including destruction, reuse, and even past interpretations.

Heritage, Conservation, and Archaeology

Heritage and conservation have become important themes in recent discourse on place, cultural identity, and presentation of the past, yet few archaeological projects have included site conservation as a viable strategy in addressing these issues either before or during excavation (Berducou 1996:250). This has been due in part to archaeology's neglect of the long history and tradition of conservation theory and practice and the general misperception of conservation as an exclusively off-site, postexcavation activity associated with technical issues and remedial solutions. On the other hand, specialists in conservation and heritage management have been largely absent in the recent and rapidly expanding discourse on the meaning, use, and ownership of heritage for political and economic purposes. Both professions have avoided a critical examination of their own historical and cultural narratives pertaining to the construction of sites through excavation, analysis, conservation, and display.

The primary objective of conservation is to protect cultural heritage from loss and depletion. Conservators accomplish this through both preventive and remedial types of intervention (fig. 1). In so doing, conservation embraces the technical means by which heritage may be studied, displayed, and made accessible to the public and scholar alike (Sivan 1997:51). In this way, the conservation of archaeological sites is like other heritage conservation. Implicit in conservation's objectives is the basic requirement to remove or mitigate the causes of deterioration. For archaeological sites, this has a direct and immediate effect on visual legibility and indirectly conditions our perceptions and notions of authenticity. Among the repertoire of conservation techniques applied to

archaeological sites are structural stabilization, reconstruction, reburial, protective shelters, and myriad fabric-based
conservation methods. Each solution affects the way archaeological information is preserved and the site is experienced
and understood, resulting in a push and pull of competing
scientific, associative, and aesthetic values.

   Conservation as an intellectual pursuit is predicated on
the belief that knowledge, memory, and experience are tied to
material culture. Conservation—whether of a landscape,
building, or archaeological site—helps extend these past
places and things into the present and establishes a form of
mediation critical to the interpretive process that reinforces
these aspects of human existence. Recently such intervention
has expanded beyond the immediate material requirements of
the object and site to a more open values-based approach that
attempts to place them into contemporary sociocultural contexts (see, e.g., Demas 2000; Matero 2000).

   The practices of archaeology and conservation appear
by their very nature to be oppositional. Excavation, as one
common method by which archaeologists study a site, is a
subtractive process that is both destructive and irreversible. In
the revealing of a site, structure, or object, excavation is not a
benign reversal of site formational processes but rather a trau-
matic invasion of a site's physicochemical equilibrium, resulting in the unavoidable deterioration of associated materials

(fig. 2). Conservation, on the other hand, is predicated on the
safeguarding of physical fabric from loss and depletion, based
on the belief that material culture possesses important scientific and aesthetic information as well as the power to
inspire memory and emotional responses. In the first case, the
informational value embodied in the materiality of objects
and sites has been expressed in conservation rhetoric through
the concept of *integrity.* Integrity can manifest in many states
as purity (i.e., free from corruption or adulteration) or com-
pleteness of form, physicochemical composition, or context. It
has come to be an expression of authenticity in that it conveys
some truthfulness of the original in time and space, a quality
constructed partly in response to the unnatural interventions
perpetrated by us in our effort to preserve.[1] Whereas archaeology decontextualizes the site by representing it *ex situ,* in site
reports and museum exhibits, historic preservation represents
and interprets the site *in situ.*

   But archaeological sites are also places. If we are to identify and understand the nature and implications of certain
physical relationships with locales established through past
human thought and experience, we must do it through the
study of *place.* Places are contexts for human experience, constructed in movement, memory, encounter, and association
(Tilley 1994:15). While the act of remembering is acutely
human, the associations specific places have at any given time

FIGURE 2 Çatalhöyük, Turkey. Structural collapse and plaster surface delamination occur almost immediately on exposure and require both large- and small-scale temporary treatments during and after excavation. Photo: Frank Matero

will change. In this last respect, conservation itself can become a way of reifying cultural identities and historical narratives over time through valorization and interpretation. In the end, all conservation is a critical act in that the decisions regarding what is conserved, and who and how it is presented, are a product of contemporary values and beliefs about the past's relationship (and use) to the present. Nevertheless, technical intervention—that is, what is removed, what is added, what is modified—is the concrete expression of a critical judgment thus formed in the course of this process. What, then, does it

mean to conserve and display an archaeological site, especially when what is seen was never meant to be displayed as such, or at least in the fragmented manner viewed?

Archaeological sites are what they are by virtue of the disciplines that study them. They are made, not found. Archaeological sites are constructed through time, often by abandonment, discovery, and amnesia (figs. 3–6). As heritage they are a mode of cultural production constructed in the present that has recourse to the past (Kirstenblatt-Gimblett 1998:7). Display as intervention is an interface that mediates and therefore transforms what is shown into heritage, and conservation's approaches and techniques have always been a part of that process.[2] Beginning with the Sixth International Congress of Architects in Madrid in 1904 and later with the creation of the Charter of Athens following the International Congress of Restoration of Monuments (1931), numerous attempts have been made to identify and codify a set of universal principles to guide the conservation and interpretation of structures and places of historic and cultural significance.

Despite their various emphases and differences, all these documents identify the conservation process as one governed by absolute respect for the aesthetic, historic, and physical integrity of the structure or place and requiring a high sense of moral responsibility. Implicit in these principles is the notion of cultural heritage as a physical resource that is at once valuable and irreplaceable and an inheritance that promotes cultural continuity in a dynamic way.

Summarized from the more recent documents, these principles can be outlined as follows:

- The obligation to perform research and documentation, that is, to record physical, archival, and other evidence before and after any intervention to generate and safeguard knowledge of structures and sites and their associated human behavior;
- The obligation to respect cumulative age-value, that is, the acknowledgment of the site or work as a cumulative physical record of human activity embodying cultural beliefs, values, materials, and techniques and displaying the passage of time through weathering;
- The obligation to safeguard authenticity, an elusive quality associated with the genuine materiality of a thing or place as a way of validating and ensuring authorship or witness of a time and place;

FIGURES 3-6 Coronado State Monument (Kuaua), New Mexico. The discovery and excavation (fig. 3), reconstruction as a ruin (figs. 4 and 5) and subsequent neglect and erosion (fig. 6) of an earthen ancestral puebloan village, ca. 1934–2000. Figures 3, 4, and 5 reproduced by permission of the Museum of New Mexico. Figure 6 photo: Frank Matero

- The obligation to perform minimum reintegration, that is, to reestablish structural and visual legibility and meaning with the least physical interference; and
- The obligation to perform interventions that will allow other options and further treatment in the future. This principle recently has been redefined more accurately as "retreatibility," a concept of considerable significance for architecture, monuments, and archaeological sites given their need for long-term high-performance solutions, often structural in nature.

Every conservation measure is a dialectic that engages in the definition, treatment, interpretation, and uses of the past today. Often historical arguments for or against the designation and retention of cultural property are based on an epistemology of scholarship and facts. Facts and scholarship, however, are explanations that serve the goals of conservation and are a product of their time and place.

Out of this dilemma, our current definition of conservation has emerged as a field of specialization concerned primarily with the material well-being of cultural property and the conditions of aging and survival, focusing on the qualitative and quantitative processes of change and deterioration. Conservation advocates minimal but opportune interventions conducted with traditional skills as well as experimentally advanced techniques. In contemporary practice, it has tended to avoid the renewal of form and materials; however, the level of physical intervention possible can vary considerably even under the current doctrinal guidelines. This includes even the most invasive methods such as the reassembly of original elements (i.e., anastylosis) and the installation or replication of missing or damaged components. Such interventions, common on archaeological sites, are often based on the desire or need for greater visual legibility and structural reintegration (fig. 7). These interventions become even more critical if they sustain or improve the future performance or life of the site or structure in its environment.

Obviously, for archaeological sites, changing or controlling the environment by reburial, building a protective enclosure or shelter on site, or relocating selected components such as murals or sculpture, often indoors, are options that allow maximum physical protection and thus privilege the scientific value inherent in the physical fabric. However, such interventions significantly affect the contextual meaning and associative and aesthetic values, an aspect already discussed as significant for many such sites. Conversely, interventions

developed to address only the material condition of objects, structures, and places of cultural significance without consideration of associated cultural beliefs and rituals can sometimes denature or compromise their power, "spirit," or social values. In this regard, cultural and community context and dialogue between professionals and stakeholders are crucial.

FIGURE 7 Convent of Mission San Jose, San Antonio, Texas. Stone consolidation and mortar repairs were identified as the most minimal interventions necessary to stabilize and reinstate the form but preserve the original fabric of this unique column on site. Photo: Frank Matero

If we accept the premise that the practice of conservation began with the relational study of the underlying causes of deterioration and the refining of an etiological approach, then it was in 1898, with the publication of Freidrich Rathgen's handbook of conservation for antiquities and the earlier founding of his conservation laboratory at the Berlin Museum, that the field was born (Rathgen 1898). Yet within the understood limitations of the scientific method to generate certain kinds of data, conservation still begins and ends as an interpretation of the work. One is not only dealing with physical artifacts and structures, but with complex cultural questions of beliefs, convictions, and emotions, as well as with aesthetic, material, and functional significance. Science helps to interpret, but it cannot and should not create meanings or singularly represent one truth.

Archaeological Sites

The conservation and management of archaeological sites is a field of increasing interest, as evidenced by a growing number of professional conferences, published proceedings, and international projects (Matero et al. 1998:129–42). Archaeological sites have long been a part of heritage and its display, certainly before the use of the term "heritage" and the formal study of tourism. However, current concern can be attributed to the perception among the public and professionals that archaeological sites, like the natural environment, represent finite nonrenewable resources deteriorating at an increasing rate. This deterioration is due to a wide array of causes, ranging from neglect and poor management to increased visitation and vandalism, from inappropriate past treatments to deferred maintenance and treatment renewal. No doubt the recent pressures of economic benefit from tourist activities in conjunction with increasing communication and mobility have caused accelerated damage to many sites unprepared for development and visitation.

Despite the global increase in the scale of these problems, issues of recovery, documentation, stabilization, interpretation, and display have been associated with many important sites since the late nineteenth century.[3] In the U.S. Southwest, preservation and archaeology were inextricably intertwined from the beginning. Indeed, the earliest preservation legislation in the United States—the American Antiquities Act of 1906—and methods of stabilization and interpretation were promoted and developed by some of the leading American archaeologists of the day: Edgar Lee Hewett, Frederic Ward Putnam, Victor Mindeleff, and Jesse Walter

Fewkes. All became involved early on in their careers in the excavation, preservation, and display of archaeological sites such as Casa Grande, Mesa Verde, and the Pajarito Plateau for the American public. This close interest in site preservation and interpretation by American archaeologists and ethnologists was fostered by their belief in portraying the Southwest as a region of cultural continuity, peopled by descendants of the ancestral cliff-dweller communities and equal to the ancient sites of the Old World.

As a result of these early interests, sites such as Mesa Verde quickly became the country's first federally sponsored aboriginal theme park, with stabilization and interpretation leading archaeology and settings constructed with contextual buildings to help tell the story. Conservation practices, including the use of compatible, reversible materials and techniques, clear differentiation between original and stabilized fabric, and protective shelters and wall capping, were implemented during the first generation of site preservation in the U.S. Southwest and thus represent unique and sophisticated approaches for their day, especially when compared with many Old World sites.

One of the first coordinated attempts to codify international principles and procedures of archaeological site conservation was formulated in the Athens Charter of 1931 where measures such as accurate documentation, protective backfilling, and international interdisciplinary collaboration were clearly articulated. In 1956 further advances were made at the General Conference on International Principles Applicable to Archaeological Excavations adopted by the United Nations Educational, Scientific, and Cultural Organization (UNESCO) in New Delhi where the role of a centralized state administration in administering, coordinating, and protecting excavated and unexcavated archaeological sites was advocated.

Other charters such as the ICOMOS (Venice) Charter of 1964 extended these earlier recommendations through explicit recommendations that included the avoidance of reconstructions of archaeological features except in cases in which the original components were available but dismembered and the use of distinguishable modern techniques for the conservation of historic monuments. The Australia ICOMOS (Burra) Charter of 1979 expanded the definition of "archaeological site" to include the notion of place, challenging Eurocentric definitions of value, significance, authenticity, and integrity to include context and traditional use, an idea important for culturally affiliated indigenous groups. Finally, in 1990, the ICOMOS (ICAHM) Charter for the Protection and Management of the Archaeological Heritage was adopted in Lausanne,

FIGURE 8 Tumacacori, Arizona. Stabilization and early partial reconstruction of the church facade. Photo: Frank Matero

Switzerland, formalizing the international recognition of many archaeological sites as living cultural landscapes and the responsibility of the archaeologist in the conservation process.

In addition to these various international attempts to address the issues of archaeological site conservation through the creation of charters and other doctrinal guidelines, a conference to discuss the realities of such standards was held in Cyprus in 1983 under the auspices of ICCROM and UNESCO. In the context of the conference subject, that is, archaeological sites and finds, conservation was defined as traditionally concerned with the preservation of the physical fabric in a way that allows maximum information to be retrieved by further study and analysis (fig. 7), whereas restoration involves the representation of objects, structures, or sites so that they can be more visually "accessible" and therefore readily understood by both scholars and the public (fig. 8) (Foley 1995:11–12).

From the scholar's position, the maximum scientific and historical information will be obtained through recording, sampling, and analysis immediately on exposure or excavation. With each passing year, except under unique circumstances, sensitive physical information will be lost through exposure and weathering. It is true that when archaeologists return to existing previously excavated sites, they may collect new information not previously identified, but this is often the result of new research inquiries on existing finds and archived field notes. Exposed sites, depending on the nature of the materials, the environment, and the state of closure of the site, will yield limited, certainly diminished archaeometric information, especially for fragile materials or features such as macro- and microstratigraphy, surface finishes, impressions, and residue analysis. Comprehensive sampling programs, instrumental recording, and reburial maximize the preservation of the physical record both indirectly and directly. Sites with archi-tectural remains and landscape features deemed important to present for public viewing require quite different strategies for conservation and display. Here the record of approaches is far older and more varied, both in method and in result (e.g., Knossos, Casa Grande [Arizona], Pompeii, and the Stoa of Attalos).

Not to distinguish between the specificity of what is to be conserved on site, or retrieved for that matter, given the impossibility of doing so, makes for a confused and often compromised archaeological program and interpreted site. Too often conservation is asked to address the dual require-ments of an archaeological site as *document* and *place* without explicit definition and identification of what is actually to be preserved. The results have often been compromised physical evidence through natural deterioration—or worse, through failed treatments meant to do the impossible. On the other end, the need to display has sometimes resulted in confused and discordant landscapes that deny the entire story of the site and the natural and sublime state of fragmentation all ruin sites possess.

This last point is especially important on the subject of interpretation and display. In an effort to address the eco-nomic benefits from tourist development, many archaeologi-cal sites have been directly and heavily manipulated to respond to didactic and re-creational programs deemed nec-essary for visual understanding by the public. In many cases this has resulted in a loss of place, accompanied sometimes by accelerated damage to those sites unprepared for development and visitation. To balance this growing trend of seeing archae-ological sites as predominantly outdoor museums, shaped by current museological attitudes and methods of display, it would be useful to approach such sites instead as cultural landscapes with phenomenological and ecological concerns. A more balanced combination of approaches could also mediate the often difficult but powerful overlay of subsequent histories visible on archaeological sites, including destruction, reuse, abandonment, rediscovery, and even past interpretations.

Conclusion

Like all disciplines and fields, archaeological conservation has been shaped by its historical habit and by contemporary con-cerns. Important in its development has been the shifting, even expanding notion of site conservation to include the sta-bilization and protection of the whole site rather than simply in situ artifact conservation or the removal of site (architec-tural) features. The public interpretation of archaeological sites has long been associated with the stabilization and dis-play of ruins. Implicit in site stabilization and display is the aesthetic value many ruin sites possess based on a long-lived European tradition of cultivating a taste for the picturesque. With the scientific investigation and study of many archaeo-logical sites beginning in the late nineteenth century, both the aesthetic and the informational value of these sites was pro-moted during excavation-stabilization. In contemporary practice, options for archaeological site conservation have included reconstruction, reassembly (anastylosis), in situ preservation and protection including shelters and/or fabric consolidation, ex situ preservation through removal, and excavation or reburial with or without site interpretation.

Despite the level of intervention, that is, whether inter-pretation as a ruin is achieved through anastylosis or recon-struction, specific sites, namely, those possessing monumental masonry remains, have tended to establish an idealized approach for the interpretation of archaeological sites in gen-eral. However, earthen tell sites such as Çatalhöyük in central Turkey at once challenge these ingrained notions of ordered chaos and arranged masonry by virtue of their fragile materi-als, temporal and spatial disposition, and sometimes conflict-ing relationships among foreign and local professionals and traditional communities. Moreover, changing notions of "site" have expanded the realm of what is to be interpreted and pre-served, resulting in both archaeological inquiry and legal pro-tection at the regional level. These aspects of site conservation and interpretation become all the more difficult when consid-ered in conjunction with the demands of tourism and site and regional development for the larger physical and political contexts.

Archaeological sites, like all places of human activity, are constructed. Despite their fragmentation, they are complex creations that depend on the legibility and authenticity of their components for public meaning and appreciation. How legibility and authenticity of such structures and places are realized and ensured must be carefully considered and under-stood for effective conservation. Certainly conservators, archaeologists, and cultural resource managers need to know well the theoretical concepts and the history of those concepts pertaining to conservation; they need to know something of the historical and cultural context of structures and sites, archaic or past building technologies, and current technical solutions. They need to familiarize themselves with the polit-ical, economic, and cultural issues of resource management and the implications of their work for local communities, including issues of appropriate technology, tradition, and sustainability.

The basic tenets of conservation are not the sole responsibility of any one professional group. They apply instead to all those involved in the conservation of cultural property and represent general standards of approach and methodology. From the broadest perspective, archaeology and conservation should be seen as a conjoined enterprise. For both, physical evidence has to be studied and interpreted. Such interpretations are founded on a profound and exact knowledge of the various histories of the thing or place and its context, on the materiality of its physical fabric, on its cultural meanings and values over time, and its role and effect on current affiliates and the public in general. This implies the application of a variety of specialized technical knowledge, but ideally the process must be brought back into a cultural context so that the archaeology and conservation project become synonymous.

Notes

1   Integrity is a common requirement for heritage found in many conservation charters and codes of ethics. See AIC Code of Ethics and Guidelines for Practice, in *AIC Directory* (Washington, D.C.: American Institute for Conservation of Historic and Artistic Works, 1995), 22–29; Australia ICOMOS (1999) 38-47; IIC-CG and CAPC, Code of ethics and guidance for practice for those involved in the conservation of cultural property in Canada, in *US/ICOMOS Charters and Other International Doctrinal Documents, US/ICOMOS Scientific Journal* 1, no. 1 (1999): 55–59; UKIC, *Guidance for Conservation Practice* (London: Institute for Conservation of Historic and Artistic Works, 1981), 1; The Venice Charter, International Charter for the Conservation and Restoration of Monuments and Sites, *US/ICOMOS Charters and Other International Doctrinal Documents, US/ICOMOS Scientific Journal* 1, no. 1 (1999): 7–8.

2   One of the earliest publications on display is M. W. Thompson's *Ruins—Their Preservation and Display*.

3   For a general summary, see Schmidt 1997; Stubbs 1995.

References

Berducou, M. 1996. Introduction to archaeological conservation. In *Historical and Philosophical Issues in the Conservation of Cultural Heritage*, ed. N. P. Stanley-Price, M. K. Talley Jr., and A. M. Vaccaro, 248–59. Los Angeles: The Getty Conservation Institute.

Demas, M. 2000. Planning for conservation and management of archaeological sites: A values-based approach. In *Management Planning for Archaeological Sites*, ed. J. M. Teutonico and G. Palumbo, 27–54. Los Angeles: The Getty Conservation Institute.

Foley, K. 1995. The role of the objects conservator in field archaeology. In *Conservation on Archaeological Excavations*, ed. N. P. Stanley-Price, 11–19. Rome: ICCROM.

Kirstenblatt-Gimblett, B. 1998. *Destination Culture.* Berkeley: University of California Press.

Mason, R., and E. Avrami. 2000. Heritage values and challenges of conservation planning. In *Management Planning for Archaeological Sites*, ed. J. M. Teutonico and G. Palumbo, 13–26. Los Angeles: The Getty Conservation Institute.

Matero, F., et al. 1998. Archaeological site conservation and management: An appraisal of recent trends. *Conservation and Management of Archaeological Sites* 2(3):129–42.

Rathgen, F. 1898. Die Konservirung von Alterthumsfunden. Berlin: W. Spemann. [First English translation: Auden, G., and H. Auden, trans. *The Preservation of Antiquities: A Handbook for Curators.* Cambridge: Cambridge University Press, 1905.]

Schmidt, H. 1997. Reconstruction of ancient buildings. In *The Conservation of Archaeological Sites in the Mediterranean Region*, ed. M. de la Torre, 41–50. Los Angeles: The Getty Conservation Institute.

Sivan, R. 1997. The presentation of archaeological sites. In *The Conservation of Archaeological Sites in the Mediterranean Region*, ed. M. de la Torre, 51–59. Los Angeles: The Getty Conservation Institute.

Stubbs, J. 1995. Protection and presentation of excavated structures. In *Conservation on Archaeological Excavations*, ed. N. P. Stanley-Price, 73–89. Rome: ICCROM.

Thompson, M. W. 1981. *Ruins—Their Preservation and Display.* London: British Museum Publications.

Tilley, C. 1994. *A Phenomenology of Landscape.* Oxford: Berg.

Decision Making for Conservation of Archaeological Sites: The Example of the Laetoli Hominid Trackway, Tanzania

Martha Demas and Neville Agnew

Abstract: The 3.6-million-year-old hominid tracks at Laetoli, Tanzania, excavated in the late 1970s and reburied, were being destroyed by tree growth by the early 1990s. The decision-making process for conserving the site included methodological assessments of significance, physical condition, and the management context. Each of these was multidimensional and examined issues such as the scientific and symbolic values of tracks, the interests of stakeholders, causes of deterioration and current threats, and factors to be considered in managing the site to ensure a sustainable solution. The process led unequivocally to the decision to rebury the site while providing interpretive materials and a replica at the nearby Olduvai Museum. The systematic methodology used at Laetoli is universally applicable in that it offers the best options for preservation of a site's values.

It is perhaps not surprising that as archaeology evolved into a formal discipline, conservation of the material record, both recovered and revealed, lagged behind. Archaeologists' interests lie in information and knowledge of the past; conservators', with preservation of the physical remains for the future. In the absence of solutions to address the formidable problems of deterioration, archaeology simply moved to fulfill its own needs and make do with whatever ad hoc solutions seemed appropriate for protection and preservation of the remains. Nor could conservation offer a systematic or cogent methodology for deciding how and for whom archaeological sites and their immovable remains should be preserved in a sustainable manner.

In recent years, however, there has been acceleration in the theory and practice of archaeological site conservation and management, and increasingly, conservation professionals have adopted a decision-making process that has at its core the values and significance ascribed to a site. This values-based approach has a number of steps and a sequence: preparation and background knowledge of the site; assessment of values and significance, taking into account the interests of stakeholders; assessment of the physical condition of the site and causes of deterioration; and assessment of the context in which the site has and will be managed, used, and protected.[1] Based on the assessments, decisions are taken, objectives established, and strategies developed for implementation such that the values and significance of the place are protected and preserved.

Systematizing and formalizing a methodology of what previously was an implicit, vague, and at best inchoate process for conservation and management of sites has proved a powerful tool to serve the needs of both archaeology and preservation.

The Process through Example: The Laetoli Hominid Trackway

In the case of the 3.6-million-year-old Laetoli hominid trackway (Site G) in Tanzania (figs. 1, 2), the result arrived at through the decision-making process was reburial after reexcavation and conservation. This famous site had been excavated by Mary Leakey and shallowly reburied in 1978–79 (Leakey and Harris 1987:553). By the mid-1980s trees had grown on the mound, raising concerns that their roots were destroying the footprints. Reburial was the option chosen by the Tanzanian Department of Antiquities (DoA) and the Getty Conservation Institute (GCI) because it was the only one that offered hope of long-term preservation of the footprints. But acceptance of the decision was not universal.

FIGURE 2 The remote landscape of the Laetoli site, at the southern limit of the Serengeti, looking north. Photo: John C. Lewis. © The J. Paul Getty Trust

FIGURE 1 The hominid trails of the southern section of the trackway as reexcavated in 1995. (Hipparion tracks cross the hominid trail.) Trees have been removed, and the trackway is ready for reburial. The northern section, shown here still under Mary Leakey's original reburial and protective covering of rocks, was undertaken in 1996. Photo: Neville Agnew. © The J. Paul Getty Trust

Recognizing, negotiating, managing, and reconciling the differing agendas and perspectives that emerged, as well as designing the technical requirements of the reburial, were all integral to the decision-making process.

This paper discusses these issues and how they were resolved in the course of planning and implementation, with emphasis on the assessments and their role in making decisions and developing implementation strategies.

The Assessment Process

Assessments of significance, condition, and management context took place mainly over a two-year period (1993–94), although information gathering and assessment continues even after a decision is made and may result in modifications. The assessments were concomitant with extensive background research on the site, its environs, previous interventions, and identification of the persons, institutions, and groups who had an interest in the site, that is, the stakeholders.

Assessment of Values, Benefits, and Stakeholders

This assessment involved review and analysis of background information, commissioning a statement of scientific significance from an eminent palaeoanthropologist, and discussions with numerous stakeholders. Not surprisingly, palaeoanthropologists were the most vocal stakeholders, and the scientific values they attributed to the site were brought forth prominently. The statement of scientific significance articulates an essential attribute of Laetoli—its uniqueness: "The hominid footprints at Laetoli comprise one of the most unique and important discoveries in the history of human palaeontology. It is most unlikely that any similar resource will be discovered and recovered in the foreseeable future, if ever again. This singular discovery plays a crucial role in our understanding of the evolution of our own species" (Lovejoy and Kelley 1995:28).

What is Laetoli's role in understanding the evolution of our species? Principally, the Laetoli footprints, unlike fossil bones, uniquely preserve soft tissue anatomy of the hominid foot—the great toe, arch, and heel—providing proof of an adducted big toe and a well-developed arch more than three million years ago (fig. 3). Because the trackway preserves the sequence and distance between steps, it also provides a means of understanding gait. The prints thus afford direct evidence, in a well-dated context, of fully bipedal hominids long before the development of the brain and the use of stone tools.[2]

The hominid and faunal prints at Site G comprise only one of dozens of fossilized print sites exposed through erosion in the Laetoli region (Leakey and Harris 1987:451–89). These record thousands of prints of animals, many now extinct, as well as plant impressions. They provide us with an unparalleled understanding of life in the savanna of East Africa at the time and therefore also the ecological context of the hominids. Site G should be seen in the context of the immense research potential of these nearby exposures, containing also fossil bones of animals and the hominid *Australopithecus afarensis.*

Assessment of a site's values requires consideration of the significance ascribed to it when discovered (usually the time when it received most prominence), its current significance (which may have changed), and its research potential (i.e., its potential to yield new information). In the course of the assessment of Site G, it emerged that the prints had not been studied in sufficient detail during their brief excavation in 1978–79 and there were still outstanding questions and disagreements about interpretation. Research potential became a pivotal issue, but the need for additional research opened old wounds, and academic divisions emerged anew, spurred by earlier accusations of poor excavation techniques on some of the prints. Thus the need for restudy became entangled with statements about the perceived mistakes of the past.[3]

Government authorities responsible for a site are principal stakeholders, who have legal mandates to serve and official priorities to consider. The DoA has legal responsibility for the site, but Laetoli is within the Ngorongoro Conservation Area (NCA), managed by a quasi-governmental body (the NCA Authority, or NCAA). The NCA is a World Heritage

FIGURE 3 The anatomy of the hominid foot is shown in this image of 1992 in which a photographic print (on the left) from Mary Leakey's original excavation is compared with the same footprint, demonstrating also the efficacy of reburial. Photo: Guillermo Aldana. © The J. Paul Getty Trust

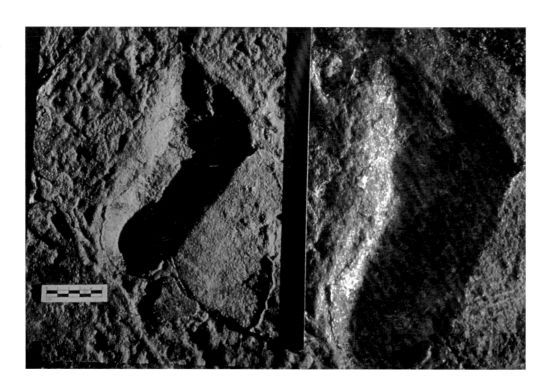

Site, nominated principally for its natural and wildlife values, and these values form the basis of management decisions and priorities of the NCAA.

Unlike scientific significance, expressed in academic publications imbued with the authority of the discipline, spiritual and symbolic values are often voiced through informal channels. One has only to peruse the Laetoli offerings on the internet to discern the wide-ranging attraction that the prints exert on the general public and the media. Spiritual and symbolic values derive from emotional response to the footprints. For Laetoli, these values follow from the affinity to modern footprints of these earliest imprints of our lineal ancestors on the earth's surface. Laetoli furthermore epitomizes universal symbolic values: the footprints offer a unifying and potent symbol of our species and our beginnings. The enduring fascination of the general public with human evolution also translates into tourism potential, and there was strong interest among many stakeholders to develop the site for visitors.

Another potential stakeholder was the local Maasai community. For the Maasai, Laetoli was, at best, a memory of the presence of Mary Leakey and her team in their landscape for a short time. Their interest insofar as the site was concerned related mainly to grazing their cattle.

Assessment of Condition

The assessment of the physical condition and threats to Site G required an understanding of its environment, including drainage patterns, use of the area by the Maasai, the presence of large mammals, and the condition of the trackway surface and individual prints.

At the level of the trackway, the tuff into which the prints were impressed was revealed in a test excavation to be fractured and fragile, and especially where it had weathered into clay, it was subject to cracking and powdering on exposure and widespread penetration by small roots of weeds and grasses and by larger roots from acacia trees (Agnew and Demas 1998; Demas et al. 1996).

Assessment of Management Context

The assessment of management context examined opportunities and constraints, specifically, the capabilities, resources, motivations, and limitations of the two authorities with responsibility for the site (DoA and NCAA); its location and accessibility; the economic and political context in which decisions needed to be made; and the potential of opening the site to visitation.

The assessment revealed few opportunities and many constraints. The principal opportunity lay in the ready-made tourist market that existed. In many developing countries, the archaeological heritage is a prime resource for tourism-generated revenue. With a wildlife tourism industry already well developed in the Serengeti and Ngorongoro Crater, it is understandable that the trackway, which is quite close to these areas, would present itself as an important site for visitation and educational purposes.

The constraints were formidable. The Tanzanian Department of Antiquities had few staff members, resources, or facilities. Laetoli is remote, without infrastructure (roads, electricity, and water), and often inaccessible during the rainy season; the nearest DoA staff were stationed at Olduvai Gorge without easy access to Laetoli. The Tanzanian experience with protecting and maintaining open sites had not been successful (Tillya 1996; Waane 1986). Furthermore, there was a history of poor cooperation between the NCAA and the DoA that reflected not only the professional nature-culture divide but also the dominance of the far larger and better staffed and resourced NCAA.

The Maasai were the only people with a regular presence in the region, which is set aside for their use by the NCAA and not open to public access. They were indeed curious about the goings-on, but ultimately their interest focused on grazing cattle, access to water, and, opportunistically, any materials being tested on site, particularly geosynthetics, which were frequently removed after the team's departure.

Finally, the politics of palaeoanthropology revealed itself in multifaceted ways. These emerged in the context of research agendas, project leadership, and the resurrection of old rivalries and the creation of new ones. Moreover, that conservation professionals should be making decisions about a site of such significance was regarded by some in the scientific community as presumptuous. Opportunistically, the Laetoli project also afforded a platform for contending political factions within the DoA.

Response to the Assessment

As is frequently the case, alternatives for conservation and use of Site G had been under discussion by various constituencies (mainly palaeoanthropologists and those interested in tourism), and two proposals had been floated long before the project began (see, e.g., Ndessokia 1990). The two options were removal of the footprints to a museum or sheltering the trackway and allowing visitation by researchers and the public. Removal to a museum would have destroyed much of the significance of the prints (study of gait, context of the prints, symbolic value of the trackway, future research potential and use of the site) and preserved only a narrow slice (evidence of soft tissue anatomy). In addition, there were constraints to museum curation, storage, and display similar to those that pertained at the site. Keeping the site open and sheltering it would have been the best means to reveal its significance but would not have been sustainable even in the short term. Given the management context and the physical condition of the trackway, both these options would have resulted in irreversible damage to the footprints.

A third option, reburial of the trackway after conservation, offered a way to preserve the footprints for the long term that was sustainable in the existing management context. As a form of long-term "storage" for archaeological sites, reburial holds their integrity and values in trust for future generations. When preservation techniques have improved or resources become available, or when new research questions arise, the reburial can be reversed and the site once again exposed, although reexcavation poses risks of damage and further deterioration.

The decision-making model was not one of building consensus among stakeholders but rather of joint decision making among the partners and consultation with various constituencies (scientists, NCA authorities, and the local Maasai community). Recognizing that no single decision would satisfy the interests of all the stakeholders, a strategy was developed to address multiple stakeholder issues while making the decision-making process transparent. A consultative committee was created (fig. 4), which included Mary Leakey; government authorities from the DoA and the Ministry of Culture; a regional UNESCO representative; representation from the Tanzanian and international scientific community; NCAA representatives; and a non-Tanzanian, African conservation professional to advise on and vet proposals, secure cooperation between the DoA and the NCAA for future management and protection of the area, and address specific issues such as the scientific restudy of the trackway.

Development of an Implementation Strategy

To implement the decision to rebury the trackway, there were particular opportunities and constraints and a host of considerations (stakeholder, technical, and management) to take into account. The assessments provided the basis both for making the decision that reburial was the most appropriate and sustainable method of preserving the trackway and for developing the implementation strategy.

Stakeholder Considerations

Opposition to the decision was voiced by small but vocal constituencies within the scientific community (international and local) and the DoA. It was channeled mainly through the press but was also brought before the Tanzanian parliament. Predictably, lack of access to the trackway was the ostensible reason, as expressed in a communiqué by a group opposed to the plan on the grounds that it was "incompatible with a long-term conservation strategy that involves displaying the footprints for educational, tourism and future scientific use" (Wilford 1995:C11). The press, ever alert to the controversies that seem endemic in palaeoanthropology, was quick to pick up the trail at Laetoli. The project became a cause célèbre, with accusations and rumors of various kinds bruited about: the project was a moneymaking venture or a colonialist undertaking, the environment was being poisoned by the use of chemicals, and so on.[4]

It became vital, therefore, to develop communication strategies for active press involvement, such as holding press weekends on site in 1995 and 1996; maintaining contact and sharing information with scientists, including publishing an article after the first conservation season in a journal targeted at that audience (Feibel et al. 1995); and opening the site during conservation to government officials, academics working in the region, and local Maasai and school groups. To enhance understanding of the reburial, a "dummy" reburial was created that showed the reburial stratigraphy and was effectively used to explain the technical aspects to press and visitors (fig. 5).

Importantly, to satisfy the research needs of the scientific community, it was desirable to compensate for lack of access to the trackway after its reburial. This involved restudy of the trackway (after excavation in 1995 and 1996) by three invited scientists nominated by senior palaeoanthropologists proposed by the consultative committee (fig. 6). Given the research agendas and politics, it is not surprising that the selection was contentious. More surprising, however, is that those scientists selected by their peers to undertake what was considered critically important research (on microstratigraphy, morphological description, and hominid gait) have been so slow to publish their findings.[5]

For future researchers, emphasis was placed on producing high-level documentation. Excellent casts made in 1978–79 of individual prints and sections of the trackway remain the most accurate documentation of the prints as originally excavated. Archival (epoxy) and museum-quality copies were made to ensure their existence in the future. Scientific-quality photography and high-resolution photogrammetry of the

FIGURE 4 Some members of the Laetoli consultative committee: *(left to right)* Mary Leakey, Desmond Clark, Webber Ndoro, and Mambiran Joof. Photo: Neville Agnew. © The J. Paul Getty Trust

FIGURE 5 The "dummy" demonstration of the reburial stratigraphy during a press and visitor day at the site. Photo: Frank Long. © The J. Paul Getty Trust

FIGURE 6 Mary Leakey on the reexcavated trackway during the scientific restudy with the palaeoanthropologist Bruce Latimer and Peter Jones who originally excavated the site with Mary Leakey. Photo: Angelyn Bass. © The J. Paul Getty Trust

trackway was carried out and the condition of individual prints recorded graphically. The intent was that the scientific restudy would complement the documentation by providing interpretation of ambiguous features of the tuff.

The tourism and educational potential lost by reburying the trackway was compensated for by producing an exhibition at the Olduvai Museum, on the tourist circuit from Ngorongoro Crater to the Serengeti. The museum's three rooms

FIGURE 7 The Laetoli exhibition at the Olduvai Museum displays a cast of the best-preserved part of the trackway together with artwork depicting hominids walking through the newly fallen volcanic ash. Photo: Neville Agnew. © The J. Paul Getty Trust

offer an orientation to the region and displays on Olduvai Gorge and Laetoli, which include a cast of the trackway and the story of its conservation. Text information is in both Swahili, for local people, and English, for international visitors (fig. 7).

Technical Considerations

The technical strategy developed for the reexcavation, conservation, and reburial of the trackway is not discussed here. There were numerous requirements that had to be met so that the reburial would best protect the trackway, including the use of specialized materials and stabilization and drainage measures, and these are published elsewhere (Agnew and Demas 1998; Demas et al. 1996).

Management Considerations

Strategies to ensure the sustainability of protection measures were devised to meet the issues that emerged from the management assessment. Communication and outreach to the Maasai community were among the most elaborated strategies, since their role in the long term was felt to be critical. The traditional religious leader of the Maasai in the region was

consulted about security and disturbance to the site that had occurred between fieldwork and about how to make the site meaningful. At his suggestion, blessing ceremonies were held at the trackway, and its importance was explained to the gathered community (fig. 8). Casts of the trackway were made for local schools, and visits to the site by schoolchildren were organized. Site security was strengthened by creating permanent posts for resident Maasai guards (paid by the DoA).

Maintenance, the lack of which led to the growth of acacia trees after 1979, was crucial. Of particular importance, therefore, was the development of a feasible monitoring and maintenance plan, to be undertaken by Olduvai staff, training in its application, and the development of a means of off-site, long-term monitoring of the condition of the trackway (Agnew and Demas 2004). Efforts were made to establish a liaison with NCA officials through the consultative committee and to involve NCA staff in joint meetings with project and DoA personnel. A long-term management plan for the NCA was in development during the project, and it proved possible through these contacts to emphasize the importance of Laetoli and other sites in it.

But what of the trackway's future? During the management assessment, scenarios of possible long-term threats to the trackway were discussed, for example, a political decision

FIGURE 8 Maasai gathering at the site during the blessing ceremony conducted by the traditional religious leader of the area. Photo: John C. Lewis. © The J. Paul Getty Trust

to uncover the trackway and develop the site for tourism. Such pressures should not be underestimated. As a site powerfully symbolic of humankind's rise, Laetoli will continue to attract interest from many quarters. Another scenario involves vandalism of the site or its abandonment followed by eventual growth of vegetation. Were staffing and government funding cuts to happen, the site could suffer this fate. A long-term threat apparent during the course of the project is the change in lifestyle of the Maasai. Increasingly they are settling and becoming reliant in part on agriculture, although cattle remain at the core of their culture. Already a dam has been built near the site to store seasonal flow for cattle. With increasing population, erosion and disturbance will likely be a grave threat to the unprotected exposures and ultimately to Site G itself. The regular presence of researchers in the area is one effective antidote to such threats. For this reason, it was advocated that the DoA encourage research and scientific surveys of the area by palaeoscientists. Although these met with conceptual approval, no sustained initiatives have been forthcoming.

Conclusion

Laetoli was challenging on all fronts. The project encompassed a spectrum of issues that far transcended the technicalities of reburial. As a holistically conceived and executed conservation project, it can stand scrutiny. The conservation strategy for the trackway had to consider all issues that

emerged in the assessments. In particular, the condition and management assessments placed constraints on the options available, yet provided an imperative direction—reburial—for the project. As a lesson in the multiplicity of values and complexities, issues and agendas that attend a high-profile site such as Laetoli, it demonstrates the strength of the assessment and conservation decision-making process. The aim of conservation is to preserve all the values of a site and not to privilege certain values at the expense of others. Without such a methodology to guide the process, the trackway was in danger of being held hostage to exclusive interests and values. This systematic, holistic methodology offers the best possibility of representing and balancing all stakeholder interests and values and achieving a well-conserved site.

Notes

1   For a fuller explanation and analysis of the decision-making process, see Palumbo and Teutonico 2002; and as applied specifically to reburial, Demas 2004.

2   The literature on Laetoli is extensive; we cite only Leakey and Harris 1987 and White and Suwa 1987 to represent the scientific literature and Reader 1988 to represent literature aimed at educated laypersons.

3   For published references to the controversies about excavation of the footprints, see Clarke 1985; Tuttle et al. 1990:359–60; Torchia 1985; White and Suwa 1987:491.

4   For a range of international and local press coverage in English referring to the controversies, see Ambali 1995; Hotz 1995; Reader 1993; Vablon 1996; Wilford 1995. Much of the Tanzanian press was published in Swahili in Motomoto (Dar es Salaam, Tanzania).

5   Schmid 2004 is the only publication to date of the work done on the trackway in 1995–96.

References

Agnew, N., and M. Demas. 1998. Preserving the Laetoli footprints: The discovery of hominid footprints in East Africa reshaped the study of human origins. Now conservators have protected the fragile tracks from destruction. *Scientific American* 279, no. 3 (September):44–55.

———. 2004. Monitoring through replication: Design and evaluation of the monitoring reburial at the Laetoli trackway site. *Conservation and Management of Archaeological Sites* 6 (3–4):295–304.

Ambali, E. 1995. Experts caution against chemical use. *Daily News (Tanzania),* 6 December.

Clarke, R. J. 1985. Comments on the Laetoli footprints. Taung Diamond Jubilee International Symposium (Mmabatho, South Africa, 2 February 1985). [Taped commentary]

Demas, M., N. Agnew, S. Waane, J. Podany, A. Bass, and D. Kamamba. 1996. Preservation of the Laetoli hominid trackway in Tanzania. In *Archaeological Conservation and Its Consequences, Preprints of the Contributions to the Copenhagen Congress, 26–30 August 1996,* ed. R. Ashok and P. Smith, 38–42. London: International Institute for Conservation of Historic and Artistic Works.

Demas, M. 2004. "Site unseen": The case for reburial of archaeological sites. *Conservation and Management of Archaeological Sites* 6 (3–4):137–54.

Feibel, C. S., N. Agnew, B. Latimer, M. Demas, F. Marshall, S. A. C. Waane, and P. Schmid. 1995. The Laetoli hominid footprints: A preliminary report on the conservation and scientific restudy. *Evolutionary Anthropology: Issues, News, and Reviews* 4 (5):149–54.

Hotz, R. L. 1995. Detective work that leaves no footprints. *Los Angeles Times,* 16 November, A1.

Leakey, M., and J. M. Harris. 1987. *Laetoli: A Pliocene Site in Northern Tanzania.* Oxford: Clarendon Press.

Lovejoy, C. O., and C. A. Kelley. 1995. The Laetoli footprints: A review of their scientific status. Unpublished report prepared for the Getty Conservation Institute, 1 March.

Ndessokia, P. N. S. 1990. The mammalian fauna and archaeology of the Ndolanya and Olpiro Beds, Laetoli, Tanzania. Ph.D. dissertation, University of California, Berkeley.

Palumbo, G., and J. M. Teutonico, eds. 2002. *Management Planning for Archaeological Sites. (Proceedings of an International Workshop Organized by the Getty Conservation Institute and Loyola Marymount University, May 2000, Corinth, Greece).* Los Angeles: The Getty Conservation Institute.

Reader, J. 1988. *Missing Links: The Hunt for Earliest Man.* London: Penguin.

———. 1993. Prints of darkness. *The Guardian (London),* 2 December, Features, 12–13.

Schmid, P. 2004. Functional interpretation of the Laetoli footprints. In *From Biped to Strider: The Emergence of Modern Human Walking, Running, and Resource Transport,* ed. D. J. Meldrum and C. E. Hilton, 49–62. New York: Kluwer Academic/Plenum.

Tillya, D. 1996. Preservation of the Stone Age site of Isimilia, Tanzania. *Conservation and Management of Archaeological Sites* 1(4):243–46.

Torchia, A. 1985. Mary Leakey made mistake in ape-men prints, anthropologist says. Associated Press, 2 February.

Tuttle, R. H., D. Webb, E. Weidl, and M. Baksh. 1990. Further progress on the Laetoli trails. *Journal of Archaeological Science* 17:347–62.

Vablon, K. 1996. Tiptoe through the turmoil: Is scientific colonialism alive and well in Tanzania? *Outside* 21, no. 3 (March): 30.

Waane, S. A. C. 1986. Roofs and shelters: The Tanzanian experience. In *Preventive Measures during Excavation and Site Protection (Conference Ghent, 6–8 November 1985),* 245–56. Rome: ICCROM.

White, T. D., and G. Suwa. 1987. Hominid footprints at Laetoli: Facts and interpretations. *American Journal of Physical Anthropology* 72:485–514.

Wilford, J. N. 1995. Dispute erupts on plans for ancient footprints. *New York Times,* 20 June, C11.

Conservation qua Archaeology at Tell Mozan/Urkesh

Giorgio Buccellati

Abstract: Increasingly, conservation is considered a necessary component of archaeological fieldwork. However, there are considerable differences in the way in which its presence affects the conduct of the work. Typically, it is an intervention that occurs apart from the excavation, whether it pertains to objects or to architecture. In a temporal sense, this often means that conservation takes place after the excavation: one may have, for instance, a "conservation season" following an "excavation season." But even when the two activities take place concurrently, they are in most cases conceived as parallel activities, where conservation is viewed as a technique that is brought to bear from the outside on results that are obtained quite independently. This paper makes a case, instead, for conservation to be inscribed in the very strategy of archaeology, not so much logistically as conceptually. Archaeologists gain a better "archaeological" understanding of their universe if they act as conservators; conversely, conservators will be even better at their work if they gain a sensitivity for stratigraphy. Conservation at Tell Mozan, ancient Urkesh, is presented as a test case of this approach, which has yielded very positive results. In particular, a new approach to the conservation of mud-brick architecture at the site is presented.

Conceptual Goals

The theme developed at the 5th World Archaeological Congress—"Of the Past, for the Future: Integrating Archaeology and Conservation"—has a clear programmatic valence. First, a moral imperative: we must save the past so that future generations may draw on it at least as amply as we do. Then, the way this can happen: conservation must be integrated with archaeology, and vice versa.

I would like to underscore here the conceptual underpinnings of our central theme. It seems to me that one has to ask anew the very question, Why conservation? The reason is that even when integrated in an archaeological project, conservation generally remains extrinsic to the archaeological process as such. At best, one generally wants an excavation to entail a clear conservation program, in such a way that the excavation strategy is modified as needed to take fully into account the needs of conservation. But I would go one step further. For even in such an ideal situation, it is my observation that conservation remains an intervention not only *a posteriori* but also *ab exteriori*. This means that conservation is a technique invoked, and the degree of "integration" is correlative to the time frame within which such invoking takes place—coherently as a planned intervention at best, or, at worst, as a salvage operation after the fact, aimed at repairing damage that has occurred. The latter situation was prevalent in the past; today, happily, the pendulum is swinging in the other direction: conservation is more frequently associated with the ongoing process of excavation. Yet even so, it remains extrinsic. Are there ways, and is there merit, in going beyond such "extrinsicism"?

My answer—and this is the answer of an archaeologist, not of a conservator—can be stated in simple terms: conservation is intrinsic to the excavation process because it teaches us about excavation. It is a fact that conservators understand better than anyone else the physical and mechanical properties of the original artifact of which we find the relics. This understanding is as critical in shaping strategy as the identification of emplacement, the attribution to a given typological class, the awareness of historical conditions, or the recognition of function. Hence it follows that the conservator is not just an expert to be consulted, even before excavation starts, with a view toward maintaining the relic and possibly reconstructing it after the fact. Rather, the conservator is an intrinsic voice in the dialogue that shapes understanding while the excavation takes place. So viewed, conservation *is* archaeology.

If that is so, it follows that conservation must be inscribed, in the most direct way, into the very process of excavation—not just after we realize that a building is important, not just when we are faced with a particularly delicate object. It must be simultaneous with excavation. Apart from considerations of cost and availability of resources, this must always be the goal, at least conceptually. From such general presuppositions that speak not just to the desirability but in fact to the necessity of "integrating archaeology and conservation," there ensue some practical consequences.

It is not only a matter of decisional and hierarchical structures. It is rather a matter of *forma mentis:* the archaeologist must think as conservator and, conversely, the conservator as archaeologist. Since conservation is not just an appendix but an intrinsic facet of the excavation process, it follows that archaeologists need conservation professionals to improve on their own work as archaeologists. Of course, conservation remains an expertise with its own unique technical competence, but its summons are not just for something additive after the fact. In other words, it is necessary for the archaeologist to not just turn to the conservator for outside input, however well planned and integrated into an operational strategy; the archaeologist should also think as a conservator while doing the archaeologist's work.

Conversely, it is just as critical that the conservator not be a mere technician providing extrinsic support but rather that he or she think as an archaeologist. Practically speaking: if courses in chemistry are required in conservation training, shouldn't courses in stratigraphy be of exactly the same importance? The depositional process through which the "relic" has originated is just as important for a conservator's understanding of the "relic" as the material matrix that defines the components on which the conservator works. The conservator must develop a sensitivity for this through hands-on experience in the field.

In this light, "integrating archaeology and conservation" does not mean so much developing a proper respect between two different individuals operating apart from one another but rather adding an educational component in the professional training of both archaeologists and conservators, so that each can operate with the sensitivity of the other.

To include such training in a conservator's curriculum means above all that the conservator must develop a special sensitivity for that unique nexus of time and space that is so central to archaeology. In other words, the conservator must understand full well what stratigraphy is, at the very moment that it is being exposed through excavation. This can only be learned in the field, and that is the component that should be an integral part of an archaeological conservator's schooling. One has to learn to touch time, to appreciate the physical interface that time assumes in the ground. Conversely, the archaeologist who has this sensitivity must develop the conservator's eye for proposing for preservation critical stratigraphic moments.

We must, then, aim for a concrete and proper conservation of important stratigraphic junctures. Consider the difference vis-à-vis the conservation of objects and even of monuments. Though timely intervention on delicate objects soon after their exposure is important, they can often undergo conservation in a museum-type environment. In this respect, object conservation is static, in the sense that the effort may often be carried out independently of the object's emplacement in the ground. In the case of architectural monuments, this is already more difficult, but in current practice the end result is the same. Walls and structures are conserved long after their initial exposure, and thus also statically—the only difference being that monuments, unlike objects, are tied to the ground. The goal that I am proposing is that the conservator be involved upstream of all this, at the very moment when exposure takes place, not so much and not only to better understand how to "save" the artifact but in order to help to understand and preserve a given stratigraphic moment.

When so implemented, conservation emerges as an important form of publication. That conservation adds to the documentary value of our work goes without saying. But in the case of architectural monuments and of stratigraphic moments, this documentary dimension is all the more significant and unique. So much so, in fact, that it becomes at times impossible to provide an alternative to visual inspection. To a certain extent, this is of course true of any artifact: no analogical representation can adequately and fully replace visual inspection. But it is especially true in the exposition of complex stratigraphic relationships, where a narrative description, a drawing, a photograph cannot do justice to all the concomitant elements that come into play. A digital three-dimensional model may indeed come one step closer to the ideal analogical rendering of such a situation, but it is still not applicable on a large scale, especially not for situations that, however important from a scholarly point of view, are not monumental in nature.

Conservation may in such cases yield the best documentation of a key stratigraphic nexus, retaining it for an independent assessment by visiting scholars. Also, the very effort that goes into conservation of such a document serves as a powerful heuristic tool for the ancillary documentation that remains, of course, as necessary as ever. In other words, thinking about conservation directs the mind of the archaeologist in the direction of a fuller set of correlations than may otherwise be perceived when limiting one's attention, myopically, to the stratigraphic argument rather than to the stratigraphic document.

Virtual and Other Realities

To illustrate how this can work, I want to use as a concrete example our own work at Tell Mozan, ancient Urkesh, with particular reference to architectural preservation. One of the largest third-millennium mounds in Syro-Mesopotamia (almost 150 hectares in size), it is located in northeastern Syria just below the slopes of the Taurus mountain range, which is today in Turkey. It was the most important urban center of early Hurrian civilization, contemporary with the Sumerian Early Dynastic and the Old Akkadian periods in the south. It remained famous in Hurrian mythology as the seat of the ancestral god of the Hurrian pantheon, and it was also known to have been the seat of an important kingdom. Our excavations have brought to light two major structures—the Royal Palace, built around 2250 B.C.E., and an earlier temple that rests on a high artificial terrace dating to at least 2700 B.C.E.

From the beginning of the excavations of what turned out to be the Royal Palace, in 1990, I became concerned with the preservation of the mud-brick walls and developed a simple protective system that has proven quite effective, as shown by our ongoing monitoring, under the supervision of our director of conservation, Sophie Bonetti. The system consists of a metal structure that closely follows the outline but not the top profile of the walls and of a tightly fitting canvas cover, tailor-made by a local tent maker. As of 2003, a total of some 400 linear meters of walls were so covered, corresponding to the entire set of the palace walls excavated so far.

The primary benefit is the protection of the walls. After thirteen years since the start of excavations in the palace, the condition of the walls remains as it was when they were first exposed. Over this relatively long period, the damage has been minimal, and the causes leading to it have been

identified and corrected. This is noteworthy because at other excavations in our area, walls that were not so protected have collapsed entirely, forcing a reconstruction that retains only the layout of the ancient structure and none of the original fabric.

It is important to emphasize the total reversibility of the process. The full protective system (metal and canvas) can be removed without leaving a trace. It is also relatively rapid. In 2003 the entire system was removed in two days by a crew of some fifteen people, and it takes about the same effort to set it back in place.

Obviously, it is not necessary to remove the protective gear on a yearly basis. Inspection of individual walls is effortless since the canvas can be easily lifted for any portion of the wall at any time (figs. 1, 2). This is a special instance when the goal of conservation as publication is achieved: visiting scholars can view such details as consistency of the bricks, faint traces of plaster, or arrangement of the mortar in ways that no photographic documentation can adequately render.

The system is fully modular, each wall being treated as a single unit, subdivided into smaller components as needed (fig. 3). This means that each new wall is covered immediately upon excavation. To wait for an eventual future season to be devoted to conservation has the disadvantage that intensive damage will inevitably occur in the meantime, and conservation can easily become little other than wholesale reconstruction. Another advantage of modularity so conceived is that excavated areas are protected while excavation is taking place in adjacent areas: for instance, the evacuation of dirt from ongoing excavations often follows a route that has an impact on earlier excavated areas, and in such cases our system affords protection from our own traffic.

But another advantage of this approach is that it is modular in a temporal as well as in a spatial sense: by protecting each wall as it is exposed, the interaction between archaeologist and conservator takes place at that critical moment when walls are exposed. The archaeologist is forced to consider more concretely the wall as an architectural unit, and the conservator to consider more sensitively the dynamics of the excavation process and the concerns of stratigraphy. Unexpectedly, modularity is one way in which the integration of archaeology and conservation takes place. Strategy decisions about the extent to which excavation should proceed are guided by considerations of how much opportunity will be available to set in place the protection system for new walls immediately following excavation. In this way, conservation is truly and properly built into the act of excavating.

FIGURE 1 Palace with walls covered, and with the canvas covering lifted to show one of the walls. Photo: J. Jarmakani

FIGURE 2 Close-up of two walls when covering is lifted. Photo: G. Buccellati

FIGURE 3 Sabah Kassem, the local smith who produces and maintains the iron structure. His dynamic participation in our work is emblematic of how conservation aids in developing an ideal collaboration between the stakeholders and the archaeologists. Photo: G. Buccellati

Conservation helps us to see each new wall not just as a fragment that is an end in itself but as the component of a larger whole that is concretely in front of us and perceivable as a real overall structure.

Modularity also means that costs are contained. This is in part due to the fact that they are spread out over a period of years. But actual total costs are also relatively low. The total spent for the portion set in place through 2002 amounted to some U.S. $5,000, including materials (metal and canvas) and labor.

It is important to note that this collaboration goes well beyond issues of costs. The enthusiasm and intelligence that local people bring to the project enhance our own work and in some important ways even our understanding of the archaeology. The conservation effort is one of the major ways in which the stakeholders are brought to a dynamic confrontation with the past that has unfolded in their own territory: as they share in re-creating its perceptual reality, they provide significant pointers toward an understanding of the monument. The notion of stakeholders' participation in "their" archaeology is a current theme today. At Mozan, we

have been applying this concept in a very concrete way since the inception of our work there.

A major benefit of our protective system has been the sharper definition of architectural spaces and volumes—the goal of all architectural restoration. In our case, this is coupled with a degree of reversibility that is not afforded by other systems. It is as if we had two archaeological sites existing contemporaneously side by side—or rather, one within the other (figs. 4, 5). One is the site that consists of the ruin—the walls as excavated. The other is the site that consists of the architecture —the walls as they once were. The rendering of volumes and spaces corresponds to the ideal of a three-dimensional rendering on the computer. Hence the concept "virtual and other realities": the wrapping provides, as it were, a real virtual reality. Except that the perception on the ground is of course infinitely richer than the one on the screen. A telltale sign of this was the realization, once the protective system was set in place, that we could no longer walk over low walls or foundations. Even though we, the excavators, were so familiar with the floor plan of our building, it was as if suddenly we had discovered, perceptually, a new dimension that until then was

FIGURE 4 Two sites in one: the palace "as ruin." The walls are documented as first excavated and preserved in their original state. Kite photo: G. Gallacci

FIGURE 5 Two sites in one: the palace "as monument." The walls are shown as volumes in their original layout. Kite photo: G. Gallacci

known to us only through the abstraction of a drawing. This perceptual enrichment of fieldwork is one of the significant results of the integration of conservation and archaeology as we practice it at Mozan: conservation helps the archaeologist to perceive the physical reality of the monument as nothing else can do. No matter how intimately the excavators know every brick of "their" walls, as soon as the protective covering goes up, they invariably see relationships that were wholly unexpected.

Obviously, such a wrapped reconstruction of the walls adds significantly to the goal of presenting and interpreting the site to the outside visitor. We have further enriched our "sitescape" through a variety of other means that help to visualize the architectural and functional elements of the structure. For instance, signs and posters can easily be added in such a way that they are visible also from a distance, where I have built a viewing station with interpretive posters. In 2003 we painted the major wings of the palace in different colors (see fig. 1)—green for the service wing and gold for the formal wing (as yet only partly excavated). This was occasioned by the realization that the modular approach described above resulted in the less desirable effect that the canvas had different shades each year. These were so noticeable that the original pleasant appearance of a light brown color, rather close to that of mud-brick, was dissipated by the motley look of the wrapping (especially in places where patches were added to reinforce older canvas). Painting the canvas over seemed like an obvious solution. And as long as we were doing that, it seemed worth trying to have colors match the functional differentiation that we already have in the floor plans. The jury is out on this approach. Aesthetically, opinions are divided between those who prefer the uniform light brown earth tone over the brilliant colors that identify functional areas. Also, it remains to be seen how the paint will resist the winter rains and the harsh summer sun. But indirectly this underscores the beauty of the system. None of these solutions is irrevocable, and experiments can be carried out without any danger to the original "document" and with low expenditures—hence with altogether limited risk. These experiments also consolidate the close concomitance of the work of archaeologists and conservators because they are both present, as it were, at the time of creation.

Technical Details

The system's simplicity is one of its major virtues. It can be applied and maintained whenever there is a smith who can assemble the metal structure, and a strong sewing machine that allows the fashioning of the tarp covers. The process of mounting the metal trellises is delicate (one must be careful not to affect the walls) but can be managed with normal supervision. Similarly, the tarps have simple geometrical shapes, and they can be sewn together without any special tailoring skills.

Also, the system in no way intrudes on any of the ancient structures: the metal structures simply rest on the floor, or in most cases on our own backfill, and the uprights are kept at a distance of some 10 centimeters from the face of the walls. While the segments of a wall cover are modular, they are all interlocked, and this, given the weight of the metal, provides adequate stability to the entire system.

In our specific context, there are two main factors that have a negative impact on conservation: rain and wind. Wind poses the greatest danger in those portions of the walls that were least well preserved. Here the hollow space contained within the covering can be considerable, and the resulting effect is that the wind has greater play inside the protective structure, rendering it more vulnerable. In such instances the very virtue of the system becomes its worst defect: since the covering is a seamless whole, a small tear can easily extend to a large portion of the structure. We are trying to overcome this problem by adding light and open wire mesh at the critical junctures. During the winter rains of 2003–4, we also removed the covering altogether in those few portions where nothing is left of the wall but only the negative trace left by the stone foundations after the stones were quarried in recent times. The fabric was set in place again once the winter was over.

To minimize the danger of water seeping through the canvas, we at first put a sheet-metal cover on the trellis, or, as a less expensive alternative, a sheet of plastic (fig. 6). But condensation trapped between the canvas and either the plastic or the metal caused the tarp to deteriorate rapidly, that is, within a couple of years. We are now trying two other alternatives. 1) A metal basin suspended from the top. This is more expensive, but it has the added advantage that one can put water in the basin to maintain an even level of humidity during the extremely hot and dry summers. 2) A loose sheet of plastic held in place by sand in plastic bags, placed directly on top of the walls.

To make visual inspection possible at any time, the coverings are not sewn at the corners of the walls. Rather, the two vertical edges overlap slightly, and they are kept tight by a set of laces that can easily be untied, and by Velcro borders that protect the metal eyelets through which the laces pass. At the

FIGURE 6 Loose plastic cover placed directly on mudbrick, with small sandbags holding it in place, and metal basin at the top to gather water seeping through the tarp (also to hold water in the summer to provide uniform humidity). Photo: G. Buccellati

bottom of each section, there is a metal bar that also keeps the fabric taut, both when it is in place and when it is lifted.

Important structural elements and significant stratigraphic documents are protected with metal boxes or glass panels to differentiate them from the covering that identifies the walls exclusively. A decision as to which of these items is to be so protected is made by archaeologists and conservators in close collaboration, in an effort to assess fully the relative feasibility and costs.

We have also addressed the question of preservation and display of the floor areas. Some of the floors were covered in antiquity with a thin layer of limestone plaster. These we have covered with plastic sheets, which are in turn covered by a thin layer of dirt, in the standard way of backfill. But this layer of dirt favored the growth of grass and thorny weeds. Rather than resort to herbicides, the backfill was covered with tiles made of recycled sherds embedded in cement. The tiles are individually placed, so they can be removed at will. We have used three different arrangements: (1) a single line to mark a path, (2) a spacing between tiles to allow a minimum growth, and (3) a tight arrangement to eliminate growth altogether. In

the formal part of the palace the floors are more elaborate; they consist of flagstones in the open areas and, in the roofed areas, of either a thick, cementlike plaster or brick pavers (fig. 7). Here we have added, to the system just described, large metal boxes that are embedded in the backfill and cover a portion of the pavement that is left free of backfill. By opening the box, a visitor can have a clear idea, from the visible detail, of the nature of the whole pavement.

Where vertical fissures have developed in the walls, we use consolidation in those cases that seem to pose the greatest risk. But our primary goal is to reduce physical and chemical intervention to an absolute minimum, and so we prefer, where possible, to apply a light stretched and weighted canvas: this simple system holds the wall in place by exerting a gentle pressure on the two sides (fig. 8).

Many issues remain under consideration, and the continuous interaction at the site between archaeologists and conservators produces a host of new ideas and experiments. The feedback we receive from a variety of sources (colleagues, visitors, staff, and workmen) helps us to fine-tune our approach. And the continuous monitoring will include all of

FIGURE 7 Modern pavers in loose and tight arrangement on top of backfill.
Photo: G. Buccellati

FIGURE 8 Vertical fissures on same wall in 2002, two years after excavations.
Note the stretched canvas, weighted down by pockets of sand on either side.
Photo: G. Gallacci

this information in what will continue to be an interesting experiment in professional interaction, in substantive conservation, and in more enlightened archaeology.[1]

Notes

1   For a few references pertinent to conservation at Tell Mozan, see G. Buccellati, "Urkesh: Archeologia, conservazione e restauro," *Kermes* 13 (2000):41–48; S. Bonetti, *Gli Opifici di Urkesh: Papers read at the Round Table in Florence, November 1999*, Urkesh/Mozan Studies 4 (Malibu: Undena, 2001) (online at http://www.urkesh.org); G. Buccellati and S. Bonetti, "Conservation at the Core of Archaeological Strategy: The Case of Ancient Urkesh at Tell Mozan," *Conservation: The Getty Conservation Institute Newsletter* 18 (2003):18–21 (online at http://www.getty.edu/conservation/resources/newsletter /18_1).

Excavations at Tell Mozan are currently supported by grants from the National Geographic Society, the Catholic Biblical Association, the L. J. Skaggs and Mary C. Skaggs Foundation, the Cotsen Institute of Archaeology at the University of California, Los Angeles (UCLA), Syria Shell Petroleum Development B.V., and the Urkesh Founders who contribute to the Urkesh Endowment. Conservation and restoration has been suppported through special grants from the Samuel H. Kress Foundation. Publication of the excavation reports has benefited from special funds from the Council on Research of the Academic Senate, UCLA, and the Cotsen Family Foundation. For the most recent excavation reports, see G. Buccellati and M. Kelly-Buccellati, "Die Große Schnittstelle. Bericht über die 14. Kampagne in Tall Mozan/Urkeš: Ausgrabungen im Gebiet AA, Juni-Oktober 2001," *Mitteilungen der Deutschen Orient-Gesellschaft* 134 (2002):103–30. Refer also to the website http:/www.urkesh.org.

PART FOUR

Finding Common Ground: The Role of Stakeholders in Decision Making

Introduction

Brian Egloff

Stakeholders are those individuals, groups, enterprises, agencies, professional organizations, or institutions that in one way or another have an interest in a place or an action. That interest can relate to tangible things or to the implementation of ideas. Implicit in this definition is the notion that there is a sense of shared concern, ownership, or belonging expressed in part as a common value system. Throughout much of the brief history of conservation and archaeology, the involvement of stakeholders has been on a limited and ad hoc basis, with some projects being relatively inclusive and others exclusive. It is fair to say that archaeologists and conservators in many instances are not trend-setters, but in some cases they have gone beyond the limits of contemporary protocols to form inventive relationships with stakeholders. Heritage specialists from Australia, Europe, Latin America, Oceania, and Southeast Asia present their experiences dealing with the diverse and sometimes conflicting plethora of stakeholders and illustrate how conservation outcomes can be achieved and sustained when situated within a framework of shared decision making.

Pisit Charoenwongsa provides us with an example from the Nan Valley in northeastern Thailand of "living heritage," where protection versus tourism in a pending World Heritage locale is all-important. The cultural aspect is considered the thrust of the exercise, but there is an underlying economic imperative to produce returns for villagers in a context of limited resources. Here the conservation of ancient pottery kilns excavated by archaeologists illustrates the need for sustainability that is closely linked to appropriate community training. It is of considerable concern that economic growth and cultural decline often go hand in hand. Of particular interest is the requirement instituted by the king of Thailand that arti-facts "should be kept at the place to which they belong." In a similar vein, the *China Principles* recommend that scientific information relating to an archaeological site should be maintained at that place, recognizing that true sharing of decision making is based on equal access, not only to economic resources but to intellectual property as well.

Stakeholders to some extent have always been part of heritage conservation projects; however, all too often they have been involved only in carrying out the manual labor or logistical support, or as interested bystanders. Most noticeable examples of the genuine sharing of decision making have occurred when research that was undertaken in foreign climes required partnerships with nationals of the host country, such as in Mexico.

Rodney Harrison, in the context of a former Aboriginal reserve in New South Wales, focuses on the particular values ascribed to what many would call ordinary sites and artifacts, though these places and things are especially evocative to the dispossessed and their descendants who wish to reassert their heritage. Richard Mackay, in the urban context, advocates that historical archaeology should follow a "values-based approach" and, like Harrison, stresses the tactile and "memory-scape" significance of artifacts.

Invariably, if a place is valued by one stakeholder group for a particular set of qualities, then it will be considered significant by other groups for different reasons. Nowhere is this seen more clearly and intensely than with national and international heritage icons. World Heritage as exemplified by the petroglyphs at Côa Valley in Portugal illustrates many of the conservation challenges that arise from stakeholder involvement with large-scale conservation projects, no matter where they are in the world. António Pedro Batarda Fernandes and Fernando Maia Pinto question how heritage specialists deal with decision making when hostility to the initiation of the conservation project is likely to continue into the foreseeable future. Local tensions among competing stakeholders, academic jealousies over who will reap the intellectual benefits, conflicting national and regional economic imperatives, and perceptions of an archaeological approach as elitist are just a few of the stereotypical challenges that emerged during the conservation of the Côa Valley archaeological site.

Central to this discussion is the notion of values within the tension-fraught world of land use, urban development, and resource exploitation and the attendant relocation of populations. Increasingly the cultural heritage resource manager has to tread a very narrow line indeed between the needs of government, the development industry, the international funding body, their professional requirements, and, more important, the ethical commitment to the local population. Growing expectations of archaeology to provide financial returns in a world driven by economic rationalism are being realized, as sacred landscapes are returned to Aboriginal communities in southeastern Australia. Brian Egloff is involved in heritage conservation in communities such as these, where the financial stakes are increasing and there is every likelihood that there will be both strong external opposition and dissension within the community if there are not open, established, and transparent avenues of communication.

The archaeology of environmental impact assessments contracted by companies concerns Ángel Cabeza when the projects have the potential to destroy heritage. How heritage specialists in Chile meet the needs of indigenous peoples—be they rural, such as the Aymaras and Atecamenos to the north, or urban dwellers, such as the Mapuche—as a feature of developmental projects is difficult to predict. A transborder situation involving environmental factors and local community needs, including food production, is described by Anabel Ford. Here on the border between Belize and Guatamala, a community group, the Amigos de el Pilar, is committed to the effective management of the Mayan archaeological site within an environmentally sustainable paradigm. Increasingly we see the conservation of cultural heritage being linked to sound natural resource management. Nelly Robles García's telling account of the encroachment of indigenous communities onto the World Heritage landscape at Monte Albán demonstrates another facet of the economic paradigm, where a substantial portion of the population lives in poverty and is seeking to encroach on heritage resources just to meet the daily needs of food and shelter.

From an international perspective, the transfer of power and decision making to stakeholders takes many forms. Recently there has been the realization that groups, particularly indigenous peoples, having been dispossessed in the past, require not only a recognition of their authority but also, and more important, positive economic outcomes. To conserve the heritage, archaeologists, anthropologists, and conservators must meet the challenge of dealing effectively with the shift from providing only short-term employment to a genuine sharing of decision making with diverse communities, including the provision of long-term sustainable economic outcomes.

Conservation, Researchers, and Aboriginal Heritage:
A Perspective from Coastal Southeastern Australia

Brian Egloff

Abstract: *Over the past two hundred years Europeans have observed and conducted research with Aboriginal communities and Aboriginals have studied "white fellas." From the perspective of the Aboriginal community at Wallaga Lake on the south coast of New South Wales, it is instructive to chart the various relationships that have obtained between researchers and indigenous groups from 1880 to the present. Commencing with the work of A. W. Howitt, who promoted the revitalization of ceremonial activities, to that of Norman Tindale and Joseph Birdsell in the 1930s that was set within a eugenics paradigm, to more recent research dealing with protected area land management, the various relationships can be demonstrated to provide if not immediate, then certainly long-term information that facilitates the meeting of community heritage conservation needs. The stakes are becoming ever higher as archaeologists and anthropologists provide advice to governments on the return of commercially valuable heritage landscapes to indigenous communities. This paper describes the strengths and weaknesses of recent experiences in Australia when dealing with community heritage conservation in the context of widely publicized legal cases.*

From the inception of anthropological and archaeological field studies in Australia, researchers from various academic disciplines have contributed to Aboriginal studies and the conservation of significant and sacred places through an intimate relationship with indigenous stakeholders. This paper focuses on an Aboriginal community on the south coast of New South Wales in a region of Australia that was affected in the 1830s, early in the colonization process. Until relatively recently it was assumed that the "remnant populations" living on Aboriginal reserves and in the surrounding countryside had little if any understanding of traditional practices or beliefs and could contribute only marginally to conservation efforts. However, due perhaps to a reserve system that placed generations in close proximity to each other, traditional knowledge was transmitted to select younger adults (Egloff [1979] 1981; Lampert and Sanders 1973). It is the retention of this traditional knowledge that supports the assertion by Aboriginal communities that they must be entrusted with the conservation of sacred places, which at times comprise entire landscape systems. Since the 1990s the aspirations of Aboriginal groups have coincided with the intention of the native title agenda of the Commonwealth of Australia and the land rights legislation of New South Wales, both of which seek to restore lands to indigenous groups as a social and economic basis for community betterment. The challenge is to demonstrate that contemporary Aboriginal community members are the rightful inheritors of significant landscapes, as many indigenous groups were either dispersed or translocated en masse from their traditional areas.

In 2001 the Office of the Registrar of Aboriginal Land Rights in New South Wales commissioned a study by Egloff, Peterson, and Wesson (2001) to find out if there were individuals who qualified under the Aboriginal Land Rights Act to be entered on the list of Aboriginal owners of two cultural landscapes, Biamanga and Gulaga National Parks, which were of significance to the Yuin peoples of Wallaga Lake. From that list of Aboriginal owners, the minister administering the act will appoint a panel to negotiate the terms for the return of lands to the community. Once the ownership of the lands is transferred, the Aboriginal council will lease the lands back to the New South Wales National Parks and Wildlife Service for park purposes. The Board of Management of the parks will have a majority of Aboriginal owners. As members of the board, the owners will have the authority to set community-driven goals that may conflict in some instances with natural heritage conservation objectives. This process is similar in intent to that of the Commonwealth government with respect to Kakadu and Uluru-Katajuta National Parks.

Australian archaeologists and anthropologists are required by the ethical standards of their professional associations as well as by the established protocols of government agencies to work with indigenous communities as an integral part of their research, and thus they are in intimate and prolonged contact with Aboriginals. I argue here that it is an almost unconscious reaction to seek social justice when working closely with indigenous communities that have been demonstrably disadvantaged through historical processes. In more and more instances, archaeologists and anthropologists are called on to provide "expert" services in the expectation that their findings will positively influence the outcome of native title or Aboriginal land rights judicial hearings and will secure social and economic benefits for indigenous communities while also conserving valuable heritage resources. Archaeologists and anthropologists have often sought to balance their work through interdisciplinary perspectives. What is required is a process that both fulfills the requirements of the research project and meets the needs of the indigenous communities, without the outcomes being inadvertently influenced by a social justice agenda. There are instances in which the recommendations of expert heritage specialists, when put to the test, have fallen short, leading to the destruction of heritage resources. Heritage conservation specialists must take steps to ensure that their involvement with stakeholders will not lead to outcomes that jeopardize heritage resources while delivering highly sensitive research results.

Wallaga Lake Aboriginal Community

On the south coast of New South Wales, in the early 1800s, explorers, entrepreneurs, and settlers recorded Aboriginal activities. Systematic census surveys were also undertaken, in some instances by the various Protectors of Aborigines, from the 1830s onward in conjunction with the distribution of blankets on the birthday of Queen Victoria. In the 1880s, ninety years after first contact, the institutionalization of indigenous groups commenced when Aboriginal families were "encouraged" to live at the then isolated reserve at Wallaga Lake. This community is situated adjacent to a coastal lagoon between two dominant landscape features (fig. 1). Gulaga Mountain directly to the north features in the peoples' origin myth;

Mumbulla Mountain, to the south, is said to be the dreaming place of Biamanga, a historical elder also known as Jack Mumbler (for photograph, see Egloff [1979] 1981:11). Both mountains hosted secret and sacred ceremonies; they are widely believed to be the ancestral forces that bind the community together and give it strength to survive (Byrne 1984).

In 1893 the Wallaga Lake community played a pivotal role in an initiation ceremony fostered by A. W. Howitt (1904), at that time the police magistrate of Gippsland in eastern Victoria (Mulvaney 1970; 1989:221). Although there is no doubt that his ethnographic studies were unethical by today's standards (Peterson 1990), his voluminous papers, available at the Latrobe Library in Melbourne and the Australian Institute of Aboriginal and Torres Straits Islander Studies in Canberra, provide ample opportunity for scholars and community representatives to reinterpret his data.

Norman Tindale's first fieldwork in 1918 was in northern Australia, where he sketched the boundaries of Aboriginal "tribes." When his work was submitted for publication, the editor removed the boundaries as at that time it was widely believed that Aboriginal bands wandered aimlessly over an unbounded landscape. This affront led Tindale throughout his career to pursue the demarcation of "tribal" lands through his continent-wide compendium of Aboriginal group boundaries (Tindale 1974). Tindale arrived at Wallaga Lake shortly after Christmas in 1938 with the then Harvard-based biological anthropologist Joseph Birdsell. Birdsell measured the physical attributes of the residents, and Tindale compiled genealogies while taking photographs of the informants. Their research aimed to document the intermingling of Aboriginal populations with the British settler society. Peterson (1990) puts forward a persuasive case that this research was undertaken in the context of the general concern with eugenics that dominated biological anthropology thinking in the 1920s and 1930s. Today, Tindale's maps of tribal and language distributions are frequently referred to in land claim cases by Aboriginal communities. His genealogies form the basis for family history projects, and the photographs he archived are in many instances the only surviving visual record of previous generations.

Both Howitt and Tindale recorded songs, dances, and phrases in the local dialect during their research, but it was not until the 1960s that linguists systematically recorded the remnants of languages that the elders possessed. This research by Diane Eades (1976), Janet Mathews, and Luise Hercus has been published only in part but is available on computer disc from the Australian Institute of Aboriginal and Torres Strait

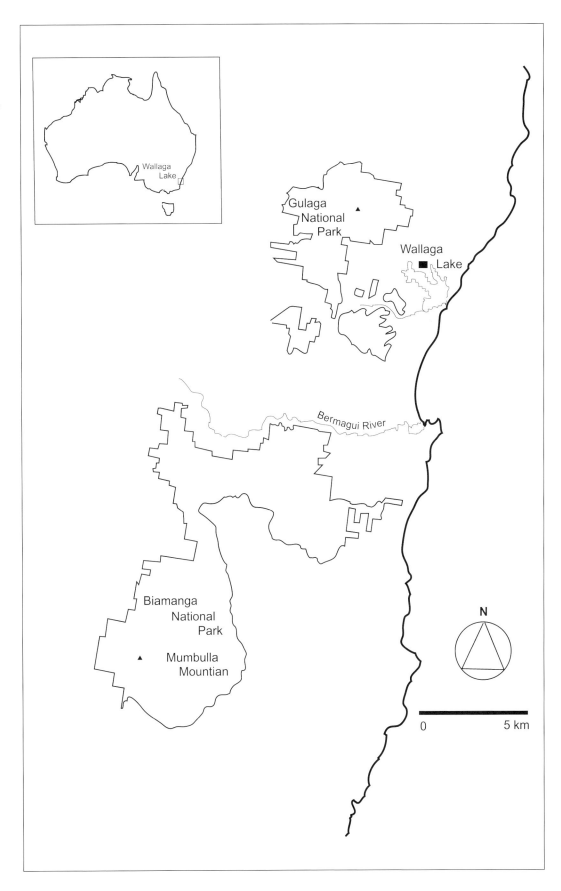

FIGURE 1 Wallaga Lake Aboriginal community with Gulaga National Park and Gulaga Mountain directly to the north and Biamanga National Park and Mumbulla Mountain to the south; far southeastern coast of Australia. Map by Brian Egloff

Islander Studies. The linguistic recordings are being used by Aboriginal elders to revive an interest in the language as it was spoken in the linguistic area that incorporates the Wallaga Lake community.

Traditional Knowledge and Landscapes of Significance

In the late 1970s the National Parks and Wildlife Service in New South Wales, the agency charged with recording and protecting Aboriginal sites, commenced not only the mapping of archaeological sites but also the documentation of sites of particular cultural significance to Aboriginal communities. This work was undertaken by an anthropologist, Howard Creamer (1984), and an Aboriginal park ranger, Ray Kelly (1975), under the direction of Sharon Sullivan, an archaeologist. Their study was continued by an indigenous team from Wallaga Lake led by Ted Thomas, a community elder. By the close of the 1970s, Aboriginal interests also had begun to correspond with the concerns of the green environment movement, although the two forces remained distinctly separate and at times politically opposed. The decade saw increasing pressure on the state government to protect landscapes with high natural and cultural values. One of the first confrontations between the timber industry and Aboriginal and green interests was at Mumbulla State Forest, a short distance south of the Wallaga Lake community. Ted Thomas, who had been working with the Park Service to record and conserve places of significance to the Wallaga Lake community, asserted that Mumbulla Mountain was a place where male initiation ceremonies had been held. This assertion was supported by both anthropological and archaeological research, as well as an archival search that located an unpublished map by Howitt of the 1883 initiation that matched the location and terrain of Mumbulla Mountain (Egloff [1979] 1981; Mulvaney 1970).

In 1980 the culturally significant south-facing side of the mountain and the summit were declared an "Aboriginal Place" and a "Protected Archaeological Area" within the state forest, and in 1994 the site was designated a national park with the addition of various other lands. Mumbulla Mountain was then the central feature of an extensive protected area. This series of events happened in the context, perhaps overly romantic, that for forty thousand or more years Aboriginal people were the "original" conservators of the Australian landscape and that today they should take on this role for the wider community (see Feary and Borschmann 1999).

The Calling of the Spirits (Morgan 1994) is an illustrated account of the life of a member of the Wallaga Lake Aboriginal community who lived in a nearby rural town. Eileen (née Thomas) Morgan is but one of many Aboriginal authors who in the 1990s wrote an account of what it meant to be Aboriginal. Autobiographies were augmented by biographies of notable Aboriginal personages. Lee Chittick, a local photographer, and Terry Fox, a former priest and community worker, produced a profusely illustrated and fascinating account of Percy Mumbler, a revered elder of the Wallaga Lake community (Chittick and Fox 1997). For the first time there were published accounts by or featuring local Aboriginal people that put a human face on heritage conservation issues. Deborah Rose (1990) drafted a report on the cultural significance of Gulaga Mountain for the Forestry Commission of New South Wales and the New South Wales National Parks and Wildlife Service, focusing on the female component of the community at Wallaga Lake and discussing their interests in the mountain.

Damaged Families and Biased Researchers

Two national inquiries added momentum to the movement to involve indigenous communities in heritage conservation: the Royal Commission into Aboriginal Deaths in Custody (Wootten 1991) and the National Inquiry into the Separation of Aboriginal and Torres Strait Islander Children from Their Families (Link-up and Wilson 1997). As we move toward transferring the control of substantial heritage landscapes, the political, economic, and social stakes are raised. When the researcher working with the community has seen informants grow from children into adults, strong personal commitments and bonds—and, more important, implied obligations—are forged. Working with Australian Aboriginal communities at times places the researcher in a social environment where the extraordinary imbalance of the haves versus the have-nots is painfully if not tragically apparent. The profound poverty and economic despair that grip families and damage entire generations cannot but influence the researcher. When called as expert witnesses, heritage specialists are presumably to provide fearless and untainted advice. Yet these archaeologists or anthropologists are aware of the injustices of the past and the inability of the legal system to correct those wrongs and provide "social justice" retrospectively. The courts and tribunals have found that heritage specialists may package the past to meet with a perception of community needs. In one instance an overzealous description of an alleged heritage place was described by a tribunal as "puffery."

Returning National Parks

In New South Wales the National Parks and Wildlife Act 1974 (NSW) and the Aboriginal Land Rights Act 1983 (NSW) facilitate the return of protected areas to local Aboriginal land councils. Only Aboriginals meeting the following criteria can have their names listed on the register of Aboriginal owners: the individual is directly descended from the original inhabitants of the culture area in which the land is situated; has a cultural association with the land that derives from traditions, observances, customs, beliefs, or history of the Aboriginal inhabitants of the land; and has consented to the entry of his or her name in the register (Egloff, Peterson, and Wesson 2001:2). The kind of information required to demonstrate direct biological descent from an original inhabitant is sensitive to say the least. Legitimate concerns as well as malicious rumors are raised with respect to the pedigree and the right to "speak for country" of individuals who seek to be listed as Aboriginal owners. It goes without saying that we live in litigious times. Only legally sound research processes will lead to positive outcomes should the findings be tested in court. Heritage conservation issues can be compared to an accordion that expands and contracts. At times the local Aboriginal community can deal with the issue, but in some instances the matter expands and becomes of national or international concern. Inclusive processes and communication are the essence of good heritage conservation practice.

David Ritter, principal legal officer of Yamatji Land and Sea Council, has written extensively on proof and evidence in native title proceedings (Ritter n.d.:at 1850). He stresses that it is not fatal to the case if archaeologists or anthropologists act as advocates, but they must stay within the realm of their expertise. However, at times the court has been critical, as in *De Rose v. South Australia* (at 352) where O'Loughlin states that the researcher providing the expert advice was "too close to the claimants and their cause: he failed to exhibit the objectivity and neutrality that is required of an expert who is giving evidence before the court. Rather he seemed—too often—to be an advocate for the applicants." Ritter emphasizes that the court wishes to hear directly from the bearers of the Aboriginal culture and that the role of experts should not supplant the testimony of community members. On the south coast of New South Wales, the landmark case *Mason v. Tritton,* testing native title and rights to the sea, had been lost to the Aboriginal defendants. In this instance the archaeological report was considered by the magistrate to be in a "strange form," as if "wishing to please the person who had asked for the opinion" (Egloff 2000:202; Strickland 1994).

At the commencement of the Biamanga and Gulaga Aboriginal owners research project, it was considered imperative by the registrar that the researchers not appear to be advocates for any segment of the community. The author, a historical archaeologist who had worked specifically with the Wallaga Lake community since 1978, and Sue Wesson, a geographer with extensive genealogical and family location data, were seen to be associated with certain factions and obviously were emotionally involved with the community. It thus seemed prudent to include in the research team Nicolas Peterson, a social anthropologist who had extensive experience with indigenous land rights in the Northern Territory since the 1970s. A research design seems to have worked wherein the multidisciplinary team consisted of some researchers who were personally close to the Aboriginal community and some who had no previous dealings with the informants or factions of the community.

In Australia there are instances when reports have been drafted by researchers but permission to publish the study has been withheld by Aboriginal communities, rendering the material unavailable for study. Neither the registrar who commissioned the report nor the researchers wanted that to happen with the Biamanga and Gulaga report. Copies of the report have been with the community for two years; issues have been raised, but by and large the questionable parts of the report have been matters of detail that were readily corrected. It was subsequently decided to make the report user-friendly by including historical photographs of members of the Wallaga Lake community. Seeking written permission from the descendants to publish the photographs has entailed numerous visits with members of the community scattered along the south coast. It is apparent that the more contact researchers have over a longer period, the less likelihood there is of their work becoming divisive and controversial (Egloff, Peterson, and Wesson 2005).

Sarah Colley (2002), in an exploration of the recent history of Australian archaeology, documents the ability of some archaeologists to work with communities and promote the objectives of conservation, while other archaeologists have failed, and the heritage resource has either been destroyed or abruptly returned to the community under court order. In the 1980s and 1990s the repatriation of skeletal material and artifact collections raised real questions and divided the Australian archaeological community. Initially the concern was with collections of Pleistocene-dated human remains. A controversial case was taken to court by the Tasmanian Aboriginal community to have La Trobe University return recently excavated archaeological material. The court order was challenged by the university but was upheld, and the archaeological materials were returned to Tasmania (Colley 2002:xii–xiii).

Conservation Agenda

Once they are deeded to the local Aboriginal land councils, Gulaga and Biamanga National Parks will be leased to the New South Wales National Parks and Wildlife Service to continue as public protected areas. For the most part, the Parks Board of Management will comprise Aboriginal owners who no doubt will adopt a conservation agenda that differs in some respects from current management practices. In anticipation of community needs, the park service has adopted an inclusive management process and has fostered the employment of Aboriginal rangers and park workers. Biamanga and Gulaga National Parks are used for a variety of community purposes, from culture camps to dreaming ceremonies and tourism-linked cultural and natural tours. Yet to be resolved is the extent to which Aboriginal people will be allowed to hunt, fish, and gather wild plants in national parks, contrary to present regulations.

Heritage conservation specialists, be they anthropologists, ethnoarchaeologists, geographers, or historical archaeologists, have long recognized the need for dialogue and partnerships with the people they are studying. Although indigenous communities were involved to some extent with surveys and the excavation of archaeological sites, they did not necessarily determine what was significant about the heritage place or decide how it should be conserved. And seldom have archaeological conservation projects been specifically designed to contribute to the social and economic needs of indigenous communities. Today there is a shift in the power balance as heritage specialists are required to share their knowledge and authority. With the value of heritage conservation still being worked through by Australian communities, it is likely that the specialist will be called on to participate at one time or another in court proceedings. However, a key role of heritage conservation specialists is to keep their employers and Aboriginal community members out of unnecessary court proceedings. Ideally this is best dealt with by having an open, transparent, and inclusive process that extends over an appropriate period. Heritage conservation must be viewed as a process that does not necessarily seek closure or resolution but that is always open-ended and in fact welcomes change. Expanding from sites to places and then to broader landscapes

while at the same time being inclusive is difficult at times, as every community speaks with a different voice.

Acknowledgments

I thank Nicolas Peterson of the Australian National University and fellow researcher Sue Wesson for their contributions to this paper. The research project leading to this paper was commissioned and supported by Warick Baird, Rachel Lenehan, Stephen Wright, and Adam Black of the Office of the Registrar, Aboriginal Land Rights Act (NSW), members of the Bega Local Aboriginal Land Council and the Merrimans Local Aboriginal Land Council. Both John Mulvaney and Nicolas Peterson have given considerable intellectual thought and published articles on the role of anthropologists in Aboriginal studies. Sarah Colley has done the same with respect to archaeologists. The Getty Conservation Institute invited me to attend the Fifth World Archaeological Congress. The University of Canberra facilitated attendance at the congress.

References

Byrne, D. 1984. *The Mountains Call Me Back: A History of the Aborigines and the Forests of the Far South Coast of New South Wales.* NSW Ministry of Aboriginal Affairs, NSW NPWS: Equus Publications.

Chittick, L., and T. Fox. 1997. *Travelling with Percy: A South Coast Journey.* Canberra: Aboriginal Studies Press.

Colley, S. 2002. *Uncovering Australia: Archaeology, Indigenous People and the Public.* Crows Nest, NSW: Allen & Unwin.

Creamer, H. 1984. *A Gift and a Dreaming: The New South Wales Survey of Aboriginal Sacred and Significant Sites, 1973–1983.* Sydney: New South Wales National Parks and Wildlife Service.

Eades, D. 1976. *The Dharawal and Dhurga Languages of the New South Wales South Coast.* Australian Aboriginal Studies, Research and Regional Studies, 8. Canberra: Australian Institute of Aboriginal Studies.

Egloff, B. J. [1979] 1981. *Mumbulla Mountain: An Anthropological and Archaeological Investigation.* Occasional Paper no. 4. Sydney: National Parks and Wildlife Service.

————. 2000. "Sea Long Stretched Between": Perspectives of Aboriginal fishing on the south coast of New South Wales in the light of *Mason v. Tritton.*" *Aboriginal History* 24:200–211.

Egloff, B. J., N. Peterson, and S. Wesson. 2001. *Biamanga National Park and Gulaga National Park Aboriginal Owners Research Project.* Report to the Office of the Registrar, Aboriginal Land Rights Act 1983 (NSW). Canberra: University of Canberra.

———. 2005. *Biamanga and Gulaga: Aboriginal Cultural Association with Biamanga and Gulaga National Parks.* Sydney: Office of the Registrar, Aboriginal Land Rights Act 1983 (NSW).

Feary. S., and G. Borschmann. 1999. "The first foresters: The archaeology of Aboriginal forest management." In *The People's Forest: A Living History of the Australian Bush,* ed. G. Borschmann, 13–21. Blackheath, NSW: Peoples' Forest Press.

Howitt, A. W. 1904. *The Native Tribes of South-East Australia.* London: Macmillan.

Kelly, R. 1975. Investigations of Aboriginal sites in the Wallaga Lakes area of New South Wales. Report of the New South Wales National Parks and Wildlife Service, Sydney.

Lampert, R. J., and F. Sanders. 1973. Plants and men on the Beecroft Peninsula, New South Wales. *Mankind* 9:96–108.

Link-up (NSW) Aboriginal Corporation and J. T. Wilson. 1997. *In the Best Interest of the Child?, Stolen Children: Aboriginal Pain/White Shame.* Aboriginal History Monograph No. 4. Canberra.

Morgan, E. 1994. *The Calling of the Spirits.* Canberra: Aboriginal Studies Press.

Mulvaney, D. J. 1970. The anthropologist as tribal elder. *Mankind* 7:205–17.

Peterson, N. 1990. "Studying man and man's nature": The history of the institutionalisation of Aboriginal anthropology. *Australian Aboriginal Studies* 2:3–19.

Ritter, D. n.d. Native title claims before the court: Proof and evidence. Butterworths Lexis Nexis Native Title Service (looseleaf) .

Rose, D. B. 1990. Gulaga: A report on the cultural significance of Mt Dromedary to Aboriginal people. Forestry Commission of New South Wales and the New South Wales National Parks and Wildlife Service.

Strickland, P. 1994. Mason v. Tritton (NSW Sup Ct, Young, J). In *The Australian Criminal Reports, 1993–1994,* ed. F. Rinaldi, 70:28–45.

Tindale, N. B. 1974. *Aboriginal Tribes of Australia: Terrain, Environmental Contacts, Distribution, Limits and Proper Names.* Canberra: Australian National University Press.

Wesson, S. C. 2000. *An Historical Atlas of the Aborigines of Eastern Victoria and Far South Eastern New South Wales.* Monash University, Geography and Environmental Science Monograph No. 53. Melbourne.

Wootten, J. H. 1991. *Royal Commission into Aboriginal Deaths in Custody. Regional Report of Inquiry in New South Wales, Victoria and Tasmania.* Canberra: AGPS.

"It Will Always Be Set in Your Heart": Archaeology and Community Values at the Former Dennawan Reserve, Northwestern New South Wales, Australia

Rodney Harrison

> Yesterday I was at Dennawan and the little bit of a [house] frame is still standing there and I got a bit emotional. . . . I was out there with Arthur Hooper and we went over and he said, "I think this is the place here now, this is where you fellas used to live," and when I walked and stood there I said, "Yes, Arthur, this is the place." You don't feel that just anywhere. You only feel that in special places, and Dennawan is a special place. It will always be set in your heart.
>
> —JUNE BARKER, speaking to the author about the significance of the archaeology
> of the former Dennawan Reserve, Lightning Ridge, 11 April 2002

Abstract: *This paper presents a perspective of an archaeological site gained through medium- to long-term community-based participatory research with one local Australian Aboriginal community. It is radically different from that which may have emerged from either a social or an archaeological significance assessment, had each been carried out in isolation. At the ruin of the former Dennawan Aboriginal Reserve in far northwestern New South Wales, the living and the dead interact through the humble physical remains of tin cans, broken bottles, and tumbled-down house frames. Drawing on oral accounts of community participants and fine-grained archaeological recording of the remains of the site, this paper reveals the complex relationship among archaeological "relics," local communities, ancestors, and the role of archaeological sites in contemporary local identity building. The participation of community members in archaeological research provided an opportunity for the sensuous nature of local people's active (re-)creation of locality to come into view. This paper argues that archaeologists must engage with those local communities that have custodianship of the places they study to adequately understand and hence manage and conserve the significance of the places.*

Archaeological Sites as Dead Places?

For many archaeologists, it is a common assumption that archaeological sites are "dead" places. The very qualities that define the "Western" aesthetic appreciation of archaeological sites—ruin, decay, fragmentation (Lowenthal 1985; Pearson and Shanks 2001; Shanks 1992)—are the hallmarks of places left behind. Archaeological sites, metaphorically and literally, form artifact crypts, coffins that we reinter for analysis and investigation. To this way of thinking, not only are archaeological sites dead, but they should ideally be static. Hence the concern among archaeologists about understanding and documenting archaeological site formation processes, which are often seen as processes that are destructive of the archaeological record. In 1983 Lewis Binford argued that "the challenge that archaeology offers . . . is to take contemporary observations of static material things and . . . translate them into statements about the dynamics of past ways of life" (20). Archaeologists, following Binford's dictum, have often seen their role as that of expert and interpreter, translating the traces of long-dead sites to educate a passive if not unreceptive public. While archaeological value has been seen to lie in the ability of a site to address technical research questions, the contemporary social value of such places has become increasingly disassociated from archaeologists' assessments and conservation of their heritage value. In cases in which archaeological sites are actively visited, interacted with, and used, there is the potential for such purely "archaeological" conservation agendas to come into conflict with the needs and wishes of stakeholders and local communities.

But as anyone who has ever seen George A. Romero's 1968 horror film, *Night of the Living Dead,* will know, the dead *walk.* In this paper I consider the example of an ephemeral and largely unremarkable archaeological site that plays an active role in the social world of one Australian Aboriginal community. I argue that a "classic" approach to assessing the scientific values associated with this archaeological site would be insensitive to the dynamic and active role that it plays in the life of this local community. A combination of detailed, fine-grained archaeological investigation and deep, participant-observation ethnography precipitates a more holistic understanding of the heritage values associated with the site. Routine archaeological assessments would be inadequate to describe, and hence manage, the significance of such a place.

An Archaeology of Attachment to the Former Dennawan Aboriginal Reserve, Northwestern NSW, Australia

The name "Dennawan" describes a multiplicity of spatially concurrent places (fig. 1). It is principally associated with an unsupervised Aboriginal Reserve, gazetted in 1913 on the site of an earlier camp that had provided an Aboriginal labor force for surrounding sheep ranching properties (fig. 2). At the turn of the nineteenth century Dennawan was a bustling village; built at the junction of two traveling stock routes on the edge of the western NSW pastoral frontier, it contained a hotel and an inn, a shop, a post office, a police station, and a resident Aboriginal population of several hundred people. Dennawan was also an Aborigines Inland Missionary outpost, where the fondly recalled missionary, Miss Ginger, taught children to read and write. Dennawan is an archaeological site on the edge of Culgoa National Park (fig. 3), a place visited and recalled in the present. Dennawan is a place from which Aboriginal people were removed in the 1940s—a symbol of the broader "spatial story" (de Certeau 1984) associated with the

NSW Aborigines Protection Board's concentration and segregation strategies of the late 1930s and the 1940s (e.g., Goodall 1996). Dennawan is simultaneously all and more than any of these things. It is an entanglement of genealogies, a place where past, present, and future collapse (for a full description of the history and archaeology of the former Dennawan reserve, see Harrison 2003, 2004; Veale 1997).

My first experiences at Dennawan occurred during a visit to the site with several local Aboriginal people who had either lived or had ancestors who lived at the site in the 1930s. The first thing that struck me was the way people interacted and articulated their relationship with the place in an "archaeological" manner. By this, I mean that it involved interrogating, touching, and talking about the material traces of the former settlement. People also interacted with the place in a formal, performative (Butler 1993) way, which suggested it was more than a dead memorial to the past. Instead, Dennawan emerged through the course of my involvement in recording it not as a dead place but an active site for the contemporary creation of locality, community, and collective identity. While I was mapping the remains of the Reserve, I developed a parallel investigation into the significance of the remains to local Aboriginal people and the way in which that significance manifests itself during visits to the site.

The Living and the Dead

For descendants of the Aboriginal people who used to live on the Dennawan Reserve, the dead often visit the living in dreams. Contemporary Muruwari people have a number of beliefs about relics and their relationship with ancestors that have contributed to the development of Dennawan as a place of pilgrimage. Physical contact of the body or skin with artifacts is considered a way of making a connection with the ancestral past. During visits, especially to precontact archaeological sites, Muruwari people like to rub artifacts such as those of flaked stone against their skin. Vera Nixon explained in an interview:

> When you're rubbing the stones over your skin you can get the feel of—you sort of get the feeling of the spirits coming into your skin somehow or another. I dunno, it's a strange feeling, but it's a good feeling.
> (DENNAWAN, 18 November 2001)

The belief that ancestors' spirits are associated with the objects they used during their lifetimes structures people's interactions with the remains of the former settlement. A trip

FIGURE 1 Location map showing Culgoa National Park and
Dennawan in western New
South Wales, Australia.
Redrawn from a map prepared
by Peter Johnson and pub-
lished in Harrison 2004

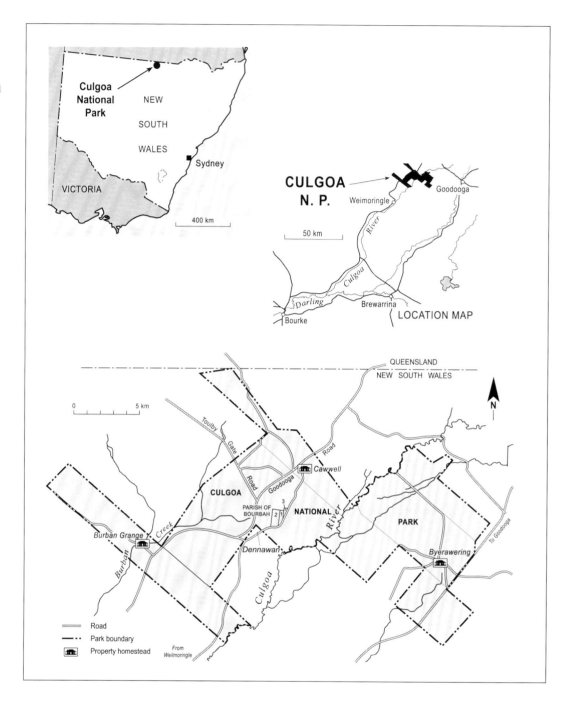

to Dennawan, then, is much more than just an opportunity to learn about the past; it is an opportunity to make direct and intimate contact with it. Josey Byno said:

> When we go and visit the place and see the artifacts that they used to use and the fire there, the oven, we get very emotional. Not only that, there is a special

feeling in the air that surrounds us. We can feel that spiritual feeling wherever we go, and we know that they are with us. (DENNAWAN, 18 November 2001)

While it is important for people to be able to touch and interact with the artifacts on site, it is considered dangerous to remove them. People who do this are tormented with bad

FIGURE 3 The remains of "Granny Bailey's house" on the former
Dennawan Reserve in 2002. *(Left to right):* Project collaborators
Josey Byno, Arthur Hooper, Dorothy Kelly, and Vera Nixon.
Photo: Rodney Harrison

FIGURE 2 The Ferguson family at Dennawan in 1936. Standing
at rear, Duncan; seated, his wife, Blanche, holding baby
Cheeko, with children Gloria, June, and Fred. Reproduced with
kind permission of June Barker.

dreams or sickness. In contrast, just being at the site is considered to make Muruwari people feel physically healthy.
Arthur Hooper, now in his seventies, noted:

> Ever since I've been coming out here, doing a little
> bit of work for people, I've been feeling really great.
> I'm really happy to see the old place again. And my
> feelings—inside me it's a very glad feeling, I have no
> worries about anything else. No aches and pains, I
> just walk around the place for hours and hours
> without getting tired. (DENNAWAN, 18 November
> 2001)

The ability of the place to effect change on the bodies of
Muruwari people is an important facet of the spirituality and
significance of the former Dennawan Reserve. These corpo-
real influences are intimately tied to various spiritual associations with the former settlement, in particular, the slippage
between post-1930 associations with Aborigines Inland Mission Christian missionaries and older, deeper associations

with *wiyrigan* (medicine men) and *miraaku* and *miraga* (spirits). This slippage creates a certain denseness of experience
that is felt by Muruwari people in the present when visiting
the archaeological site, which they have increasingly done on
a regular basis, especially over the past ten to twenty years.

Archaeology

Technical detail obtained from fine-grained differential GPS
recording is being integrated with anecdote and memory in
the mapping of the archaeological remains at Dennawan to
produce a multivocal, textured representation of the archaeological record and to provide insights into a shared past (figs.
4–7). An artifact database linked to a hand-held computer and
differential GPS has been used to record all of the eight thousand artifacts and structural features at the site to a horizon-
tal accuracy of ±4 centimeters. Digital audio recordings taken
in the field have been captured as a separate layer and integrated into the GIS. Oral accounts and archaeological mapping have been combined to develop integrated data sources
on which to base an interpretation of the archaeology of the
former Reserve. The site recording was undertaken during

FIGURE 4 GIS map showing the locations of features recorded during the archaeological survey in 2001–2. Features include broken bottle glass, tin cans, wooden posts, and corrugated iron sheeting (for more detail, see Harrison 2004:chap. 8). Courtesy of Rodney Harrison

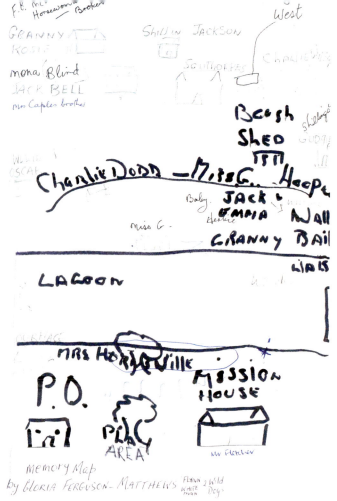

FIGURE 5 Gloria Matthews's "memory map" of the former settlement, drawn in late 2002. Gloria lived at Dennawan during the late 1930s and has vivid memories of the settlement as it existed at that time. Reproduced with kind permission of Gloria Matthews.

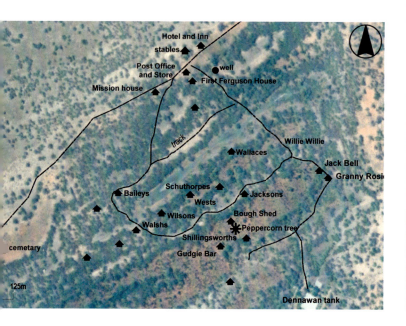

FIGURE 6 The information from Gloria Matthews's map combined with the results of archaeological field survey reveals an individual memoryscape. The physical remains of the settlement serve for contemporary Muruwari people as a mnemonic for remembering the dead and a focus for the active creation of locality and collective identity. Courtesy of Rodney Harrison

FIGURE 7 Detail of the scatter of archaeological remains near one of the former residences at Dennawan, showing tin can, enameled milk jug, and kerosene tin. These humble archaeological remains are imbued with immense emotional and spiritual significance for Muruwari people. The significance of such artifacts emerges only in dialogue between archaeology and oral history. Photo: Rodney Harrison

multiple field trips over a period of approximately eighteen months. This relatively protracted period of investigation was important for allowing the community the longer time frames they required to engage collaboratively and in a considered way with the research, and it was an important part of the project methodology.

Understanding the Significance of the Former Dennawan Reserve

The archaeology of the former Dennawan Reserve has much information to contribute regarding the relatively hidden histories of Aboriginal pastoral labor camps in the nineteenth and twentieth centuries in Australia. However, the ruins of the former Reserve are much more than a source of information to local Muruwari people; they represent instead the focus for a program of shared, collective memorialization of the past. The artifacts that remain on the former Reserve are invested with intense emotional and spiritual power. They form the conduit for controlled interactions between the spirit and human worlds and between past and present. Instead of ceasing to exist after its abandonment, Dennawan continues to hold power and fascination for Muruwari people as a place where local traces and memories persist, challenging and actively assisting in the creation of the past and the present. It does this as much through the mutual involvement of people and objects, which both evoke and create collective memories, as through their absence or decay. Place and trace provide creative opportunities for citation, quotation, and montage (Pearson and Shanks 2001). For Muruwari people, Dennawan is past *and* future. Each trip to Dennawan represents an opportunity to excavate a "place of buried memory" (Küchler 1999; Leslie 1999:108).

This social-archaeological significance of Dennawan is unlikely to have registered under a conventional archaeological significance assessment. Though that approach may have involved community consultation (Byrne, Brayshaw, and Ireland 2001), leading to a recognition of the historical significance of Dennawan to Muruwari people, I think it is unlikely that the intimate, sensual relationship between people and objects at Dennawan would have become evident in the absence of either the detailed archaeological study or deeper ethnographic research. This emerged in the context of detailed archaeological fieldwork and the protracted engagement of the community with the archaeological project and participant observation in moving across and interacting with the place. Other authors have described the protracted

engagement of local community members with archaeologists recording sites in a region as "story-trekking" (e.g., Green, Green, and Neves 2003), and this marriage of the recording of individual "landscape biographies" (Harrison 2002), oral history, and field survey is emerging in community-based archaeological research as an integral method for articulating the role of archaeological resources in contemporary local social relations (see also Byrne and Nugent 2004). This provides a challenge to heritage managers, who make routine archaeological and social significance assessments but tend not to investigate the significance of these areas in tandem with one another.

Outcomes of Increased Stakeholder Participation in Archaeology in Australia and Implications for Conservation

The outcomes of increased stakeholder participation in archaeology in Australia have important implications for conservation in ways that are broadly relevant to archaeology worldwide. I would argue that the kind of collaborative community archaeological research discussed here has real conservation outcomes in terms of developing a more holistic understanding of the contemporary values of archaeological sites. Dennawan's significance lies neither in its scientific significance as an archaeological site nor in its historic or social significance to the local community but at the interface of archaeology and community. It is the deep layering of memory and attachment, and the complex structuring of the archaeological record that emerges in dialogue with contemporary accounts of local people, from which the significant values of Dennawan can be surmised.

There are a number of more general outcomes of increased stakeholder participation in archaeology in Australia, a point that has been noted by a number of authors over the past ten years, during which time communities have become increasingly vocal about their rights to be involved in the conservation of archaeological places (e.g., Byrne 2002, 2003; Byrne, Brayshaw, and Ireland 2001; Clarke 2000, 2002; Davidson, Lovell-Jones, and Bancroft 1995; Davison 1991; Godwin and L'Oste-Brown 2002; Greer 1996; McIntyre-Tamwoy 2002; Ross and Coghill 2000). I have summarized a number of these outcomes in a paper written with two of my colleagues (Greer, Harrison, and McIntyre-Tamwoy 2002). Where community stakeholders have been involved in setting the research agenda for archaeological research projects, focus shifts to

- the recent, remembered past and the "entangled," "cross-cultural" nature of historic heritage places;
- the role of "locally significant" heritage places as part of the active creation of community and as integral components of local, social identity (as opposed to the "national" heritage of the state, which archaeologists and other heritage practitioners might emphasize);
- understanding what local communities actually "use" heritage for and how archaeology specifically can be used by communities; and
- the way in which the past is socially constructed, and contested, by different stakeholders.

All of these approaches that community stakeholders bring to archaeology not only benefit heritage conservation through the development of a more holistic understanding of the significance of places but also challenge archaeology to produce new research to meet community needs and interests. I think such a diverse mix of approaches is healthy for the discipline of archaeology, not only in stimulating new and often exciting lines of research, but also in reminding archaeologists of the various stakeholders who hold interests in the pasts they study (e.g., Layton 1989a, 1989b; McBryde 1991).

In the case of Dennawan, social beliefs about the relationship between objects and the dead also dictated, to a large extent, that archaeological investigation should be nonintrusive. Communities are increasingly calling for archaeologists to develop new, innovative, nondestructive ways of working with archaeological sites. At Dennawan, I was able to employ some of the new spatial technologies associated with differential GPS and GIS. Again, I think such calls from stakeholders also have positive spin-offs in challenging archaeologists to develop methods of archaeological investigation that conserve the archaeological resource but still answer archaeological research agendas.

Conclusion: Rubbish or Relic? Object Lessons and the Archaeology of the Tin Can

The humble archaeological remains at Dennawan belie the intensity of the local people's emotional attachments to the site and its relics. With its ephemeral archaeological remains and piles of tin cans and other "rubbish," Dennawan is clearly not the sort of archaeological site that would have attracted much attention under an archaeological or cultural heritage management discourse that focuses on the deep prehistoric

past or prominent built structures such as the remains of early pioneering infrastructure. I would argue that people throughout the world have similar, hidden relationships with the archaeological sites we assess regularly as dead places. But we cannot presume to manage the multitude of values that communities attribute to these places by considering them "dead." Local communities create archaeological sites as much as we create them through our archaeological interpretations. Sometimes the dead walk among us.

References

Binford, L. 1983. *In Pursuit of the Past.* New York: Thames and Hudson.

Butler, J. 1993. *Bodies That Matter: On The Discursive Limits of "Sex."* London: Routledge.

Byrne, D. 2002. An archaeology of attachment: Cultural heritage and the post-contact. In *After Captain Cook: The Archaeology of the Recent Indigenous Past in Australia,* ed. R. Harrison and C. Williamson, 135–46. Sydney University Archaeological Methods Series 8. Sydney: Sydney: Archaeological Computing Laboratory, University of Sydney.

———. 2003. The ethos of return: Erasure and reinstatement of Aboriginal visibility in the Australian historical landscape. *Historical Archaeology* 37 (1):73–86.

Byrne, D., H. Brayshaw, and T. Ireland. 2001. *Social Significance: A Discussion Paper.* Sydney: NSW National Parks and Wildlife Service.

Byrne, D., and M. Nugent. 2004. *Mapping Attachment: A Spatial Approach to Aboriginal Post-Contact Heritage.* Sydney: NSW National Parks and Wildlife Service.

Clarke, A. 2000. Time, tradition and transformation: The negotiation of cross cultural engagements in Groote Eylandt, northern Australia. In *The Archaeology of Difference: Negotiating Cross Cultural Engagements in Oceania,* ed. R. Torrence and A. Clarke, 142–81. One World Archaeology, 33. London: Routledge.

———. 2002. The ideal and the real: Cultural and personal transformations of archaeological research on Groote Eylandt, northern Australia. *World Archaeology* 34 (2):249–64.

Davidson, I., C. Lovell-Jones, and R. Bancroft, eds. 1995. *Archaeologists and Aborigines Working Together.* Armidale: University of New England Press.

Davison, G. 1991. A brief history of the Australian heritage movement. In *A Heritage Handbook,* ed. G. Davison and C. McConville, 14–27. Sydney: Allen & Unwin.

de Certeau, M. 1984. *The Practice of Everyday Life.* Berkeley: University of California Press.

Godwin, L., and S. L'Oste-Brown. 2002. A past remembered: Aboriginal "historic" places in central Queensland. In *After Captain Cook: The Archaeology of the Recent Indigenous Past in Australia,* ed. R. Harrison and C. Williamson, 191–212. Sydney University Archaeological Methods 8. Sydney: Archaeological Computing Laboratory, University of Sydney.

Goodall, H. 1996. *Invasion to Embassy: Land in Aboriginal Politics in New South Wales, 1770–1972.* Sydney: Allen & Unwin in association with Black Books.

Green, L. F., D. R. Green, and E. G. Neves. 2003. Indigenous knowledge and archaeological science. *Journal of Social Archaeology* 3 (3):366–98.

Greer, S. 1996. Archaeology, heritage and identity in Northern Cape York Peninsula. In *Australian Archaeology '95: Proceedings of the 1995 Australian Archaeological Association Annual Conference Tempus,* vol. 6, ed. S. Ulm, I. Lilley, and A. Ross, 293–99. St Lucia: University of Queensland.

Greer, S., R. Harrison, and S. McIntyre-Tamwoy. 2002. Community-based archaeology in Australia. *World Archaeology* 34 (2):265–87.

Harrison, R. 2002. Ngarranganni/Ngamungamu/Jilinijarra: "Lost places," recursiveness and hybridity at Old Lamboo pastoral station, southeast Kimberley. Ph.D. dissertation, University of Western Australia.

———. 2003. The archaeology of "lost places": Ruin, memory and the heritage of the Aboriginal diaspora in Australia. *Historic Environment* 17 (1):18–23.

———. 2004. *Shared landscapes: Archaeologies of Attachment and the Pastoral Industry in New South Wales.* Studies in the Cultural Construction of Open Space, 3. Sydney: University of New South Wales Press.

Küchler, S. 1999. The place of memory. In *The Art of Forgetting,* ed. A. Forty and S. Küchler, 53–72. Oxford: Berg.

Layton, R., ed. 1989a. *Conflict in the Archaeology of Living Traditions.* One World Archaeology, 8. London: Routledge.

———. 1989b. *Who Needs the Past? Indigenous Values and Archaeology.* One World Archaeology, 5. London: Routledge.

Leslie, E. 1999. Souvenirs and forgetting: Walter Benjamin's memory-work. In *Material Memories: Design and Evocation,* ed. M. Kwint, C. Breward, and J. Aynsley, 107–22. Oxford: Berg.

Lowenthal, D. 1985. *The Past Is a Foreign Country.* Cambridge: Cambridge University Press.

McBryde, I., ed. 1991. *Who Owns the Past?* Oxford: Oxford University Press.

McIntyre-Tamwoy, S. 2002. Places people value: Social significance and cultural exchange in post invasion Australia. In *After Captain Cook: The Archaeology of the Recent Indigenous Past in Australia,* ed. R. Harrison and C. Williamson, 171–90. Sydney University Archaeological Methods, 8. Sydney: Archaeological Computing Laboratory, University of Sydney.

Pearson, M., and M. Shanks. 2001. *Theatre/Archaeology.* London: Routledge.

Ross, A., and S. Coghill. 2000. Conducting a community-based archaeological project: An archaeologist's and a Koenpul man's perspective. *Australian Aboriginal Studies* 1:76–83.

Shanks, M. 1992. *Experiencing the Past: On the Character of Archaeology.* London: Routledge.

Veale, S. 1997. Culgoa NP land use history. Unpublished report to the NSW National Parks and Wildlife Service, Sydney.

Community-based Archaeological Resource Management in Southeast Asia

Pisit Charoenwongsa

Abstract: *This paper emphasizes the importance of implementing a community-based approach to heritage management for projects in Southeast Asia. With reference to living heritage, it is vital that the people have substantial input into how their cultural heritage is maintained. This point is illustrated in a case study of a new project in Nan province, northern Thailand, in which a community-based approach is being applied in both the excavation and postexcavation processes. By designating much of the province an integrated cultural and natural landscape with Thai National Heritage Site status, the archaeological and geographic features can be protected for generations to come. Main issues include the ongoing debate about preservation versus tourism and development; stressing methods of protection rather than ownership of cultural property; and the relationship between practical archaeology and preservation of the archaeological resource through stakeholder involvement in Southeast Asia. As a number of countries in Southeast Asia lack funding and material resources, it is imperative that they apply sustainable systems for successful heritage management. This discussion could be broadened to encompass social and economic approaches to heritage preservation across Southeast Asia.*

The destruction and depletion of cultural heritage is easily understood as a consequence of rapid development. Accordingly, conservation—the safeguarding of sites—is viewed as a process contradictory to development. The inclusion of the Nan and Wa Basin Integrated Cultural and Natural Landscapes of Northern Thailand on the country's tentative World Heritage List by the Thai Committee on the Convention for the Protection of the World Cultural and Natural Heritage provided an encouraging opportunity to bring awareness of the built and material heritage and its significance to the local people.

For the first time in Thailand, Nan province played host to an archaeological program initiated by a broad range of people: community members, with technical assistance from staff of SEAMEO-SPAFA (Regional Centre for Archaeology and Fine Arts in Bangkok, Thailand) and UNESCO, university professors, private sector employees, and government officers, including the provincial governor. Another interesting project, involving the excavation of a site initiated by a Thammasat University professor, is the focus of this paper. It is hoped that this project, in a lesser-known area of the Royal Kingdom of Thailand, will prevent damage to and the loss of other endangered heritage resources.

The Nan Project: Secrets of Its Success

At Bo Suak, Nan province, excavations were conducted in 1999 by Sayan Prishanchit, a Thammasat University lecturer, on private land with the consent of the owner. Two mounds turned out to be ceramic kilns dated between 500 and 750 B.P. Fortunately, the kilns were in perfect condition and provided a great deal of information. Therefore, as this was archaeologically rich terrain and acknowledging the fact that Nan is one of the poorest provinces in Thailand, it was agreed that a community-based archaeological project would be set up in the area.

The aim of this project was the creation of "living heritage," named after ICCROM's Living Heritage Sites program, whereby a community-based approach is applied to heritage site management. In this case, the provisional "Nan Project" includes the following:

- providing people with the appropriate in-community training to become on-site participants with archaeologists; and
- continuity of indigenous culture to be maintained through the promotion and trade of handicrafts, textiles, foods, and other local products.

In both cases, decent incomes and higher self-esteem should be gained in the long term, which can develop local people's confidence in offering skills and knowledge of their own accord.

The sustainability of preserving Nan province's cultural heritage is being reviewed by the Office of the National Committee on the Convention for the Protection of the World Cultural and Natural Heritage of Thailand. In the Nan project there had to be a relationship between preservation and the ways in which practical archaeology is carried out. Not only was it fortuitous in being able to secure permission to excavate on private land, but the owner was enthusiastic at every stage of the development, taking a cultural rather than a financial interest.

The Nan project has been successful for the following reasons:

- Volunteers were welcome at any time to work with archaeologists.
- Working with archaeologists has given local people greater understanding of this practical skill and has also created an appreciation of heritage issues, such as development and conservation.
- During excavation, the site was made accessible to the public to view the archaeological work.
- The land, originally privately owned, is now in the public domain, so that there are greater opportunities for decision making with regard to the cultural and natural aspects of Nan.

The site area was gradually improved. First a shelter was placed over the kilns; then a wooden building, disassembled from old wooden houses by local workers, was constructed to house some ceramic collections and was used as a venue for seminars. It was designed by an architecture student and built according to the local Lanna (northern Thai) style as instructed by local experts.

In addition, the site became better known and was used as a teaching and learning center for ceramics and the general archaeology and history of northern Thailand, especially after the visits of HRH Princess Galyani, the king's elder sister, in 1999, and HRH Crown Princess Maha Chakri Sirindhorn in 2001.

After five interesting and productive years at Nan, the site remains a small-scale and innovative project. No outstanding problems have been encountered. A subdistrict administrative organization saw the possibility of developing another community-based archaeological center when another kiln site was located nearby; however, this plan has not received public support.

Factors in the Implementation of the Nan Project

Three groups prompted this new community-based approach to archaeological resource management. All needed to be redirected in their attitudes toward this subject.

The Community

Previously, local people would have been sidelined in the sociological and environmental decisions made concerning their land. Poverty is a prominent problem in Southeast Asia. One crucial step in creating awareness and instilling appreciation of cultural heritage was to promote its economic and educational benefits for the community. With the assistance of major institutions such as the World Bank, conservation should become a welcome activity in the province, as it will help to alleviate poverty and rescue people from social exclusion.

Developers

Modern development, on and in heritage sites or areas, is expanding in Southeast Asia at an alarming rate. This trend is the prime suspect in the damage and disappearance of heritage resources in this region. Those Southeast Asian countries with the money and materials to engage in modern development are striving for economic growth; the inadvertent result is a cultural decline. This scenario can be observed elsewhere in the world. The most blatant ignorance encountered in this situation is the attitude of the developer who can see only an "ancient pile of bricks" standing in the way of a new multimillion-dollar shopping complex.

Economics are the guiding force in modern development, but heritage issues and the views of the local community should also be highly valued. Currently, archaeology is expected to deal with much of this emphasis on conservation. In fact, heritage resources, when managed appropriately, can also be used for economic benefit, since they may have much longer life spans than modern structures and materials.

As communities in heritage areas are inevitably affected by modern development, they can provide the necessary link of understanding between conservators and developers. More important, they can participate in projects by contributing valuable personal information on matters of heritage.

Academics

Academics tend to have an insular and narrow view of archaeological resource management. Moreover, generally they do not seek interaction with the community involved, and they have a limited view of the cultural issues that are at stake. In Southeast Asia, this occurs because of an education system that fails to teach the value and significance of the built heritage such as temples and other ancient monuments and material heritage such as ceramics, textiles, and ancient artifacts.

However, direct and fulfilling approaches to conservation issues were achieved at Nan with the necessary interaction provided for the community by SEAMEO-SPAFA and UNESCO.

Final Comments

In addition to developing an appreciation for the history and value of a heritage site, the Nan people were imbued with a sense of pride in the archaeological work conducted at Nan and enjoyed talking with television and radio media about it. They were impressed with the detective work and felt that touching the artifacts was a special experience. They felt a greater sense of ownership and wanted all finds to be kept in Nan as testimony of their local history. Without knowing it, their sentiment coincides with the statement made by His Majesty King Bhumibol Adulyadej in 1957 that "artifacts and art objects should be kept at the place to which they belong," despite the fact that such finds have to be relinquished to the appropriate authority.

The Antiquity Act of Thailand states in chapter 24 that no one can claim ownership of any finds either buried or concealed and/or abandoned at any place in the country or its specified economic zone. Moreover, finds automatically become state property regardless of who owns the land on which they were found. The finder of such artifacts has to deliver them to a competent authority, either an administrative officer or a police officer under the criminal procedure code. The finder is entitled to a reward of one-third of the value of such property. In this case, the owner is considered the legal custodian.

What does the future hold for Nan archaeology? Among other developments, a postgraduate student from Thammasat University is now conducting his own research into the use of the site as an informal educational center.

Finally, the Nan community, with typical Thai warmth and courtesy, welcomes visitors. And the community now understands the term *boraanakhadii* (archaeology).

Adaptive Management and the Community at El Pilar: A Philosophy of Resilience for the Maya Forest

Anabel Ford

Abstract: *Resource management and conservation are palpable themes of the day. Nowhere is this more keenly felt than the Maya forest, one of the world's most biodiverse areas and among the last terrestrial frontiers. Over the next two decades this area's population will double, threatening the integrity of the tropical ecosystems with contemporary development strategies. Curiously, the Maya forest was once home to a major civilization with three to nine times the current population of the region. The forest survives and demonstrates resilience to the impact of human expansion. This paper discusses the El Pilar Program, which argues that there are lessons to be learned from the past. Over the past ten years, the program has forged new ground in testing novel strategies for community participation in the conservation and development of the El Pilar Archaeological Reserve for Maya Flora and Fauna. The program touches major administrative themes of global importance: tourism, natural resources, foreign affairs, and rural development and education. Yet its impacts go further. Working with traditional forest gardeners affects agriculture, rural enterprise, and capacity building. There are few areas untouched by the program's inclusive sweep, and more fields have the potential to contribute to its future.*

The El Pilar Archaeological Reserve for Maya Flora and Fauna is a site that spans the contemporary borders of Belize and Guatemala (fig. 1); it involves a number of partnerships, the most important of which is that with the communities surrounding the site. The primary objectives of the El Pilar Program are research, development of a binational tourist destination of Maya history and environmental education, support of local and community leadership from enterprise development to sustainable growth, and promotion and preservation of the living legacy and history of the Maya and

how the forest became a garden. The El Pilar Program argues there are lessons to be learned from our past, particularly with respect to managing natural resources.

Understanding the Culture of the Maya Forest

The issue of resource conservation has accompanied humankind throughout time. Resource limits have been identified in the archaeological record and recorded in historical documents and are measured exhaustively today. Archaeological research on prehistoric civilizations, including that of the Maya forest, has provided an appreciation of past strategies of managing resources.

The magnificent Maya civilization of Mesoamerica was once a flourishing farming society. The Maya prospered over many millennia by using forest-dwelling animals and plants and adapting domesticated crops to their tropical habitat. By doing so, they met their basic needs and managed environmental assets while recognizing environmental limitations.

Today, population increase, deforestation, monoculture farming strategies, and Old World methods of pasture and plow are bringing the Maya forest to yet another threshold. The Maya forest of Mesoamerica is a biodiversity hot spot, ranked second of twenty-five endangered regions by Conservation International (Mittermeier, Myers, and Mittermeier 2000), and current projections for the region are ominous. The population is predicted to double over the next twenty years, further straining resources. Yet this region was home to the ancient Maya civilization, whose population was three to nine times the current level, a civilization that has left clues that hold great potential for developing a strategy to manage the complex habitats of today's forest.

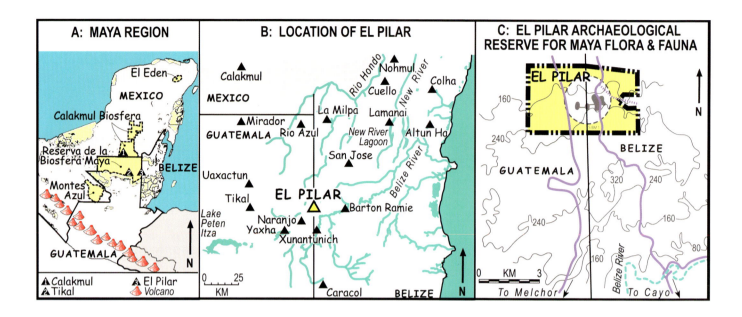

FIGURE 1 Regional, local, and site-specific scales of El Pilar.
Courtesy of BRASS/El Pilar Program

The Maya Forest as a Garden

The composition of the Maya forest today is reminiscent of the Maya people's complex relationship with nature. More than 24,000 types of plants have been identified in the region, 5,000 of which are endemic. This diversity combined with evaluations of species similarity suggest a homogeneous composition wherein widely spaced areas share 53 to 71 percent of the plant species (Campbell et al. 1995). This is dramatically different from the Amazon, where study plots rarely have more than 10 percent of species in common (Balée and Campbell 1998; Campbell 1989, 1994, 1998). The Maya forest's great diversity and general homogeneity are combined with a high economic component, with up to 90 percent of the plants listed as useful (Campbell, Walker, et al. 1995; Campbell, Ford, et al. in press). This suggests that human systems played an important role in the development and maintenance of the Maya forest (Atran 1990, 1993; Moran 1993).

Linguistic terms in the Mayan language speak to traditional knowledge of the forest and describe a continuum of its economic qualities (Barrera Vásquez 1995). *Kanan K'ax* describes a "well cared for" forest, evoking the concept of management, yet the verb *kanan* signifies both "care for" and "learn" in the Yucatecan Mayan language family, a recognition of the changing dynamics of an adaptive cycle in ecology. *Ka'kab K'ax* indicates a forest with good agricultural soil quality, reflecting a subtle appreciation of the environment (Atran 1993; Atran et al. 1999). If human interventions selectively graded the species' composition of the Maya forest to favor economic needs over four millennia, how might an understanding of this relationship shape conservation efforts today?

The first step is to study the rise of the Maya civilization in light of the traditional farmers of the forest today. An analog of forest structure itself (Senayake 2003), traditional poly-cultivation in the tropics minimizes instability and degradation and integrates labor techniques that maximize production (Bray 1994; Gomez Pompa 1990; Gomez Pompa and Kus 1998; Mollison 1988). The result is a mosaic land use strategy tailored to local economic needs: the Maya forest as garden (Nigh 1995, 1997). Heterogeneous and biodiverse, tropical forest gardens constituted the strength of the Maya community in the past, as they do today (Tzul 2001), by relying on the traditional knowledge of local farming households. The El Pilar Program is working alongside communities to explore and promote the traditional forest garden as an alternative to extensive land-use strategies.

Community Participation and the Development of the El Pilar Archaeological Reserve for Maya Flora and Fauna

Deep forest jungle sequestered the vestiges of Maya city monuments and houses after their demise around A.D. 900, until the 1830s when curious Western explorers entered the region (Stephens 1969). Since then, the area has drawn scholars who have been conducting research that fills university library bookshelves. Regional leaders, schools, and organizations in the Maya forest have come to recognize the educational vacuum that exists with regard to their own area and history. The El Pilar Program focuses on this void and is encouraging local communities to use, protect, and understand how they contribute to the Maya forest's evolution (Ford and Miller 1994, 1997; Wernecke 2000–2001; cf. Fagan 2003) as well as participate in and learn from the archaeological research at El Pilar.

The El Pilar Vision Unfolds: Community Involvement

In 1992 the Belize Department of Archaeology spearheaded the initial investigations at El Pilar. With the government's support, in 1993 the El Pilar Program commenced a full-scale investigation (see Appendix 1). Insights gained from detailed surveying, mapping, and extensive excavations over ten seasons have established the foundation for an innovative approach to participatory conservation and development efforts in the Maya forest (Ford 1998; Ford and Montes 1999; Ford and Wernecke 2001; Girardin 1999).

As work at the site gained momentum, local community members in Belize expressed interest in the research and investigations at El Pilar. In 1993, with the El Pilar Program's assistance, the local villagers established Amigos de El Pilar (AdEP). AdEP identified its mission: foster community partnerships in the creation and management of El Pilar, develop new livelihood opportunities, promote sustainable income generation geared to the growing ecotourism industry, and promote education on the preservation of natural and cultural resources (see www.interconnection.org/elpilar).

Since its inception AdEP has made significant strides. Working with national and international leaders, AdEP participated in the creation of protected area boundaries in 1995, and applauded the official designation as the El Pilar Archaeological Reserve for Maya Flora and Fauna (EPAR) in Belize and Guatemala in 1998. This new legal status would have significant influence over the future of El Pilar and the community and was vital in expanding local involvement and support.

With Ford Foundation funds, regional program advocates were formally incorporated as the El Pilar Program (Appendix 1). In Belize, Anselmo Castañeda, a natural resource conservationist, focuses on local and regional environmental issues. In Guatemala, José Antonio Montes, an international lawyer, concentrates on legal and political processes. Castañeda's interest in ecological sustainability and Montes's appreciation of international law transformed the team into the binational program it is today. This new dynamic infused AdEP with new internal organizational ability and external visibility. The El Pilar Program helped to develop a website for El Pilar in 1997 that highlights the community's collaborative efforts and provides updates of research and management activities.

As the community's relationship with the El Pilar Program matures, AdEP is focusing its activities on its mission and becoming independent (Awe 2000a, 2000b). Not only does AdEP have its own vision of how its relationship with El Pilar should develop, it is gaining the capacity to translate its vision into tangible results. As an income-generating strategy related to environment and tourism, AdEP developed the Masewal Forest Garden Trail in 1999. This 1.5-kilometer visitor trail, which highlights ornamental and medicinal plants as well as the nursery, was created with the assistance of Raleigh International volunteers (fig. 2).

Through their own spirit and dedication and grants and support from the network of the El Pilar Program, AdEP opened the Be Pukte Cultural Center in 1998 (fig. 3), a forum for AdEP's meetings and a place to feature handcrafted items, publications, and information on El Pilar. The center has evolved to host community activities related to education, ceremonies, presentations, and meetings, as well as cultural events and natural resource training.

Education in the Maya Forest

Educational outreach is an important way to build both a foundation of community support and a leadership base for AdEP. The El Pilar Program, now fully composed of community, research, and management entities (see Appendix 2), coordinates a variety of field and community endeavors and has made it a priority to develop local environmental and conservation education curricula.

Community education got under way during the early years with meetings and workshops in which various aspects of conservation and development were addressed. In 1995 three workshops were arranged to train the local community

FIGURE 2 Community collaborators Raleigh International at the Masewal Forest Garden and Reinas El Pilar Lakin and Chikin. Courtesy of BRASS/El Pilar Program

in resource development and management. To familiarize AdEP with other archaeological sites, a series of mobile workshops, or *talleres,* were organized. Participants visited six major archaeological sites in the Mundo Maya (Maya World, a transnational concept encompassing Mexico, Guatemala, El Salvador, Belize, and Honduras) in 1999–2000 to evaluate community and reserve strategies and development options.

Through a series of workshops between the government and AdEP, innovative education programs at the university level have also begun.

Managing One Resource in Two Countries

One of the challenges facing the El Pilar Program is its binational character. Local education has increased El Pilar's visibility within the community and acted as a catalyst for AdEP to begin building a presence at the regional, national, and international levels. In 1995 AdEP President Marcos Garcia discussed the group's interests with key officials in ministry and department offices in the Belize capital of Belmopan. In 1996 Garcia represented the community at a binational government-sponsored workshop, Encuentro El Pilar. As part of this first region-wide workshop focused on El Pilar, participants had the opportunity to visit El Pilar and see its potential. They identified goals aimed at the formal protection of El Pilar in both Belize and Guatemala.

The collaboration of communities, nongovernmental organizations (NGOs), and students has borne results. In 1998 AdEP joined with a Belizean NGO, Help for Progress, to develop a successful partnership between Belize and Guatemala, as well as the improvement of conservation endeavors at El Pilar (www.helpforprogress.org).

By 1998 protective reserves had been established around El Pilar in both countries. During successive international roundtable workshops (Mesa Redonda I, II, and III; fig. 4), the administration and management of the contiguous reserves was established. A permanent organization on the Guatemalan side, Amigos de El Pilar, Melchor, was officially registered in 2000 to set the institutional framework for true cross-border management.

To further the spirit of the cross-border alliance, a cooperative association was established between AdEP-Belize and AdEP-Guatemala to undertake full organizational responsibility for the Fiesta El Pilar. Under their administration, new ideas are being incorporated into the fiesta. In 2001, for example, two Reinas El Pilar were selected to pose as El

FIGURE 3 Growth of the Amigos de El Pilar cultural center. The
1995 *galeria (top left)*, the 1998 Be Pukte *(top right)*, the 2000
interior *(bottom left)*, and the 2003 Cultural Center and Café
(bottom right). Courtesy of BRASS/El Pilar Program

Pilar Chikin and Lakin (see fig. 2), or West and East, symbol-
ically dissolving political boundaries (Awe 2000a, 2000b). As
of 2002, members of AdEP refer to themselves as "AdEP
Lakin" and "AdEP Chikin," further transcending boundaries
and affirming new alliances.

The Way Forward
There is reason to look forward to greater opportunities.
Major international agencies have invested resources in the El
Pilar process (Ford 2001). As the visibility of El Pilar increases,
new interests and opportunities are emerging, and regional
and international agencies are now looking to increase their
stake in El Pilar.

Demonstrating and advocating the conservation-
tourism model is only the beginning of a larger process.
Rethinking traditional and even progressive strategies aimed
at providing local communities with entrepreneurial skills
will need to be addressed in the ongoing project of sustainable
and profitable ecotourism development. Although well established, the institutional framework of the El Pilar vision is still
fragile. As investments are made and risks are appreciated, the
unity between AdEP and the local community creates opportunities for El Pilar. Each new external link that is forged reinforces AdEP's internal organizational structure. The process is
deliberate, however, and needs attention if AdEP is to keep
pace with faster marketing schedules.

FIGURE 4 Consensus building with the Mesa Redonda El Pilar. The core group of MRII in 1998 at Rum Point Belize *(top)* and MRIII at Remate Guatemala *(bottom)*. Courtesy of BRASS/El Pilar Program

Reflections

The achievements and progress that have been made at El Pilar since its beginnings in 1992 are the result of an ever-expanding network of collaborators. Supported by annual funding efforts, the El Pilar Program has established an eclectic base (see Taylor-Ide and Taylor 2002).

The El Pilar vision is not static. As EPAR and its surrounding communities evolve, there will be adjustments; as more people visit the site each year, the vision grows. A commitment lies at the core of the El Pilar Program—the commitment to uphold the integrity of the cultural and natural resources it was formed to protect. To be genuine, that commitment needs to be wholly embraced by the local community, towns, and cities. Participation is what makes the El Pilar Reserve for Maya Flora and Fauna dynamic, infusing it with the ability to educate, reform, and transform.

Acknowledgments

The work at El Pilar owes much to the people of the Maya forest and the governments of Belize and Guatemala who had the foresight to explore an innovative development scheme. They have explicitly given the El Pilar Program the privilege to demonstrate the many different ways to view the ancient Maya monuments. Imagining the Maya forest as one region, appreciating El Pilar as one site, and collaborating with cheerful skepticism—these have provided a new dimension to include El Pilar among the novel destinations of the Mundo Maya. Our work is dedicated to all who know that they are part of this story and to all who will be.

Appendix 1. A History of El Pilar

1972	El Pilar recorded by the Department of Archaeology (DoA) Government of Belize
1984	Belize River Archaeological Settlement Survey (BRASS) initial mapping of the site
1993	DoA conservation at El Pilar with BRASS project
1994	Help for Progress NGO begins participation with Amigos de El Pilar
1995	Official boundaries of El Pilar established in Belize
	Model Maya House created at Tzunu'un; El Pilar listed on World Monument Watch
	Master map of site core completed, including Pilar Poniente, Guatemala
1997	El Pilar certified as a *monumento cultural* (cultural monument) in Guatemala
1998	El Pilar developed as a contiguous reserve in Belize and Guatemala
2000	Rolex Award for Enterprise-Cultural Heritage recognition for El Pilar vision
2001	Publication of *El Pilar Trail Guide*
	Both AdEP groups sign Declaration of El Pilar International Community Participation
2002	8th annual Fiesta El Pilar held, organized by AdEP Chikin and Lakin
2003	Collaboration with Counterpart International, Washington, D.C.
2003	National Institute of Culture and History Belize begins collaboration with AdEP Lakin
	Consejo Nacional de Areas Protegidas endorses the master plan for El Pilar

Appendix 2. Collaborative Team Organization

El Pilar Program

University of California, Santa Barbara, Main Office: Anabel Ford, Director

Exploring Solutions Past: Nonprofit organization based in California (www.espmaya.org)

Counterpart International: Megan Havrda

Belize Advocate: Anselmo Casteñeda, Regional Environment

Guatemala Advocate: José Antonio Montes, International Law

Community Participation

Amigos de El Pilar: Lakin/Chikin (Belize/Guatemala)

Community Accompaniment

NGO Program Partners: Community and Conservation Management

Help for Progress/Belize: Elias Awe, Rick August

Canan K'aax and Naturakeza para la Vida/Guatemala: Ramon Zetina, Suamy Aguilar

References

Atran, S. 1990. *Cognitive Foundations of Natural History.* New York: Cambridge University Press.

———. 1993. Itza Maya tropical agro-forestry. *Current Anthropology* 34 (5):633–700.

Atran, S., D. Medin, N. Ross, E. Lynch, J. Coley, E. Ek'Ukan, and V. Vapnarsky. 1999. Folkecology and commons management in the Maya lowlands. Paper presented at the Proceedings of the National Academy of Sciences of the United States of America.

Awe, E. A. 2000a. *Regional Community Action and the El Pilar Archaeological Reserve for Maya Flora and Fauna.* Belmopan: Help for Progress, Belize.

———. 2000b. *Trans-Boundary Initiative for Cooperative (Joint) Management of El Pilar Archaeological Reserve for Maya Flora and Fauna and the Promotion of Community Based Ecotourism and the Development of Sustainable Agricultural and Forestry Practice in Belize.* Belmopan: Help for Progress, Belize.

Balée, W., and D. G. Campbell. 1998. Evidence for the successional status of liana forest (Xingu River Basin, Amazonian Brazil). *Biotropica* 22 (1):36–47.

Barrera Vásquez, A. 1995. *Diccionario Maya.* 3d ed. México, D.F.: Editorial Porrúa.

Bray, F. 1994. Agriculture for developing nations. *Scientific American* 271 (1):18–25.

Campbell, D. G. 1989. The quantitative inventory of tropical forests. In *Floristic in Tropical Countries,* ed. D. G. C. H. D. Hammond, 523–33. New York: New York Botanical Garden.

———. 1994. Scale and patterns of community structure in Amazonian forests. Paper presented at "Large-Scale Ecology and Conservation Biology: 35th Symposium of the British Ecological Society with the Society for Conservation Biology," University of Southampton.

———. 1998. Signature of the classic Maya on the tropical forests of Belize. Paper presented at the American Anthropological Association, Philadelphia.

Campbell, D. G., A. Ford, K. S. Lowell, J. Walker, J. K. Lake, C. Ocampo-Raeder, A. Townesmith, and M. Balick. In press. *The Feral Forests of the Eastern Petén: Time and Complexity in the Neotropical Lowlands,* ed. C. Erickson and W. Balée. New York: Columbia University Press.

Campbell, D. G., J. Walker, V. Castillo, J. Lake, C. Ocampo-Raeder, and S. Smith. 1995. The signature of the classic Maya empire on Belizean tropical forests. Paper presented at the American Association for the Advancement of Science, Atlanta.

El Pilar Program. 2003. www.marc.ucsb.edu.

Exploring Solutions Past. 2003. www.espmaya.org.

Fagan, B. 2003. A responsibility for the past: Integrating conservation and archaeology. *Conservation* 18 (1): 4–10.

Ford, A., ed. 1998. *The Future of El Pilar: The Integrated Research and Development Plan for the El Pilar Archaeological Reserve for Maya Flora and Fauna, Belize-Guatemala.* Washington, D.C.: Bureau of Oceans and International Environmental and Scientific Affairs.

———. 2001. El Pilar: Gateway between Belize and Guatemala. *Washington Report on the Hemisphere* 21 (1–2):4–5.

Ford, A., and C. Miller. 1994. Arqueología de acción en la selva: Creación de la Reserva Arqueológica de El Pilar, Guatemala-Belice. *Utzib* 1 (7):19–21.

———. 1997. *Creación de la Reserva Arqueológica El Pilar en Guatemala y Belice.* Guatemala: Museo Nacional de Arqueología e Etnología, Guatemala.

Ford, A., and J. A. Montes. 1999. Environment, land use, and sustainability: Implementation of the El Pilar Archaeological Reserve for Maya Flora and Fauna, Belize-Guatemala. *Mesoamérica* 37 (June):31–50.

Ford, A., and D. C. Wernecke. 2001. *Trails of El Pilar: A Comprehensive Guide to the El Pilar Archaeological Reserve for Maya Flora and Fauna.* Santa Barbara, Calif.: Exploring Solutions Past: Maya Forest Alliance.

Girardin, A. 1999. *The El Pilar Archaeological Mapping Project: A Geographic Information Systems Objective.* Le Mans: École Supérieure des Géomètres et Topographes.

Gomez Pompa, A. 1990. Maya sustainability project annual report to the MacArthur Foundation. University of California, Riverside. Submitted to Summary Report.

Gomez Pompa, A., and A. Kus. 1998. Taming the wilderness myth; environmental policy and education are currently based on Western beliefs about nature rather than on reality. *BioScience* 42 (4):271–79.

Mittermeier, R. A., N. Myers, and C. Goettsh Mittermeier. 2000. *Hotspots: Earth's Biologically Richest and Most Endangered Terrestrial Ecoregions.* México, D.F.: CEMEX.

Mollison, B. C. 1988. *Permaculture: A Designer's Manual.* Tyalgum, Australia: Tagari Publications.

Moran, E. F. 1993. *Through Amazonian Eyes: The Human Ecology of Amazonian Populations.* Iowa City: University of Iowa Press.

Nigh, R. 1995. Animal agriculture and the reforestation of degraded tropical rainforests. *Culture and Agriculture* (Bulletin of the Culture and Agriculture Group, American Anthropological Association) 51–52 (Spring–Summer):2–6.

———. 1997. Organic agriculture and globalization: A Maya associative corporation in Chiapas, Mexico. *Human Organization* 56 (4):427–36.

Senayake, R. 2003. *Analog Forestry.* www.forestgarden.org/franalog.htm.

Stephens, J. L. 1969. *Incidents of Travel in Central America, Chiapas and Yucatan II.* 2 vols. New York: Dover Publications.

Taylor-Ide, D., and C. E. Taylor. 2002. *Just and Lasting Change: When Communities Own Their Futures.* Baltimore: Johns Hopkins University Press in association with Future Generations.

Tzul, A. 2001. First meeting of farming communities in the Maya forest for the design of an agroforestry model—El Pilar: Retrieving old traditions. Unpublished manuscript. Help for Progress, Belize.

Wernecke, C. 2000–2001. El Pilar: A Maya rainforest refuge. *Explorers Journal* (Winter):22–25.

Social Landscapes and Archaeological Heritage in Latin America

Nelly Robles García

Abstract: *This paper addresses the urgency of understanding the multiple elements that make up the contemporary social setting of archaeological sites in Latin America, elements that in their totality create the social landscape. This concept helps us to outline the social dimensions of phenomena that are more commonly the province of anthropology and sociology and are rarely approached from the perspective of heritage conservation. In practice, our lack of understanding of these phenomena creates severe constraints in developing proposals to support the conservation of heritage sites. Study of the social landscape is crucial to a complete understanding of the relationship between heritage conservation and regional development, which unfortunately in Latin America is a negative one.*

Despite the paucity of social research regarding the relationship between archaeological heritage or heritage sites and society at large, in recent years there has been an undeniable advance in such studies. Without exception, society emerges as a heterogeneous entity, made up of a multiplicity of actors and situations that overlap and interact around specific sets of interests.

Heritage sites reflect a mix of tangible and intangible interests, as well as material and ephemeral resources. The contemporary view of such sites is that they consist of both ancestral and modern values. Archaeologists, as those responsible for managing sites and as interpreters of traditional societies, tend to be sensitive to and value the ancestral over the modern, whereas for government and associated institutions the reverse tends to be true. Most field experience reveals the pressure that a lack of understanding of and capacity to balance these factors generates with respect to site conservation and the context for technical work (Hoopes 1997; Robles 1998).

It is therefore extremely important to define a basis for analyzing this context, recognizing that the tension between these two points of view may spill over into political demands. In Latin America such demands may result in mass movements that promote non-negotiable agendas, where the pressures of circumstance mean that the decisions taken are not necessarily the best for the conservation of cultural heritage.

Background

In Mexico and other countries in the region, the emergence of archaeology coincided with a certain attention to indigenous roots as a manifestation of nationalism. Archaeology offered nation builders a way to link the descendants of a noble and accomplished past to visions of a proud and prosperous future.

By 1939 Mexico had institutionalized broad-based oversight of archaeological heritage, which placed control of all modalities of archaeological research and protection in the hands of the state. Nominally the state left room for some participation in conservation efforts by creating the possibility of neighborhood or community councils (INAH 1972). In practice, however, state tutelage constrained the liberty of action by a wide range of actors, especially in relation to land use (INAH 1972). This created a tension or antagonism over both the process of decision making and the substance of conservation policy that continues to bedevil conservation efforts.

From 1962 to 1964, when Mexico made a concerted effort to create what would become the National Museum of Anthropology, there emerged a series of debates over the decision to display simultaneously evidence of past and present material cultures, that is, the archaeology and ethnography, of indigenous peoples. Although a broad-based spirit of nationalism supported the establishment of the monumental museum, this did not silence the voices of discontent that objected to the combination of archaeological heritage and contemporary ethnography in a single collection under a common roof, in effect linking pre-Conquest with contemporary landscapes.

More recently, efforts by the Committee of the Americas of the Society for American Archaeology have revived hopes for a better understanding between archaeology and heritage preservation in Latin America (Drennan and Mora 2001). Nevertheless, this convergence continues to fall short as it lacks insights and methodology from social and economic anthropology that would produce a more complete picture of the social complexities that shape heritage management. In effect, one of the most persistent dilemmas has been the reluctance of traditional specialists and practitioners to recognize the changing context of their work. Without such recognition, pleas for more broadly based approaches to heritage management appear to have little hope of prospering.

Contemporary Complexity

Today a more open academic environment facilitates discussion regarding different elements and processes in site management or the myriad tasks of conservation. Attention has shifted to trying to understand the elements of society and the conditions that generate the persistent stress affecting sites (Demas 2000; Hoopes 1997; Robles 1998; Robles and Corbett 1995).

Using an anthropological or sociological lens, it is possible to identify those actors who shape the social context of a specific archaeological site and to calculate their level of influence over the processes of conservation or degradation affecting it. We can also calculate the benefits the site condition may distribute to those actors (Robles 1998). Without undermining archaeologists' research in different areas, we need to understand that independent of the scientific values that may permeate a heritage site, at any moment—but especially once a site's significance is established—that very process may trigger or revive an array of interests associated more closely with its status as a resource than as a focus of scientific study.

Today social research tends to document indigenous affairs related to cultural heritage in general and to archaeology in particular. We see, nevertheless, that social considerations in their broadest sense include a wide array of societal

environments. Thus we can find an extensive assortment of challenges linked to urban, city-country, modern, traditional, political, or other interests that form part of the mix that has been put into play. In this sense we understand the need for social research focused on heritage matters, as it permits a more reliable assessment of the range of conditions that characterize the relationship between a site and the larger society of which it is a part (Robles and Corbett 1995).

The *social landscape* may be understood as a complex concept that elaborates not only the list of actors present at a site or area but also the relationships that exist between the actors and the site, with the concept of heritage, and among the actors themselves. The concept also captures the array of interests centered on the site and on cultural heritage, which generally prove more extensive than we first imagine.

In this respect a heritage site may be known but may remain unexplored for generations without any alteration in its relationship with the social environment. Archaeological research removes the site from anonymity, and a successful project generates value by converting the site to an attraction; this in turn can trigger a struggle of economic interests linked to several sectors, particularly tourism. This occurs independent of and often without explicit recognition of other dimensions of social complexity such as property, land tenure, values, or other constructs.

Taking Monte Albán (fig. 1) as a case study to demonstrate what the concept of social landscape can mean for most archaeological sites in Mexico or elsewhere in Latin America, several levels of analysis are necessary to understand the variety of stakeholders that interact with the site. The result has been a fascinating complex of overlapping social groups, individuals, and interests clearly differentiated from one other, a complexity in which heritage resources play a central role, not only in a scientific sense. For some of these actors, this site can be understood as simply an enormous piece of earth and as such can be treated according to the rules of the free market and speculation. Others may see it as a large open space for recreation and outdoor activity; still others see it as part of an ancestral heritage whose grandfathers set it aside to be preserved and appreciated. Meanwhile scientists see it as an important setting for understanding a culture stretching back centuries or even millennia.

The Monte Albán Experience

Experience gained in working at Monte Albán, a World Heritage Site in Oaxaca, Mexico, has enhanced sensitivity to social

FIGURE 1 The central plaza of Monte Albán. Courtesy of Archive of the archaeological site of Monte Albán, INAH

realities in the context of heritage sites. These become as important as understanding historical events, physical conditions of structures, or other elements such as chronologies. A site such as Monte Albán, immersed in a physical context of urban marginality and poverty, demonstrates the need to mobilize social science methodologies to understand the social complexity of the site (fig. 2). Some of the levels of analysis used in this study are discussed below.

Social Actors

Information collected directly in the field reflects the diversity of actors playing a role in the setting of the site. These include site workers, scientists, visitors, and students, as well as those who, without being present at the site on a daily basis, nevertheless generate demands on it, such as hotel owners, travel agents, neighbors, property owners, shepherds, and others, including institutions.

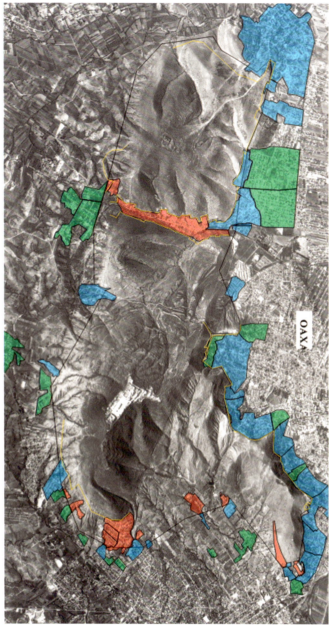

Scale 1:12,500

FIGURE 2 Aerial photo of Monte Albán, showing surrounding human settlements. Courtesy of Archive of the archaeological site of Monte Albán, INAH

■ Colonies within the polygon

■ Colonies in the areas adjacent to the polygon

■ Colonies having one section within the polygon

— Netting placed inside the polygon to demarcate urban growth

Source: INEGI 1995. Digitalization of image: Araiga Adrian Salinas.

Institutions

In Mexico, based on a single law, the federal government has control of heritage resources, including archaeological resources as they are considered part of the national heritage (INAH 1972). The National Institute of Anthropology and History (INAH) was established to study, preserve, and interpret for the public different elements valued in archaeological sites. This monolithic character makes INAH an institution almost without parallel in the archaeological world and at the same time shows that the Mexican public accepts the notion that heritage is a responsibility of the state. Elsewhere in Latin America, institutional counterparts of the Mexican model have been created, for example, in Guatemala, Peru, Cuba, and Colombia. Nevertheless, these culturally oriented institutions are not the only ones that may play an active role in the conservation of archaeological resources. This role now stretches across institutions that address tourism, public works, urban planning, and the management of land and ecological resources, in addition to others with the capacity to affect the archaeological heritage. To date, none of these offers an agenda that addresses heritage conservation, given the Latin American political tradition that assumes that heritage issues are complicated, delicate, and exclusive.

Political Jurisdictions

In Latin America social relations structured around land historically have been of exceptional importance given its status as the central resource sustaining communities and cultures. In Mexico, as in most Latin American countries with a history of conquest, the problems of land tenure go much further and deeper than the simple relationship between land and property. Independent of the type of land tenure, the law referenced above and the Mexican Constitution recognize the municipality as the legally sanctioned institution with the power to decide on the future of archaeological remains within their political jurisdiction.

In the case of Monte Albán one must deal with four municipalities on these issues, even though there are constant internal contradictions regarding who should make decisions, especially when dealing with different socially defined properties. These are widely recognized and distributed in Mexico, and they complicate decision making as municipalities claim their authority over available resources, whether natural or cultural (fig. 3).

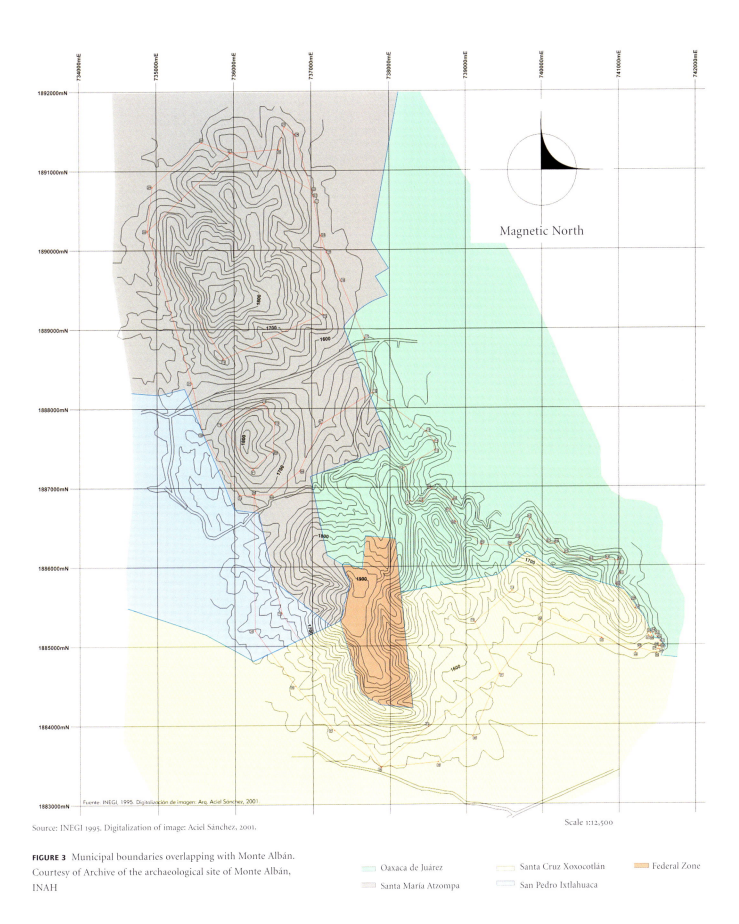

Source: INEGI 1995. Digitalization of image: Aciel Sánchez, 2001.

Scale 1:12,500

FIGURE 3 Municipal boundaries overlapping with Monte Albán.
Courtesy of Archive of the archaeological site of Monte Albán,
INAH

Oaxaca de Juárez   Santa Cruz Xoxocotlán   Federal Zone

Santa María Atzompa   San Pedro Ixtlahuaca

Magnetic North

Land Tenure and Speculation

Much more important than the recognition of ancestral values and appreciation of cultural heritage are values related to land and access to potential economic resources generated by the archaeological sites. In Mexico, values associated with land are deeply grounded in the various indigenous and mestizo cultures. *Ejidos* (common lands), communities, private property, and federal property appear to be legally and legitimately differentiated by specific institutions. However, in practice there may be unwritten, yet locally recognized, values that a narrow technical perspective may omit or overlook but that form important parts of the local value system. In the case of the protective boundary around Monte Albán, there are four types of land tenure, each clearly represented by different social groups and leaders. Stakeholders may find that INAH presents an obstructive presence, limiting their capacity to behave as they see fit in the management of resources they consider to be theirs rather than under the control of the federal government.

In this sense, landownership and its defense has been such a long-standing condition across Mexico and Latin America that it has generated, besides bloody internal struggles, the emergence of a complex system of power parallel to the official political structures (Stephen 2002). In this way, discussions necessary to further the goals of conservation within the boundaries of the Monte Albán archaeological zone, whose priority is the control of speculation on community and ejido lands, have had to focus on representatives of agrarian interests rather than on the municipal authorities who, according to law, are the agents formally charged with addressing land conflicts (fig. 4).

Speculation on lands having a specific social character (ejidos and communities) represents a threat to the integrity of cultural heritage within the Monte Albán archaeological zone for two reasons. First, excavation to create foundations for modern buildings presents an ongoing danger in the form of destruction of materials and disturbance of the subsoil. Second, during excavation, the likelihood of illegal extraction and trafficking in archaeological materials is also heightened.

The history of Monte Albán as a site open to the public reflects a permanent struggle to resist the proliferation of irregular, marginal settlements overlapping the boundaries of the protection zone. The complexity of land tenure, the lack of commitment on the part of local and state governments, lack of clarity regarding alternatives, and budget scarcities in the agencies responsible for heritage values combine to create an environment that is ideally suited to the encouragement of speculation on community and ejido lands, nuclei that on the

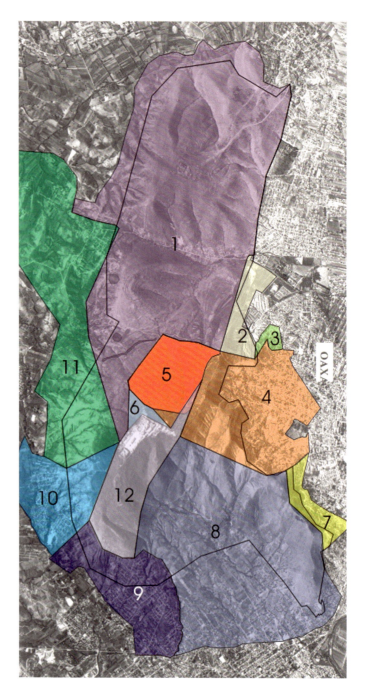

FIGURE 4 Land tenure complexity in Monte Albán. Courtesy of Archive of the archaeological site of Monte Albán, INAH

1 Ejido of Santa María Atzompa
2 Bustamante family private property, Montoya Agency, city of Oaxaca de Suárez
3 Ejido of San Martín de Mexicapan, city of Oaxaca de Suárez
4 Communal property of San Martín de Mexicapan, city of Oaxaca de Suárez
5 Communal property of San Martín de Mexicapan, area claimed by the Peasants Union of San Martín de Mexicapan
6 Ejido of San Martín de Mexicapan, area recognized by co-owners and neighbors
7 Communal property of San Juan Chapultepec, city of Oaxaca de Suárez
8 Communal Property of Santa Cruz Xoxocotlán
9 Ejido of Santa Cruz Xoxocotlán
10 Property of private agency, San Javier, city of Santa Cruz Xoxocotlán
11 Ejido of San Pedro Ixtlahuaca
12 Area under the guardianship of INAH

Source: INEGI 1995. Digitalization of image: Araiga Adrian Salinas.

whole belong to small-scale speculators whose uncoordinated activities have the effect of promoting a constant invasion of supposedly protected spaces. And this takes place at the archaeological site that is the single most important tourist attraction in Oaxaca, whose renown generates more than half a million visitors annually and serves as the engine of the tourist economy in the state (Robles and Corbett 2002).

Nevertheless, this problem cannot be resolved simply by having the state take absolute control of all land showing evidence of archaeological materials, as the social unrest that would create would be enormous. The governments of the region will never have the resources to acquire so much land: the official archaeological zone of Monte Albán covers 2,078 hectares, of which approximately 10 percent has been opened to the public. Even if they could acquire the land, there would not be sufficient funding to support archaeological exploration, restoration, services, and protection. The undeveloped lands would continue to draw squatters and looters. The central issue is land tenure and the speculative activities associated with it. These conditions and all that flows from them in terms of stakeholder activity and competition for advantage must remain the central focus of any social analysis supporting conservation (Olea 1997:153–56).

Land Use

The different actors and interests provoke a flow of decisions regarding land use and access to related resources. In governmental models addressing the conservation of heritage sites in the region, there is no possibility of formal expropriation giving the state absolute control over the land. Therefore, archaeological research and heritage protection, or tourism and interpretation, are simply uses to be added to those already associated with diverse features of the site, for example, agriculture, grazing, collecting and gathering, and other extractive uses. At Monte Albán, some of these uses have relatively low impact on the archaeological remains, but others, for example, house or road construction, clearly result in continuing erosion or drastic alteration of a variety of significant features of the site (fig. 5). Different stakeholders clearly pursue conditions such as tenure security, access to agriculture and grazing, extractive rights, and general control over access to resources in ways that assure the rights of use and disposal. Land use rights may be so grounded in custom and practice that they rarely exist in written form, but this does not reduce their powerful hold on notions of justice and legitimacy. In this respect, no matter how valued and reasonable heritage protection appears to the archaeologist, to many stakeholders it will

simply be a rather new arrival among the long list of claimants to land use.

Indigenous Land Claims

A critically important aspect of the social landscape in archaeological heritage consists of claims by indigenous groups over possession, access, gain, and values flowing from different archaeological sites and museums. This element is exceptionally delicate in that two streams of discourse flow from it, each subject to logic grounded in the ways in which interest groups define and legitimize their values.

First, there are the historic claims of indigenous groups to use traditional and ancestral lands in ways consistent with their values and accustomed practice. Marginalized from the period of the Conquest to the present, indigenous people in Mexico and elsewhere in Latin America seek recognition of rights long ignored. These claims, which above all refer to the rights of indigenous communities for access to their culture— a right stipulated in Article 2 of the Constitution of the United Mexican States—concern the right to continue exercising their worldview, which attaches the highest values to ancestral sites, to continue practicing traditions and beliefs, and to shape practice in ways that are far from the utilitarian perception imposed by the state, which regards diverse archaeological sites as tourist attractions to generate income (fig. 6).

This legal component raises a serious challenge to Latin American governments in the sense that historically they have accepted ancestral values as ideological instruments that legitimize accession to power or other behaviors within the group, but they segregate contemporary indigenous populations from decision-making processes related to the future of cultural heritage or the control of other resources. This practice of exclusion, which in Mexico is a long way from resolution in spite of serious efforts over the past decade, contains the potential for disruptive and destabilizing confrontations.

However, indigenous groups may also demand dominion over heritage sites for reasons distant from ancestral concerns or a desire for cultural continuity. To the extent that "in many communities there is a belief that archaeological zones are big business" (Martínez and Bader 1998), the central concern may be economic, not ethnocultural.

A second, very different perspective on indigenous claims has to do with the extent to which they have been borrowed or reshaped to serve the interests of specific groups who seek to legitimize their claims on heritage resources by linking them to presumed indigenous interests. Indigenous discourse serves to justify and mask claims on the state that in reality draw on a clear economic interest such as commercializing

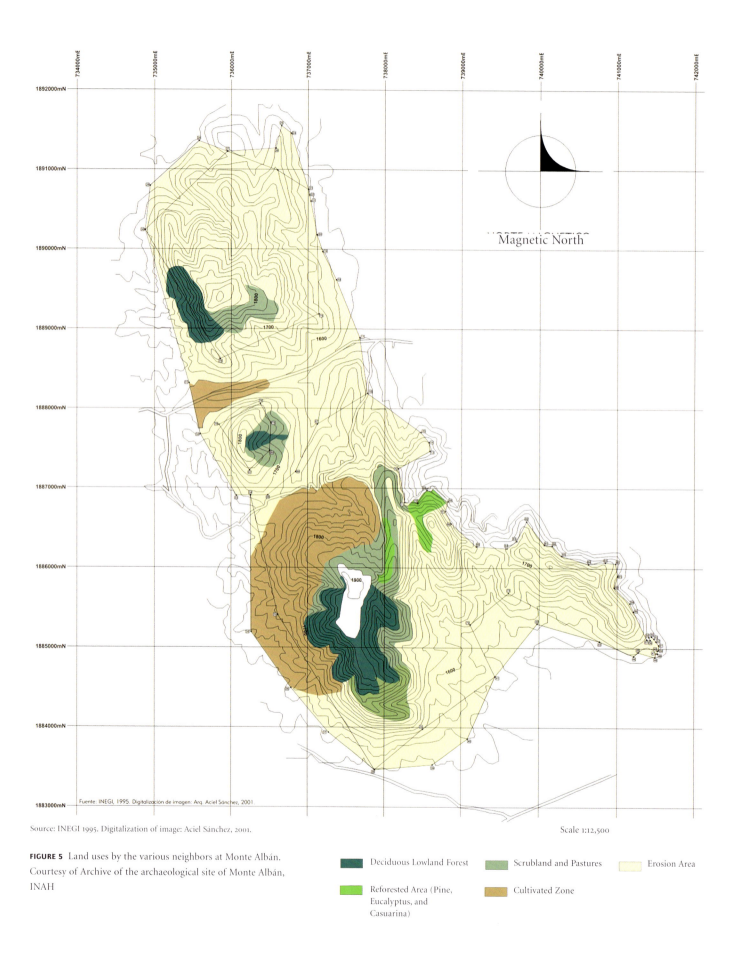

Magnetic North

Scale 1:12,500

Source: INEGI 1995. Digitalization of image: Aciel Sánchez, 2001.

FIGURE 5 Land uses by the various neighbors at Monte Albán. Courtesy of Archive of the archaeological site of Monte Albán, INAH

Deciduous Lowland Forest

Reforested Area (Pine, Eucalyptus, and Casuarina)

Scrubland and Pastures

Cultivated Zone

Erosion Area

FIGURE 6 Rally at the central plaza. Courtesy of Archive of the
archaeological site of Monte Albán, INAH

heritage sites either through provision of services or by treating them as commodities to be bought and sold, in effect engaging in disguised speculation. This subtle difference, not readily recognized by the inexperienced, traps anthropologists, conservation professionals, archaeologists, and those generally sympathetic to indigenous causes.

Even leaders of indigenous movements may fall prey to this. In 2001 Subcomandante Marcos, the EZLN moral leader, passing through Oaxaca, publicly defended "indigenous" claims to parts of Monte Albán, unaware that the group requesting his support was in fact a group of speculators cloaking themselves in indigenous rhetoric. Some of the most assertive participants in efforts to secure control over lands within Monte Albán's boundaries on the grounds that they should be under the control of neighboring indigenous communities are in fact migrants from other parts of the state seeking a tactical advantage in negotiations with INAH.

Urban Growth

The increased concentration of urban housing is probably among the most damaging forms of land use to protected areas. While planned settlements certainly generate damage, much more damage comes from the spontaneous settlements commonly associated with poverty and marginalization across Latin America. Some of the region's most important heritage sites are vulnerable to such pressures. Irregular settlements involve all kinds of excavation, from foundations to terracing. These destroy and bury archaeological materials as well as important elements of the natural and cultural heritage (fig. 7).

The concentration of population also generates a demand for public services. Streets, schools, water lines, and other services require excavation and/or burial. The affected populations, however, are much more concerned with access to services than any damage their provision might cause.

FIGURE 7 Settlement growth toward
Monte Albán. Courtesy of Archive
of the archaeological site of Monte
Albán, INAH

Around Monte Albán spontaneous growth and the formation of poor settlements is part of contemporary reality.
More than one hundred thousand people live on the fringes
of the archaeological zone in at least fifty unplanned, poorly
serviced *colonías* (Corbett and Gonzalez Alafita 2002). This
situation opens the door to politicians inclined to promise
all kinds of services or improved conditions in return for
political support. The politician or agency manager who is
reluctant to respond may quickly become a target of marches
and demonstrations. But the extension of services only
encourages further settlement and the process becomes self-
perpetuating.

Quality of Life

It is worth noting the tendency toward a negative relationship
between successful heritage sites—defined in terms of annual
visitors—and the quality of life in the settlements that sur-
round them. As more major sites in the region become
engulfed by the growth of metropolitan areas or even their
own service populations, the sharp contrast between local
conditions and the apparent prosperity of heritage site visitors
becomes more apparent. The average income of the majority
of families living in the immediate area of Latin American
heritage sites is at the poverty level, on occasion well below
minimum wage. Monte Albán represents an extreme case in
which many families live in extreme poverty without basic
services such as education, access to health care, or urban
infrastructure (fig. 8). The great majority of the economically
active population work at casual labor or in the informal

economy, with low incomes, no benefits, and few prospects.
The consequences for families are predictable: poor diets, bad
health, and minimal services. The average level of education
in communities around the archaeological zone is less than six
years of primary school.

Today the surroundings of heritage sites such as Monte
Albán and others in Mexico reflect poverty, social marginality,
and conditions hardly conducive to an appreciation of the values of heritage conservation. This description, regrettably, is
not an exception, as we can see by comparing Monte Albán to
other well-known heritage sites in Latin America. Teotihua-
can, Tula, and Mitla in Mexico; Machu Picchu and Chan Chan
in Peru; Kaminaljuyu and Quirigua in Guatemala, to name a
few, present similar profiles.

When speaking of the relationship between society and
heritage in Latin America, we describe a series of conditions
that overlap in diverse ways to create the social landscape that
characterizes the contemporary life of the site in question.
Unfortunately, in Latin America these landscapes all too frequently refer to settings of conflict over resource access and
control linked to a low quality of life, urban poverty, and
social problems such as drugs, assaults, pollution, congestion,
and other indicators of a highly stressed existence. Meanwhile,
the heritage sites themselves become the targets of looting,
vandalism, depredations, and other behaviors very much at
variance with what we hope they will convey about human
aspirations and accomplishments. Both the sites and the populations around them become targets for opportunistic, even
corrupt, behavior.

FIGURE 8 Housing quality in the surrounding neighborhoods of Monte Albán.
Courtesy of Archive of the archaeological site of Monte Albán, INAH

Without a doubt, in Latin America we see a clear association between cultural heritage conservation in general and archaeological protection specifically and levels of development. It is essential to find research methods adequate to produce a clear understanding of the social setting of heritage protection in order to formulate alternatives for inclusion in development planning. The goal must be to generate development programs that create positive environments for efforts to protect the archaeological heritage.

Acknowledgments

I wish to thank the Getty Conservation Institute for the opportunity to participate in the sessions on the conservation of archaeological heritage during the Fifth World Archaeology Congress, the source for the original draft of this paper. I also want to thank Jack Corbett for rich discussions on the central ideas of this paper and for his translation into English and Adrian Salinas for the preparation of the photographs that illustrate the text.

References

Corbett, J., and O. Gonzales Alafita. 2002. Crecimiento urbano, deterioro ambiental, y el futuro de Monte Albán. In *Patrimonio arqueológico y sociedad en el Valle de Oaxaca*, 337–47. Memoria de la Segunda Mesa Redonda de Monte Albán, INAH. México, D.F.: INAH.

Demas, M. 2000. Planning for conservation and management of archaeological sites: A values-based approach. In *Management Planning for Archaeological Sites*, ed. J. M. Teutonico and G. Palumbo, 27–54. Los Angeles: The Getty Conservation Institute.

Drennan, R., and S. Mora. 2001. *Archaeological Research and Heritage Preservation in the Americas*. Washington, D.C.: Society for American Archaeology.

Hoopes, J. W. 1997. El Cayo Project. *SAA Bulletin* (Society for American Archaeology) 15 (4):20–21.

Instituto Nacional de Antropología e Historia (INAH). 1972. *Ley Federal sobre Monumentos y Zonas Arqueológicos, Artísticos, e Históricos.* México, D.F.: INAH.

Martínez, M. A., and C. Bader. 1998. Patrimonio arqueológico: Su administración y manejo. In *Memoria, 60 años de la ENAH,* coord. Eyra Cárdenas Barahona, 443–46. México, D.F.: INAH.

Mason, R., and E. Avrami. 2000. Heritage values and challenges for conservation planning. In *Management Planning for Archaeological Sites,* ed. J. M. Teutonico and G. Palumbo, 13–26. Los Angeles: The Getty Conservation Institute.

Olea, O. 1997. Conclusiones. In *Especulación y patrimonio: 4º Coloquio del Seminario del Estudio del Patrimonio Artístico, Conservación, Restauración y Defensa,* ed. A. E. De Anda, 153–56. México, D.F.: Universidad Nacional Autónoma de México, Instituto de Investigaciones Estéticas.

Robles Garcia, N. 1998. Management of archaeological resources in Mexico: Experiences in Oaxaca. *SAA Bulletin* (Society for American Archaeology) 16 (3):22–25.

———. 1998. *El manejo de los recursos arqueológicos: El caso de Oaxaca.* México, D.F.: CONACULTA-INAH.

Robles Garcia, N., and J. Corbett. 1995. Land tenure systems, economic development, and protected areas in Mexico. In *8th Conference on Research and Resource Management in Parks, Sustainable Society and Protected Areas Management and on Public Lands,* 55–61. Hancock, Mich.: George Wright Society.

———. 2002. Land use, regulatory failure, and public policy in Mexico. Unpublished paper prepared for the Lincoln Institute of Land Policy Seminar on Speculation, Boston, Mass., 7–9 March 2002.

Stephen, L. 2002. *Zapata Lives! Histories and Cultural Politics in Southern Mexico.* Berkeley: University of California Press.

Reflections on Archaeological Heritage and Indigenous Peoples in Chile

Ángel Cabeza

Abstract: This article is an attempt to awaken archaeologists to the new demands from different groups of society, especially indigenous peoples, regarding the preservation and appropriate use of their archaeological heritage. It analyzes the New World context of heritage policies and the way in which archaeologists have had to adapt and focus their objectives and methods. It presents a brief comparative analysis and explains the Chilean situation, especially as regards the conditions that have resulted from recent legislation on indigenous and environmental topics, and how, from the state's perspective, work has been done with indigenous people.

The onset of the twentieth century was marked by the imperialism of a handful of states that controlled most ethnic cultures and minorities in their territories. This situation, combined with two world wars and a cold war lasting several decades, led to the disappearance of many cultures and, with them, their centuries-old wisdom. The twenty-first century has begun differently, with an explosion of cultural diversity and a strengthening of cultural identities that were either hidden or almost extinct. Our world is very different from the one we knew two decades ago. Different groups of people have made great strides in economic and political integration that hitherto had seemed impossible. At the same time, intensive migrations over the last decades have radically changed the ethnic map of many cities and regions in the world due mainly to inequalities in access to development and increased poverty in many countries.

Archaeology, as a concept and as research, has been affected both positively and negatively by these events. On the one hand, archaeology has incorporated in its work much of the technological progress made and has torn down old theoretical precepts. Furthermore, it has drawn a group of professionals open to creating and participating in new theoretical and methodological orientations and willing to face the new realities that are affecting their research. On the other hand, the new value that many societies have placed on cultural diversity has enabled many cultures to regain their past and heritage, generating a new and constantly changing situation that is at times in conflict with the development of archaeology.

This paper offers reflections, from the Latin American perspective, based on two decades of experience with different indigenous groups and communities, as well as participation in various debates on the subject.

Ethics and Governance with Regard to Heritage

Culture may be defined as a series of distinct spiritual, material, intellectual, and emotional features that mark a particular society or social group. Cultural heritage is a legacy from our forebears and a testimony to their very existence. The importance of heritage stems, fundamentally, from its contribution to forming a culture's identity. Identity consists of the essential element that enables people to gather together around a common project, this being understood as a civil community that may include different peoples who share basic principles and values. A proper relationship among cultural heritage, national identity, and a national project is key to achieving harmonious and long-lasting development. Heritage results from different cultural and historic traditions; it expresses the diversity of the land and its people. Knowledge of and respect for cultural diversity enriches people's lives and contributes to strengthening tolerance, valuing differences, and fostering fraternity between human beings. For that reason, we must learn to value cultural diversity and avoid confrontation so as to foster a profound and fruitful coexistence.

In this sense, it is necessary to broaden an understanding of heritage that is still dominated by aesthetic and historic criteria while excluding some groups. In many cases, priority has been given to heritage linked to power groups, to masculinity and supremacy, to the detriment of the everyday and mundane, with more attention paid to what has been written than what was spoken, and greater heed paid to the ceremonial and sacred than to the secular.

Research into identifying and exporting heritage, especially archaeological heritage, has been a topic of widespread discussion. Doubtless, the majority of persons acknowledge that a society is heir to all cultural accoutrements that its ancestors created and which belong to its culture. But societies have a history, one that concerns a territory whose borders change as do its occupants, either with migration or the arrival of other peoples with whom there follows integration, assimilation, or overt domination. Heritage has frequently been considered war booty or has been deliberately eliminated to destroy all trace of the existence of earlier societies that occupied that particular territory. Hardly any society, past or present, has been free from such practices.

Nowadays, more individuals and states share certain principles of mutual respect that must be extended to all societies. The Universal Declaration of Human Rights and, more recently, the Conventions of UNESCO point that way. However, the task is not easy, and there exist very complex historic and philosophic aspects: ethnic rivalry, religious struggles, political confrontations, and historical debts for past wars that are a difficult burden to shoulder and resolve.

For decades, with certain exceptions, archaeologists have been building up a pleasant academic refuge that has been respected by the community. It was a time of discovery and exotic trips motivated by a desire to understand the past and to collect archaeological objects for exhibition in national museums. Curiosity for what was familiar and foreign was the dominant factor that fed the scientific appetite and the community's imagination.

However, the reality is different for archaeologists today, depending on the location of their work. At least two basic processes are involved in the change. First, a portion of archaeologists have had to take part in the debate from the viewpoint of the environment, the economy, and development related to archaeological heritage, where decisions are taken by teams of professionals from different disciplines, at times with great circumstantial pressure brought to bear on

them. These decisions may lead to the substantial modification of certain projects under development, or the abandonment of the projects, or to the destruction of the heritage itself. It is the archaeology of environmental impact studies; it is archaeology contracted by companies or by public services; it is archaeology with deadlines (Cabeza 2001; Neumann and Sanford 2001).

Second, the power of indigenous peoples is reemerging, as is that of diverse nonurban communities, whose identity was ignored by the government and by society. Knowledge of their heritage provides force and sustenance for the political projects of these groups, strengthening their social cohesion and differentiating them from a nation's society in general and leading to economic initiatives such as tourism, arts, and crafts. In this context, a number of archaeologists have been surprised to find that they are not as welcome as before or that they are rejected outright; that their projects come to a full stop and their scientific interpretations are criticized because they contradict local beliefs.

Some archaeologists have refused to acknowledge such changes. Others have realized that they are not capable of dealing with the situation, that they were not trained for field archaeology marked by social, ethnic, political, and economic contingencies. Still others, as a result of more failures than successes, have had to walk this tightrope alone, facing their colleagues' mistrust and the conflicts that heritage research and conservation hold today. The challenge is this: how do we exchange information and viewpoints? how do we face this matter constructively from the perspectives of the academic, governmental, and indigenous world and of the communities that are nowadays claiming the right to take part in these decisions (Pearson and Sullivan 1995; Stapp and Burney 2002)?

Experiences in Australia and Canada are very important but little known by other countries as yet, especially with regard to participation by native communities. The situation in the United States is very valuable because of the contradictions that exist between public and private archaeological heritage and, especially, because of its accomplishments in interpreting and managing archaeological sites in protected areas. In Europe the situation is different but no less interesting with respect to the way in which local identities have been able to take over their heritage and the state has taken a backseat with regard to its administration. In Latin America, always a hotbed for innovation or unabashed copying, the situation is very diverse, but the initiatives already begun by Mexico, Peru, Argentina, and Brazil are of utmost importance for understanding what is happening in the region.

The underlying question should not be who the owner is or who is the more legitimate heir to various cultural assets but rather how we will be capable of recognizing the diverse values of such assets and use them properly so that everybody's identity is reproduced in an atmosphere of respect and harmony for all concerned. Rather than center discussion on the ownership of heritage, what should be considered is how we can better conserve that archaeological heritage for everybody and at the same time ensure that it provides cultural sustenance, force, and acknowledgment for its closest heirs. For that, the establishment of common policies of conservation, research, education, and diffusion is of vital importance, and we must move toward that goal in spite of the inevitable conflicts that arise (Zimmerman, Vitelli, and Hollowell-Zimmer 2003).

Archaeological Heritage and Indigenous Peoples

Chile's heritage is subject to a large number of the problems and conditions discussed above. Since Chile's settlement thousands of years ago, many human groups have inhabited it, developing their own cultures over the centuries. Several of them have since disappeared; some were displaced, while others were annihilated or conquered. In the sixteenth century a new invader and colonizing force came as a deep shock to the American continent. Conquest and colonization were dramatic; ancient cultures disappeared; and millions of persons died as a result of this contact, which led to the interbreeding of peoples and cultures that form the mosaic of what America is today.

It is in this context that the complexity of archaeological heritage must be understood as regards its origins, ownership, functions, and conservation. In fact, pre-Hispanic archaeological heritage was created by and therefore belongs, first of all, to the legitimate heirs of the original cultures in Chile. But if we understand Chile as a civil community of different cultures all living in the same territory and whose inhabitants are mostly mixed-race, the concept of ownership widens to include an entire population that is heir to and accountable for such an archaeological heritage. Here we encounter a noticeable demographic difference when we compare ourselves to the United States or Australia, for instance, where there was never racial mixing to the extent that it existed in Chile or in any other country in Latin America, where the indigenous population is in the majority.

In this context Latin American states, led by groups of European origin, have fought continuously to build up nation-states, ignoring—save for a few exceptions—the ethnic diversity and the ancient past of the populations they found. For that reason, both in colonial times and during the Republic, there has been an attitude and even a policy of contempt for and destruction of that past and all it represents. Independence gave way to a new political scene and the search for or creation of our own roots on which to build a different future. For many years, intellectuals idealized a romantic view of indigeneity, but the contradiction between "savagery" and "civilization" was inevitable, and the policy of extermination and conquest was reinforced in the interests of building a national society that was as culturally homogeneous as possible. In some countries such as Mexico, the ideal of a Spanish-indigenous nation was embellished; in others, such as Argentina, a nation of European immigrants devoid of any indigenous peoples was conceived.

In Chile the state set about the task of building a nation where the indigenous populations would be assimilated into a Western way of life; education was one of the pillars of that initiative. The large number of indigenous peoples—the Mapuche—combined with four centuries of Spanish coexistence with that culture produced a special concoction that has been simmering until the present day. These people are now vigorously demanding the political clout that for decades had been unanticipated. A somewhat similar occurrence took place with other indigenous cultures that have survived despite all efforts toward miscegenation, such as the Aymaras and Atacameños in the north and the Rapanui on Easter Island who, through territorial annexations, were incorporated into Chile at the end of the nineteenth century.

The recent upsurge in archaeology in Chile has been marked by environmental impact studies and the ever-increasing influence of indigenous cultures on day-to-day archaeology and on decision-making processes regarding the future of the archaeological heritage. The state has had to face these matters directly and pragmatically with differing results, few resources, and decisions handed down by some authorities rather than as a result of consistent and well-planned public policies. With a few exceptions (Navarro 1998), universities have remained on the sidelines, surprised by what has happened, by the force of the indigenous movements and by the evolution of the private archaeological market. Responses in the form of analysis of the situation, action that should be taken, and training of future professionals in archaeology have come from individuals rather than from the university system per se.

In this context, some archaeologists have been tempted to split archaeology into two unequal categories: one scientific and the other motivated by development projects. Also, some have preferred to distance themselves from the conflicts of indigenous peoples and their claim over control of archaeological sites on their land or anywhere else in the country. On the other hand, some researchers who have devoted their lives to archaeology have been unjustly criticized by indigenous peoples who ignore the role that they and their research have had in revitalizing their past and cultural identity.

The return of democracy to Chile in the 1990s made its mark on this situation with the enactment of two laws: one concerning indigenous peoples and the other the environment. Both laws created their own administrative structures and ways in which to handle citizen participation, hitherto nonexistent. In the first case, it was thought better to handle the indigenous movement and its representative structures at the level of individual cultures that were recognized through a national council that would formulate public policies and take the main decisions. Consolidating such institutionalism has been difficult, both because of its rejection by some indigenous sectors wishing to take a more radical approach to recovering land and territorial independence and because of the more obvious political, cultural, and economic contradictions between society and the state. The most frequent clashes were those stemming from forestry industries, the construction of dams, and the control of water and land rights.

The National Service for Indigenous Development and the National Monuments Council of Chile

The National Monuments Council (CMN) and the National Service for Indigenous Development (CONADI) are responsible for protecting Chile's heritage, both legally and technically. The two institutions signed an agreement of cooperation in 1996, aimed at working out joint strategies and projects related to the heritage of indigenous people. United in facing a common challenge, they can achieve the objectives defined in their respective legislations: the Law concerning National Monuments (1970) and the Law concerning Indigenous Peoples (1993). (For further information, see www.monumentos.cl.)

This agreement covers the preparation of a survey of archaeological, architectural, historic, and symbolic heritage of all indigenous peoples; a complete study of what indigenous cultural assets have to be protected by the National Monuments Law; and policies for protection, conservation, and preservation for all time of such heritage. It enables each to obtain advice on matters relating to cultural heritage. There is also an understanding within each institution that although archaeological finds belong to the state according to law, their administration could be in the hands of different institutions and even in the hands of the indigenous peoples themselves or the institutions they set up for that purpose.

However, there are problems, such as permits for undertaking archaeological digs, that are not duly coordinated with the indigenous communities, or unauthorized encroachments by the communities onto archaeological heritage that negatively affect it. In the majority of these cases, no harm was intended; rather, it was a question of ignorance of the regulations, a lack of advice, or the way in which the persons or institutions involved were handled politically.

This agreement has been maintained despite changes in the CONADI authorities. This new institution's work has been difficult because it must respond to indigenous demands, ranging from support for local development projects and the acquisition of land and water rights to resolving serious conflicts concerning squatters on land and political demands for territorial or cultural independence. At the same time, the approach to relations with indigenous people by the previous few governments has been affected by differing internal views of the problem and of solutions to potential conflicts such as the claiming of more lands, as well as political opposition to decisions taken. Indigenous people need to be consulted in the development of economic projects on Indian lands, such as the use of rivers for power plants, building of new highways, and exploitation of natural resources.

CMN's own actions have been affected by these often contradictory views. Its activities have been aimed at applying a policy whose grounds were ethical, opening up conversations in stages and gradually transferring responsibilities within prevailing legislation. This meant having to face romantic notions from within both the indigenous communities and the state, as well as having to face indigenous groups who thought that their political objectives could be attained only by bringing pressure to bear on the state. There are also groups of businessmen or landowners as well as indigenous communities who believe that defending their own interests—even to the extent of using force—is legitimate if the state or the courts of justice are unable to settle their demands satisfactorily. Interesting discussions on these problems at a global cultural, political, and economic level can be found in documents published by the Getty Conservation Institute (de la Torre 2002; de la Torre and Mason 1998).

We find an example of such conflicts and their possible resolution in San Pedro de Atacama in the north of Chile. This place has a complex situation that is in permanent flux—an immense cultural heritage and a local community that is being ethnically revitalized. There, the concept of appropriating heritage as one element of identity has been used to integrate the community, by claiming that the community must control and manage its own archaeological sites. However, the conflicts have gradually been subdued; the community was invited to take an active part, action was agreed on among the different institutions dealing with heritage, such as the local museum, CONADI, the communities, and the Chilean Forest Service (CONAF), which administers national parks. This meant developing projects for administering archaeological sites by the communities in consultation with the CMN, CONAF, and CONADI, undertaking archaeological research projects, and properly protecting such heritage. Over time, the communities themselves have discovered that the search for joint solutions was more satisfying and long-lasting than any conflict could ever be.

In the case of the Mapuche peoples located in urban areas and in the south of Chile, the focus has been on approaching with patience and much discussion the core topic surrounding their cultural identity—defending their ritual sites and burials. Because these were not legally protected as archaeological or historic monuments, they might be affected by infrastructure projects such as dams, roads, or electricity lines. Due to the large population, its dispersion, and its distrust of the state, many meetings have had to be held that included indigenous professionals acting as mediators within the communities. Fortunately, several of these ceremonial sites are now national monuments, and the communities thus endowed have discovered certain benefits that they have shared among themselves. Achieving this required time and determination.

On Easter Island, whose archaeological heritage is known worldwide, the situation has been very difficult because of its location in Polynesia, almost 4,000 kilometers from continental Chile. Its inhabitants feel the great cultural and geographic divide with Chile. The local community has known how to revitalize its culture based on its archaeological past and the oral memory or record of its traditions made by researchers. Also, more so than elsewhere, the community's archaeological heritage is the basis for its economy, so it is conscious of the need to protect and control it. There, the strategy has been to create a local structure with the help of the island authorities and the participation of the community,

which also takes part in decision making. This decentralization has been generally positive, with specific problems arising when certain leaders have wished to go forward more quickly than is politically possible.

Conclusion

The world context and the greater political influence of indigenous peoples, communities, and interest groups must be faced by those who devote time and effort to the archaeological heritage, for reasons of research or administration. From an ethical, cultural, and economic point of view, communities have rights over their heritage that must be respected. Therefore, those who are working toward getting to know and protect such cultural assets cannot take refuge in science, legislation, or the state. Their role is to foresee these problems and seek creative and all-encompassing solutions. They must understand the conflicts and their causes; keep dialogue going; and accept the fact that proposals could be rejected or may fail in the short term but once corrected with the help of the local community, might be successful. Those who work in the heritage area have to tread carefully and not exacerbate disagreements but remain firm in their convictions that peaceful understanding is the best way to resolve demands that, sometimes and for many years, had been put off or, at times, silenced.

It is not an easy task, and there are different views as well as contradictory political, ethnic, and economic interests involved. Cultural assets and especially archaeological heritage is riddled with such interests. For that reason, professionals working in heritage, archaeologists and conservators, have an increasingly important role in planning and decision making wherein different persons must have room to express themselves and share ideas. They must also bear in mind that the community does not have one sole voice, that there are different interest groups that often go as far as fighting for the supremacy of their approaches. For that reason, education and proper public information are very valuable. Many problems result from ignorance of our projects by the communities and to a certain haughtiness and standoffishness on our part that has led to the attitude that we know what is best for heritage. Archaeological heritage has different values; scientific value is one of them, but there are also cultural and religious values that a community places on it. It is essential to find the common ground where all can coexist.

Archaeological heritage can be a bridge for understanding between cultures with mutual respect and within the guidelines of universal principles. There are no special recipes; every situation is different, and peoples' experiences are vital when it comes to resolving conflicts and acknowledging the different values and interests that harmonize or contradict heritage.

Finally, it is worth mentioning that peace and cooperation are stronger than resentment or ignorance; discovering our heritage and using it respectfully and jointly enables us to grow. Although the past is full of injuries that still separate us, we nevertheless have a future to be shared.

References

Cabeza, A. 2001. Evaluating the environmental impact of development projects on the archaeological heritage of Chile. *Conservation and Management of Archaeological Sites* 4 (4):245–47.

de la Torre, M. 2002. *Assessing the Values of Cultural Heritage.* Research report. Los Angeles: The Getty Conservation Institute.

de la Torre, M., and R. Mason. 1998. Economic and heritage conservation. A meeting organized by the Getty Conservation Institute, December.

Navarro, X. 1998. *Indigenous Archaeological Heritage in Chile: Reflections and Proposals for Handling It.* Temuco, Chile: Universidad de la Frontera.

Neumann, T., and R. Sanford. 2001. *Cultural Resources Archaeology.* Walnut Creek, Calif: Altamira Press.

Pearson, M., and S. Sullivan. 1995. *Looking after Heritage Places.* Melbourne: Melbourne University Press.

Stapp, D., and M. Burney. 2002. *Tribal Cultural Resource Management.* Walnut Creek, Calif: Altamira Press.

Zimmerman, L., K. Vitelli, and J. Hollowell-Zimmer. 2003. *Ethical Issues in Archaeology.* Walnut Creek, Calif: Altamira Press.

Whose Archaeology? Social Considerations in Archaeological Research Design

Richard Mackay

Abstract: A worldwide trend toward greater recognition and empowerment of stakeholders in archaeological investigation and conservation is reflected in outcomes that range between formal roles for stakeholders in ongoing management to genuine control of and inclusion in processes for identification of heritage values. Concurrently, archaeological investigation and heritage management projects are increasingly reaching out to wider communities, providing opportunities for participation or innovative means of communicating project outcomes. Debate continues about the role of archaeology and archaeologists. Those who focus on "humanist" perspectives consider the contextual aspects of sites and their values in a social and community setting. Others view such an approach as outside the realm of real archaeology. This paper argues that finding common ground requires archaeology to move in two directions: toward traditional owners and other stakeholders so as to adopt a holistic approach to value identification and inclusive management and, concurrently, outward to the wider community, connecting place and knowledge with people through structured communication and events. If there is to be common ground in archaeological heritage management, it is in a values-based approach that facilitates an inclusive and interpretive archaeology.

The worldwide trend toward greater recognition and empowerment of stakeholders, especially indigenous stakeholders, was illustrated during the Fifth World Archaeology Congress when Gary Pappen, a traditional owner of the Lake Mungo World Heritage Site in Australia, told participants, "If you want to work on this site, you will do it on our terms. We are the culture bearers." Pappen's message, though bluntly delivered, was well received and provides a salient parallel for other archaeological sites and their stakeholders.

Stakeholder involvement was a dominant theme in the "Finding Common Ground" session of the conservation program organized by the Getty Conservation Institute at the congress. The case studies presented showcased diversity and developing practice in inclusive involvement of culture bearers for important archaeological places across the globe.

As António Pedro Batarda Fernandes and Fernando Maia Pinto, whose paper immediately follows in this volume, point out, in Côa Valley in Portugal, formal roles have been defined and the involvement of stakeholders legitimized. However, while such processes are clearly a move in the right direction, active stakeholder participation seems to be an implementation of a management goal, or rather formalization of a process, rather than an integral element of the process itself.

Half a world away, on Rapanui (Easter Island), concerns about the imperialist impact of nonindigenous values and practices have ensured greater and earlier control and the vesting of authority in culture bearers, although inevitable change to places and their community values is recognized. Sergio Rapu's paper focused on the role of the entire community as partner with government in conservation (Rapu 2003). While this is an evolving process, the integral role of culture bearers is clearly at the core of successful values-based management that reflects and responds to the significance of traditions and meanings, as well as the physical fabric of the place itself.

The importance of intangible values to a comprehensive understanding of heritage is illustrated by Rodney Harrison in his paper on Dennawan Reserve (see in this volume). The cultural resource management process at Dennawan recognizes the danger that as archaeologists focus on technical research, social values become disassociated. The Dennawan case study turns this dilemma around, emphasizing event-based experience of remains so as to refresh the "memoryscape" of stakeholders. Here the meaning, rather than the fabric or resulting science, is seen as significant, and there is a strong contrast with the traditional archaeological obsession of recording fabric. The management technique used to record significance in this case is to "map" event behavior through graphic recording of intangible values, that is, marking the "meanings" on maps or plans.

The principles highlighted in each of these case studies (and the others presented in an earlier part of the session) are relevant to the wider practice of archaeology and in particular to archaeological investigation and research design. Much of the role of archaeology worldwide and its relationship with history and traditions hinges on perceptions of the value and role of material culture. However, in doing so, the discipline tends to focus on physical evidence as the data set, rather than on other values that the place may have for its constituent stakeholder communities. Archaeologists have long trumpeted the potential of the discipline to contribute to history. But does archaeological investigation and analysis enrich the community? Is it a public good? Is there not a real danger that in fulfilling obligations that may arise from statutory controls or in pursuing evolving technology and science, archaeology can become introspective, derivative, and little more than self-serving, rather than provide a wider public or community benefit?

In my field, colonial archaeology in Australia, it is increasingly accepted that archaeology contributes major thematic evidence that can disprove or question traditional clichés about issues such as convict history and nineteenth-century "slums." The late-eighteenth- and early-nineteenth-century colonial settlement sites in Sydney and Melbourne are of significance to the geopolitical history of the world, as they provide tangible evidence related to the process of colonial settlement through forced migration that was the precedent to the cadastral boundaries and structure evident today.

The Cumberland/Gloucester Street site in The Rocks, Sydney (Godden Mackay and Karskens 1999; Karskens 1999), sheds new light on nineteenth-century working communities, putting paid to traditional myths that these areas were simply "slums." A similar picture has recently emerged in Melbourne at the Little Lonsdale/Casselden Place site excavated over the past fifteen years (Murray and Mayne 2001).

Significantly, with both of these projects the impetus for archaeological investigation has been development pressures or management issues, but the conduct of the investigations and the project outcomes have had a wider community effect. In both cases, levels of public participation were high, with opportunities to excavate on site, attend tours, or enjoy extensive media coverage. There have been a number of academic papers and books and even a schools education kit (Astarte Resources 2001). Interestingly, in the case of the Cumberland/Gloucester Street site, now known locally as the "BIG DIG," the very act of archaeology and the extent of media coverage and political interest have imbued the place with a late-twentieth-, early-twenty-first-century layer of meaning and resulting social value. The site remains vacant, stabilized as excavated, and discussions continue about the prospect of its long-term conservation as a Historic Place.

These Australian archaeological investigation projects illustrate the prospect that there is an important wider stakeholder community than traditional culture bearers. For many places, there is also an interested public who can acquire a legitimate stake in archaeological heritage management through participation and communication. The wider community is therefore a stakeholder for many archaeological places because it is the wider community that directly or indirectly pays for archaeological investigation or management, is itself part of the history and may be eager to participate, be involved or informed. Of course, this can only happen where the archaeologists or resource managers involved provide an appropriate opportunity to do so.

If archaeology is to engage with stakeholders, the obligation is not only to include culture bearers but also to look to delivery of a wider community good—realizing the legitimacy of social context, as well as the potentially self-serving needs of archaeology.

Recent dialogue in the U.S. literature has directed archaeology toward such a humanist approach and proactive stakeholder engagement. This dialogue is relevant to urban archaeologists, like me, whose major projects attract thousands of visitors and hundreds of community participant diggers but which are still managed (in the statutory sense) on the basis of recovering "research value." The reality is that for many sites, this is the game: any prospect of conserving remains is often already removed by management decisions or statutory consent (allowing total excavation and removal), well before the on-site archaeology begins.

Archaeology is, however, gaining ground in the tussle to be relevant to society. The American debate and projects like the BIG DIG highlight diverse views on what may be regarded as archaeological data. Cleland's article in *Historical Archaeol-*

ogy, "Historical Archaeology Adrift?" (2001a:1–8), for example, has spawned a rugged debate and questioning of the role of history. This in turn draws in contextual considerations:

> A tension has thus arisen between the science which is inherent in the basic method, which constitutes archaeology, and a humanistic component of historical archaeology. Moreover, many believe that it is the latter which gives the field its freshness, imagination and adventure. (CLELAND 2001b:28)

Storytelling, and its role, not to mention even more outrageous "archaeological events" are derided by some and praised by others in a related series of discussions. Odell's article, "Research Problems 'R' Us," moves toward an engagement and humanist position that without telling stories and engaging the public, the future of the discipline of archaeology is insecure (Odell 2001:679–85).

Traditionally, archaeological investigation, even if undertaken as part of cultural resource management or salvage archaeology, has tended toward an academic research framework, often structured through geographic models: global, neighborhood, or household, as reflected in some of the WAC-5 session papers. However, we should perhaps be asking additional contemporary questions. Perhaps the question is not what do we want to know, but what do *they* want to know? In other words, how do we connect with an eager, interested, and often enthusiastic wider community? They may come to the digs; they may attend lectures; they participate at one level, but is the discipline becoming increasingly sophisticated in its technical analysis and theoretical models at the front end while neglecting the public deliverable at the back end?

Jones (2002) perspicaciously observes that these issues—archaeology as science versus archaeology in its human context—divide the discipline: objectivity versus subjectivity, rationality versus relativism, processualism versus postprocessualism.

He observes also that "one of the major strengths of an interpretive archaeology that embraces a variety of post-structural approaches is the rigorous nature of its theoretic framework" (22).

In other words, we can and should, perhaps, conduct archaeology as science in a social context, by constructing research frameworks that engage more directly with archaeology as "heritage" in its community setting. Such an approach sits well with the conservation ethos of the Getty Conservation Institute and international conservation orga-

nizations such as the International Council for Monuments and Sites (ICOMOS). Consistent with current best practice in wider heritage management, archaeology needs to move more decisively toward a values-based approach in which all significant aspects of the place or site are assessed as input to management decisions—including local economic issues, for example, or intangible aspects of culture, such as meaning or association. Stakeholder values, needs, wants, and desires must be part of the site management context; to paraphrase the views of the Lake Mungo traditional owners, the archaeology must be done on "their" terms.

Figures 1 through 3 endeavor to summarize this progression. Figure 1 presents a linear model in which the filter of research design may be used to ensure that investigation of physical evidence (i.e., the archaeology) contributes to the bank of knowledge by being undertaken within problem-oriented parameters, cognizant of existing theory and knowledge. The science and logic are apparent, but the people are sadly absent.

FIGURE 1 The relationship between theory and evidence, reflected in traditional archaeological research design.

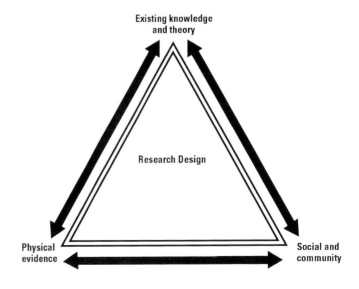

FIGURE 2 Research design reflecting broader issues, such as social and community context.

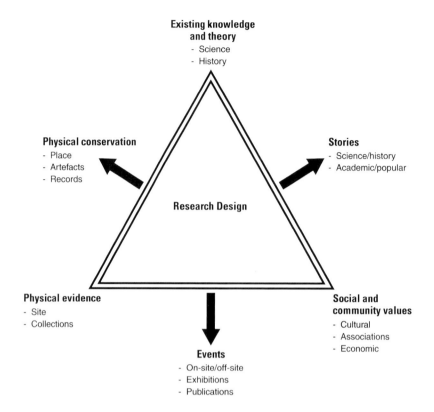

By contrast, figure 2 provides a triangular representation in which existing theory and knowledge and physical evidence are counterbalanced by social and community values. In other words, the conceptual framework for archaeological research design is expanded and can also respond to cultural practices, associations, meanings, or even the economic values of a particular place—to ensure that decisions about archaeological investigation or site management address all of the values of the place and the needs of its stakeholders.

Figure 3 builds on the representation in figure 2 by suggesting some potential outcomes. Physical evidence considered in relation to existing knowledge and theory is thereby focused on management issues and physical conservation needs for the place, its artifacts and records. The information or "stories" coming out of the investigation relate not only to existing knowledge and theory but also to the social and community context. The stories, therefore, may be academic or factual material or less formal storytelling of the type advocated by Praetzellis (1998) and others.

There is a third set of outputs, however, arising from the physical evidence of the place itself and its social and community context—the "archaeological event." This may take the form of participation in an excavation, a site tour, a website, an exhibition, media coverage, or even a book launch. In other

words, where the value of the site is embodied more in its social context than in its potential contribution to theory and knowledge, it may well be that the appropriate outcome from archaeological investigation and management is the event itself rather than a report or publication. This notion, of course, provides more fodder for the derisive commentary in some of the U.S. literature about event-based archaeology, and therein lies the tension between traditional science-based models and the more humanist, inclusive approach advocated in this paper.

If twenty-first-century heritage management is about conserving all identified values and making them available to both contemporary communities and future generations, then there is a need for a less academic, less patronizing approach to archaeology; one that is more inclusive of both culture bearers and wider community stakeholders. Effective archaeological management involves moving beyond consultation, beyond tokenistic participation in projects, beyond new management involvement, and even beyond events, to an integrated approach to archaeology in its contemporary social context. The process must work both ways, with stakeholder input for values identification and management and output that connects the results of archaeological processes to their constituent communities. In doing so, cultural resource managers will better recognize and realize the importance of archaeology in providing opportunities for an emotional response to the community's tangible history. If there is to be a common ground in archaeological heritage management, it is in a values-based approach that facilitates an inclusive and interpretive archaeology.

Acknowledgments

I wish to acknowledge the Getty Conservation Institute for its foresight in including a conservation theme in the Fifth World Archaeology Congress. I thank Brian Egloff and Ángel Cabeza Monteira for thoughtful guidance and for chairing the "Finding Common Ground" sessions, as well as the presenters cited in the text above. My thinking about event-based archaeology has developed through a project titled Exploring the Archaeology of the Modern City, undertaken by La Trobe University, and I thank my colleague Tim Murray for stimulating critique of some of these ideas. Penny Crook has provided research assistance related to this paper and my general consideration of archaeological research design.

References

Astarte Resources. 2001. *The BIG DIG Education Kit.* www.astarte.com.au.

Cleland, C. E. 2001a. Historical archaeology adrift? A forum. *Historical Archaeology* 35 (2):1–8.

———. 2001b. Reply to Douglas V. Armstrong, Lu Ann de Cunzo, Gregory A. Waselkov, Donald L. Hardestry, and Roberta S. Greenwood. *Historical Archaeology* 35 (2):28–30.

Godden Mackay Pty Ltd. and G. Karskens. 1999. *The Cumberland/Gloucester Street Site, The Rocks, Archaeological Investigation, Volumes I–IV.* Redfern, NSW, Australia: Godden Mackay Logan Pty Ltd., Heritage Consultants.

Jones, A. 2002. The archaeology of two cultures. In *Archaeology Theory and Scientific Practice,* 1–22. Topics in Contemporary Archaeology. Cambridge: Cambridge University Press.

Karskens, G. 1999. *Inside The Rocks: The Archaeology of a Neighbourhood.* Alexandria, NSW, Australia: Hale and Iremonger Pty Ltd.

Murray, T., and A. Mayne. 2001. Imaginary landscapes: Leading Melbourne's 'Little Lon'. In *The Archaeology of Urban Landscapes: Explorations in Slumland,* ed. A. Mayne and T. Murray, 89–105. Cambridge: Cambridge University Press.

Odell, G. H. 2001. Research problems 'r' us. *American Antiquity* 66 (4): 679–85.

Praetzellis, A. 1998. Why every archaeologist should tell stories once in a while. *Historical Archaeology* 32 (1): 1–13.

Rapu, S. 2003. The changing meaning of the heritage management challenge: Rapanui, Chile. Paper presented in the "Finding Common Ground: The Role of Stakeholders in Decision Making" session, Fifth World Archaeology Congress, Washington, D.C.

Changing Stakeholders and Community Attitudes in the Côa Valley World Heritage Site, Portugal

António Pedro Batarda Fernandes and Fernando Maia Pinto

Abstract: *Because of its responsibility for managing a World Heritage Site, the Côa Valley Archaeological Park (PAVC) has a specific policy with regard to its stakeholders. Most local stakeholders and a large segment of the community have not yet realized that the region's achievement of sustainable development will rest on general upgrading of the socioeconomic structure. The aim of this paper is to explain why the PAVC advocates that the ability of the region to provide high-quality products and services, which match the inestimable significance of the Côa Valley rock art, will determine the success of a development project for the region based on cultural tourism. After an introductory overview of global cultural heritage management guidelines, we examine the challenges the PAVC faces in trying to establish specific management, preservation, and development strategies in this area of Portugal. We also discuss how, in certain cases, following completely "politically correct stakeholder and community-friendly" guidelines can endanger the preservation of our common cultural heritage.*

Over the past few decades, the international archaeological community has paid increasing interest to conservation heritage management (CHM) problems, as one can see from the vast literature concerning this matter (for references on the subject, see Matero et al. 1998). This has occurred for two reasons. Initially archaeologists realized that every research project should take a holistic approach to the site or sites under investigation and that preservation and presentation matters should be viewed in the same manner. Later it was believed that if archaeologists or professionals from related disciplines did not manage (i.e., preserve and present) cultural heritage resources themselves, perhaps responsibility for them would be given to administrators who lacked a preservation perspective.

To fully appreciate and understand stakeholders, we need to know how to identify, assess, and establish the best methods of communication with them. A brief discussion aims to highlight the important role that stakeholders play in the implementation of CHM processes. To some extent it also provides a basis for questioning a "politically correct" view of the involvement of community and stakeholders that underlies some authors' approaches to this issue. These approaches sometimes overemphasize the importance of stakeholders when implementing cultural heritage conservation projects. The notion that everything in the management implementation process must be done in accordance with or respecting stakeholders' demands or needs is advocated by some authors. This line of thought has made its way, unquestioned, into the mainstream of CHM thinking.[1]

The involvement of stakeholders is crucial to the success of any given CHM project. Nevertheless, we seek to demonstrate that in specific circumstances local stakeholders' and communities' ambitions should not jeopardize the higher aim: the preservation of cultural heritage resources.

Stakeholders can be located far from a particular region and still have an interest in the development or preservation of its resources. This concern may stem from their desire to preserve something valuable to them as members of the wider community. In this sense, all those who have proved themselves committed to the preservation of humankind's common legacy may have a legitimate stakeholder interest in the management or defense of the preservation of Côa Valley rock art. Local Côa stakeholders need to be aware that the significance of the valley's rock art makes it an invaluable testimony to all humankind. The fact that it is located in "their" region does not intrinsically make them the sole or even the most decisive voices when discussing the management and tourism use of the rock art and overall development strategies.

Identification of Stakeholders

There are several different kinds of communities and stakeholders. The community can be local, national, international, or specific, such as the archaeological community. They all constitute different "stakeholders," the term being understood as individuals or groups of individuals who, whatever their location, have a specific interest in the way any given resource (in this case, cultural heritage) is managed. The number of stakeholders could be endless.[2] Because of their interest, stakeholders can either directly or indirectly affect CHM, in ways ranging from everyday decisions to long-term resolutions.

Open Attitudes and Wide-Ranging Discussion

The adoption of an open attitude by CHM organizations, what Hall and McArthur (1998) describe as "being the facilitators," will certainly foster their relationship with stakeholders. Naturally this does not mean that CHM managers should concede to every demand, as we discuss below. Nevertheless, a wide-ranging iterative process of discussion with the community and the many stakeholders on relevant matters (objectives, strategies, overall philosophical conservation and preservation approaches, etc.) must be established in order to secure the medium- and long-term success of a CHM project.

Assessing the socioeconomic and cultural status of the community can be a helpful tool in adjusting communication strategies so that the information CHM organizations transmit will be reasonably well understood. This will avoid time-consuming misinterpretations and will clarify positions so that all parties know what they can expect from one other.

Communication Processes

The local community needs feedback, whether it realizes it or not, from involved organizations in order to fully appreciate and judge the significance of its own cultural heritage. At the same time, even allowing for different communication strategies, the discourse of managers is often biased by their own beliefs, interests, or views and even, regrettably, is sometimes "bought by the highest bidder" (Hall and McArthur 1998:55), which is not very helpful when trying to gain the trust of communities. Managers must understand that CHM organi-

zations do not work in a void or for themselves. These organizations, as any others, are integrated in a given society and are, in fact, the most empowered of stakeholders. Nevertheless, they need to be aware that it is society that delegates to CHM organizations the authority and the obligation to protect something that possesses important values to that given society.

Suitable communication methods must be established to ensure that the message is delivered effectively to communities and stakeholders. This can be achieved by promoting innovative and extended educational programs or by well-targeted information and promotion campaigns. It can also be accomplished by engaging influential and popular individuals within the community, establishing them as proficient communication channels for reaching the population. CHM organizations have to be active rather than reactive, trying actively to reach stakeholders and communities since they must be involved in the planning process from the start.

The Côa Valley Case Study: Changing Roles of Stakeholders and Community

The Côa Valley Archaeological Park (PAVC) was created in 1997 and given the responsibility to "manage, protect and organize for public visits, including the setting up of museum facilities, the monuments included in the special protection zone of the Côa Valley" (Zilhão 1998). A year later UNESCO classified the Côa Valley rock art as World Cultural Heritage. The roughly 1,200 engravings inscribed in schist, ranging in age from the Upper Palaeolithic to the present and located mostly along the banks of the final 17 kilometers of the Côa River, form the core of the cultural heritage management project in the Côa Valley (figs. 1–3).

The Côa Valley Archaeological Park was born of the need to preserve an invaluable assemblage of open-air rock art that was threatened by the construction of a dam. In this context, the creation of the park encountered fierce resistance from the supporters of the dam who believed that the dam was going to bring progress and development to the region (see Fernandes 2003). Therefore, from the beginning, a significant part of the local population did not endorse the implementation of an alternative project governed by wide-ranging conservationist, nature-friendly policies, which aimed to value heritage and to incorporate into regional development the concept of World Heritage.

For a majority of the local population and stakeholders, the creation of the park was considered a defeat, as they

preferred the dam, the construction of which assured them a steady flow of income for at least two years. Local stakeholders felt that an urban elitist minority (stakeholders themselves, nevertheless) who had never paid any attention to that underdeveloped rural interior area of Portugal had imposed the creation of the park and subsequent halt in the dam construction (Gonçalves 2001a). Within the Portuguese administrative and political system, the creation of an archaeological park of roughly 200 square kilometers under the Ministry of Culture caused evident turmoil in the relationships between public institutions. Divergences occurred among the existing agriculture, land management, and environment agencies but mainly with the local administrations, who were heirs to a strong municipal tradition in Portugal.

Hence, it is no surprise that much of the regional population regarded the park with animosity. Adding to the situation, some important national government investment projects were postponed or delayed, an example of the latter being the construction of a museum devoted to the valley's rock art that would expand the region's capacity to receive visitors. But the chief complaint, especially on the part of the municipality, concerned the visitation system, which, in order to preserve the authenticity and integrity of the engravings and their surroundings, allows only a limited number of visitors per day (for a detailed consultation and review of this sys-

tem, see Fernandes 2003; Zilhão 1998). Nevertheless, in the seven years the park has been open, 130,000 individuals have already visited the engravings (information provided by the PAVC's accountant's office).

Influential local stakeholders fancied questionable thematic parks and wanted to offer completely free access to the engravings. Their concept of development for the area included the creation of low-investment Disneyland-esque tourist structures such as on-site souvenir shops, food outlets, parking facilities, and amusement attractions—as if more than the rock art was needed to provide a quality visitor experience appealing to a broad cross-section of the general public. The main concern was to try to capture huge visitor numbers that could generate "astronomic" income flows while bypassing large private investments and the upgrading of socioeconomic and cultural structures. It is plain to see that this development concept[3] would endanger the preservation of the Côa Valley rock art in its full integrity and authenticity, especially if one considers the quite untouched context in which the engravings had survived hitherto. The most heeded local stakeholders and therefore an important part of the community give little value to the engravings—usually referred as "doodles done by the millers" who worked on the riverbanks until the 1950s. From their perspective, the only benefit would have been economic by taking the approach

FIGURE 2 View of Penascosa rock art site. One can imagine the negative impact that ill thought and intrusive mass tourism structures would have on this quite unspoiled and picturesque landscape. Photo: © Luís Luís, Parque Arqueológico do Vale do Côa

FIGURE 3 The entwined horses of the Ribeira de Piscos rock art site. Photo: CNART (Centro Nacional de Arte Rupestre). © IPA (Instituto Português de Arqueologia)

FIGURE 4 The garbage cans of Vila Nova de Foz Côa. Photo © António Pedro Batarda Fernandes, Parque Arqueológico do Vale do Côa

advocated above in which tourism development came first and only afterward preservation and holistic management of the Côa Valley rock art resource.

In the Côa Valley case, we believe it is important to clarify what is understood by the type of sustainable development that incorporates public presentation of the rock art. Our model, which determined the implementation of the "low-impact" visitation scheme (see Fernandes 2003), agrees with that of the World Commission on Environment and Development, which defines this concept as "development that meets the needs of the present without compromising the ability of future generations to meet their own needs" (WCED, cited in Lélé 1991:611). In this sense, the rock art cultural resource must

be seen as a fundamental but nonrenewable element of a sustainable development vision for the region.

It was precisely the prominence and importance of all that the World Heritage concept encompasses that began to reverse the situation, causing a growing number of stakeholders to change their minds and start supporting the park and its policies. In fact, the prestige, visibility, and publicity associated with the "Côa Valley World Heritage brand" is finally being used by locals in the promotion of their products, as they seek to certify them as authentic quality items and services. Some cases are more successful than others (fig. 4).

Instrumental to the success of this slow but steady process of changing mentalities was the PAVC's standpoint. Although seeking the active involvement of all stakeholders, the park strongly supports national, international, and especially regional or local stakeholders who maintain as a goal of their management philosophy the offer of quality products and services. In the long run only a culture of excellence (based either on already existing "products"—rock art, Port wine, olive oil, gastronomy, or landscape—or on new, genuine, and socioecologically sound products) will determine and maintain the success of sustainable development for the region. Among the examples of stakeholders using this approach are local and national government institutions, restaurants, cafés, teahouses, hostels, olive oil producers, tour operators, and Port wine farmyards, some with hosteling facilities or small on-site museums. The above-mentioned stakeholders are experiencing good results as a consequence of upgrading their offerings and also of their association with the Côa rock art World Heritage brand (fig. 5) (see Fernandes 2003:103–4).

FIGURE 5 Some of the local traditional agricultural products that the PAVC sells in its reception centers: port wine, honey, and olive oil. Photo © António Pedro Batarda Fernandes, Parque Arqueológico do Vale do Côa

In addition to promoting a first-rate overall cultural tourism offering in the area, beginning with a quality experience visiting the rock art sites (small groups of visitors viewing rock art in a relatively untouched environment located in a characteristic landscape), the PAVC aims through this policy to lead the way in improving most stakeholders' procedures by demonstrating the long-term benefits of such a change. Hall and McArthur (1998:54) believe that "stakeholders set definitions of quality that managers work towards." In the case of local stakeholders, this is what is taking place in the Côa, although here, conversely, it was the management principles established by the PAVC that established new definitions of quality for stakeholders.

As stated, the political and social circumstances of the Côa Valley created an environment that was somewhat hostile to the implementation of the park's management policies. This climate is being dissipated slowly but gradually as stakeholders begin to see and plan for the long-term, sustainable, culturally based development of an area where illiteracy levels are high, especially among the numerous aged population (see Fernandes 2003:96–97). Instead of opting for an entirely stakeholder-friendly approach, the PAVC deliberately chose to demonstrate the justness of its management and development policies. However, this is a slow process, and it will take time for stakeholders to fully understand that the future of this region lies in sustainable tourism that takes advantage of the region's invaluable heritage coupled with the provision of prime commodities and services.

Conclusion: Anti-Development Fundamentalism or Just Plain Good Sense?

We are aware that some may accuse the park of conducting a somewhat elitist or fundamentalist approach to the management of the Côa Valley in a socioeconomic context not fully prepared to understand the reach of most of the implemented conservation and development strategies. We do not believe that rock art or cultural heritage in general should be fully accessible to or appreciated by only a few chosen connoisseurs. Nor do we consider that it "belongs" only to a local community that descends more or less directly from the makers of a given cultural heritage feature. We do not feel that planning for or attempting to assure the sustainable future of the rock art and subsequently of the development of tourism and other economic avenues in the area is an elitist or fundamentalist approach. We believe it to be just plain good sense.

Another criticism sometimes heard is that archaeologists are preservation fundamentalists who turn up their noses at any development project. As the Côa Valley case study demonstrates, when most local stakeholders have an everyone-for-himself approach to CHM and when their proposals, needs, or development concepts endanger the preservation of cultural heritage, a line has to be drawn.

CHM bodies have a preservation pact with all humankind that must be kept. Rational and reasonable preservation policies—such as the ones implemented in the Côa Valley—"dictate" that some stakeholders' ambitions cannot be taken into account if we want to safeguard cultural heritage properties. As Jacobs and Gale (1994:1–8) point out, there is a profound difference of approach and management goals between what they define as "heritage industry" and "sustainable tourism." Although the involvement of stakeholders in cultural heritage management is essential, sometimes less conciliatory decisions have to be taken. These situations can arise when stakeholder interests are impossible to reconcile, when a specific stakeholder's demand is incompatible with the preservation of heritage, or when a substantial portion of local stakeholders favor the construction of dams over the preservation of significant cultural heritage sites. In the case of the Côa, if the most influential local stakeholders and the considerable part of the community that favored the dam had their way, the rock art sites would not have been saved from flooding. However, political decisions such as the one that stopped the construction of the dam as well as the implemented management strategies have to be clearly explained so that all parties understand why some demands, wishes, or ambitions cannot be met and to assure that the entire process is transparent.

The Côa Valley case study demonstrates the difficulties of the holistic, open, modern approach to cultural heritage management. Nevertheless, a well-integrated and productive set of organizations devoted to the preservation and public presentation of global cultural heritage must be aware that the conflict between development and preservation with all that it entails may force them, at times, to take a stand, to draw a line. Although the arguments presented in the introductory section and in the Côa case study may be somewhat contradictory, we believe that politically correct stakeholder and community-friendly guidelines might not sometimes serve long-term preservation needs or sustainable development options. In our opinion, the long-term preservation of the Côa Valley rock art is dependent on the success of the park's implemented management strategies. At the same time, the possibility for successful sustainable tourism development in the area lies in the endurance of the rock art. Since the two are utterly entwined, it is clear that any disproportion in the tourism development/preservation equation would have a tremendous and perhaps irreversible impact. Even if we agree with Liwieratos's (2004) statement that "there is a greater chance of achieving sustainable conservation through development if responsibilities are shifted to the public," we also believe that, before such a change, it is vital to make sure that the public and the stakeholders, especially local ones, are truly prepared to deal wisely with the responsibility of contributing decisively to the management of a World Heritage Site.

Acknowledgments

We wish to thank João Zilhão and Alexander Gall for useful suggestions and commentaries on early drafts. We would also like to thank the latter for proofreading the text.

Notes

1   For a general approach on this, see, for instance, Hall and McArthur 1998: chaps. 3, 4; McManamon and Hatton 2000; Start 1999. For an example of a politically correct Portuguese approach, see Gonçalves 2001a, 2001b.

2   See Hall and McArthur 1998: 46 for a hypothetical but thorough list of stakeholders in any given situation.

3   For an assessment of the negative impacts that this kind of development triggered in the Algarve region after the creation of Portugal's number 1 mass tourism destination, see Tourtellot 2005:67.

References

Fernandes, A. P. B. 2003. Visitor management and the preservation of rock art: Two case studies of open air rock art sites in northeastern Portugal: Côa Valley and Mazouco. *Conservation and Management of Archaeological Sites* 6:95–111.

Gonçalves, M. 2001a. Introdução geral. In *O caso de Foz Côa: Um laboratório de análise sociopolítica*, ed M. Gonçalves, 9–26. Lisbon: Edições 70.

———. 2001b. Da "pré-história" à história do caso de Foz Côa. In *O caso de Foz Côa: Um laboratório de análise sociopolítica*, ed. M. Gonçalves, 27–64. Lisbon: Edições 70.

Hall, C. M., and S. McArthur. 1998. *Integrated Site Management: Principles and Practice*. London: The Stationery Office.

Jacobs, J., and F. Gale. 1994. *Tourism and the Protection of Aboriginal Cultural Sites*. Canberra: Australian Government Publishing Services.

Lélé, S. 1991. Sustainable development: A critical review. *World Development* 19 (6):607–21.

Liwieratos, K. 2004. Introducing the competitive advantage theory/strategy in heritage management. *Public Archaeology* 3(4).

Matero, F., K. L. Fong, E. del Bono, M. Goodman, E. Kopelson, L. McVey, J. Sloop, and C. Turton. 1998. Archaeological site conservation and management: An appraisal of recent trends. *Conservation and Management of Archaeological Sites* 2:129–42.

McManamon, F. P., and A. Hatton. 2000. Introduction: Considering cultural resource management in modern society. In *Cultural Resources Management in Contemporary Society: Perspectives on Managing and Presenting the Past*, ed. F. P. McManamon and A. Hatton, 1–5. London: Routledge.

Start, D. 1999. Community archaeology: Bringing it back to local communities. In *Managing Historic Sites and Buildings: Reconciling Presentation and Preservation*, ed. G. Chitty and D. Baker, 49–60. London: Routledge.

Tourtellot, J. B. 2005. Destinations Scorecard: 115 Places Rated. www.nationalgeographic.com/traveler/scorecard/115_destinations_article.pdf.

Zilhão, J. 1998. The rock art of the Côa Valley, Portugal: Significance, conservation and management. *Conservation and Management of Archaeological Sites* 2:193–206.

PART FIVE

Issues at World Heritage Sites

Introduction

Sharon Sullivan

Many famous World Heritage Sites have been discovered by archaeological investigations (Troy, Knossos, and the Willandra Lakes are three notable examples), and many more have had their cultural value increased or more clearly demonstrated by archaeological work. Eugenio Yunis in his paper points out that there are one hundred eighty sites on the World Heritage List whose primary world heritage values are related to their archaeological resource.

The criteria for World Heritage listing, however, do not include archaeology as such. Cultural sites are listed because they illustrate or possess outstanding features expressive of human history, culture, or technical achievement. These outstanding features need to be discovered, assessed, recognized, and compared with other like sites in order to be listed as World Heritage Sites. Therefore, though the archaeological resource is often the very basis of listing, there are no World Heritage Sites listed for their archaeological values; rather, they are listed for the heritage qualities that archaeology, along with other research methods, has uncovered. The position of archaeology as a crucial methodology—in some cases the only methodology capable of uncovering and articulating the significance of World Heritage Sites—but not as a specific World Heritage value in itself, raises a number of issues relating to the interpretation and protection of the archaeological resource at World Heritage Sites.

Giorgio Buccellati addresses some of these issues. In a clear and thoughtful discussion of the importance of archaeology to World Heritage listing and the necessary role of the archaeologist in the site's consequent interpretation and presentation, as well as its discovery, he points out that in many

cases the excavator is the creator of the cultural values of the site and consequently must work from the beginning with a view to the final presentation and explanation of the site's values in a way to which the general public will respond. He likens the archaeologist-interpreter to an orchestra conductor: the listeners do not know the details of the score or the intricacies of the orchestra, but they can appreciate the music because the conductor knows these things and transmutes them into music that the audience can appreciate. Without the conductor the music remains uninterpreted, the story untold. Buccellati goes on to discuss this role in more detail, with a series of examples and parables that deal with these issues elegantly and poetically. He points out that the nature of the archaeological resource makes it especially important that the archaeologist intelligently and sensitively interpret the site, consider the views of key stakeholders, and popularize and spread the underlying story that the site has to tell. By this process, the archaeologist ensures that the key values of the site are known and that the archaeological resource that created them is respected and conserved.

A second issue that emerges in the conservation of the archaeological resource at World Heritage Sites is the potential for conflict between the methodology of archaeology and other cultural values that the site may have. For example, the archaeological resource at Willandra Lakes in western New South Wales is considered of immense research value by archaeologists and is included on the World Heritage List because it tells us a great deal about very early populations of *Homo sapiens sapiens*. However, the human remains of these ancient people are of great significance to the contemporary Aboriginal community, which has strongly objected to their being treated as "scientific specimens," and the management of the site purely for its research value conflicted with some of these other values. Gamini Wijesuriya takes up this theme from an interesting angle. He discusses the differences between the traditional archaeological practice, as evolved in the West and spread to the rest of the world, in particular, to Southeast Asia, and the development of the World Heritage Convention and World Heritage Criteria. He argues that recognition of community values and a community voice in management has been inimical to the inherited archaeological bureaucratic practice in Southeast Asia but that recognition of World Heritage values by these countries has considerably broadened and deepened the archaeological tradition and has led to recognition of the humanistic as well as the research values of significant World Heritage Sites in the region. The increasing emphasis by the World Heritage Committee on the management of World Heritage Sites as living sites, of significance to their present inhabitants, has helped to change traditional, rather restrictive and bureaucratic archaeological research mores.

At World Heritage Sites with substantial archaeological remains, another issue relates to the actual conservation of these remains, especially where they have been exposed. There is often a great deal of pressure to exhibit them to the public, since they are the physical evidence of the story being told and the reason that many people actually visit the site. Such remains are often subject to gradual attrition by weathering, inadequate protection, and overuse. There is often a potential conflict between their conservation (which may indicate the need for reburial) and their exposure—used to explain the site to the visitor but often very damaging in the long term.

Also, often at World Heritage Sites only the excavated, described, or assessed portion of the resource is recognized, protected, and interpreted. The future archaeological potential of the site is often not officially recognized, and major parts of the archaeological resource are often excluded from the designated World Heritage area, because their significance is not recognized at the time of listing. An example of this is Angkor in Cambodia, a World Heritage area that includes all the major temples and water management systems that made up the great Khmer settlement, discovered and conserved over almost two centuries, initially by the French and later by the international community and the Cambodian government. The designated World Heritage Site is of outstanding beauty and displays breathtaking examples of craftsmanship and technical achievement. However, much of the settlement of greater Angkor—where people lived and worked—is not included in the World Heritage Site, and until recent archaeological investigations, including the use of satellite imagery, its extent and importance have not been recognized. So often much of the archaeological resource and the heritage landscape, which are crucial for conserving the site's World Heritage values, are not included in the designated World Heritage Site.

Douglas C. Comer's paper addresses this issue from the point of view of monitoring. He describes a rigorous and carefully designed monitoring system for World Heritage Sites with archaeological values, focusing on Petra as an example. His work is values based and uses systematic monitoring to identify change at all levels of the landscape and consequent remedial management action to conserve the key features of the World Heritage Site. Monitoring systems are designed to range from broad ecological characteristics and values through entire ancient landscapes (including those around the World Heritage Site) to specific structures and features—with the whole treated as an integrated system for management purposes. Comer points out that this broad yet detailed approach not only gives us the tools to protect the present resource but also provides fresh insights into the working of ancient landscape systems. Such a system makes it possible to record systematically and in detail changes to specific exposed features and to carry out remedial work to conserve them if necessary, and it can be applied to landscapes surrounding the designated site that will affect its significance.

Eugenio Yunis specifically addresses the issue of tourism at World Heritage Sites and its effect on archaeology, pointing out that many sites suffer from extensive overuse and crowding. He emphasizes that demand management, destination management, and site management are all necessary methods of tourism control. Although these methodologies may seem distant from the everyday concerns of archaeologists, they are crucial for the ongoing conservation of the resource. He points out that other World Heritage Sites (especially in sub-Saharan Africa) suffer from neglect and lack of resources and management. At these sites, in contrast to those with overcrowding, he points out that well-planned promotion and visitation could help to rectify the neglect and could in fact contribute to conservation by providing the necessary funding and resources through visitor contributions and by raising the national and international profile of these sites and consequently support for their conservation among the international community.

Taken together, these papers provide an interesting and stimulating picture of some of the challenges and responses relating to archaeological conservation at World Heritage Sites. Perhaps above all they make us realize the crucial role of the archaeologist, not only in discovering World Heritage values, but also in ensuring that the archaeological resource, which often forms the basis for these values, is duly recognized and protected in World Heritage conservation and management practice.

Sustainable Tourism at Archaeological World Heritage Sites

Eugenio Yunis

Abstract: *High tourist numbers at archaeological World Heritage Sites (WHS), mostly in developed countries, can create numerous problems that affect their culturally valuable structures or elements. Measures to ease the problems derived from tourism congestion at these sites are urgently needed. This paper argues that strategies and management plans aimed at site maintenance and conservation also need to include the management of visitors, specification of the corresponding interpretation and management techniques concerning group and individual visitors, seasonal flows, zoning, and capacity limits. A complementary approach to reducing tourism pressure on existing and often crowded WHS is to diversify the heritage designation process, including wider heritage-rich regions. Also, cultural tourism opportunities could be expanded through the inclusion of wider regions in tourism development plans and promotional programs in and around WHS. In developing countries, where most archaeological sites suffer from abandonment, looting, and decay as a result of insufficient protection due mainly to the extreme shortage of public funds, tourism can offer an excellent opportunity to achieve two objectives: safeguard their archaeological heritage and generate job and income opportunities to alleviate poverty in the sites' surrounding areas.*

There are certainly many issues regarding archaeological World Heritage Sites, but I neither intend nor pretend to cover them all in this brief paper. The approach adopted here is from the socioeconomic development perspective, including environmental and conservation issues. It focuses particularly on the contribution that tourism, as a contemporary socio-cultural phenomenon and vibrant economic sector, can make to sustainable development. I make special reference to the potential of tourism in the developing world while not ignor-

ing the problems frequently associated with mass tourism in more developed destinations.

The focus of this paper is on tourism at archaeological World Heritage Sites, although most of the conclusions and guidelines proposed for these are also applicable to other types of cultural heritage properties. And when looking at archaeological heritage sites, I distinguish between two extremes: highly visited sites, most of them located in developed nations and usually suffering from high flows of visitors; and sites in developing countries, generally with low levels of visitation and often suffering from lack of financial resources for their conservation.

Tourism in Today's World

The impressive growth of tourism over the past fifty years is one of the most remarkable economic and social phenomena of this period. International tourist arrivals grew, in real terms, from a mere 25 million in 1950 to 698 million in 2000. This represents an average annual growth rate of 7 percent over a period of fifty years. The revenue generated by these arrivals—excluding air fares and not taking into account income from domestic tourism—has increased at 12 percent a year over the same period, well above the average annual economic growth rate. Revenue reached U.S. $476 billion in 2000 and today represents the number one item in world trade in services (32.1 percent). Tourism represents 6 percent of total international trade, including goods and services.

Reasonable and relatively conservative forecasts by the World Tourism Organization indicate that this trend will continue, in spite of temporary crises due to wars, epidemics, and other political or economic events, and that tourism will grow steadily in the foreseeable future. International arrivals are expected to increase to more than one billion in 2010 and attain over 1.5 billion by 2020. These data relate to the whole tourism sector, but it is reasonable to assume that tourism at World Heritage Sites will develop along parallel lines, or even faster.

Indeed, cultural and natural world heritage sites are becoming favored destinations for an increasingly larger number of tourists. According to a study by the European Commission, 20 percent of the total tourist visits in Europe, both intra-European and from overseas, are culturally motivated, while 60 percent of European tourists are interested in cultural discovery during their trips, whether within Europe or to other destinations. Current habits of shorter but more frequent holidays will particularly favor cultural, natural, and generally specialized destinations.

Although this type of tourism is not new, the progressive increase in numbers has taken place in the late twentieth century and is likely to grow even faster in the new century. Many factors explain this trend, among which are

- a more sophisticated tourist, in search of different cultural backgrounds and expressions;
- a growing number of local authorities looking at tourism as a source of income and employment opportunities;
- a growing awareness among conservation, cultural, and natural heritage authorities about the possibility offered by tourism to generate financial resources; and
- a continued growth in global tourism demand, both international and domestic, that pervades all types of destinations, including World Heritage Sites.

At the outset, it is important to state that, over and above the economic benefits that tourism can bring to nations and communities, the main value of tourism at heritage sites lies in that it serves as an introduction to the historical and cultural background of a country or place that people might otherwise never approach.

Tourism at Archaeological World Heritage Sites in Developed Countries

There are currently about 180 archaeological sites on the UNESCO list of World Heritage Sites, of which some 60 to 65 are located in the developed countries of Europe, North America, Japan, and Oceania. These forty or so countries have a huge domestic tourism market and were host to nearly 500 million foreign tourists, or approximately 70 percent of the international tourism market in the year 2000.

Many of these tourists, both domestic and foreign, visit World Heritage Sites and generate substantive income for the sites themselves and for many local residents living in the surrounding areas. At the same time, the problems created by high tourism visitation to these archaeological sites are numerous, and in many cases they have an impact on the valuable remaining structures or components that make up the site and that give significance to it. Measures to ease the problems derived from tourism congestion at these sites are, therefore, urgently needed. Three basic models are generally proposed to manage tourism congestion, each dealing with demand management, destination management, and site management. The first two fall under the responsibility of public authorities and the tourism industry, while the third is of particular relevance to the issues dealt with in this volume.

At the root of most of the problems derived from tourism at highly visited sites is the absence of a suitably balanced site management plan that integrates the four main objectives, conservation, research, education, and public visitation. Furthermore, when such a plan does exist, it is common to find that it has not taken into consideration the fact that the site is to be, or indeed needs to be, visited by tourists of different ages, interests, nationalities, and requirements and at different times throughout the year.

Management plans must, in the first place, provide for the right type of measures to ensure the necessary conservation of the site and to preserve its different values. But plans should also involve the local community in site management, and of course also in the economic benefits that can be derived from it. This is the only way to ensure the community's commitment to and cooperation in protecting the site, through a better understanding of its cultural and historic values and the realization that it is not renewable.

Together with a strategy for site maintenance and conservation, there is an imperative need to formulate a strategy for the management of visitors at each archaeological site, with specification of the corresponding interpretation and management techniques concerning group and individual visitors, dealing with seasonal flows, establishing special zones with different protection measures according to their fragility and vulnerability, and with different capacity limits, and so on.

A key condition for success in the implementation of site management plans is stakeholders' participation in the plan's formulation. In addition to the local community, it is essential to involve tour operators, other tourism-related companies, and their staff. Cooperation and coordination between site managers and tourism businesses is a determinant in achieving the smooth handling of visitors, including large numbers of them when the site permits it. The opposite is also true: even a small number of uncontrolled visitors at a site can result in damage to it. This usually happens when there is no coordination between site managers, on the one hand, who feel unconcerned about tourism flows, and tour operators, on the other, who are only interested in short-term economic gains for their business. Both attitudes combined may lead to serious damage to the site's physical structures and its values, and of course to a reduction in visitors' satisfaction and learning.

But beyond site management, there is another issue in connection with highly visited sites. While it has been generally beneficial for these sites to be inscribed on the World Heritage List, since it has helped to develop further awareness of the value of heritage and the need to preserve it, it may be argued that it has also meant adding a further element of risk, due to the appeal that such inclusion and the resulting media coverage exerts on the public at large and especially on private tourism operators.

This is why it seems reasonable and convenient to consider alternative approaches to site designation, perhaps extending the concept of "sites" to include wider heritage "areas" or even "regions." Indeed, attractive and culturally rich monuments, villages, or archaeological sites that are equally representative of a given culture or historical period for which a site has been designated often remain outside the tourist circuits and do not benefit from the positive effects of tourism development. Thus, in order to reduce the tourism pressure on existing and often overcrowded World Heritage Sites, there is a need to diversify the heritage designation process. At the same time, there is a need to expand the cultural tourism offer through the promotion and inclusion of wider regions in tourism development plans and promotional programs in and around the World Heritage Sites.

In summary, in the face of increased pressure from a higher proportion of the population in the developed world wanting and having the right to travel, to experience and learn about foreign cultures, and to visit their built and natural heritage, it is necessary to

- strengthen conservation efforts at archaeological heritage sites likely to be visited by high numbers of tourists;
- establish, in consultation with the local community and with the tourism industry, advanced management plans for archaeological sites, including regulations for their visitation, and strictly enforce them; and
- identify new archaeological and cultural heritage attractions near World Heritage Sites and develop them for tourism visitation, so that demand can be better spread out, thus reducing the pressure on existing sites.

Archaeological World Heritage Sites in Developing Countries

Let us now look at the other extreme. More than one hundred archaeological World Heritage Sites are located in developing countries, many of them in the so-called least developed nations, where tourism is only incipient. Most archaeological sites in these countries are suffering from abandonment, looting, and decay as a result of a total lack of protection and conservation due, among other factors, to the extreme shortage of public funds for such purposes. Few of these sites receive visitors, and if they do, it is usually in small numbers. Yet tourism can offer an excellent opportunity to these countries to achieve two objectives: safeguarding their archaeological heritage and generating job and income opportunities to alleviate poverty in the sites' surrounding areas.

A good example of this type of situation is sub-Saharan Africa, where extreme poverty is the norm. There are twenty-eight archaeological sites registered or candidates to the UNESCO World Heritage List in thirteen African countries south of the Sahara, which represent about 8 percent of all such sites in the world. These thirteen countries have a total population of 192 million, with an average GDP per capita of less than U.S. $300. Worse than this average is the crude fact that over 80 percent of these people, that is, more than 160 million persons, are living on less than one dollar per day.

The same thirteen countries received only a combined total of 1.55 million tourists in the year 2000, with an average per country of about 150,000 tourists per annum. This is barely 0.22 percent of total international tourist movement. And what is happening to their archaeological World Heritage Sites? They are generally in danger because of an understandable lack of attention by the public authorities, which are financially unable to cater for the most essential needs of the local population. The local communities, for their part, are perhaps unaware of the cultural, archaeological, and historic values embodied in those sites, and as they do not receive any benefit from them, they are also unaware of their potential economic value. A similar situation can be found in several countries in Asia, the Middle East, and Latin America, even if they are not in the least developed category.

National determination by governments of these countries, as well as generous and concerted international action, is required to assist them in developing heritage tourism around their archaeological and other World Heritage Sites in a sustainable way. This will allow them to achieve conservation and economic objectives at the same time. Cooperation among national governments, their cultural and tourism authorities, international organizations, and the international tourism industry is urgently needed. Also, the cooperation of archaeologists, conservation professionals, and managers of highly visited sites in Europe and North America would help to transfer their experience in research and interpretation, in site management, protection, and conservation, in tourism development and marketing, among other areas.

This issue could represent a tangible way for the archaeology and conservation professions to show their commitment to the main challenges of our world today—reducing shameful poverty levels in a world of affluence and contributing to social harmony and peace.

Presentation and Interpretation of Archaeological Sites: The Case of Tell Mozan, Ancient Urkesh

Giorgio Buccellati

Abstract: *Management of archaeological sites should not be viewed as an additional layer that is imposed from without but as something that issues from the intrinsic value of the monument. From this perspective, the best management practice is one that reflects the strategy that has brought the site back to light in the first place. As part of management, the excavator ought to communicate the motivation behind the recovery, because that is the same motivation that governs any effort at conserving and presenting. Only then can the excavator legitimately leave the site and turn it over to others for protracted management. The thrust of this article is that the archaeologist-excavator must work with a view toward final presentation from the very beginning of the excavation process. Such an effort will remain inscribed in the monument in ways that could never be proposed again later and will make a broader fruition of the monument flow seamlessly from its intrinsic value as progressively perceived through the excavation. This conviction is developed not out of theory but rather out of the practice of archaeological work at a particular site, which is at the basis of the conclusions proposed here. It may be said that if ancient Urkesh lay buried under what came to be known as Tell Mozan, we as excavators are the ones who have once again turned Mozan into Urkesh. This paper seeks to describe how we have gone about this task.*

Archaeological "Localization"

Let me propose a metaphor, taking my cue from a neologism. The term "localization" has come to be used regularly in information technology and related domains to refer to what we might normally call "translation." There is a whole industry built around this concept: it addresses the particular need to make commercial websites accessible not only and not so much in different languages, but in different cultures. How to advertise bathing suits to Eskimos might be a reductio ad absurdum of this process. The point is that to sell a product one has to make it "locally" relevant; one has to translate not just words but a whole mind-set and the material embodiments by which it is represented. You might say that localization is the commercial side of semiotics.

So it should be, I would argue, with the presentation and interpretation of archaeological sites. We seek to convey understanding. In a commercial venture, understanding is seen primarily as appeal: it is not so much that a firm wants customers to understand the inner workings of its product; it only wants them to understand what can appeal to them so that a potential customer becomes an actual one. In a cavalier, and ultimately patronizing, approach to the presentation of an archaeological site we may fall prey to the same syndrome: whatever the *vulgus* can accept, that's what we'll provide them. But this attitude, and any shade thereof, must be avoided—for three good reasons.

First, there is an intrinsic value to presentation and interpretation—to archaeological "localization," if you will. Culture is a continuum, and there should be no hopeless rift between the technical aspects of archaeology and the interests of the layperson. Gradual transitions in the kind and amount of detail, yes. But a sharp break—no. When presenting and interpreting, the archaeologist must be like an orchestra conductor: few if any people in the audience may be able to read the score, but the music performed *is* the score, not a watered-down semblance of it. It is such a profound respect for the continuity of culture that will save us from any form of paternalism, whether vis-à-vis stakeholders or tourists. And note that just as a conductor is first and foremost a musician, so must archaeological "localization" remain in the hands of the archaeologists. It should not become a job that we gladly relinquish to outsiders, leaving it for them to decide what the rhythm should be or where the crescendos should go.

Second, presentation and interpretation are an extension of our teaching mission. We must be able to gauge the common ground between our technical knowledge and the degree of readiness in our audience. We must be in touch with the concerns of our audience, and address them—not in order to sycophantically modify our data for the sake of pleasing but rather in order to present what we perceive as real values in such a way that they can be truly appropriated. The other side of paternalism is a "take it or leave it" attitude: this is what we offer, too bad if you don't like it. Instead, we must identify with legitimate interests, stir them, and provide answers.

Third, presentation and interpretation should enrich our own archaeological horizon. We must become better archaeologists precisely through the effort of explaining. After all, the whole of scholarship is a form of translation. As archaeologists, we translate a mound of dirt into a pile of paper or its digital counterpart. And this process develops in a capillary sort of way from the most synthetic to the most analytic. But the data so understood and so presented remain always a single whole: answering the broadest question has implications for the most remote detail. This is also why we archaeologists must be the presenters. Trained, there is no doubt, by the skills that show us how to help the audience appropriate the intended target, but also trained to bear in mind the nature and value of this same target.

In this light, "popularization" is not a secondary endeavor with which the archaeologist cannot be bothered. It is rather an intrinsic aspect of our task. In the few remarks that follow I deal with a few instances that may help to show how this can happen in a concrete situation, using as a test case our own work at Tell Mozan, ancient Urkesh, in northeastern Syria. In so doing, I plan to address the concerns of the overall theme in this session of WAC from a perspective that is only seemingly tangential. It goes to the core of the problem, I submit, if we view management (at least as far as it pertains to an archaeological site) not as an additional layer that is imposed from without but as something that issues from the intrinsic value of the monument. From this perspective, the best management practice is one that reflects the strategy that has brought the site back to light in the first place. The excavator ought to communicate the motivation behind the recovery, because that is the same motivation that governs any effort at conserving and presenting. Thus the thrust of my argument is that the archaeologist-excavator must work with a view toward final conservation and presentation from the very beginning of the excavation process. Such an effort will remain inscribed in the monument in ways that could never be proposed later and will make a broader fruition of the monument flow seamlessly from its intrinsic value as progressively perceived through the excavation. For better or for worse, that has been my concern at the site about which I am speaking here. It may be said that if ancient Urkesh lay buried under what came to be known as Tell Mozan, we as excavators are the ones who have once again turned Mozan into Urkesh. Here, then, I seek to describe how we have gone about this task.

What Popularization Can Do for Scholarship

In our effort at protecting the mud-brick walls of a royal palace that is undergoing long-term excavation, we have aimed at combining conservation with reconstruction (see my article in Part III of this volume). This makes the ruins much more understandable to even the occasional visitor, particularly with the addition of color schemes and signs that explain the function of the various rooms through which one can in fact walk with a newly acquired sense of appreciation for such things as circulation patterns or size of rooms, which remain abstract when just laid out on paper. But unexpected results quickly become apparent for the archaeologists as well. No matter how well trained one is to read floor plans and sections, the danger is always present to perceive them as they are on our reading medium (whether paper or the computer screen), that is, as planes rather than as indices to volumes. The effort at "reconstructing" our walls by means of metal and canvas coverings could not be justified only in the function of correcting this misperception. But, having embarked on a reconstruction program that aims at presenting the architecture to the public in an understandable way, there is the unquestionable benefit that the archaeologist, too, can perceptually relate to volumes rather than just planes. Here is a very telling example of the continuum about which I was speaking earlier: the effort of visualizing serves the same function that biofeedback does, because the volumes one reconstructs for public presentation elicit a new understanding of the very premises on which the reconstruction is based in the first place.

It also quickly emerges that only the team of archaeologist and conservator could accomplish this. One cannot subcontract the task to outsiders, because the questions that arise in the process require a full understanding of the stratigraphic premises on the one hand (archaeology) and of the limits of intervention on the other (conservation). An apt parallel can be found in the textual sphere. A "good" translation is not the "translation of a translation," that is, the reworking of a "literal" translation. Rather, a "good" translation is one that transfers the syntactical, semantic, and semiotic valence of the original text—hence one that requires an even greater understanding of the source language than is needed for a "literal" translation, that is, a rendering of mere morphological and lexical features. Thus in the case of our palace, every detail of the reconstruction is assessed both in terms of its stratigraphic and functional relevance as understood by the archaeologist and in terms of its susceptibility to preservation.

Virtual reality reconstructions are another good example of how important it is that archaeologists be directly involved in the technology. No such project can be handed to an outsider the way we give a manuscript to the printer. We do not want to just present an aesthetically attractive rendering to the public. Rather, the presentation ought to serve as a vehicle for an in-depth consideration of spatial relationships that may not be immediately apparent, even after the walls are restored to their original dimensions. A three-dimensional model elicits questions from the archaeologist that have an important heuristic function, in that it directs attention to aspects of connectivity that one might not otherwise suspect.

Ultimately, a thorough effort at presentation and interpretation becomes involved in matters of semiotics that can also be surprising. Signs were dynamic and easily perceived by the culture from which the monuments arose. Palace and temple were endowed with a richness of meaning that is only dimly hinted at in the meager remnants we bring back to light. The very words *palace* and *temple* may in fact be more evocative than the ruin. But we must assume that the ancients would instinctively have had a full semiotic perception—that is, an awareness of the valence a monument can have as a sign. Perhaps no amount of reconstruction and explanation can ever again elicit such a perception, but a committed effort to a reconstruction and explanation so directed can endow the ruin with a resonance it lacks when we, the archaeologists, stop after we have laid bare the skeleton. The effort to communicate the value of ancient signs to the public forces scholars to think more deeply about just what such value was. In this respect, presentation and interpretation, resting on stratigraphic understanding and conservation skills, serve as the conduit for a proper humanistic approach to archaeology. The overriding concern of such an approach to the past lies in the

appropriation of past experience, an appropriation not based on fantasy but rather on a controlled reflection about what the ancient experience in fact was. We may say that the archaeologists' first task is to establish, with the tools and the sensitivity of a social scientist, the patterns that are recognizable in the physical record. At which point, they continue with the tools and the sensitivity of the humanist to reach beneath the simple clustering of patterns and to inquire after the meaning that gave them origin in the first place.

What Popularization Can Do for Conservation

More specifically, we may now consider the effect on conservation of popularization taken in the sense of proper presentation and interpretation. An effort to promote understanding of a site is a two-way street. On the one hand, a site that is well understood encourages people to preserve it. On the other hand, eliciting meaning for others, even the occasional others, raises the archaeologist's awareness for meaning *tout court.*

As for the first point, pride in one's heritage is the best guarantee against looting, or even casual damage. But such pride can only derive from an understanding of the intrinsic value of a site. Archaeological ruins are not always immediately evocative of grandeur, hence education is as critical a component as conservation and reconstruction. The second point is the reverse. As scholars, we are not engaged in empty advertising. We don't make up meaning; we find it. And any effort to convey it to others—from peasants to politicians—helps us to see it in a different light. Culture is a continuum not only because it can be explained, but because the explanation rebounds on the explainer.

At Mozan, we have pursued these goals in a commonsense sort of way, that is, not so much out of a predetermined program that we had set out to implement but rather responding to needs as they were perceived little by little. This is not to say that we stumbled into action casually and haphazardly. There was from the beginning a strong commitment to the basic principles that I have been outlining, and what developed slowly were only the specific forms that our concrete implementation of these principles took over time.

For instance, we found that the best way to integrate the "stakeholders" (we did not then have a name for them), and at the same time the best way to avoid any form of paternalism (or neocolonialism, if you wish), was to develop our own sense of commitment to values. In this manner, the effect of our actions was to co-opt and be co-opted at the same time. To co-opt—because we assume that the values we believe in have an independent pull on the "others." And to be co-opted—because we are eager to appropriate the values they in turn believe in. It is then clear that we want to share something that we consider valuable in its own terms. In this way we have communicated the need to conserve the nonspectacular as well as the spectacular—and this is no small feat in archaeology. We have nurtured an atmosphere of great care for the maintenance of the past by showing how even small details are essential to understand the larger picture. As a result, there is a sense of pride not just in the fruition of the finished product as presented but also in its maintenance. And conversely, the stakeholders nurtured in us an appreciation for responses that we did not expect—poetic addresses, for instance, on the part of what turned out to be innumerable poets among our neighbors, or drawings, or even musical compositions inspired by "our" shared archaeological site that looms so large on all our various horizons.

Importantly, along these lines, our early start on conservation showed how we are professionally involved in conservation. Walls were preserved when first exposed, not after they were known to be the walls of a palace. This communicated our commitment to the exposed relic as such, regardless of its potential public relations value. It communicated, in other words, a degree of professional integrity and coherence that was not lost on the audience (again, our "stakeholders"). In return, we were strengthened in our resolve, because their embracing our effort underscored for us the intrinsic worth of the effort, almost as much as receiving an additional grant!

The presentation we provide as a finished product (reconstructed walls, posters, handouts, even an audiotape that accompanies a visitor when we are not present at the site) is the major avenue for our message. But another very important channel of communication has been the talks we give in more or less formal settings. We begin with our own workmen, who number up to two hundred in some seasons: we give general overviews with slides and now computers, but we also give, to the crews of the individual excavation units, periodic assessments of the goals, the progress, the strategy. We provide them with handouts that spell out dates and names. Our workmen and other local collaborators, who are all from neighboring villages and towns, come back with their families and friends and begin to explain not just about walls and buildings but about events and history. We also give more formal presentations in the local towns, whether in cultural centers or schools, and of course receive groups and individuals who come for an occasional visit. The newly found understanding of their own territorial past is a source of great

energy, and it obviously provides a firm lever on which rests the long-term protection of the site.

Some episodes attest to the far-reaching benefits of this approach. Our site was used as a burial ground for neighboring villages. That this can no longer be the case was accepted with good grace, but beyond that we have also started working on the removal of existing burials, with the full cooperation of the families. In the case of the village of Mozan itself, we established a common cemetery where the human remains that we have studied are reburied along with the bodies of newly deceased members of the village. Also, in the lower portion of the tell, which corresponds to the ancient outer city (for a total of almost 150 hectares), there are fields that are owned by local farmers who cultivate them on a regular basis. A change from wheat to cotton culture has stimulated the construction of industrial-type wells. When one is planned, the owner waits for the expedition to return, at which time we do a sounding and submit a recommendation to the Directorate General of Antiquities and Museums as to whether a permit may or may not be granted. And even when our recommendation is negative, it is accepted without grudge. Finally, the urban growth of neighboring towns has been chartered by the various local governments in ways that respond to the requirements of archaeology as we have been presenting them. The positive result is that the ensuing regulatory plans take into full account the landscape in which the site is located and seek to protect it by steering the development away from it.

Conclusion: "Localization" as Semiotics

As in the case of conservation, presentation and broad interpretation for the public, or archaeological "localization," must not be viewed as an outside intervention that takes place apart from, independently of, and long after the archaeological work proper. "Localization" must be inserted in the archaeological work itself, avoiding the tendency to see it as something which is both *a posteriori* and *ab exteriori*. The main reason, I have argued, is that archaeology as such benefits from the effort, that is, that we learn about our side of archaeology by seeking to present it and explain it to the local and the wider public. Unquestionably, better archaeology results from proper localization.

In our experience, this means that pertinent concerns must be inscribed in the excavation process itself and not left for a distant, later, and extrinsic intervention. It is, to some extent, a matter of sensitivity more than of procedures or staffing. In a broad sense, this touches on the question of meaning. For the archaeologist, meaning can easily be reduced to technical control, more or less defined by metrical data, and reinforced by statistical correlations among seemingly infinite masses of data. And it is indeed important that we master this aspect of our trade. For in the absence of full control, there can only be fantasy. But it is important that we seek the meaning beyond, or rather behind, the patterns, that is, the meaning that ultimately gave rise to the patterns when the "data" were embedded in the stream of life. It is in this sense that I have referred to localization as "semiotics." Properly, we seek to identify the value that signs had for the ancients. But an invaluable support to this effort is the parallel endeavor to identify the value that the same signs ought to have for our contemporaries. In this way, we all—archaeologists working at the site, modern inhabitants of the area, and outside visitors—become stakeholders of our common past.

Are We Ready to Learn? Lessons from the South Asian Region

Gamini Wijesuriya

Abstract: Although with Western colonization, traditional practices of caring for heritage began to disappear from South Asian countries, strong conservation traditions based on Western knowledge started to develop. Over the years, issues specific to local and regional situations were identified and innovative solutions were found. The World Heritage system brought new ideas and demanded the fulfillment of certain requirements with its nomination process. This was difficult within the existing institutional and legislative structures. As a result, conflicts arose but the outcomes were promising. The results also demonstrated that the World Heritage system can be used as a platform for sharing knowledge for the better protection of South Asian heritage.

Two major movements of heritage conservation can be seen in South Asia. The first has a regional outlook and originated more than one hundred fifty years ago. In the mid-nineteenth century, British colonial administration introduced "archaeology" into their public sector management regimes in South Asia. Soon "conservation" became a major activity in this management system, as an integral part of archaeology. Including conservation within the domain of archaeology in these countries was a very useful model at the time, when the colonial administration concentrated on protecting major archaeological sites that had been neglected for centuries and required state protection. At this time, however, archaeology in this part of the world was a management discipline rather than an academic discipline (Wijesuriya 2003a). Systems that had originated in India and Sri Lanka were later extended to Nepal as well as to Bangladesh and Pakistan after the latter two separated from the mainland. This reflects a common thread in the approach to archaeology and conservation that is deeply rooted in all these countries.

The second movement is universal in its outlook; it affected the region through World Heritage activities. The concept of World Heritage and its operations over the past three decades brought, even demanded new definitions as well as new approaches to the conservation of heritage. The concept required a reassessment of heritage values, a broadening of conservation approaches, a demarcation of buffer zones, and above all new management structures.

The two movements are in conflict, not necessarily with regard to the end objectives, but to the way in which they operate. This paper attempts to explore some of the conflicts that have emerged in managing World Heritage archaeological sites in the region. World Heritage Sites provide a common platform to debate and to learn from these issues, both for the international community that exercises jurisdiction over the World Heritage Convention and for those at the local level who are responsible for the protection of heritage. Examples presented here are from the author's experience of working in five countries—Sri Lanka, India, Pakistan, Bangladesh, and Nepal—on a number of issues together with the World Heritage Centre, ICOMOS, and ICCROM.

Conservation in the Past

The past indeed lives in the present in South Asian societies and plays a significant role in the lives of the people (Wijesuriya 2003a). One remarkable result is the transmission of heritage, dating from the sixth century B.C., to the present generation with its original values and associated communities (Wijesuriya 2003b). This continuity of heritage, mostly of religious traditions, was possible because of highly sophisticated principles and processes of conservation developed by these societies. *Mayamatha,* a treatise on architecture written in the sixth century, provides evidence:

> Those temples whose characteristics are still [perceptible] in their principal and secondary elements [are to be restored] with their own materials. If they are lacking in anything or have some similar type of flaw, the sage wishing to restore them [must proceed in such a way that] they regain their integrity and are pleasantly arranged [anew]; this [is to be done] with the dimensions—height and width—which were theirs and with decoration consisting of corner, elongated and other areas, without anything being added [to what originally existed] and always in conformity with the initial appearance [of the building] and with the advice of the knowledgeable. (Quoted from Dagens 1985)

It is also evident that such principles have been complemented by the infrastructure and resources provided by the rulers and the public. Chronicles refer to the rulers who appointed special officers and even ministers to oversee conservation work (Wijesuriya 1993). A ninth-century inscription from Sri Lanka quoted below documents the level of skills that were available for conservation.

> [There shall be] clever stone-cutters and skilful carpenters in the village devoted to the work of [temple] renewal.
>
> They all . . . shall be experts in their [respective] work.
>
> Means of subsistence of the [same] extent [as is] given to one of these, shall be granted to the officer who superintends work.
>
> Moreover, when thus conferring maintenance of the latter person, his work and so forth shall [first] be ascertained, and the name of him [thus] settled [with a livelihood], as well as his respective duties, shall be recorded in the register.
>
> Those of the five castes who work within the precincts of the monastery shall receive [their] work after it has been apportioned; and they alone shall be answerable for its correctness.
>
> The limit [of time] for the completion of work is two months and five days.
>
> Blame [shall be attributed to] the superintendents, the *varikas* and the labourers who do not perform it according to arrangement.

> Those who do not avoid blame, [and] do not do [the work] or cause it to be done [as arranged], shall be deprived of their share. (De Zilva Wickremasinghe 1912:8–9)

Conservation and Archaeology under Colonial Rule

The above systems began to disappear with the beginning of Western colonization. The first major conservation movement began with the arrival of the British in the nineteenth century. British colonial administration introduced "archaeology"—as a management discipline—in India, which included Bangladesh and Pakistan, in the mid-nineteenth century and two decades later in Sri Lanka (Wijesekera 1990) with the establishment of departments of archaeology (Archaeological Survey of India and Archaeological Survey of Sri Lanka). These departments were in the domain of public administration, and the original intention of the work was to record the archaeological ruins of the respective countries.

These departments began the identification and recording of individual monuments and, in some instances, large areas with surface ruins, as well as the process of state protection. Within a decade or two, the authorities were compelled to undertake rescue operations to protect some of the significant monuments that were in a bad state of repair. The public works departments' services were obtained for the stabilization of structures, under the guidance of civil engineers. With the exception of Sri Lanka, such structural conservation work was continued by engineering professionals (designated as archaeological conservators) even after responsibility for such work was fully taken over by the respective departments of archaeology. In terms of resources, conservation work began to absorb much of the annual government allocations.

In the early stages of colonial administration, departments of archaeology were headed by civil servants, but they were gradually replaced by professional archaeologists who possessed academic, field, and managerial experience. Thus, in theory, an archaeologist was always in command of all the conservation work carried out by the respective departments. In addition, again with the exception of Sri Lanka, all conservation professionals (engineers) functioned under the immediate supervision of an archaeologist (designated superintending archaeologist, assistant director, etc.). The majority of conservation work in the form of consolidation of ruins was guided by Marshall's conservation manual (Marshall 1923) and similar documents adopted by each country.

Even today, archaeology and conservation management systems are centrally controlled and highly bureaucratic, with hardly any focus on the general public as their main customers, and they are often subject to political interference. Over the past decades in some countries, archaeologists have been replaced by civil servants as heads of departments. The systems operate with strong legislative mandates but under archaic government procedures most of which are nonflexible and internally focused. Although many senior-level staff have access to current knowledge in archaeology and conservation, its application is not as simple as one would like to see.

For more than a century and a half, knowledge transmitted mostly from the West has directed the activities of conservation and heritage management in general. In the end it has generated a great wealth of knowledge about heritage conservation. Many sites have been documented and action has been taken to protect and maintain them on a regular basis by means of on-site monitoring systems. Although conservation issues specific to this part of the world had been addressed and innovative solutions found by local professionals, these drew little or no attention from the rest of the world. It was a one-way information flow and therefore natural that such systems conflicted with new movements such as world heritage conservation practice. There are, however, many positive outcomes as a result of the conflict between the two movements.

Conventional versus World Heritage Approaches

The second conservation movement came to this part of the world with the introduction of the World Heritage Convention. The convention shifts from the concept of cultural property to cultural heritage, thus capturing a much broader spectrum of human traces of the past (ICCROM Newsletter 2003). This has resulted in greater recognition of the diversity of the heritage and intangible dimensions of the past. For instance, the concept of cultural landscape brought recognition to places that have significance to societies but do not necessarily contain tangible remains. The World Heritage system, headed primarily by Western scholars, began to define monuments and sites in a much broader geographic and cultural context and to develop conservation approaches accordingly. These new ideas, together with certain explicit requirements for inscribing sites on the World Heritage List, were imposed on conservation professionals in the Asian region as well.

Initially, professionals in Asia had to absorb and translate these new ideas and requirements into their local and institutional cultures. They also faced the task of educating and convincing politicians and the general public about the new developments as these groups began to express more interest in the subject. Some of the examples discussed below explain the nature of the conflicts and the final outcomes that have been or are yet to be achieved.

In the case of the archaeological World Heritage Site of Hampi in India, the Department of Archaeology had identified fifty-six individual buildings for protection long before the convention came into effect. However, these are only the major and visible ruins of a unique and massive city center of the fifteenth century, with clear boundaries covering a geographic area of more than 30 square kilometers. For the purpose of the convention, and with the help of provincial government heritage legislation, the site definition now exceeds the fifty-six monuments. Conventional legislation, which defines what heritage will be protected, and management approaches need revision so as to facilitate World Heritage operations.

Archaeological sites are generally considered ruins, for the most part buried and dead or "not in use." Many archaeological sites in the Asian region, however, do not fit this view. For example, Anuradhapura in Sri Lanka, Lumbini in Nepal, Bodhgaya in India, and many other sites are still places of worship and pilgrimage and are considered sacred by millions of Buddhists. These places contain archaeological remains dating back to the third century B.C.E., but their sacredness adds a different set of values and conservation challenges. Although these values are included in the criteria for selection of World Heritage, their consequences are yet to be understood by the professional conservation community. It should be understood that the conservation of these sites as presently undertaken is in direct conflict with general approaches to archaeological sites. Some of the practices in this region could be further refined and adapted to deal with issues of archaeological sites associated with living religions (Wijesuriya 2003b).

The test of authenticity of materials, form, and design as required by the convention was in direct conflict with some existing conservation practices in the region due to the lack of recognition of the cultural context and the diversity of different countries. For instance, many religious buildings demand the replacement of decayed materials in order to retain spiritual and other cultural values attached to them. The spiritual significance of a stupa in Sri Lanka as reflected by its outer appearance is more important to Buddhists than the materials replaced or added during conservation. The old material remains are respected in Buddhist culture but in a somewhat contradictory manner. The practice of renewal by replacing decayed materials guarantees continuity and also helps to retain the spiritual significance of a temple. Disregard for such practices in different geographic regions and cultures has been highlighted previously. It is worth quoting Ito (2000):

> Authenticity is a European word originating from ancient times. In contemporary days, it appears in the text of the Venice Charter. In [the] European concept, conservation methods applied in Roman ruins, namely, conservation with minimum interventions, would be evaluated as meeting authenticity in material. However, in most Asian languages we do not have any proper word corresponding to authenticity. . . . We Asian experts in charge of conservation were embarrassed by this method of minimum intervention. We thought that we have had other ways of conservation and should keep the essence of these ways even in future. We were much troubled.

This conflict has resulted in the Nara Document on Authenticity, which has provided a useful framework for recognizing diversity and considering conservation practices in the cultural context of a given society when it is desirable.

On the other hand, the Nara Document does not give license to conservators to disregard or undervalue the authenticity of material remains of the past. Thorough documentation, research, analysis, and wider consultation in decision making in the conservation of materials, be they part of a building or otherwise, are some of the important practices demanded today that were also practiced in Asian countries. But the increased deterioration of systems within the departments of archaeology in South Asian countries has tended to result in deviation from these practices. The replacement of over one thousand terra-cotta plaques at the World Heritage Site of Paharpur in Bangladesh is a case in point. The archaeological conservator–project leader of the conservation program decided to replace ancient terra-cotta plaques with replicas and to preserve in a museum those that were removed. This was well intentioned and well documented, but the conservator and his team were unable to capture the difference between the original work and the replicas, thus sacrificing authenticity. Current practices—contrary to the original intent of having conservation be an integral part of archaeology under the purview of an archaeologist—do not

ensure wider consultation among colleagues within or outside the department. If that had occurred, a disastrous situation would have been averted. Involvement of the World Heritage Centre in this matter was considered a conflict, but it can be seen as an incentive for local professionals to avoid such situations in future and to embark on widely advocated multidisciplinary team work in conservation.

Linking heritage conservation with land use planning was the single most powerful tool used in the recent past. This is particularly relevant to the management of large archaeological sites. The conventional departmental system has neither a legislative mandate nor the required staff for this purpose. A major paradigm shift is required in heritage management approaches for these conventional systems to be able to work with relevant authorities who have legal mandates. Had this sort of approach been used as advocated by the experts involved in the World Heritage missions, some of the major threats to the sites could have been avoided. Building the massive bridge across the World Heritage Site of Hampi in India led the site to be included in the List of World Heritage in Danger. This easily could have been avoided if heritage protection authorities had reviewed the infrastructure needs of the area with the planning agencies. On the other hand, the sacred area planning scheme prepared for the archaeological World Heritage Site of Anuradhapura, with the help of the town and country planning legislation and many agencies, is the principal management tool being used for its conservation. The region has some of the best-practice examples to share and adapt to particular situations. The World Heritage system could be an open platform for this purpose.

Working within civil society, let alone respecting its views, is a phenomenon generally in conflict with the prevailing practices of public service in South Asia. However, it is important that the responsibilities of protecting heritage be shared with the wider community. Civil society can include the private sector, nongovernmental organizations, volunteers, and local communities that are in favor of and useful in heritage conservation. Not only is the current public service in conflict, it does not provide any opportunities for making new alliances. To overcome this situation and facilitate conservation of large archaeological sites, several new initiatives are under way in Asian countries. The Sigiriya Heritage Foundation that was established by the government of Sri Lanka provides for public-private partnerships in protecting the Sigiriya World Heritage Site. The Lumbini Development Trust has taken responsibility for managing Lumbini, while the Department of Archaeology retains supervisory powers. A number of similar initiatives have been taken in India for the management of their archaeological sites, some of which have been active from the nomination stage. The effectiveness of these initiatives in protecting World Heritage Sites needs closer examination and adaptation.

The management plan is another important instrument demanded under the World Heritage Convention. This requires the analysis of outstanding universal values and the formulation of long-term strategies not only for conservation but also for other relevant aspects such as presentation, visitor facilities, tourism, future research, monitoring, and maintenance. Annual operational programs are intended to stem from these management plans. Such plans demand very high skills from the preparation to the implementation stage, and require evaluations and revisions at regular intervals. Preparation of management plans, which also require wider consultation with different professional groups and with civil society, are not practices familiar to the public service sector.

The system provides only limited conservation planning at central offices where some management capabilities exist. Low-ranking staff based at the site level can make little if any contribution to the preparation of management plans. By way of comparison, a person in charge of a World Heritage archaeological site in Asia could be a very low-ranking staff member with little education but long years of experience, while a manager based at a similar site in a Western country could be a professional with postgraduate qualifications. It is, however, worth recording that as a result of pressure from the World Heritage operation, management plans for many sites are being developed with the help of professional communities outside the public sector, and sites are being managed by professionals. The transition to having a professional heritage manager at the site level and the preparation of comprehensive management plans are experiences that can be shared with the international community.

There is a strong monitoring component for all sites protected by the respective governmental agencies (departments of archaeology) in Asia. Some sites are guarded twenty-four hours a day by permanent staff members who are expected to report any minor or significant changes to the remains, based on the monitoring results. Another level of monitoring is conducted by senior staff members of the regional or head office who visit sites on a regular basis. The terminology used may differ, but the ultimate objective is to observe changes to the heritage. Though information collected in this manner is qualitative, it is adequate for the preparation of annual maintenance or conservation plans. It

may not be sufficient, however, for the requirements of periodic reporting. Nevertheless, it is important that existing practices be given due consideration in developing modern monitoring methods.

Conclusion

Cultural heritage, with its many diverse and composite cultures, plays an important role in the political arena as well as in the day-to-day lives of many people in the region. The number of World Heritage Sites in the region is rising, as it ought to, which adds new dimensions to consciousness of the past. However, the notion that protection of heritage is the role of government is deeply rooted in the minds of many people because of the prevailing practices of government-controlled archaeology and conservation. The importance given to the World Heritage List and relevant matters by the respective governments as well as increasing awareness among professional groups and the general public, and their willingness to be partners in heritage protection, has opened conservation approaches and management practices to wider debate. The conventional government-controlled system, with strong, deeply rooted conservation approaches and management practices, was in conflict with World Heritage operations when the latter began in these countries.

These conflicts have raised interesting issues relevant to the conservation and management of World Heritage Sites that are also applicable to heritage conservation in general. As a result, new initiatives have emerged and local conservation professionals and agencies have opted to revive their conventional approaches, management practices, and even legislation and to share best practices at the regional and international level. Similarly, the World Heritage system has begun to acknowledge the importance of issues in South Asia, thus demonstrating that there are some gaps in current knowledge and that there are areas for improvement. The process of knowledge expansion should give due consideration to issues at heritage sites in their own cultural, social, and organizational contexts. The World Heritage system provides a useful platform to discuss new and improved approaches to conservation and management practices while sharing knowledge from local, regional, and international experiences. However, the ultimate objective should be to use World Heritage as a vehicle for the conservation of heritage in general (Wijesuriya 2001). As the director-general of UNESCO has urged, "This concept of heritage calls upon each and every one of us to respect the trans-historical significance of the sites, not only those inscribed in the lists, but also those which, while possessing comparable significance, have not been listed and perhaps never will be. World Heritage sites should serve as an example and become models of conservation for all sites, including those of more local interest" (Matsuura 2003).

References

Cleere, H. F., ed. 1989. *Archaeological Heritage Management in the Modern World.* London: Routledge.

Dagens, B., trans. 1985. *Mayamatha—An Indian Treatise on Housing, Architecture and Iconography.* New Delhi: Sitaram Bharatiya Institute of Scientific Research.

De Zilva Wickremasinghe, D. M., ed. and trans. 1912. Jetavanarama Sanskrit Inscription. In *Epigraphia Zeylanica: Being Lithic and Other Inscriptions of Ceylon,* vol. 1, 8–9. London: Oxford University Press.

ICCROM. Newsletter. 29 June 2003.

Ito, N. 2000. World cultural heritage and self-enlightenment of conservation experts. In *Report on Consultative Meeting on Regional Co-operation in Cultural Heritage Protection in Asia and the Pacific,* 15–17. Nara: Asia Pacific Cultural Centre for UNESCO.

Larsen, K. E., ed. 1995. *Nara Conference on Authenticity in Relation to the World Heritage Convention.* Paris: UNESCO.

Marshall, J. 1923. *Conservation Manual.* Calcutta: Superintendent Government Printing.

Matsuura, K. 2003. World heritage: The challenges of the 21st century. In *World Heritage 2002: Shared Legacy, Common Responsibility.* Paris: UNESCO.

Wijesekera, N., ed. 1990. *History of the Department of Archaeology.* Colombo: Department of Archaeology.

Wijesuriya, G. 1990. Conservation and maintenance. In *Monuments and Sites—Sri Lanka,* ed. G. Wijesuriya, 95–113. Colombo: ICOMOS Sri Lanka.

———. 1993. *Restoration of Buddhist Monuments in Sri Lanka: The Case for an Archaeological Heritage Management Strategy.* Colombo: ICOMOS Sri Lanka.

———. 2001. Protection of sacred mountains: Towards a new paradigm in conservation. In Final Report of UNESCO Thematic Expert Meeting on Asia-Pacific Sacred Mountains, Japan, 47–62.

———. 2003a. Are we reinventing the wheel? Archaeological heritage management under the British colonial rule in Sri Lanka. In *Archaeologies of the British,* ed. S. Lawrence. London: Routledge.

———. 2003b. The past lives in the present: Perspectives in caring for Buddhist heritage sites. Paper presented at ICCROM Forum on Living Religious Heritage: Conserving the Sacred, Rome, October.

Wijesuriya, G., E. Wright, and P. Ross. 2002. Cultural context, monitoring and management effectiveness (Role of monitoring and its application at national levels). Paper presented at the Workshop on Monitoring World Heritage Sites, Vicenza, Italy, 11–12 November 2002.

Monitoring of Landscape Change at World Heritage Sites: Prologue to Proactive Management

Douglas C. Comer

Abstract: *This paper argues that rigorous programs of monitoring key resources, visitor experience, and community conditions should be established at World Heritage Sites. Thoughtfully structured monitoring can greatly reduce the time needed to develop effective and efficient management programs and sustainable site improvement projects that are informed by science and public participation. It can also alert decision makers and the concerned public to ongoing natural and cultural processes that will destroy key resources in the absence of intervention. Monitoring is described at two scales: of the integrated landscape in which the site is located and of management zones established within the site. Monitoring programs must be based on (1) an understanding of the natural and cultural resources at the site that make it worth preserving in the first place and (2) explicit statements of desired uses and conditions at the site. That is, monitoring programs must be based on both scientific study and social understanding. The first of these should be accomplished through an inventory and evaluation of site resources and of practical knowledge of the natural and cultural systems that affect those resources. The second must be developed through negotiation with stakeholders, which at World Heritage Sites include groups based both locally and globally.*

The Advent of Protected Area Monitoring

Protected area management in most places has developed largely by repeating the patterns of human organization that are familiar to those charged with establishing a management organization at a particular site. Most often, this has been done uncritically. However, we now have a history for the management of protected areas, including archaeological sites, stretching back about a century that we can use to improve and develop site management.

A key moment in that history was the passage, in 1970, of the National Environmental Policy Act (NEPA) in the United States. In response to this act, the U.S. National Park Service, the oldest of the organizations that manage archaeological sites and other protected areas, began to keep careful records of environmental change produced by management activities. Soon, monitoring protocols and programs were being developed at many parks.

After about a decade, it became clear that the protocols developed for monitoring provided the basis for a more effective and efficient way to manage parks. Management zones had been an essential element of general management plans for parks for half a century. Now, biologists, ecologists, and archaeologists were brought in to define management zones with much more attention to the distribution of the natural and cultural resources that parks had been established to protect. Many park managers enthusiastically embraced this style of management, originally instituted as a result of an increasing demand for management transparency and accountability, because it provided a better way to use funds and staff. Thus the policy to establish a program for each park to monitor the conditions of natural and cultural resources in a more formal and precise way than had been done previously evolved to link the results of monitoring to management decisions.

In a monitoring program, the site to be protected is treated as a system. A system contains specialized parts that must function and interact in ways that sustain the system as a whole. Communication and coordination of these parts is essential to systemic sustainability. The agency by which communication and coordination is accomplished must, minimally, be able to

- establish system requirements, that is, identify essential system components and standards for those components.
- survey component standards (characterize the condition for each component).
- plan and organize efforts to maintain and improve system health based on a solid evaluation of component conditions and the ways in which they operate to affect the system as a whole.
- monitor the condition of key system components and the effectiveness of steps taken to maintain and improve system health.
- revise plans and reorganize efforts in a timely manner.

Monitoring programs make explicit several of the capabilities essential to the executive functions of effective communication, coordination, planning, and decision making. Site managers in developed countries with mature administrative support systems for protected areas functioned relatively well for decades without a monitoring program. They were able to do so because the five capabilities listed above were in place, and they were able to use these capabilities by emulating the seasoned managers with whom they worked in their formative years. By making these capabilities explicit, however, we make them accessible to managers who do not have the benefit of the training and support that those in established systems enjoy. A monitoring program is also a shortcut to effective planning, and it retains the necessary ingredients of public involvement. Finally, it provides site managers not only with the information they need to make decisions but also with the substance of arguments they can deploy to explain those decisions and to acquire funding, equipment, and personnel.

Essential Elements of a Monitoring System

The purpose of monitoring is to identify undesirable change occurring at strategic loci. The object is more than to arrest deterioration at these loci before it becomes irreversible; it is to reverse deterioration before it precipitates system collapse. Monitoring is employed in many fields, including medicine and natural resource preservation. As the principles of transparency and accountability have become more prominent in government and business, monitoring has emerged in those areas as well.

In every field, monitoring involves first identifying *indicators*. Indicators are the things to be measured. An elegant monitoring system selects things to be measured that are most pertinent to the overall condition of the system to which they belong. In medicine, for example, one monitors, among other things, blood pressure and cholesterol. In natural resource conservation, one monitors the health of indicator species or those species that are most sensitive to generally deleterious environmental change. An often-cited indicator from a practical realm is the canary in the coal mine. If the canary dies, it becomes urgent to understand why and to take swift corrective action for the safety of the miners.

The second step in monitoring is to decide on or devise *instruments*. In medicine, these include an inflatable cuff and a stethoscope in the case of blood pressure. In ecology, we might count occurrences of indicator species in a certain area to measure species health.

The third step is to set standards. When what we measure exceeds those standards, we take corrective action. Deciding on the corrective action usually involves discussion, even debate, and perhaps testing to understand why standards have been exceeded.

At protected areas, monitoring can be thought of as being of two types. The first of these involves monitoring not only the protected area itself but also the entire region in which changes that occur might affect resources, experiences, and conditions inside the protected area. This type of monitoring can be termed "integrated landscape monitoring." The other kind of monitoring is of change occurring in zones that have been established at protected areas. These zones are established in ways that are described more fully below, but they are generally determined by the desired uses and conditions suggested by the distribution of cultural and natural resources within the protected area. This type of monitoring can be called "management zone monitoring."

In what follows, occasional reference is made to ongoing efforts at Petra Archaeological Park in Jordan to establish a monitoring system in order to distinguish integrated landscape monitoring from management zone monitoring. The Petra experience also serves to highlight some specific considerations and tools that are appropriate to each scale.

Integrated Landscape Monitoring

Crucial here is the use of a broad landscape analysis in order to identify indicators, select instruments, and establish standards. This regional perspective will reveal encroachment on core resource areas by ongoing development that changes viewshed, drainage, and vegetative patterns. The most practical and cost-effective means of accomplishing this is sometimes to use satellite remote-sensing technology. This technology can be employed as a key tool in a preliminary landscape analysis that helps to yield indicators, instruments, and standards. Satellite imagery also provides a synoptic view of landscape change, one that shows how changes in one area of a large landscape affect other areas. In addition, it compensates for the chronic shortage of personnel at protected areas in developing countries that would otherwise be needed to inventory, characterize, and evaluate the landscape by on-the-ground inspection.

Efforts now under way at Petra Archaeological Park to establish a monitoring program illustrate uses of satellite imagery for integrated landscape monitoring. At Petra, as at many other cultural and natural World Heritage Sites, destruction and deterioration of specific resources is often produced by altering the balance between cultural and natural processes, which leads to the instability of structures that we wish to conserve. Most destructive systemic changes involve encroachment by modern development, and the immediate degradation of experience is often far from trivial.

Topography is the framework for human occupation of a landscape: people can reside and work only where slope and aspect are suitable and where water, the occurrence of which depends to a large degree on topography, is present. Existing satellite technology can be used to produce a digital elevation model (DEM), the basic tool by which topography can be analyzed, represented, and understood. This technology includes ASTER imagery and data collected by the space shuttle radar technology mission (SRTM). Both sources can be used to obtain data that will provide a DEM with 30-meter accuracy. Such data are inexpensive. Acquiring more precise DEMs may be necessary for some applications, although these are usually more expensive. They include the analysis of aerial stereo pairs obtained with aircraft. Alternately, Space Imaging Corporation can acquire, for almost any location on earth, stereo pairs that can be used to produce DEMs accurate to 6 meters horizontally and 2 meters vertically. Such a DEM is being acquired for a portion of Petra, and the utility of the DEM will be tested there. What must be kept in mind, however, is that satellites are being launched continually, and these will provide data of increasing precision and utility.

Viewshed Analysis

Modern developments such as hotels and roads are jarring when seen by visitors who are walking through ancient cities and landscapes. Digital elevation models can be used to high-light those areas that would intrude on views from historic areas (see fig. 1). The degree of development in these areas can serve as indicators; protocols, including those involving remote-sensing technologies, to detect degree (in particular, height) of development can be instruments; and height restrictions and lux levels at night can be incorporated into standards.

Vegetative Change

Encroachment also sets in motion changes in topographic, hydrologic, and vegetative patterns that over longer periods can destroy cultural resources. A history of vegetative change can be constructed using what is now well-known technology of LANDSAT and SPOT satellites, which have been collecting multispectral data for twenty-five years. The history can first provide a baseline and then tell us how vegetation has changed in type and distribution. Certain types of vegetation can produce damage to cultural resources, and degree of vegetative growth is easily observable in multispectral and hyperspectral imagery. The ASTER satellite can, among other uses, serve as an instrument (fig. 2). High-resolution (approximately one meter per pixel) satellite near-infrared imagery (such as that acquired from IKONOS and Quick Bird satellites) has become readily available over the past few years and can now provide even more precise tracking of vegetative change. Standards must be developed with reference to a ground inventory of resources sensitive to vegetative change. Not only vegetation, but also the lack of vegetation, can constitute a threat because erosion develops more easily and proceeds more rapidly as vegetation disappears. Standards should be established in indicator areas for acceptable type, density, and distribution of vegetation.

Hydrologic Change

Erosion is more directly produced, of course, by water. Water at many archaeological sites is the greatest single threat to cultural resources. It destroys belowground sites through erosion; and as surely, though sometimes more slowly, it damages and eventually destroys architecture, whether of wood, earth, or stone.

Hydrological flow models show how water would flow, assuming that all rain became runoff and there was no interception, evapotranspiration, or loss to groundwater. Figure 3 displays such a model. The area in which the majority of tombs and the ruins of freestanding structures at Petra are contained is outlined in red.

An example of interception in a flow model is a water management system. Therefore, the baseline for hydrological

FIGURE 1 Viewshed analysis of Petra. Areas visible from the historic core are indicated in light green. Courtesy of CSRM and Space Imaging

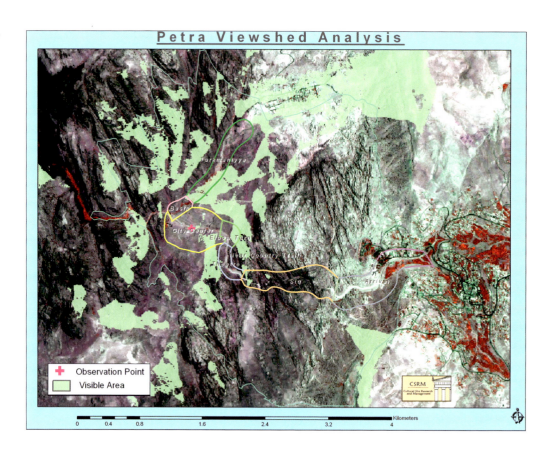

FIGURE 2 ASTER (advanced space-borne thermal emission and reflection radiometer) satellite image draped over DEM produced through stereoscopic analysis of the two data sets collected simultaneously by the satellite. Courtesy of CSRM and Space Imaging

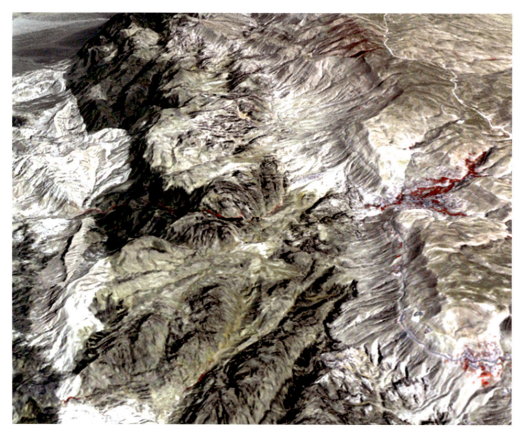

FIGURE 3 Flow accumulation analysis based on 10-meter accuracy digital elevation model produced by Talal Akasheh, vice president for development and planning, the Hashemite University, through the analysis of black-and-white aerial stereo pair photographs. The analysis indicates the location and volume of streams (most of them intermittent) that contribute to flooding in Petra. A solution to flooding can be devised by redistributing water flow upstream from the ancient city. Courtesy of Talal Akasheh

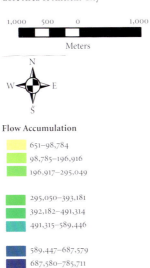

Core Area of Ancient City

1,000   500   0   1,000
Meters

N
W ← → E
S

Flow Accumulation

651–98,784
98,785–196,916
196,917–295,049

295,050–393,181
392,182–491,314
491,315–589,446

589,447–687,579
687,580–785,711
785,712–883,844

change at archaeological sites often should include features in such systems. One function of the water management system at Petra was to direct water to agricultural fields. By draping high-resolution IKONOS satellite imagery over a digital elevation model, we can see clearly for the first time what eludes the observer on the ground, a field system that is placed optimally in the watershed (fig. 4). While the field system here is obviously intact, where field systems have been destroyed elsewhere, flash flooding downstream is common. The prime example of this is the area into which the modern town of Wadi Musa, adjacent to Petra, has spread over the past fifteen years.

FIGURE 4 Field system above the Beidha area of Petra that distributes water to terraced fields. Given the similarity in plan to Nabataean fields elsewhere, it seems likely that this field system originated in Nabataean time. Courtesy of CSRM and JPL/NASA, with special thanks to Mike Abrams

Figure 5 shows the results of the removal of the field irrigation system that once acted to buffer flash flooding. This photograph was taken on 14 January 2004. Floodwaters are seen coursing through the heart of the ancient city, eroding archaeological sites and tombs. Floodwaters running down-slope and through the sandstone canyon system pick up salts. When the sandstone from which the famous tombs of Petra were cut absorbs the water, it absorbs the salts. When the water evaporates, the salts crystallize, forcing sandstone grains apart in a process known as "salt-wedging." Water also runs

FIGURE 5 Flash flood waters among tombs in the core area of Petra on 14 January 2004.

down the facades of tombs. Limestone dust from nearby high-lands has settled on the exterior of the tombs, forming a hard but brittle crust. When water finds its way into cracks in the crust, it eventually wears away the softer sandstone beneath. The exterior, on which decoration has been carved, falls away.

The ancient water management system also directed water into channels that led to cisterns or reservoirs. Cisterns were usually carved into stone and out of the rays of the sun. This was important because the system also shunted water away from the tombs cut into the walls of the sandstone canyon system in which Petra is located.

What is needed is the identification of indicators in the form of areas where development would most compromise the ancient water management system, instruments by which to detect and gauge development in these areas, perhaps including the use of satellite imagery, and standards that would discourage development likely to produce damage to the cultural resources of Petra. A monitoring system of this sort at Petra could be a model for such systems at other World Heritage Sites.

Management Zone Monitoring

Monitoring also occurs at zones within a protected area. Management zones should be discrete (nonoverlapping) areas determined by

- distribution, type, and sensitivity of resources present.
- environmental parameters that affect resource condition, visitor flow, and visitor experience.
- infrastructure design and standards that affect visitor flow and experience.
- desired use. Uses essential to accomplishing management objectives for the protected area are assigned the highest priority.
- desired condition. Desired condition is determined not only by local and international resource management standards and guidelines but also by management objectives.
- boundaries suggested by existing landscape features. These features can be natural (e.g., rivers and ridges)

or produced by human alteration of the landscape (e.g., roads and treelines). Ideally, an observer located anywhere in the landscape would find it possible to determine the zone by noting prominent landscape features.

It is important to note that desired uses and conditions for the integrated landscape should be formulated with the participation of stakeholders. Once these have been determined for the entire landscape in which the protected area is located, specific uses and conditions can be allocated to individual management zones. Indicators can then be established for those conditions that are most informative about and representative of the overall desired conditions for the zone. As with integrated landscape monitoring, the instruments selected must be practical, as well as provide the appropriate degree of precision. Standards are often best set with input from scientific and technical experts, as well as from groups

that will be affected by the results of monitoring. Petra management zones are shown in figure 6. Desired uses and conditions for these zones are presented in table 1; table 2 presents sample indicators, instruments, and standards for each zone.

Management Response

An essential element of effective monitoring is that it be integrated into site management procedures so as to trigger management action if standards are not met. Therefore, the 2000 Petra Operating Plan provides for the management organization and operating procedures necessary to ensure that destructive actions are documented and that this documentation is used as the basis for management action. At full staffing levels, Petra Archaeological Park will have three monitoring specialists with expertise in stone conservation and geology, archaeology, and cultural anthropology.

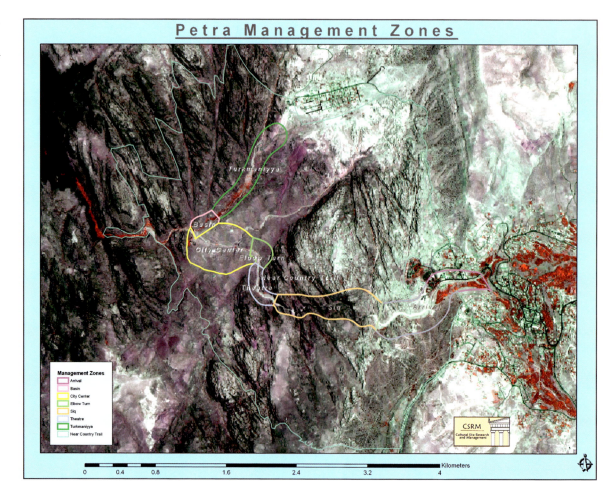

FIGURE 6 Management zones at Petra Archaeological Park, Petra World Heritage Site. Courtesy of CSRM and Space Imaging

Table 1 Desired uses and conditions for management zones at Petra. These will be reevaluated by stakeholders each year for three years.

Management Zone	Desired Use	Desired Condition
Arrival	Basic visitor orientation, transition from modern to ancient world. Must provide list of possible experiences, locations of essential amenities (rest rooms, food, refreshments) map, and orientation film (7–17 min.).	Order and cleanliness, clarity of message, effective presentation to visitor of options and the location of basic services. Inviting and engaging atmosphere, friendliness and hospitality. Opportunity to rest and renew before entering Siq.
Siq	Interpretation of natural forces that produced Siq, use of Siq in ceremonies, hydrological role of Siq, instilling a sense of expectant awe.	Quiet, natural smells and sounds, clear but non-intrusive interpretive media.
Theater	Establish connection with Greco-Roman city planning tradition, discussion of Nabbataean stone-working mastery, discussion of role of Nabbataeans in Greco-Roman world (e.g., four Roman emperors were of Arab descent).	Clear but nonintrusive interpretive devices that do not degrade resource.
Elbow Turn	Rest areas, comfort stations, transition to central portion of ancient town and orientation of visitor to city center layout, role of Petra in trade, flow of water into city and into agricultural fields above city.	Clean rest rooms, opportunities for comfortable rest, opportunities to rehydrate, clear but non-intrusive interpretive devices, opportunity to acquire additional interpretive media.
City Center	Explanation of probable layout of Edomite, Nabbataean, Roman, Byzantine, Crusader, and Bedouin occupation of the area.	Clear explanation and depictions of ancient city-scape that do not depend upon destructive research or devices.
Basin	Review of experience, rest and renewal.	Clean rest room and dining facilities. Clear instructions as to options for returning to modern world.
Turkmaniyya	Return route to modern world, enhancement of experience by using traditional modes of transport, opportunities to acquire authentic handicrafts, viewing of additional tombs from perspective of mode of transport, overall perspective of ancient city as one gains elevation.	Traditional but comfortable modes of transport offered in nonaggressive fashion, interpretive devices for features along Turkmaniyya, summary of experiences in park, and suggestions for additional ones (e.g., Ad-Dayr, High Place, Wadi Sabra, etc.).
Near Country Trail	Specialized tours (e.g., High Place of Sacrifice, Um Alp-Biyara, Crusader Castles) on well-marked and patrolled paths.	Opportunities for more intimate experience with nature and culture, patrols to ensure that undesirable activities are not allowed.

Every incident of observation will generate a written document, whether the observation is by Petra site personnel on their daily rounds or by technical specialists visiting the site. Monitoring observation forms will be prepared for use by park staff during regular rounds at the park. These will call for information about the exact location of the observance; the date and time; what was observed, including any activities or conditions that have produced or may produce damage or deterioration; any preliminary recommendations; and the name of the observer. Observations made by technical experts will include a summary that can be easily used by Petra site management for taking steps to correct the observed problem.

It will be the responsibility of the Petra Archaeological Park director to review each written monitoring observation,

eventually with the assistance of the chief, Branch of Research and Monitoring. The park will keep a file of every written monitoring observation and staff will discuss each one with the director and prepare a yearly report that includes each observation, actions taken to correct observed problems, and further actions required. The director will also have the responsibility for requesting resources adequate to correct observed problems.

Iteration

Monitoring is an inherently iterative exercise. Monitoring reports reviewed and discussed annually by stakeholders provide the basis for modification of indicators, instruments,

Table 2 Sample indicators, instruments, and standards for Petra management zones. These will be reevaluated by stakeholders each year for three years.

Management Zone	Sample Indicator	Sample Instrument	Sample Standards
Arrival	Degree of visitor orientation	30-second interviews at entrance to Siq of random sample of visitors	80% of visitors know four key monuments or sites, three tour routes, locations of rest rooms, locations of food and drink, are aware of need for sun protection and necessity of staying on pathways in central area of site
Siq	Graffiti	Reporting with digital cameras and GPS	Any occurrence of graffiti or vandalism
Theater	Visibility of remaining mason's marks	Bimonthly inspection	Any erosion of mason's marks
Elbow Turn	Condition of rest rooms	Two inspections per day conducted at different times each day	Rest rooms are open, clean, and have all necessary supplies
City Center	Degree of visitor orientation	30-second interviews at center of Colonnaded Street of random sample of visitors	80% of visitors know locations of rest rooms, locations of food and drink, are aware of need for sun protection and necessity of staying on pathways in central area of site; 75% know that visible monuments and sites are from different time periods, and that other tour routes exist that would require at least one more day at Petra; 60% can name at least three visible key monuments and sites
Basin	Visitor satisfaction	Survey form	80% of visitors rate dining and rest facilities good or better
Turkmaniyya	Availability and adequacy of transportation	30-second interviews in Umm Sayhun of random sample of visitors	No injuries, no reports of visitor harassment, wait time of less than 15 minutes at Basin and at Umm Sayhun for transport back to Wadi Musa
Near Country Trail	Inspection of tombs	Reporting form	No incidents of use of tombs as rest rooms or reports of graffiti
Integrated Landscape	Percentage of landscape covered by field systems watered by runoff	High-resolution satellite imagery	No decrease in percentage of landscape covered by field systems watered by runoff

standards, and reporting procedures. At Petra, it is anticipated that it will be three years before a monitoring program will be fully effective. Other iterations are sure to follow as recurring problems are addressed and solved and new concerns take center stage. Once the program is in operation, however, it will provide transparency and accountability in management—a way to explain and make available for public discussion management decisions and requests for staff, funding, equipment, and other resources necessary to effective and efficient site management.

PART SIX

Archaeology and Tourism: A Viable Partnership?

Introduction

Eugenio Yunis

The relationship among archaeology, conservation, and tourism is attracting more attention from scholars in archaeology and conservation and from managers of archaeological sites as tourist movement around the world—especially to famous sites—continues to grow at a rapid pace. Several questions arise in connection with this issue:

- Can tourism activities be permitted within archaeological sites, and if so, under what conditions?
- Can the risks associated with tourism be controlled at archaeological sites? How?
- To what extent can tourism contribute, financially or otherwise, to the conservation of archaeological sites?
- Should there be limits on tourist numbers at archaeological sites, and if so, how should these limits be established?
- How should local communities living close to archaeological sites be associated with tourism activities, and what should be their role in conservation of the sites?
- Is there a role for archaeologists in the development of sustainable forms of tourism?

The Fifth World Archaeological Congress addressed these issues in a special session in which leading specialists presented their views, based on their experiences at various locations in the Americas, Europe, and the Middle East. The session was jointly organized by the Getty Conservation Institute and the World Tourism Organization.

A generally agreed-upon initial premise of this discussion was that tourism is an unavoidable sociocultural and economic phenomenon of affluent contemporary societies. It was similarly agreed that tourism is likely to continue to grow throughout the world, as new strata of consumers gain access to the tourism market and as worldwide communications continue to improve, awakening the desire to visit historical, natural, and other attractive sites and landscapes. It was also generally accepted that visiting archaeological and other historic sites has, in principle, a positive effect, in the sense that it can help to educate people about their own past or that of particular societies and in so doing can improve intercultural understanding and eventually lead to a more peaceful world.

But at the same time, it was amply recognized that uncontrolled tourism can severely and irreversibly damage fragile sites, deteriorating their physical fabric, destroying their values, and not effectively transmitting their importance to the visitor. The presentations on specific cases in different parts of the world—by three members of the archaeological profession and a tourism planner—and the debates that followed served to draw some interesting conclusions that could enlighten both immediate actions to be taken by site managers and tourism operators and future research and policy making. The most salient conclusions are summarized here.

A first, fundamental condition for making tourism at archaeological sites sustainable from the economic, social, and cultural standpoints is to involve local communities, for being guardians of the sites enables them to reap benefits from the tourism activity that takes place there. Community-based cultural tourism and ecotourism can provide one answer, as demonstrated in the case of the Eastern Desert in Egypt. As Willeke Wendrich puts it beautifully, "By involving the local population directly in the excavation and adding a training component as well as a site management plan to the archaeological work, an unglamorous mudbrick site might change from a useless section of off-limits land at the fringe of a community to a source of pride and potential income."

Complementing the above approach, it was suggested that expanding tourism to lesser-known sites in the vicinity of a major site, the values of which are equally representative of a given culture or period, would ease the pressure exerted by high volumes of visitors to famous sites. Thus it was found necessary to develop a "narrative of the region" from scratch by combining the history, natural environment, and local attractions into a coherent presentation.

One risk of tourism-based economic development is the marginalization of the local population. The local community is vulnerable and easily can be exposed to outside influence; they often welcome development opportunities with the promise of benefits but without the experience to foresee likely negative consequences to their social well-being and lifestyle. The hazards in this case are multifaceted: rapid development, lack of political will to safeguard the community's interests, greed and corruption, lack of legislative controls (or implementation of those laws), and the impact of the transient tourist.

In a similar vein, using the example of Maya sites in the Yucatán Peninsula of Mexico and Central America, Wolfgang Wurster stresses the need to adopt a global perspective, both in archaeological research and excavation as well as in tourism, relative to the larger cultural area of civilizations, not just to individual sites. Until recently, the causes of deterioration to sites in this region have been the extreme rainfall, which disintegrated mortar structures, and aggressive vegetation, which destroys roofs and walls. During recent decades, a third factor of destruction has prevailed: illicit digging by looters that precipitates the collapse of the entire structure.

A global, sustainable view requires a multidisciplinary team of experts: architects, archaeologists, civil engineers, forestry officials, tourist managers, and economists, united in drawing up a master plan for the entire Maya region or other settlements that are to be made accessible to controlled tourism. Wurster further emphasizes that "times have changed, and they bring about a change of thinking, not just in methods of conserving monuments, but also in the expectations and pretensions of tourism."

In her presentation on the Altamira caves, Pilar Fatás Monforte states that "the purpose of heritage conservation should be to allow responsible use, applying criteria of sustainability, so that present exploitation does not exhaust future utility." This is the approach applied in the management of public visits to the cave of Altamira. In describing the advantages of the approach adopted at this Palaeolithic site—where a replica of the cave and a didactic museum with modern interpretive techniques were built—she underlines an additional benefit: the new museum helps to arouse people's interest in the fragility of heritage and the need to restrict visits to the original cave. She points out that the primary task is to preserve the cave from risk, but staff are also trained in communication, dissemination, and provision of scientific information to all interested parties.

Finally, Scott Cunliffe, adopting the perspective of tourism planner, proposes a planning and management tool, "cultural risk management" or risk management for cultural resources, to provide a means for a productive, effective, and viable partnership of archaeology and the tourism industry. He stresses the need for the presentation and interpretation of archaeological conservation to link the protection of the resource (conservation) to its use, understanding, and business potential: "This direct link to tourism could and should be at the heart of the partnership between archaeological conservation and tourism."

In conclusion, it was agreed at the session that tourism is a key determinant of the future of archaeological sites worldwide, and it cannot be left to occur without sensible and careful planning and continuous monitoring and control. Social, cultural, and economic impacts from tourism must be compatible with the principal objective of long-term conservation of archaeological sites. Sustainable tourism offers the opportunity to move from potential conflict to cooperation among tourists, the local population, and conservation and archaeology professionals.

The New Museum of Altamira:
Finding Solutions to Tourism Pressure

José Antonio Lasheras Corruchaga and Pilar Fatás Monforte

Abstract: *Since its discovery in 1879, the cave of Altamira has attracted large numbers of visitors. In 1979 the National Museum and Research Center of Altamira was established to preserve and manage the cave. In 1982 annual visitorship was fixed at 8,500 people. The new Museum of Altamira, inaugurated in 2001, offers an alternative—a replica—to visitors that does not compromise the preservation of the original cave. Heritage is a fragile, nonrenewable resource. The purpose of heritage conservation should be to allow responsible use, applying criteria of sustainability, so that present exploitation does not exhaust future utility. The replica of Altamira allows the cave to be experienced with absolute fidelity. It is a large three-dimensional "open book," scientifically sound and original in its museological concept. The reproduction is part of a huge permanent exhibition about the Paleolithic period that is intellectually accessible to all; it fosters intelligent interaction and pleasure in learning through its analogy to present-day life. The cave of Altamira is known worldwide as a milestone in the history of art. Its symbolic, social, and tourist implications position it among those sites having a notably positive impact on their regional environments.*

History of the Cave of Altamira

The paintings of Altamira—the first to be cataloged as Paleolithic—were discovered in 1879 by Marcelino Sanz de Sautuola. Since then, Altamira has become a symbol of prehistoric art throughout the world because of its antiquity and, above all, the magnificence of its art. It constitutes a milestone in an art form that proliferated in Europe, from Gibraltar to the Urals, more than twenty thousand years ago.

Throughout time, Altamira suffered many natural and artificial transformations. The difficulty of preserving the cave soon became evident. There were several rock falls from the ceiling. In addition, an interest in allowing public visits began in the early twentieth century. In 1924 the authorities in charge began to make the cave more accessible by providing paths and steps and illuminating it with spotlights. A road was built leading to the cave, and the esplanade next to its entrance was turned into a parking lot.

In 1939 the authorities focused on increasing tourism, and in 1955 Altamira was visited by more than fifty thousand people. This began a critical period for preservation of the cave: experts in charge of its conservation wanted to reduce visitor numbers, but politicians thought large numbers of tourists were an economic boon of vital importance to fostering tourist activity in Cantabria generally.

This disastrous cultural policy led to visitor numbers of more than 177,000 in 1973. At that time the cave was the main tourist attraction in the region and one of the most frequently visited sites in Spain. The situation was so bad that if the number of visitors had increased, the paintings would probably have disappeared as a result of extreme changes in humidity and temperature causing physical, chemical, and microbiological problems (fig. 1).

In 1978 the cave was given to the Spanish government, which since then has been responsible for its management. In 1979 the National Museum and Research Center of Altamira was created by the Spanish Ministry of Culture to preserve and manage the cave. That same year the cave was closed to the public, and a team of specialists began to study environmental parameters. On conclusion of the study, a fixed daily

FIGURE 1 Visitors flocked to the cave of Altamira during the 1970s. Courtesy of Museo de Altamira

number of visitors was determined that would not alter its inner climatic environment, and in 1982 Altamira was reopened for a reduced daily-maximum number of visitors, with an absolute limit of 8,500 people a year. The aim was to maintain its microclimate and to ensure the preservation of the paintings and engravings.

Altamira and Tourism: Finding Solutions

As a general philosophy, the fundamental aim of conserving heritage should be to enable its use. When we talk about using heritage, we have to consider its sustainability, because present exploitation should never exhaust its future use. This is the approach applied in the management of public visits to the cave of Altamira. Visits are not restricted to specialists; the general public may, by prior request, visit the cave, and this will continue as long as conservation conditions permit. The only condition governing their selection is that visitors must be over twelve years old; the order of appointments is based on a waiting list.

The temporary closure of the cave in the 1980s was hotly disputed since it had a profoundly negative effect on tourism.

On the one hand, there was the need for proper management of the cave; on the other, a large demand to visit. The cave's fragility left no doubt that the two situations were incompatible. The solution was to offer a high-quality alternative.

The idea of reproducing Altamira became a much discussed topic. Of course, outside cultural circles, the main motivation was to relieve the crisis suffered by the tourist industry. Many arguments were advanced to support this: economic, political, social, and educational. All were in agreement that a solution must be found that served all parties and interests involved.

Since 1982 the main preservation problems have been addressed. However, some outstanding issues affecting the cave were yet to be resolved: (1) it was necessary to repeat and complete the research work carried out in 1979; (2) there was no permanent recording system that might allow the verification of preservation parameters; and (3) environmental risks, such as sewage and traffic, had not been totally resolved. These concerns, combined with the availability of modern techniques for data recording and the application of new approaches, were reasons to search for a solution from a broader perspective.

In 1992 this solution materialized as a museum project for Altamira that was approved by the museum consortium and begun in 1993. Since then the Ministry of Education and Culture has invested significant funding in scientific equipment and in research agreements with other institutions, as well as in the purchase of the land above the cave. The multifaceted project included measures to improve conservation of the cave art and other heritage held by the museum, planning of a multidisciplinary research project to advance scientific knowledge about Altamira, and various communication strategies to popularize this knowledge. In other words, the project responds to the three main functions of a museum: conservation, research, and communication.

The aims of the project were (1) to satisfy the great demand to visit Altamira; (2) to improve the preservation of the paintings and engravings in the cave; and (3) to create a focal attraction that could contribute to the development of the regional tourist sector. The tools needed were a protection plan; construction of new infrastructure (supply and sewage systems, roads, paths, etc.); and a new building to house the reproduction of the cave, a large permanent exhibition on the Paleolithic period in Cantabrian Spain, new areas for laboratories, research, and administration, and any other public or semipublic facilities that the museum as a whole may require.

The Altamira project encompasses all of these. The cultural offerings of the new Museum of Altamira include not only the reproduction of the cave but also a permanent exhibition, *The Times of Altamira,* and many other activities such as workshops, conferences, and guided visits (fig. 2).

The project has solved the problems of preservation by carrying out a diagnosis of preventive preservation requirements and increasing the amount of land owned around the cave by 80,000 square meters, enabling traffic and supply and sewage systems to be moved more than half a kilometer from the cave. It has answered the demand for knowledge about and visits to Altamira by constructing a replica, creating the exhibition *Times of Altamira,* and reshaping the landscape. And, of course, it has helped to regenerate regional tourism.

The Neocave of Altamira

The name "Altamira" creates high expectations because it is a landmark in the history of art and has become a legend throughout the world. This implies a responsibility on the part of the museum not to disappoint those expectations.

Using a replica could be a problem because of the tendency to attribute value exclusively to originals and to reject copies and reproductions (sometimes the term "falsification" is even used, confusing quite disparate concepts). The solution was to ensure that the project's conception, design, and execution were of the highest quality and based on scientific research.

Using the results of this research, the replica of Altamira re-creates the original cavern space as it was during Paleolithic habitation rather than as it is today: that is, natural rock falls, supporting walls, paths, and other arrangements made in modern times have been suppressed.

By applying computerized modeling to the cave's topography, more than 40,000 sample points per square meter were measured and shaped; the reproduction has an accuracy of one millimeter. The paintings have been reproduced using the same techniques and natural pigments employed by Palaeolithic artists. Thus high technology and artisan techniques were combined to achieve the best results (figs. 3, 4).

This high-quality alternative to visiting the original cave does not compromise preservation of the original, yet it allows it to be known with absolute fidelity. It is an "open book" about Altamira based on scientific data and an original museological concept based on quality and singularity. The new museum provides an interesting opportunity for everyone to experience this heritage, and it allows Altamira to be shown without restriction to a larger number of visitors. More than one million people have visited the new Museum of Altamira since 2001; the number of visitors is expected to stabilize at over 200,000 per year, which is more than the number that came to the original cave during the 1970s (figs. 5–7).

FIGURE 3 Ortho-image of the polychrome ceiling. Produced by the National Geographic Institute. Courtesy of Museo de Altamira

FIGURE 4 Process of reproducing the paintings. Courtesy of Museo de Altamira

FIGURE 5 The Neocave: vestibule. Courtesy of Museo de Altamira

FIGURE 6 The Neocave: ceiling with paintings. Courtesy of Museo de Altamira

FIGURE 7 The Neocave: paintings of bison. Courtesy of Museo de Altamira

The Neocave of Altamira is part of a huge permanent display on the Paleolithic consisting of original pieces from various museums as well as multimedia presentations; it is intellectually accessible to all and motivates intelligent interaction and pleasure in learning through analogy to present-day life (fig. 8). The new museum has become a model of visitation for other heritage sites; many requests for technical information have been received for use by other museums and cultural spaces.

Other Tourism-related Implications

The tourism industry has recovered in Santillana del Mar and its surroundings. Tourism pressure justified the important investment in this multifaceted project, because it helped to guarantee not only the cultural and economic profitability of the project and the surrounding environment but also a departure from seasonal visitation patterns. That is why the project has been linked to tourism and was attached to a European Union Support Framework, "Valuation of Cultural Resources of Tourist Interest," wherein it responds to the third defined strategy: "aspects relating to the recovery and maintenance of cultural resources of tourist interest." The project revalues Altamira by making tourist use possible.

There is another collateral benefit: the new museum helps to arouse people's interest in the fragility of heritage and the need to restrict visits to the cave. For example, in September 2002 the cave was closed again in order to restudy conservation conditions. This time the public reaction was very different from that in 1979; the reasons for closure were well understood by the general public, and they have access to an extremely interesting alternative, the Neocave.

Another key to appropriate management of the cave is entrusting it to museum technicians, basically curators. While the main task is to preserve the cave, staff are also trained in communication, dissemination, and provision of scientific information to all interested parties.

The Museum of Altamira is a cultural reference point for the tourist destination of Cantabria and "Green Spain" in general. The museum and Paleolithic art are used to portray Cantabria in the current tourist campaign of "Green Spain." The bison of Altamira are among the themes selected by Turespaña in its international campaign, "Spain Marks," which promotes Spain as a cultural and tourist destination. The regional government of Cantabria includes the Museum of Altamira in its promotional efforts. The museum collaborates in this promotion; its communication department personally welcomes tourism and travel journalists sent by the

Promotion of Tourism Service of the Cantabrian government and tour operators referred by the Regional Society of Tourism. Through its booking department, the Museum of Altamira pays special, personalized attention to visits organized by travel agencies, booking centers, and hotels.

The Museum of Altamira disseminates information about its cultural offerings and sends a quarterly newsletter published by the Friends of the Museum Assocation to tourism offices. In summer 2003 the Museum of Altamira made available a new brochure edited especially for tourist establishments: hotels, tourist offices, travel agencies, and so on.

A final consideration is the professional relationship between the museum and tourism, which is difficult because no relationship existed between the Spanish Ministry of Tourism and the Ministry of Culture. In 2002 the "Plan to Promote Cultural Tourism" was presented to the Ministry of Culture. This was developed by the Secretary of State for Tourism to promote the heritage resources of Spain as tourist attractions. The first general aim outlined was the creation of a cultural tourism offering (a cultural offering becomes a cultural tourism offering when the rights to its use and enjoyment are available for acquisition in the tourist market),

which involved measures designed to increase information on cultural products and to reinforce the promotion and support of the commercialization of cultural products.

Step by step, the results of the campaign are being seen. At present, museums are listed on the official website of Turespaña, cultural icons have been incorporated in the campaign "Spain Marks," and museum activities have been included in the cultural calendar. Recently, the Museum of Altamira participated in another initiative designed to meet the goals of sensitization to and structuring of the cultural tourism sector. A number of training sessions were held, aimed at cultural and tourism technicians, agents of archaeological venues, civic groups, parks, and cultural landscapes, to analyze Altamira as a cultural tourism resource. However, in most cases, each museum must establish its own relationship with tourism institutions and companies, and this usually depends on the goodwill of the professionals in charge of communication departments, where they exist. Broader collaboration is recommended in the future between the cultural and tourism sectors in order to obtain cultural products of high quality.

Archaeology and Sustainable Tourism in Egypt: Protecting Community, Antiquities, and Environment

Willeke Wendrich

Abstract: *This paper explores how archaeologists should consider getting involved with sustainable tourism in order to communicate their findings to the public, protect the sites that they are working on, improve fund-raising for the archaeological project, and contribute to an economically viable system for the population of the area. Two examples illustrate the benefits of working closely with the local community. The Eastern Desert Antiquities Protection Project (EDAPP) involves a training program and the creation of a collection of present-day material culture by the Ababda nomads from the Eastern Desert in Egypt. The Fayum ecotourism project is a first step in defining the development needs for an area of Egypt that has an extremely interesting history but does not attract the mass tourism that the Giza pyramids and the monuments of Luxor do.*

Egypt is a country with immensely impressive and well-known archaeological remains that draw approximately 2.5 million tourists annually. These visitors spend an average of $1,100 each, which amounts to 6 percent of Egypt's gross national product (GNP).[1] Based on World Bank data, it appears that in 2002 almost 50 percent of Egypt's gross domestic product was generated by the service sector, with tourism providing the largest percentage of revenue. An estimated 2.2 million people (3.5 percent) of a population of 62 million find employment in the tourism sector.[2] In spite of the large number of people employed in tourism, most of the tourism industry revenue benefits the large (often international) tour and hotel companies and the Egyptian government.

Most tourists who visit Egypt follow a standard itinerary, from the pyramids at Giza, near Cairo, to the temples of Luxor and nearby Karnak, often combining the cultural experience with relaxation at the Red Sea coast where beach and dive tourism has developed at a rapid pace (fig. 1). Archaeologists and conservators are worried about the threat to the ancient remains posed by the increase in the number of visitors. The rise in temperature and humidity and physical attrition in the tombs and pyramids have a direct causal relation to the large numbers of tourists visiting these monuments, and at several locations the number of visitors has had to be reduced. In 1995 the number of visitors to the tomb of Nefertari in the Valley of the Queens in Luxor was limited to 150 per day. Since 2003 the tomb of Nefertari has been closed to regular visitors. In the same year the maximum number of daily visitors to the pyramids of Khufu and Khafra was set at 300. At times these monuments are closed completely so as to allow the temperature and relative humidity to return to acceptable levels. Not only the enclosed spaces are under threat: backpacks brush past limestone walls, thousands of feet climb the soft stone of the ancient thresholds and stairs—the wear and tear is apparent.

Large crowds are by no means the only danger to Egypt's antiquities. By defining protocols for conservation and site management, the Egyptian Supreme Council of Antiquities is attempting to protect the archaeological monuments and sites from threats varying from town expansion, soil harvesting, and extensive or intensive visitation by tourists to looting and the effect of environmental changes resulting from the artificially high level of the water table and air pollution.

Whose Cultural Heritage?

World Heritage Sites, many of them monumental tombs or religious complexes built by the elite, are under close scrutiny. Egypt has a wealth of less glamorous antiquities, dispersed in

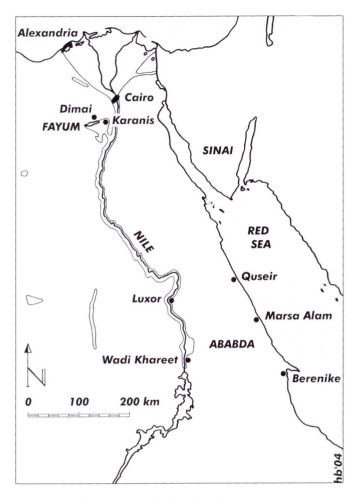

FIGURE 1 Map of Egypt. Drawing by Hans Barnard

the landscape of the Nile Delta, strung out along the edges of the desert, and buried under modern cities, towns, and villages. School programs bring Egyptian children into the museums and monuments, creating an awareness of Egypt's glorious past. It is, however, a very selective past. For most visitors, Egyptians and tourists alike, "antiquities" are the awe-inspiring stone structures found in Luxor and Giza, not the mudbrick remains at the edge of the village.

Ironically, the ancient remains built of modest mudbrick, rather than the built-in-stone provisions for the afterlife of the elite, provide the most important information about the lives of the ancient Egyptians. They represent residential areas, workshops, and even palaces. These ancient settlement sites, some of them of enormous proportions, are often located in remote rural areas that are plagued by adverse economic circumstances. Poverty tempts the inhabitants of these areas to mine every possible source of income, be this the fertile soil that is conveniently concentrated in ancient mudbrick or antiquities that can be sold into the illegal market. These problems are by no means new. The *sebakhin,* or soil diggers, have been farming ancient mudbrick sites for generations, sometimes at an industrial scale. At the site of Karanis, in the Fayum depression just southwest of Cairo, railway tracks once led to an enormous void at the heart of an ancient Greco-Roman city (fig. 2). In the process of digging for fertile soil, the sebakhin came across papyri, statuettes, and other interesting finds that could be sold to antiquities dealers. In the case of Karanis, it was the persistence of archaeologists from the University of Michigan that finally put an end to these destructive activities in about 1925. Today, the poorer

FIGURE 2 *Sebakhin* involved in "mining" the ancient town of Karanis on an industrial scale for fertile mudbrick, papyri, and other antiquities. Courtesy of the Kelsey Museum of Archaeology, University of Michigan, Kelsey Museum Archive 5.2465

segment of the population still ventures out to archaeological sites to dig for treasure. An equal lack of awareness exists among wealthy Egyptians, and this results in the expansion of building projects, industrial quarrying enterprises, and large-scale land reclamation and irrigation projects that destroy the ancient sites.

That these activities result in the destruction of cultural heritage is mostly lost on the persons who make use of the additional source of income. The question should be asked: whose cultural heritage are we trying to protect? And under which circumstances does cultural heritage become jointly "ours"?

The Role of the Archaeologist

In the history of the archaeology of Egypt one might also point a finger at the early archaeologists who certainly contributed their share to the destruction of ancient sites, a fact that did not go unnoticed by the Egyptian authorities.[3] In the nineteenth and twentieth centuries the most common attitude of Western archaeologists to Egyptians was colonialist: a paternalistic attitude of the *effendi* (lord) to the ignorant *fellaheen* (peasants) who were hired as workmen, and this was combined with an elitist attitude of the Western scholar to Egyptian colleagues. What the great scholars left behind was in many cases an unsystematically excavated, unpublished site, abandoned and left open to the elements. Archaeologists of the second half of the twentieth century became aware that they had a responsibility for conservation, site management, and protection. Paradoxically, as soon as a foreign archaeological team shows interest in an archaeological site, this arouses or strengthens the interest of the local population; and the result may well be an increase in illicit digging activities as soon as the excavation team has left the area.

Can this phenomenon be turned into a win-win situation? It potentially can, if a direct link can be made between income, knowledge, and preservation. That link could be formed by alternative forms of tourism such as ecotourism or cultural tourism. Ecotourism and cultural tourism are forms of sustainable tourism that are responsible, are sensitive to the local environment and culture, and directly improve the welfare of the local population. In the literature the number of terms for and definitions of sustainable tourism is enormous, but the goals can be summarized as follows:

- To develop greater awareness and understanding of the significant contributions that tourism can make

to the cultural and natural environment and the economy.
- To promote equity in development.
- To improve the quality of life of the host community.
- To provide a high-quality experience to the visitor.
- To maintain the quality of the cultural and natural environment on which the foregoing objectives depend (see Dowling and Fennell 2003:5).

Is there a role for archaeologists in the development of sustainable tourism? Archaeologists traditionally (and caricaturally) consider tourists and tourism with mild contempt—as an ignorant nuisance, as a threat to the ancient remains, or at best as a potential funding source. A more productive stand is taken by archaeologists who are aware that interaction with tourism can be an important asset on several different levels.

Stimulating the interest of the local population in nearby antiquities and creating a heightened awareness of their cultural value will help to preserve the ancient remains. Direct economic interest of the local community in the local antiquities will strengthen this effect considerably. For archaeologists, important issues are at stake. To have the support of the local population in the protection of an archaeological site is as important as legal and government protection. Archaeologists can have an important role in stimulating such support by aiding the development of sustainable tourism. They can provide the knowledge to make an unglamorous archaeological site into a fascinating narrative. Through their familiarity with multiple cultures, they are able to help translate the expectations of the visitors and the hosting culture. The yield for the archaeologist, apart from rapport with the surrounding population and better protection of the ancient sites, is that his or her work will have a much broader audience (and potential donors).

By involving the local population directly in the excavation and adding a training component and site management plan to the archeological work, an unglamorous mudbrick site might change from a useless section of off-limits land at the fringe of a community to a source of pride and potential income. Is this too optimistic? I use two examples to illustrate the benefits and potential of working closely with the local community. The Eastern Desert Antiquities Protection Project (EDAPP) involves a training program and the creation of a collection of present-day material culture of the Ababda nomads from the Eastern Desert. The Fayum ecotourism project is a first step in defining the development needs for an area of Egypt that has an extremely interesting history but does not attract the mass tourism that the Giza pyramids and the monuments of Luxor do.

Eastern Desert Antiquities Protection Project

Although the Egyptian Eastern Desert and the Red Sea shore are located in an extremely arid environment, there are nevertheless many remains of past human activities. These are concentrated at quarrying or mining sites; along the shore, where the harbor towns were founded; and along the routes from these harbors to the Nile Valley, transport routes protected by a string of fortified watering stations. The dates range from the prehistoric to the present, with the height of activity in the early Roman period (first and second centuries B.C.E.).

In 1994 a team comprising experts from the University of Delaware, Leiden University, and the University of California, Los Angeles, started work in Berenike, a Greco-Roman harbor from which ships left for the Indian Ocean basin (Sidebotham and Wendrich 1995, 1996, 1998, 1999, 2000). The team worked under the auspices of the Egyptian Supreme Council of Antiquities and hired approximately sixty members of the local community, which in this region is not a static but a mobile entity. The Ababda are a nomadic group living in the southern part of the Egyptian Eastern Desert. Part of the group has settled along the Red Sea in villages such as Marsa Alam and Quseir and in a large village in the Nile Valley, Wadi Khareet. The people who have settled in Wadi Khareet have mostly given up their pastoral nomadic lifestyle and have become agriculturalists or laborers. A substantial group that still lives in the desert follows the rainfall to find good grazing for their herds of sheep, goats, and camels (fig. 3). The relations between the settled and mobile Ababda are close knit, and the change from one lifestyle to the other is fluid. An Ababda family can decide to live in the village, but as long as they have livestock, they can leave on a moment's notice. Members of different clans are found in specific areas of the desert but also in the villages. The composition of the group of Ababda working on the excavation project was equally mixed. Men from different Ababda clans came from a settlement and several encampments nearby; others came all the way from Wadi Khareet in the Nile Valley, a distance of approximately 250 kilometers.

Apart from working on the excavation, several of the older Ababda were hired as guides for the survey of the hinterland. During their life of roaming the desert, they regularly came across ancient remains, often near the same water sources that are used today. These Ababda were able to show where in the vast area of the Eastern Desert antiquities could be found, although they usually did not discern British camps of World War II from Roman or Pharaonic settlements. During the mapping and excavation of the ancient remains, the discussion with the Ababda would often center on the people living in the desert two thousand years ago. When it became apparent from the excavated material that during its latest phase (fifth and sixth centuries C.E.) Berenike had been inhabited by a settled group of nomads, the Ababda became even more enthusiastic. The cooperation prompted a discussion on cultural change, the eternal demands of life in the desert, and the preservation of culture—both the ancient remains and the rapidly changing culture of the Ababda.

The latter was uppermost in many minds because change was imminent. From 1990 onward there was rapid development of beach and diving tourism along the Red Sea coast. In 1998 the first effects of this development could be noticed in the south, where the Ababda live. A brand-new asphalt road had been built, and the bus service that used to pass through the area once a week was expanded to four times a week and, in 2000, to six buses a day. The first hotels were built just north of Marsa Alam. At the same time the government tried to convince the Ababda to lead a more settled life by building villages, water tanks, schools, and clinics.

FIGURE 3 Ababda dwelling in the region of Berenike. Photo: Willeke Wendrich

Reactions among the Ababda varied widely. Some Ababda were ready to settle and adapt to a "modern" way of life, to find employment as truck drivers or builders. Others abhorred the developments and said that they would withdraw deeper into the desert. A third reaction, mostly from people who had been settled for approximately twenty years, or were "second-generation" settled Ababda from the Nile Valley, was one of resignation and also pride. Their identity was Ababda. It was this group especially that was interested in preserving not only ancient but also present-day Ababda culture. Through their contacts during the excavation with men who were still living in the desert, they realized how little they knew about Ababda culture and how much there was to know.

With the help of the Cultural Fund of the Netherlands Embassy in Cairo, the Eastern Desert Antiquities Protection Project was initiated. This comprised a training program for the Ababda in preserving the desert sites and understanding the ancient use of the desert, but it also included a component that concentrated on the present-day desert dwellers and the cultural heritage of the Ababda. In the context of EDAPP, a group of Ababda created three exhibitions on Ababda culture: one in Berenike, one at the visitors' center in the Ottoman Fort at Quseir, and a traveling collection that has been on display for a year at the Museum of Ethnology (Wereldmuseum) in Rotterdam.

Related to the rapidly changing circumstances along the Red Sea shore, another focus of discussion became how the Ababda could contribute to and benefit from the increasing tourism. The dive centers and hotels are owned by large national and international companies. The desert safaris, however, can benefit greatly from direct involvement of the Ababda community. At present there is one company that has initiated this close cooperation, one in which the Ababda have real input.[4]

In several areas of Egypt, experiments have been done with training the local population to be involved in an official capacity in the protection of the natural and cultural habitat. Locally recruited rangers are active in the Sinai[5] and the Wadi Rayan area in the western part of the Fayum (see below).

In 2000 an initiative of the University of Southampton set out to involve the local community of Quseir in the development of a heritage center, which, apart from involving the town in the excavations, also had the explicit purpose of stimulating tourism.[6] The role of archaeologists in the development of sustainable tourism in the Eastern Desert could be expanded, however. In the first place, by making results of archaeological work available in both English and Arabic, the information will be much more accessible. Their involvement in training programs for inspectors of the Supreme Council of Antiquities, local guards, and rangers would highlight the importance and most recent information on the archaeology. Expansion of training initiatives for guards would ensure the direct involvement of the Ababda and would help to preserve the vulnerable cultural and natural resources of the Egyptian Eastern Desert.

Fayum Ecotourism Project

On the initiative of the Egyptian Tourism Development Authority (TDA) and the Fayum Governorate, a team of specialists researched the viability of developing an ecotourism program in the Fayum (Wendrich 2000). This is an area of Egypt with a fascinating history but without impressive tourist magnets such as spectacular temples, tombs, and pyramids. The objective of the local authorities and the TDA was to attract tourists to this region by promoting a different kind of tourism. The Fayum, about 100 kilometers southwest of Cairo, combines an impressive desert landscape with important natural and cultural resources. As one of the resting places for migratory birds, it could be advertised as an important birding area. Rural tourism could include visits to the many craftsmen who are active in the villages that dot the fertile Fayum basin. The desert landscape surrounding the Fayum depression is extremely impressive and a geologic paradise. In addition, the region has important paleontological resources.

On top of that, the Fayum boasts many archaeological sites. It is the region where we have the earliest evidence of agriculture in Egyptian prehistory (ca. 5500 B.C.E.). It was later transformed from a large swamp into well-organized agricultural fields during the Egyptian Middle Kingdom (ca. 1975–1640 B.C.E.). The Fayum was one of the most important sources of the wealth of the successors of Alexander the Great: with the wheat grown in Egypt they could finance alliances with cities around the eastern Mediterranean. All these historically important developments are reflected by a ring of ancient settlements that can still be found today surrounding the Fayum basin. These archaeological remains, unimposing perhaps in comparison to the famous stone monuments, are witness to the occupations, worries, and successes of the ancient inhabitants (fig. 4). Their story needs to be spelled out by scholars who study the settlements in all their aspects and are willing to share their fascination by explaining in accessible language what is special about them.

FIGURE 4 The Fayum region, the Greco-Roman village of Dimai. Photo: Willeke Wendrich

In the last ten years the desert around the Fayum depression has seen an enormous increase in visitors. Expatriates living in nearby Cairo venture out into this vulnerable area with their four-wheel-drive vehicles on weekends. In 2003, while working in the area, we were visited at least twice a week by groups of off-road adventure tourists, organized by a Cairo-based tour operator. Most of the visitors are environment-conscious, well-meaning citizens who do not realize that this form of tourism is very destructive to the delicate desert environment and the equally delicate paleontological and archaeological remains. There is a great need for information and more controlled access to the area, which should at the same time generate income for the local population and authorities.

The Fayum Governorate and the TDA are in favor of developing ecotourism. Their definition of ecotourism differed, however, on two important points from that of the team researching ecotourism potential. In the recent past, plans for the development of ecotourism in Egypt have always involved the construction of luxurious ecolodges in gorgeous natural settings. The research team concluded that a better rationale

was to make use of (upgraded) existing accommodations, as the occupancy rate of hotel rooms in the Fayum is only 15 percent. The involvement of and direct benefit for the local population is another aspect that was not immediately associated with ecotourism by Egyptian policy makers. This situation is slowly changing, however. Experience with local rangers and guides in the Wadi Rayan area, who help to preserve the landscape and at the same time provide information to visitors, proved positive. The community is given a direct stake in preserving the cultural and natural landscape by providing a group of inhabitants of the Fayum with an additional source of income. The continued efforts to develop sustainable tourism in the Fayum seem to be slowly focusing more attention on the grassroots stakeholders.

Conclusion: Safely Experiencing the Adventure of Discovery

There is a growth market for tourists who are not satisfied with the mass tourism offerings but style themselves as travelers. Their goal is not to have a relaxing, lazy time. Instead they want to experience the genuine culture of a country and its regions by traveling off the beaten track. While some travelers are content with no-star hotels, most travelers want to have comfortable, even luxurious lodgings and good meals. Most important, the excursions have to be exciting, adventurous, safe, and interesting.

Involvement of the local community is a key feature in the development of sustainable tourism. This poses a challenge and creates the need for training in the regions that want to develop this form of tourism. Training should first provide a community with insight into guests' expectations. Language training for at least a portion of the community is equally indispensable. Another important point is to provide relevant information on the area for guards, guides, and rangers. For most geographic areas, a "narrative of the region" has to be developed from scratch by combining the history, the natural environment, and the local attractions into a coherent presentation.

Most archaeologists work in the same region for a considerable period each year over several years, and through employing members of the local communities, they have built relationships of mutual appreciation, understanding, goodwill, and trust. Members of the community who have worked at an archaeological site can work together with the archaeologists to develop the narrative and accompanying exhibits. The combined experience of the local population and the archaeologists, consisting of a thorough knowledge of local circumstances, the region, its landscape, and its history, is an important resource in developing training programs for guides and rangers. Bringing out the narrative and providing high-quality information is something that archaeologists working in the region could do incomparably with little extra effort. The archaeological work might itself be part of the narrative, and local guides who have worked on the excavation could take guests to the "archaeologists at work."

The advantage of this type of sustainable tourism for the population of the region is that the proximity of antiquities will no longer be a source of neglect but a source of income. The advantage for the archaeologists is that a good relationship with the people living on or near an archaeological site will help to protect sites, and this is even more likely to be the case when the local population has a direct and real stake in their preservation. Archaeologists can use information disseminated to tourists to highlight the results of their work and attract additional financial support. The main advantage is accrued by the antiquities: making the local population stakeholders in preservation will provide better long-term protection of the sites than posted signs or hired guards.

Tourism is an unavoidable and potentially positive fact of our times. Sustainable tourism is a way to move from potential conflict to cooperation among tourists, the local population, and conservation and archaeology professionals.

Notes

1   Encyclopedia of the Orient, http://i-cias.com/e.o/egypt_2.htm.

2   United Nations Development Programme, www.undp.org.eg/profile/egypt.htm.

3   Mohamed Ali, in a decree of 15 August 1835, blamed the European treasure hunters for the large-scale destruction of antiquities. See Reid 2002.

4   This is the Red Sea Desert Adventures initiative. See www.redseadesertadventures.com/.

5   Listed in evaluation documents for UNESCO and the World Heritage Site of Saint Catherine's monastery. See http://whc.

unesco.org/archive/advisory_body_evaluation/954.pdf; www.sinaiparks.gov.eg/; www.cairotimes.com/content/issues/envir/jujob3.html.

6   Further information on the community archaeology project can be found at www.arch.soton.ac.uk/Projects/projects.asp?Division=3&SubDivision=0&Page=0&ProjectID=20.

References

Dowling, R. K., and D. A. Fennell. 2003. The context of ecotourism policy and planning. In *Ecotourism Policy and Planning,* ed. R. K. Dowling, 1–20. Cambridge: CABI-Publishing.

Reid, D. M., ed. 2002. *Whose Pharaohs? Archaeology, Museums, and Egyptian National Identity from Napoleon to World War I.* Berkeley: University of California Press.

Sidebotham, S. E., and W. Z. Wendrich. 1995. *Berenike 1994: Preliminary Report of the 1994 Excavations at Berenike (Egyptian Red Sea Coast) and the Survey of the Eastern Desert.* Leiden: Leiden University Research School of Asian, African and Amerindian Studies CNWS.

———. 1996. *Berenike 1995: Preliminary Report of the 1995 Excavations at Berenike (Egyptian Red Sea Coast) and the Survey of the Eastern Desert.* Leiden: Leiden University Research School of Asian, African and Amerindian Studies CNWS.

———. 1998. *Berenike 1996: Report of the 1996 Excavations at Berenike (Egyptian Red Sea Coast) and the Survey of the Eastern Desert.* Leiden: Leiden University Research School of Asian, African and Amerindian Studies CNWS.

———. 1999. *Berenike 1997: Report of the 1997 Excavations at Berenike and the Survey of the Egyptian Eastern Desert, including Excavations at Shenshef.* Leiden: Leiden University Research School of Asian, African and Amerindian Studies CNWS.

———. 2000. *Berenike 1998: Report of the 1998 Excavations at Berenike and the Survey of the Egyptian Eastern Desert, including Excavations at Wadi Kalalat.* Leiden: Leiden University Research School of Asian, African and Amerindian Studies CNWS.

Wendrich, W. Z. 2000. *Travelling with Bedouin, Farmers and Fishermen: Ecotourism for Sustainable Development in the Fayoum Oasis.* Cairo: Tourism Development Authority/North South Consultants Exchange, May.

Maya Cities and Tourism

Wolfgang Wurster

Abstract: *This paper treats Maya cities in the tropical rainforest—their investigation, conservation, and preparation for tourism. The geographic area of Maya cities in Central America encompasses southeastern Mexico, especially Yucatán, the lowlands of Guatemala, where Maya culture had its origins in the Petén, and part of Belize and Honduras. The time frame of the ruins in question is roughly the first millennium C.E. The author was involved for fifteen years in a project to conserve Maya cities in the northeast of Petén on behalf of the German Archaeological Institute. The project, called the Cultural Triangle, embraces an area of some 400 square kilometers east of Tikal toward the border with Belize and contains the large ancient cities of Yaxhá, Nakúm, and Naranjo and some fifty minor sites. In this area, the Guatemalan National Institute of Anthropology and History, in collaboration with the German Archaeological Institute, planned and implemented a project to document, conserve, and maintain endangered Maya sites. As of June 2003 it had been financed substantially by the German federal government as part of a regional development program aimed at the conservation of the rainforest and the nondestructive use of natural resources, which includes tourism. This paper presents a summary of experiences related to traditional conservation and possible alternatives. It also emphasizes a global perspective related to the larger cultural area of Maya civilization, not just to individual sites.*

Maya cities had their classical period between 300 and 900 C.E. They functioned as individual city-states with their surrounding dependent settlements, thus transforming an inhospitable area of forest and swamps into a densely populated cultural landscape with intensive agriculture. The urbanistic design of Maya cities follows astronomical and cosmological precepts, involving also the surrounding topography. Its architectural elements contain massive terraced structures, stepped pyramids with towering temple buildings atop, and multistory palaces. These elements are arranged around plazas and squares and are connected by enormous causeways that were used as processional roads.

The most characteristic feature of this stone-and-mortar architecture is the Mayan vault, made of protruding stone slabs and lime mortar. And the most stunning invention of the Maya was a hieroglyphic writing system, handed down to us in carved script on stone slabs that recorded the history of the rulers, their wars, and their alliances.

All these features, together with the unique setting in the tropical rainforest, called special attention to Maya sites and since the end of the nineteenth century incited the interest of adventurers, scientists, and then tourists. An additional romantic attraction was the fact that most of the sites had not been destroyed or reused by later settlers or other civilizations but simply covered up by the tropical jungle.

Today, after so many centuries of abandonment, most of the Maya sites—and there are hundreds of them just in the lowlands of Petén—are in immediate danger of being destroyed. Until recently they had been damaged mainly by the extreme rainfall that disintegrated the mortar structures and by the aggressive vegetation, which tore apart roofs and walls. During recent decades, a third factor of destruction prevailed: illicit digging by treasure hunters. In search of rich tombs and archaeological objects, the looters excavated enormous tunnels and ditches inside the monumental architecture and thus precipitated the collapse of entire structures.

The early excavations of Maya sites, mainly undertaken by U.S. institutions, usually did not involve conservation: one would cut down the rainforest completely and then record and excavate the monument, leaving all trenches open. Later, all great excavations, including those of the Carnegie Foundation, powerful U.S. universities, and then the Mexican government, were combined with programs of reconstruction of monumental architecture. Chichen Itzá, Uxmal, and Palenque were such sites. In his *History of Mexican Archaeology* (1980), the renowned Mexican scholar Ignacio Bernal defines his operational guidelines: "Most archaeology is funded with public money, in Mexico at least. The State is concerned not so much with the increase of knowledge as with the creation, by excavating and restoring of suitable ruins as foci of national pride, of a greater feeling of continuity with the people's own past and the encouragement of tourism."

In the Petén lowlands, the University of Pennsylvania started a twelve-year research program in 1957 at Tikal, the greatest Maya city of all, with enormous efforts and five hundred workmen. Some of the most important architectural monuments, especially the great pyramids, were partially reconstructed. Since the outer retaining walls of the buildings had decayed, leaving the massive interior core of filling material open to further destruction, the containing walls were replaced by new masonry of stone and cement.

In terms of the UNESCO Charter of Athens, anastylosis should not be used in the conservation of Maya monuments; they are constructions made of solid core filling and exterior containing walls of mortar-masonry. The re-creation of such an exterior wall by means of new construction is not reversible since the new shell cannot be separated from the old core. It is a durable solution, no doubt, but it leaves little or nothing of the original monument. And since the procedure is extremely expensive and time-consuming, it was applied to few monuments and mostly only in one part of the original structure, the prominent facade with the staircase. This Tikal procedure created a striking contrast between the few reconstructed monuments and the enormous number of urban structures that could not be addressed and remain simply as mounds of earth and fallen debris covered with vegetation.

The reconstruction methods of the University of Pennsylvania at Tikal were setting an overwhelming example of restoration throughout Central America, and ever since they have been applied universally: total or partial reconstruction of very few important buildings on a site, leaving the rest untouched. No doubt this method saved important buildings, but the appreciation of a Maya city as an urbanistic creation is thereby neglected. The visitor appreciates solitary, single monuments only.

A real boom in the reconstruction of Maya ruins started about twenty-five years ago, as publications such as *National Geographic* called attention to them. Slogans such as "Mayan World" and "Mayan Route" became the trademark of increasingly intense touristic promotion in Central America, especially in Mexico and Belize. Tourism to archaeological ruins turned out to be big business, usually run as an ever-increasing industry by multinationals. In 2002 Mexico counted 20 million tourists, most of them exclusively to archaeological sites. Tikal had more than 150,000 visitors. We may rightly infer that the national economy of most Central American countries depends in great part on revenues from tourism to archaeological sites. This creates increasing pressure for monumental reconstructions at the sites. And the methods of the school of Tikal still prevail: partial reconstruction of selected buildings, much use of white cement, and touristic installations and hotels within the site.

In the case of the Cultural Triangle Project, which covers an enormous area of tropical forest and many dozens of sites abandoned and in danger of collapsing, the first task was to safeguard the monuments with scaffolding and to control vegetation, followed by the consolidation of walls and vaults and the refilling of looter tunnels and trenches.

For the conservation of exposed interior cores of pyramidal structures that had lost their exterior retaining walls, the director of the Triangle Project, Oscar Quintana, and his chief conservator, Raul Noriega, both architects, developed a unique conservation method: the missing exterior retaining walls are re-created using tapia, mud walls of earth, with an interior structural enforcement made by a netting of lianas. With this technique, the exterior volume of buildings is regained, and the vertical walls of the structure are protected from erosion by small grasslike plants growing on the outside. This new system is extremely economical and ecological; it does not require cement or stone materials; it uses the fallen debris within the monumental precincts of Maya cities; and it has been tested successfully since 1998. With this system of mud-wall construction, many more structures of Maya sites can be addressed than would be the case using the procedures of the Tikal school—and at much lower cost, in far less time, and using a completely ecologically sound procedure.

But the most important change of attitude in conserving Maya sites in the Cultural Triangle program is the new way of viewing sites. A Maya city is considered not just a group of prominent buildings to be restored—mainly pyramids—but rather an intricate urban creation whose main feature, after investigation by archaeologists, can be rendered to the visitor by the control of vegetation according to a master plan. The intention is to visualize plazas and causeways and buildings and their connection with one other by a kind of landscape gardening. Even if most of the monuments remain earth mounds without restoration, the urbanistic scheme can be made visible by accentuating its traits through the control of vegetation. For the sake of creating an overall impression for visitors, it is helpful to build outlooks or viewpoints on elevated areas of the urban topography and to convey additional information using urbanistic models of the site and replicas of stelae in situ.

Such a global view requires a multidisciplinary team of experts, architects, archaeologists, civil engineers, forestry officials, tourist managers, and economists, united in drawing up a master plan for the entire region of Maya settlements that is to be made accessible for controlled tourism. The visitors are meant to experience it as the habitat of an ancient civilization, with its combination of archaeological sites and untouched rainforest with its flora and fauna—as a cultural landscape. The entire area will be declared a national park by the Guatemalan Congress. This includes the planning of access roads, itineraries, and visitor centers, and it requires the involvement of the adjacent communities: their inhabitants have to perceive benefits from the development of tourism. Such a master plan excludes excesses of reconstruction at ruins as well as the construction of luxury hotel installations and restaurant zones within the archaeological sites.

It is strange that the experts of financing agencies in particular, such as the Inter-American Development bank (IDB), still adhere tenaciously to obsolete details of reconstruction according to the old school of Tikal. We believe that times have changed, and they must bring about a change of thinking, not just in methods of conserving monuments, but also in the expectations and pretensions of tourism. A visitor coming to see Maya cities in the untouched tropical rainforest does not necessarily have to find an air-conditioned hotel with French cuisine; he or she will be just as happy in a well-designed and comfortable jungle lodge of a suitably light construction adapted to the tropical environment. For the tourist manager, that would suggest the planning of a high-quality touristic infrastructure in keeping with the natural surroundings and according to ecological principles, situated in the area but not at the archaeological sites.

There is no doubt that in the case of Maya sites, archaeology and tourism are closely related. They are not enemies; they are partners. Almost all archaeological investigation and conservation depends on funding with a view to future tourism. However, the traditional points of view of touristic management and site preservation remain the old-fashioned principles and their emphasis on reconstruction.

The problem is one of authenticity of historic monuments. Authenticity is lost through excessive reconstruction. If we, the well-intentioned but economically powerless archaeologists, could convince the top tourism managers and financing agencies that the authenticity of a historical monument in its tropical environment is in itself a profitable asset in terms of its future touristic use, we could perhaps save more original Maya cities from destruction by restoration. A Maya city represents a cultural resource of high commercial value, for its touristic potential. It is a unique historic monument and belongs to a species in danger of extinction. To kill such a rare bird would be economically unwise. Instead, its use ought to be sustainable and guided by principles of maintaining its authentic features, for the sake of golden eggs, of future touristic profits.

References

Bernal, Ignacio. 1980. *A History of Mexican Archaeology: The Vanished Civilizations of Middle America*. London: Thames and Hudson.

Tourism and Cultural Risk Management

Scott Cunliffe

Abstract: *This paper is a brief compilation of material given in response to papers presented in two sessions dealing with tourism, archaeology, and World Heritage Sites. Tourism is a key determinant of the future of archaeological sites worldwide. Risks at historic sites are assessed by the likely hazards that may have an impact on the site or artifact, the exposure of those elements at risk of damage or destruction, and the vulnerability of the resources to damage or destruction of all kinds. A planning and management tool, cultural resource risk management, is proposed to provide a working tool for a productive, effective, and viable partnership between archaeology and the tourism industry.*

The session titled "Archaeology and Tourism: A Viable Partnership?" was one of the few at the Fifth World Archaeological Congress dealing with the business of archaeology. Case studies and examples given in the session clearly underline the importance and value of collaboration, cooperation, and support between archaeologists and tourism professionals at historic sites. The ultimate endeavor for both parties is to conserve and protect these attractions from risk of damage of all kinds, particularly those risks arising from the hazards associated with tourism.[1] Risk management for cultural resources is proposed as a mutually beneficial working tool for systematically managing future risks and uncertainties at historic sites, especially those risks derived from the uncontrolled impacts of tourism.[2]

Risks at historic sites are described by the likely hazards (including the adverse affects of tourism) that will have an impact on the site or artifact, the exposure of those elements at risk of damage or destruction, and the vulnerability and resilience of the resources to damage or destruction of all kinds. Cultural risk management is then a planning and management tool defined as "a systematic approach to making decisions under conditions of uncertainty, and dealing with the total risks by anticipating possible opportunities and accidental losses, and designating and implementing procedures that minimize (1) the occurrence of loss and/or (2) the socio-cultural, economic, or environmental impact of the losses that do occur" (Cunliffe 2004).

Tourism at fragile archaeological sites is inevitably accompanied by both positive and negative impacts. It is hoped that by illustrating and advocating the use of this planning and management tool, there can be additional opportunities to build an increasingly viable partnership between tourism (businesses, policy makers, and tourists themselves) and archaeology (consultants, academics, policy makers, and the archaeological resources) to identify, assess, and manage natural and anthropogenic hazards that pose risks to archaeological resources.

The Past: Friend or Foe

Nelly Robles García from the Instituto Nacional de Antropología e Historia (INAH) in Mexico described an age-old conflict in Monte Albán, Oaxaca. After many years of constructive effort at this archaeological site, there has been a generally positive response from visitors to the upgrading of interpretation and maintenance and the improvement of visitor services. At the same time, there has been a lack of political will and capacity to counter the local corruption, to enforce laws of heritage protection, or to solve the deeper social problems of poverty and continued low levels of provision of basic quality-of-life needs for the local population.

In this case, the "friend" is the growing positive relationship between site and visitor, which is at the same time the "foe" for the locals as they see benefits accruing to a small number of individuals and businesses (not always local) while their overall standard of living has improved little. This is not uncommon to historic sites around the world, particularly in developing countries. One of the risks of economic development, in this case tourism development, is the marginalization of the local population. The local community is both vulnerable and exposed to outside influence, often welcoming development opportunities with the promise of benefits, without the capacity to forecast likely (negative) consequences to their social well-being and lifestyle. The hazards of tourism development are multifaceted: rapid development, lack of political will, greed and corruption, lack of legislative controls (or weak implementation of those laws), and the impact of the tourist.

While tourism is by nature a destructive industry, there is rarely deliberate malice on the part of tourists themselves. To the contrary, they are generally well intentioned and are often unaware of certain negative impacts they may be causing to sites and artifacts. A lack of adequate guidance provided on site to minimize tourists' impacts is often to blame. International conservation charters provide basic principles of cultural resource protection, but these documents need to be interpreted for site-specific use and application.

For example, the Charter of Athens for the Restoration of Historic Monuments (1931) included seven brief resolutions called "Carta del Restauro." In those first seven sentences, there was clear recognition of the need to agree on an internationally accepted means of protection of excavated sites, taking into consideration problems and mistakes of the past. This was a significant turning point for twentieth-century archaeology in terms of the need for protection. It did not, however, mention tourism as an agent of deterioration of ancient monuments. This was to come much later. Nevertheless, the Charter of Athens was the first international instrument recognizing the risks associated with poor planning and poor management at archaeological sites. As such, it can be seen as one of the first attempts at risk management for cultural sites and objects as it contains descriptions of vulnerability, exposure of the elements at risk, and the hazards—the circumstances which may cause harm—with the objective of mitigating damage and unwanted impacts of change.[3]

International charters covering cultural tourism have developed considerably in the past thirty years. The Charter of Cultural Tourism (ICOMOS, November 1976, Brussels) was revised over a period of twenty-two years until the eighth draft, titled "International Cultural Tourism Charter, Managing Tourism at Places of Heritage Significance," was accepted in October 1999 (8th Draft, for adoption by ICOMOS at the 12th General Assembly, Mexico, October 1999). At the same time, the profile of visitors to archaeological sites, their means of transportation, and their demands for access to sites have changed significantly.

Whereas before the 1950s adventure tourism often consisted of organized scientific and historical discovery expeditions, the jet (among other things) has provided the means for modern tourists to travel the globe to experience our great monuments of the past. As new areas are opened up and new archaeological resources are uncovered, it is the backpackers who are the most prolific adventure tourists, forging new frontiers of accessible sites. Changes in the practice and conventional wisdoms of archaeological investigation and conservation have also adapted to modern demands of tourism for increased access to sites, more information, and greater freedom to experience archaeology firsthand.

The work of the early-twentieth-century archaeologists in Central America, described by Wolfgang Wurster as "the old Tikal school," progressed from scientific exploration and investigation (excavation) to abandonment (rarely inclusive of conservation), followed by periods of monumental reconstruction. Chichen Itzá, Uxmal, and Palenque, for example, rely on the allure of archaeological resources to attract international tourists accompanied by their growing appetite for a learning experience, a sense of discovery, and, more recently, the need for adequate safety and security.

The changing demands of visitors for more information, more opportunities for discovery, more of everything that constitutes a quality experience, mean that the stories of conservation need to be told. Good design is good business for both archaeology and tourism. The story of archaeological conservation is a story worth telling, although one not frequently told. The presentation or interpretation of archaeological conservation links the protection of the resource (conservation) to its use, understanding, and business potential (how it is presented and interpreted to the general public). This direct link to tourism could and should be at the heart of the partnership between archaeological conservation and tourism.

The Future: Uncertain and Risky

The ancient cave in Altamira, Spain, provides a good example of a site and its managers responding to the need to ensure that future generations of visitors can explore, learn, and contribute to the conservation of the archaeological resource. The site faced the risk of grave destructive consequences from uncontrolled and excessive visitation; in 1973 the annual rate of 177,000 tourists was virtually destroying the fragile cave paintings at the site. The carbon dioxide in the breath of visitors was severely damaging the wall paintings. Adaptations to the site, starting in 1982, provided a creative range of visitor experiences that have taken the pressure off the in situ resource, ensuring its preservation. The bold new plan cut visitor numbers to 8,500 per year, reducing income significantly (the entire facility was closed for most of the period 1979–82). While the site was then protected adequately in 1982, it was not until 1992 that the museum project at Altamira dealt comprehensively with managing tourism at the site. Other environmental risks continued, however, from excessive traffic volumes and inadequate sewage and solid waste disposal. Potential disaster is always a strong motivation for policy change.

The significant risks of the future (Howell 1994) will derive from the direct and indirect impacts of tourism, not just in terms of physical damage, already obvious at many high-volume sites, but also in terms of the indirect impacts of tourism on social conditions, changing income patterns, societal values, social dislocation, and so on. Looting persists and is likely to persist, particularly where poverty exists in the world. Mention of future damaging elements would be incomplete without recognizing the destructive results of corruption. This can be one of the most damaging aspects or consequences of tourism development, not only in developing countries.

The *Heritage at Risk* publication from ICOMOS (Bumbaru, Burke, and Petzet 2000) provides an excellent summary of the threats facing various specific cultural sites around the world. The report is descriptive and not analytic. Risk management is not mentioned, and the types of responses to the threats identified are necessarily broad based. Tourism is described largely as a source of negative impacts: "Threats to archaeological heritage resources on the international level are perceived as deriving from three primary sources: cultural tourism, international development programs, and the degradation of the environment through natural process or by human-induced environmental change. Tourism now consti-

tutes six percent of world trade. Heritage, be it cultural or natural, is the major focus of much tourism. The shaping of archaeological resources to meet the demands of tourism has had a major impact which for the most part has been negative" (Bumbaru, Burke, and Petzet 2000).

The government of British Columbia in Canada takes a more positive overview of risk and the potential impacts of a variety of hazards. "An archaeological resource impact may be broadly defined as the net change between the integrity of an archaeological site with and without the proposed development. This change may be either beneficial or adverse" (Province of British Columbia 1996). Looking toward the future, there needs to be a balanced view of both the costs and benefits of any strategic planning. This is a prerequisite to successful cultural risk management.

Cultural Risk Management

Thorough and comprehensive forward planning and risk management can help to avoid or minimize loss and damage to archaeological resources. Catastrophic events at archaeological sites come most often from a lack of forward planning. To use an old but relevant maritime acronym, all catastrophes can be traced to poor execution of the Seven Ps of life: Proper Planning and Preparation Prevents Particularly Poor Performance (Cunliffe 1995b). Archaeological conservation planning should clearly plan for all identifiable future uncertainties and catastrophic events, natural and man-made. Cultural risk management is aimed at sustainable practices "minimizing losses, avoiding, sharing and mitigating risks of all kinds" (Bowden, Lane, and Martin 2001).

Risk management is not new to the world of heritage conservation. We are seeing this type of risk analysis more and more in an increasingly litigious world (*Economist* 2001) where public safety is becoming an increasingly high priority at cultural sites. The Australian National Parks planners, for example, are using a variety of risk management tools for forward planning of maintenance needs, damage repair, accessibility assessment, public liability needs, and especially health and safety needs analysis. Elements of risk management are inherent in the conservation process and have been for a long time. What has changed is the need to single out this planning tool, to identify the characteristics of the site where risks are present for the purpose of minimizing potential loss (damage to the heritage resource, financial loss, personal injury, loss of life or property), and to develop appropriate treatment strategies.

The following formula provides a simple way of illustrating the relationship between the main identifiable components of a total risk assessment:

$$Risk_{(Total)} = Vulnerability \times Exposure_{(Elements\ at\ risk)} \times Hazard \text{ (Granger 1998)}$$

Assigning a value to each identified risk can provide an objective means of setting priorities, identifying what is immediately urgent and what requires the utmost care, and establishing budget and conservation priorities. The objective of this model is not necessarily the quantification of risk in numeric terms but rather to provide a means of identifying risks in terms of both likelihood and consequences, resulting from the product of the three variables vulnerability, exposure, and hazard. Each individual risk identified in the model includes the necessary element of time, as each risk identified has a unique time (or period of time) and place of occurrence. The incidence of simultaneous multiple hazards, as is often the case at times of disaster or catastrophe, raises those cumulative risks to a higher priority for risk treatment.

A treatment strategy can then follow with four simple steps. A residual-risk evaluation should be made after the treatment has been implemented to monitor the effectiveness of the treatment (Cunliffe 1995a). A residual risk is simply what risks remain after a certain treatment (Beck 1992).

- Identify the risk priorities (use worse case scenarios if it is useful, measure priorities in terms of both likelihood and potential consequences).
- Conduct a first-cut assessment by assigning a value to the risks by identifying, with best available information:
  - i) all likely hazards, vulnerability or resilience to those hazards, and the level of exposure of those elements at risk to damage or decay;
  - ii) the probability of that event occurring; and
  - iii) the potential severity of that risk, or the severity of the potential consequences.
- Develop a treatment strategy for dealing with the risks with available resources of manpower, finances, and so on.
- Assess what risk remains (residual-risk assessment), monitor and evaluate the effectiveness of treatment strategies.

These basic steps are a good starting point to assign a measure or value to identified risks (Lupton 1999). The same need for adaptability and using basic principles exists with the application of conservation planning and management techniques—there is no one formula, but rather a box of tools with which to work. Risk management is one such tool.

Conclusion

The tourism industry recognizes that the conservation of cultural resources is critical to destination attraction and to the successful long-term viability of the industry as a whole. There have been some catastrophes along the way; however, recent events in the world have heightened awareness of the need for crisis management and risk management planning for all places where crowds gather, moving or stationary (Cunliffe 2002).

Tourism is a key determinant of the future of archaeological sites worldwide (Howell 1994). Social, cultural, and economic impacts must be compatible with the principal objective of long-term preservation. Other determinants include financial support, available expertise, safety and security of the site and visitors, accessibility, and political stability.

Risk management for cultural sites should be aimed at identifying future policy needs to guide site protection and to identify and plan for all possible future risks and uncertainties to avoid potential disasters, to protect the archaeological resources, and to maintain a sustainable tourism product. Such foresight will be a basic requirement of conservation and presentation of fragile archaeological resources in the future. Risk management and crisis management for cultural resources should become a working tool in the everyday conservation and presentation of archaeological resources. To prepare for the future, we need immediate action to identify and to manage risk and uncertainty; we owe it to our children to plan as comprehensively as we can for the future of our past.

Acknowledgments

I would like to acknowledge in particular four speakers in the sessions to which I am responding as they have provided the impetus and some detail for this paper: Pilar Fatás, Nelly Robles García, Wolfgang Wurster, and Willeke Wendrich. It would be remiss to not acknowledge the courage and foresight of the Getty Conservation Institute and the World Tourism Organization to facilitate the staging of this dialogue.

Notes

1   "Risk" is defined as the chance of something happening that will have an impact on objectives. It is measured in terms of consequences and likelihood (Standards Association of Australia 1999). As a product of vulnerability, exposure, and hazard, risks can be identified as having a unique time (or period of time) and place of occurrence.

"Hazard" is defined as a source of potential harm or a situation with the potential to cause loss. In cultural risk management, it is a situation or condition with potential for loss or harm to the historic resource, the community, or the environment (Cunliffe 2004). The impact of a hazard may be immediate (occurring at a unique time) or cumulative (occurring over a period of time) and will have an effect on a specific location.

2   "Risk management" refers to the culture, processes, and structures that are directed toward the effective management of potential opportunities and adverse effects (Standards Association of Australia 1999).

3   "Vulnerability" is defined as the susceptibility to loss, damage, or injury, and the capacity to cope with recovery from such losses from natural and anthropogenic hazards.

"Exposure" is the position of being exposed to potential harm or loss (physical, financial, or other), including the specific parts or elements that are exposed and therefore vulnerable (Cunliffe 2004).

References

Beck, U. 1992. *Risk Society: Towards a New Modernity.* London: Sage.

Bowden, A. R., M. R. Lane, and J. H. Martin. 2001. *Triple Bottom Line Risk Management.* New York: John Wiley.

Bumbaru, D., S. Burke, and M. Petzet, eds. 2000. *Heritage at Risk: ICOMOS World Report 2000 on Monuments and Sites in Danger.* Paris: K. G. Saur.

Charter of Athens. www.icomos.org/docs/athens_charter.html.

Cunliffe, S. 1995a. Monitoring and evaluation as practical management tools. *ICOMOS Momentum* 4(3).

———. 1995b. *Protection through Site Management.* Hue, Vietnam: UNESCO Principal Office for Asia and the Pacific.

———. 2002. Forecasting risks in the tourism industry using the Delphi technique. *Tourism* 50(1):31–41.

———. 2004. Some risks are worth taking: Tourism risk management in tropical coastal areas. Thesis, James Cook University, Australia.

Government of the Province of British Columbia. 1997. "Archaeological Impact Assessment Process." Archaeology Branch Operational Procedures. Ministry of Sustainable Resource Management, Archaeology and Forests Branch, Ministry of Sustainable Resource Management, Vancouver.

Granger, K. 1998. Geohazards risk and the community. In *Disaster Management: Crisis and Opportunity: Hazard Management and Disaster Preparedness in Australasia and the Pacific Region,* vol. 1, ed. D. King and L. Berry, 140–48. Centre for Disaster Studies. Cairns, Australia: James Cook University.

Howell, B. J. 1994. Weighing the risks and rewards of involvement in cultural conservation and heritage tourism. *Human Organization: Journal of the Society for Applied Anthropology* 53:150–59.

Lupton, D., ed. 1999. *Risk and Sociocultural Theory.* Cambridge: Cambridge University Press.

Standards Association of Australia. 1999. *AS/NZS 4360: Risk Management.* Strathfield, NSW: Standards Association of Australia.

PART SEVEN

Challenges in Conserving Archaeological Collections

Introduction

Jerry Podany

Archaeological excavation is often compared to peeling an onion, since the progress of both activities is measured layer by distinct layer. But there is at least one significant difference that is relevant to the long-term responsibilities of those who dig the earth and penetrate the oceans for knowledge of the past. An onion is reduced in size and complexity as it is peeled, whereas an archeological site expands as the layers are progressively exposed. As the site is fully brought to light and recorded and as to some degree the context of each feature is both revealed and destroyed, the site and the volume of material finds become larger. The cumulative knowledge gained, new questions that surface, challenges that must be faced, and of course the responsibilities for its organization and care also expand in volume, depth, and complexity. This expansion includes the collections gathered and the records created. These are crucial resources for the future, since they serve as primary sources for understanding the past as well as the processes that were undertaken to expose it. Future interpretation depends on the survival of the material artifacts as records that will be reread. But this cannot happen if the text has been erased.

It has been argued that what gives relevance to an artifact is the context in which it is found; primarily this is seen to be "the site." But what gives the site context? What provides the crucial evidence that enables us to determine what the site was, what happened there, who might have occupied it, and, of course, when? To a degree it is the artifacts that provide context to the site; hence their survival is crucial to a full understanding of it.

Archaeologists are increasingly called into partnerships to meet the obligation of providing long-term care for these heritage resources. And as archaeologists work in tandem with preservation professionals, they support broader use of the archaeological record by a larger and more diverse audience. In this session four speakers were asked to consider the challenges faced in the conservation and preservation of archaeological collections. The word *collections* is being defined in the broadest manner possible, but clearly it is concerned directly with the material finds removed from the site and the records and archives created in the process of excavation. This is not meant to enhance the now out-of-date and increasingly tenuous divisions between movable and immovable but rather to bring attention to archaeological collections at a time when they are suffering neglect, even as concepts of site management are gaining ground.

The burden, if one can properly call it that, is large—and growing with each trench that is opened. Like some magical well, there seems to be an endless flow from the ground. We keep pumping but have made little progress in our methods of adequate storage, productive distribution, and full use of what has been recovered. All around the world one can find masses of excavated material in bags, boxes, and crates. The quantities in some instances become so large that they are described only by the weight of each container holding them. The material sits in conditions that encourage corrosion, degradation, and decay. Finds are often said to be "warehoused," a word less than conducive to the idea of repeated and valued access. One is left to wonder if the local, state, or national regulations were the only motivation for the artifact's retention and how, given such neglect, we could have become so short-sighted. And how, in light of the way collections are neglected, we could fail to recognize archaeology as an activity not of any given moment, or even of a series of defined seasons, but as an ongoing process, a never-ending search for knowledge through discovery, interpretation, and rediscovery. While we may have accepted, or perhaps gotten used to, the fact that destruction is the price we pay for knowledge through excavation, it must be asked if we have done all we should to examine the price tag, to make sure that we are getting the best deal. Have we done all we can to lower the cost, to minimize the destruction?

The situation is the more critical given the incalculable value of archaeological collections. They form, as Terry Childs tells us, a "new frontier" for the archaeological research of the twenty-first century and beyond. It would be pure hubris to assume that only one interpretation of these finds is sufficient, or even correct. And it is inexcusable not to recognize that some percentage of these finds have enduring value for future scholars who will apply new knowledge and analytic tools to reconsider or expand previous conclusions.

Childs presents a number of plausible recommendations that will, if adopted, advance the cause of preservation and assure the long-term survival of archaeological resources. The call going out to archaeologists is to take a more proactive role in the promotion and care of existing collections. They are asked to be more vigilant in their recognition and support of the *full* value of the material they have brought to light. Kirstin Huld Sigurðardóttir reminds us, however, that what is not realized, what is not taught, cannot be valued. She sees the solution in education and the transfer of preservation concepts and conservation methodologies at every stage of the archaeologist's training. At present such opportunities are rare in the academic world, and this must change.

Hande Kökten also emphasizes full and proper training, as well as ongoing support, for professional conservators rather than the disastrous "recipe book" approach undertaken by those who, although well meaning, are less than fully and professionally trained. But Kökten also rightly points out that it is not just a matter of academic opportunity, already rare enough, or the number of training programs for professional conservators, equally rare internationally. It is also a matter of support from national authorities and a more complete understanding of the nature of the conservation profession by those authorities and allied professions. This is particularly true with regard to the conservation of more neglected "movable" finds. Even when educational programs are in place, Kökten reminds us, the lack of legislative recognition of the conservation profession and insufficient budgetary support can dramatically stifle the preservation of heritage resources.

Kökten agrees with Childs and Huld Sigurðardóttir about the need to educate archaeologists but points to the need for further education of conservation professionals as well. This new generation of field conservator, working hand in hand with informed archaeologists who themselves can make significant contributions to the effective stabilization of finds on site, will provide more in-depth knowledge of longer-term and more complex treatments. Such a team will be far more effective at establishing fully appropriate storage conditions and use guidelines. One would also hope that opportunities for conservators to work directly with archaeologists before as well as during excavations will increase, as will the commitment to conservation facilities and funding for collections stabilization beyond the excavation season's time frame. It is only through such support that the resources already unearthed will find their full potential and serve a broader set of functions.

Archaeological collections have an increasingly diverse set of functions—as research tool, educational resource, and gateway to cultural identity. The cultural values placed on objects, and the interaction with those objects, by groups whose ancestry lays specific ownership claims, is continually being redefined and expanded. Jessica Johnson, Bruce Bernstein, and James Pepper Henry have shown how collections at the National Museum of the American Indian invite reinterpretation not only by future archaeologists but also by the many whose cultural ties lay claim to significant (and significantly different) interpretations born of a cultural continuum. The unique preservation challenges they face in meeting the needs of all the new shareholders are impressive. Balancing these justifiable needs with the overall desire to retain the physical integrity and analytic worth of the objects can be difficult, but use of the collections in this way allows us to look outside of constructed academic boundaries and find new perspectives, new knowledge, and new answers.

Accessibility requires careful management planning if preservation needs are to be effectively met. An excellent and relatively recent example of proper curation and management planning, leading to a more accessible and hence more valued archaeological archive, is the London Archaeological Archive and Research Centre discussed by Hedley Swain. The archaeological records and finds held at the Centre are considered a crucial research and heritage asset that is put to use for both ongoing research and educational programming. As a result, the collections have what might be thought of as "self-generating value" and ongoing support as they become an integral part of cultural, scientific, and educational life.

In most instances reality presents our efforts with slim resources. It is through collaboration, creative thinking, and long-term commitment to bring the appropriate value and support to our archaeological collections that we can achieve our goal of preserving these resources. It is also through the proactive lobbying of those who provide funding and who write legislation that preservation and use are achieved together.

It is an honor for the American Institute for the Conservation of Historic and Artistic Works (AIC) to collaborate with the World Archaeological Congress and the Getty Conservation Institute to coordinate this session, "Challenges in Conserving Archaeological Collections." It is our hope that the discussions begun during the session and in this volume will encourage archaeologists and conservators from many countries to engage in the dialogues so critical to the preservation of archaeological materials and records. Among the AIC membership are conservators who specialize in the treatment and preservation of archaeological sites and finds. There are also those who focus on collections care and those trained to undertake preservation in archives. Their work to preserve such material for future study and enjoyment is guided by and reflected in the concerns presented by the speakers at this session. And their ongoing willingness to partner with archaeologists is embodied in the AIC's continual efforts at interdisciplinary outreach.

Archaeological Collections: Valuing and Managing an Emerging Frontier

S. Terry Childs

Abstract: *The artifacts, excavation records, photographs, laboratory notes, and increasing amounts of digital data are all that remain of an archaeological project and sometimes are the only existing record of a past culture. Instead of being highly valued, carefully cataloged, and properly stored for future research, interpretation, and heritage needs, many archaeological collections and associated records have not received the attention they deserve, especially by archaeologists. In fact, many collections around the world have never been washed or received preliminary analysis. Collections are often lost, or when their location is known, they are not properly preserved and stored. Nor are they readily accessible for use. This paper reviews the reasons for the poor state of archaeological collections in the United States to provide an example of the current situation in a country with a long history of archaeology, active cultural resources management programs, and good historic preservation laws. It then examines a few key issues that require more active involvement by archaeologists worldwide. Archaeological collections could be an emerging frontier for research, public education, and heritage use if individual archaeologists and the archaeological profession as a whole take more responsibility for the collections they create.*

Preservation and conservation—these two words are widely used among professional archaeologists but usually regarding archaeological sites, not the unique, permanent, and irreplaceable collections recovered from them. Once an archaeological site is excavated or destroyed by development or looting, collections of artifacts and the equally crucial associated documents become an irreplaceable record of the past. Without these, archaeologists cannot adequately conduct further research, interpret the past, or manage the resources in informed ways.

Archaeological collections, however, are in a state of crisis worldwide despite the recognition by some that they are the new frontier for research (de Grooth and Stoepker 1997:299; Mabulla 1996:209). There is inadequate space to store them, inadequate funds to conserve and protect them over the long term, poor training opportunities, and inadequate professional staff to ensure their care, accessibility, and use (see Kibunjia 1996; Mabulla 1996; Pearce 1990; Seeden 2000; Sullivan and Childs 2003).

The archaeological profession must take some degree of responsibility for this state of affairs. Archaeologists have learned to value their trowels and shovels more than the collections they create. They are outraged when objects are looted from sites but ignore the rampant loss of systematically collected objects and records in repositories. They have an ethical responsibility for the stewardship of their collections (Childs 2004), yet this tenet is only beginning to be actively discussed and supported (Barker 2003; Trimble and Marino 2003). Archaeologists must learn how the decisions made during project planning, budgeting, and fieldwork intimately relate to long-term collections care, accessibility, and use.

This paper begins with a brief summary of the current status of archaeological curation in the United States as a plausible example of global trends. It must be acknowledged, however, that many differences exist between countries based on how the archaeological discipline developed, including the influence of colonialism, who owns the movable objects of the past, and how heritage management legislation developed (Andah 1990; Ndoro and Pwiti 2000; Pearce 1990). The second section focuses on key responsibilities of archaeologists worldwide that affect the care and management of their collections. With improved professional education and responsibility, well-preserved and conserved collections may become more viable products of our profession.

Synopsis of the Current State of Collections Management in the United States

Beginning in the late 1960s, several federal laws were enacted that forever influenced the future of American archaeology. Archaeological investigation (often called compliance work) was now required when development occurred on federal lands. This meant that the resulting collections began to accumulate at a rapid pace. A few archaeologists became alarmed by this unanticipated growth (Marquardt 1977; Marquardt, Montet-White, and Scholtz 1982), and several studies were conducted in the 1970s and 1980s to examine the status of the existing collections (Ford 1977; GAO 1987; Lindsay, Williams-Dean, and Haas 1979). They found inadequate care and visible deterioration of existing collections because of lack of professional staff, funding deficiencies, insufficient storage space, and poor protection against theft, fire, and other disasters. The collections were inaccessible for use as a result of poor or nonexistent inventories or catalogs. They noted, too, that many archaeologists took inadequate responsibility for the collections they generated.

The need for professional policy and standards for the curation of archaeological collections was a key recommendation of these studies. In 1990 the federal regulations "Curation of Federally Owned and Administered Archaeological Collections" (36 CFR 79) were finally promulgated. They were an important step toward improved collection care, particularly by acknowledging that it involves real costs. The regulations also assign responsibility for funding collection care to the federal agency on whose land the collection was recovered. In coordination with the Archaeological Resources Protection Act of 1979 (ARPA), it is now expected that each project research design identify a repository where the collections will be curated and that the related costs be covered in the budget.

The Native American Graves Protection and Repatriation Act (NAGPRA) was also enacted in 1990 (McKeown, Murphy, and Schansberg 1998) and influenced some positive actions to achieve better archaeological collections management (Sullivan and Childs 2003). In particular, repositories that had to comply with NAGPRA were required to summarize their collections since most did not know what they held. Also, each federal agency had to determine what it owned and where its collections were located.

The long-standing underfunding by archaeologists who "forgot" to budget for archaeological collection management in their grant applications and government agencies that inadequately funded compliance work has had profound impacts on collections today. Many collections are seriously degrading and have inadequate professional staffing to improve conditions. Unfortunately, there are also limited funding sources for the upgrading of existing collections and the repositories that care for them.

Furthermore, the costs of archaeological curation have been rising since the promulgation of 36 CFR 79 because these regulations mandate standards for the long-term management of and access to collections. These standards cover the curatorial services that are to be provided and the environmental and security conditions of the repository. Many nonfederal institutions have adopted these standards and incurred significant costs to do so. As a result, more and more repositories charge fees for curating collections they do not own (Childs and Kinsey 2003), which increases the cost of archaeological projects. Increasing costs also are leading to more compliance projects, particularly surveys, that do not collect artifacts. This, in turn, may skew the archaeological record for future researchers.

Moreover, the lack of storage space for existing and incoming collections has caused a number of U.S. repositories to close their doors to new collections. With the current decrease in state and federal budgets, state museums and state university museums are becoming targets for serious reduction of basic functions and staff. Since many of these museums and repositories care for federal and state collections and provide excellent public education through exhibits, the collections that U.S. taxpayers support and visit are in jeopardy.

Fortunately, some positive things have happened in recent years. First, many states, tribes, and local governments have instituted policies for the care of archaeological collections, including funding responsibilities. Federal entities, such as the U.S. Army Corps of Engineers Mandatory Center of Expertise in Archaeological Curation and Collections Management, have been established. The Army Corps of Engineers center helps to assess and rehabilitate existing collections and identify, upgrade, and support repositories that meet the standards in 36 CFR 79, among many other things (Marino 2004; Trimble and Meyers 1991). Several federal agencies have pooled their resources to build and support regional repositories, such as the Anasazi Heritage Center in Colorado, that excel in both collection care and public education. Here, and at other repositories across the United States, curated materials are being brought to the attention of local people, including schoolchildren, Native Americans, and retired persons.

Managing Archaeological Collections: Some Critical Responsibilities

Archaeologists must take more responsibility for the collections they generate as more graduate students use these collections for research (Nelson and Shears 1996) and culture groups increasingly care about and value the preservation of and access to the materials of their past (see Ardouin 1997; Neller 2004). In the United States the public is demanding to know how their taxes are being spent on archaeology. This need for responsibility is especially poignant in the context of overcrowded repositories and inadequate long-term funding to support and professionally staff repositories worldwide. At a minimum, archaeologists must be stewards of the collections they create by designing, budgeting, and implementing field projects with the collections in mind. But first there is the issue of how to promote the value of collections for research, public outreach and interpretation, and heritage purposes. Both the profession as a whole and individual archaeologists must take active roles.

Valuing Archaeological Collections

Little effort has been expended on encouraging the archaeological profession to value its collections as much as the sites from which they are derived. If existing collections are not valued as a whole, they are not regularly accessed and used to advance archaeological theory and method. When collections are ignored, they often degrade. This downward spiral largely stems from woefully inadequate training in archaeological collections management and conservation for upcoming archaeologists and little attempt to value and use collections in coursework (Childs and Corcoran 2000; Longford 2004; Sullivan and Childs 2003). Also, there are very few reports on best practices for dealing with collections management and care to aid in the education process. Although the International Council of Museums and other organizations valiantly assist in educating professionals about curation and conservation worldwide, they simply cannot meet all the needs.

As a result, there is little professional impetus for accountability and for long-term interest in the research collections created largely by academics. In general, university-based archaeologists have not learned to deal with the long-term management of the collections they create when

they work anywhere in the world. They often split up collections by taking some or all from the location of origin for further study (Asombang 2000:26; Fatunsin 1997:70). When a collection is left fully or partially intact in the place of origin, the associated documentation rarely accompanies the objects to make them usable for future research. Few or no funds are budgeted for the next critical steps: cataloging, conservation, labeling, packing, and storage.

To alleviate these problems, the profession should

- encourage every graduate program to require a course on the management of collections from project planning through fieldwork and analysis to the repository;
- encourage research on existing collections, including thesis and dissertation work, and give out annual awards for the best research conducted;
- advocate for the need to rehabilitate and rehouse existing collections in order to increase their usability for research, education, and heritage activities;
- encourage use of the Internet to provide summaries of collections, object catalogs, and images of objects and documents for potential users (this is happening, although slowly because of the related costs and expertise required);
- promote the development of guidelines and best practices on such issues as budgeting for curation, the management of associated records, and field collection practices.

Individual archaeologists should promote the value and use of collections by

- teaching these issues at the undergraduate and graduate levels, including the need to maintain long-term value through proper conservation treatments;
- using collections in teaching, interpretive activities, and personal research (graduate research projects that use collections help students to learn about discoveries that can be made [Barker 2004]);
- depositing in the repository a complete set of associated records created during project planning, fieldwork, lab work, and report writing, together with the recovered artifacts;
- identifying and working with a repository or archive to curate an archaeologist's professional papers, photographs, and data (Silverman and Parezo 1995).

Managing the Growth of Collections

A field archaeologist's primary concerns before going to the field are to plan a research design or scope of work and obtain funding support for the work, whether for compliance or research. Often, archaeologists are not aware that key components of a research design directly affect the resulting collections over the long term. Collections growth is affected in particular; it has not been managed by the archaeological profession worldwide. There is little understanding of the quantity and range of collection types that currently exist in the United States, for example, or the condition they are in for research, interpretation, and heritage uses. All indications are that basic collection-level inventories are lacking worldwide. This deficiency jeopardizes the development of appropriate policies and best practices to improve collections care, obtain adequate space for storage and use of collections, and determine how best to handle the current outcry to deaccession collections.

To better manage the growth of collections, the profession should

- advocate for the development of a survey instrument and database to collect basic information on existing collections across a nation. Data should minimally include associated time period(s), current condition, ownership, primary material types, and storage location. The profession should help to obtain funding for the survey and then maintain it by collecting data about new collections. The resulting database should be made available on the Internet for widespread use.
- develop a policy on deaccessioning, "the process used to remove permanently an object from a museum's collection" (Malaro 1985:138). There is a growing push to deaccession redundant objects and soil samples that occupy significant storage space in repositories, yet any action taken must be done responsibly to ensure future usability of what is curated (Childs 1999; Sonderman 2003).
- develop standards for field collecting to consider during project planning, including a collecting strategy and methods to sample redundant material types.
- encourage all funding organizations, whether governmental or nonprofit, to require that all applicants identify the repository where the resulting collection will be curated.

Individual archaeologists must help to manage collections growth by

- developing all research designs and scopes of work with the following in mind:
  - a collecting strategy based on the theoretical or compliance focus of the work, the phase of work (i.e., survey, testing, excavation), and, whenever possible, the long-term research plans for a region (Childs and Corcoran 2000; Sonderman 2004; Sullivan 1992).
  - when appropriate, a strategy to sample redundant and bulky object types, such as undecorated body sherds, fire-cracked rock, and shell, before they are accessioned in overcrowded, understaffed repositories (Sullivan and Childs 2003). Sampling requires careful typological sorting and analysis by a materials expert to determine appropriate sampling categories and sizes.
  - a formal curation agreement, which recognizes the obligations of the repository that will curate the objects and records of the collection owner, often represented by an archaeologist.
  - a project budget that covers the expenses of preparing the resulting collection for long-term curation, including appropriate containers, labels, cataloging, and conservation work, as well as any curation fees charged by the selected repository (Childs and Corcoran 2000; Sonderman 2004).
- identifying where all project collections are curated in project reports, articles, and books so that future researchers, educators, and heritage communities can find and use them.
- identifying the ownership of each collection created so that long-term responsibility for the collection is known. A collection is rarely owned by an individual archaeologist.

Understanding Curation Costs

Given the current need for funding support to help curb the archaeological collections crisis, it is crucial that archaeologists understand the costs involved in collections care. While fieldwork primarily involves onetime costs, except for some long-term artifact analysis, collections care involves costs "in perpetuity" (Woosley 1992). The many costs of curation revolve around five major items, which need to be shared by the archaeological and museum communities to ensure future access and use: (1) initial processing of new collections, including necessary conservation, cataloging, labeling, boxing and storing of the objects and records, and inventorying; (2) periodic inspection of existing collections and any necessary rehabilitation, conservation, and inventorying; (3) creation or upkeep of repository space and appropriate facilities; (4) hiring, training, and retaining of professional staff; and (5) education of the public who use the collections, which should involve input from local communities with heritage interests or that are located near the originating excavations.

Many repositories around the world are full to the brim, have little means to expand both in terms of space and staff, have little support to make improvements, and have poorly trained staff (Kibunjia 1996; Mabulla 1996). Although the above costs are recognized, there are few funding sources to meet the needs. By the late 1970s, U.S. repositories and museums began to implement some solutions to these problems. Repositories began to charge curation fees for various services on collections they could not own, such as those from federal or state land. Usually it is a "onetime only" fee per standard box size to process and curate new collections, and the amount varies depending on local differences in salaries, cost of materials, land and building costs, and utilities (Childs and Kinsey 2003). Many repositories also have collection submission requirements that state exactly how a collection must be prepared before deposition. These solutions are beginning to have a positive effect on the long-term sustainability of many repositories and might be viable options in other parts of the world.

To better manage the costs of caring for and managing archaeological collections, the individual archaeologist must budget for and handle the initial processing of the collections he or she creates. The archaeological profession must

- advocate for a clear understanding of collection ownership in each country, so that it is known which institutions, such as university museums or government agencies, are accountable and financially responsible for existing and new collections.
- advocate for granting processes that focus on upgrading repositories to meet existing national standards, rehabilitating existing collections, and inventorying current collections by time period, condition, ownership, and so on.
- advocate for a system to accredit repositories that meet national standards for managing archaeological collections. Accreditation, perhaps similar to the

program of the American Association of Museums in the United States, would enable agencies, contractors, and researchers to make better decisions about the long-term care of new collections and to budget for standardized services. It also would enhance the professional credibility and visibility of each accredited repository.
- assist in the development of partnerships between appropriate organizations in a country to build or expand repositories for mutual benefit.

Conclusion

There is much to do to preserve and protect archaeological resources. The job is so big that every archaeologist needs to be involved—whether on the front line in a cultural resources management company, teaching ethical responsibilities in the classroom and the field, or overseeing collections in a repository. All of these efforts are equally necessary, valuable, and require coordination. Most important, all professionals are responsible for leading by example so that new generations of archaeologists learn appropriate attitudes, values, and practices for the stewardship of both sites and collections. Archaeological collections and the associated documentation are a growing frontier for researchers, public educators, and heritage communities if their growth and costs are well managed.

References

Andah, B. W. 1990. The museum and related institutions and cultural resource management. In *Cultural Resource Management: An African Dimension.* Special issue, *West African Journal of Archaeology* 20:148–56.

Ardouin, C. D., ed. 1997. *Museums and Archaeology in West Africa.* Washington, D.C.: Smithsonian Institution Press.

Asombang, R. N. 2000. The future of Cameroon's past. In *Cultural Resource Management in Contemporary Society,* ed. F. P. McManamon and A. Hatton, 20–30. London: Routledge.

Barker, A. W. 2003. Archeological ethics: Museums and collections. In *Ethical Issues in Archaeology,* ed. L. Zimmerman, K. D. Vitelli, and J. Hollowell-Zimmer, 71–83. Walnut Creek, Calif.: Altamira Press.

——— 2004. Stewardship, collections integrity, and long-term research value. In *Our Collective Responsibility: The Ethics and Practice of Archaeological Collections Stewardship,* ed. S. T. Childs, 25–41. Washington, D.C.: Society of American Archaeology.

Childs, S. T. 1999. Contemplating the future: Deaccessioning federal archaeological collections. *Museum Anthropology* 23 (2):38–45.

————, ed. 2004. *Our Collective Responsibility: The Ethics and Practice of Archaeological Collections Stewardship.* Washington, D.C.: Society of American Archaeology.

Childs, S. T., and E. Corcoran. 2000. *Managing Archeological Collections: Technical Assistance.* Electronic document, www.cr.nps.gov/aad/collections/. Accessed 1 March 2004.

Childs, S. T., and K. Kinsey. 2003. Costs of curating archeological collections: A study of repository fees in 2002 and 1997/98. *Studies in Archeology and Ethnography 1.* Washington, D.C.: Archeology and Ethnography Program, National Park Service. Electronic document, www.cr.nps.gov/aad/tools/feesstud.htm. Accessed 1 March 2004.

de Grooth, M. E., and H. Stoepker. 1997. Archaeological finds in depots and museums: The end of the line or the beginning? In *Archaeological Heritage Management in the Netherlands,* ed. W. J. H. Willems, H. Kars, and D. P. Hallewas, 296–315. Amersfoort: Van Gorcum.

Fatunsin, A. K. 1997. The case of Jos Museum. In *Museums and Archaeology in West Africa,* ed. C. D. Ardouin, 68–76. Washington, D.C.: Smithsonian Institution Press.

Ford, R. I. 1977. *Systematic Research Collections in Anthropology: An Irreplaceable National Resource.* Cambridge, Mass.: Peabody Museum, Harvard University for the Council for Museum Anthropology.

General Accounting Office (GAO). 1987. *Problems Protecting and Preserving Federal Archeological Resources.* Washington, D.C.: General Accounting Office, RCED-88-3.

Kibunjia, M 1996. The status of archaeological collections and resources in Africa. In *Aspects of African Archaeology: Papers from the 10th Congress of the Pan-African Association for Prehistory and Related Studies,* ed. G. Pwiti and R. Soper, 783–86. Harare: University of Zimbabwe Publications.

Lindsay, A. J., G. Williams-Dean, and J. Haas. 1979. *The Curation and Management of Archaeological Collections: A Pilot Study.* Publication PB-296. Springfield, Va.: National Technical Information Service.

Longford, N. 2004. Cutting through the dirt: Training archaeologists to identify their roles in the preservation and conservation of archaeological materials. In *Our Collective Responsibility: The Ethics and Practice of Archaeological Collections Stewardship,* ed. S. T. Childs, 149–68. Washington, D.C.: Society of American Archaeology.

Mabulla, A. 1996. Tanzania's endangered heritage: A call for a protection program. *African Archaeological Review* 13 (3):197–214.

Malaro, M. C. 1985. *A Legal Primer on Managing Museum Collections.* Washington, D.C.: Smithsonian Institution Press.

Marino, E. 2004. Back from the brink—Renewing research potential. In *Our Collective Responsibility: The Ethics and Practice of Archaeological Collections Stewardship,* ed. S. T. Childs, 43–51. Washington, D.C.: Society of American Archaeology.

Marquardt, W. 1977. *Regional Centers in Archaeology: Prospects and Problems.* Research Series No. 14. Columbia: Missouri Archaeological Society.

Marquardt, W., A. Montet-White, and S. C. Scholtz. 1982. Resolving the crisis in archaeological collections curation. *American Antiquity* 47 (2):409–18.

McKeown, C. T., A. Murphy, and J. Schansberg. 1998. Complying with NAGPRA. In *The New Museum Registration Methods,* ed. R. A. Buck and J. A. Gilmore, 311–19. Washington, D.C.: American Association of Museums.

Ndoro, W. and G. Pwiti. 2000. Heritage management in southern Africa: Local, national and international discourse. *Public Archaeology* 2:21–34.

Neller, A. J. 2004. The future is in the past: Native American issues in archaeological collections care and management. In *Our Collective Responsibility: The Ethics and Practice of Archaeological Collections Stewardship,* ed. S. T. Childs, 125–35. Washington, D.C.: Society of American Archaeology.

Nelson, M. C., and B. Shears. 1996. From the field to the files: Curation and the future of academic archeology. *Common Ground* 1 (2):35–37.

Pearce, S. M. 1990. *Archaeological Curatorship.* Washington, D.C.: Smithsonian Institution Press.

Seeden, H. 2000. Lebanon's archaeological heritage on trial in Beirut: What future for Beirut's past? In *Cultural Resource Management in Contemporary Society,* ed. F. P. McManamon and A. Hatton, 168–87. London: Routledge.

Silverman, S., and N. J. Parezo. 1995. *Preserving the Anthropological Record.* 2d ed. New York: Wenner-Gren Foundation for Anthropological Research.

Sonderman, R. C. 2003. Deaccessioning: The archaeologist's conundrum. *SAA Archaeological Record* 3 (4):8–9.

————. 2004. Before you start that project, do you know what to do with the collection? In *Our Collective Responsibility: The Ethics and Practice of Archaeological Collections Stewardship,* ed. S. T. Childs, 107–20. Washington, D.C.: Society of American Archaeology.

Sullivan, L. P. 1992. *Managing Archaeological Resources from the Museum Perspective.* Technical Brief No. 13. Washington, D.C.: Archeological Assistance Division, National Park Service.

Sullivan, L. P., and S. T. Childs. 2003. *Curating Archaeological Collections: From the Field to the Repository.* Walnut Creek, Calif.: Altamira Press.

Trimble, M. K., and E. A. Marino. 2003. Archaeological curation: An ethical imperative for the 21st century. In *Ethical Issues in Archaeology,* ed. L. Zimmerman, K. D. Vitelli, and J. Hollowell-Zimmer, 99–112. Walnut Creek, Calif.: Altamira Press.

Trimble, M. K., and T. B. Meyers. 1991. *Saving the Past from the Future: Archaeological Curation in the St. Louis District.* St. Louis: U.S. Army Corps of Engineers, St. Louis District.

Woosley, A. 1992. Future directions: Management of the archaeological data base. In *Quandaries and Quests: Visions of Archaeology's Future,* ed. L. Wandsnider, 147–59. Occasional Paper No. 20. Carbondale: Center for Archaeological Investigations, Southern Illinois University.

Archaeological Archives in Britain and the Development of the London Archaeological Archive and Research Centre

Hedley Swain

Abstract: Although the importance of records, finds, and archives from archaeological excavations is continually stressed in the literature, it is the norm in Britain and Europe for them to be underresourced, undervalued, and underused. The Museum of London, through the creation of the London Archaeological Archive and Research Centre (LAARC), is attempting to redefine the value of archives not just by emphasizing the importance of proper curation but also by linking it to access and research. The LAARC is already being used as a model of good practice in Europe and, we hope, will lead to a new approach to archaeology that places archives in a more holistic approach to the discipline.

As long ago as 1904 archaeologists in Britain were expressing concern about the ability of museums to store and curate the material from archaeological excavations. In that year Flinders Petrie (1904:134) suggested the provision of a national repository: "A square mile of land, within an hours journey from London, should be secured; and built over with uniform plain brickwork and cement galleries at a rate of 20,000 square feet a year, so providing 8 miles of galleries 50 feet wide in a century, with room yet for several centuries of expansion space."

Three elements of this description are worth noting: "within an hours journey from London" suggests the need for rapid access; "20,000 square feet a year" suggests a large mass of material; and "several centuries of expansion space" suggests that the rate of deposition will be continuous. These observations remain true for British and indeed European archaeology today. There is a lot of it, it keeps coming, and we believe that we should provide ready access to it.

Archaeological archives (the term normally used in England for the collective records and finds and associated reports and data from an excavation) should represent a prime research and heritage asset; yet they have been underresourced and underused. For many years British museums have struggled to find the resources to properly store archives, never mind maximize their research and educational value. This situation has been made worse by the organization of archaeology in Britain today whereby the practitioners are primarily commercial organizations whose peripatetic activities are quite separate from the museums that are expected to curate archives (see, e.g., Merriman and Swain 1999).

In London in the past thirty years this situation has become acute. The unprecedented level of excavation in the historic urban core has resulted in the largest body of archaeological records and finds of its kind. This is an immense research resource, making London one of the best-understood historical cities in Europe (Museum of London Archaeology Service 2000). However, it has brought with it huge logistical problems for the Museum of London, which takes and cares for the archives from excavations.

The London Archive and Research Centre

In the last few years the Museum of London has attempted to embrace the need for an easily accessible and sustainable home for the material from previous London excavations. Since its foundation in 1976 the Museum of London has acted as the home for archaeology in the capital (Ross and Swain 2001; Sheppard 1991). The museum's field units, in their different incarnations, have carried out the vast majority of excavations in Greater London. The museum's main galleries tell London's story from prehistory to the twentieth century and draw heavily on archaeology, as have some of its recent temporary exhibitions such as *London Bodies* (Werner 1998),

FIGURE 1 The *London Bodies* exhibition, which used human skeletons from the archive. Courtesy of Museum of London

which used human skeletons to demonstrate how the appearance of Londoners has changed through the ages (fig. 1), and *High Street Londinium* (Hall and Swain 2000a), which focused on how excavations had helped to reconstruct the appearance of Roman Londinium. Behind the scenes the museum also cares for the archives from excavations in Greater London. It has long been realized that this material offers both great challenges in terms of its sheer quantity and an incredible untapped resource for research. In creating the London Archaeological Archive and Research Centre (LAARC) the museum has tried to meet these challenges.

The LAARC was opened in February 2002; it is housed in the museum's Mortimer Wheeler House resource center, about two miles from the main museum building and its galleries. It shares the building with the offices of the museum's archaeology service and much of the museum's social and working history collections. A grant from the Heritage Lottery Fund (the U.K.'s national lottery) provided about 50 percent of the funding. Other funds came from central government, the Getty Grant Program, and many other organizations, archaeological societies, and individuals. Two new large storage areas have been created, as well as a visitor center and two

FIGURE 2 The interior of the LAARC. Only the proper curation of the vast resource of material from London excavations will unlock its research potential. Courtesy of Museum of London

study rooms (fig. 2). State-of-the-art roller storage has been installed, and computerized index and access systems (the latter available on the Internet) have been developed. The LAARC project, which included building and equipping the new spaces, designing the computer systems, and undertaking a minimum standards program on the archive, cost about £2.5 million. Funds for the six-person team that manages the LAARC are found from the museum's recurrent costs.

The core staff for the LAARC is adequate for day-to-day management and curation. Extra project funds are sought to undertake specific enhancement and research projects. These currently include a major project funded by the Wellcome Trust to produce an online database of the human skeletons held in the archive.

The London archive is by far the largest in Britain. It currently contains about 150,000 individual boxes of finds stored on 10,000 meters of shelving and includes finds and records from about 5,200 individual excavations from Greater London. And, of course, these figures are growing every year. Therefore, about twenty years' expansion space has been built into the plans. This will be achieved partly through current spare space but also by the rationalization of existing material. For example, a current program entails recording and then discarding some assemblages of mundane

and repetitive ceramic building materials from past excavations that would not have been retained under modern excavation methodologies.

The museum has set rigorous standards for the preparation of new archives resulting from excavations and expects the archives from all excavations in Greater London to be deposited in the LAARC. It has taken a while for the twenty or so archaeological contractors who regularly operate in London to become accustomed to this new, disciplined approach, but the will seems to be there, and material is now being deposited at an increased rate.

Meanwhile, the LAARC has also turned its attention to material that is already in its care. This material was generated over about one hundred years by many different archaeologists working for many different organizations. Currently, this material is not compatible and often not easily accessible. A huge effort is being made to bring all this material up to an acceptable level of care and accessibility, not only for its long-term well-being but also to encourage research.

Research has been spearheaded by the publication of a London archaeological research framework (McAdam et al. 2002) and a series of partnerships with London's archaeologists and universities. The international research potential of material held at the LAARC is also being recognized. The

FIGURE 3 A Roman School Box. Material deaccessioned from the archive is used in these boxes that are delivered to London schools. Courtesy of Museum of London

museum already has formal partnerships in place with La Trobe University in Melbourne to study eighteenth- and nineteenth-century assemblages and with Pennsylvania State University to study DNA from some of the skeletons held in the archive.

Another key part of the London archaeological community is its local societies; the museum is working with these groups to encourage research and use of the LAARC. Several societies were actively involved in the planning of the LAARC and donated funds for its creation. It is hoped that society projects either researching London's past or helping with collections management in the LAARC will allow local members to feel actively involved in London's archaeology—something that has been very difficult in the past ten years as more and

more archaeology has been funded commercially by developers. Under another initiative, the LAARC is hosting the Central London Young Archaeologists Club for children and teenagers.

The LAARC is not an alternative to the museum's galleries, and it is fully appreciated that archives may not be the best way to introduce the general public to archaeology. There are public weekend events at the LAARC, but its main value is as a foundation for other activities. The *London Bodies* exhibition would have been impossible without the museum's archive of human remains; other such projects will follow. The sorting and rationalization of material in the archive has also made possible the museum's Roman Boxes for Schools scheme, whereby unstratified material has been turned into teaching collections (Hall and Swain 2000b) (fig. 3). Such material was also used in *The Dig*, a re-created excavation using real artifacts, which was the museum's summer family event in 2001 (Martin 2002).

The LAARC's philosophy is simple, but it calls on the archaeological community to refocus its priorities. Over thirty years we have become expert at excavating and recording archaeological material in the face of threats from development. But we have been not sufficiently used the results of excavation to further public knowledge and appreciation of the past. A vast unrealized resource has slowly accumulated. By its proper curation, we are now ready to put it to a variety of uses, led by research. It is hoped that the LAARC will develop as a strong foundation for archaeological activity in London and a model for similar endeavors elsewhere.

The Wider Challenge

The challenges posed by the curation of archaeological archives are not restricted to London. A number of reports and surveys have highlighted the plight of archaeological archives throughout Britain (Swain 1998). Archaeological digging units have been slow to transfer archives to museums, and museums in their turn have struggled to find the space and resources to care for them to acceptable standards. There has also been a poor record of dialogue between museums and archaeologists.

The initial success of the LAARC hides underlying contradictions in British archaeology that undermine much of the philosophical basis for archaeology. As archaeologists we have long learned that excavation is destruction and that it is imperative therefore that we properly preserve and "archive" our records and finds and publish the results. Developing from the idea of archiving is the concept that the archive should be a valuable research tool, allowing archaeologists to "test" the conclusions made—in the same way that a scientific experiment is valid only if it can be repeated—but also allowing new research by comparing the results from more than one dig or studying a different aspect of the archive.

Experience has shown that professional archaeologists, and the archaeological community in general, have been reluctant to archive material and to use archives as a valid research resource—obviously, by so doing undermining the original premise for preservation in the first place. There is a tendency in the profession to fall back on the argument that material must be preserved because it is part of our heritage and is unique. This will not do. It is not justifiable to spend large amounts of money and resources preserving something just because it was dug up and is old. It must have a demonstrable value to society now and be valued as a resource for future research, display, and education.

In Britain much progress has been made in the past five years to recognize the poor state in which archives are being curated and the threats so posed to them. However, the profession still has some way to go in realizing that the material is of real value and to demonstrate this by using the archives, thus demonstrating the need for care. We hope that the LAARC can play an important part in this task by demonstrating how archives can be used once they are valued.

It is not enough simply to keep archives because they are a record of excavations. They must be put to use. Archives must be properly curated. If they are properly curated they can be used for research and as a foundation for other archaeological endeavors: display, education, management. It is only worth curating them if they are used in these ways.

References

Hall, J., and H. Swain. 2000a. *High Street Londinium*. London: Museum of London.

———. 2000b. Roman Boxes for London's Schools: An outreach service by the Museum of London. In *Archaeological Displays and the Public*, ed. P. M. McManus. London: Archetype Publications.

Martin, D. 2002. Great excavations. *Museum Practice* 7 (1):21–23.

McAdam, E., T. Nixon, H. Swain, and R. Tomber, eds. 2002. *A Research Framework for London Archaeology 2002*. London: Museum of London.

Merriman, N., and H. Swain. 1999. Archaeological archives: Serving the public interest? *European Journal of Archaeology* 2 (2):249–67.

Museum of London Archaeology Service. 2000. *The Archaeology of Greater London*. London: MoLAS.

Petrie, W. M. F. 1904. *Methods and Aims in Archaeology*. New York: Bloom.

Ross, C., and H. Swain. 2001. *Museum of London: 25 Years*. London: Museum of London.

Sheppard, F. 1991. *The Treasury of London's Past*. London: HMSO.

Swain, H. 1998. *A Survey of Archaeological Archives in England*. London: Museums & Galleries Commission.

Werner, A. 1998. *London Bodies*. London: Museum of London.

Working with Native Communities and the Collections of the National Museum of the American Indian: Theory and Practice

Jessica S. Johnson, Bruce Bernstein, and James Pepper Henry

Abstract: *The Smithsonian's National Museum of the American Indian (NMAI) takes the attitude that it is the steward, not the owner, of the collections entrusted to its care. This is codified in its mission statement. Therefore, a flexible approach is required to develop new methods that allow it to work collaboratively with NMAI's primary constituency, native peoples of the Western Hemisphere. This paper describes three areas (loans to native communities, conservation, and repatriation) in which the NMAI has been working to transform traditional museum practices to better support its mission.*

The National Museum of the American Indian (NMAI) Act instituted the museum in 1989 and mandated its three sister facilities: the George Gustav Heye Center (GGHC) in the U.S. Custom House in New York City, which opened in 1994; the Cultural Resources Center (CRC) in Suitland, Maryland, which opened in 1999; and the National Mall Museum in Washington, D.C., which opened in 2004. Collections are housed in the purpose-built CRC in Suitland, just southeast of Washington, D.C. The CRC provides state-of-the-art resources and facilities for the proper conservation, protection, handling, cataloging, research, study, and use of the museum's collections, library holdings, and photo and paper archives. The CRC also serves as a hub for the museum's community services, educational outreach, technology and Web development, and information resources. The Mall museum and the GGHC serve as the exhibit facilities and the public face of the museum.

George Gustav Heye, a wealthy New Yorker, assembled the original collections of NMAI in the early twentieth century. He started collecting in 1894, but it was not until 1922 that he opened his museum on 155th Street and Broadway in New York. Following a period of extraordinary growth in the 1920s, the museum fell on financial hard times, which were exacerbated by Heye's death and increasing operating costs. The years of inadequate funding began to be corrected in 1990, when the Heye Museum was absorbed by the Smithsonian Institution.

The collection currently numbers approximately 800,000 objects from across the Western Hemisphere and encompasses archaeological, ethnographic, contemporary, and historic objects and archives. Heye himself collected and purchased extant collections of ethnographic and ancestral objects, but he also relied on his curators and other hired collectors. The archaeological holdings include the important Hawikku collection made between 1917 and 1923 by the museum-sponsored Hendricks-Hodge expedition and the large, well-documented C. B. Moore collection from the southeastern United States. Many of the archaeological objects were not collected systematically, but among them are spectacular Mexican stone sculptures and Mixtec turquoise mosaics and gold ornaments. Field notes, photographs, films, and other records are housed in the museum's archives.

NMAI acknowledges native cultures as its living, first-person voice. NMAI takes the attitude that it is the steward of the collections, not the owner; and its mission is to affirm to native communities and the non-native public the cultural achievements of the indigenous peoples of the Western Hemisphere in collaboration with native cultures and to support the perpetuation of native culture and community.[1] The museum is actively working to develop procedures and policies that will preserve both the tangible and the intangible represented by the collections. Because of its mission, the uses of its archaeological collections are likely to be somewhat different from traditional archaeological repositories. Nonetheless, the collections of ancestral artifacts will no doubt also serve traditional archaeological uses such as research, as well as provide evidence of the history of the discipline. NMAI views the inclusion of native people in the recounting of and decision-making regarding their own ancestral past as a means to increase and broaden its understanding of native cultures.

NMAI acknowledges the diversity of cultures and the continuity of cultural knowledge among the indigenous peoples of the Western Hemisphere by incorporating their traditional methodologies for the handling, documentation, care, and presentation of collections. NMAI is actively striving to find new approaches to the study and representation of the history, materials, and cultures of native peoples. Its challenge is to transform traditional institutional practices to better support its mission. This paper presents three examples where the museum is working to transform typical museum practices in ways that directly support its mission: loans to native communities, conservation treatment, and repatriation.

Zuni Loan

An illustration of why and how the museum supports both the tangible and the intangible heritage in collaboration with native communities is a loan of objects to Zuni Pueblo. Zuni representatives selected two hundred pieces that were returned to Zuni Pueblo to be exhibited and used by the Zuni. In August 2001 the A:shiwi A:wan Museum and Heritage Center at Zuni Pueblo in northern New Mexico opened the exhibition *Hawikku: Listening to Our Ancestors.*

The objects were returned to Zuni Pueblo because they had been excavated from Hawikku, a Zuni ancestral village, by the Hendricks-Hodge expedition. These excavations recovered more than twenty thousand objects, which were taken to the museum facilities in New York. Though extensive restoration and cleaning was done to the objects, they were never exhibited, and detailed site reports and analysis were never completed.[2] This circumstance made the pueblo venue the first exhibition of the Hawikku collections since their excavation some eighty years earlier. The exhibition was not what the archaeological community had anticipated but rather the Zuni people's own recounting about their contact with Europeans. Their first contact was with the Spanish in 1542 at Hawikku, the site where the Spanish would build a mission church and at which the Zuni, on three occasions, attempted to remove the

foreign presence from their village. They finally succeeded in 1679 and 1680, with the Spanish abandonment of the mission and the Pueblo Revolt. But relations between the Zuni and outsiders were never simple, as evidenced by the Zuni allowing a new Catholic mission church to be built in the eighteenth century in the consolidated village of Holana.

Hawikku was not to be a final resting place for the Zuni people's ancestors; instead it became, in the excavations of 1917–22, the focus of research and removal of burials and funerary objects by Heye Foundation archaeologists. It was this history the Zuni people recounted in their 2001 exhibition.

The first group of objects, about fifty pots, was loaned to the museum at Zuni Pueblo as a "handling collection" that could be used by students, potters, and others in the community. The standard loan document was altered slightly to acknowledge the potential risks involved in handling. Zuni potters and cultural experts took the lead in the pueblo, providing direction for the handling of the pottery. A second group of objects, mostly bone, stone, basketry, wood, and other nonpottery materials, was sent out at a later date to be used in the 2001 exhibition. Throughout the loan preparation, NMAI staff sought to acknowledge the Zuni people's ascendant role as the best caretakers and interpreters of Zuni-made objects. To this end, Zuni representatives came to Washington, D.C., to direct the type and amount of conservation treatments for the objects to be returned to the village.

It should also be noted that the objects were received at the pueblo without the involvement of the museum or its staff. Rain fell the day the truck arrived; it was believed to be the blessing of the ancestors.

Since the original exhibition was mounted in 2001, the cultural center staff has modified and changed the exhibition several times. In addition, Zuni staff have continually sought advice from traditional Zuni knowledge bearers, recording their understanding and information about the objects for use in Zuni classrooms and tours. Clearly, on the return of the objects, the Zuni people have worked diligently to return the collection to a Zuni context. Although the people of Zuni Pueblo certainly understand the archaeological context of the collection (the pueblo has a successful and long-standing archaeological program), their success with the project derives from making Zuni interpretations more broadly known, without the usual overlay of academic interpretation. Zuni contexts thus take their place alongside other interpretations, increasing, diversifying, and improving understanding for all of us.

Conservation Consultations

The Zuni loan was an opportunity to expand the development of an approach to conservation treatment that is now becoming standard in the NMAI conservation laboratory. Like the museum as a whole, the conservation unit identifies its primary constituency as the native peoples of the Western Hemisphere whose communities hold the knowledge and expertise to properly determine how objects should be cared for and conserved. Conservation consultations are carried out directly with representatives of the community to identify appropriate treatments for the objects that will be used for exhibit (Johnson et al. 2004).

The practical aspects of these consultations are evolving. They have been done on an ad hoc basis for some time (Heald and Ash-Milby 1998). Preparation for the new Mall museum and support from the Andrew W. Mellon Foundation have given the museum the opportunity to develop a more standardized approach to the consultations and methodologies for documentation at the museum facility. To date, most consultations have been held at the CRC, but more recently they have also been carried out at or near the communities themselves.

This process has given the conservation staff the opportunity to evaluate many personal and professional assumptions about how and why treatments are carried out. With the guidance of curatorial and other staff, individuals have learned to be inclusive and to avoid taking the leading role in discussions. Conservators act as receivers of information; they are receptive to new and different approaches to the work. This shift in authority is essential for demonstrating the museum's commitment to the idea that the tribal consultants are the experts regarding the care of their cultural material. Often the consultants are elders, artists, and craftspeople or community or political leaders. The goal of this dialogue is to understand how the consultants want the objects to look when they are exhibited. Other consultations occur throughout the museum in all departments to guide many other NMAI programs.

Sometimes consultants ask the conservators to undertake treatments that the latter feel will cause damage in the long term. In addition, the conservators have been asked to make repairs that they do not have the skills to carry out. In such cases, the approach is to try to understand if the material proposed for cleaning or consolidating is really important or whether it is the appearance or the effect that matters. Alternative materials are suggested that may achieve the same effect. Continued discussion leads to solutions that are acceptable to all. When the conservators feel they do not have the skills to execute the level of restoration that is requested, consultants have been asked to carry out the treatment while conservators document what is done.

For the Zuni loan, two consultations with Zuni community representatives were held at the CRC. In this case, the consultants were potters and tribal governmental representatives. Topics included how and if the objects should be cleaned, appropriate ways to mount objects to protect them from physical damage during shipping and handling, appropriate means to exhibit the objects at the pueblo, previous restoration that had been done and whether removal or repair was needed, how to stabilize fragile surfaces, and ways to stabilize a burnt wooden column from the mission church so it could safely travel and be mounted upright.

A great deal of information was shared by the consultants among themselves; most of this discussion was privileged and not accessible to NMAI staff. Nonetheless, as decisions were made, they were relayed—in English—to NMAI staff. Some decisions were explained further and a cultural context was provided; others were taken by NMAI sui generis.

When the exhibition opened at the pueblo, the Zuni governor, Malcolm Bowekaty, reminded people, "We have waited over eighty years to bring back the pots. . . . [That] these pots are finally home, we consider a blessing, that our ancestors are coming to bless us." Jerome Zunie, a tribal archaeologist commented, "It's a good history that we have, . . . and it's a good thing these pieces return to Zuni."

Repatriation Policies

The NMAI Act, which legislated the formation and development of the physical structures of the museum, also established provisions for the Smithsonian Institution to implement and facilitate the repatriation of specific kinds of objects and materials to tribes in the United States. This act predates the Native American Graves and Repatriation Act (NAGPRA), which applies to other relevant institutions in the United States.

Through repatriation policies, NMAI is committed to the disposition, in accordance with the wishes of native peoples, of

- human remains of known individuals;
- human remains of individuals who can be identified by tribal or cultural affiliation with contemporary native American groups;

- funerary objects;
- objects of cultural patrimony;
- ceremonial and religious objects; and
- objects transferred to or acquired by the old Museum of the American Indian illegally or under circumstances that render invalid the museum's claim to them.

NMAI has voluntarily taken steps beyond the repatriation provisions of the NMAI Act, its subsequent 1996 amendment, and NAGPRA. As noted previously, the museum's mission embraces its special responsibility to protect, support, and enhance the development, maintenance, and perpetuation of native culture and communities throughout the Western Hemisphere. Where the provisions of NAGPRA are limited to federally recognized native governments, the NMAI has taken a broader approach to repatriation, acknowledging the spirit of the legislation and extending these provisions to all of its indigenous constituencies in North, Central, and South America. For example, NMAI repatriated objects to the Taino community of Caridad de los Indios in Cuba and to the Siksika First Nation in Canada.

Conclusion

Through repatriation consultations, exhibition collaborations, and other museum activities with native community members, museum staff members are made aware of general and specific cultural sensitivities associated with collections in the museum's possession. The museum understands it cannot foster trust and long-term collaborative relationships with its primary constituency if it does not recognize that these constituents have an inherent interest in the management, interpretation, and disposition of collections. Pursuit of understanding of the cultural contexts and perspectives of native community members leads to the concept that museum staff are the stewards of these collections and not the owners. With stewardship comes the responsibility and burden of managing collections in unconventional ways in accordance with the wishes and concerns of the affiliated native community.

This paper illustrates several ways staff who work directly with the archaeological collections are using the mission of NMAI to best serve its primary constituency. This is a constant struggle, which will evolve as the museum moves forward. Each project takes the museum closer to ways of developing policies and procedures that better support its mission.

There are a number of serious problems that are currently being addressed, such as pesticide contamination (e.g., arsenic, mercury, and para-dichlorobenzene) of the collections that are being repatriated (Johnson and Pepper Henry 2002) and the best means for the museum of record information gathered during consultations so that others in the institution who have not been present may also follow the wishes of the community. There is a lot yet to do. But with the help of native communities and individuals, the museum is finding its way.

Notes

1   NMAI Mission Statement: "The National Museum of the American Indian shall recognize and affirm to Native communities and the non-Native public the historical and contemporary culture and cultural achievements of the Natives of the Western Hemisphere by advancing—in consultation, collaboration, and cooperation with Natives—knowledge and understanding of Native cultures, including art, history, and language, and by recognizing the museum's special responsibility, through innovative public programming, research, and collections, to protect, support, and enhance the development, maintenance, and perpetuation of Native culture and community."

2   Frederick Hodge wrote several short papers (e.g., Hodge 1937), and Watson Smith, Richard Woodbury, and Nathalie Woodbury published *The Excavation of Hawikuh by Frederick Webb Hodge: Report of the Hendricks-Hodge Expedition, 1917–1923*, in 1966.

References

Heald, S., and K. E. Ash-Milby. 1998. Woven by the grandmothers: Twenty-four blankets travel to the Navajo Nation. *Journal of the American Institute for Conservation* 37:334–45.

Hodge, F. W. 1937. *History of Hawikuh New Mexico: One of the So-Called Cities of Cibola.* Los Angeles: Southwest Museum.

Johnson, J. S., S. Heald, K. McHugh, E. Brown, and M. Kaminitz. 2004. *Practical Aspects of Consultation with Communities.* AIC Object Specialty Group Postprints, vol. 9, Proceedings of the American Institute for Conservation Objects Specialty Group Session, June 2003.

Johnson, J. S., and J. Pepper Henry. 2002. Pesticides and repatriation at the National Museum of the American Indian. In *ICOM-CC 13th Triennial Meeting, 22–28 September 2002,* ed. R. Vontobel, 673–78. London: James and James.

Smith, W., R. B. Woodbury, and N. F. S. Woodbury. 1966. *The Excavation of Hawikuh by Frederick Webb Hodge: Report of the Hendricks-Hodge Expedition, 1917–1923.* New York: Museum of the American Indian/Heye Foundation.

Challenges in Conserving Archaeological Collections

Kristín Huld Sigurðardóttir

Abstract: *This paper offers a perspective different from that presented by Childs, who suggests that archaeologists are to blame for the inadequate storage of objects from archaeological sites and thus for their degradation. I suggest that there are other forces that are guiding the actions of archaeologists, such as archaeology programs offered by universities, which until recently have not been object oriented. I suggest further that there is inadequate training in how to treat objects from the time they are discovered until they are handed over to conservators or collections care managers. It is also necessary to take into account societal forces that influence which archaeology projects are undertaken and that therefore steer archaeologists toward fieldwork instead of objects studies.*

When viewed together, the papers by Childs, Swain, and Johnson, Bernstein, and Pepper Henry suggest that in spite of some universal problems such as inadequate storage areas and lack of funding, we are all influenced by our different cultural approaches to archaeology. What some perceive as the cause of a problem, others do not.

Childs maintains that it is primarily archaeologists who are responsible for the fact that archaeological remains are degrading in our storage facilities. Or as she states, "The archaeological profession does not value its collections as much as the sites from which the collections derive." Storage facilities would improve and some conservation work would be carried out if archaeologists and archaeology students were to show more interest in studying the objects instead of putting their emphasis on fieldwork. This is a harsh generalization that needs a response. In defense of archaeologists, I want to focus on two main points: the education offered in the

discipline of archaeology and some of the forces that affect archaeological research.

Education in the Discipline of Archaeology

There is tremendous variation in the archaeology programs offered at universities and colleges around the world. However, the trend during the past few decades has been to favor socially or theoretically oriented courses at the expense of object-based courses. In some countries, students must hold a degree in archaeology at both the undergraduate and graduate level to call themselves archaeologists. Other countries offer archaeology as part of a one-year postgraduate program for which students do not need any previous education in the subject. As a result, the knowledge and ability of archaeologists varies greatly. Although many have a good fundamental knowledge of objects, some have gone through programs that do not include object-based courses. As a result, they look for research material that matches their interests and knowledge.

Object studies are an essential part of archaeology programs; no student of archaeology should be able to graduate without taking courses dealing with objects, starting with basic programs at the undergraduate level and moving on to in-depth programs at the graduate level. These should focus not only on styles, typology, and dating but also on various analytic methods. Training students in elementary chemistry, materials science, and the use of basic instruments such as the microscope ought to be part of all programs from the undergraduate level onward.

The generalization that the archaeological profession does not value its collections is thus unrealistic from my point of view. The problem we are dealing with is not that archaeologists are not interested in the objects but that far too many lack the type of education and training needed to study the objects to any useful depth.

We must also take into consideration the archaeologists' professional environment, which itself might shift over time. Archaeologists may be working at an institution such as a museum where they are in proximity to an objects collection, at a university where the emphasis might be on theoretical studies, or in a freelance capacity so that they must compete for projects.

Forces That Affect Archaeological Research

The time has passed when archaeologists could decide without any restrictions what they wanted to excavate or research. There are many different forces affecting their work today. Two of these forces are addressed here: political and social.

Let me begin with a discussion of political forces. In most parts of the world, political decisions have both a direct and an indirect influence on the professional environment of the archaeologist, through antiquated legislation or various agreements and, more clearly, through funding. In some countries, the funds available for archaeological research are established by the state and thus are subject to political decisions. Although politicians have advisory groups of specialists who have some say about what to support, those groups are working along lines set by the politicians. The majority of projects that have been favored in recent years are those aimed at the information society and public awareness, which promote the uniqueness of local sites in various countries. Object studies are simply not a priority at present, and good storage areas are not considered important by most people. To effect change in the kinds of projects that receive financial support, archaeologists and conservators need to talk to their politicians and emphasize the objectives of those types of projects.

The problems caused by the complicated and weak, outdated legislation in both the United States and Britain have been discussed in this conference. In the United States, legislation varies from state to state. British archaeology is currently run on a free-market basis; in a way, it is controlled by property developers, as there is minimal legislative control and weak powers of enforcement.

By comparison, all five Scandinavian countries have relatively strong heritage legislation and strong powers of enforcement. The acts vary somewhat among the countries, but there are common trends in legislation, the most important one being that all excavated objects are the property of the nation and there is a central authority that takes all major decisions regarding the objects and the sites. This authority decides in which museums the objects will be housed. Landowners do not own the objects found on their property, although they might get a reward for some finds such as gold or silver. In all five countries, there are strict regulations regarding excavation permits. In most of them, excavation authorization is limited to museums or universities connected to museums; however, this is not the case in Iceland and Sweden, where privately owned firms are in charge of archaeological excavations. But all excavators have to work according to regulations set by the central authorities. In Iceland, archaeologists have to finish all their work within a fixed time. All their archaeological archives, whether objects, original drawings, field notes, photographs, or diaries, must be handed over to the central agency within a year after the excavation has finished, and the objects must have received conservation treatment. Therefore, a prerequisite for being granted an excavation permit is a signed statement from a conservator who will treat excavated objects. Conservation costs are thus included in the budget plan submitted with the application for an excavation permit.

The needs and demands of society are among the main forces that steer archaeological research. Whether because of local planning or construction projects, archaeologists must be prepared to undertake many different projects each year. They must be ready to come at short notice to excavate and record as thoroughly as possible the cultural layers in question, often being allowed only a relatively short period to undertake the work, frequently in bad conditions. They are required to record as much information as possible before a road is built or a power plant is erected. It is thus societal pressures that far too often dictate the type of research the archaeologist undertakes. In far too many countries, developers do not understand the need for comprehensive research after the fieldwork is completed. They pay for the excavation needed but less willingly for the research required as a consequence of the excavation work or for conservation of the objects. As a result, objects are left in inadequate storage, without being conserved or thoroughly studied.

The need to thoroughly record an archaeological find in order to use the information for various purposes is one of the social forces guiding the work of the archaeologist. This is the case in Iceland, where, according to the Planning and Building

Act, the prerequisite for agreeing to a local planning proposal is that the area has been surveyed and all the archaeological sites mapped and GPS coordinated.

In connection with preparing for this paper, I conducted a short survey to determine whether conservation of objects in the field and collections care were offered to archaeology students by universities in England and Scandinavia. Twenty-two universities were contacted in Scandinavia and Britain. The questions were simple: Was field conservation or collections care offered at either or both the undergraduate and the postgraduate level, and were the subjects offered as a whole unit, or as a part of a unit; and were either or both of these subjects offered as a diploma course? The results were as follows:

- Of the twenty-two universities, only four offered courses in collections care. Those were whole-unit courses at both the undergraduate and the postgraduate level, a part-unit course at the undergraduate level, and a diploma course (fig. 1).
- Eight universities offered some courses in field conservation of objects. In some cases, the same university offered some or all of the courses included in the survey. All eight universities included some teaching of field conservation in their undergraduate

program; only one offered a complete unit at the undergraduate level. Two of the universities offered field conservation as part of their postgraduate program, one as a whole unit and the other as part of a unit.

When extending the research a bit further to include eight universities from Australia and the United States, the result was even worse. Of the eight universities chosen, none offered courses in the above subjects.

Childs suggests in her paper that postgraduate students ought to be trained in collections care and field conservation. I would like to take her idea a little further and propose that field conservation of objects and the elements of preventive conservation be made obligatory subjects at the undergraduate level in all university archaeology programs, along with courses in object studies. Objects are among the main sources on which archaeologists base their interpretation of the sites. There is not much point in training students in good field techniques without teaching the proper handling and interpretation of objects. Imparting a thorough understanding of proper handling and of the various material groups from the very start of archaeology studies is essential to preserve the documentary value of the objects. It is thus not enough to offer postgraduate students courses in field conservation or

FIGURE 1 Courses offered in field conservation and collections care.

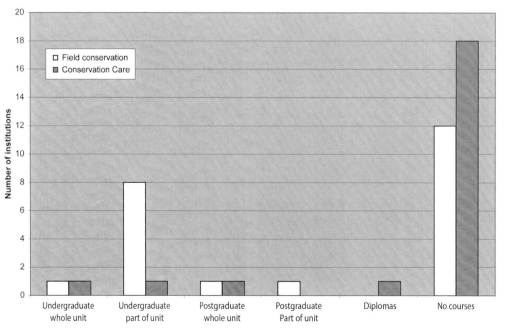

objects studies. How to handle objects, from the moment they are excavated until they are placed in an appropriate storage or display area, must be among the first subjects taught to the archaeology student.

It is therefore not the archaeologist who is to blame for the degradation of objects in storage but the professional who has the basic knowledge of the needs of the objects—that is, the conservator—who ought to be promoting the importance of the subject and working to get it included in the archaeology programs offered at universities and colleges worldwide. One cannot state, therefore, that the archaeological profession does not value its collections as much as the sites from which the collections derive. It is the political and social forces and requirements of the world we are living in that determine what kind of research is undertaken. The courses available in the various archaeological programs greatly influence the research interests and abilities of archaeologists. Conservators ought to promote the importance of object studies, as well as training to enhance field conservation, preventive conservation, and collections care, as a part of all archaeology programs at the university level.

Archaeological Conservation in Turkey

Hande Kökten

Abstract: This paper describes the development of archaeological conservation as a field of study in Turkey, with special reference to the preservation of movable cultural property. Documents from various institutions concerned with archaeology (conservation laboratories, museums, excavations, foreign archaeology institutes, etc.) indicate that conservation has previously been a secondary interest for archaeologists. This has affected the development of both conservation centers and training programs, to the detriment of archaeological sites and collections. However, with the progress that has been made in modern archaeology and the use of scientific research methods provided by other disciplines, archaeologists and museum professionals have come to recognize the necessity and importance of archaeological conservation, which has contributed to the development of current preservation policies in Turkey.

Research into the development of archaeological conservation in Turkey and attempts to collect relevant information from different excavations have proven difficult because conservation applications related to movable cultural property have not been properly recorded. At the same time, projects dealing with the restoration of monuments and other immovable cultural property (i.e., mosaics, wall paintings) have been considered part of the archaeological or architectural research and therefore have been included as references in publications. The information gained during the research for this paper is not sufficiently extensive or detailed to put forward a clear conclusion about the influence of early excavations and foreign archaeological institutions[1] on the development of conservation policy and practice in Turkey. Therefore, this paper describes the general evolution of conservation at

archaeological excavations in the context of archaeological fieldwork and archaeological museums, as well as conservation training programs, and legal issues. A comparison of the development of archaeology and archaeological conservation in Turkey indicates that these fields have not yet been equally embraced by the authorities, in part because of a lack of knowledge about the aims, principles, theory, and methodology of conservation as a field of study. Instead, it was (and in many cases still is) recognized as a "craft" that could be applied by talented and enthusiastic archaeology students, trainees, and museum staff. Therefore, the need for trained conservation professionals—conservators and conservation technicians—has not been yet clearly acknowledged by excavators, museum specialists, or bureaucrats responsible for the management of the archaeological heritage. This neglect has affected both the structure and the evolution of archaeological conservation in Turkey, and only recently has preservation been acknowledged as a scientific field.

During the early years of archaeological research in Turkey, the conservation of objects was limited to basic cleaning treatments and restoration work at excavation sites and in museum workshops, undertaken by a combined team of foreign and local professionals who were not necessarily trained in conservation. There were cases in which small objects were taken abroad for conservation purposes and returned to Turkey after the treatments were completed.[2]

The first attempts at conservation practice in Turkey were of a rather primitive and nonscientific nature, although they were no doubt motivated by goodwill. Begun in 1937, the first "conservation workshop," containing a chemical investigation laboratory, a sculpture workshop, and a fumigation chamber, was established in the İstanbul Archaeology Museum. From the early 1940s until the initiation of short-term training programs for the museum staff, attempts to protect art objects and archaeological finds were inconsistent and insufficient.[3] In 1968 the Ministry of Culture initiated a scientific approach to the preservation of cultural property by running training programs for the museum staff at the Museum of Anatolian Civilization, and courses on in situ preservation of wall paintings were organized by ICCROM at Göreme Valley (Cappadocia). Finally, in 1984, the Central Conservation-Restoration Laboratory in İstanbul was founded as a research unit to deal with the conservation problems of collections in state museums (İzmirligil 1995). However, because of insufficient financial resources and the limited number of trained conservators, this institution was gradually turned into a laboratory where conservators provided conservation treatment for hundreds of objects in poor condition from almost any museum in the country. Thus, although the Central Laboratory still has an important role and function in the preservation of archaeological collections, its scope and facilities are far from adequate to meet the needs of state museums.

Legal Issues

The first code of laws (Asar-ı Atika Nizamnamesi) concerning the care of Turkey's cultural heritage went into effect in 1869; its purpose was to issue excavation permits for foreign archaeologists and prevent illicit trafficking of antiquities (Umar 1981). This legislation was expanded and revised in subsequent years; the most important development was the establishment of the Higher Committee of Monuments in 1951 (Akozan 1977). This committee was responsible for determining principles that would guide the preservation of historic monuments and sites in Turkey, as well as guide the oversight and supervision of restoration projects. The current legislation governing the care of cultural property was enacted in 1983[4] and responds to the section concerning protective measures in the Recommendation Concerning the Protection, at National Level, of the Cultural and Natural Heritage by UNESCO, which states that "Member States should, as far as possible, take all necessary scientific, technical and administrative, legal and financial measures to ensure the protection of the cultural and natural heritage in their territories. Such measures should be determined in accordance with the legislation and organization of the State."[5] However, it contained very little specific

reference to the conservation and restoration of movable cultural property. The articles from the code of laws quoted below concern the archaeologist specifically and the conservator indirectly. They serve here to illustrate the problems of conservation policy in Turkey.

In Part I, Article 3.a, "conservation" is defined as "treatments of preservation, maintenance, repair, restoration, and functional modification of immovable cultural and natural property, as well as preservation, maintenance, repair, and restoration of movable cultural property." As for the "administration and supervision" of cultural property, Article 24.a states, "Movable cultural and natural property is state property and will be kept and preserved by the state in museums. According to the principles described in the legislation, the Ministry of Culture and Tourism may control the registration and maintenance of these properties." Article 26 continues, "The establishment and improvement of museums to preserve natural and cultural property that are within the scope of this legislation are among the obligations of the Ministry of Culture and Tourism."

Article 41 states, "At the end of each excavation campaign, all excavated movable cultural and natural property will be transferred to a state museum that is designated by the Ministry of Culture and Tourism." And finally, under the title "Preservation and Disposition of the Site," Article 45 states, "Excavation directors are responsible for the maintenance, repair and arrangement of the immovable cultural and natural property, as well as the maintenance and repair of the movable cultural property that is uncovered at the excavations." This article responds to the UNESCO recommendation on the preservation of archaeological remains: "The deed of concession should define the obligations of the excavator during and on completion of his work. The deed should, in particular, provide for guarding, maintenance and restoration of the site together with the conservation, during and on completion of his work, of objects and monuments uncovered. The deed should moreover indicate what help if any the excavator might expect from the conceding State in the discharge of his obligations should these prove too onerous."[6] However, because there are few conservation professionals, this obligation cannot be fulfilled in most Turkish excavations. At the present time, either a great number of archaeological finds are transferred to local museums without receiving conservation treatment, or they are treated by archaeologists who use basic recipes for certain problems without exploring the reasons for the initial deterioration processes.

Conservation at Archaeological Excavations

As stated in the Turkish legislation, excavation directors are responsible for the conservation and maintenance of archaeological finds, including the small objects and materials remaining at archaeological sites (architectural and decorative elements, trench sections, etc.). In many instances, the issue of preservation has been solved by archaeologists themselves, using practical methods that can be described as neither permanent nor scientific. This is in part the result of a scholarly negligence that originates from the habit of self-reliance: when archaeology was a young and developing field in Turkey, Turkish archaeologists, as well as many of their colleagues abroad, had to be content with the knowledge and circumstances of their time. In many cases this meant being both creative and pragmatic, since conservation practice was not yet fully in the service of archaeology. With the passing years, in contrast to interdisciplinary approaches that are employed in the United Kingdom and the United States that require partnerships between archaeologists and conservators, Turkish professionals have insisted on their "conventional" methods of "restoring" objects. Because of these unprofessional attempts to restore objects without preserving them and the unfathomable resistance to establishing conservation practice in Turkey, not only has the development of preservation lagged behind, but many archaeological collections in museums and remains at archaeological sites have been adversely affected.

However, since many foreign archaeological expeditions in Turkey (i.e., Sardis, Kaman, Pergamon, Miletos, Sagalassos expeditions) consider conservation a major part of their fieldwork, they have started field laboratories for the treatment of movable cultural property, included conservators in their teams, and trained some of the Turkish team members in archaeological conservation, albeit at an elementary level. This approach had a positive influence on Turkish excavators, as it gave them an opportunity for comparison and helped them to realize the value of the partnership between archaeologists and conservators. An undesirable result of this development has been the unexpected and rather irrational misuse of the experience. Instead of establishing conservation programs based on proper training, archaeologists have preferred to use "conservation treatment recipes" for certain problems (i.e., the use of electrochemical cleaning methods for copper-alloy coins, cleaning of calcareous layers by soaking the object in acid solutions, gluing potsherds with industrial and often irreversible adhesives, etc.). The unavoidable result was certainly destructive, and when irreversible damage to archaeological collections was discovered, archaeologists and art historians finally admitted the urgent need for conservation science and training programs in Turkey.

Unfortunately, the strategy of field conservation in Turkey is linked to the status of state museums, where conservation professionals and facilities do not exist. As a result, the treatments that are undertaken during excavation become the only treatments that the excavated objects receive. This strategy requires that all conservation work be completed in the field laboratory, which is contrary to the principles of preservation and minimal intervention. Equally distressing is the fact that this approach is valid only for ongoing excavations; there is no such opportunity for treatment at salvage digs.

Conservation in Archaeological Museums

As mentioned in Article 24.a, "movable cultural property is state property and will be kept and preserved by the state in museums." This principle points us to a directive issued in 1983 for museums by the General Directorate of Monuments and Museums.[7] According to this directive, museum objects (including the archaeological and ethnographic collections) in storage will be preserved properly and storage areas will be arranged to enable scientific research. "Museum specialists" are in charge of "collecting, excavating, classifying, and certifying objects"; their duties also include the "repair of exhibits, arrangement of storage areas, and preservation and mechanical cleaning of museum objects." They are also in charge of observing the condition of the museum objects and reporting those that need treatment in the laboratory. However, the curricula of the programs from which museum specialists have graduated do not include active or preventive conservation techniques for museum objects. These circumstances are reminiscent of the situation mentioned in the United Kingdom Institute for Conservation (UKIC) report, published in 1974, which draws attention to "the unacceptably high proportion of conservation work in United Kingdom museums and art galleries then being carried out by curatorial and technical staff who had received no specific training to undertake it" (Cannon-Brookes 1994:47). Unfortunately, in spite of the establishment of conservation training programs in universities that provide education at different levels (two-year programs for conservation technicians and four-year diploma programs for conservators), the situation has not yet changed sufficiently in Turkey. For the most part, this lack of change is due to deficiencies in the legislation concerning the definition of conservation professionals and the lack of a realistic financial management program for using this potential in museums.

With the exception of several regional museums, such as the Museum of Anatolian Civilization in Ankara, most Turkish museums have neither conservation laboratories nor workshops to perform treatments. This situation, as well as the delayed awareness of archaeological conservation in Turkey, has caused the following problems:

Nonprofessionals who have attempted to "restore" archaeological objects rather than to preserve them have caused damage to those objects.

There is a vast amount of excavated material in museums and field storage depots accumulated from long-standing archaeological projects and short-term salvage excavations. Museums and archaeological sites lack preventive conservation methods.

Conservation Training

Because archaeologists have responsibility for ensuring that the required conditions are met for the preservation of excavated material, both during and after excavation and both in the field and in the museum (where archaeologists are often assigned as museum specialists), conservation training should be considered at two levels: (1) preventive conservation training for archaeologists, art historians, and other professionals who participate in archaeological digs; and (2) conservation education for conservation technicians and conservators.

Because of the absence of professional conservators and/or conservation technicians in field laboratories, excavators need to be equipped with all relevant information concerning lifting, packing, and storage techniques as well as to be made conscious of the importance of monitoring and maintenance of their sites. On the other hand, since all the excavated material is to become part of museum collections and its conservation treatment cannot be fully completed during the excavation campaign, museum specialists need comprehensive knowledge enabling them to apply preventive preservation methods to their collections.

Preventive conservation courses are being added to the curricula of archaeology, art history, and anthropology programs at the undergraduate level. Training in the restoration of immovable cultural property (architectural remains, historic towns, and monuments) was first started in 1972 at the Middle East Technical University (Ahunbay 1996; Yavuz 1994) as a graduate program in the architecture department. It was later followed by similar programs in various universities in

Turkey; training in the conservation of movable cultural property was not considered until 1989.

Meanwhile, conservation training programs in Turkey offered at the preundergraduate level by vocational schools do not appear to have uniform curriculum content due to differences in their objectives. The selection of courses by individual programs is based on the preservation needs of traditional architecture and monuments in different regions. This local quality complies with the main characteristics of two-year programs, which encourage cooperation between the conservation technician and the craftsman (Ülkücü 1999). In this way, the knowledge and experience of the local craftsman is shared, taught, and documented in a systematic manner by the conservation professional. As a result, information about different materials, production techniques, and aging processes will be available to future generations. However, the duration of these programs is inadequate to assure comprehensive training, since the students have to learn the theory of conservation as well as gain practical skills within a two-year period (Ersoy 2000).

Due to the small number of educated conservation faculty in Turkey, as well as the delayed awareness regarding the need to provide training in archaeological conservation and the conservation of movable cultural property, preundergraduate, undergraduate, and graduate programs are not as prevalent as the architectural restoration programs (Ersoy 1999).[8] However, there is a growing need for archaeological conservators in the field and in museums, and archaeologists are beginning to realize that the assistance of a professional conservator during and after the excavation can make an important difference. And although it seems to be a very slow process, a new and more rational approach is being developed in Turkey that includes conservation at the professional level.

Conclusion

It is realistic to admit that in spite of the goodwill of archaeologists, conservation science in Turkey has not yet reached the level hoped for or needed. There is a great need for a clear and sincere conservation policy addressing both short- and long-term goals. There is no doubt that greater preventive conservation measures in archaeological excavations and museums will improve the condition of collections and enable archaeologists to gain more information from finds. Increasing the number of conservation training programs, as well as developing their content to respond to the variety of archaeological materials excavated, will foster the growth of a well-prepared and experienced generation of conservation professionals who can cooperate with archaeologists in excavations and museums. We owe it to our future to make every effort to promote the conservation of Turkey's cultural heritage.

Notes

1   The British Institute of Archaeology in Ankara (est. 1948), Deutsches Archaeologisches Institut—İstanbul Abteilung (est. 1929), and Institut Français d'Etudes Anatoliennes in İstanbul (est. 1930) are the three major institutions that undertook excavations in the early years of archaeological research in Turkey.

2   Jürgen Seeher, who directs the current excavations at Bogazkoy, states, "During the early years of the Bogazkoy excavation (Hattusas) most of the cuneiform tablets found prior to World War II were taken with the permission of the Turkish authorities to the Berlin Museum for professional conservation and study. Pottery was usually cleaned and restored at the site by specialists or in the Ankara Museum."

3   A report compiled by the Ministry of National Education in 1961 mentions that because of the damage caused by devastating environmental conditions at the Museum of Fine Arts in İstanbul and İzmir, the Committee of Fine Arts considered it necessary to send two members of the museum staff to Italy for conservation training and to establish "restoration workshops" in these museums.

4   Legislation for the Preservation of Cultural and Natural Property of Turkey, Legislation No. 2863, T. C. Resmi Gazete, Sayı. 18113, 23.7.1983.

5   "Recommendation Concerning the Protection, at the National Level, of the Cultural and Natural Heritage," V. Protective Measures, Article 18, General Conference of the United Nations Educational, Scientific and Cultural Organization, Paris, 17th session, 1972.

6   "Recommendation on International Principles Applicable to Archaeological Excavations," General Conference of the United Nations Educational, Scientific and Cultural Organization, New Delhi, 9th session, 1956.

7   Müzeler İç Hizmet Yönetmeliği, Ankara, 1990.

8   The two-year preundergraduate conservation program of Ankara University, at Baskent Vocational School, has offered courses in the conservation of movable cultural property since 1990. The curriculum consists of the characteristics of historical and archaeological organic and inorganic materials, manufacturing techniques of ethnographic and archaeological objects, their deterioration processes, and conservation of movable objects (archaeological objects in particular). Graduates of this program are qualified as conservation technicians.

The four-year undergraduate program of İstanbul University, in the Faculty of Literature, was established in 1993 and aims to provide training in the conservation and restoration of movable cultural property.

References

Ahunbay, Z. 1996. *Tarihi Çevre Koruma ve Restorasyon* (Preservation of the Historical Environment and Restoration). İstanbul: YEM Yayın.

Akozan, F. 1977. *Türkiye'de Tarihi Anıtları Koruma Teşkilatı ve Kanunlar* (Laws and Organization for the Protection of Historical Monuments in Turkey). İstanbul.

Cannon-Brookes, P. 1994. The role of the scholar-curator in conservation. In *Care of Collections,* ed. S. Knell. London: Routledge.

Ersoy Kökten, H. 1999. Educational opportunities for Turkish conservators. *Field Notes: Practical Guides for Archaeological Conservation and Site Preservation,* No.7. Japanese Institute of Anatolian Archaeology.

———. 2000. *Türkiye'deki İki Senelik Konservasyon ve Restorasyon Eiitiminin Sorunları ve Çözüm Önerileri* (Problems and Solutions for the Two-Year Conservation-Restoration Program in Turkey). Ankara Üniversitesi, Başkent Meslek Yüksekokulu, I.Ulusal Taşınabilir Kültür Varlıkları Konservasyonu ve Restorasyonu Kolokyumu. Mayıs.1999, Ankara.

İzmirligil, Ü. 1995. *Koruma ve Onarım* (Conservation and Restoration). Sayı.1, İstanbul, 1.

Ülkücü, M. C. 1999. *Ara Eleman Yetiştirmede Duvar Teknikleri Eiitiminin Yeri ve Önemi* (The Importance of Masonry Techniques Training for Vocational Schools). Zonguldak Karaelmas Üniversitesi, I. Ulusal Restorasyon Eğitimi Sempozyumu, Safranbolu 3–5. Ekim.1996, Özköse A., ed. Zonguldak.

Umar, B. 1981. *Eski Eserler Hukuku* (Law of Antiquities). İzmir, 6.

Yavuz, A. 1994. Türkiye'de Koruma Eğitimi (Conservation Training in Turkey). Taç Vakfı Yıllığı II, İstanbul.

PART EIGHT

Preserving the Cultural Heritage of Iraq and Afghanistan

Introduction

Claire L. Lyons

During an international congress at which the thematic banner of conservation formed a major component, it was inevitable that marquee events on archaeology and war took center stage. Warfare and its collateral effects are, of course, the ultimate worst-case scenario that preservationists confront. For many who are engaged in the recuperation and stewardship of the archaeological record, the Fifth World Archaeological Congress offered an opportune moment to discuss the intersections—or more accurately collisions—of archaeological and military interests. Still very much a matter of debate and dissension within the professions of archaeology and conservation, the topics ranged from eyewitness reportage of looting to practical interventions and legislative strategies.

The four years since WAC-4 in Cape Town have witnessed the U.S.-led invasion of Afghanistan and deepening conflicts over sites of historical and religious significance in other parts of the world. Jerusalem is an example but is not the only flashpoint of divisions that currently enmesh archaeologists and conservators in the Realpolitik of culture. Planning for WAC-5 coincided with the inexorable march toward a second war in Iraq. Its Washington, D.C., venue added a disturbing irony and urgency to the presentations. For these reasons, a number of symposia and plenary sessions were organized to discuss what had happened, what was being done in response, and what lessons might be learned for the future.

The following papers represent a cross section of those offered in three symposia on Afghanistan and one on Iraq, which joined plenary addresses, impromptu remarks, and council resolutions on the crisis. Only ten weeks before the congress, Baghdad had fallen to coalition forces and television broadcast images of museums looted, libraries burned, hospitals ransacked, and the "cradle of civilization" despoiled by pillagers. Written and revised over the course of eighteen months, the essays represent a snapshot of tragic events, subsequent actions, and critical reactions in the wake of two equally chaotic but fundamentally different invasions. Although the situations continue to evolve, some remedial lessons may be taken in hindsight from these instructive accounts.

The picture painted by the contributors is not optimistic. Combined efforts to document and map heritage, train local staff, and draw up the sort of preventive and emergency plans that were advocated after the first Gulf war (Stanley-Price 1997) are laudable. The impulse to *do something* for countries under occupation, however, necessarily entails ethical dilemmas that walk a fine line between aid and collaboration: are we making things right, or just making things seem right? A palpable tension exists between the ideals of professional best practices and what can feasibly be accomplished under the mantle of coalition politics and military security. The tension and ambiguities that such concessions breed can be read between the lines that follow. They mirror larger questions posed by WAC members who attended these sessions and who challenged the premises of archaeologists' and conservators' participation in the scenarios of war on humanitarian grounds.

Potential dilemmas were not so apparent during the three panels on Afghanistan. Philip L. Kohl and Rita Wright assembled an impressive roster of distinguished specialists to address the intentional destruction of collections and monuments, which for the most part has been underreported once the shock of the Bamiyan Buddha's demolition receded into memory. Candid accounts offered by Omara Khan Masoodi,

Abdul Wassey Feroozi, and Osmund Bopearchchi of the plight of museums, not to mention the virtual erasure of little-known sites, make it difficult to encompass the personal sacrifices that Afghan colleagues have endured, or to ignore their calls for assistance. Admirable projects to restore and rebuild have been initiated by individual conservators, international agencies, and sister museums, as described in papers by Christian Manhart and Jim Williams and Louise Haxthausen, all from UNESCO. It is clear, however, that even in Kabul the needs are overwhelming and security has yet to be extended to rural areas where narcotics and artifacts are now the main cash crops. Afghanistan is a paradigm of collateral damage, attributable to a chain of causes and effects that decades of war set into motion. Yet audiences on hand to hear their accounts at WAC were unaccountably sparse. Is the loss of history in a signally important region at the crossroads of East and West of less consequence than that suffered in Mesopotamia? Or, as Kohl and Wright underscore, is the problem a lack of political will and the failure of promised funding to materialize when attention shifted to Iraq?

Overflow audiences attended the Iraq session, which featured the perspectives of art law, conservation, cultural property, and Mesopotamian archaeology. The goal was to share information, particularly on the status of monuments outside the capital as of June 2003. Much has changed since those reports were aired. While the spotlight was on the museums in Baghdad, some of the most famous archaeological ruins, including Nineveh and Babylon, were in harm's way from organized looting for the antiquities market and the abusive construction of military installations. Patty Gerstenblith analyzes deficiencies in international conventions that fail to cover the responsibilities of occupying forces in circumstances like this. Gaps and loopholes undermine efforts to respond swiftly when archaeological heritage is threatened by conflict. Law has proven an effective disincentive to consumers of stolen cultural property. Legislation that aims to restrict the import of Iraqi antiquities into the United States and to amend the current legislation that implements the 1970 UNESCO Convention was introduced in Congress, to help authorities react more flexibly. However, it stalled under intense lobbying by representatives of the art market community. The bill that was finally passed (Emergency Protection for Iraqi Cultural Antiquities Act of 2004) represents a compromise that moves things forward but not as far as they need to go. The legislation does not cover countries that are not party to the 1970 UNESCO Convention, for example, Afghanistan, because it is not currently considered politically

expedient to acknowledge anything less than success in that country.

The issue of postconflict occupation and reconstruction and its deleterious effects on archaeological zones has recently come to the fore. Zainab Bahrani, an Iraqi American scholar who served for several months as archaeological adviser to the Iraqi Ministry of Culture, considers the physical and symbolic damage sustained at Babylon, by any account a site of global significance. Though apparently unscathed during hostilities or by wholesale looting, Babylon was selected as the location of a U.S. military installation. Construction plans excluded archaeologists and Iraqi officials on security grounds, and as a result the integrity of the site has been severely, perhaps irreversibly damaged. Bahrani sees the coalition's occupation of Iraq's historical fabric here and in other archaeological areas as a seizure of conceptual territory and a form of iconoclasm not so different from that perpetrated in the name of religion in Afghanistan.

These cases call out for action, but they also call into question the wisdom of embedding with the military. Is there a risk that archaeologists and conservators will be perceived as placing the rescue of monuments and artworks at a higher priority than safeguarding lives and basic human resources? In the situation of Afghanistan, as Kohl and Wright point out, heritage is a facet of human rights, and its destruction is inseparable from other sociopolitical problems. It constitutes a shared tradition and is therefore essential to long-term stability. Theirs is a valid concept, but it becomes murkier in the case of Iraq, which was viewed much less favorably from the outset and has worsened over time as reports of military mismanagement like that at Babylon circulate. The willingness of professional archaeologists and conservators to act as government advisers is viewed skeptically by some colleagues, who question why protest "limited itself to the broken china—and ignored the broken lives of the war's victims" (Ascherson 2003:65; see also Hamilakis 2003:104–11). Few of those who volunteer their efforts in postwar Afghanistan and Iraq, or for that matter in Lebanon or the Balkans, do so without genuine concern for people and their heritage. The following papers offer no easy answers. They point to the need voiced at the congress for a renewed engagement with the professional, political, and ethical aspects of fieldwork in the context of war. Independent archaeological and conservation organizations have a very important stake in the outcome. Doubtless, the opportunity to test convictions will present itself in the not too distant future.

References

Ascherson, N. 2003. Editorial. *Public Archaeology* 3:65.

Hamilakis, Y. 2003. Iraq, stewardship, and "the record": An ethical crisis for archaeology. *Public Archaeology* 3:104–11.

Stanley-Price, N. 1997. War and the conservator. *Museum Management and Curatorship* 16, no. 2 (June):155–91. [See also articles by B. O. Roberts, V. Dauge, I. Skaf, and K. Norman in this issue.]

The Law as a Tool for Cultural Heritage Preservation: The Case of Iraq and Afghanistan

Patty Gerstenblith

Abstract: *As the subject of cultural heritage has grown and expanded with the awareness of the need to preserve cultural heritage for the benefit of future generations, so the law that addresses the problems of preservation has grown. Law, both national and international, is the primary mechanism for controlling and shaping human behavior in order to maximize the public good. However, recent experiences of both intentional and unintentional damage, destruction, and other threats to the cultural heritage in Iraq and Afghanistan demonstrate the shortcomings of the national and international legal systems in their attempts to reduce and eliminate these losses. This paper examines some of these shortcomings and briefly proposes modifications to these legal regimes that would make the law more responsive to contemporary threats to cultural heritage and would impose mechanisms for providing more effective cultural heritage resource management and preservation.*

Cultural Heritage in Time of War

It is perhaps ironic that, so far as we know, direct military action during the second Gulf War posed relatively little danger to the Iraqi cultural heritage. The conduct of war with respect to cultural heritage is now governed by the 1954 Hague Convention on the Protection of Cultural Property in the Event of Armed Conflict.[1] Among other provisions, it calls on nations that are party to the convention to avoid the targeting of cultural sites and monuments, except in cases of military necessity (Art. 4). The main drawback is that the primary partners in the coalition that led the invasion of Iraq, the United States and the United Kingdom, are not parties to the convention (although the United Kingdom has since announced its intention to ratify it). The United States signed the convention in 1956 and President Bill Clinton transmitted it to the Senate for ratification in 1999, but it has been held hostage to domestic politics and the perception that it is not very important. Both the United States and the United Kingdom are party to the Hague Conventions of 1899 and 1907, which have some provisions for the safeguarding of cultural property during war. These nations also recognize parts of the 1954 convention as customary international law. However, given the minimalist provisions of the earlier conventions and the failure to ratify the 1954 convention, major military powers such as the United States and the United Kingdom are able to pick and choose which parts of the 1954 convention they will follow and which parts they reject. This leads to considerable uncertainty as to the conduct of these nations during war and occupation. Whether the recent war in Iraq will serve as a catalyst or disincentive for ratification also remains to be seen.

Even if more nations were to become parties to the convention, this would not solve all of the difficulties, because the convention itself is inadequate in many respects. The 1954 convention was written in reaction to the massive cultural heritage displacement that occurred in Europe during World War II. The threats posed to cultural heritage during warfare have multiplied, and more needs to be considered than just intentional or collateral damage from the targeting of cultural sites. In 1999 the Second Protocol to the convention was drafted to respond to some of the issues that arose during the Balkan wars of the early 1990s. Recent experiences in Iraq demonstrate that still more changes are needed.

Cultural Heritage in the Aftermath of War and during Occupation

The Hague Convention addresses conduct during occupation, as well as during active warfare (Art. 5 and Second Protocol). However, there are many aspects of the occupation of Iraq that the convention fails to address, probably because this occupation is very different in character from the occupation of Europe by German forces during World War II. It is also not clear when some of the obligations, in particular the obligation to maintain peace and security, are triggered (Art. 4, par. 3). Much of the looting and destruction in the Baghdad cultural institutions occurred after the U.S. forces were in control of Baghdad, between approximately 8 and 20 April 2003, and before the coalition's occupation was formally recognized by the U.N. Security Council, on 22 May 2003 (UNSCR 1483).[2]

During the period of occupation and even after the end of formal occupation in June 2004, the U.S. military has engaged in conduct that has been harmful and even destructive to the cultural heritage of Iraq. One example is the building of a military base on the site of Babylon, which, according to Zainab Bahrani (see this volume), has damaged the ancient site located there (Curtis 2004). Other military actions taken in the attempt to defeat the insurgency and in the aftermath, particularly the clearing of buildings in the old city of Najaf, have reportedly harmed Iraq's cultural heritage. The U.S. military is engaging in the controlled detonation of ordnance in the immediate vicinity of the World Heritage Site of Hatra, which may be destabilizing the structures at the site (Crawford 2005), and is using the minaret of the ninth-century al-Mutawakkil mosque in Samarra (known as the Malwiya because of its spiral minaret) as a sniper position because it provides an excellent view of the surrounding area (Harris 2005). However, as there is no consistent method of monitoring these actions or assessing their effect, the nature and extent of any damage cannot be determined at this time.

The Hague Convention does not seem to envision the long-term occupation of territory. For example, the convention should require that a cultural heritage damage assessment be carried out under the auspices of either the national authorities or a nongovernmental organization, such as UNESCO, within a limited time following the cessation of hostilities. The convention needs to clarify that the occupying power has an obligation to prevent looting and vandalism of cultural sites and institutions not just by its own forces but also by the local population.

Article 1 of the First Protocol of the 1954 Hague Convention, written at the time of the main convention, regulates the disposition of movable cultural objects. It prohibits the removal of cultural objects from occupied territory and requires the return of any objects that are removed for safekeeping at the end of the occupation. Unfortunately, this protocol has not received the same degree of international acceptance as has the main convention, and it is not clear whether the United States regards the First Protocol as part of customary international law.

The failure to accept the principles of the First Protocol is problematic in terms of the theft of antiquities for sale on the international market, which is discussed below. It is also problematic for other reasons. For example, an exhibition of Mesopotamian antiquities that would travel to Europe or the United States has been proposed several times during the occupation of Iraq (Weir 2004). While some laud the possibilities of such an exhibition to increase awareness of Mesopotamian culture and history and to perhaps raise funds for cultural heritage reconstruction, it is unclear whether trained professionals have had much involvement in the drafting of the plans. More significantly, the failure to involve Iraqis in these decisions exacerbates the concerns and suspicions of not only the Iraqis but also the professional archaeological and conservation communities, which have already been alarmed by events in Iraq.

Finally, the failure of the United States to acknowledge the First Protocol creates difficulties when the United States removes cultural materials from Iraq for purposes of emergency conservation, as it has done with a trove of Jewish manuscripts found waterlogged in the basement of the Iraqi security police headquarters (Myre 2003). While the removal for purposes of conservation seems justified under the Hague Convention and the First Protocol, both the general public and the heritage conservation community could more willingly countenance such removal and cooperate if there were confidence that the materials will be returned in due course.

Neither the various national nor international legal systems are able to provide adequate disincentives to the looting of cultural institutions, as occurred in Baghdad in April 2003. Some of the vandalism, especially the burning of manuscripts, books, and documentation, and looting, especially the taking of computers and other types of equipment, was either random or for the purpose of obtaining desired supplies by the local population. Other aspects of the looting, such as of the museums, were more likely targeted at supplying antiquities and other cultural objects for sale on the international art market. The Hague Convention and its First Protocol are not directly relevant here, other than through the obligation to prevent looting and vandalism, because the prohibition on removal of cultural materials refers to removal by states and not by individuals.

The 1970 UNESCO Convention on the Means of Prohibiting and Preventing the Illicit Import, Export and Transfer of Ownership of Cultural Property is, however, more directly relevant to this circumstance (O'Keefe 2000).[3] Article 7(b) of the convention calls on state parties to prevent the import of "cultural property stolen from a museum or a religious or secular public monument or similar institution . . . , provided that such property is documented as appertaining to the inventory of that institution," and to return any such material imported to the state party of origin. Many art-importing nations, including France, Italy, Australia, and Canada, have been parties to the UNESCO convention for many years; the United Kingdom, Japan, and Switzerland have joined more recently. The United States joined the convention in 1983 and implemented Article 7(b) through section 308 of the Convention on Cultural Property Implementation Act (CPIA).[4] While this provision automatically prohibits importation of cultural materials stolen from the museums and libraries of Baghdad, the requirement that such material be documented can be a significant impediment when the documentation in the Baghdad institutions was so severely compromised (Russell 2003).

The reaction of the world community to the events in Baghdad demonstrates that it can respond quickly and effectively to cultural crises when the political will and sufficient public pressure, primarily through the media, are present. However, the uniqueness of the response to the Iraq situation and the total failure of the international community to respond to the equally devastating cultural crisis in Afghanistan demonstrate the overall ineffectiveness of the international legal system. Of greater efficacy in the case of Iraq, but again an unusual circumstance, were the sanctions on the import of Iraqi goods in place since 1990. Therefore, the import or dealing in such goods was already prohibited before the second Gulf War began. This circumstance applies neither to Afghanistan nor to most of the other nations of the world where looting and destruction of archaeological and other cultural sites is rampant.

On 22 May 2003 the U.N. Security Council called on U.N. members to prohibit the trade in illegally removed Iraqi cultural materials in Resolution 1483, paragraph 7. Of particu-

lar interest is the reaction of the British government, which, in response to UNSCR 1483, enacted an administrative prohibition on dealing in illegally removed Iraqi cultural materials.[5] This prohibition criminalized such dealing and reversed the typical burden of proof in criminal cases by requiring that an individual handling such materials establish that he or she did not know or have reason to know that such materials were illegally removed. UNSCR 1483 and the British provision are broader than the 1970 UNESCO Convention because they apply not just to materials stolen from institutions but also to materials taken from any location in Iraq, including archaeological sites. Switzerland, which only recently ratified the UNESCO Convention and is, along with the United Kingdom and the United States, among the more significant market nations, enacted special provisions for prohibiting trade in illegally removed Iraqi cultural heritage materials.[6]

Like the U.S. action to maintain the prohibition on importation of Iraqi cultural materials through the system of sanctions that had been in place since 1990,[7] the British action is administrative in nature. The British action will automatically terminate if UNSCR 1483, paragraph 7, is rescinded. Although helpful in the short term, these restrictions are not an effective deterrent to looting because they are not likely to last for an extended time. However, a recent study of the London market in Iraqi antiquities indicates that the market has dropped dramatically since 2003 (Brodie 2005). Based on our experiences of artworks stolen during World War II and other examples of looted cultural materials, we can conclude that some collectors, dealers, and middlemen in the art market are willing to hold stores of cultural materials or trade them privately out of the public eye for long periods, waiting for temporary import restrictions to expire and statutes of limitations to bar actions by true owners to recover their stolen cultural materials.

Looting of Undocumented Materials

Of even greater concern than the theft of objects and manuscripts from museums and libraries is the looting of undocumented artifacts from archaeological sites. When sites are looted and the context and associated materials of the artifacts are lost, their historical, cultural, and scientific information is irretrievably destroyed (Brodie, Doole, and Renfrew 2001). From the legal standpoint, it is also much more difficult to trace undocumented materials and recover them. This in turn means that there is greater incentive to loot such objects because they are relatively easy to sell on the international market. Major museums in the United States and elsewhere are sometimes willing to purchase such undocumented artifacts because there is no direct evidence of their theft and it is less likely that the acquirer will lose the investment in the object. The looting of archaeological sites began early in the war in Iraq with the withdrawal of the Iraqi military, particularly in the south (Gibson 2004). The looting of sites in Afghanistan has gone on for many years, and the lack of centralized government control means there is little possibility of preventing it (Feroozi 2004).

Besides the U.N. Security Council resolution that deals exclusively with Iraq, the only international instrument to address this problem is the 1970 UNESCO Convention, which in Article 3 states that the import of illegally exported cultural property is illicit and in Article 9 calls on states parties to render assistance to other state parties in cases in which their "cultural patrimony is in jeopardy from pillage of archaeological or ethnological materials." The United States implements Article 9 through two sections of the CPIA, sections 303 and 304.[8] However, the structure of the CPIA poses several obstacles to swift and effective action to prevent the import of undocumented artifacts into the United States. These obstacles include the following: the other nation must be a state party and must have diplomatic relations with the United States to present a request; the request must provide documentation that would support both a bilateral agreement with the United States (including, for example, that the nation is taking actions consistent with the convention to protect its cultural patrimony) and emergency action, which the United States can take in certain circumstances to impose import restrictions without the need to negotiate a bilateral agreement; the request must be reviewed by the Cultural Property Advisory Committee (CPAC), which recommends whether the statutory criteria for either (or both) an emergency action or a bilateral agreement are satisfied; the president must then determine whether the statutory criteria are met. During the years of the sanctions against Iraq, it was not possible for Iraq to bring an Article 9 request to the United States because the two countries did not have diplomatic relations. At the time of this writing, the lack of clear governing authority in Iraq, the security situation, and the difficulty of assembling the required materials continue to make such a request unlikely for some time. Afghanistan cannot bring such a request because it is not a party to the UNESCO Convention.

In May 2003 legislation was introduced in the U.S. House of Representatives (H.R. 2009) that would have imposed an immediate import restriction on illegally removed Iraqi cultural materials and would have amended the CPIA in several crucial respects.[9] It would have allowed the president to impose import restrictions in emergency situations without need for a request from another country and without need for review from the CPAC. These amendments also would have extended the duration of bilateral agreements and emergency actions to ten years (rather than the current five) and would have allowed emergency actions to be renewed an unlimited number of times (rather than the current maximum of eight years). This bill met with overwhelming opposition through the lobbying efforts of lawyers representing the National Association of Dealers in Ancient, Oriental and Primitive Art and coin dealers and collectors, and this legislation died at the end of the 2004 congressional session.

In November 2004 Congress enacted different legislation (S. 671; H.R. 1047) as part of a miscellaneous trade bill.[10] This legislation gives the president the authority to impose import restrictions under the CPIA without need for Iraq to bring a request to the United States and without need for review by the CPAC. The language of the bill largely tracks that of UNSCR 1483 and is the fulfillment by the United States of its obligations under that resolution. The main drawback of this legislation is that it does nothing to assist Afghanistan or to simplify the process for imposing import restrictions in case of emergencies in the future. This is a significant shortcoming in the legal protection that the United States could offer to assist in the reduction of looting of archaeological sites.

It is ironic that Switzerland, which has lagged behind the United States for many years in the effort to prevent the illicit trade in antiquities, is now taking significant steps in that direction. Switzerland joined the UNESCO Convention in October 2003 and has enacted legislation that will allow it to enter into bilateral agreements with other state parties.[11] The Swiss system will be much simpler than that used in the United States, and, once an agreement is in place, it will last for an indefinite period. This long duration is necessary in order to provide a sufficient disincentive to looters, middlemen, and dealers who would otherwise be willing to keep material for many years in the hope that, at some point in the future, it will be possible to sell them in the markets of Western countries.

Cultural Resource Management

Perhaps the most unusual threat to the cultural heritage of Iraq has arisen from the efforts that the United States is undertaking to rebuild Iraq's infrastructure, which suffered both during the years of sanctions and during the war itself. There is no international instrument that imposes a direct obligation on occupying powers to avoid damage to cultural sites and monuments during construction projects. This demonstrates again the shortcomings of the Hague Convention, which is largely limited in its vision to the situation of World War II.

In many countries, including both Iraq and the United States, cultural resource management provisions contained in relevant statutes require that any area that will be affected by a project be surveyed and then efforts taken to mitigate damage to cultural resources located there. Mitigation may include relocating a project or carrying out salvage excavation before the project can proceed. While there are many differences in the details and such requirements are limited in the United States to government-funded projects and those located on government-owned or managed land, the principles are basically the same.

The occupation of Iraq presents an unusual circumstance in that it is not clear whether either Iraqi domestic law or U.S. law controls. U.S. domestic law (the National Historic Preservation Act)[12] requires the avoidance or mitigation of harm from federal undertakings in foreign countries at sites that are on the World Heritage List or on the country's equivalent of the National Register, which might cover as many as 3,500 to 5,000 sites in Iraq. The archaeological community has brought pressure to ensure that the U.S. construction contracts incorporate cultural heritage resource management principles, but the success of this pressure is not yet certain.

The silence of the Hague Convention on this point is puzzling, except for the fact that it was written in 1954 when concepts of cultural heritage resource management were relatively unknown. The provisions of the convention and even the Second Protocol that deal with this situation are frustratingly meager. The convention seems premised on the notion that the occupying power should do nothing to interfere with the cultural heritage of the occupied territory. Article 5, paragraph 2, requires that the occupying power take "the most necessary measures of preservation" to protect cultural property damaged by military operations and does not seem to envision the need to protect cultural property from other types of damage. Article 9 of the Second Protocol permits an occupying power to undertake archaeological excavation only "where this is strictly required to safeguard, record or preserve cultural property." This provision arguably permits the carrying out of survey and salvage work by an occupying power,

but it does not require it. Similarly, international norms and customary international law establish general principles for the protection of cultural property during occupation and require cooperation to the fullest extent feasible with the local national authorities in doing so. However, none of these instruments imposes a direct obligation on an occupying power to undertake survey and salvage work in an attempt to prevent or mitigate damage to cultural resources during the types of construction projects now being planned by the United States.

Modern principles and standards of cultural heritage resource management should be embodied in a new protocol to the Hague Convention that would directly impose these obligations on occupying powers. It should be a relatively uncontroversial provision, one that would attract many ratifying nations or one that would quickly be recognized as part of customary international law. Such an accepted norm of international law would avert difficulties when an occupying power is undertaking large-scale construction projects and has suspended many of its own domestic rules for the awarding of construction contracts, as the United States has done. Widespread acceptance would do much to assure protection for the world's cultural heritage if comparable situations were to arise in the future.

Conclusion

While the events in Iraq and Afghanistan have been dramatic and have caught the attention of the media and the public as few other comparable events have done in recent years, the experiences of these two nations serve as a microcosm of threats to heritage throughout the world. The impact of war on the cultural heritage of Iraq and Afghanistan demonstrate the shortcomings of both the international and domestic legal regimes to serve as a sufficient disincentive to both intentional and inadvertent harm to cultural heritage resources. The Hague Convention of 1954, written against the backdrop of Hitler's cultural destruction and intended to avert similar events in the future, can be seen today to be inadequate both to deal with looting carried out by individuals (rather than by nations) and to accord respect for cultural resources that is commensurate with our contemporary understanding of cultural heritage resource management and preservation. Domestic legal regimes, particularly that of the United States, need to be made more responsive to emergencies in cultural heritage protection that will likely result in the future from similar political, economic, and military upheavals.

Notes

1   Hague Convention on the Protection of Cultural Property in the Event of Armed Conflict, 14 May 1954, 249 U.N.T.S. 240. Available at http://portal.unesco.org/culture/en/ev.php@URL_ID=8450&URL_DO=DO_TOPIC&URL_SECTION=201.html.

2   United Nations Security Council Resolution 1483, 22 May 2003. Available at http://ods-dds-ny.un.org/doc/UNDOC/GEN/N03/368/53/PDF/N0336853.pdf? OpenElement.

3   UNESCO Convention on the Means of Prohibiting and Preventing the Illicit Import, Export and Transfer of Ownership of Cultural Property, 14 November 1970, 823 U.N.T.S. 231. Available at http://portal.unesco.org/en/ev.phpURL_ID=13039&URL_DO=DO_TOPIC&URL_SECTION=201.html.

4   Convention on Cultural Property Implementation Act, 19 U.S.C. §§ 2601–13.

5   United Kingdom Statutory Instrument 2003 No. 1519, sec. 8. Available at http://www.hmso.gov.uk/si/si2003/20031519.htm.

6   Swiss Ordinance on Economic Measures against the Republic of Iraq of 28 May 2003, SR 946.206. Available at www.kultur-schweiz.admin.ch/arkgt/kgt/e/e/_kgt.htm.

7   Iraqi Sanctions Regulations: Some New Transactions, 31 C.F.R. 575.533(b)(4) (23 May 2003).

8   19 U.S.C. §§ 2602–3.

9   The Iraq Cultural Heritage Protection Act, H.R. 2009, 108 H.R. 2009 (2003). Text available at http://thomas.loc.gov/cgi-bin/query.

10   Emergency Protection for Iraqi Cultural Antiquities Act, S. 671, 108 S. 671 (2004). Text available at http://thomas.loc.gov/cgi-bin/query.

11   Federal Act on the International Transfer of Cultural Property. Available at www.kultur-schweiz.admin.ch/arkgt/files/kgtg2_e/pdf.

12   National Historic Preservation Act, 16 U.S.C. §§ 470a–2 et seq.

References

Brodie, N. 2005. The plunder of Iraq's archaeological heritage, 1991–2004, and the London antiquities trade. In *Archaeology, Cultural Heritage, and the Trade in Antiquities*, ed. N. Brodie, M. Kersel, C. Luke, and K. W. Tubb. Gainesville: University Press of Florida.

Brodie, N., J. Doole, and C. Renfrew, eds. 2001. *Trade in Illicit Antiquities: The Destruction of the World's Archaeological Heritage.* Cambridge: McDonald Institute for Archaeological Research.

Crawford, H. 2005. Turning a blind eye. *Museums Journal* 105, no. 2 (February).

Curtis, J. E. 2004. Report on meeting at Babylon, 11–13 December 2004. Available at www.thebritishmuseum.ac.uk/newsroom/current2005/Babylon_Report04.doc.

Feroozi, A. W. 2004. The impact of war upon Afghanistan's cultural heritage. Available at www.archaeological.org.

Harris, L. 2005. U.S. snipers on Samarra's spiral minaret. *Art Newspaper,* 25 February. Available at www.theartnewspaper.com/news/article.asp?idart=11727.

McGuire, G. 2002–3. Nippur and Iraq in time of war. *Oriental Institute Annual Report* 2002–3 (updated 14 April 2004). Available at http://listhost.uchicago.edu/pipermail/iraqcrisis/.

Myre, G. 2003. After the war: Reunion. *New York Times,* 28 July, A10.

O'Keefe, P. 2000. *Commentary on the UNESCO Convention 1970.* Leicester: Institute of Art and Law.

Russell, J. M. 2003. A personal account of the first UNESCO Cultural Heritage Mission to Baghdad, 16–20 May. Available at www.archaeological.org.

Toman, J. 1996. *The Protection of Cultural Property in the Event of Armed Conflict.* Brookfield, Vt.: Dartmouth Publishing; Paris: UNESCO.

Weir, W. 2004. Artifacts tour: A cradle of debate. *Hartford Courant,* 10 March, A1.

Babylon: A Case Study in the Military Occupation of an Archaeological Site

Zainab Bahrani

Abstract: This paper addresses the current occupation of Babylon and other archaeological sites in Iraq by U.S.-led military forces and its physical and psychological ramifications for the cultural heritage and people of Iraq. Not unlike the bombing of the Bamiyan Buddhas by the Taliban, a well-known and widely publicized case of religious iconoclasm, the occupation of cultural and historic sites in Iraq is another method of cultural warfare. Given concern with the lack of attention to this area of archaeological theory, this paper proposes a close study and analysis of the way in which occupation, demolition, and construction at ancient sites and historical urban centers have become instruments of war.

The Occupation of Babylon

Babylon, one of the most prominent and important cities in Mesopotamian history, has been seriously damaged as a result of war and occupation by U.S.-led coalition forces.[1] Before the 2003 air campaign in Iraq, archaeologists and scholars of Near Eastern antiquity were well aware of the possible dangers to Iraq's archaeological sites and spoke out publicly and with a united voice regarding the need to protect Iraq's museums, monuments, and heritage sites in the case of war.[2] What the scholarly community had not foreseen was that the greater part of the damage to cultural heritage would not occur as a result of the bombing campaign or early ground war against the Iraqi regime. Instead, it was to be the result of the subsequent occupation by the coalition forces. This series of events in Iraq ought to be heeded by the World Archaeological Congress, the scholarly community, conservationists, and heritage management professionals because it is an example of cultural destruction of a kind that is not often addressed in discussions

of the protection or treatment of cultural property during war. In particular, the Iraq war has brought to the fore significant issues regarding military use of the historic fabric of the enemy's land. If military conflict implies, at least in part, an aspect that is heavily territorial, then the historic environment as enemy terrain or the territory of conquest is a subject that needs to be addressed more directly by archaeological theory. In hostilities such as the 1990s Balkan wars and territorial conflicts in Palestine-Israel and Cyprus, the use of heritage sites in the formation of identities and territorial disputes has been addressed (Abu El-Haj 2001; Kohl and Fawcett 1995). However, these lessons have not been applied to the practices of the coalition forces in Iraq, either by the popular press and media or in academic writing. The conceptual territory of antiquity and the uses of the past in nineteenth-century imperialist discourse is an area that has been discussed specifically in my earlier work (Bahrani 1998, 2003). Here I address a similar semiotic use of the past, but in this case, it is not limited to a conceptual historic terrain. In the example of Babylon (as well as a number of other archaeological sites in Iraq), this symbolic use of the past has taken on a material reality in the physical occupation of antiquity, a reality that has extensively damaged the archaeological remains.

The destruction of the Bamiyan Buddhas by the Taliban regime, as a form of direct iconoclasm, was met with international cries of outrage. Yet there has been relative silence in response to the destruction of standing monuments and heritage sites in Iraq. What are the factors that make one type of cultural destruction (iconoclasm of figural images) seem horrendous and unacceptable and another (destruction of nonfigural archaeological sites or standing monuments) more readily acceptable as part of the collateral damage of war?

240

Here I examine the case of Babylon, an ancient city whose fame is of legendary proportions, and consider its treatment as a result of armed conflict, as well as what ought to have been done to avert the extensive damage that has taken place. I also argue that the occupation and destruction of a legendary site such as Babylon can be read along the same theoretical lines as iconoclastic acts.

Through his renowned study, *The Power of Images,* David Freedberg has shown that acts of destruction we call iconoclasm reveal a belief in the power of the image rather than a disregard for it (Freedberg 1989). In response to the destruction of the Bamiyan Buddhas, he wrote convincingly that this was a perfect indication of the Taliban's fear of the power of these magnificent colossal images (Freedberg 2001). The occupation and consequent destruction of Babylon by coalition forces, it can be argued, reveals a similar ambivalence to that manifested in the destruction of more direct forms of pictorial iconoclasm. The destruction of the site takes place, not because of a disregard or lack of interest in Babylon or Mesopotamian antiquity, but precisely because Babylon is recognized by its military occupiers as a powerful sign of the occupied land. In the case of the 2003 Iraq war, Babylon as "sign" became a locus of the investment of military aggression as a form of display. That use of the site reveals an ambivalence not completely unlike that displayed by the Taliban's response to the Buddhas, in that the legendary city associated with decadence, despotism, and evil in the biblical Christian tradition was deliberately chosen as a military base, not despite the fact that it is Iraq's most famous, legendary heritage site, but because of its fame and mythical values. The occupation damages the site, seemingly without any respect or concern for its values as a historic site or as cultural property; yet this very same destructive occupation makes use of the efficacious and potent symbolic power of the site.

The bombing campaign of March and April 2003 did not directly hit any museums, religious buildings, or archaeological sites. It was only in the aftermath, during the occupation, that the destruction began. At first, the destruction was considered the result of activities of a mob of local people, even if some blame was initially placed on coalition forces for not guarding civil buildings. The looting of museums and libraries in spring 2003 was well publicized in the media, but it was only the beginning of a more general destruction that was about to take place. It soon became clear that there would be systematic occupation of heritage sites by the military; however, the extensive damage to cultural property that has occurred throughout Iraq since the fall of Baghdad has

remained mostly unrecorded and unrecognized because, unlike other recent conflicts such as that in the Balkans, there has been no survey of war damage by international observers or scholars. When the United Nations, the Red Cross, and other international aid organizations pulled out of Iraq in fall 2003 because of the worsening security situation, it spelled an end, in effect, also to international efforts to assist Iraq's museums, libraries, and cultural property in general.

The worst aspect of the cultural disaster is at archaeological sites. Iraq is referred to as Mesopotamia, the so-called cradle of civilization in traditional archaeological terminology. It comprises over ten thousand listed archaeological sites as well as hundreds of medieval and Ottoman Muslim, Christian, and Jewish monuments, making it one of the world's richest countries in terms of ancient heritage. While some looting has always gone on in countries rich in antiquities, the archaeological sites of Iraq are now being looted to an extent that was previously unimaginable anywhere. The looting supplies the appetites of a large international illicit trade in antiquities as many objects end up in places such as Geneva, London, Tokyo, and New York. The lack of border control under the occupation has only added to the ease with which the illegal trade in Mesopotamian artifacts functions, and there is now no real effort, either by coalition forces or by the interim government, to stop the plunder that is taking place.

The destruction of sites by looting is widely known to the world archaeological community. What is not well known is that the coalition military forces now occupy a number of important ancient Mesopotamian cities, Babylon being only the most famous example. The military occupation of archaeological sites is causing ongoing daily destruction of some of the most important heritage sites in Iraq. The structures built for the military camps are dug into the archaeological layers. Heavy equipment tramples across and destroys ancient remains. For example, helicopter flights have rattled the brick walls of Babylon to the point that at least two temple structures of the sixth century B.C.E. have collapsed (fig. 1). There has been no statement or response from UNESCO or any other cultural nongovernmental organization calling for a halt to this occupation of heritage sites or to their destruction by the military. The terms of the Geneva Convention and the Hague Convention, however, would make the occupation of such sites illegal under international law.

Babylon was first occupied by the U.S. Marine Corps in April 2003 (figs. 2, 3). The camp, known as Camp Alpha or "The Ruins" in military terminology, was ceded to the Polish military command in fall 2003. Much of the infrastructure of

FIGURE 1 Helicopter over Babylon. U.S. military helipad built into the site between the palace of Nebuchadnezzar and the Hellenistic Theater. Photo: Zainab Bahrani

this extensive camp, the headquarters of South Central Command, had been installed under U.S. command, for example, the bulldozing and paving of an area for a helicopter pad in the heart of the ancient site. But construction work continued throughout the ancient site under Polish command. Although the United States and Britain have not ratified the Hague Convention of 1954, Poland has signed and ratified it. Article 28 allows for the prosecution of those breaking the convention.

There was initially a tremendous international response to the looting of institutions in April 2003. International meetings were called and pledges were made to assist the museums and libraries of Iraq in restoring and renovating their collections. Plans to protect archaeological sites were discussed by a number of cultural NGOs in Europe and the United States, but few of the international pledges have come through, and international experts, conservators, archaeologists, and cultural organizations have been unwilling to risk going into Iraq. Therefore, meetings on Iraq have shifted, usu-

FIGURE 2 Soldiers in the reconstructed area of the Palace of Nebuchadnezzar, sixth century B.C.E. Photo: Zainab Bahrani

FIGURE 3 Soldiers in Babylon, at sixth-century B.C.E. remains of
the Ishtar Gate. Photo: Zainab Bahrani

ally to Amman, where Iraqi scholars are then requested to
travel out by land to meet with the international experts at
this safer location. As a result, the world's archaeological and
scholarly community has not seen the extent of destruction
that has taken place in Iraq. Because places like Babylon are
military camps and security is invoked as a reason for limiting
access, the international press has had little to say about this.
In Iraq itself, as a rule, archaeologists from the State Board of
Antiquities and Heritage (SBAH) are not allowed onto sites
that have been taken over as military camps. No permission is
sought by the coalition forces before any construction work,
movement of earth, or changes in the topography are made by
the military. Although the Antiquities and Heritage Law of
Iraq requires that any construction work at a heritage or
archaeological site be authorized by the SBAH, this law has
been ignored by the military, whose spokesmen have stated

that, for security purposes, all such laws are suspended during
the war and the occupation.

Nature of the Site Before and After the Occupation

Although knowledge of Babylon had survived in the Western
tradition through references in the Bible and by classical
authors, its location was unknown. In the region of Iraq itself,
however, the place always retained its name and was called
Babil by the locals. Among the names for the grouping of
mounds in the area, "Babil" was still in use locally during the
Ottoman era. From 1811 to 1817 Claudius James Rich conducted early excavations at Babylon. Robert Koldewey, the
German archaeologist, began extensive work there in 1899.

Excavation by Koldewey revealed a city of tremendous proportions. The southern citadel, the processional way, the Greek theater, and a number of temples and residential quarters were all unearthed, and Koldewey's team removed parts of the ancient glazed brick walls, including the Ishtar Gate, to take to Berlin. The ancient city encompassed about 900 hectares; it was the largest city in antiquity before imperial Rome. Babylon was considered a city of such vast proportions that nothing else could compare. According to Herodotus (*The Histories* 1.191), people in the inner city remained unaware when its outskirts were captured by Cyrus. Aristotle stated that because the city was so large, it took three days for news of the conquest to reach the center (*Politics* 3.1.12).

U.S. military reports, and even statements by representatives of UNESCO in the past year, indicate that there is a lack of awareness with regard to the extent of the site. Military reports and press accounts state that ancient Babylon is limited to the small area where reconstruction work took place under the previous regime. The military's public affairs office thus uses the argument that any damage to Babylon was already done by Saddam's regime and that by the time the U.S. Marines arrived at the site, little ancient heritage remained.

In the 1980s a team of Iraqi archaeologists, under orders from Saddam Hussein, reconstructed the lateral wall of the processional way near the palace, the Greek-Hellenistic theater, and parts of the palace of Nebuchadnezzar. Saddam Hussein also had a palace of his own built on the ancient riverbed, after bringing in earth from outside Babylon to form a large mound or artificial tell (no doubt as a mock ancient site) as a base for the palace. The reconstruction was loudly disapproved of by the world's archaeological and scholarly community because it was located in the ancient area. It was this project that notoriously included bricks inscribed with Saddam's own name in the reconstructed walls of the palace of Nebuchadnezzar II.

Nevertheless, the damage that has occurred as a result of turning Babylon into the South Central headquarters of the multinational coalition force, the largest military camp in the area, is far more extensive than any damage that occurred as a result of the additions ordered by Saddam. The military camp has conducted projects that have required the bulldozing and compacting of earth across the site and in numerous areas. Sandbags and large barrel-like containers used for barricades have been filled with ancient earth from the site. Colossal concrete blocks have been positioned everywhere, compressing the layers below. Tanks and other heavy military vehicles drive across the ancient pavement of the processional way, destroy-

ing the surface. A large helicopter landing zone was constructed in the heart of the ancient site, between the palace and the Greek theater. This area was bulldozed and leveled, then paved with asphalt. Dozens of helicopters fly in and out of this area on a daily and hourly basis, over ancient palace and temple walls. The military also began construction of two more helicopter landing zones in Babylon, which were eventually turned into parking lots for large military vehicles and machinery.

When asked why the site of Babylon had been decided on as a military camp, no official was able to give an answer. The modern town of Hilla, where the coalition has another helicopter landing zone and which is close to Babylon, could have been used instead as a location for the camp. In April 2003 press reports stated that U.S. troops likened their entrance into Babylon to that of Alexander the Great and his troops in the fourth century B.C.E. Tanks drove along the ancient processional way and occupation ceremonies took place that were photographed and published by the media. This behavior suggests that the occupation of Babylon was a deliberate symbolic expression of power over Mesopotamia. The occupation of sites such as Babylon and the images of military force at the ancient ruins can be described as an aesthetic of occupation, a display of force that uses the sign of history and its control as a statement of victory.

International Response

Some form of international response by the world archaeological community can still take place, but for Babylon and other occupied archaeological sites in Iraq, there can be no solution now. The lack of response may in part be due to the fact that as a military base, Babylon has not been open to either scholars or journalists. As noted earlier, the military cites general security concerns as a reason for both the occupation of Babylon and prohibiting access to the site. Access to the site by archaeologists or by the SBAH director in charge, Maryam Omran Moussa, and her assistants, was considered unnecessary since the Polish troops had brought along their own military civil military cooperation (CIMIC) archaeologists. The U.S. military also has a section called CMO (civic military operations). These officers can be well intentioned, but they themselves were at times responsible for damage to Babylon, because they felt that they could take decisions on construction despite the Antiquities and Heritage Law or requests from the SBAH representative that they do no work at the site.

There have been varied responses from the international academic community. Some intellectuals are reluctant to make statements about the destruction of cultural property in Iraq by the coalition while so many people are losing their lives in the violence of war. Other scholars state a desire to remain politically neutral in the conflict. Remarkably, the Archaeological Institute of America and the College Arts Association of the United States have been more critical and outspoken than have scholarly organizations that specialize in the Middle East. But the occupation of archaeological or heritage sites during war, as a practice or an act of war, still has to be addressed seriously in the archaeological literature. The use of archaeological sites, the deployment of modern architectural construction, and the demolition of older city centers in the name of modernization are well-known tools of colonial occupation. The issue has been discussed by numerous anthropologists, architectural historians, and architects (e.g., Abu El-Haj 2001; Segal and Weizman 2002). Archaeologists must also come to understand that the demolition and the reconstruction of ancient sites and older traditional city centers in the name of modernization and security are not purely aesthetic or historical issues. They are related directly to human rights because the manipulation and destruction of the historic and architectural fabric of the occupied land is an instrument of war.

Destruction of cultural property in armed conflict can take several forms. In "Cultural Warfare," John Yarwood points to four types of such destruction (Yarwood 1998). In the first case, damage is collateral in operations where an enemy occupies an area that includes historic monuments. In the second case, there is deliberate destruction of monuments with the intention of ethnic cleansing. The third type of damage occurs through looting, ultimately for connoisseurs who reside outside the occupied country. While a great deal of looting in Iraq fits into this third category, this form of damage and the illicit antiquities trade are more readily discussed by the archaeology profession. Instead, I am concerned here with the fourth type of cultural warfare: the deliberate destruction of the enemy's patrimony in situations in which, in Yarwood's (1998) terms, this assists neither military nor ethnic cleansing operations. Such destruction can be a result of an uncontrolled, unplanned attack, or often, a deliberately planned psychological operation (Yarwood 1998).

After two years of military occupation and martial law, the ancient heritage of Iraq can be classified as seriously endangered. Whereas the extensive looting and damage to sites has been described in the press and in the world archaeological community as falling, more or less, into the category of collateral damage, it can be demonstrated that the occupation of iconic heritage sites such as Babylon are psychological operations of military occupation. That at least six heritage sites have been taken over as coalition military camps indicates that this is not a random choice but the preplanned and systematic use of heritage sites for military operations. It is a psychological operation of warfare because it appears to be a deliberate choice to occupy a famous and iconic site of local cultural mythology. Babylon's symbolic mythical value is not lost here; instead, it is incorporated into the process of the occupation, and its symbolic significance is subsumed in a display of power over this ancient terrain.

Perhaps what is needed now is a new protocol for the protection of cultural heritage during war and occupation. This protocol might underscore the fact that the use of a heritage site as a military base qualifies as a form of direct cultural destruction, directly related to other forms of cultural warfare and ethnic cleansing. Furthermore, since the current political situation has rendered UNESCO an ineffective voice for the protection of cultural heritage in Iraq (and perhaps elsewhere), a nonaligned cultural organization made up of archaeologists and conservationists could be called together, perhaps under the auspices of the World Archaeological Congress, to take on that responsibility. A survey of war damage ought to be conducted as soon as possible under this independent professional group. Finally, an academic study of the practices of the uses of the past and the systematic occupation of heritage sites by the U.S.-led occupation of Iraq could be the subject of future archaeological-theoretical studies on the relationship of archaeology and politics and, more generally, of ideological uses of the past.

Notes

1   This essay is based on my own fieldwork, assessment, and documentation of the damage to Babylon under coalition occupation. The work was conducted jointly with Maryam Omran Moussa, director of the site of Babylon, on site, over the course of three months in summer 2004. Reports of this damage were made known by us to the Iraqi Ministry of Culture, to the U.S. Civil Military Affairs Office in Baghdad, to the U.S. Department of State, Office of Cultural Property, and to the British Embassy in Baghdad in July 2004. Requests and negotations for the removal of the camp, and outlines for the correct procedures to accom-

plish the removal, were also made over the course of the summer in a joint effort by Dr. Moussa and me. As a result of these negotations, the coalition authorities agreed to remove the camp by the end of 2004. In preparation for the final removal, John Curtis of the British Museum was called to Babylon for a three-day trip, 11–13 December 2004, as a witness and to verify reports of damage. The British Museum posted his eight-page preliminary report on damage to the site, "Report on Meeting at Babylon 11th–13th December 2004," at www.thebritishmuseum.ac.uk/ newsroom/current2005/Babylon_Report04.doc. It is important to note that the eight-page document does not cover all the damage but was intended as a list of the types of damage that have occurred.

A full account of the struggle for Babylon will appear at a later date, elsewhere. This essay presents some preliminary observations only. It is dedicated to Maryam Omran Moussa, with profound admiration.

2   See http://users.ox.ac.uk/~wolf0126/petition.html.

References

Abu El-Haj, N. 2001. *Facts on the Ground: Archaeological Practice and Territorial Self-Fashioning in Israeli Society.* Chicago: University of Chicago Press.

Aristotle. 1995. *Politics.* Loeb Classical Library Edition. Cambridge, Mass.: Harvard University Press.

Bahrani, Z. 1998. Conjuring Mesopotamia: Imaginative geography and a world past. In *Archaeology under Fire*, 159–74. London: Routledge.

———. 2003. *The Graven Image: Representation in Babylonia and Assyria.* Philadelphia: University of Pennsylvania Press.

Freedberg, D. 1989. *The Power of Images: Studies in the History and Theory of Response.* Chicago: University of Chicago Press.

———. 2001. The power of wood and stone: The Taliban is not the first to fear the mysterious lure of art. *Washington Post,* 25 March.

Herodotus. 1954. *The Histories.* Trans. A. de Selencourt. Harmondsworth: Penguin.

Kohl, P. L., and C. Fawcett. 1995. *Nationalism, Politics and the Practice of Archaeology.* Cambridge: Cambridge University Press.

Segal, R., and E. Weizman. 2002. *The Civilian Occupation.* Tel-Aviv: Verso.

Yarwood, J. 1998. Cultural warfare. Paper presented at "Art, Antiquity, and the Law: Preserving Our Global Cultural Heritage: An International Conference." Rutgers University, New Brunswick, N.J.

The National Museum and Archaeology in Afghanistan: Accomplishments and Current Needs

Abdul Wassey Feroozi and Omara Khan Masoodi

Abstract: *This paper reviews the history of the Institute of Archaeology in Afghanistan and the recent history of the National Museum in Kabul. It suggests concrete steps that need to be taken to strengthen both these institutions and to preserve and promote Afghanistan's cultural and national heritage.*

Archaeology in Afghanistan: History and Structure of Support and Current Needs

Throughout its history, Afghanistan has played an indispensable role in the growth and development of human culture and has functioned as a crossroads of civilization.[1] Afghanistan's ancient civilization and culture are also of special importance to the history of world religion. Studies of the pre- and proto-historical periods of Afghanistan from the Palaeolithic, Neolithic, and Bronze and Iron Ages up to the Greco-Bactrian, Kushan, Sassanian, and Hephtalite periods, as well as during Islamic times, testify to the fact that Afghanistan possesses a rich and greatly important past. Afghanistan has also been known as a meeting place of important civilizations of the East and West, and it has drawn the attention of scholars and researchers from around the world.

Officially, archaeological activities were initiated in the country in 1922, when the first contract was signed between the Afghan state and the Délégation Archéologique Française en Afghanistan (DAFA). After World War II, in 1949–50, an American mission headed by Louis Dupree started prehistoric research in the south, at sites that included Deh Morasi and Dashti Nower. Later, archaeological activities were carried out by missions from Germany, Italy, Japan, Greece, Great Britain, India, and Russia, which also signed protocols, conducted excavations, and surveyed different sites in Afghanistan up to 1978. As a result, hundreds of ancient sites were discovered and excavated, and numerous objects were unearthed.

With the establishment of the Institute of Archaeology in 1963, all archaeological activities were promoted and certain sites, such as Hada (Tepe Shutur, Tepe Tup-e Kalan), Tepe Maranjan, and Kham-e Zargar, were independently excavated by Afghan experts. Among these outstanding sites are the Great Temple in Shotor Hada and the Buddhist Temple of Maranjan Hill. As a result of political destabilization and lack of security, from 1978 to 1992 the only excavation carried out was at Tepe Maranjan in Kabul, and the Institute of Archaeology concentrated its efforts on archaeological publications, dissertations, and articles.

From 1992 onward, after the government of Dr. Najibullah was toppled and the Mujahidin government was installed, chaos and irregularity took over the state system. Looting and vandalism began; the country lost its infrastructure, and all state departments experienced extreme difficulties. More than 70 percent of the objects in the National Museum collections and 100 percent of the objects deposited in the Archaeological Institute were plundered and exported to neighboring countries for sale. Clandestine excavations were conducted throughout the country, and through illicit traffic, historical objects found their way to international markets.

During the period of the Taliban, a majority of Afghanistan's cultural heritage, which was precious and unique, was demolished. Such remains as the colossal Buddha statues in Bamiyan and smaller images in the Kabul Museum were destroyed. Extremely difficult conditions and uncertain security, combined with day-to-day difficulties and budget shortages, further hindered archaeological activities and caused a brain drain from Afghanistan.

Since the collapse of the Taliban regime and the establishment of the new government, it is hoped that, with the help and cooperation of friendly countries, the Institute can resume archaeological activities and research and start joint projects at important sites such as Bamiyan, Kabul, Kharwar, and Mes Ainak (in Logar province). To promote all facets of archaeology in Afghanistan, the following needs should be addressed:

- Training of staff in the fields of archaeology, architecture, conservation, photography, and management;
- Protection, preservation, and conservation and restoration of archaeological sites and monuments;
- Fostering of relations with foreign research institutions;
- Excavation of certain endangered sites;
- Exchanges of scholars and students from Afghanistan with other countries;
- Publication of scientific books, dissertations, and articles;
- Rebuilding and rehabilitation of the National Museum in Kabul;
- Provision of a new building for the Institute of Archaeology (to replace the one destroyed, which should become a monument to destruction);
- Nomination of important ancient and historical sites to the World Heritage List;
- Preparation of a national inventory of sites and monuments and archaeological maps;
- Ratification of the 1970 UNESCO Convention on the Means of Prohibiting and Preventing the Illicit Import, Export and Transfer of Ownership of Cultural Property and the 1995 UNIDROIT Convention;
- Computerization of the archaeological archives;
- Enrichment of the National Institute of Archaeology library, the photographic laboratory, and modernization of the restoration laboratory; and
- Procurement of equipment for the various departments of the National Institute of Archaeology.

Last, it is hoped that world communities interested in Afghanistan's cultural heritage will contribute to these projects.

Overview of the National Museum: Events during the Past Two Decades

Situated at an important junction on the ancient Silk Roads, Afghanistan has been a crossroads of cultures since time immemorial. Its unique cultural heritage reflects a history that is marked by complex indigenous encounters with Achaemenid Persia, China, and Alexandrian Greece, as well as with Buddhism, Hinduism, and Islam. The collections representing this rich and unique cultural heritage were displayed in various museums in the larger cities of Afghanistan, especially in the National Museum in Kabul.

King Habibullah (1901–19) brought together collections of wooden sculptures previously brought from Nuristan by his father, King Abdur Rahman, and carpets, silk and wool embroidery, metalwork, manuscripts with miniature paintings, and other luxury objects that had belonged to former royal families, to create the royal collection in his father's former palace pavilion at Bagh-e Bala. These collections were moved to the Kot-e Baghcha palace pavilion, located in the Arg (citadel), in 1925. In an effort to modernize Afghanistan and Kabul, King Habibullah's successor, Amanullah Khan, built the suburb of Darulaman, which included a European-style museum, installed in what had been the municipality building, just below his palace. In 1931 this museum was inaugurated by his successor, Nadir Khan, with the collections from the Kot-e Baghcha palace pavilion and enriched with the archaeological finds of the DAFA. Based on an agreement between the governments of Afghanistan and France, the excavation of archaeological sites was begun. The museum in Darulaman was twice renovated and enlarged, in the mid-1940s and in the mid-1970s. After the political complications that followed, during the period of Daoud and the Soviet occupation, the museum suffered from its location in this distant suburb, which was on the front line of much of the fighting. Nevertheless, the collections were preserved.

During the years that followed the collapse of the Soviet-backed government, the Kabul museum was directly in the theater of the looting and destruction that went on in Afghanistan. Until 1992 more than one hundred thousand objects belonging to periods ranging from prehistory to the twentieth century were conserved in the museum. Unfortunately, as a result of the civil war that raged in Kabul from 1992 to 1995, especially on the south side of the city where the National Museum is located, much was damaged. In May 1993 a heavy rocket crashed into the upper floor of the museum and set it on fire. In 1995, when the war intensified in the area, the Ministry of Information and Culture decided to protect the remaining collections. The objects were registered, photographed, put in cases, and moved to the center of the city. This effort was undertaken by the personnel of the National Museum and of the Archaeological Institute with the financial support of the Society for the Preservation of Afghanistan's Cultural Heritage (SPACH).

Efforts to account for the collections have shown that 70 percent of the objects were destroyed by fire, stolen, or plundered. Of the 30 percent of the original collections that remain, most are in need of repair.

An intensive traffic in cultural heritage objects has developed. The culmination of this traffic occurred during the occupation of the Taliban, who destroyed anything that resembled an animate figure and that could not be carried away for sale. In 2001 they smashed the sculptures of the National Museum collections. In March of the same year they also destroyed the colossal 38- to 55-meter-high Buddha statues at Bamiyan.

The often-quoted sign over the museum's entrance door reads, "A nation can stay alive when its culture stays alive," but the National Museum had become a ghost museum. Until 2003 the building was without windows or a roof. Objects stolen from the National Museum have shown up for sale on markets around the world. However, the museum staff's efforts to preserve the collections have been, and are today, exemplary; thanks to their perseverance, large numbers of objects, although many are damaged, are stored at the museum and in the Ministry of Information and Culture. Despite the destruction and the looting, the National Museum in Kabul today remains culturally rich and unique.

After the fall of the Taliban regime and the installation of the interim and transitional governments, plans were made to protect and reconstruct the culture of Afghanistan. These plans included the reconstruction of the National Museum building, the repair of the remains of the National Museum collections, the reactivation of the various departments of the museum, the establishment of an exact inventory of the collections of the National Museum and of the museums in the provinces, and the training of young professionals in the making of a database system for the museum. These are the tasks that the museum is painfully undertaking today.

International pledges were made to rebuild and rehabilitate the museum, but ten months after the fall of the Taliban regime and the establishment of a new government, no work had yet begun on the museum building. Collections remain stored in precarious situations, and the restoration of objects had to begin in bombed-out rooms without water or electricity. As the pledges and promises had yet to give concrete results, UNESCO Kabul decided to prepare the museum for winter by providing electricity, water, and window panes. These repairs at least permitted the museum staff to continue to work during the deadly cold and protected some of the collections from the rigors of winter. The British Museum funded a new restoration department that includes a wet and a dry room. The restoration department was built with the support of the British International Security Assistance Force (ISAF). The Greek government has given funds for the restoration of several rooms and the electrification of the museum; the U.S. government donated $100,000 for structural repairs. The major problem that remained was the lack of a roof over the museum structure. Currently, SPACH is making a donation of $40,000 to finish the roof. These funds are from the UNESCO Funds-in-Trust from the government of Italy. The Japanese government has given the photographic material necessary for the establishment of a new photographic department, and with the assistance of the National Federation of UNESCO Associations in Japan, a photographic exhibition was organized and the museum photographers trained. The photographic exhibition, *Work in Progress: The Rebirth of the Kabul Museum,* was the first exhibition in the museum for over twenty years and was intended to increase awareness of the problems facing the museum. Training has been undertaken by both the Italian and French governments. With the assistance of the Musée Guimet in Paris, several statues that had been smashed by the Taliban have been repaired, including the famous statue of Kanishka from Surkh Kotal. The restoration teams have also brought with them equipment and chemical treatment solutions. The French NGO Patrimoine sans frontières has donated additional materials for restoration.

The museum is in a dangerous area, and in fact, the area is no longer serviced by public transport, which is a tremendous burden on the museum staff. The isolation of the museum in the far suburb of Darulaman was one of the factors that contributed to its deteriorated state. If the museum had been in the city center, it would not have experienced so much looting, as the neighbors would have seen the looters and protected their cultural heritage. There has been a plan for more than two decades to build a new museum. However, the land that was allotted to the Ministry of Information and Culture for this purpose is situated near the Arg, which today is a no-man's land, occupied by the Ministry of Defense. This location is not suitable for a museum, as it is exposed to great risks. A more appropriate site should be identified. In fact, the Ministry of Information and Culture owns the land adjacent to the National Archives. If a new museum were to be built here, it would become a museum complex, sharing a common restoration laboratory for manuscripts and other museum objects. During the past conflict, the National Archives did not suffer damage, as its site is protected from both missile fire and looting by the proximity of the mountains and the local population. However, the city zoning plan has classified this land for commercial use.

As the rehabilitation of the present museum has just begun, there can be no safe storage of cultural heritage objects, which are kept in various locations around Kabul and in the provinces. The Ministry of Information and Culture required the space that had been occupied on the ground level by the stored objects as work space for its staff. The storage situation in the Ministry is very precarious, as was demonstrated by the bomb that exploded in 2002 just across the street. Along with the perilous condition of the stored cultural heritage objects, there is an associated problem, that of not being able to take in objects from excavations. The minister of culture has said that today Afghanistan's number one problem in the cultural sector is illicit excavation and looting. Fortunately, many objects have been stopped from leaving the country, but where are they to be kept? If there were museum space to protect and restore these objects, scientific archaeological excavation could begin. At the same time this would help put to an end to much of the illicit excavation, as it has done in Iraq.

It is impossible to speak about the museum without mentioning the human factor. The National Museum in Kabul has one of the most dedicated staffs in the country. They have done their utmost, and the seemingly impossible, to save what could be saved of the museum collections. This dedication should be repaid, but in fact, because the museum is isolated in a far suburb of Kabul that lacks public transportation, the museum staff is in one of the most dangerous situations in the country. Also, until very recently, working in a building without electricity or water was excruciating, especially during the winter months. The museum staff is just beginning to receive the benefits of training and up-to-date methods of inventory and restoration. For the past two decades, they have not been in contact with their colleagues around the world and have missed the exchange of ideas and methods that accompanies these contacts. If the museum is to continue to attract and retain such dedicated staff, training opportunities and exchange must be provided. Not only should short-term training be organized for the dedicated staff, but long-term training for the younger generation must be foreseen and organized, in the near future, to ensure the continuation of quality work in the museum.

Estimates of reconstruction and rehabilitation time for the Darulaman area range from ten to twenty years. In the meantime, the museum and its collections must be rehabilitated and exhibitions organized for the edification of the public. Education of the younger generation in Afghanistan, and those returning to Afghanistan, is of the highest importance to the country and to the future understanding of its unique cultural heritage, which has been shrouded by the last years of obscurantism.

Kabul today is in search of cultural direction. Attempts to create venues for popular culture have met with resistance from the conservative elements of society. One example, among others, is the musical concert that was planned for the Nauruz (New Year) celebration in the Olympic Stadium in 2002 but canceled at the last moment without explanation. Artists have not found exhibition facilities. There has been much discussion of the intangible cultural heritage of Afghanistan, but until now popular expressions of art and culture have not been encouraged. The ideal National Museum would become a place of study and artistic expression. There is a great need for a museum complex having archaeological, ethnological, and popular components.

Notes

1   The first section of this paper was written by Dr. Feroozi, the second section by Dr. Masoodi.

Preserving the Cultural and National Heritage of Afghanistan

Philip L. Kohl and Rita Wright

> If the culture of a nation dies, its soul dies with it. It's not enough to eat and clothe yourself. You have to have some sense of identity.
>
> —NANCY H. DUPREE, Society for the Preservation of Afghanistan's Cultural Heritage

Abstract: *This paper describes the various forms of destruction to which the rich archaeological remains of Afghanistan have been subjected over the past quarter century: they have been plundered for the antiquities market, obliterated by incessant fighting, and even deliberately demolished by governmental decrees. It suggests that many countries, including the United States, bear certain responsibilities for this destruction and urges greater financial support to protect the archaeological sites and architectural monuments of Afghanistan and to rebuild the national museum and research institutions devoted to the promotion of Afghanistan's unique pre-Islamic and Islamic pasts. It also discusses the recent reemergence of the looting of sites and the trading of antiquities on an unprecedented scale and urges international efforts to prevent these activities.*

The Cultural, National, and Cold War Heritage of Afghanistan

Three consecutive sessions were presented at the Fifth World Archaeological Congress (WAC-5) titled "Preserving the Cultural and National Heritages of Afghanistan." This title was chosen to emphasize the complexity and diversity of Afghanistan's past, to acknowledge that its heritage and legacy from different periods are multiple, and to distinguish and highlight both its cultural and its national heritage. In the context of contemporary Afghanistan, this last distinction is crucial. Today Afghanistan has an essentially 100 percent Islamic cultural heritage (i.e., its numerous different peoples almost exclusively profess Islam), but it also has a national heritage comprising all the remains from different periods and cultures that are found within its borders and, literally, in its earth. One wants to preserve both the cultural and the national heritage of Afghanistan and to never repeat the deliberate destruction of monuments deemed non-Islamic or culturally alien, such as was perpetrated by the Taliban. Given this recent history, the argument can be made that initial restoration and archaeological efforts should perhaps principally focus on the remains of Afghanistan's Islamic cultural heritage, such as the current UNESCO-sponsored projects to restore the Timurid mosques and minarets of Herat and the minaret of Jam nestled deep in the Hindu Kush (see, in this volume, Manhart; Williams and Haxthausen). As civic nationalism takes root, Afghans should be made aware and proud of the incredibly rich archaeological remains of all the periods and cultures interred in the Afghan soil.

Afghanistan also has the dubious distinction of sharing another heritage or legacy as one of the worst victims of the Cold War, the decades-long standoff between the Soviet Union and the United States to achieve global hegemony. Already poor and underdeveloped throughout the 1970s, Afghanistan descended into a state of warfare and perpetual political insta-bility as a consequence of the Soviet invasion in December 1979, a condition of fighting and insecurity that arguably has prevailed more or less continuously until the present. The tragedy that led to the rise of the Taliban and ultimately to the support it provided for Al-Qaeda was neither inevitable nor fortuitous. All sides must bear responsibility for the tragedy that unfolded and left Afghanistan so devastated. Equally, it is obvious that the entire world benefits from a secure, econom-ically restored, and peaceful Afghanistan. There is no question that very basic needs must be met—security, subsistence, health, education, and the reconstruction of basic infrastruc-ture—and that all must be provided as quickly as possible.

Given this scheme of things, what priority should be accorded the restoration and preservation of Afghanistan's cultural and national heritage? The question is impossible to answer definitively, though two basic points should be made. First, all the ongoing problems Afghanistan confronts today are interrelated. The resurgence in the looting and pillaging of sites, the ongoing rape of Afghanistan's pre-Islamic and Islamic archaeological monuments that has occurred during the past two years, is often ultimately orchestrated by entrenched warlords interested in maintaining their local con-trol and resisting central authorities. Political stability and the pillage of archaeological sites are inversely related. The war-lords would not engage in such activities if they were not profitable, nor would local peasants willingly dig up sites at

FIGURE 1 Local villagers "excavating" the mound of Tepe Zargaran within the walled precinct of ancient Balkh. Note the armed "supervisor." Courtesy of Ronald Besenval, Director, Délégation Archéologique Française en Afghanistan (DAFA)

warlords' requests if they too were not financially benefiting, at least to some degree, from doing so (fig. 1). The profitabil-ity of looting, of course, depends directly on the nearly insa-tiable demands of the antiquities market, and it is the collectors in western Europe, Japan, and the United States that somehow must be stopped from purchasing Afghanistan's stolen antiquities. Archaeological materials are nonrenewable resources, and every time sites are plundered, information about the past is irrevocably lost.

Second, a country's cultural and national heritage is basic to a country's sense of self and, consequently again, to its security and stability. Despite all the centrifugal forces at work, Afghanistan has held together as a viable nation-state during the recent conflicts and chaos. A shared sense of his-tory and pride in a collective past—both pre-Islamic and Islamic—potentially unites different ethnic groups on either side of the Hindu Kush. The restoration of a national museum and the preservation and legitimate excavation of archaeolog-ical sites promote this sense of a shared past and, thus, can be considered essential for the reconstruction of the country. Afghanistan has multiple priorities: roads, hospitals, and schools need to be built; at the same time, the different peo-ples of the country need to think of themselves as sharing a unique and rich historical tradition.

Reconstruction and Heritage

The protection and preservation of Afghanistan's heritage is part of a larger effort involving competing needs that include military and humanitarian efforts and reconstruction pro-jects. The United States and other governments have appro-priated significant funds for each of these, but the greatest attention has been to military and humanitarian needs, mat-ters of basic security, counternarcotics programs, and relief and refugee assistance. Reconstruction projects, the category that presumably includes heritage concerns, have focused pre-dominantly on basic infrastructure, such as road building.

Barnett Rubin (2003), in testimony to the Committee on International Relations, House of Representatives, stated that although significant programs have been undertaken, the progress of reconstruction has been "patchy and slow," and, as the statistics he cites demonstrate, this slowness is even more apparent for cultural projects. Rubin notes significant short-falls in the overall funding for reconstruction promised and disbursed and for projects that include culture, heritage, and media; estimates of funding needs compared to disburse-ments make a poor showing. Figures from the World Bank,

Deutsches Bank, and United Nations Development Program estimate that more than $10 million were needed for a single year and $20 million for two and a half years. When compared to figures from the Afghan Assistance Coordination Authority and the Donor Assistance Database,[1] only $6.9 million, or roughly 69 percent, had been dispersed by the time of his report. These figures sharply contrast with funds for urban development and transportation, where 270 percent of the estimated needed expenses was disbursed for the first year.

Figures for funding specific to cultural heritage are hard to come by. Christian Manhart (this volume) lists the dollar amounts entrusted to the UNESCO Funds-in-Trust program for cultural projects in Afghanistan. Donor countries include Italy, Japan, Switzerland, and Germany, as well as private foundations, such as the Aga Khan Trust Foundation for Culture (AKTC). The specific restoration and conservation projects for which these funds have been allocated are discussed in more detail in his contribution. Other funding has come from the United States, Greece, the United Kingdom, and the Society for the Preservation of Afghanistan's Cultural Heritage (SPACH). SPACH was established by Nancy Dupree and other volunteers and funded by private individuals and European governments. Direct exchanges with European museums, specifically directed to salvage excavations, rehabilitation of the National Museum in Kabul, and training programs there have been implemented by the Musée Guimet and the British Museum.

The United States has contributed significant funding for reconstruction efforts but very little to projects related to Afghanistan's cultural and national heritage. The two major U.S. funding initiatives for heritage projects abroad are the State Department, Office of Cultural Property, and USAID. In 2003 approximately $1 million was allocated to the Office of Cultural Property, a sum that may increase in the future. Project funding is based on proposals submitted by U.S. ambassadors either in "partnership between the U.S. Embassy and the country's Ministry of Culture or local non-profit organization . . . [overseen] . . . by the Embassy's Public Affairs Section. . . . Organizations wishing to suggest projects for consideration may contact the Public Affairs Office at the American Embassy in the eligible countries" (U.S. Department of State, Cultural Property 2003a).

Three grants were awarded to Afghanistan through the Ambassador's Fund for Cultural Preservation in 2003 and two from other State Department funds. Ambassador's Fund grants included $33,310 to restore the seventeenth-century Mullah Mahmud Mosque in Kabul, a surviving example of late Mughal vernacular architecture; $25,000 for restoration of the tomb of Jamaludin Al-Afghani, a nineteenth-century Islamic reformer; and $37,000 for repair, restoration, and rehabilitation of the Bagh-e-Babur Gardens. The Mogul emperor Babur was a descendant of Genghis Khan, and the sixteenth-century shrine and garden were dedicated to him. Other funds allocated through the State Department were $14,000 for an inventory of the National Museum to reestablish an accurate record of cultural artifacts and $100,000 for the rehabilitation of the main building of the museum (approved in May 2003) through basic structural repairs, including repair of the then-nonexistent roof. These figures may sound impressive—until one considers how much money in total is being directed toward reconstruction efforts in Iraq (tens of billions of dollars) vis-à-vis Afghanistan and how much is relatively available or allocated to the reconstruction of heritage and cultural patrimony in Iraq compared with Afghanistan. One example will suffice. In tacit admission of some responsibility for the looting of the Baghdad Museum and the pillaging of sites that ensued in the wake of the American-led Coalition of the Willing invasion of Iraq in spring 2003, the federally funded National Endowment for the Humanities (NEH) announced a new program to support projects exclusively concerned with "recovering Iraq's past."[2] This program has a rolling deadline and has been receiving applications since August 2003; it expected to announce its initial round of grantees during late winter 2004. Nonprofit institutions (i.e., individual scholars associated with such institutions) may apply for research grants of up to $100,000. Needless to say, no similar program has been established for Afghanistan. In other words, individual American scholars can receive grants to help recover Iraq's past as large as the single largest U.S. government grant to Afghanistan for this purpose in 2003. From this relative perspective, the two situations are totally incomparable.[3]

Falling out of Sight

Reconstruction efforts geared to Afghanistan's heritage have not stayed in the public eye. Since the fall of the Taliban, very little interest has been shown by the U.S. government, by the American public as a whole, or by the archaeological community. This lack of interest demonstrates a poor understanding of the relevance of cultural and national heritage in creating the civil society envisioned, or at least promised, in preparation for the invasion of Afghanistan. (See the epigraph at the beginning of this essay; a sign proclaiming essentially the same message—"A nation stays alive when its culture stays alive"—has hung in front of the National Museum in Kabul.) Administration rhetoric and the public press took strong stands against the Taliban's destruction of its pre-Islamic artifacts and monuments, fueled by newspaper coverage of the Bamiyan statues. These events elicited a public and governmental outcry over their destruction, but this enthusiasm for Afghanistan's national and cultural heritages has all but disappeared from the government's and the popular media's agendas.

The relative lack of interest among archaeological colleagues is more perplexing. The international scholarly community and archeological professional organizations have been particularly restrained. One would expect the same type of active engagement in heritage issues as has been exhibited by the Society for American Archaeology (SAA) Government Affairs Committee and efforts of other professional groups and museums with respect to Iraq to have parallels in monitoring heritage issues in Afghanistan. At the Fifth World Archaeological Congress sessions on Afghanistan, it was disappointing to find that approximately thirty colleagues (in a large ballroom set up for 300+) stayed throughout the daylong seminar and perhaps twenty others wandered in and out. This number was in stark contrast to the 300 or more attending sessions on Iraq and voicing their loud, clear, and justifiable concerns.

In fact, attention to heritage issues in Iraq has dominated media coverage worldwide since April 2003 when news of the extensive looting of the Baghdad Museum first became known. This diversion has led to a shift in focus away from equally compelling heritage projects in Afghanistan. The SAA and the Archaeological Institute of America (AIA) have closely and appropriately monitored legislation directed toward Iraq, some of which could have benefited Afghanistan as a "tag-on." The Senate bill that was adopted (see Gerstenblith, this volume) could have included protections for imported antiquities from nations like Afghanistan that were not party to the 1970 UNESCO Convention on Cultural Property, but unfortunately these provisions were not adopted because of opposition from the trading and collecting communities.

Steps toward a Future

When the United States went into Afghanistan to remove the Taliban government, there was the hope that the country would be restored to a certain level of stability with a new representative government. However, as is well known, pock-

ets of Taliban and Al-Qaeda sympathizers continue to undermine these efforts. The effectiveness of insurgent groups is partially due to the country's difficult terrain and its porous border with Pakistan. Antigovernment groups can move back and forth across the borders with relative ease. The Pakistani government and military have worked with the United States and coalition forces to eliminate these groups, but they have little power in remote tribal areas, making the situation difficult to secure.

This lack of security is inextricably linked to protecting and conserving Afghanistan's cultural heritage. As Omara Khan Masoodi points out in his contribution to this volume, the National Museum is located in a distant suburb of Kabul, a factor that may account for its current "forgotten" condition. He makes a persuasive argument for building a new structure closer to the center of Kabul, where a museum complex could serve as a cultural center for the city and where materials would be more secure. Whatever strategy is followed, the museum is a critical piece in restoring the country's heritage. Without a secure place in which to house objects, all current and any future collections are in jeopardy, since the museum is the country's major repository for archaeological and ethnographic collections. Its condition is more urgent, though—as we have emphasized—it is less in the public eye than the Baghdad Museum. It has neither a sound structure nor adequate storage space, not to mention sufficient numbers of trained personnel to ensure security. Masoodi's suggestion that the National Museum be located in a museum complex near the National Archives is sensible because it would provide a visible presence for the country's rich national and cultural heritage and promote public education on issues of stewardship and preservation.

An equally pressing problem is the pillaging and looting of archaeological sites. Here, there is a direct link between the military hazards and the country's cultural and national heritage. The looting in the country clearly is a critical problem. Sayeed Raheen, minister for culture and information in Kabul, stated, "[The looting of sites is the] worst of my country's problems. . . . For the criminals the profit margins are bigger than those of opium, and it's getting worse by the day" (cited in *Times [London]* 2002). In central Afghanistan a seventh-century city has been discovered at Kharwar, which, given its exceptional state of preservation, has been referred to—perhaps somewhat dramatically—as the Pompeii of Central Asia. Drug barons and warlords are currently excavating it. This theft at archaeological sites is yet another form of destruction of the country's heritage, beyond issues related to the National Museum and its holdings. To illustrate this destruction of Afghanistan's archaeological sites, we show two photographs of the world-famous site of Ai Khanoum in northeastern Afghanistan, the easternmost Hellenistic city ever discovered and meticulously excavated by French archaeologists during the 1960s and 1970s. The first image shows some of the exposed monumental public architecture at Ai Khanoum during the original French excavations (fig. 2); the second image shows what the site looks like today, revealing a landscape that can only be described as lunar (fig. 3). Osmund Bopeararchchi (this volume) has estimated that hundreds of ivory pieces, jewelry, intaglios, plaster medallions, and bronze items from Ai Khanoum have reached Pakistani bazaars and private collections.

As recent news reports have confirmed, the looting and pillaging of the country's heritage are to some degree funding the continued resistance to supporting a legitimate national government by filling the pockets of "warlords." The Hague Convention specifies that during an occupation, if national authorities are unable to safeguard and preserve the country's cultural property, necessary measures of preservation should be taken by occupying forces. Although the United States has not passed the enabling legislation that would make it a U.S. law, these considerations still ought to be reason enough for U.S. and coalition forces to take an active role in safeguarding Afghanistan's national and cultural property.

In his testimony to the House of Representatives, Rubin argued that as long as the reconstruction efforts are ignored, Afghanistan will remain a refuge for Al-Qaeda and other

FIGURE 2 The palace at Ai Khanoum as seen during the excavations of the French Archaeological Mission (DAFA). Courtesy of Délégation Archéologique Française en Afghanistan (DAFA)

FIGURE 3 The site of Ai Khanoum today after its near-total destruction. Courtesy of Délégation Archéologique Française en Afghanistan (DAFA)

militant groups. Abdul Wassey Feroozi put it another way. Looting, he said, is "another bead in the necklace. . . . To stop it, you must do the same things as to stop the drugs and other crime: strengthen the government, build up the police and the national army, [and] break the power of the warlords. Unfortunately we are still waiting for all these things" (*Guardian* 2003).

These considerations aside, there is much to be done in our own "homeland" to secure Afghanistan's and the world's cultural heritage. We cannot forget that the major benefactors of the illicit digging and theft of antiquities are the dealers and collectors, many of whom conduct their trade in the United States. Their complicity in fostering the commercialization of Afghanistan's heritage deserves greater attention. For some collectors, stolen antiquities comprise substantial portions of their investment portfolios, acquired at the expense of the cultural patrimony of individual nations. Traffickers supply looted artifacts to dealers who establish their monetary value and distribute them to the principal consumers of antiquities, the collectors (Coe 1993). Implementation of existing laws and new ones that are being proposed and debated should be a top priority for the U.S. government and professional organizations, individual archaeologists, and local and national

officials who need to take a more active role in protesting the complicity of dealers and collectors in the pillaging of a country's national and cultural heritages. Current conditions in Afghanistan are dire, but they can be turned around with appropriate attention, commitment, and support.

Postscript: On 24 May 2005, at a meeting in Washington, D.C., attended by President Hamid Karzai and other officials from the Islamic Republic of Afghanistan, the National Endowment for the Humanities announced an agency-wide initiative, "Rediscovering Afghanistan," to promote research, education, and public programs on Afghanistan's history and culture.

Acknowledgments

We are grateful to Joan Gero, academic secretary for WAC-5, to the Getty Conservation Institute (GCI) for their invitation to participate in the congress, and to Claire Lyons of the Getty Research Institute for organizing the subtheme, "Preserving the Cultural Heritage of Iraq and Afghanistan." Generous support from both the GCI and the National Geographic Society made it possible for us to organize these sessions. Specifically, their support allowed us to bring Omara Khan Masoodi, director of the National Museum in Kabul, and Abdul Wassey Feroozi, director general of the National Institute of Archaeology of Afghanistan, to Washington, D.C., for the WAC-5 meetings. In addition to Masoodi and Feroozi, Jim Williams from UNESCO in Kabul, Osmund Bopearachchi, and Bertille Lyonnet of CNRS in Paris, Ute Franke-Vogt of the German Archaeological Institute (DAI), and Nadia Tarzi of the Association for the Protection of Afghan Archaeology also received support and took part in our sessions. Other participants were Najim Azadzoi, Juliette van Krieken-Peters, Andrew Lawler, and Sanjyot Mehendale. Deborah Klimburg-Salter and Frederick Hiebert also were invited to participate, though their contributions were received subsequently. We also wish to acknowledge here the helpful comments of William Fitzhugh of the Smithsonian Institution who kindly functioned as the discussant at the end of the three sessions. During their stay in Washington, D.C., Masoodi and Feroozi visited the Museum Support Center of the Smithsonian Institution and discussions began about possible future conservation assistance to the National Museum in Kabul by the Smithsonian. The interest and support of Natalie Firnhaber at the Smithsonian Support Center was especially appreciated. Participants in the Afghanistan symposium also visited the National Geographic Society headquarters in Washington, where Masoodi and Feroozi and Bopearachchi made short presentations, illustrating the current conditions of Afghanistan's archaeological monuments and remains. Again considerable interest, including possible future assistance, was expressed during this meeting, and John Francis and John Hall of the Committee for Research and Exploration at the National Geographic Society, who organized these presentations, must also be warmly thanked for their support.

Notes

1 For information on DAD, see www.cic.nyu.edu/conflict/conflictproject4.html#Aid.

2 See www.neh.gov/grants/guidelines/iraq.html.

3 We confess that one of the principal reasons we decided to proceed with organizing the sessions on Afghanistan at WAC-5 was the lack of comparable attention and concern for Afghanistan relative to Iraq. Specifically, as the United States geared up in fall 2002 to invade Iraq, it became increasingly clear that Afghanistan's plight would soon be overshadowed. The cultural costs of waging war would still be apparent, but now the focus would turn to Iraq, and Afghanistan once again would be forgotten. It was also clear that there were many interesting parallels, as well as contrasts, between the destruction of Afghanistan's heritage and that of Iraq, particularly with the looting of the Baghdad National Museum in April 2003 and the subsequent extensive pillaging of Sumerian sites in southern Mesopotamia. Such comparisons and contrasts can be drawn from the essays collected in this volume.

References

Coe, M. D. 1993. From huaquero to connoisseur: The early market in pre-Columbian art. In *Collecting the Pre-Columbian Past,* ed. E. H. Boone, 271–90. Washington, D.C.: Dumbarton Oaks Research Library and Collection.

Frontline. 2002. Vandalized Afghanistan. 16–19 March.

Guardian. 2003. Plunder goes on across Afghanistan as looters grow ever bolder. 13 December.

NEH Program: Recovering Iraq's Past. 2003. www.neh.gov/grants/guidelines/iraq.html.

Rubin, B. R. 2003. Testimony of Dr. Barnett R. Rubin, Director of Studies, Center on International Cooperation, New York University. Presented before the Committee on International Relations, House of Representatives, 19 June.

Times (London). 2002. Afghans' lost city plundered for illegal London art trade. 7 December.

U.S. Department of State. International Information Programs. 2002. Ambassador's Fund preserves cultural heritage. usinfo.state.gov/regional/nea/sasia/afghan.

———. 2003a. Ambassador's Fund for Cultural Preservation. exchanges.state.gov/culprop/afcp/info.htm.

———. 2003b. House of Representatives for H.R. 2009. See www.thomas.loc.gov.

UNESCO's Mandate and Activities for the Rehabilitation of Afghanistan's Cultural Heritage

Christian Manhart

Abstract: UNESCO plays a major coordinating role in international activities directed to safeguarding Afghanistan's cultural heritage. In Bamiyan a major effort has been undertaken to consolidate the cliffs and niches where the statues once stood and to conserve remaining fragments. Other projects coordinated by UNESCO include preservation of mural paintings in the Buddhist caves and the rehabilitation of minarets in Jam and Herat. Efforts continue in Kabul to restore the National Museum and to provide training of museum staff. This paper chronicles the strong commitment by Afghan authorities to safeguarding their cultural heritage, the importance of cultural heritage in the reconstruction process, and the major role of UNESCO in these efforts.

UNESCO has responded to the challenge of rehabilitating Afghanistan's endangered cultural heritage, which has suffered irreversible damage and loss during the past two decades of war and civil unrest. The safeguarding of all aspects of cultural heritage in this country, both tangible and intangible, including museums, monuments, and archaeological sites and music, art, and traditional crafts, is of special significance for strengthening cultural identity and national integrity. Cultural heritage can become a mutual focal point for former adversaries, enabling them to rebuild ties, engage in dialogue, and work together to shape a common future. UNESCO's strategy is to assist in the reestablishment of links between the populations concerned and their cultural history so that they may develop a sense of common ownership of monuments that represent the cultural heritage of different segments of society. This strategy is linked directly to the nation-building process within the framework of the United Nations mandate and concerted international efforts to rehabilitate Afghanistan.

With reference to the U.N. secretary-general's dictum, "Our challenge is to help the Afghans help themselves," policies and activities for safeguarding Afghanistan's cultural heritage focus on training and capacity building. As the U.N. Program Secretariat for Culture, Youth, and Sports, UNESCO is entrusted by the Afghan government to coordinate all international efforts aimed at safeguarding and enhancing Afghanistan's cultural heritage. In this context, UNESCO organized several meetings in close cooperation with the Afghan Ministry of Information and Culture, notably the International Seminar on the Rehabilitation of Afghanistan's Cultural Heritage in Kabul, which was the first international seminar in Kabul after the fall of the Taliban regime.

In attendance were 107 specialists in Afghan cultural heritage and from donor countries and institutions. The seminar, chaired by H. E. Makhdoum Raheen, minister of information and culture of the Afghan government, offered presentations on the state of conservation of cultural sites, existing programs, and coordination of the first conservation measures. The amount of U.S. $7 million was pledged for priority projects and allocated through bilateral agreements and UNESCO Funds-in-Trust projects. The need to ensure effective cooperation was emphasized. Bearing in mind the enormous need to conserve sites at immediate risk of collapse, it was clearly stated and approved by the Afghan government that the Bamiyan statues should not be reconstructed.

Following the Afghan authorities' request to UNESCO to coordinate all international efforts for the safeguarding of the country's cultural heritage, UNESCO established the International Coordination Committee for the Safeguarding of Afghanistan's Cultural Heritage (ICC) in October 2002. It includes Afghan experts, international specialists from the most important donor countries, and organizations providing funds or scientific assistance. The first plenary session of the ICC was held in Paris in June 2003, chaired by H. E. Makhdoum Raheen, in the presence of His Highness Prince Mirwais. Seven representatives of the Afghan Ministry of Information and Culture and more than sixty international experts participated as members of the committee or as observers.

Concrete recommendations allowed the efficient coordination of actions at the highest international conservation standards. Key areas of concern were development of a long-term strategy, capacity building, implementation of the World Heritage Convention and Convention on the Means of Prohibiting and Preventing the Illicit Import, Export and Transfer of Ownership of Cultural Property, national inventories, documentation and rehabilitation of the National Museum in Kabul, and safeguarding of the sites of Bamiyan, Jam, and Herat. Several donors pledged additional funding for cultural projects in Afghanistan during and following the meeting.

Bamiyan

Following the collapse of the Taliban regime in December 2001, UNESCO sent a mission to Bamiyan to assess the condition of the site, cover the remaining large stone blocks, and provide protection from harsh winter conditions. In July 2002 another mission, organized with the International Council on Monuments and Sites (ICOMOS) and directed by its president, Michael Petzet, was undertaken to prepare conservation measures.

A project preparation mission to Bamiyan composed of German, Italian, and Japanese experts was undertaken in late September 2002. The experts noted that over 80 percent of the mural paintings in the Buddhist caves dating from the sixth to the ninth century C.E. had disappeared, through neglect or looting. In one cave, experts found the thieves' tools and the remains of freshly removed paintings. Consequently, the Afghan Ministry of Information and Culture arranged protection with the local commander, who provided ten armed guards for permanent surveillance of the site. No further thefts have been noted since. Of additional concern were large cracks in and around the niches where the Buddha statues had been situated, which could lead to the collapse of parts of the niches and inner staircases. Experts carried out complementary measures and advised on appropriate actions. The Japanese Foreign Ministry approved a UNESCO Funds-in-Trust

grant for safeguarding the Bamiyan site with a total budget of U.S. $1,815,967. ICOMOS financed the restoration of a Sunni mosque and another building, located in close proximity to the niche of the large Buddha.

A working group on the preservation of the Bamiyan site, comprising twenty-five Afghan and international experts, was jointly organized by UNESCO and ICOMOS in Munich in November 2002. The group recommended certain conservation measures and clearly reiterated that the statues should not be reconstructed. After delays caused by the Iraq war and resulting lack of security in the area, a three-week mission by the architect Mario Santana from Leuven University was undertaken in June 2003 for scientific documentation of the niches and the remaining fragments from the Buddhas.

Recommendations by the ICC in June 2003 included consolidation of the extremely fragile cliffs and niches, preservation of the mural paintings in the Buddhist caves, and preparation of an integrated master plan. A large scaffolding, donated by the German Messerschmidt Foundation, was transported to Afghanistan by the German army in August 2003. The Italian firm RODIO successfully implemented the first phase of the emergency consolidation of the cliffs and niches (fig. 1). In July, September, and October 2003, as well as in June–July 2004, specialists from the Japanese National Research Institute for Cultural Properties (NRICP) were fielded to Bamiyan to safeguard the mural paintings and prepare a master plan for the long-term preservation and management of the site. The NRICP submitted a preliminary master plan to UNESCO and the Afghan Ministry of Information and Culture in early 2005. It is expected to be finalized in close cooperation with the Afghan authorities by the end of 2005. Furthermore, a Japanese enterprise has prepared a topographic map of the valley and a 3-D model of the niches and the cliffs.

In December 2003 the second UNESCO/ICOMOS expert working group convened to evaluate the progress of consolidation, conservation, and archaeological activities. The twenty-five experts present notably appreciated the consolidation method and work of the Italian firm RODIO, which had recently succeeded in preventing the collapse of the upper eastern part of the Small Buddha niche. Recommendations for a 2004 work plan included final consolidation of the Small Buddha niche, conservation of the fragments of the two Buddha statues, preservation of the mural paintings, and coordination of the archaeological activities undertaken by the Délégation Archéologique Française en Afghanistan (DAFA) and the NRICP.

FIGURE 1 Mountain climbers repairing Small Buddha. Courtesy of P. Maxwell, UNAMA

A third expert working group meeting, organized by UNESCO and NRICP, was held in Tokyo in December 2004. Participants at the meeting expressed their deep appreciation for the activities already undertaken to consolidate the Buddhas' niches, preserve the statues' remains, protect the mural paintings, map the site, prepare the master plan, and train local personnel. For the first time, experts were able to use carbon-14 dating technology to ascertain the age of the two Buddha statues, as well as of the mural paintings: the Small Buddha was shown to date from 507 C.E.; the Great Buddha, from 551; and the mural paintings, from between the late fifth and early ninth century C.E. The participants agreed on the need to pursue the activities undertaken during the first phase of the project, which focused on emergency measures, and emphasized that longer-term measures were urgently required to ensure the continued preservation of the site. The approval of the recommendations by the group marks the end of the successful two-year UNESCO-Japan project and determines the future goals of its second phase.

Jam and Herat

In March 2002 the architect Andrea Bruno and the structural engineer Marco Menegotto assessed the state of conservation of the Jam and Fifth Minarets, the Gawhar Shad, the Citadel, the Friday Mosque, and other monuments in Herat and drafted project documents for their conservation. Later, Bruno and a hydrologist carried out a mission to advise on the consolidation of the Jam Minaret's foundations, the stabilization of its overall structure, and the water flow of the two rivers. They recommended protective measures for the archaeological zone of Jam, which was threatened by illicit excavations. Although the dramatic high floods of April 2002 had damaged the gabions installed by UNESCO in 2000, these remained efficient in protecting the monument, which has perhaps survived only as a result of this measure. In June 2002 the Jam Minaret was inscribed as the first Afghan property on the UNESCO World Heritage List.

From mid-October to early November 2002 Mario Santana and Tarcis Stevens, also an architect from Leuven University, carried out detailed metric documentation of the five minarets of the Gowhar Shad Musalla in Herat and the Jam Minaret. A preliminary training session on the use of a surveying total station donated by UNESCO was conducted for Afghan experts.

In January 2003 an expert working group was held on the preservation of Jam and the monuments in Herat. Among the twenty-three participants were Minister of Information and Culture Raheen; Zahir Aziz, Afghanistan's ambassador to UNESCO; Omara Khan Masoodi, director of the National Museum in Kabul; and Abdul Wassey Feroozi, head of the Afghan Institute of Archaeology. The working group evaluated the present state of conservation of the site of Jam and the Fifth Minaret, the Gawhar Shad, the Citadel, the Friday Mosque, and other monuments in Herat and addressed the

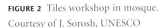

FIGURE 2 Tiles workshop in mosque.
Courtesy of J. Sorosh, UNESCO

problem of illicit excavations. They compared conservation methods and emergency and long-term conservation and coordination proposals with reference to identified priorities. Recommendations were made, allowing the commencement of emergency activities in 2003.

In November 2002 Swiss authorities approved a UNESCO Funds-in-Trust project for emergency consolidation and restoration of the site of Jam, budgeted at U.S. $138,000. Italian authorities granted U.S. $800,000 through the UNESCO Funds-in-Trust for emergency consolidation and restoration of monuments in Herat and Jam. The first activities under these projects began in April 2003 with the construction of a project house in Jam, the clearing of the Jam riverbed, and the repair and reinforcement of the wooden and metal gabions damaged by floods in 2002.

From late July to mid-August 2003, Andrea Bruno, Giorgio Macchi, Mariachristina Pepe, and a representative of UNESCO began preliminary work on a geological soil investigation at the minarets and made recommendations for their long-term consolidation. The Fifth Minaret in Herat received temporary emergency stabilization by means of steel cables designed by Macchi. This intervention was successfully carried out by the Italian firm ALGA, under very difficult security and logistical conditions. The minaret is now secured and stabilized, though it is probably not resistant to serious earthquakes. Three archaeologists from the Italian Institute for Africa and the Orient (IsIAO), under a UNESCO contract,

carried out safeguarding excavations on the site of Jam in August 2003. Additional protective measures for the foundations of the Jam Minaret were undertaken in 2004; the geophysical soil study and consolidation of the base of the minaret will be carried out in 2005.

In 2002 UNESCO, with the Society for the Preservation of Afghanistan's Cultural Heritage (SPACH), revived the tile-making workshop in Herat (fig. 2). Sixty Afghan trainees are learning the production of traditional tiles. In December 2003 the German authorities approved a U.S. $59,890 UNESCO Funds-in-Trust project for the retiling of the Gowhar Shad Mausoleum. The necessary tiles are being produced by the workshop in Herat.

National Museum of Kabul

Immediately after the collapse of the Taliban regime in December 2001, a UNESCO mission identified and gathered the remains of various statues and objects in the National Museum in Kabul to prepare for their restoration. In November 2002 UNESCO took emergency measures in preparation for winter. New windows were installed in several rooms on the ground and first floors, as well as a deep-water well with a pressure tank and plumbing to ensure water connection for the conservation laboratory. In addition, a large generator was donated to supply electricity. In 2003 UNESCO, through the Society for the Preservation of Afghanistan's Cultural

Heritage (SPACH), contributed U.S. $42,500 to complete the museum roof.

In January 2003 the Greek government began restoration of the National Museum in fulfillment of its commitment, made in May 2002, to donate approximately U.S. $750,000. UNESCO provided the Greek specialists with drawings and plans of the Kabul Museum that were produced by Andrea Bruno. The U.S. government contributed $100,000 to this project. In addition, the British contingent of the International Security Assistance Force (ISAF) installed a new restoration laboratory composed of a wet and a dry room, funded by the British Museum. The French Centre d'Etudes et de Recherches Documentaires sur l'Afghanistan (CEREDAF) donated conservation equipment and the newly created French DAFA, together with the Musée Guimet in Paris, carried out training courses for the museum's curators.

General Activities

In September 2002 UNESCO contracted with the French nongovernmental organization Agence d'Aide à la Coopération Technique et au Développement (ACTED) for emergency repair of the protecting roof of the nine-dome Hadji Pyada mosque in Balkh—the oldest mosque in Afghanistan—to protect it from the harsh winter conditions.

Funding and other forms of assistance, exceeding the U.S. $7 million pledged during the May 2002 seminar, have been given for cultural projects in Afghanistan. The UNESCO Funds-in-Trust program has been entrusted with the following amounts (in U.S. dollars) from donor countries:

- $1,815,967 from the government of Japan for the conservation of Bamiyan;
- $1,674,685 from the government of Italy for the monuments of Herat, Jam, and the National Museum, as well as the museums of Ghazni;

- $138,000 from the Swiss government for Jam and $250,000 for Bamiyan;
- $59,890 from the German government for retiling the Gowhar Shad Mausoleum in Herat.

Bilateral contributions include

- $5 million from the Aga Khan Trust for Culture for the restoration of the Babur Gardens and the Timur Shah Mausoleum in Kabul and the rehabilitation of traditional housing in Kabul, Herat, and other cities;
- $850,000 from the government of Germany in 2002, through ICOMOS Germany and the German Archaeological Institute, for restoration of the Babur Gardens and training of Afghan archaeologists;
- $750,000 earmarked by the Greek government and $100,000 from the U.S. government for restoration of the National Museum building;
- DAFA: preventive excavations in Bactria and Aï Khanum;
- Musée Guimet: several training courses for the staff of the National Museum;
- British Museum: restoration of three rooms at the National Museum for the installation of a conservation laboratory.

Furthermore, $400,000 under UNESCO's regular budget for the biennium 2002–3 and $480,000 for the biennium 2004–5 have been utilized for the implementation of cultural activities in Afghanistan.

All UNESCO activities are being implemented in accordance with the recommendations of the ICC. It should also be emphasized that these cultural funds come from specific cultural budgets. As such, they are in no instance taken from humanitarian funds but constitute an addition to them.

Recovery from Cultural Disaster: Strategies, Funding, and Modalities of Action of International Cooperation in Afghanistan

Jim Williams and Louise Haxthausen

Abstract: This paper discusses the rehabilitation of Afghanistan's cultural heritage following the fall of the Taliban regime. It addresses the transitional government's commitment to the preservation and protection of this heritage, and its urgent need for resources to carry out that goal. The International Coordination Committee (ICC) has played a key role in mobilizing funding, providing policy recommendations to the Afghan authorities, and reviewing technical options for specific interventions to preserve and rehabilitate sites and monuments, among other forms of assistance. This paper addresses these programs and other specific projects, particularly the rehabilitation of the National Museum in Kabul, that are under way or being planned.

Rehabilitating the cultural heritage of Afghanistan is a central element in giving the Afghan people a sense of historical continuity and national unity. The transitional Afghan authorities have acknowledged this fact by committing themselves "to create an environment where the cultural heritage is preserved, protected and handed on to young generations of Afghans as a record of the rich experience and aspirations in their country, so as to foster cultural creativity in all its diversity."[1]

What must Afghanistan do to make this commitment into reality? After twenty-three years of war, the cultural heritage of the state of Afghanistan has been described as a cultural disaster. Historic monuments were severely damaged, through deliberate destruction or progressive degradation. Archaeological sites and the National Museum in Kabul were massively looted. Cultural professionals were isolated from international cooperation and exchanges that provide training and research opportunities to upgrade skills.

Currently, resources in the country to address these needs are virtually nonexistent. As H.E. Hamid Karzai stated at the Tokyo Conference in January 2002, "It is an almost unprecedented situation, where an administration has no immediate source of revenue. We will rapidly lose credibility if we cannot pay our staff or deliver services to the people. . . .We see it as essential that the pledges are promptly materialized." Since the Tokyo Conference, international aid has been channeled to Afghanistan, but pledges made there and at subsequent donor meetings for the reconstruction of Afghanistan are insufficient to address existing needs and painfully slow in coming into the country.

This lack of aid is equally true with regard to funding to preserve and promote Afghanistan's cultural heritage. The Ministry of Information and Culture of the Islamic Transitional State of Afghanistan is facing the overwhelming challenge of reviving a tradition of international cultural cooperation established in the early twentieth century. This cooperation took the form of numerous partnerships with scientific institutions from around the world. Notable results of this cooperation were interventions to protect Afghanistan's major cultural monuments and sites as well as a series of important archaeological discoveries that have fundamentally deepened knowledge of Afghanistan's history and culture. From 1979 on, as the security situation in the country progressively deteriorated, international cooperation in the area of culture became more and more limited and eventually, during the Taliban regime, essentially stopped.

Priorities and Modalities of Action

Slow progress in achieving tangible improvement in the overall situation of Afghanistan's cultural heritage makes it easy to lose sight of the substantial progress that has been made. Since the fall of the Taliban regime, strategies have been devised, coordinating mechanisms have been put in place, and funding has begun to reach the country to allow programs to move from assessment to genuine implementation.

At the seminars and commissions discussed in Christian Manhart's paper, dialogues were initiated, plans of action developed, and emergency measures designed. At the June 2003 meeting, specific problems were identified, such as the modification of the 1980 law on cultural heritage and the need to sign the two conventions concerning the illicit traffic of culture heritage.

The International Coordination Committee (ICC) serves as a forum to keep the attention of the international community focused on the importance of rehabilitating Afghanistan's cultural heritage and to mobilize funding. It also provides policy recommendations to the Afghan authorities on priority issues. At the same time, it reviews and validates technical options for specific interventions to preserve and rehabilitate sites and monuments. Finally, the ICC plays a critical role in providing strategic input to the program on culture, media, and sport contained in the annual National Development Budget (NDB), the overall framework for development aid in Afghanistan.[2]

In the area of culture, the NDB is an overall investment program for the rehabilitation of the country's public services. It concentrates on the preservation and protection of cultural and historic monuments and sites, the rehabilitation and modernization of public cultural institutions, and the establishment of an enabling environment for creativity and civil participation in cultural activities. The overall objective is to ensure that Afghans enjoy improved access to culture. For fiscal year 1382 (March 2003–March 2004), the following seven priority projects were identified:

- Rehabilitation of the National Museum
- Rehabilitation of the National Archives
- Rehabilitation of the Kabul Theater
- Emergency consolidation and conservation of cultural monuments and sites
- Rehabilitation of the Public Library
- Prevention of illicit excavations and traffic of cultural property
- Revival of traditional Afghan music

These projects, identified and monitored through a series of government-led consultations, seek to balance stakeholder participation and strong national ownership, with the government "in the driving seat" of the reform, as President Karzai put it.

The UNESCO Kabul office plays a facilitating role. When the Ministry of Finance established consultative groups as forums for a government-donor dialogue on NDB formulation and monitoring, the UNESCO Kabul office was requested to act as coordinator for the consultative group on culture, media, and sports. This is fundamentally a role of institutional capacity building in strategic programming and monitoring by the Ministry of Information and Culture, as the government has given individual ministries the responsibility to deliver their respective NDB programs. The Ministry of Information and Culture has the ultimate responsibility for delivering the NDB projects, whoever the implementing agency and/or donor may be.

Achievements and Lacunae

International cooperation in the field of culture is progressively reviving; however, given the magnitude of the needs, the general sentiment among Afghan authorities is one of frustration. First, the mobilization of the international community to safeguard the Bamiyan Buddhas against destruction had raised hopes of massive help once the Taliban regime fell. Second, much of the initial funding received has not yet generated visible changes, as much preparatory work—in particular, updated scientific documentation of monuments and sites—was needed before concrete rehabilitation activities could start.

The National Museum continues to be an urgent priority. Thanks to funding from Greece, the United Kingdom, the United States, UNESCO, and the Society for the Preservation of Afghanistan's Cultural Heritage (SPACH), its physical rehabilitation has begun. Several of the statues from the Kushan period that were smashed to pieces by the Taliban have now been restored and are on display in the entrance hall of the museum.

But support to cultural institutions remains limited. The most striking example is that of the Kabul Theater. The theater is in the same stage of devastation that it was when the Taliban regime fell. More positive is the situation of Afghan Films, the Public Library, and the National Archives, where rehabilitation work is in progress.

A major challenge in reversing the tragic process of impoverishment of Afghanistan's cultural heritage is to stop the continuous looting of archaeological sites and the illicit traffic of cultural property outside of the country. The Ministry of Information and Culture of Afghanistan estimates that ongoing looting and illicit traffic are of a magnitude comparable to that endured during the Taliban regime. The means available to counter looting remain excruciatingly limited, especially in provincial areas where the security situation remains volatile. In early 2004 the Ministry of Information and Culture requested the deployment of five hundred armed guards to the most exposed archaeological sites in the country, but resources have been insufficient to meet this demand. The reinitiation of scientific excavations is another strategy to counter looting that was adopted by the Ministry of Information and Culture with the support of international cooperation, in particular, Italy and France. Here again the lack of security at most archaeological sites has limited the opportunity for such interventions.

Meanwhile, the Afghan authorities are taking steps to ratify the two international instruments protecting cultural property against illicit traffic, the 1970 UNESCO Convention on the Means of Prohibiting and Preventing the Import, Export and Transfer of Ownership of Cultural Property and the 1995 UNIDROIT Convention on Stolen or Illegally Exported Cultural Objects. With assistance from UNESCO, the 1980 Law on Cultural Heritage is under review and being harmonized with the international standards stipulated in the two conventions. The ratification of these two international instruments will give Afghan authorities legal means to claim the restitution or return from abroad of its cultural property.

The demonstrated commitment of the Afghan authorities to safeguarding their cultural heritage as part of the reconstruction process has catalyzed an immediate revival of international cooperation in the field of culture. However, whether Afghanistan will recover from the cultural disaster it has experienced remains uncertain. This will depend, to a large extent, on the willingness of the international community to engage in long-term partnerships and capacity-building efforts.

Notes

1   National Development Budget, Programme 1.5: Culture, Media and Sports. Full text is available at www.af, the website of the Islamic Transitional State of Afghanistan.

2   Current figures on NDB funding are available at www.af, donor database.

Preserving Afghanistan's Cultural Heritage: What Is to Be Done?

Osmund Bopearachchi

Abstract: *Over the past ten years countless antiquities, including statues, jewelry, bronze, faience, ivory carvings, and thousands of coins, have been discovered accidentally or as the result of clandestine digging. Planned destruction of archaeological sites and museums, illicit digging, and vandalism in pursuit of material gain have completely destroyed the sculptures and paintings of the region. Traces of a glorious past have disappeared forever. In the midst of the continuing human suffering in Afghanistan, it is impossible to suppress pain, despair, and above all anger at the destruction of the cultural heritage of a land that was one of the great meeting points of East and West. This paper argues that as the reconstruction effort begins in Afghanistan, there is the need for global custodians of cultural heritage to step in to assess the magnitude of the destruction thus far and to catalog the surviving elements that need to be preserved and restored on a priority basis.*

The civilized world woke up from a long sleep to see clouds of smoke rising above the Buddha statues in Bamiyan. The threat so often dismissed as inconsequential had become a ghastly reality in early March 2001. It took the Taliban's destruction of the colossal statues of Buddha, which dated to the fifth and sixth centuries C.E., for the world to take an interest in a long forgotten and abandoned country. Spent artillery shells, lined up like sentries, stood at the base of the mountain alcove where the world's tallest Buddha statues once stood. The Buddha's outline and piles of rubble are all that remain today (fig. 1). Broken pieces of the statues and fragments of the beautiful paintings that once decorated the niches were briefly offered for sale in the Peshawar bazaar.

Although aesthetically the Bamiyan statues—the largest Buddhist statues in the world—are considered by art histori-

ans to constitute an experimental phase and thus are not the most beautiful works of art that Afghanistan, once the cradle of many civilizations, ever produced, their destruction is especially notable as an act of sheer barbarism. Unfortunately, this act marks neither the beginning nor the end of the long history of Afghanistan's cultural heritage in peril.

The destruction of the Afghan patrimony is no longer a problem that concerns only the Afghan people, who over the years have suffered the devastation of a civil war caused by both international policies and disputes between rival factions. When the Taliban came to power in 1996, the National Museum in Kabul had already been destroyed, and the ancient sites of Aï Khanoum, Hadda, Tepe Shotor, Bactres, and Tepe Marandjan, which had been explored by French and Afghan archaeologists, had already been ransacked (fig. 2). The pillaging took place before, during, and after the Taliban regime. And today, in fact, the destruction of ancient sites has reached its apogee.

In May 1993 the National Museum was destroyed by several rockets and subsequently looted. Explosives pulverized the roof, the top floor, and most of the building's doors and windows (fig. 3). The nearby Institute of Archaeology was also severely damaged. More than four thousand objects deposited in the storerooms of the museum were stolen. When the area was cut off by the fighting and the staff was unable to reach the suburb of Darulaman, where the museum is located, the looters took everything humanly possible. As Philippe Flandrin aptly described it:

> Three quarters of the collections that have been found were removed without any iconoclastic intent. The pillaging of the museum follows the same surgical rules as the looting of castles. It is carried out with method

and order, under the guidance of professional thieves who take care to salvage, along with the valuables, the corresponding catalogs and inventories that identify the stolen items. (2001:43; my translation)

Not a single coin is left in the cabinets where coins were stored. Apart from the specimen stored in the Royal Palace prior to the destruction of the museum, all the coins from the Kabul hoard, from the Kunduz hoard (627 Greco-Bactrian coins and their imitations), and from the excavation of Aï Khanoum were looted. Most of the artifacts stolen from the National Museum, which had originally been excavated in Herat, Bactra, Aï Khanoum, and Hadda, surfaced a few days later in the Peshawar bazaar and from there found their way to private collections. Among them are the invaluable ivory plaques excavated at Begram by French archaeologists in 1937. A month later, UNESCO and the UN Office for the Coordination of Humanitarian Assistance to Afghanistan began reinforcing the building to prevent additional damage.

Thirty percent of the remaining artifacts were rescued by the museum authorities and were kept at the Ministry of Cultural Affairs. The museum was partially restored and inaugurated in summer 2000 by the Taliban minister of cultural affairs. The large statues and especially the statue of Kanishka and the seventh-century Bodhisattva image from Tepe Marandjan, which looters could not move, were among the exhibits.

The destruction of the collections that had escaped the looting began long before the Buddhas were dynamited in early March 2001. Already, on 4 February, a line of cars had stopped in front the museum. Carrying hammers and axes, the minister of finance, the minister of culture with his adjunct, and the notorious Mollah Khari Faiz ur-Rahamn, who slapped the Bodhisattva in summer 2001, ordered that the storeroom be opened. According to a staff member who witnessed the scene, "As they entered the storeroom, they snarled in excitement and started to smash everything while chanting 'Allahu Akbar'" (Flandrin 2002:211). Throughout history, the destruction of a nation's cultural treasures has been the consequence of religious fanaticism, political ideology, or mere ignorance, yet never before had the madness reached such magnitude. On 22 March 2001, three weeks after decreeing that all the statues of Afghanistan should be destroyed, the Taliban briefly opened the National Museum to journalists, revealing a gloomy, near-empty labyrinth of rooms missing virtually all its treasures. The statue of Kanishka and the Bodhisattva image of Tepe Marandjan were reduced to tiny pieces. It turns out that in February the Taliban had started to

destroy even the artifacts stored for safekeeping at the Ministry of Cultural Affairs.

The head of Durga, exhumed in Tepe Sardar, escaped the wreckage thanks to the astonishing cleverness of Dr. Masoodi and his colleagues. They gave a collection of sixty copies of Greco-Buddhist statues, made before the war for use by archaeology students in Kabul, to the enraged Islamic students who arrived the following day to complete the destruction and who continued to ransack the storerooms of the Ministry of Culture and Information, where they found the coffers that had been brought there by Najibullah in

FIGURE 1 Destroyed colossal statue of Buddha at Bamiyan.
Photo: Osmund Bopearachchi

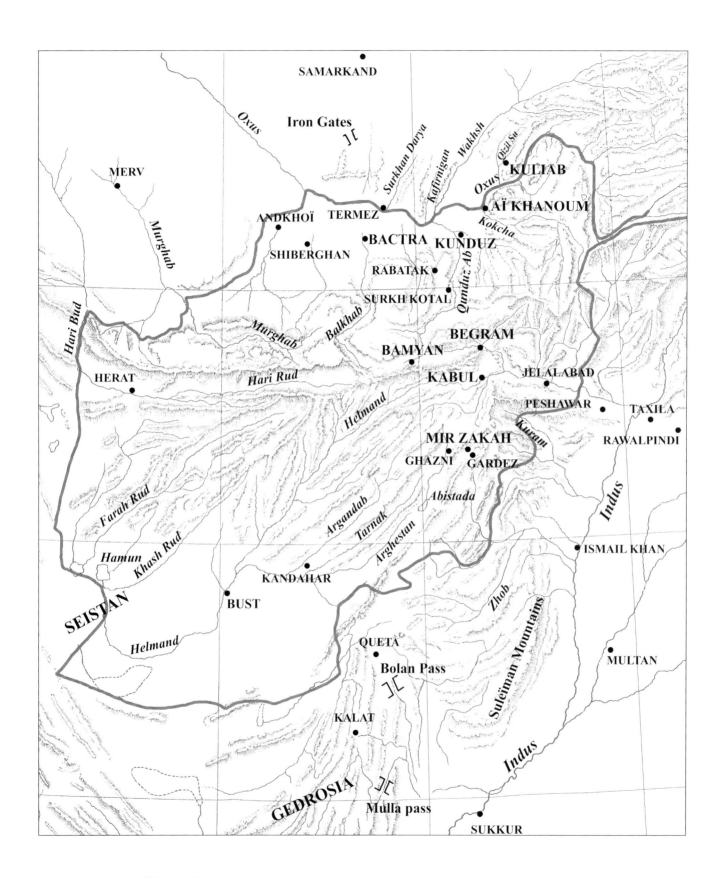

FIGURE 2 Ancient sites in Afghanistan. Drawing by François Ory

FIGURE 3 Destroyed National Museum in Kabul.
Photo: Osmund Bopearachchi

1989. If today the princely couple of Fundukistan and the sublime paintings of the Kakrak grottoes near Bamiyan remain intact, it is thanks to the deadly game played against the Taliban by the curators of the museum, who deserve our sincere admiration.

Begram is one of the rare sites that still remains undisturbed—and this only because it is littered with land mines (fig. 4). All the statues left by the Afghan archaeologists of the excavations at Tepe Marandjan during the pro-Russian government were stolen by the villagers.

The Minari-i-Chakari, the Buddhist pillar, also called the Alexander pillar, dating to the first century C.E., was hit by a rocket and tumbled to the ground in March 1998. No one will see its eternal beauty again. The monastic complex of Hadda is situated in present Jalalabad, halfway along the road from Kabul to Gandhara. The ruins of this ancient site, with its Buddhist stupas and caves, were extensively excavated by the French archaeological delegation in Afghanistan under Barthoux. A large and well-preserved monastic complex near Hadda, at Tepe Shotor outside the northern edge of the plateau, was excavated between 1974 and 1979 by Afghan archaeologists. They were able to unearth a beautiful stupa complex decorated with magnificent stucco figures dating to the second century C.E. depicting the Naga king in the Fish Porch and a realistic figure of Heracles. Looters have by now systematically pillaged and destroyed Tepe Shotor. Huge statues that could not be removed were smashed, and small statues were taken to Pakistani bazaars for sale (see Tarzi 2001).

For the past ten years, the ancient site of Aï Khanoum has been the target of systematically planned illicit digs (see

FIGURE 4 Ancient site of Begram.
Photo: Osmund Bopearachchi

Bernard 2001; Bopearachchi 2001). One of the most significant contributions to an understanding of the Greek presence in Bactria was made through the Aï Khanoum excavations led by French archaeologists under Paul Bernard. This remarkable city, which bore the distinctive imprint of cultural currents from the days of Greek glory, no longer exists. The prospectors for treasure appear to have used the metal detectors that were originally brought into the country to detect Russian land mines for quite another purpose. Photographs taken by Hin Ichi Ono show the lunarlike appearance of the city (see Bernard 2001:figs. 3, 5, 6, 10, 13; see also Kohl and Wright, this volume, fig. 2). The lower city is completely devastated. The place where the big temple once stood is a crater. Some of the Corinthian and Doric capitals unearthed by the French archaeologists were taken away; they now serve as the base for the columns of a teahouse in a nearby village (see Bernard 2001:fig. 7).

It is in this unfortunate situation that one of the largest deposits of coins known in the history of currencies was discovered by chance sometime between 1992 and 1995, in Mir Zakah, located in Afghan territory in Pakhtia province, near the Pakistan border (Bopearachchi 2001, 2002). No one is able to relate exactly how the treasure was discovered; we only know that it was found at the bottom of a well. Clandestine Afghan excavators, at the price of disputes that cost several lives, found a true cave of Ali Baba. This coin deposit is calculated to contain more than four tons of minted metal—close to 550,000 coins, mostly silver and bronze, and 350 kilograms of gold pieces. During visits to bazaars in Peshawar, Pakistan, in February 1994, I was able to hurriedly examine six bags containing 300 kilograms of minted metal, that is, about 38,000 pieces from the treasure of Mir Zakah. The fairy tale built around the second deposit of Mir Zakah has now become an unending nightmare. According to some reliable sources, two and a half tons of coins from the second Mir Zakah deposit had been taken to Switzerland for sale.

Response to Illicit Trade

What stance should we adopt concerning antiquities unearthed accidentally or illicitly? We are obviously confronted with an extremely delicate problem. Should we or should we not make records of these items? An object of art, once removed from its archaeological context, loses more than half its historical value. If its origins are unknown, a work of art is a mere object without a soul. For this reason, I have struggled to learn, where possible, the origin of pieces

from clandestine excavations before they appear in sale catalogs. However, whether this work is done or not, it is impossible to divert them from their final destinations—sale catalogs, where they are listed with impunity. It is certain that these recent discoveries add much to our knowledge of the political and economic history of Bactria and India from the conquest of Alexander the Great to the end of the Kushan period. It is well known that the reconstruction of the history of the Greeks and their nomadic successors in Bactria and India depends mainly on numismatic, archaeological, and epigraphic evidence.

It is in this context and in the course of my research on the history of Greeks and their successors in Bactria and India that I concentrated my efforts to obtain the best information I could about coins and other significant antiquities and make records of them. The objects that I have seen personally in Pakistani bazaars do not represent one-tenth of the artifacts that have been dispersed in international art markets. Hundreds of ivory pieces, jewelry, intaglios, plaster medallions, and bronze items from northern Afghanistan have reached Pakistani bazaars and private collections.

Many ivory items were unearthed from the legal excavations of Aï Khanoum, especially in the palace treasury, which have already been documented by Claude Rapin (1992: pl. 118). To this list, illegal excavations have probably added the following items: hairpins, votive sculptures, and perhaps part of a sword case. Gold and silver jewelry similar to the pieces found in legal excavations have reached the market. They comprise rings, bracelets, pendants, and earrings. Hundreds of carnelian and agate cut stones, similar to those already published by Rapin (1992), were seen in the bazaars.

A faience head of a Greco-Bactrian king was found in June 1998 in unrecorded circumstances in the ancient Greek city of Aï Khanoum. It certainly belongs to an acrolithic statue. On close examination, it becomes obvious that the horizontally cut border at the bottom of the head was meant to fit into a wooden structure. The fragments of the cult statue found in the *cella* of the main temple of Aï Khanoum and the faience head, also from Aï Khanoum, are the only examples of acroliths that have so far been found in Bactria.

The discovery of hundreds of manuscripts written in Greek (see Bernard and Rapin 1994), Bactrian, Prakrit, and Aramaic have revolutionized our understanding of the socioeconomic and political history of ancient Bactria. A notable discovery in recent years was scrolls written in Aramaic dating to the fourth century B.C.E. According to a reliable source, they were found accidentally by a villager who took refuge in a cave one winter night. Feeling cold, he unknowingly started to burn scrolls and parchments of ancient manuscripts that he found in the vicinity. Only on awakening in the morning did he realize that he had burned more than 75 percent of the documents. The remaining ones give precious information about the socioeconomic history and practices of cults during the Achaemenid period. It is fortunate that at least these documents have been saved and scholars have an opportunity to study them.

As regards the vandalized National Museum, I share the view that a new museum should be constructed in a central location. At least 30 percent of the former collections, which had miraculously escaped the looting and destruction, are now kept safely in two places. The 20,000 objects in gold and silver, which had been excavated from the six tombs of Tillya-Tepe, had been kept at the Central Bank and have now reappeared. The statue of Kanishka and the Bodhisattva image from Tepe Marandjan, which were reduced to pieces by the Taliban, have been restored by the conservators of the Musée Guimet in Paris. The conservators of the National Museum have made studious efforts to restore little by little the remaining 2,748 statues destroyed by the Taliban (fig. 5).

Some individuals abroad acquired objects stolen from the National Museum without knowing their origins, and some of them are willing to return the items to the museum. In June 2003 I learned that the third-millennium B.C.E. silver vase from the Fullol hoard, which had been exhibited in the Museum, had entered a private collection in London. At our request the private collector agreed to return the piece to UNESCO. Today it is kept in the Archaeological Museum of Lattes under the custody of UNESCO. The time has come to encourage private collectors and dealers who keep these stolen objects knowingly or unknowingly to return them to UNESCO.

There are also benefactors who took the initiative to buy items as they appeared on the art market with the intention of returning them to Afghanistan. Hirayama, for example, purchased the famous marble foot belonging to the cult statue of the main temple, excavated by French archaeologists in the 1970s from Aï Khanoum. He also has in his possession paintings from the Kakrak valley. The Society for the Preservation of Afghanistan's Cultural Heritage (SPACH) also purchased some statues of the National Museum. All of these items will be returned to Afghanistan one day. Only UNESCO and the international community can determine when the restitution should take place. Various items were bought by collectors with the intention of selling them at a higher price. It is impossible to make any money from well-publicized stolen

FIGURE 5 The conservators of the National Museum restoring artifacts destroyed by the Taliban. Photo: Osmund Bopearachchi

property. These collectors have a moral obligation to take a courageous step and return them to UNESCO. The road will be long and painstaking.

Response to Illicit Excavation

Finally, what is to be done regarding the illicit digging? As a period of reconstruction begins in Afghanistan, it is time to reflect on Afghanistan's vulnerable legacy. The looting of ancient sites, including Aï Khanoum, Bactres, and Hadda, is still taking place. There is a tremendous need for global custodians of cultural heritage to step in to assess the magnitude of the destruction thus far and to catalog the surviving elements that need to be preserved and restored on a priority basis. It is depressing to admit that in spite of efforts by the present Afghan minister of cultural affairs, illicit digging has reached its apogee. There are two types of illicit digging in Afghanistan. The first is done by well-organized diggers supported by powerful men whose ultimate goal is to furnish the international market with antiquities. Only competent authorities, conscious of their cultural heritage, can put an end to this practice. The present government understandably has many other priorities. Peace in Afghanistan remains very fragile, as the ongoing violence reminds us. The second type of illicit pillaging of sites is more innocent. This plunder is done by villagers hoping to find a few pieces of gold to nourish their families. The world owes its profoundest sympathies to the Afghan people, who were chased from one frontier to another and who have suffered the vicissitudes of civil war, famine, and drought. They have been the hapless victims of political ideologies, which reduce the human condition to a position subordinate to international economic interests. But in promoting the cynical game of Realpolitik in Afghanistan, humankind itself has lost part of its collective cultural heritage. That is a loss for which the entire world bears collective responsibility. The struggle against the destruction of Afghanistan's cultural heritage is intrinsically linked to the political and economic stability of the country.

Today Afghanistan needs food, doctors, and schools to fight famine, disease, and ignorance. Perhaps we should leave the Buddha statues as they now are to show how far religious fanaticism, ignorance, and intolerance can go. We will not permit the forces of evil to destroy human dignity. We cannot save or restore what has been destroyed, but we can fight to preserve what remains. We will not allow political and economic interests to defile the sovereignty of the Afghan

state. The cultural heritage of all humanity is at stake, not solely that of an often-forgotten and abandoned country.

Acknowledgments

My contribution to this volume is based in part on the UNESCO reports and those of Carla Grissmann, consultant for the Society for the Conservation of the Afghan Cultural Heritage, and Nancy Dupree; on books and articles by Emmanuel de Roux, Roland Pierre Paringaux, Pierre Centlivres, Philippe Flandrin, and Andrew Lawler; and on a trip I made to Afghanistan in summer 2002.

References

Bernard, P. 2001. Découverte, fouille et pillage d'un site archéologique: la ville gréco-bactrienne d'Aï Khanoum en Afghanistan. In *Afghanistan: Patrimoine en péril. Actes d'une journée d'étude*, 71–96. Paris: Centre d'Études et de recherches documentaires sur l'Afghanistan.

Bernard, P., and R. Besenval. 2002. Hier et aujourd'hui, Aï Khanoum l'Alexandrie de l'Oxus. In *Afghanistan: Une histoire millénaire*, 85–87. Paris: Réunion des Musées nationaux.

Bernard, P., and C. Rapin. 1994. Un parchemin gréco-bactrien d'une collection privée. *Comptes Rendus, Académie des Inscriptions et Belles-Lettres*, 261–94.

Bopearachchi, O. 2001. Quelle politique adopter face à la dispersion du patrimoine? Le cas de l'Afghanistan et du Pakistan. *L'Avenir des musées*, Paris, 289–306.

———. 2002. Vandalised Afghanistan. *Frontline, India's National Magazine* 19 (March):66–70.

Centlivres, P. 2001. *Les Bouddhas d'Afghanistan.* Paris: Éditions Favre.

Dupree, N. 1999. Recent happenings at the Kabul Museum. *SPACH Newsletter*, July, 1–7.

Flandrin, P. 2001. *Le trésor perdu des rois d'Afghanistan.* Paris: Éditions du Rocher.

———. 2002. *Afghanistan: Les trésors sataniques.* Paris: Éditions du Rocher.

Rapin, C. 1992. *Fouilles d'Aï Khanoum, VIII. La trésorerie du palais hellénistique d'Aï Khanoum. L'Apogée et la chute du royaume grec de Bactriane. MDAFA* 33, Paris.

Tarzi, Z. 2001. Le site ruiné de Hadda. In *Afghanistan: Patrimoine en péril. Actes d'une journée d'étude*, 60–69. Paris: Centre d'Études et de recherches documentaires sur l'Afghanistan.

PART NINE

Archaeology and Conservation in China Today: Meeting the Challenges of Rapid Development

Introduction

Neville Agnew

The wealth of China's cultural heritage is astounding but not unexpected, given the antiquity, size, and diversity of the country. Its civilization has been unbroken for five thousand years, and its large, inventive population has created a vast archaeological heritage.

With China's rapid emergence as an economic and world power since the late 1970s, aggressive development has been occurring. Almost daily, important archaeological finds are made, often as a result of major infrastructure projects. And, with the increase in wealth and disposable income, internal tourism is on the rise. These factors, combined with greater regional autonomy, create new and powerful threats to add to the traditional ones of deterioration and decay.

The panel organized by the State Administration of Cultural Heritage of China (SACH) and the Getty Conservation Institute (GCI) discusses Chinese archaeology and conservation in this climate of rapid development and economic growth from a number of perspectives: existing relevant laws and regulations and their application and, sometimes, lack of enforcement; the management of archaeology and cultural heritage conservation; urban development and rescue archaeology; the discovery of sites and their conservation; and the lack of well-trained personnel to conserve and manage archaeological sites and materials.

China's transition into the mainstream of international thinking and practice in heritage conservation through initiatives such as the development of professional guidelines for the management and conservation of heritage sites is recognized here. The policy for archaeological research is discussed in order that the international community may better understand conditions in China today regarding the implementation of archaeology and the practice of conservation.

It seemed appropriate, given the GCI's conservation work in China and its long collaboration with SACH, to include a Chinese delegation in the theme of integrating conservation and archaeology, particularly since there appears not to have been a substantial presence from China at previous World Archaeological Congresses, or much opportunity at conferences, given the language barrier, for sustained interaction with the international archaeological and conservation community. Eight delegates from a variety of geographic regions in China, from government policy makers to site managers, planners, and an academic, participated in the congress. Prior translation of the papers into English and simultaneous translation during the sessions enhanced communication. Six of the eight papers presented are included in this volume.

Yang Zhijun's paper reviews the legal and policy aspects governing the four hundred thousand sites and twelve million artifacts in state-owned museums. He points out that the 1982 Law on the Protection of Cultural Relics was revised in 2002 and that China has signed all the international treaties concerned with heritage. His paper provides a concise overview of the structure of the legal and heritage administration system and differentiates the hierarchy of laws, regulations, rules, and measures, the last two being quite specific, for example, *Rules for the Work of Field Archeology* issued by the Ministry of Culture on 10 May 1984.

A void has existed in China between the legal system and professional practice in heritage conservation and management until recently, when China ICOMOS (with SACH approval) issued the *Principles for the Conservation of Heritage Sites in China* (the *China Principles*). Yang Zhijun points out that this bridge will, in time, be seen as a milestone.

Of particular interest in Yang's paper is the open acknowledgment of serious problems in China's heritage protection: pressure from development for rescue excavation and the infractions of developers; the vast national tourism industry, with the stress it puts on sites; and illicit dealing in antiquities. These and other problems precipitated the 2002 revision of the law, the main elements of which are reviewed in his paper.

Guan Qiang discusses in greater detail some of the problems in a fast developing country, which, as he says, looks "like a vast construction site," and pose a challenge to the work of both archaeological excavation and the protection of cultural heritage. He touches on the archaeological rescue activities as a consequence of the much-debated Three Gorges Dam project and claims that a clear picture of the original culture in the Three Gorges area has been obtained as a result. Guan does not skirt the difficult issues that are being faced because of these capital construction projects and points out the conflicts and stresses they can create, particularly underfunding of rescue and preservation activities and inadequate personnel and professionals in preservation work.

Guan proposes a number of measures to address these problems. These include stricter enforcement of the law, utilization of methodological guidelines such as the *China Principles,* and better and more comprehensive planning. One senses that this is an uphill struggle: as Guan points out, there are ten universities in China with archaeological institutes, but over half the graduates currently go on to work in other occupations, presumably better-paid ones. Among the measures proposed by Guan is the encouragement of a higher standard of multidisciplinary research, such as the introduction of methods and technologies including dating, DNA sequencing, palaeoclimate studies, and computer simulations to enhance and revitalize archaeological investigation and promote more rigorous standards of preservation. Finally, Guan points out that there is more openness on the part of authorities in China to international collaboration and exchange. There is a great potential still to be tapped in partnership with foreign countries and professionals, and SACH endorses and promotes cooperation of this kind.

Chen Tongbin describes the significant challenges faced in the conservation of large-scale archaeological sites, such as Liangzhu. She identifies urbanization as the main destructive factor and seeks to balance the needs of the inhabitants to earn a livelihood and the need to find ways to protect the heritage resource. Her approach is that of a regional planner: to reassign land use, redirect transportation networks to avoid

key preservation zones, freeze certain construction projects, and move industrial and mining firms out of the region, as well as relocate and financially compensate a large portion of the population. As she implies, these are hard decisions to make; they must balance the legitimate needs and concerns of the local inhabitants with those of a very significant site in the history of Chinese civilization. Furthermore, funding has not yet been secured for the integration of this large-scale conservation planning with the Hangzhou City (within which Liangzhu falls) socioeconomic development plan. Two further issues are of interest here. One is Chen's observation that conservation of excavated artifacts from the site cannot move forward at this time because of these macro-scale preservation plans. The other is that the local inhabitants are clearly ambivalent: they feel threatened by the archaeological park because it will undoubtedly have an impact on their personal economic situations but believe it may bring income from tourism. It will be interesting to track the evolution of this enormously complicated and large-scale initiative.

Wu Xiaohong discusses the graduate program in conservation science that was established in the Archaeology Department at Peking University in 1995. She also mentions programs in conservation science at other universities and their importance in training conservation professionals. A deficiency, she points out, is that these programs emphasize the technological aspects of conservation, and this compromises the ability of graduates to deal with the complexities of archaeological site conservation. Her critique of conservation practice in China with regard to archaeological excavation projects is a familiar one in other parts of the world: that is, conservation is not routinely included in the planning or execution of an archaeological excavation project, and certainly not with site management. As she states, conservation is usually thought of as an exclusively off-site, postexcavation activity, concerned with technical problems or remedial treatment.

Being well aware of the need for conservators to understand archaeology more deeply, and certainly for archaeologists to be cognizant of their obligation to the site and the artifacts they excavate, Wu Xiaohong urges a more integrated approach to conservation in the academic arena and in the practice of field archaeology.

Yuan Jiarong, like Chen Tongbin, is concerned with an early site, specifically, an archaeological rescue project in the Liyie River basin, Hunan province. The project led to a sensation in academic circles in China because of the large number of bamboo and wooden slips found, containing writing from the Qin dynasty (221–206 B.C.E.). Yuan brings forth in detail problems referred to in the paper by Guan Qiang, in which pressure from development tends to override rescue archaeology. As he points out, Article 31 of the Law of the People's Republic of China on the Protection of Cultural Relics stipulates that the expense and workforce needed for rescue excavation must be included in the investment and work plans of the construction companies. Apparently a disregard for this legal requirement led to damage to the site, despite the budget requirements for the excavation and protection of the sites in the Liyie Basin having been submitted to the authority in charge of construction in a timely manner. This submission was ignored, and construction proceeded until it was stopped by the Hunan Provincial Institute of Cultural Relics.

Yuan points out that funding for archaeological excavation is a core issue in all these controversies. The law clearly stipulates one thing, but construction entities try to postpone compliance with all kinds of excuses, especially when the schedule for construction is urgent. As he states, bulldozers remain on the scene to put pressure on archaeological work until the funding issue is finally resolved. He urges that change be brought to the current situation. The reader infers from this that many sites must be lost to development because they are either small or do not attract attention through the discovery of major archaeological finds and are out of the oversight of a vigilant provincial or local archaeology and heritage authority.

Wang Jingchen's paper discusses two sites in Liaoning province in northeastern China: the very early and important Niuheliang site and the Qin dynasty site of Jiangnushi, a coastal site associated with the imperial visits of the First Emperor to that region of China.

As with the other sites discussed by the panel, Niuheliang and Jiangnushi are enormous in size. The former is concerned with the Hongshan culture, and Wang discusses the methods that are being used to endeavor to protect particularly the earth and mud sculpture remnants in a severe climate. Notably, his organization has reburied the so-called Goddess Temple as a protective measure. By contrast, at Jiangnushi, where most of the material excavated is earthen, and because of the extraordinarily large size of the site, he and his staff so far have been unable to develop an effective and comprehensive conservation approach but have undertaken interesting interpretive aspects by marking surface features after reburying exposed structures. As Wang notes, this is experimental to some degree, and he has used plantings of different kinds—grasses, trees, and other shallow-rooted plants—to outline the now-buried features. This, together with nonoriginal colored sand, is being tried as interpretive and presentation techniques.

The papers presented in this panel provide insights into the complexities of preserving archaeological heritage in the face of rapid development and economic growth. They point to the magnitude of the challenges facing authorities and cultural heritage professionals in China in their attempts to safeguard this vast legacy for future generations. It is hoped that the publication of these presentations, together with the participation of the Chinese delegates at WAC-5, will underscore the important initiatives that are under way in this country and will pave the way for further dialogue and collaboration with the international community.

China's Legal Framework for the Protection of Its Material Cultural Heritage

Yang Zhijun

Abstract: *China has a rich and extensive cultural heritage spanning five thousand years. This paper describes the legal framework that had been established to protect the material cultural heritage, ranging from international treaties to domestic legislation enacted at different levels of government. It outlines the main distinctive features of the recently revised Law of the People's Republic of China on the Protection of Cultural Relics and lists other relevant legislation that complements this law.*

China is a unitary multinational state with a five-thousand-year history of civilization. It is extremely rich in material cultural heritage (immovable and movable cultural relics) aboveground, underground, and underwater. There are approximately four hundred thousand sites at which immovable cultural relics have been found, and approximately twelve million cultural artifacts have been collected in state-owned museums. To protect these items of humankind's cultural heritage, China has now established a legal framework for their protection that is well suited to the conditions of the country. This framework has developed through decades of effort and exploration since the founding of the People's Republic of China. A brief outline of this legal system is presented below.

1   *Legislation at various levels in accordance with the functions and powers of the different levels of government.*
     Under the constitution, basic laws, special laws, and international conventions are promulgated for approval by the National People's Congress, by its Standing Committee, or by the State Council.

     The National People's Congress passed the Constitution of the People's Republic of China in December 1982. Article 22 of the constitution stipulates that it is the state's responsibility to protect famous scenic places, ancient sites, precious cultural relics, and other important historic and cultural heritage. Under this article, the National People's Congress established the Law of the People's Republic of China on the Protection of Cultural Relics in 1982 and revised it in 2002.

     To date, China has signed all international treaties regarding the conservation of world heritage, including Conservation of World Cultural and Natural Heritage (by the Standing Committee of the National People's Congress in November 1985); Prevention of Illicit Import, Export, and Transfer of Ownership of Cultural Property (by the State Council in September 1989); UNIDROIT Convention on Stolen or Illegally Exported Cultural Objects (by the State Council in March 1997); and Protection of Cultural Property in the Event of Armed Conflict (by the State Council in 2000).

     Administrative laws and regulations, which are normative documents, formulated or promulgated by the State Council or administrative organizations at the national level, are the following:

     - Provisional Regulations on the Administration of Areas of Scenic and Historical Interest (State Council, 7 June 1985);
     - Notice of the State Council Concerning Further Improvement of the Work on Cultural Relics (24 November 1987);
     - Regulations of the People's Republic of China on the Administration of the Protection of Underwater Cultural Relics (State Council, 24 October 1989);

- Measures of the People's Republic of China for the Administration of Foreign-related Issues in Archaeology (adopted by the State Administration of Cultural Heritage and approved by the State Council on 22 February 1991);
- Detailed Rules for the Implementation of the Law of the People's Republic of China on the Protection of Cultural Relics (adopted by the State Administration of Cultural Heritage and approved by the State Council on 30 April 1992);
- Detailed Ordinances for the Implementation of the Law of the People's Republic of China on the Protection of Cultural Relics (Premier of the State Council, Wen Jiabao, 13 May 2003);
- Enforcement and Improvement of the Cultural Relics Work (State Council, 30 March 1997); and
- Enforcement of Protection and Management of Cultural Relics during the Development of the Western Region (State Council, 31 August 2000).

Local regulations are normative documents formulated, deliberated, and promulgated by the standing committees of people's congresses of the provinces, autonomous regions, and municipalities directly under the central government in accordance with state laws and adapted to the actual conditions of the localities. In accordance with the Law of the People's Republic of China on the Protection of Cultural Relics, all the provinces, municipalities directly under the central government, and autonomous regions have formulated and promulgated corresponding local regulations.

Administrative rules are formulated and promulgated by central state administrative organizations and local state administrative organizations. These have a certain legal force, but they are positioned below laws, administrative laws and regulations, and local regulations. They are easily implemented as they have clear aims and are relatively detailed and concrete:

- Rules on the Work of Field Archaeology (trial implementation) (Ministry of Culture, 10 May 1984);
- Measures for the Administration of Museum Collections (Ministry of Culture, 19 June 1986);
- Measures for the Administration of Projects for the Protection of Cultural Relics (Ministry of Culture, 17 March 2003);

- Measures for Investigation, Design, and Resource Management of a Conservation Intervention Project and Measures for Quality Control of the Conservation Intervention Project (trial implementation) (State Administration of Cultural Heritage, 11 June 2003);
- Notice of the People's Government of Henan Province Concerning the Improvement of the Work of Protecting Cultural Relics in Economic Development Zones (14 December 1992);
- Measures of Beijing Municipality for the Administration of the Protection of the Site of the Fossils of Peking Man in Zhoukoudian (People's Government of Beijing Municipality, 1 February 1989); and
- *Principles for the Conservation of Heritage Sites in China* (China ICOMOS, October 2000).

Special mention must be made of the *Principles for the Conservation of Heritage Sites in China* (the *China Principles*), which were the result of three years of work, begun in 1997, by the State Administration of Cultural Heritage of China, the Getty Conservation Institute in the United States, and the Australian Heritage Commission. The *China Principles,* which combine successful Chinese conservation experiences with advanced international conservation concepts and practices, including the Burra Charter, have been successful guidelines for conservation practitioners in China. Although the *China Principles* were formulated recently, they have received a great deal of attention from the international conservation field and in time will be acknowledged as a milestone.

2 *The newly revised Law of the People's Republic of China on the Protection of Cultural Relics.*
It has been twenty years since the Law of the People's Republic of China on the Protection of Cultural Relics was established. The policy of reform and opening to the outside world has taken root in the hearts of the people. The national economy has achieved sustained development at a supernormal rate, and the level of people's material, spiritual, and cultural life has been raised significantly, offering a great opportunity for the conservation of physical cultural heritage but also great challenges. The challenges arise from several factors:

- Large-scale capital construction projects have greatly increased. Some planning departments and construction entities, without asking for permission from cultural relics departments, have initiated construction projects that cause damage to relics, especially those that are underground. Archaeologists are under pressure to conduct rescue excavation. It is no longer news that archaeologists must compete with bulldozers in order to rescue cultural relics. It is a very serious matter when legal entities violate the law.

- The process of urbanization and infrastructure construction has been accelerated. Many Chinese cities embody several hundreds or thousands of years of history. Many people think that modernization consists of high-rise buildings and widened streets. Consequently, some cities have torn down buildings that exhibited local characteristics and/or ethnic style. Some cities have replaced their entire historic precincts with modern buildings.
- The tourist industry is thriving. To promote tourism, some sites are treated merely as moneymaking ventures. The number of visitors far exceeds the capacity of sites. Some protected places have implemented restoration measures but changed the status of the cultural sites or made the old places like new. Some sites, managed by tourism companies, whose interest is primarily the pursuit of profit, have been damaged.
- The market for cultural relics is brisk. Relics stores and auction businesses for antiquities are booming. Some business owners conduct under-the-table deals using their legal businesses. Some sell excavated artifacts illegally.
- The fever for collecting cultural material has intensified as even companies, entities, and private collectors are involved in relics collection. The sources and channels of traffic in relics have not been identified.
- Illicit excavation, theft, speculative buying and selling, and smuggling of cultural relics are rampant.

The nation's economy needs to be developed, city infrastructures need to be improved, and people's standard of living needs to be raised, but material culture cannot be sacrificed for these purposes, even though not all problems can be prevented during society's progression from a planned economy to a market economy. In the face of these new conditions and situations, in order to deal with the relationships among productive construction, urban devel-

opment, tourism, personal productivity and living standards, and cultural relics conservation, one needs to make adjustments, restrictions, and standardizations within the legal framework. This was the reason for the recent revisions to the Law on the Protection of Cultural Relics.

The work of revising the Law on the Protection of Cultural Relics started in 1996. The Standing Committee of the National People's Congress passed these revisions on 25 October 2002. During this period, the State Administration of Cultural Heritage, the Legislative Office of the State Council, the Education, Science, and Culture Committee, and the Legislative Committee of the National Congress conducted consultations and investigations. Experts from all fields were invited to attend some twenty meetings for discussions and evaluations focusing on improving management, standardizing the circulation of relics, and enforcing the policing power of cultural relics administrations.

The revised Law on the Protection of Cultural Relics expands the original law from eight chapters and thirty-three articles to eighty articles, covering many areas. The revisions are precise, specific, and visionary. The most significant revisions cover some aspects of immovable cultural relics:

- The policy of "focusing on protection, giving first place to rescue, achieving reasonable utilization and improving management" of cultural relics has been upgraded to a law.
- Governments at all levels are responsible for the protection of cultural relics in the areas under their jurisdiction. Protection of cultural relics shall be incorporated into the plan of economic and social development and the necessary financial resources should be included in the government budget. The conservation plan for each cultural site should be incorporated in the urban or rural development plan. Capital construction, development of tourism, and so on, shall not cause damage to cultural relics.
- The revision clearly defines the nature of ownership of cultural relics. State ownership of immovable cultural relics shall not be altered owing to any change in ownership of the land on which they are located, nor shall it be transferred, mortgaged, or operated as enterprise assets.

- Measures for strengthening the administration of the protection of cultural relics include the following:
  — Sites not yet determined as protected shall be registered and announced to the public, and measures shall be formulated for their protection.
  — Immovable cultural relics that have been completely destroyed shall not be rebuilt on the original sites.
  — Conservation plans should be specially formulated for registered historically and culturally famous cities, historical precincts, villages, or towns.
  — Repair of protected cultural sites for moving or rebuilding purposes shall be undertaken by entities certified to do the projects.
- Legal liabilities are revised and administrative powers of law enforcement strengthened in regard to cultural relics and specific, clearly defined acts which are in violation of the law on the protection of cultural relics. Departments for administering cultural relics have the power to order corrections or to impose economic or administrative penalties.

3 *Mutual complementarity with other relevant laws and regulations of the State.*
China's constitution stipulates that protection of cultural relics is the common duty of the nation, society, and every citizen. From the legislative point of view, the laws for the protection of cultural relics are relatively complete. Among the other relevant laws and regulations are laws on mineral resources, customs, city planning, environmental protection, and the protection of military facilities that clearly stipulate the protection of cultural relics. Criminal law stipulates that violation of the Law on the Protection of Cultural Relics is a crime and may carry specific punishment. In reality, however, it is not an easy matter to effectively enforce the laws and regulations regarding the protection of cultural relics. In recent years, the frequency of violations has increased. Some local governments wish to improve the appearance of cities and the living conditions of their residents but lack the money; therefore, often, it is the investors who control urban real estate developments. Many cases have occurred in which governors or mayors have neglected cultural relics protection in favor of engineering projects. It is very difficult to deal with issues related to the damage or destruction of cultural relics.

At present, the situation cannot be completely controlled. Nonetheless, protection of the national cultural heritage is the obligation of every citizen. Laws and regulations are needed to protect cultural relics tenaciously, though the burden is heavy and the road is long.

Acknowledgments

I would like to express my sincere gratitude to the Getty Conservation Institute for inviting me to participate in the Fifth World Archaeological Congress.

Archaeology, Cultural Heritage Protection, and Capital Construction in China

Guan Qiang

Abstract: *China has an unparalleled legacy of cultural and historic sites, which span a continuous time frame from one million years ago to the present. Rescue archaeology is very much in evidence as the pace of capital construction in China today is a major factor driving archaeological fieldwork. An especially successful example is the work undertaken in conjunction with the Three Gorges Dam project. This paper outlines the difficulties in conducting archaeological excavations and preservation efforts during capital construction projects and proposes strategies for dealing with these challenges.*

China is an important part of the world where humans have lived and flourished for millennia. Archaeological findings indicate an abundance of cultural and historic sites within China's boundaries. The fossil and archaeological record of human remains and activities from one million years ago to the present is continuous. The main areas of distribution of remains are concentrated along the basins of the Yangtze and Yellow Rivers; deposits can be found as far north as the basins of the Heilongjiang and the Liao Rivers and as far south as the Lancang and Pearl Rivers. Therefore, as many scholars have stated, all of China is a huge site of cultural relics, and this judgment, in the author's opinion, is by no means an exaggeration. The scale of Chinese cultural and historical sites is extremely rare in the world in terms of distribution, eras, and abundance. These sites are valuable legacies belonging to the Chinese nation and to humankind as a whole.

The major branches of Chinese archaeological study are fieldwork, underwater archaeology, and remote sensing from the air, among others. Archaeological fieldwork can be subdivided into proactive archaeology (for scientific research) and that undertaken in the course of capital construction and for rescue purposes. Work in recent years has been mostly proactive and has been carried out by various foreign colleagues. Archaeological fieldwork can be implemented only with the approval of the State Administration of Cultural Heritage of the People's Republic of China and in accordance with the law.

China, it is well known, is a developing country. With its fast-growing economy, it has the appearance of a vast construction site; and these construction activities result in more changes to cities and rural areas with each passing day. This development poses a great challenge to the work of archaeological excavation and the protection of the cultural legacy.

In China, archaeological work is normally a consequence of large-scale construction projects. For many years, archaeological work and protection of cultural relics have occurred in tandem with capital construction; thus this has been one of the main tasks of Chinese archaeologists. In this respect, remarkable results have been achieved that have captured the world's attention. For example, for the archaeological work and relics protection in conjunction with the Three Gorges Dam project, the Chinese government has invested several hundred million yuan (RMB) and the State Administration of Cultural Heritage of the People's Republic of China has organized some one hundred teams to do the archaeological excavation and protection work at 1,087 sites in the area above- and belowground. Prior to June 2003 when the water level in the reservoir reached a height of 135 meters, excavation and protection work on 531 underground and 302 aboveground sites was affected, and some 60,000 artifacts were unearthed. Thus a clear picture of the original culture in the Three Gorges area has been obtained, and for the most part, the sequence of prehistoric cultural development in the reservoir area has been mapped. In the meantime, a number of significant historic and cultural resources have been identified for sustainable economic development in the reservoir area. Other contributions in this volume address urban archaeological work in Liye in Hunan province, Liangzhu culture in Zhejiang province, and Jiangnushi and Niuheliang ruins in Liaoning. Most of these are projects of archaeological and cultural protection undertaken in coordination with capital construction.

Of course, there have been difficulties and problems while conducting archaeological excavations and preservation work during capital construction. They are mainly as follows:

- Archaeological and cultural departments are not able to participate prior to the filing for approval of the construction project; they play a reactive role after construction has begun.
- There exists an inherent conflict between the discovery and protection of important ruins and the implementation of the construction project, so some ruins and possible traces cannot be protected.
- The timing and funding needed for archaeological and cultural protection work cannot be sufficiently guaranteed when they depend on the capital construction schedule. Importantly, some academic questions cannot be resolved within this time frame.
- Some large-scale cultural ruins and sites are seriously threatened with each passing day by construction in cities and rural areas and the development of the tourism industry.

The reasons for the problems incurred are mainly as follows:

- Some persons are not sufficiently mindful of the law, nor is enforcement always adequate.
- The speed of economic development tends to overwhelm the process of evaluation of heritage sites by government officials.
- As a developing country, China does not have enough economic strength, and development takes priority.
- Existing personnel specialized in archaeological and cultural protection work in China do not have sufficient knowledge of cultural ruins and sites; hence, their knowledge and professionalism must be enhanced.
- Because of the shortage of professionals in archaeological and cultural protection work, they rush here and there like a fire brigade, endeavoring to cope with the work.

The above-mentioned difficulties, problems, experiences, and lessons no doubt occur in other countries and regions of the world, but they are handled and solved in different ways; therefore, the outcomes are different.

Facing the challenges of rapid economic development, the archaeological and cultural relics protection fields are adopting the strategies listed below. There is a need to shift from the passive mode and take the initiative, focusing on protection of important sites and objects of cultural heritage that belong to humanity as a whole. Specifically, we must

- establish a more comprehensive and operational system of laws and regulations and a team to strictly enforce the law for protection of cultural relics. The Law of the People's Republic of China on the Protection of Cultural Relics, revised in 2002, stipulates that when conducting a large-scale capital construction project, the entity in charge should report beforehand to the administration of cultural relics at the provincial government level and carry out an investigation and survey by archaeological organizations within the construction area where cultural relics may exist. If relics are found, the provincial administration should, in consultation with the construction unit, work out measures for protection of the relics in compliance with the requirements stipulated by law. When important finds are discovered, a timely report must be submitted to the State Administration of Cultural Heritage for action. The construction entity should include funds for archaeological work in the project budget in the event that an archaeological investigation, survey, and excavation are needed. Regulation of construction activities in the protection area and the buffer zone must be imposed. In particular, legal penalties should be specified in detail in cases in which cultural relics are not protected, with some rights of punishment authorized to the cultural relics administrative department. This will strengthen the administrative function of the department for the protection of cultural relics and make the execution of the law more effective. On this basis, a specialized contingent for the execution of cultural heritage protection laws must be set up or strengthened in every region, thus changing completely the current situation in which there is a law to abide by but nobody to enforce it.

- establish comprehensive principles and guidelines, and an evaluation system, for the conservation of cultural relics and historic sites. The *China Principles* were promulgated as professional guidelines. These will further help to regulate many activities for the protection of cultural relics.

- strengthen the protection and interpretation of cultural ruins. In November 2000 the State Administration of Cultural Heritage put forward the "'Tenth Five-Year Plan' for Protection of Large-Scale Cultural Ruins." It is hoped that under this plan, not only will the protection of several hundred important cultural sites be possible, but through cooperation between construction projects and archaeological investigation, survey, and excavation, the location of the ruins will be made clear and the area to be protected—where construction must be controlled—will be further defined. Moreover, it is required that all regions develop master plans for the protection of sites of importance. In the meantime, archeologists are encouraged to complete archaeological reports expeditiously and disseminate the findings. The State Administration of Cultural Heritage will publish annual newsletters on findings of important cultural relics to enhance awareness among government officials and the Chinese people about the importance of protecting and interpreting the cultural heritage. By doing so, it is hoped that the construction of a number of parks for protected sites (National Parks for Cultural Sites) can be completed before the year 2015 and attempts be made to solve existing difficulties and problems. So far, the compilation of most master plans for protection work has been started and some plans have been completed. When these are approved by the State Administration of Cultural Heritage they will be published for implementation by the local government. For instance, protection is under way of large sites such as the Mausoleum of the First Emperor of the Qin Dynasty, the Yangling Mausoleum for Emperor Jing of the Western Han Dynasty in Shaanxi, Yuanmingyuan Garden in Beijing, and some other important ruins in Guangzhou and Chengdu. Protection includes many important elements such as assessment, environment, usage, engineering work,

management, classification, and estimation. It also addresses a great number of scientific and technical problems in the areas of archaeology, history, anthropology, ethnology, sociology, and museology as well as physicoecology, new technology, and the application of new materials. Therefore, the work of protecting these important ruins has become more scientific and operational, thus promoting overall improvement in the protection of cultural ruins in China.

- train high-quality personnel for archaeological work. According to initial statistics based on a general survey, it has been preliminarily determined that there are some 400,000 registered places and sites with a valuable cultural legacy, of which more than 100,000 are ruins and tombs from ancient times. The number of those yet to be discovered plus recently found sites resulting from capital construction may be even greater. Effective protection of so many cultural sites depends to a large extent on the establishment of a group of high-quality personnel. At present there are only several tens of thousands of people engaged in the work of archaeological excavation, cultural protection, and museology in China. Obviously this is insufficient to handle the great amount of work, especially since less than one-third are specialists in cultural protection and archaeology. In China, there are more than ten universities with archaeological (cultural relics protection and museology) departments, but over half of the graduates every year have gone to work in other occupations. Therefore, the State Administration of Cultural Heritage has developed a strategy to cultivate the needed professionals, for example, by actively organizing and assisting all these universities in training professionals. In addition, it encourages all science and technology organizations to retrain personnel in specialized subjects that support research in the preservation of cultural relics.

- further encourage multidisciplinary and comprehensive research and protection of cultural relics and historic sites. Archaeological work in China today is carried out mainly in conjunction with capital construction according to an accelerating schedule, with a short time frame and inadequate funding; to a great extent, this has restricted the application of multidisciplinary science and technology research.

ARCHAEOLOGY, PROTECTION, AND CAPITAL CONSTRUCTION

Nevertheless, archaeological workers everywhere increasingly are introducing methods and technologies from the natural sciences in order to acquire comprehensive information. These include dating techniques, DNA sequencing for research in ethnology, remote-sensing techniques, computer simulation, and research on palaeoenvironmental settings, paleogeography, and paleoclimate. Much research and testing has been undertaken with regard to archaeological sites and ruins, such as the protection of earthen ruins and in situ protection of large wooden structures and ancient mines. Good results have been achieved in all these areas. Great attention has also been paid to the study of excavated artifacts, such as lacquered woodenware, silk fabrics, ivories, and stone. Notwithstanding, there is still much to be done in relation to multidisciplinary study and the implementation of effective protection of excavated cultural heritage.

· expand exchanges with foreign countries. By 1990 the State Administration of Cultural Heritage had published the "Administrative Regulations of the People's Republic of China on Archaeological Work Involving Foreign Countries," which regulate archaeological and research activities by foreigners, thereby giving foreign archaeologists and cultural relic protectionists more opportunity to take part in investigation, excavation, and protection of cultural remains. Since the 1990s Chinese organizations for archaeological and cultural preservation have been engaged in relatively extensive cooperation of this kind with the United States, Japan, and Europe, and they have achieved outstanding results. For example, the project of the State Administration of Cultural Heritage in cooperation with the Getty Conservation Institute on the protection of the Mogao Grottoes at Dunhuang in Gansu has proven a model of success. At present there is still great development potential to be tapped by China in partnering with foreign countries. The State Administration of Cultural Heritage will make efforts to continuously support and promote cooperation of this kind.

Planning for Conservation of China's Prehistoric Sites: The Liangzhu Site Case Study

Chen Tongbin

Abstract: This paper focuses on the general status of conservation planning for prehistoric archaeological sites in China, taking the Liangzhu archaeological site as a typical case study. The site is an important one for Chinese archaeological study of the Neolithic period in the downstream region of the Yangtze River. The cultural remains and ruins, scattered over an area of 60 square kilometers, are located primarily in the developed areas south of the Yangtze River, which in 2001 were incorporated in the Hangzhou urban area. There has been dynamic development of urban and town construction and industrial growth in the area, and the protection of the site has a direct bearing on the lifestyle and production activities of the local people, as well as on the city's socioeconomic development plan. In preservation planning for protection of the Liangzhu site, a host of policies have been devised in response to specific issues in compliance with the Law on Cultural Relics and employing the guidelines of the Principles for the Conservation of Heritage Sites in China *(the* China Principles*). These policies take into account the local socioeconomic development plan in order to preserve the authenticity and integrity of the remains and ruins. This paper also lists several critical issues still in need of solution.*

Overview of Prehistoric Site Preservation Planning in China

Status of Site Preservation

China's economy is in a state of robust development that has been accompanied by unprecedented nationwide urbanization since the 1990s. This is endangering a great number of archaeological sites, in some cases to the point of destruction. In the absence of effective protective measures, unforeseeable consequences could result within the next ten years. Hence the urgency to develop policies and plans to ensure the preservation of all the archaeological sites.

Professional and Legal Framework for Preservation Planning

In accordance with Article 9 of the *Principles for the Conservation of Heritage Sites in China* (the *China Principles*, issued by China ICOMOS with the approval of the State Administration of Cultural Heritage), there are six steps prescribed for the preservation of cultural relics: (1) investigation; (2) research and assessment; (3) implementation of the four legal prerequisites; (4) determination of objectives and preparation of the conservation master plan; (5) implementation of the master plan; and (6) periodic review of the master plan and action plans. The preservation plan constitutes the backbone of protection, and it constitutes a statutory document for the implementation of protection measures for each site in China.

In view of the nonrenewable nature of heritage sites, planning for their preservation should be given priority in China's current development plans for economic construction:

- Preservation plans should precede the tourism development plan and become its raison d'être.
- Development plans should be the basis for preservation planning for famous historical and cultural cities.
- Development plans should be incorporated as an essential part of the planning system for urban and town development and overall urban plans.
- The central role of planning in the protection procedure as prescribed in the *China Principles* is clearly defined. However, it has not been given the attention

and support it deserves in China's prevailing system of laws and regulations.

Challenges in the Protection of Ancient Sites

Twenty-two and a half percent of the 1,271 national-priority protected sites in China, that is, 286 sites, are archaeological sites, of which 103 are prehistoric. These sites are much larger in scale than many other sites in terms of the area of land they occupy. The long history of Chinese civilization and the many sites scattered over the vast expanse of territory pose varied challenges, both human and natural, to planning for their protection.

Human destructive factors include large-scale urban and rural economic construction projects, development for tourism, high population density, and extensive farming. Natural destructive factors are erosion resulting from loss of vegetation, erosion from wind and rain, weathering, and freeze-thawing.

Basic Concepts for Preservation Planning

Compliance

- Law of the People's Republic of China on the Preservation of Cultural Relics
- Law of the People's Republic of China on Urban Planning
- *Principles for the Conservation of Heritage Sites in China*

Basic Criterion

- The principle of keeping cultural relics in their original state must be adhered to.

Preservation Objectives

- To keep the remains and ruins and their surroundings authentic, intact, and undisrupted

Basic Tasks

- To identify sites for preservation and determine their boundaries
- To demarcate protection zones and devise rules for management
- To work out protection measures
- To develop specific subplans for interpretation, use, management, and maintenance
- To formulate plans for periodic implementation and cost estimates.

Planning efforts in recent years for the preservation of Cheng-toushan, Niuheliang, Dadiwan, Qianjianglongwan, and Liangzhu prehistoric archaeological sites and other ancient sites originating from other historic periods, in compliance with the Laws and Principles, have identified protection zones, devised management rules, worked out protection measures, and developed specific plans for interpretation, use, and management with a view to keeping the sites authentic and intact. Of these cases, the Liangzhu site is of particular concern because of its strong potential for economic development.

Overview of the Liangzhu Site

Description of the Site

Liangzhu is one of the most significant sites in the Yangtze River basin for archaeological study from the late Neolithic period. The remains date to around 3,000 to 2,000 years B.C.E. Liang encompasses more than 130 sites discovered so far and covers an area of 60 square kilometers within which two administrative towns, Liangzhu and Pingyao, are located. The remains include a large-scale man-made terrace, architectural structures, dwelling places, a graveyard, altars, and massive construction projects. The archaeological finds are largely fine jade artwork, coupled with ceramics, stone, bone, and lacquerware.

Geographic and Climatic Conditions

The site is located inside the Yuhang district of Hangzhou municipality, Zhejiang province. This is an economically developed region of China's southeastern seaboard. It is in a contiguous area between hilly land in western Zhejiang province and the Hangjia Lake flatland. The remains are scattered in the river valley plain at an elevation of 3 to 8 meters above sea level. They are close to the low hilly land in the west and north and connect with the waterway plain in the east and south. Hence the terrain is level and open. The site is within the southern fringe of the northern subtropical monsoon region.

Significance

Liangzhu is typical of the initial period of China's civilization and is therefore an extremely important archaeological site. In terms of its large scale and advanced culture, it bears witness to five thousand years of Chinese civilization. The finest collection of jade utensils for ritual purposes so far has been excavated from Liangzhu; they are without match worldwide from the same period. Many achievements of the Liangzhu

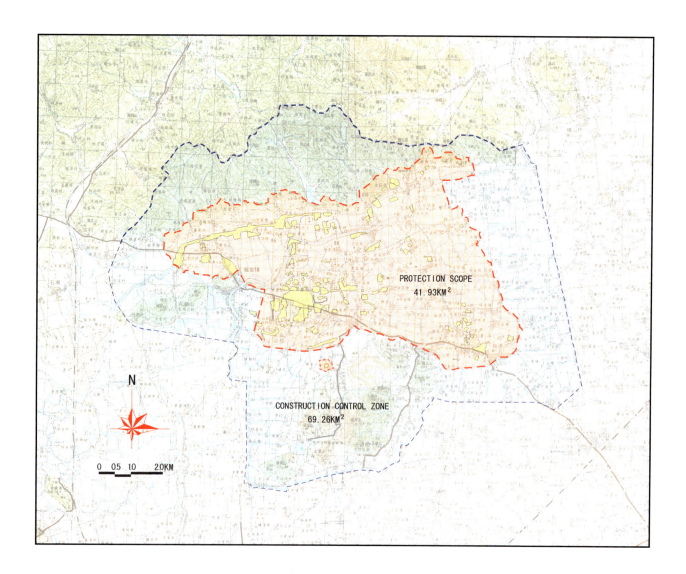

FIGURE 1 Zone division inside the Liangzhu site. Courtesy of
Architectural History Research Institute, Beijing

culture were later inherited and developed in the Shang and
Zhou dynasty cultures. Therefore, the site has played an
important role in the development and evolution of Chinese
civilization.

Case Relevance

Protection of the Liangzhu site has a direct bearing on the
productive activities and lifestyle of the local inhabitants as
well as the socioeconomic plan of Hangzhou city. Similar
cases in China are the ancient Chang'an city site of the Han
dynasty, the Qinshihuang Mausoleum, and other large archaeological sites that cover scores of square kilometers located on

the outskirts of cities. Hence, in a country such as China
where economic development is in full swing, protection of
Liangzhu is of great importance.

Challenges in the Preservation of the Liangzhu Site

The site is located in the developed area south of the Yangtze
River and northwest of Hangzhou city. This area became part
of urban Hangzhou in 2001; it borders the urban area of
Hangzhou, and its center is only 23 kilometers from down-
town Hangzhou. Given the lack of land for urban develop-

ment, it is an ideal location for construction. There are about 30,300 inhabitants on the site, scattered in four townships and twenty-seven villages. The average population density is 739 persons per square kilometer. Urban construction and industrial development within the area have experienced dynamic growth—more than 200 percent since 2000 (these data are based only on the number of investment projects)—and its periphery is attracting the attention of Hangzhou real estate developers.

Urbanization: The Main Destructive Factor
Archaeological sites such as Liangzhu are destroyed by earth moving, house building, road construction, pipe laying, and other large-scale urbanization activities. Certain agricultural activities, such as fish farming and deep plowing, also pose a considerable threat.

The population problem is a distinctive feature of China, hence the production activities and lifestyle of the inhabitants in the area put tremendous pressure on protection efforts. The desire to speed urbanization is of importance to the local economy, but at the same time it is a factor that hinders protection efforts. Therefore, the question of how to balance the needs of the inhabitants with the need to protect the large Liangzhu site figures high on the local agenda. Other challenges such as conservation treatments for cultural relics and site management will have to be addressed at a later time.

Policy Considerations regarding Protection of the Site as a Whole and Urbanization
Presentation of the authenticity of the site involves primarily interpretation, which pertains to academic and technical concerns but has little to do with the day-to-day concerns of site inhabitants. Nevertheless, efforts to keep the site intact must be closely linked to the interests of the local people.

Protection planning for Liangzhu follows the relevant laws and the *China Principles* and involves a spate of policy measures targeted at specific problems while also taking into account local socioeconomic development plans.

Essential Preservation Measures

To control urbanization within the site, it is necessary to

- put on hold transportation system development by intercepting the town and township trunk roads where they cut across the key preservation zone so as

to regulate the transportation network inside the zone;
- halt industrial construction by prohibiting new industrial projects and moving out 117 industrial and mining firms;
- place restrictions on construction activities in farmers' dwellings by means of three methods, moving, scaling down, or levying heavy taxes;
- bring agricultural activities under control by limiting tilling and planting;
- introduce ecologically sound measures aimed at retaining water bodies and maintaining the man-made wetland environment;
- reduce population density by phased moving of 806 households (10,000–20,000 persons) out of the area;
- concentrate the amount of land for construction and prepare havens for those staying behind, and keep the preservation zone tidy and clean;
- change the way the land is used by reducing by over 400 percent the amount of land approved for construction so as to have a larger proportion of land for preservation, agriculture, forest, and even barren land.

To intensify the urbanization process in areas bordering on the site, the following steps need to be taken.

- Streamline the traffic system. Main trunk roads should be planned for towns and townships bordering on the site so as to gradually do away with the heavy transit traffic and improve the traffic situation outside the zone.
- Adjust the economic structure by setting up a consolidated industrial zone and a farm-products processing base, thus enabling relocation of industrial and mining firms and the employment of farmworkers on labor-intensive projects.
- Speed up urbanization by resettling those uprooted from the zone in newly planned towns and townships.

Basic Preservation Measures

- Set up multilevel preservation zones
- Develop prioritized management plans
- Fine-tune the traffic system
- Work out a specific population control plan

- Formulate dwelling quarters control plans
- Change the way the land is used
- Incorporate all this in the overall local socio-economic development plans (fig. 1).

Existing Problems

Criteria Governing the Census of People Remaining

Ascertaining the number of people residing inside the preservation area is one of the crucial problems of the overall plan, as it is closely related to the effectiveness of the preservation effort and to the amount of funding to be invested in preservation. At this point China has no specific indicators available for acceptable population density within an archaeological area such as Lianzhu. What is taken as the parameter for reference in preservation planning for Pingyao and Liangzhu is the value of the average population density, namely, 257 to 430 persons per square kilometer. This figure is multiplied by the area of the total preservation zone—41.93 square kilometers—to derive a population ceiling. The base result is 10,800 to 18,000 persons.

The data are obtained by calculating the status of the current capacity of the area; however, this falls far short of an ideal criterion.

Earmarked Funding

The Phase I relocation plan involves 2,894 persons, or 806 households. Moving and resettlement costs are 160 million yuan (200,000 yuan on average per household). The overall size of the industries and mines to be relocated involve 16.5 thousand square miles, and the moving expenses total 333.2 million yuan (800 yuan on average per sq. m). Together, the cost is approximately 500 million yuan (493.2 million RMB, or U.S. $60 million).

This amount has to be raised from various sources. Funding sources and structures are yet to be explored, as is the availability of such a large sum for preservation.

Management

Many large-scale archaeological sites are located on the outskirts of cities and involve several administrative zones (cross-village, cross-county, and even cross-province and cross-municipality). How to establish effective site management organizations under the existing administrative system, what kinds of functions they are expected to perform, and how efficient they will be are all questions that need to be addressed in the implementation of the preservation plan, especially when this entails moving a large number of people and controlling land use.

Special Economic Policies

Measures in large-scale archaeological site preservation planning will necessarily entail compensation for relocation of people, population limits on site, and restrictions on agriculture—measures that have implications for the life and gainful activities of the local people. There is clearly a need for special economic policies. The question and challenge today concerns the need for special policies for site preservation under the prevailing government policy on the dismantling of housing and resettlement.

Interest of Local People

Local inhabitants have mixed feelings about preservation of the site. On the one hand, they hope that the park built there will bring them income from tourism; on the other hand, they are worried about the economic loss and restriction caused by the relocation and limited agricultural use. Therefore, they are as skeptical as they are expectant and await the details of special government policy and the availability of funding to implement the plan.

Conservation during Excavation:
The Current Situation in China

Wu Xiaohong

Abstract: *China's rapid economic development and concomitant development projects have affected archaeological excavation and conservation in both positive and negative ways. The increase in the number of projects provides a large amount of research material and opportunities for archaeologists and conservators; however, it also reveals the lack of experienced and qualified personnel. Current excavation and conservation techniques and research cannot cope with the problems generated by the large number of emergency excavations. Media reporting has improved and promoted conservation awareness among the general public; however, the media sometimes misrepresent the role of heritage conservation, which provokes negative responses. The attitude and degree of concern of local government also affects the quality of on-site excavation and conservation. By their very nature, excavation and conservation are in opposition. But the information embodied in the materiality of objects and sites derives from the combination of archaeological excavation and conservation. This paper argues that archaeologists and conservators should be specially trained in the examination and conservation of archaeological objects and sites during and after excavation. And whereas current training programs emphasize technological solutions in conservation, there is a need to broaden these programs to include management and decision making.*

In the past few decades China's developing economy has generated many infrastructure construction and urban development projects. A large number of emergency excavations have resulted. Some 70 percent of all archaeological projects have been initiated under these circumstances. These have affected archaeological excavation and conservation in both positive and negative ways. Because large numbers of ancient sites have been and continue to be discovered during construction and urban development, funds should be available for excavation and conservation. Currently, about 90 percent of excavation funds in all of China come from such projects. It should become possible with such funds to apply advanced scientific methods to many aspects of research and conservation work in situ. However, local governments significantly affect the quality of on-site excavation and conservation since they often control the distribution and use of funding.

The prevalence of such projects provides a large amount of research material and opportunities for archaeologists and conservators, but this also results in damage to ancient sites and remains because of a lack of experienced and qualified personnel on the project team. The situation on site has become critical.

Excavations resulting from development projects are put forward hurriedly, with little time to organize qualified and experienced experts from different fields to devise an integrated plan. In addition, the current state of excavation and conservation techniques and research cannot cope with the range of problems generated by the large number of emergency excavations, for example, the recovery of fragile deteriorated silk and the prevention of color fading on the surface of unearthed relics, which is caused by environmental changes.

Emergency excavations are undertaken at many ancient sites and cemeteries that the government may choose to expropriate. If the sites are of such importance and need to be preserved in situ to minimize damage, the construction plan may need to be changed, and this may bring disastrous economic losses. Who has the responsibility to bring such pressure to bear and how should cultural values, benefits, and stakeholder interests be balanced?

The increase in media reporting about excavation and conservation has improved and promoted conservation awareness among the general public; however, sometimes the role of heritage conservation is misrepresented, provoking negative responses.

Excavation and conservation are fundamentally in conflict. Excavation, as a physical process, is a reversal of depositional and formational processes because it exposes the stratum, objects, and the site. This kind of subtractive process is both destructive and irreversible. The cultural deposit and the history it embodies are destroyed, and the physical and chemical equilibrium of the site, established in the process of cultural deposit formation, is disrupted. The objective of conservation, in contrast, is to preserve cultural relics from loss and depletion by preventive and remedial means. Conservation applies every possible managerial and technical method to prevent or postpone the degeneration of the physical fabric.

From the perspective of the value of the information embodied in the materiality of objects and sites, archaeological excavation and conservation should be joined together. Conserving objects and sites preserves the cultural values possessed by the physical fabric. It is well presented in the conservation principle, "Keep the historic condition." This principle emphasizes the integrity and authenticity of remains, including the purity and unity of materiality and of the cultural information related to past human existence. Archaeologists study the cultural information embodied in the materiality of the site and objects to discern the thoughts and experiences of ancient peoples. Archaeological excavation makes it possible for us in the present to touch the past. Excavation is not only a physical method by which the archaeologists study a site but also an important process for estimating the value of the site and remains. Conservation aims to preserve the physical fabric and thereby the values it embodies.

The unity of the materiality and the cultural information of relics requires that conservators and archaeologists carry out research and documentation, including recording every kind of evidence during and after excavation, to safeguard all the information about the cultural beliefs, values, materials, and techniques that are embodied in the site as an aggregate record of human activity over the passage of time. In fact, conservation in China is not routinely involved in the planning, execution, or examination of the archaeological excavation project, or even in site management. Conservation is usually thought of as an exclusively off-site, postexcavation activity concerned with technical problems or remedial treatment. Few archaeological excavation projects have included

conservation as an important component from the beginning, despite the fact that excavation without a professional conservator can result in irreversible damage, such as the destruction of lacquer, silk, ivory, pigment, and plant remains. On the other hand, conservators are often reluctant to be involved in the cultural context of a site. Lacking the relevant cultural information, they may treat the objects or sites with improper interventions, such as the application of a nonreversible chemical reagent that may contaminate the surface and jeopardize important information, or they may neglect the context of the objects in the site, such as the placement of the wares and traces on the surface of artifacts.

Conservation during excavation requires that conservators understand archaeology more deeply. It is a complex, systematic undertaking involving many disciplines and many communities. It is not the sole responsibility of one professional group to make decisions. Conservation and archaeology should be completely united during excavation. Both disciplines have to study the physical evidence of the site and its contents, and the background and history of the deposits associated with human activities. The cultural context should be the basic common element that unites every method and discipline in order to preserve the site and its contents in a harmonious way.

There is a well-established system in China whereby every province and city has its own archaeology and cultural heritage institutes, but there is no national one. Most of the professional personnel are well-educated archaeologists, but there are few full-time conservators, and the conservators working in museums lack excavation experience. Therefore, archaeologists in the provincial and municipal institutes have become a major force for conservation during excavation and have become the cultural resource managers. There is an urgent need to train archaeologists in the principles of conservation and scientific method, as well as to adjust the deployment of human resources within archaeology and cultural heritage institutes by employing more conservators.

In fact, conservation training and education programs have been available at institutes and universities in China for the past twenty years, but most of these focus on conservation technology. The first academic training program in conservation science in China started at Fudan University in Shanghai in the 1980s as a two-year graduate program. It was organized by the Department of Physics, and all faculty members were professional physicists. Because the program lacked financial support and was considered inappropriate to the work of the department by the university's evaluation system, it ended after a few years. The first undergraduate student program was established at the Department of History (now the School of Archaeology and Museology) in Xi-Bei (North-West) University in Xi'an in the early 1990s. All of the faculty have science backgrounds. The basic courses of this program are chemistry, and the emphasis is on technical conservation of objects. The students are divided into groups that focus on different technologies, but not every student has the chance to practice all of them. Currently there are twenty students on average who graduate from this program each year. Many work in museums and institutes of archaeology and culture heritage. The graduate program in conservation science was established in the Department of Archaeology at Peking University in 1995. It emphasizes materials science in conservation and the preservation of materials. In 1999, supported by cooperation between China's State Administration of Cultural Heritage and Peking University, the School of Archaeology and Museology came into existence, based in the Department of Archaeology. Undergraduate programs in conservation and

ancient architecture were added to the curriculum. Other universities, such as Qinghua, Beijing Technological University, and Xi'an Jiao Tong University, also have programs in conservation science. These programs have an important role in training conservation personnel. However, almost all such programs emphasize the technological aspects. It is impossible for their graduates to manage complex systematic projects of archaeological site conservation.

A dearth of experts in the conservation of archaeological sites will continue to be a serious problem in China in the coming decades if professional conservation training and education are not undertaken as soon as possible.

Acknowledgments

I am grateful to the Getty Conservation Institute for inviting me to attend the Fifth World Archaeological Congress and to the Chinese State Administration of Cultural Heritage for their financial support.

Heritage Protection in the Liyie Basin, Hunan Province, the People's Republic of China

Yuan Jiarong

Abstract: *Archaeologists from the Hunan Provincial Institute of Cultural Relics and Archaeology successfully conducted a rescue archaeology project in the Liyie River basin in 2002 that led to the discovery of the ancient city of Liyie (300 B.C.E.) and some thirty-six thousand bamboo and wood slips containing writings from the Qin dynasty (221 B.C.E.–206 B.C.E.). The discovery caused a sensation in academic circles in China. The site and findings are now securely protected by the policies of the government of the People's Republic of China.*

The Rescue Archaeology Project at Wangmipo Hydroelectric Power Station

This project was launched after the onset of construction of the Wangmipo Dam located at the middle stream of the You River in Baojing County, Xianxi Tujia clan and Miao clan Autonomous Region. The power station project budget is 2 billion RMB, which is not a large-scale project. However, as one of the western region development projects, it is important in promoting the economy of Hunan province. The dam project was inaugurated on 18 August 2000 and was completed in 2004.

The You River is one of the largest tributaries of the Yuan River. It originates on the border between the Yunnan-Guizhou plateau and the Wuling Mountains in western Hubei province. The area is hilly, and the altitude is more than 800 meters. Lack of transportation creates an economic disadvantage. Because of the region's remoteness, archaeology has long been neglected, although it was generally held that an archaeological discovery here would be beyond expectations.

According to the People's Republic of China's law on the protection of cultural relics, "before carrying out a large-scale capital construction project, the construction entities shall first report to the department for cultural administration of a province, an autonomous region, or a municipality directly under the central government for organizing an archaeological excavation team to conduct exploration and investigation at places where such relics may be buried underground within the area designated for the project." Hunan provincial archaeologists complied with their responsibility to contact the authority in charge of construction and began an archaeological survey during May and June 1997 in the area to be submerged. Some seventy-nine archaeological sites and ancient cemeteries were discovered, ranging from the Paleolithic to Neolithic periods and from the Shan and Zhou dynasties, the Warring States period, and the Qin and Han dynasties to the Song and Yuan dynasties. The Liyie basin site has the richest cultural remains and the most important concentration of sites in the region.

In conformity with Article 31 of the laws of the People's Republic of China on the protection of cultural relics, "the expenses and workforce needed for prospecting for cultural relics and archaeological excavations, which have to be carried out because of capital construction or construction for productive purposes, shall be included in the investment and labor plans of the construction entities or reported to the planning departments at higher levels for proper arrangement." Once the archaeological survey was completed, the budget for the excavation and protection of the archaeological sites in Liyie basin was submitted to the authority in charge of construction, but no reply was received for a considerable period. The situation became urgent when, in March 2002, partial destruction of the archaeological site occurred during the construction of the flood prevention dam at Liyie. In compliance with the law, a notice was issued by the Hunan Provincial Institute of Cultural Relics and Archaeology to stop construction where the archaeological sites were located. The regional government exceeded its authority in allowing work to proceed. After many rounds of negotiations with the regional government and the authorities in charge of construction, agreement was reached. Under the principle "rescue comes first, preservation is the priority," in April 2002 archaeological excavations were begun in the area to be submerged with a focus on the ancient city site of Liyie. In June some thirty-six thousand pieces of bamboo and wooden slips containing writing were unearthed from ancient well No. 1. A proposal was put forward to the governments on the in situ preservation of the entire archaeological site. After many rounds of discussions and negotiations with the construction authorities, a plan for protecting the sites was finalized. The site was listed as a Provincial Priority Protected Site in September 2002 and as a National Priority Protected Site in November 2002.

The rescue archaeology project at Wangmipo Dam entailed a series of operations, including acquiring information about the construction project, budgeting, excavation, and preservation. There were obstacles to be overcome at almost every turn, from initial negotiations to the final settlement. The disputes centered on issues of budgeting and differing approaches concerning economic development versus heritage preservation.

China is a developing country, and economic development is a national priority. Developers and even some government officials view development as more important than the protection and preservation of cultural heritage. They feel the urgency to construct and are reluctant to acknowledge the nonrenewable nature of the treasures underground. They do not communicate with and even refuse to cooperate with heritage preservation authorities responsible for archaeological excavation, and they emphasize the superiority and urgency of their development projects. Therefore, the cultural relics and archeological entities that negotiate with the construction companies or conduct protection work at the construction sites are always subjected to difficulties and resistance. In the current circumstances, there is a long way to go before conservation awareness can be promoted effectively to the general public.

Funding for archaeological excavation and preservation of cultural remains is a core issue in all controversies. The law clearly stipulates that funding for archaeological digs must be included in the overall budget of the construction project, as

is also the case internationally. However, the construction entities often are not willing to provide the funds for archaeological excavation in a timely matter and try to postpone compliance with all kinds of excuses. Delays or the unavailability of funding for survey and excavation work add to the threat of destruction, especially when the construction schedule is stringent. The authorities in charge of the project often are not willing to provide funding for archaeology in a timely manner mainly because the planning department either did not budget for site conservation as a necessary and specific item or did not budget sufficient funds. Funding for archaeological fieldwork is therefore distributed from the "unpredictable" line item in the budget. Bulldozers remain on the scene to put pressure on archaeological work until the day the funding issue is finally resolved. Much needs to be done to bring about a change in the current situation.

Issues of Heritage Preservation and Development in the Liyie Basin

The Wangmipo hydroelectric power station archaeological work was mainly concentrated in the Liyie basin. The town of Liyie is located at the northwestern border of Hunan province; since ancient times it has been an important river port on the upper stream of the You River. It is a crossroad to Sichuan, Guizhou, and Chongqing. The basin includes Liyie township on the left riverbank and Qingshiuping, in Baojing county, on the right riverbank.

A levee was proposed to protect the important historic town of Liyie as part of the Wangmipo hydroelectric project. It was designed to be built east and south of town and to cross the ancient town of Liyie, which dates from the Warring States period to the Han dynasty. Soil for the levee was to be taken from two ancient cemeteries: Maicha cemetery from the Warring States period (300 B.C.E.) and Dabang cemetery from the Eastern Han dynasty (A.D. 100). A cemetery from the Western Han Dynasty (200 B.C.E.–A.D. 100) at Qingshuiping was proposed as the housing project site for the people removed from the area that was to be submerged. Rescue archaeology digs were conducted in the above three cemeteries.

Usually, to make sure that construction can progress normally, there are two general objectives when undertaking a rescue archaeology project. One is to excavate the site and ensure careful preservation of the finds. The other is to acquire as much archaeological data as possible for research purposes. The three cemeteries mentioned above have been dealt with in this manner. The exposure of the ancient city site of Liyie created a departure from the normal routine of rescue archaeology.

The ancient city site of Liyie is located on the grounds of Liyie's present-day primary school. The east part of the site was eroded away by the river. The site covers an area of 25,200 square meters—210 meters long and 120 meters wide. Some 2,000 square meters of the site have been excavated. So far excavation has uncovered the remains of city walls, a moat, roads, dwellings, and wells, in addition to the bamboo and wood slips. The city was of military importance during the Warring States period. The excavation of the site and the discovery of the bamboo and wooden slips with their writing greatly increased knowledge and understanding of the Qin dynasty, which represents a turning point in Chinese history. The significance of the discovery is far-reaching.

This find led to the proposal that the whole city site should be preserved. The proposal meant that the levee should be shifted closer to the You River, a revision to the design of the levee that would increase the budget significantly. The authorities in charge of the Wangmipo project vigorously opposed this change, but the sensational find itself silenced the opposition. Some thirty scholars from across China gathered in Changsha city, the capital of Hunan province, to celebrate the find as the first great archaeological discovery in China in the twenty-first century. High-ranking officials from the State Administration of Cultural Heritage of China came to Changsha and Liyie to inspect the finds and the archaeological site. Through many rounds of inspections and discussions with heritage and archaeological authorities, the Hunan provincial government approved the proposal and ordered the provincial department of construction to rework the design of the Wangmipo project. The primary school will be removed so that the site can be preserved, developed, and used in the future. Funding for archaeological fieldwork was ordered to be in place soon to ensure the smooth progress of the archaeological dig. State leaders also expressed their concerns on the issues of protection and preservation of the ancient city site of Liyie and endorsed the proposal.

Many rounds of discussions were required to reach a final settlement. The levee is to be constructed closer to the You River to ensure the preservation and protection of the entire site. The inner side of the levee base will be about sixteen meters from the No. 1 well. Seven designs for the levee were developed and evaluated, and a design with a 16-meter-deep retaining wall was selected to be built to protect the ancient city.

On 6 September 2002 the Hunan provincial government listed the ancient city site at Liyie as an important provincial cultural heritage site and made a special application to the State Council to list the city as a nationally important site requiring protection. The application was successful, and the ancient city became fifth on the list of nationally protected sites by the State Council on 22 November 2002.

Preservation and Development of the Ancient City Site of Liyie

Tourism plays an important role in China's economic development. Cultural heritage sites are the columns that support the mansion of the tourism industry. The discovery and preservation of ancient Liyie serves as a timely catalyst for the economic development of the region.

There are three ancient city sites buried around the town of Liyie, each associated with a cemetery from that period.

- The site belonging to the Warring States period and the Qin dynasty at Liyie (300 B.C.E.) is located to the east of the town along the left bank of the You river, and its associated Maicha cemetery is located 1 kilometer to the north of the town.
- The site from the Western Han dynasty at the village of Weijiazhai (200 B.C.E.–100 C.E.) is located at the upper stream of the ancient city of Liyie across the You River in Baojing county, and the associated cemetery, Qingshuiping, is located on a hill to the southeast about 1 kilometer from the village.
- The site belonging to the Eastern Han dynasty at Daban (100–300 C.E.) is situated 3 kilometers to the southwest of ancient Liyie township on the left bank of the You River. Its associated cemetery is located to the east and north of the city site at Daban. According to a preliminary investigation, this cemetery also has some four hundred ancient Ming dynasty graves.

The above sites and their associated cemeteries are unique; they reflect social and political changes over a six-hundred-year period in the valley of the You River. A practical preservation plan and good development of the sites will surely help to promote tourism and the local economy.

The issues concerning the preservation of the city sites at Liyie have drawn much attention from the central and provincial governments. The Hunan provincial government has given high priority to the preservation of the cultural heritage found at the town of Liyie and has put it high on the agenda of provincial social and economic development, with an emphasis on culturally oriented tourism. The local government has undertaken to revise the planning for the township at Liyie in order to promote mountain tourism and alleviate the poverty that has long been a regional issue.

Longshan county government has the responsibility for implementing the preservation and development plans. This includes a special administration set up to take charge of the plan. Regulations and measures concerning the preservation of the ancient city site at Liyie, Longshan county, were issued; relevant authorities have been consulted to work out a practical heritage preservation plan and a master plan for Liyie township, as well as the removal of the Liyie primary school.

Under the pressure of development and use of heritage, preservation efforts directed at the town of Liyie are facing new and growing challenges. There are two approaches concerning the preservation of heritage: "full usage of the heritage" and "reasonable usage of the heritage." The former emphasizes the pursuit of profit and views heritage as a commodity. Heritage sites are often under the threat of devastation as a result. The latter insists that the preservation of heritage is the priority and that all tourism development should be based on careful assessment. It is possible to achieve a balance between heritage preservation and economic development. The successful preservation of the heritage at Liyie depends on which approach is adopted. Excavations of the ancient city site at Liyie will continue for research purposes. The dig will be long term and systematic. The results will be on display if preservation requirements can be implemented, so that the general public can learn about its past.

Acknowledgments

I wish to thank the Getty Conservation Institute for enabling me to participate in the Fifth World Archaeology Congress.

The Conservation and Presentation of Large-Scale Archaeological Sites in Liaoning, China

Wang Jingchen

Abstract: *The prehistoric Niuheliang and Qin dynasty Jiangnushi archaeological sites in Liaoning province have important historic, artistic, and scientific value. They comprise an outstanding combination of social, architectural, and natural scenic elements. Relevant measures have been adopted to protect these cultural heritage sites appropriate to their characteristics and conservation needs. The conservation approach applied to the sites was based on selected, proven technology and materials, integrating chemical conservation, environmental treatment, and archaeological work with exhibition display. Emphasis was placed on conserving the archaeological excavation while also preserving the surroundings. Social, economic, and tourism development needs are met through the exhibition of five thousand years of Chinese civilization revealed at the sites, thereby also raising public awareness of the importance of conserving cultural heritage.*

In Liaoning, research has played a significant role in Chinese archaeology. This is not only because the province is located at the crossroads of central China, northeastern China, and the northeastern Asia region, which created a hub for cultural dissemination and exchange, but also because important sites in Liaoning province demonstrate a complete archaeological sequence with clear and unique characteristics. Two such sites are Niuheliang Hongshan Culture (near the city of Chaoyang), a large ceremonial architectural group comprising an altar, a temple, and tombs, and the Emperor Qin's Jieshi palace site located in Suizhong county on Bohâi Bay. Respectively, these sites provide proof of a five-thousand-year-old culture and two thousand years of a unified empire.

The size of the Niuheliang and Jiangnushi sites is immense. With their grand scale and contents, they possess important historic, artistic, and scientific values and represent the outstanding integration of social architecture and natural landscapes. The challenge today is to conserve them and make the best use of their social function.

General Situation of the Sites

The Niuheliang Hongshan Culture Site
This site is located in the west of Liaoning province, at the junction of Lingyuan and Jianping counties. Some twenty Hongshan culture sites have been discovered in the area. In the Niuheliang No. 1 section, with Nushenmiao (the Goddess Temple) at the center, many stone tombs were built along the slope of the surrounding hills, forming a complex of sites about 10 kilometers from east to west and 5 kilometers from south to north, covering a total area of 50 square kilometers. The main structures are the stone tombs, Nushenmiao, and the altar (fig. 1). The significance of the Niuheliang site in terms of human sociology is that it demonstrates a social complexity and religious evolution that existed long before that of other known Chinese prehistoric cultures. Its altar, temple, stone tombs, and excavated artifacts indicate a hierarchical society.

The Jiangnushi Site
The Jiangnushi site is located in the southern coastal area of Suizhong county. It is a large Qin dynasty, ethnic Han architectural complex with a monumental plaza at its center, with Zhi Miao Bay and the Heishantou site on the east and west sides. It covers the subareas of Wazidi, Zhou Jianan Mountain, and Dajinsitun, among others. This large architectural site is well preserved and has been systematically excavated. Histori-

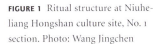

FIGURE 1 Ritual structure at Niuhe-liang Hongshan culture site, No. 1 section. Photo: Wang Jingchen

cal literature confirms the geographic location, particularly since excavation results established that it possessed the characteristics of an imperial palace. It was most likely the temporary palace for the first Qin emperor when he toured the eastern region.

Conservation of the Relics Sites

To preserve these two precious cultural heritage sites, measures have been adopted that focus simultaneously on excavation and conservation of the sites and their surroundings. The Liaoning Provincial Cultural Relics and Archaeology Research Institute has established field stations at both sites and carries out general management and conservation work. So as to meet socioeconomic and tourism development needs, exhibit five thousand years of civilization and history, and promote public awareness, the intention is to display these two sites while at the same time conserving them. The implications of this have been explored, and a few trial methods have been implemented.

The principles of conservation were to select proven technologies and reliable materials and combine chemical conservation with environmental treatment while integrating the archaeological and exhibition work. The main components of the Niuheliang site are stone architecture, including soil and mud sculptural remnants, all of which require complex conservation interventions. Although Jiangnushi is a simple earthen material site, so far it has not been possible to provide an effective and comprehensive conservation approach because of the extremely large area it covers.

Rammed Earth Protection

Jiangnushi comprises a large remnant rammed earth structure as its main architectural component (fig. 2). Erosion from rainwater has had a severe impact as the site faces the ocean and is exposed to high humidity and salt. All of these conditions pose challenges for conservation. Consequently, after excavation, the safest conservation method—backfilling the exposed features—was adopted.

At Niuheliang the main threats facing the earthen burial mounds are soil slumping and freeze-thaw deterioration. The Liaoning Provincial Cultural Relics and Archaeology Research Institute is collaborating with the China National Institute for Cultural Property, Beijing University, and the Conservation

FIGURE 2 Archaeological excavations at the Jiangnushi site. Photo: Wang Jingchen

Institute of the Dunhuang Academy to carry out experimental preservation on the No. 2 section of Niuheliang. Comparisons of various protective materials were made through comprehensive on-site and laboratory tests. It was decided to use a non-aqueous-based silicone resin reinforcement (251M) as the penetrating consolidant for the main body and potassium silicate solution with clay as the crack filler.

Stone Conservation

The No. 2 site of Niuheliang was selected for experimental conservation. The approach is to carry out preservation mainly of exposed structures and secondarily to rebury or shelter the more important relics. Portions of the stone tombs have been seriously damaged by natural causes such as temperature fluctuations, freeze-thaw, wind, and rain erosion. Reinforcement of foundations, securing of surface rocks, and stabilization of stone tombs have been done. Through experimentation, an epoxy was chosen as the adhesive for the stone.

Foundations

The stone tombs have completely settled, thus eliminating the need to reinforce large foundation areas, in accordance with common practice and architectural regulations. Furthermore, as archaeological excavation had weakened the foundations of the tombs, they were partially refilled to stabilize them. For the exposed soil and stone portions, spreading grass species with wide-spreading roots were planted to prevent structural damage due to soil loss from water erosion.

Walls

Environmental tidying up of the stone tomb walls was undertaken to show the outlines of individual tombs. Partially collapsed stone walls were restored based on scientific evidence, and during the restoration, attention was paid to the original structure by replacing the stones in their correct positions.

Reburial

The main tomb and a typical stone tomb were stabilized and restored and the openings covered for protection and display. The rest of the tombs were backfilled for protection.

Earthen Sculpture

The Nushenmiao (or Goddess Temple) has been reburied and a simple protective shelter built over it. The threats faced were that the walls of the pit had lost support through excavation, resulting in instability; and due to freezing, cracks developed in the walls, resulting in surface exfoliation. Mud sculptures were deteriorating for similar reasons. Colored motifs were fading due to exposure to the air, and parts of the low-fired colored motif clay wares were gradually breaking up.

In order to protect the Nushenmiao and its excavated artifacts, there is an urgent need to adopt the following measures for both the archaeological excavation and exhibition:

- Construction of a building for protection, excavation, and exhibition. The building, covering some 500 square meters, would require services such as lighting, temperature, and humidity control.
- Carry out research and testing to solve the adhesive, consolidation, and fading problems of the mud sculpture.

Archaeological Site Display

The principles in this case should include display of the site's overall relationship to its surroundings and the actual artifact locations. The display should make available the academic research results. All displays should be implemented without damage to the site and its surroundings.

Having been designated as an experimental site display project of the State Administration of Cultural Heritage, the Jiangnushi site has made much progress. Through consultation with specialists, it was decided that the display should include a surface outline of the restoration, the current state of conservation, and the status of the restoration in relation to the site's original condition. Due to limitations of protection techniques and research ability, the last phase has not been carried out as yet.

The outline of the site is marked by the use of different kinds of plants to show the different functions of the various architectural structures. The No. 4 section of the southwest corner of Jieshi Palace was chosen for this purpose. The surface was marked out with grasses, surrounded by cypress trees and short Dutch chrysanthemum plants to represent the width of the wall base. There are two gaps left at the southern and northern main gates; the central lane is covered with nonoriginal red sand. Three different types of plantings are used to represent different types of relics. This approach protects the site and its surroundings while maintaining its cultural ambience (fig. 3).

With support from the State Administration of Cultural Heritage a 1:1 representation of the Heishantou site (part of Jiangnushi) was made in order to display the outline of the original foundations. The result, after evaluation, has been quite satisfactory (fig. 4).

FIGURE 3 Using the marking method to restore the outline of the No. 4 section of Jieshi Palace. Photo: Wang Jingchen

FIGURE 4 The recovery of the Hei-shantou site. Photo: Wang Jingchen

Conclusion

Protection of large-scale archaeological sites is an extremely complicated and systematic engineering process that requires iterative reasoning and technical experiments, large capital input, and proven technology. However, current ability lags behind these ambitions. Therefore, international support and assistance is requested from foundations and specialists in heritage conservation.

Acknowledgments

I thank the Getty Conservation Institute for providing the opportunity to take part in the Fifth World Archaeological Congress, which enabled the exchange of ideas and the sharing of experience, technology, and methods with specialists in the same field from around the world.

PART TEN

Sharing Resources and Experience: Managing Archaeological and Rock Art Sites in Southern Africa

Introduction

Janette Deacon

The papers in this part report on initiatives that have enabled conservators and managers of archaeological sites in the region to share their experience and resources. The results have neatly encapsulated some of the hotly contested issues that challenge the standard methods used, particularly at rock art sites. They have also provided some hope for political commitment to sustainable development of rock art and other heritage sites.

All the contributors draw attention to mistakes that have been made in the past and suggest strategies that could avoid them in the future. It is interesting that the problems are seen to lie not so much with the "hardware"—the sites themselves and the conservation methods used—as with the "software"—the intangible heritage, intercommunity relationships, and the decision-making processes regarding presentation, conservation, and management.

The eternal local residents/outside experts dichotomy that planners face on a daily basis is played out time and again at heritage sites, where it is often magnified by mutual misunderstanding. In southern Africa the vast majority of rock art and other archaeological sites are in rural areas. The gap between locals and experts therefore remains wide. Webber Ndoro and George H. O. Abungu give examples of what can happen when one party acts without proper and sustained consultation with the other. In some cases it may be preferable to do nothing. As Johannes Loubser points out, there are no miracle cures, and preventive care is often preferable to intervention. The same applies to the presentation of sites to the public. Sven Ouzman warns against "freezing" artifacts and sites when a wider diachronic approach would extend their lives in the present and the future. World Heritage listing has had an impact on rock art sites in the region, and Phenyo Churchill Thebe describes the interdependence of the intangible and tangible heritage of the World Heritage Site at Tsodilo in Botswana. Where local beliefs and practices are ignored, they add to the byproducts of dissatisfaction that local people feel when they have been left out of the decision-making process.

Despite these problems, light can be found at the mouth of the cave. Benjamin Smith's paper cites initiatives in South Africa to address the presentation of rock art in a positive way by using San indigenous knowledge and ensuring that local communities benefit directly from opening sites for tourism. The lessons learned in this and other projects throughout the region have been shared in the workshops and courses offered by the Southern African Rock Art Project (SARAP) that are described in my own paper. Thanks to assistance from the Getty Conservation Institute in the initial stages of the project, it could serve as a model for other regions of the world as well. The challenge is to stay connected.

Sharing Resources: Issues in Regional Archaeological Conservation Strategies in Southern Africa

Janette Deacon

Abstract: *Many countries in southern and eastern Africa share a similar range of rock art and archaeological sites and a similar philosophy regarding their conservation and the intangible heritage related to them. It is therefore possible, at least theoretically, to apply lessons learned in one country to issues that arise in another. Several programs stimulated by the World Heritage Centre, the Getty Conservation Institute, the Norwegian Agency for Development Co-operation (NORAD), the Swedish International Development Co-operation Agency (SIDA), and the International Centre for the Study of the Preservation and the Restoration of Cultural Property (ICCROM) over the past two decades have begun to build capacity and integrate heritage research practice and conservation at a regional level in southern Africa. This paper discusses the Southern African Rock Art Project (SARAP), which has identified rock art as a shared resource in the region and has played an important role in encouraging participating countries to nominate rock art sites for World Heritage listing and to develop appropriate conservation management plans. To succeed, archaeological conservation programs require close cooperation with local communities, as well as an external stimulus, agreement on appropriate behavior toward the sites or resources, and a governmental infrastructure capable of funding, implementing, and monitoring management plans.*

Common Issues

Archaeological sites in Africa, particularly in eastern and southern Africa, cover a longer record of human history than those on any other continent. That many sites are well preserved is the result of both natural preservation factors and the philosophies of most traditional African societies, which call for conserving the intangible heritage of places and not interfering with natural processes.

The countries in the southern African region that are the subject of this paper, Tanzania, Malawi, Mozambique, Zambia, Zimbabwe, Botswana, Namibia, South Africa, and Lesotho, also shared a colonial history over the past few centuries. Except for those few countries that saw European settlement in the seventeenth century, all were colonized in the nineteenth century and by the late twentieth century had regained independence. This means that they not only have similar archaeological heritage conservation practices and challenges but also deal with them in much the same way, using principles and legal structures borrowed mainly from the United Kingdom and other western European countries. Common issues that are related more to the recent and current economic situation and that therefore also have parallels with countries elsewhere in Africa and beyond are

- the perception that archaeological sites are of low priority because they do not generate income, create jobs, or otherwise stimulate the economy;
- a consequent lack of secure long-term financial commitment from governments for archaeological heritage management;
- limited opportunities for training in cultural heritage site management;
- a resultant history of reliance on short-term, project-related donor funding for training initiatives, research, conservation projects, and the purchase of equipment; and
- a lack of institutional memory at cultural heritage institutions because of rapid staff turnover.

Conservation Issues at Archaeological Sites

All archaeological sites are protected under general legislation in southern Africa, and there is a reasonably efficient permit system that controls excavation and the collection of artifacts and, less often, environmental impact assessment. The main management issue highlighted at the Tenth Congress of the Pan-African Association for Prehistory and Related Studies in Zimbabwe in 1995 (Pwiti and Soper 1996) was the need for specialist proactive conservation at archaeological sites. Those most at risk had been affected by excavation or other forms of research, natural erosion, public visitation, and agricultural, commercial, and social development.

Sites Selected for Research

One would expect that sites selected for research would be better conserved than those that are not excavated, but this is not always the case. Whether excavation programs are undertaken by local researchers or by visiting archaeologists from abroad, the funding is available only for the period of excavation and, possibly, analysis of the materials for a year or two thereafter.

There is a real need for integration of archaeology and conservation at an early stage in all excavation projects (Deacon 1995, 1996; Deacon and Brett 1993; Pwiti and Soper 1996). This should be applied through legislation as well as other incentives. Funding agencies could insist on a description of the long-term protection measures that will be instituted, with a budget line item for the excavation to be filled in. To date there has been remarkably little documentation and monitoring in southern Africa of methods such as backfilling with and without sand bags, the use of plastic sheeting versus geotextile, hardening of exposed surfaces, roofing methods, drainage options for sites on slopes and the effects of tracing on rock paintings or engravings.

Sites Vulnerable to Natural Erosion

Archaeological deposits, dry stone walls, and especially rock paintings and engravings are vulnerable to natural erosion where they are exposed by excavation or other forms of research intervention, as well as by fire, sun, wind, or water. The challenge for conservation is to know when to intervene and what methods to use. In most cases the intervention tries to slow down the erosion or divert the causes.

Sites Open to the Public

Long-term and regular visitation at archaeological sites usually has a negative effect on the deposits and structures that people come to see. McKercher and Du Cros (2002:2) suggest that this happens when the cultural resource management and cultural tourism sectors have not formed a true partnership. Tourism values may therefore be compromised to protect the archaeological values, or the archaeological and other cultural heritage values are compromised to promote tourism. In southern Africa the latter is more often the case, although there are notable exceptions, for example, the Laetoli footprints in Tanzania (see Demas and Agnew this volume).

As Ndoro and Thebe point out in this volume, African rural communities have successfully protected sites for thousands of years by continuing to use them, controlling access to them, or avoiding them in the course of agricultural activities. The older Stone Age deposits have been protected by virtue of the fact that local communities are unaware of their significance and value.

Sites Affected by Development

Population growth that leads inexorably to land development for housing, food production, commerce, and infrastructure is taking its toll on archaeological sites in southern Africa just as it is elsewhere. Environmental impact assessments are required in some countries, but not in all. Cultural heritage conservation authorities are faced with decisions about mitigation and whether to sample sites before destruction or disturbance or to insist that they be protected regardless of the cost.

Southern African Archaeological Conservation Initiatives

Generally, southern African countries have limited financial resources and expertise for archaeological site conservation, even when legislation provides protection. They have relied heavily on donor funding for specific projects, usually initiated by a crisis. A critical issue is raising awareness among politicians and officials at all levels of government of the need for conservation of archaeological and other heritage sites. The prestige of World Heritage Sites has helped considerably in this regard.

For all the problems it may bring in terms of management, the decision by the World Heritage Centre in 1995 to pay special attention to sub-Saharan Africa has paid dividends. The purpose of their meeting, held in Harare in 1995 (Munjeri et al. 1996), was to encourage southern African countries to become signatories to the World Heritage Convention and to thereby increase the number of World Heritage Sites in the region and overcome some of the biases inherent in the listing system. As a result, in the past eight years South Africa, Botswana, and Namibia have signed the convention and submitted tentative lists, joining Tanzania, Malawi, Mozambique, Angola, Zambia, and Zimbabwe. Only Lesotho and Swaziland are not yet states party to the convention. In addition, eight new sites have been added to the World Heritage List, nomination dossiers and management plans have been drafted for five more sites, and plans are afoot to draft at least two more. Of these fifteen sites, ten have a strong archaeological component and eight include rock art.

I want to focus here on the results of an initiative to integrate the conservation needs of southern African rock art with training and networking to share expertise. The needs that were identified have been addressed through the infrastructure and encouragement provided by World Heritage listing.

The Southern African Rock Art Project

Delegates at the meeting organized in Harare by the World Heritage Centre in 1995 identified the need for a regional management strategy for rock art in southern Africa. Funded initially by UNESCO with assistance from the Getty Conservation Institute, representatives from the member countries met in South Africa in 1996 and in Zimbabwe in 1997 to plan the way forward. The first step was to conduct a survey of the existing rock art records and assess the gaps (Deacon 1997).

In May 1998, at a meeting in Pietermaritzburg, South Africa, the Southern African Rock Art Project (SARAP) was established as a collaborative program of the South African National Monuments Council, the National Museums and Monuments of Zimbabwe, the Getty Conservation Institute, and the International Centre for the Study of the Preservation and the Restoration of Cultural Property (ICCROM). The aim of SARAP was to address a perceived need for regional collaboration in rock art conservation and management, and it set out to

- raise awareness and understanding of the wealth of rock art in the subcontinent;
- enable those unfamiliar with rock art outside their own countries to get a better perspective on the rock art of the region as a whole;
- encourage southern African countries to identify rock art sites in need of protection and conservation;
- generate criteria for assessment of southern African rock art sites as tentative World Heritage listings;

- develop a collective strategy for conservation and the nomination of rock art sites for the World Heritage List; and
- assist member states to acquire the necessary skills and expertise to nominate rock art sites for the World Heritage List and draw up management plans.

To address priorities identified in Pietermaritzburg, it was decided to arrange a series of workshops and courses at rock art sites suggested for World Heritage nomination. The workshops would be attended by directors and senior heritage managers in decision-making positions for the nomination and management of World Heritage Sites. The courses would take place at rock art sites on the tentative list and participants would be drawn from staff responsible for day-to-day management of these sites to encourage networking among rock art specialists in the subcontinent and to share knowledge and experience.

It was generally agreed that

- the most pressing need was assistance in real-life situations on how to manage with limited resources and capacity;
- courses should address general issues for all levels of management, at the national, regional, and site levels;
- courses and workshops should have a cascade effect on cultural resources management and at the same time build awareness and capacity in collaboration with the projected rock art training course at the University of the Witwatersrand in Johannesburg;
- lobbying at the governmental level would be needed to encourage funding and follow-through;
- every participant would be expected to deliver a project at the end of the course, for example, the drafting of a management plan; and
- networking after the course should be built into the planning.

The first course on management plans for rock art sites—dubbed COMRASA, an acronym for the Conservation and Management of Rock Art Sites in Southern Africa—was supported by ICCROM and the Getty Grant Program and was held at the Matobo Hills in Zimbabwe in July–August 1999. There were twenty participants from all countries in the region except Angola and Swaziland. The program was led by Sharon Sullivan, former director of the Australian Heritage Commission, and focused on the development of a management plan. A manual was compiled, a library of reference works was made available, and meetings were held with local stakeholders and local and national government officials. Basic recording methods were demonstrated at a rock art site (Silozwane), and each of the four groups of participants developed a management plan for this site that was presented on the last day. After the course, each participant was expected to submit a report within six months on a project that he or she had initiated to apply management principles at a rock art site. About half the participants complied with this requirement.

In July 2000 a workshop was held in Dar es Salaam and at rock art sites near Kondoa in Tanzania for the decision-making group to assess the significance of the rock paintings and to assist Tanzania with a plan of action to survey and document the sites, write the nomination dossier, and prepare a management plan. The program was led by Sharon Sullivan with the assistance of Joseph King from ICCROM. Participants met with the relevant minister at the national level and as with the local residents who were most affected by nomination of the site. The draft documents were completed by the Antiquities Department in Tanzania in 2003 for submission in 2004.

The second COMRASA course was held in Kasama, Zambia, in July 2001 and this time focused on rock art documentation. There were eighteen participants from all the countries involved, and staff were drawn from South Africa, Zimbabwe, Zambia, and Norway.

Kasama was chosen as the venue for the course for two reasons. First, it is the rock art site that Zambia intends to nominate to the World Heritage List; second, the rock paintings are at risk from rock quarrying and forest clearance for charcoal in the area. It was hoped that by meeting there, attention would be drawn to the need for decisive action to curb the quarrying that has already destroyed several rock art sites. A site with the only painting of an elephant recorded in the 1990s had been virtually destroyed by soot from fires built in a small rock shelter to crack the rock before breaking it up for building material.

Funding for the course was generously provided by NORAD as a regional program through a cooperative program with the South African Department of Environmental Affairs and Tourism (DEAT). The implementing agent was the South African Heritage Resources Agency (SAHRA), assisted by the National Heritage Conservation Commission in Zambia and the National Museums and Monuments of Zimbabwe. In addition, ICCROM's AFRICA-2009 program, established

to train English- and French-speaking heritage practitioners in Africa between 1999 and 2009, provided funding for the writing and production of the course manual.

The course was officially opened by the minister of tourism in Zambia, the Hon. Michael Mabenga. The event was reported on national television, and Mabenga was enthusiastic about the development of Kasama rock art for tourism. The expected outcomes of the course were to enable participants to

- complete a documentation project of real use and benefit to the Zambian authorities;
- acquire general familiarity with the range of documentation methods available; determine which of these types of documentation programs would meet particular needs for varying situations; and design and carry out or commission documentary projects to meet research and management needs;
- have an understanding of how to interpret, analyze, and use different types of site documentation;
- obtain hands-on skill and experience in basic documentation techniques;
- obtain hands-on skill and experience in the development of site data systems; and
- acquire experience in consulting with local communities and addressing their needs and concerns.

About two hundred villagers (in addition to about seventy inquisitive children), five headmen, and seven members of the local Rock Art Conservation Committee met the COMRASA staff and participants at a traditional meeting place on the outskirts of Kasama. They divided into three groups according to their villages, and the participants' groups met with them and sought answers to the questions that had been drawn up the previous day.

At the end of the course each of the three groups of participants presented a proposal to potential funding agencies planning to commission a survey of the Kasama rock art in preparation for the nomination of the site for World Heritage listing. The presentations were made on the last day, and the permanent secretary for the Northern Province, Sylvester Mpishi, was the guest of honor.

In February 2002 the Botswana National Museum made use of the COMRASA infrastructure and raised funding for a two-week workshop on rock art recording and documentation that was held at the newly declared World Heritage Site at

Tsodilo. On this occasion, nineteen museum staff members attended, and the manual developed for Kasama was used a second time.

Participants gained hands-on experience of various methods of rock art recording and identified key issues for management of the rock art at Tsodilo. The results are summarized in a revised rock art site record form for Botswana and in proposals for a conservation management plan for rock art at Tsodilo that were developed by the participants.

In addition to these SARAP initiatives, workshops to assist with management planning and the nomination of rock art sites for World Heritage listing have also been held in Mozambique, Malawi, and Namibia with the assistance of staff from the National Museums and Monuments of Zimbabwe, the University of Bergen, and the Rock Art Research Institute at the University of the Witwatersrand.

New Initiatives

There has been a great deal of interest in continuing the SARAP-COMRASA program, but problems with administration of funding were experienced. An initiative spearheaded by NORAD in 2003 led to a meeting in Malawi in March 2004 to reestablish the COMRASA courses with assistance from the AFRICA-2009 program. As a result, individual countries are now responsible for identifying their needs and raising funds to run courses that will be assisted by expertise from SARAP members and ICCROM administration.

Such a partnership will be mutually beneficial. ICCROM's ten-year training strategy for the conservation of immovable cultural property in Africa, AFRICA-2009, has worked in collaboration with other African cultural heritage organizations, the UNESCO World Heritage Centre, and CRATerre-EAG. Three-month courses are held for about twenty participants in alternate years in English in Mombasa, Kenya, and in French in Cotonou, Benin. The goal of the program is to increase national capacity in sub-Saharan Africa for the management and conservation of immovable cultural heritage.

Reflections

The SARAP experience has highlighted issues at both ends of the management spectrum. At the local level, it was evident that the people living closest to sites must be recognized and involved in decision making even if they are not indigenous to the area and have no connection with the belief system that generated the rock art. Such communities need to have some tangible or intangible benefit from site conservation and management that may not necessarily be financial. It is therefore crucial to understand the sociopolitical environment of local communities and local government structures before introducing conservation methods and to identify and then apportion the benefits.

At a broader level, the SARAP program suggests three main requirements for a regional program of this kind that is aimed at the long-term conservation of archaeological sites.

An external stimulus. In this case it was the World Heritage Centre's program in Africa and the prestige associated with the nomination of rock art sites for World Heritage listing, together with the availability of donor funding to compile dossiers and develop management plans.

Guidance on how the work should be done. In the SARAP case this took the form of workshops and courses that identified the needs and provided on-site, hands-on training. Participants developed policies, guidelines, and management plans that were appropriate to their needs but that also conformed to internationally acceptable standards. In the process they were able to interact with local stakeholders, network with their peers, and compare sites and priorities in several countries.

Establishment and maintenance of an effective infrastructure for implementation and long-term monitoring of the site and the management plan. This phase received the least attention during the SARAP program and should be the focus of future initiatives. It requires close cooperation at two levels: with the local community living closest to the site who must be consulted at all stages because they will always be the most directly affected by the management program; and with the official administrative bodies responsible for the legal and practical management of sites so that long-term conservation is not neglected. This would include strategy plans, budgeting for staff salaries and ongoing training, and visitor management and professional conservation intervention when required. It is the stage that can be done only by official staff dedicated to the site(s) and suggests commitment at all levels of government.

The challenge for the future is to successfully integrate these issues regarding the conservation of archaeological sites with the plans and strategies of local, provincial, and national governments.

References

Deacon, J. 1995. Promotion of a neglected heritage at Stone Age sites in the Western Cape, South Africa. *Conservation and Management of Archaeological Sites* 1 (2):75–86.

———. 1996. Case studies of conservation practice at archaeological and palaeontological sites. In *Monuments and Sites—South Africa,* ed. J. Deacon, 53–70. Colombo: ICOMOS.

———. 1997. A regional management strategy for rock art in southern Africa. *Conservation and Management of Archaeological Sites* 2 (1):29–32.

Deacon, J., and M. Brett. 1993. Peeling away the past: The display of excavations at Nelson Bay Cave. *South African Archaeological Bulletin* 58:98–104.

McKercher, B., and H. Du Cros. 2002. *Cultural Tourism: The Partnership between Tourism and Cultural Heritage Management.* New York: Haworth Hospitality Press.

Munjeri, D., W. Ndoro, C. Sibanda, G. Saouma-Forero, L. Levi-Straus, and L. Mbuyamba, eds. 1996. *African Cultural Heritage and the World Heritage Convention. First Global Strategy Meeting, Harare, 11–13 October 1995.* Harare: National Museums and Monuments of Zimbabwe.

Pwiti, G., and R. Soper, eds. 1996. *Aspects of African Archaeology.* Harare: University of Zimbabwe.

Intangible Heritage Management: Does World Heritage Listing Help?

Phenyo Churchill Thebe

Abstract: *This paper examines selected issues regarding cultural resource management as a means of exploring the effectiveness of World Heritage listing. The Tsodilo Hills in the northwest of Botswana provide a useful case study for questioning the success or failure of World Heritage listing in the country. A key argument is that it is necessary to conduct additional consultation and public awareness programs to ensure a greater level of protection of the site. It is further argued that some aspects of intangible heritage management have a key bearing on understanding the conservation and management of the site. While the World Heritage listing is helpful to the government of Botswana, its benefits to the local community have not yet been realized. This has resulted in the community's dissatisfaction with the management of the site.*

> My ancestors have lived in Tsodilo for centuries. Throughout this time, they have looked after this area. They have not destroyed it. You and I also find an unblemished area. This is important because in future if the area is destroyed, you will have witnessed it in its original form.

These words were spoken by Kgosi Samochao in his speech at the official opening of Tsodilo World Heritage Site in 2001. They can be interpreted in two ways: as an expression of the community's desire to share the management of cultural heritage with the rest of the world and rhetorically—as an expression of the community's dissatisfaction with international methods for the conservation and management of Tsodilo.

To interpret intangible traditions, which are preserved in the Tsodilo community, we must understand their role in society. Here "intangible heritage" refers to the belief systems, behavior, folklore, oral traditions, myths, thoughts, aspirations, legends, and spiritual aspects of a people's culture. It also takes account of nonphysical elements rather than the material elements that have symbolic and spiritual connotations (Deacon 1994; Luxen 2001). "Tangible heritage" refers to various forms of material culture, including rock art, ritual objects, structures, and buildings. All of these testify to the practices pertaining to living cultures in traditional societies. These issues are also crucial in the management of archaeological sites. Saouma-Farero (2001) argues that the quest for the message of intangible heritage requires us to identify the ethical values, social customs, beliefs, and myths of which the physical heritage is the sign, the expression, in time and space. He states further that the concept of cultural representation of space is more important than the object itself.

Luxen (2001) argues that the distinction between physical heritage and intangible heritage is artificial, that physical heritage attains its true significance only when it sheds light on its underlying values. Intangible heritage must be personified in tangible representation, for instance, by visible signs, if it is to be conserved. This dialectic may prove especially fruitful in providing greater representation of cultures of the world that place more importance on oral traditions than on sophisticated artistic expression (Luxen 2001). Similarly, Turner (1967) argues that one cannot analyze ritual symbols without studying them in relation to other "events." That is, symbols are essentially involved in the social process. I extend these ideas to Tsodilo by arguing that to understand the characteristic elements of intangible heritage at the site, we have to study social institutions that have a bearing on the rock art. These include rainmaking ceremonies that are currently conducted at various parts of Tsodilo.

I attempt here to construct plausible arguments to counter those that claim to undermine the rationality of intangible heritage. I also examine closely the importance of intangible heritage to the communities at Tsodilo and challenge the claims that make such living cultures a myth. Here "myth" refers to stories, legends, and tales. I argue that contrary to the popular view, intangible heritage plays an important role in the authenticity and integrity of the site.

Geographic Setting

Tsodilo is in Ngamiland in northwestern Botswana and about 1,400 kilometers from the nation's capital, Gaborone. The mountains of Tsodilo rise majestically from the surrounding Kalahari; at 1,395 meters, they are Botswana's highest point and a sacred landmark that has been attracting people to trade, visit, and live there for thousands of years (figs. 1, 2). These

FIGURE 1 Land use map of Tsodilo. Courtesy of Botswana National Museum

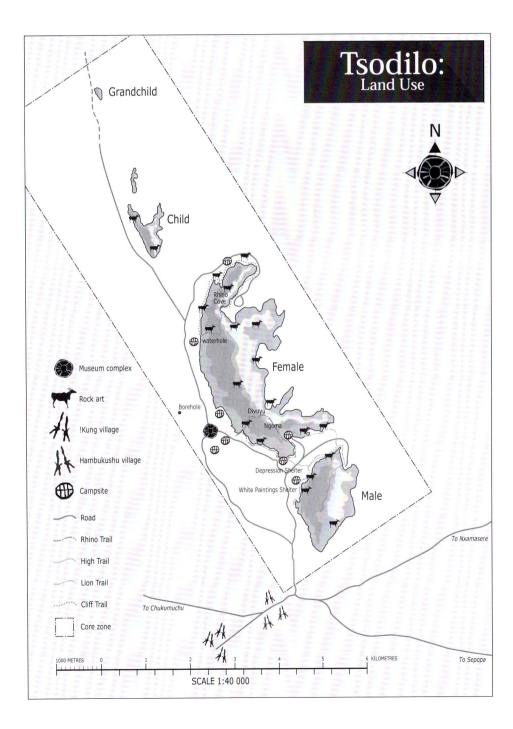

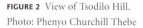

FIGURE 2 View of Tsodilo Hill.
Photo: Phenyo Churchill Thebe

mountains have been referred to as "hills," a misnomer that does little justice to their imposing presence (Munjeri 2000).

Local Communities

Two ethnic groups, the click-speaking !Kung and the Hambukushu, Bantu speakers, live at Tsodilo today in separate villages (fig. 3). The !Kung trace their ancestry to hunter-gatherers in the Nxauxau and Qangwa regions, where they still have relatives (Munjeri 2001).

The Tsodilo Hills

The Tsodilo Hills are one of Africa's premier rock art sites. More than 4,500 paintings have been painted at 400 sites, most of these dating from 850 and 1100 C.E. Consisting of red and white paintings (the red are older), they portray wild and domestic animals, geometric patterns, humans, and what appears to be a whale (Munjeri 2001) (figs. 4, 5). According to Campbell (1994), these images were finger painted and made

with pigments from hematite (red), charcoal, and calcrete (white), possibly mixed with animal fat, blood, marrow, egg-white, honey, sap, or urine. Tsodilo rock art is essentially religious in nature. It is generally accepted that the ancestors of the San, or river "Bushmen," made Tsodilo rock art. In reality the picture is much more complex: there are a number of San communities that are passionate about Tsodilo rock art that was painted by their ancestors (Walker 1998).

Archaeological Diversity

In addition to rock paintings, Tsodilo is rich in archaeological finds. Three rock shelters, White Paintings Shelter, Depression Shelter, and Rhino Cave, have been excavated. More than twenty mines and the remains of two villages, Divuyu and Nqoma, dating to 800 C.E. have been uncovered. Pots, metal spearheads, stone tools, glass beads, and fish bones have been found and help us to form a picture of ancient life at Tsodilo. Denbow (1980) argues that the artifacts indicate that local communities were involved in long-distance trade from Congo to the Kalahari.

FIGURE 3 Hambukushu village. Photo: Phenyo Churchill Thebe

FIGURE 4 White paintings, elephant and geometric shapes.
Photo: Phenyo Churchill Thebe

FIGURE 5 Red painting, rhinos. Photo: Phenyo Churchill Thebe

Flora and Fauna

Tsodilo's timeless cultural heritage is matched by its natural beauty. It is visited by many animals, including leopards, hyenas, and elephants, and is home to the diminutive Tsodilo rock gecko that is found nowhere else.

Spiritual Attributes

There are a number of reasons why the local people are attached to Tsodilo. First, it is considered home to their ancestors, which creates both emotional and personal attachments to the place—as does its beauty. Second, for a long time the place has provided sustenance: water, edible plants, and a variety of game animals. Third, many creation myths are associated with the area. And fourth, the place is used for ritual and religious purposes. Among the latter are the San trance dance, which plays an important social, political, and economic role in community life (fig. 6). It is conducted in designated places around Tsodilo. The harvesting of local fruits, such as mongongo, motsintsila, and morethwa, has a close link with the hills. Rainmaking rituals also have importance both to the community and to the site. Tradition and custom prohibit visits to rainmaking sites by the local community. This and other taboos help to protect the site and can be useful in developing laws and policies for the care and management of Tsodilo.

Tsodilo's Nomination to the World Heritage List

In order to understand whether the World Heritage listing has value to the local community at Tsodilo, it is necessary to discuss it in the context of the nomination dossier. Tsodilo is significant because of the following values:

- Spiritual: Healing waters, offering and prayer sites, creation sites, rainmaking places, and continuing pilgrimages by people of several religious denominations.
- Aesthetics: Natural beauty and isolation have made Tsodilo a Kalahari landmark. It has at least two rock art traditions.
- Scientific: Results of archaeological, rock art, geologic, seismic, zoological, botanical, paleoenvironmental, and anthropological research.
- Historical: 100,000 years of human occupation, from the middle Stone Age to the Iron Age, and mining, as well as oral histories of the villages from the 1850s to the present day.
- Traditions: Rainmaking and healing are still practiced, and local communities have strong ties to the hills.

FIGURE 6 Painting depicting the San trance dance. Photo: Phenyo Churchill Thebe

- Environmental: Its inaccessibility has helped to conserve its significance.

Methodology

Based on a number of research methods, a more comprehensive approach to intangible heritage is advocated here. Ethnographic sources were used regarding pertinent aspects of intangible heritage. Interviews with the San and the Hambukushu (twenty individuals from each group) helped to define the issues regarding intangible heritage and its continuity over time. Folklore, beliefs, and stories about the area were compiled.

Translators were not necessary as I was able to communicate with both communities in a common language, Setswana. I used questionnaires that covered personal data, views on World Heritage listing, and subsistence strategies, taking into account appropriate forms of address and the people's diverse cultural traditions and customs. Initially, the questionnaires were written in English and translated into Setswana for use in the field. This is necessary because the medium of communication is primarily Setswana.

Clearly, an ethnographic survey of this nature requires a large sample. It is therefore essential to devote considerable time and resources in the future to interviewing in detail at least one hundred people. Because there are substantial numbers of San and Hambukushu in the study area, it will not be difficult to find a large sample.

Survey Results and Analysis

Eighty percent of those who were interviewed expressed dissatisfaction with the World Heritage listing. They argued that it does not help to improve their lives because they are not in joint venture with the Botswana government. Table 1 summarizes the results of my research.

The survey attempted to assess awareness of the World Heritage listing. As mentioned above, the ethnographic survey forms were designed to elicit specific information about intangible heritage and its relevance to World Heritage listing. Sixty percent of the sample indicated a low level of understanding; 40 percent had some understanding. The most frequent criticism was that no benefits have been realized by the community. That is, all the people interviewed expressed hope regarding the economic potential of the site as a tourist destination. Generally, many were not opposed to the Botswana government's "occupation" of the site. However, they com-

Table 1. Summary of Interviews at Tsodilo Hills

Interviews	Yes (%)	No (%)
Idea of a WHS	8	40
No idea of WHS	12	60
Satisfied with World Heritage listing	2	1
Not satisfied with World Heritage listing	18	90
World Heritage listing helps	4	20
World Heritage listing does not help	16	80
Site economic potential	20	100
No economic value of site	0	0
Need a fence around site	14	70
No need for fence around site	6	30
Road from Nxamasere should be graveled	20	100
Road from Nxamasere should not be graveled	0	0

plained that there were not sufficient efforts to make people aware of the advantages and disadvantages of the listing. Some even thought that the nomination of Tsodilo as a World Heritage Site meant that the site was being "taken" from them. For instance, one of the informants, Mareko Motlhaba, remarked, "It appears that this listing business has given our monument to the rest of the world."

A related question analyzed in the surveys was to what extent national or international involvement affects local or traditional care. Respondents were given the following options: very well, quite well, and not at all. Sixty percent of the respondents stated that they were not satisfied with the involvement of the government and UNESCO. Most people claimed that they had not been given the opportunity to become involved in the management of the site. Thus the respondents agreed that the presence of national and international involvement reduces local care.

Respondents were also asked whether the local community needed the fence around Tsodilo. Seventy percent of the respondents said the fence is needed to control visitors and livestock movements. Only 30 percent said that the fence interferes with their access to the monument and with the movement of livestock and wildlife. Regarding improvement of the Nxamasere and Tsodilo access road, all respondents wanted it to be improved with gravel because that would promote development in the area.

The surveys at the Tsodilo Hills have yielded crucial information regarding whether World Heritage listing provides benefits in Botswana. Clearly, the World Heritage listing has not met the expectations of the Tsodilo community. This is not because there are no benefits but because there has been little public education on the value and the benefits.

The Tsodilo Management Plan: What Do We Seek to Preserve, and for Whom?

To protect, study, and develop the site, the Botswana National Museum formed an advisory committee and prepared an Interim Management Plan in 1992, supported by a Scheme of Implementation in 1994. Pierre de Maret (1995) conducted an evaluation of the Tsodilo Hills Management Plan and its implementation for UNESCO and the Botswana National Museum. In his view, these documents are among the "best of their kind produced south of the Sahara to date." He states also that they are both thorough and practical. The overall strategy of the Tsodilo Management Plan is to harmonize infrastructure with the surroundings. It also seeks to keep development to a minimum. The idea is to have all developments reversible where possible to allow for easy rectification should any of them subsequently prove to have been ill founded. The plan also calls for limiting development to the periphery of the site as much as possible (Campbell 1994).

Regarding ongoing activities at the site, de Maret (1995) states that the Zion Christian Church members "tramping" around the area during rituals is a matter of concern and must be addressed. On the contrary, it can be argued that we need to ask more fundamental questions: What is the meaning of the dance? How to do we conserve the site without denying people access to it? For whom are we conserving it?

A number of strategies are recommended for addressing the conservation of the natural and cultural heritage of Tsodilo. One of these is to develop a management plan that makes the local community joint owners of the site. Modalities for such a partnership should be carefully reviewed with the local community. The current organization of the Botswana National Museum (BNM) is not ideal for such a partnership. Nongovernmental organizations should also be involved. The ongoing talks with the Trust for Okavango Development Initiative (TOCADI) should also be encouraged because this will enhance the management of the site. Other benefits include shared technical and financial resources.

There should also be continuous dialogue. The San and Hambukushu communities that currently reside at Tsodilo are the real stakeholders. They have the knowledge to carry out restoration projects. They should be given authority, responsibility, and accountability. They should be part of the conservation process. They have long realized and preserved the positive, intangible aspects of their culture. But the current management plan does not discuss aspects of intangible heritage.

A study conducted by Keitumetse (2002) identifies components of cultural heritage and strategies employed in managing them at Tsodilo and Tlokweng. She argues that there is little attention to living traditions that are recognized by the local community as culture. She also points out that this approach to cultural resources management is influenced by several factors: the origins of the concept of heritage management, the disciplinary approach that determines cultural heritage, and the internationalization of cultural heritage management. She concludes that the way cultural resources are perceived and valued in most African countries is a result not only of specific government programs but also of outside factors (Keitumetse 2002).

Intangible Heritage Management

In Botswana a number of paintings were chipped in what appears to be the removal of pigments for ritual purposes. In Zimbabwe some Christians were reported to have removed paintings because they considered them devilish (Walker 1998).

In 1999 Walker and I observed that a number of paintings at Tsodilo were destroyed by what appeared to be removal of pigment for ritual purposes. All of these were eland paintings associated with rainmaking. Unfortunately, this was termed "vandalism." This is clearly a complex issue, and a better system of solving the problem has to be devised. We conducted an experiment to restore an eland painting. By the time we completed the restoration process, it started to rain. Some members of the local community argued that this was a clear testimony that Tsodilo is an ancient temple.

This brings up issues of identity—whose land and property? The fundamental issue is, should members of the community be allowed to "activate" the paintings at Tsodilo. Another question is, is it acceptable to restore the managed heritage? Members of the community argued that it was wrong, that it is against the wishes of the ancestors. I suggest that the community be consulted on this matter. A dialogue should be promoted between the BNM and the two local communities, perhaps using existing venues such as the public meetings (Kgotla), the Village Development Committee

(VDC), and the Tsodilo Development Committee (TDC). These forums will facilitate related tourism income–generating activities, for example, craft production, local transportation (by donkey cart), performances, nature trails, and tracking. Local staff should be trained to be future managers of the site. Museum staff should practice "engaged anthropology." While governments' efforts to consult and be sensitive to the needs of the people can be appreciated, it seems that more grassroots work has to be done. This should be implemented initially in the form of workshops that actively involve the community.

Another problem is that archaeological research has been concentrated on the San and rock art. More attention should be devoted to the later Iron Age, to recent history, and to the ethnography of Tsodilo communities. The Hambukushu

should be encouraged to participate in tourism-related activities at Tsodilo.

Conclusion

This paper attempts to provide an up-to-date summary and interpretation of the intangible heritage of the Tsodilo communities from a management perspective. I have argued that both the !Kung and the Hambukushu feel that they are not yet receiving the full benefit of World Heritage listing. Their concern can lead the villagers to be uncooperative regarding the management of the site.

Ten local people are employed by the museum at Tsodilo (fig. 7), but all members of the community should have opportunities and outlets to sell crafts. The villagers have also

FIGURE 7 Tsodilo Museum. Photo: Phenyo Churchill Thebe

expressed the desire to be involved in all stages of site development. There are tensions that exist between the Hambukushu and the !Kung that seem to arise from competition for resources. These tensions require delicate handling.

I have suggested that we need to be less patronizing and more inclusive. For example, we should combine training of heritage managers and the community. Learning has to be a two-way process. Although the Tsodilo Management Plan has a number of limitations, Tsodilo was hailed as a unique and innovative cultural resources management project.

There is a dialectical relationship between the government and the local community regarding the management of the site. The government has the duty to conserve the site using "modern technology"; the community sees the site as its "spiritual home." For many years, they preserved the paintings very well. Furthermore, the local community initially saw the World Heritage listing as an "apple from heaven"; now, they fail to see its benefits.

I want to conclude with a call for action. Aspects of intangible heritage must be actively incorporated in the management planning of the site. Intangible heritage should not be regarded as "myths," "superstitions," or "barbaric."

Appendix. Tsodilo Anthropological Survey (Interviews)

1. Name   M/F   Age

2. Marital status

3. Village

4. Date of interview

5. What is your main important economic activity?

6. What is a WHS?

7. What type of heritage is found at Tsodilo?

8. Who were the prehistoric painters at Tsodilo?

9. Do you know the symbolic meaning of rock art?

10. Are traditional ceremonies conducted at Tsodilo?

11. What time of the year are they conducted?

12. What is intangible heritage management?

13. Is there a particular word associated with intangible heritage management?

14. Has World Heritage listing improved/not improved economic activities at Tsodilo? How?

15. Describe how you would like the heritage at Tsodilo to be managed and shared.

16. Is the local community getting its share of benefits from World Heritage listing?

17. Is the fence around the WHS necessary?

18. Should the road from Nxamasere be graveled?

Acknowledgments

I would like to thank my wife, Thato Thebe, Greek Phaladi, and Berlinah Motswakumo for helpful comments on earlier drafts. I also want to thank James Denbow for his advice on archaeology theory. Of course, I could not have undertaken my studies without significant financial support. The Fulbright Program and the Graduate School of the University of Texas, Austin, enabled me to pursue this research. The Department of Anthropology at the University of Texas provided a research leave during summer semester 2003, at which time the initial draft of this paper was completed. The Getty Conservation Institute provided funding that made it possible for me to present the initial draft at the Fifth World Archaeology Congress. The Botswana National Museum provided photographs and a video of the official opening of Tsodilo.

References

Campbell, A. 1994. *Tsodilo Management Plan Scheme of Implementation.* Gaborone: Government Printer.

Campbell, A., and D. Coulson. 1988. Cultural confrontation at Tsodilo. *Otima* [Johannesburg].

Deacon, J. 1994. *Some Views on the Rock Paintings in the Cederberg.* Cape Town: CTP Book Printers.

Denbow, J. 1980. Early Iron Age remains from Tsodilo Hills, northwestern Botswana. *South African Journal of Science* 76: 474–75.

Keitumetse, S. O. 2002. Living and archaeological sites in Botswana: Value and perception in cultural heritage management. Master's thesis, University of Cambridge.

Lewis-Williams, J. D. 1990. *Discovering the Rock Art of Southern Africa.* Cape Town: Clyson Printers.

Luxen, J. L. 2001. The intangible dimension of monuments and sites. In *Authenticity and Integrity in an African Context,* ed. J. Saouma-Forero. Rome: UNESCO.

Maret, P. de. 1995. *Evaluation of the Tsodilo Management Plan and Its Implementation for UNESCO/NMMAG.* Gaborone: Government Printer.

Munjeri, D. 2001. *Tsodilo Dossier, 1999.* Gaborone: Botswana National Museum.

Saouma-Forero, G., ed. 2001. *Authenticity and Integrity in an African Context.* Rome: UNESCO.

Turner, V. 1967. Symbols in Ndembu ritual. In *The Forest of Symbols: Aspects of Ndembu Ritual,* 19–47. Ithaca, N.Y.: Cornell University Press.

Walker, N. 1998. Botswana's prehistoric rock art. In *Ditswammung,* ed. P. Lane, A. Reid, and A. Segobye, 206–32. Gaborone: Pula Press and Botswana Society.

Rock Art Tourism in Southern Africa: Problems, Possibilities, and Poverty Relief

Benjamin Smith

Abstract: *This paper considers successes and failures in the history of rock art management and presentation in southern Africa. It argues that public rock art sites have a key role in national identity, poverty relief, and job creation and makes a strong case for a management process in rock art tourism development based on carefully negotiated partnerships between landowners, local communities, archaeologists, and heritage managers.*

Rock Art Tourism

On 27 April 2000 President Thabo Mbeki unveiled the new South African coat of arms. At its heart is a pair of human figures derived from San rock art. President Mbeki explained that San rock art, which is found throughout southern Africa, was chosen because it unites everyone in a common humanity (fig. 1). It is also among the finest art traditions in the world, a reminder of a proud history of cultural achievement in Africa extending back to the dawn of time.

In 1864 Charles Darwin predicted that Africa would be shown to be the cradle of humankind (Darwin 1864). Today a large body of evidence suggests that he was correct. Africa has revealed the oldest hominid bones, the oldest human bones, and the oldest cultural objects. Genetic research indicates an unparalleled antiquity for the peoples of Africa (Cavalli-Sforza 2000). Blombos Cave, in South Africa's Western Cape (Henshilwood et al. 2002), has revealed the world's oldest pieces of art: two complex patterned engravings dated to 77,000 years ago. They are more than twice as old as the acclaimed earliest paintings from France, those of Chauvet Cave. And if art and culture began in Africa, so too should have language and religion.

No wonder then that President Mbeki chose to put San rock art at the heart of his new coat of arms, and no wonder that he also chose to write the new national motto—*!ke e:*

FIGURE 1 The new South African coat of arms with rock art at its heart.

/xarra //ke—in a San language. San heritage represents the nation's link to an unparalleled antiquity. In a previously divided nation, the oldest human remains evoke a time when all of humanity lived in Africa, when all people were Africans. This is the "common humanity" captured in the coat of arms and this is the "unity in diversity" that is referred to in the South African national motto.

In 2001 South Africa's most recently developed public rock art site, Game Pass Shelter, was opened in KwaZulu-Natal. This site was developed as the first of a new generation of public rock art sites that will showcase the rock art treasures of South Africa. In his opening address, Premier Lionel Mtshali spoke of the great national pride that he derives from an understanding of the San rock art of Game Pass Shelter. He referred to the deep spirituality contained in the art, a power that brought generations of earlier communities together, healing sickness, spite, and malice. It is this ancient magic that Thabo Mbeki hopes we can use to heal South African society.

This is a deeply inspiring vision. In the past, however, rock art did not unite South Africans in the way Mbeki envisages. Apartheid politics could not allow it. This paper sets out the new public rock art developments within the broader history of public rock art in South Africa, so as to show how it may be possible to develop sites in such a way that we overcome the serious problems experienced at public rock art sites in the past.

Site Protection

In 1993 Janette Deacon reviewed the history of the declared national monuments of South Africa. She noted that before 1993 of more than 3,800 declared national monuments, only 38 were precolonial sites and just 10 were rock art sites. Seven of the ten rock art sites were declared between 1936 and 1943. The sites of Nooitgedacht and Driekopseiland were two of these (Deacon 1993:122) and were among the first of all South African national monuments to be declared. Their listing was achieved thanks to the forceful personality of Maria Wilman, director of the McGregor Museum in Kimberley. Wilman saw official listing as the only practical way to protect the sites. At the time Nooitgedacht was in imminent danger of being destroyed by diamond mining. Driekopseiland was threatened by submersion under a dam. The listing of the sites and their preservation was won through a series of feisty letter exchanges with Clarence van Riet Lowe, secretary of what became the National Monuments Council. The current

national status of the sites of Nooitgedacht and Driekopseiland, even their continued existence, is thus a product of a particular historical circumstance and personality.

The motivation for the listing of the other rock art sites seems to have been similar. Most were declared for "protective" purposes: to safeguard them from destruction, vandalism, and encroachment. Schaapplaats in the Free State is a typical example. Here a fence was erected across the front of the shelter to protect the art and a National Monument plaque was installed to indicate the site's special status. The fence was more than 2 meters high and comprised multiple strands of barbed wire. Schaapplaats offers a vivid picture of the defended site: public rock art, shielded from a range of hostile forces. The need for Schaapplaats-style defenses was real; even at the ten declared sites, perhaps especially at these, graffiti and other serious damage were prevalent (Deacon 1993:123–24).

The extent to which the fences protected the rock art is unclear. Graffiti and other damage continued. Blundell (1996) has suggested that the fences may have served to increase the amount of damage because their authoritarian nature called out to be challenged. Wherever they were used, fences were breached. Some sites were then allowed to return to being unfenced; others were reinforced with dramatic cages such as those at the White Lady site in the Brandberg, Namibia, the white rhino shelter in the Matopos, Zimbabwe, and a range of sites around Kondoa in Tanzania. Heavy-duty wire mesh or iron bars were used to block off entire rock shelter frontages (fig. 2). But even the cages were violated. In Tanzania, of more than twenty cages erected, all but one were removed and reused by local communities.

Site Presentation

It was those sites that had been declared National Monuments for protective reasons that, almost by default, became the first public rock art sites. In South Africa they were marked on maps, road atlases, and signposts, and visitors were thereby channeled to them. And yet the sites were not presented; they were only protected. In cases such as Schaapplaats the ugly fence guaranteed a poor visitor experience. The rock art was scarcely visible between the wires, and photography was impossible. It is no wonder that such fences were cut and removed. For eight of the nine rock art sites declared before 1990, funding was not provided for presentation materials. The single exception was Nooitgedacht, where the McGregor Museum erected a small site display in the late 1970s. This was

FIGURE 2 The caged site of the White
Lady Shelter, Brandberg, Namibia.
Courtesy of Rock Art Research
Institute, University of the
Witwatersrand

an important precedent, and it helped to inform visitors of
the importance of the site; however, without an on-site custodian, the display was vandalized and graffiti continued
(Morris pers. com. 1989). In almost all cases, this minimalist
approach to public site management had a serious adverse
impact on site conservation.

Beyond the conservation and aesthetic problems of the
minimalist approach lie more serious intellectual problems.
Blundell (1996) argues that leaving sites unmediated cannot
be an option in South Africa. In a country where pejorative
racial misconceptions have been so prevalent, cultural heritage sites need to be explicitly interpreted so that their
sophistication is exposed and their indigenous values
revealed. For San rock art, this must involve the juxtaposition
of San indigenous knowledge with the art, because it is only
from a San understanding, an insider's view, that it is possible
to appreciate the unparalleled symbolic and metaphorical
sophistication of the art.

In the absence of mediation, one is faced with a dangerous alternative—an outsider's view. In such a view, sometimes
referred to as the colonial gaze (Blundell 1996; Dowson and
Lewis-Williams 1993), the human and animal images of San
art are often read as simple pictures of hunting and gathering:
a rendering of an old and idyllic primitive lifeway in which the
San were a seamless part of nature. This reading is, of course,

merely a mirrored reflection of the prejudices of the viewer.
Those with an insider's view of San art know that it was every
bit as complex as Western art; it is a profoundly spiritual art.
By failing to explicitly interpret San rock art, the early public
rock art sites perpetuated the colonial gaze and thereby unwit-
tingly reinforced past prejudices and misconceptions (Blundell 1996). No doubt this suited the political agenda of the
time, but this cannot be allowed to continue today. Sites must
be mediated, and an insider's view must be presented.

By using San indigenous knowledge, the colonial gaze
can be confronted, challenged, and overcome. This is an
explicit aim of the presentation at a newly opened public rock
art site in South Africa's Northern Cape Province. Wildebeest
Kuil is on land owned by the !Xun and Khwe Khoi-San communities. Visitors to Wildebeest Kuil start by viewing a twenty-
minute film about !Xun and Khwe history and indigenous
knowledge. The film seeks to create excitement and anticipation for the site visit to come. After the film a community guide
leads the visitor up the small hill on a one-hour circuit of the
site. There are many stops along the way where additional
information is provided. It is only toward the end of the tour,
when visitors have gained a detailed understanding of the history of the site, its past inhabitants, and the ancient stories and
traditions that give meaning to its rock art, that the path winds
upward to the massive concentration of rock engravings on the

summit (fig. 3). The rock art experience of Wildebeest Kuil is profoundly moving, and one takes away a genuine understanding of the magic of San culture and art.

Sites, Their Communities, and Their Management

As at Wildebeest Kuil, visitors to the Tandjesberg rock painting site in South Africa's Free State Province are also carefully managed. They access the site along a fixed route with an authorized guide who ensures that correct visitor etiquette is adhered to and that the art is not damaged by visitation. Tandjesberg was the first rock art national monument at which such visitor controls were put in place (Ouzman 2001). Within the site, visitors were guided along an elegant wooden boardwalk fronted by a handrail to protect the art. On the rail were placed lecterns showing enhanced reproductions of the rock art, thus helping visitors to view fine details in the art that

they might otherwise miss (fig. 4). The site was a model of good management until, in 1998, a wildfire wreaked havoc. The boardwalk and the lecterns burned, with such intensity that many of the paintings were seriously damaged. This damage has since been mitigated as a result of the combined efforts of professional archaeologists, conservators, and community members (Morris, Ouzman, and Tlhapi 2001). Though the fire at Tandjesberg has forced professional archaeologists to reconsider the use of wooden boardwalks at rock art sites, the experience has shown the critical importance of maintaining good relationships between archaeologists and landowners and communities. Before, during, and after the fire, the owners of Tandjesberg have acted as model custodians; that the site is still accessible to visitors, and even still exists, is largely thanks to their good efforts. Unfortunately, not all rock art sites enjoy such care and attention.

Seeking quick profits, some private guest houses, hotels, and farms have sought to exploit rock art by laying out rock

FIGURE 3 San guides sharing their pride in their indigenous knowledge and ancient heritage at the newly developed rock engraving site of Wildebeest Kuil, Northern Cape, South Africa. Courtesy of Northern Cape Rock Art Trust

FIGURE 4 The boardwalk at Tandjes-berg, Free State, South Africa, before the devastating 1998 fire. Courtesy of Rock Art Research Institute, University of the Witwatersrand

art trails. Most of these trails are self-guided, and the sites have neither presentations nor visitor controls. These sites perpetuate the minimalist approach of the early national monuments, and the resulting damage has been similarly heartbreaking: some have been reduced to pigment smears or walls of graffiti. This situation does not, fortunately, represent the majority of landowners but the actions of a few individuals who have made minimal profit at the risk of, and sadly often at the expense of, art treasures that are beyond value.

To avoid these problems requires the establishment and implementation of sensitive and sustainable management and presentation practices. The South African Heritage Resources Agency has recently laid down a set of minimum standards that must be met before a rock art site can be opened to the public. It is to be hoped that this move will bring an end to unsustainable profiteering from rock art. Truly sustainable rock art tourism requires a considerable injection of time, energy, and money. To use Wildebeest Kuil as an example, the visitor facilities are the product of more than eight thousand days of work and required an investment of R2.5 million. Even with this large investment, the construction was subsidized: most of the professionals donated their services or worked at cost. The Department of Environmental Affairs and Tourism (DEAT) funded the development as a grant, and it is only through grant funding that such a development can be viable in South Africa; a loan of R2.5 million could not have been

serviced by turnover. In practice, turnover at Wildebeest Kuil is proving barely sufficient to cover the costs of upkeep. Fortunately, DEAT has taken a farsighted perspective that looks beyond short-term profit and recognizes the huge social benefits that an investment like this produces. Wildebeest Kuil has created new, permanent jobs for people who were previously unemployed. In addition, spin-off craft production and sales provide sizable additional incomes to dozens of families. The site is not only empowering the !Xun and the Khwe communities, it is also becoming an important tourist draw for the wider Northern Cape area.

But in Zimbabwe, the case of Domboshava provides a graphic reminder that even well-intentioned government investment may not be the whole answer. Domboshava is a large painted shelter, 35 kilometers northeast of Harare. It is a national monument curated by the National Museums and Monuments of Zimbabwe (NMMZ) and one of the finest rock art sites in northern Zimbabwe. It has important economic value to the region because, like Wildebeest Kuil, it draws in local and international visitors. On 14 May 1998, the night before a large new interpretation center was due to open, a local community member broke into the site and smeared the main rock art panel with dark brown enamel paint (fig. 5). In the follow-up inquiry it transpired that there was great resentment toward the NMMZ and their management practices at the site (Taruvinga and Ndoro 2003). By the NMMZ's taking of gate revenues, the local community felt that it was stealing their revenue. The NMMZ saw the gate takings as small recompense for their large and ongoing investment at the site. Equally, they felt they had done much to assist the community: they had built a special structure at the site in which locals could sell curios.

As the investigation of the causes of the incident continued, it became clear that financial issues were only part of the problem. For many years NMMZ had received complaints that tourists were being stung by bees living in a small but deep hole in the ceiling of the main painted shelter. The bees were smoked out from time to time but always returned. NMMZ therefore took the decision to block the hole with concrete. We now know that this hole played a key role in the rainmaking ceremonies of the local community. During the ceremony, sacrifices were made in the shelter and a fire lit. If smoke passed through the hole and out of the top of the hill, then all knew that rain would come. If the smoke did not appear, then something was wrong and rain would not come until the community had identified and dealt with the cause. For a number of years before the paint incident these ceremonies had been conducted in secret. The blocking of the hole brought this broader discontent to a head.

Domboshava stands as testimony to the vital importance of consulting with and involving local communities in all aspects of site management. Pearson and Sullivan (1995) have argued convincingly that all the significances of a site should be considered in its management and that the preservation of the physical heritage at the site need not always be the first priority. Domboshava, like many sites in southern Africa, was part of a living ritual landscape every bit as important to local people as the ancient art. Pearson and Sullivan would argue that this living heritage was as important as Domboshava's San rock art and that it should have been at the heart of both the management and the presentation of the site. This need not mean that all aspects of the living heritage should be revealed to visitors; most likely, the community would not want this. It could mean, however, that the site would need to close on certain days to allow ceremonies to be conducted in private.

The management process advocated by Pearson and Sullivan was developed at Cook University to avoid the pitfalls at Domboshava. It involves the preparation of a detailed management plan that is drawn up by a facilitator but which is driven by key stakeholders. It is based on a statement of significance. This statement captures all the stakeholder significances of the site, not just the need for the protection of the physical site remains. The second phase in the process is to identify, with the stakeholders, the key issues affecting the site. The final phase is to develop

FIGURE 5 Modern brown oil paint smeared over San rock art at Domboshava, Central Mashonaland, Zimbabwe. Courtesy of Terje Norsted

strategies to address these issues and draw out as much of the site's potential as possible. This process is inevitably one of compromise. Stakeholders often want different things, and a middle path has to be found that is satisfactory to all or to most. This model of site development has proven remarkably successful in Australia, where it has often succeeded in bridging traditional Aboriginal site management requirements and the interests of archaeological conservation and tourism. If this process had been followed at Domboshava, there seems little doubt that the paint incident would have been avoided.

The Cook University management process is now starting to be implemented by rock art managers throughout southern Africa thanks to the COMRASA training workshops (Deacon 1997). Rock art managers from Tanzania southward have embraced the process, and we are now starting to see the benefits. Both Wildebeest Kuil and Game Pass were developed using this model. They are the first major public rock art sites to be developed in South Africa in full partnership with local communities. It is to be hoped that they represent the future of public rock art in South Africa, a heritage developed for the benefit of all, not just the few.

In discussing the role of local communities in rock art management at a conference in 2002, Webber Ndoro emphasized that acknowledging the role of local communities in management can, in itself, ensure the preservation of sites. He pointed out that those sites that we seek to manage survive only because they have been successfully managed and protected by a complex system of indigenous management practices. He encouraged managers to recognize the effectiveness of these traditional practices and to use them as the bedrock for modern site management plans. I support this suggestion; traditional management practices are usually those best suited to maintaining the significances of each site: they have been developed and fine tuned over many centuries. The example of Mwela Rocks outside Kasama in northern Zambia, however, offers a cautionary note.

At Mwela Rocks more than seven hundred rock art sites were protected within a sacred forest managed by a spirit guardian and various traditional leaders. In 1992 the sacred forest was intact and the rock art sites were well preserved; however, within three years, and in spite of the protests of the traditional authorities, the sacred forest had been cut to the ground and many of the rock art sites had been mined to make builders' gravel (fig. 6). This destruction occurred simply because of economic need and economic opportunity. Charcoal burners moved in from villages outside the area and

FIGURE 6 Stone quarrying prior to NHCC intervention among the rock art sites of Mwela Rocks, Northern Province, Zambia. Courtesy of Rock Art Research Institute, University of the Witwatersrand

felled the sacred forest before the local community could mobilize to stop the damage. With the sacred status of the area defiled, hundreds of rock breakers descended to quarry stone to fuel a building boom in nearby Kasama town. Without legal authority, the traditional custodians were powerless to stop the destruction. The government department with the appropriate legal authority, the National Heritage Conservation Commission (NHCC), was based at the opposite end of

FIGURE 7 Game Pass Shelter, KwaZulu-Natal, South Africa, where national government and rural communities are working together to preserve heritage and create jobs. Courtesy of Rock Art Research Institute, University of the Witwatersrand

Zambia. Once the NHCC became aware of the extent and pace of damage they acted swiftly, even setting up a regional office in Kasama, but massive and irreparable damage had already been done.

Mwela Rocks shows the terrible consequences of traditional conservation regulations losing effectiveness in a modern developmental context in the absence of active support from national government institutions. With state law superseding traditional law, the old indigenous site conservation practices, while effective in the past, are becoming difficult to enforce. In some cases they also need to adapt to deal with the unforeseen circumstances of modern times, such as global tourism. Like Ndoro, I believe that many aspects of indigenous management practices should be fostered and retained, but the most effective management process in my view will come from a Cook University–type management plan that is drawn up and implemented through a partnership between community members and appropriate heritage and conservation professionals. The community brings knowledge of the significance and meaning of the site and a wealth of experience as to how the site was protected in the past. The professionals bring broad experience of practices that have worked effectively in other places and complex scientific skills that can help to conserve the significances of the site. The challenge is to create a workable partnership between the two, one in which issues and concerns are made explicit by both sides and compromises reached and effected. To get this to work is a fine balancing act. Success often depends on the personalities involved.

It is in this spirit that Wildebeest Kuil and Game Pass Shelter have been developed. Both sites are owned and managed by nonprofit trusts made up of all the key stakeholders who are willing to serve as trustees. As these are San heritage sites, these communities have strong representation on both trusts. But because the trusts comprise a range of individuals and organizations, they cannot be manipulated by particular agendas or sectional interests; instead, they operate by the consensus of a range of stakeholders. Since a trust must be nonprofit, commercial interests cannot overpower other issues in site management and presentation, and all income from the site is ploughed back into preserving the significances of the site.

It is through this shared ownership and by embracing and celebrating indigenous knowledge both in site presentation and site management that we can achieve President Mbeki's dream of public rock art sites that help to heal society (fig. 7). There will always be room for improvement at our public sites. Presentation and management practices will continue to progress, but the premises and processes we use to build our presentation and management structures are now on a firm and stable footing. At sites such as Wildebeest Kuil we are seeing the new face of public archaeology in Africa. It is a face that will restore national pride by celebrating Africa's unparalleled history of achievement and innovation. And it is a face that will create jobs by bringing people from all over the world to see the sites where humanity, art, and culture began. These sites are symbols of this great African legacy.

Acknowledgments

The Rock Art Research Institute is funded by the National Research Foundation of South Africa (GUN2053470) and the Research Office of the University of the Witwatersrand. Additional support for this research was received from the Chairman's Fund of Anglo American, the Educational Trusts of AngloGold and De Beers, the Getty Conservation Institute, and the Ringing Rocks Foundation. I am grateful to Geoff Blundell, Janette Deacon, Catherine Odora-Hoppers, Sven Ouzman, and Adele Wildschut for their critical input. All opinions and conclusions expressed here are my own and may not reflect the views of those that have funded this research. All errors are my own. An earlier version of this paper was presented at the National Research Foundation Indigenous Knowledge Systems Colloquium in Kimberley, South Africa, in 2002.

References

Blundell, G. 1996. Presenting South Africa's rock art sites. In *Monuments and Sites South Africa*, ed. J. Deacon, 71–81. Sri Lanka: ICOMOS.

Cavalli-Sforza, L. L. 2000. *Genes, Peoples, and Languages.* Berkeley: University of California Press.

Deacon, J. 1993. Archaeological sites as national monuments in South Africa: A review of sites declared since 1936. *South African Historical Journal* 29:118–31.

———. 1997. A regional management strategy for rock art in southern Africa. *Conservation and Management of Archaeological Sites* 2:29–32.

Dowson, T. A., and J. D. Lewis-Williams. 1993. Myths, museums and southern African rock art. *South African Historical Journal* 29:44–60.

Henshilwood, C. S., F. d'Errico, R. Yates, Z. Jacobs, C. Tribolo, G. A. T. Duller, N. Mercier, J. C. Sealy, H. Valladas, I. Watts, and A. G. Wintle. 2002. Emergence of modern human behaviour: Middle Stone Age engravings from South Africa. *Science* 295:1278–80.

Morris, D. 1989. Archaeology for tomorrow: The site museum as classroom at Nooitgedacht. *South African Museum Association Bulletin* 18:291–94.

Morris, D., S. Ouzman, and G. Tlhapi. 2001. Tandjesberg, San rock painting rehabilitation project: From catastrophe to celebration. *Digging Stick* 18 (1):1–4.

Ouzman, S. 2001. The problems and potentials of developing and managing public rock art sites in southern Africa. *Pictogram* 12:4–13.

Pearson, M., and S. Sullivan. 1995. *Looking after Heritage Places.* Melbourne: Melbourne University Press.

Taruvinga, P., and W. Ndoro. 2003. The vandalism of the Domboshava rock painting site, Zimbabwe: Some reflections on approaches to heritage management. *Conservation and Management of Archaeological Sites* 6 (1):3–10.

Rock Art Management in Eastern and Southern Africa: Whose Responsibility?

George H. O. Abungu

Abstract: *Rock art is an important part of Africa's heritage and is found in most parts of the continent. However, its study has been the preserve of comparatively few professionals. Although hunter-gatherers created the majority of rock art, particularly in southern Africa, the Bantu and other groups have also contributed to this heritage. Today, the questions persist: Whose heritage? Whose responsibility? This paper views rock art conservation as the responsibility of diversified stakeholders and examines ways in which the local community can be involved in the ownership and protection of heritage. The study and practice of rock art is everybody's business; it must move away from the traditional elitist approach to encompass various voices and the apportionment of responsibilities.*

The African continent is extremely rich in terms of cultural and natural heritage. As the cradle of humankind, producing the earliest evidence of hominids and stone tools, Africa has witnessed a deep relationship between humans and the environment. Many of Africa's landscapes have been shaped by the spiritual and physical needs of the people. Its cultural landscapes are imprinted by human action; in many cases they continue to appeal to people's spiritual aspirations by functioning as sacred places for local communities, in addition to serving today's commercial needs as tourism destinations.

The spectacular cultural and natural landscapes—sacred forests, hills, caves, rock shelters—have become part of human experience. Animal life in Africa, which is unparalleled elsewhere, has played a major part in the lives of Africans; interaction with the environment and its resources has therefore shaped human thought and actions on the continent.

The results of this interaction are numerous; they include spectacular archaeological and rock art sites of varying concentrations all over the continent. Northern and southern Africa are particularly rich in rock art heritage, but nearly every part of Africa has some kind of rock art, with regional distinctions.

Rock Art of Africa

African rock art dates back 27,000 years to the so-called Apollo 9 site in Namibia. It is probably the earliest form of human communication remaining on the continent today and is much more graphic than written text. Rock art points to human social activities, cognitive systems, abstract thought, and concepts of reality that together give meaning to our lives; it tells us a great deal about how people perceived their world. It provides insight into the earliest ways in which humans thought and survived in a more or less untamed and challenging environment. Rock art is unique; once lost, it can never be regained.

African rock art has been a contested heritage, particularly in regard to its origins and creators. Today it is more or less accepted that the bulk of early eastern and southern African rock art was likely created by the ancestors of the hunter-gatherer peoples of the region. These are the ancestors of the Khoisan of southern Africa, the Sandawe and Hadza of Tanzania, and the Twa, with descendant groups in central and southern Africa.

The Khoisan were probably the earliest inhabitants of eastern and southern Africa. In eastern Africa, their descendants are the Hadza and Sandawe. In southern Africa, they came to influence many of their neighbors not only through spiritual roles but also through language as many present-day non-Khoisan groups, especially the Bantu groups, have acquired clicks in their language.

These were the people encountered by Bantu-speaking farmers and acknowledged as the original landowners; they knew the country and its resources and not only had access to its spirits but also controlled the circle of nature. They were acknowledged to have natural abilities to enter the land's supernatural environment and control natural phenomena such as rainmaking and environmental vitality. They were the people who had tamed the environment, giving it spiritual and symbolic meaning and tapping its natural resources through hunting and gathering.

It has been shown that the religious and everyday activities of groups such as the Khoisan are intertwined and that earth—from which all life springs—has mystical powers. Humans and animals can communicate but only when humans move from the physical to the intangible realm in the Khoisan's mythology. Certain animals are valued for their meat as well as for their metaphysical properties to the extent that they are seen to possess a force that helps humans to administer health, harmony, the weather, wild animals, and human rights of passage (Coulson and Campbell 2001:31). Through special dances using animal powers, men and sometimes women can achieve a trance state, then pass through stages into the supernatural realm. It has been argued that these actions dominate the rock art of Africa, particularly in southern Africa (see Lewis-Williams and Dowson 1989:91). They are of great value, for they provide not only spiritual nourishment but also an understanding of the world's intangible aspects and a way to control the otherwise inexplicable (Coulson and Campbell 2001:32).

In many places, for example, in Chongoni (Malawi), Kisami (Zambia), Matopo (Zimbabwe), and Kondoa (Tanzania), the tradition of rock art was continued by the Bantu groups. These were agropastoralists; art for them, just as for hunter-gatherers, was a means of controlling and understanding their surroundings. The role of the Bantu in creating rock art has been underestimated. Their contribution, however, has provided an important learning opportunity for rock art scholars.

Rock art has been of great importance to the well-being of Africans as far back as the prehistoric period. As a spiritual medium, it has helped them to understand their environment and the forces that interact with it and to interpret those things beyond the human realm. It ensured the ordered process of society. In some cases, rock art was used for initiation and ceremonies. It is therefore imperative to incorporate in the conservation and interpretation of rock art sites an understanding of the way in which local communities view their world. This is even more important now, in a time of changing cultures and disappearing oral history. We must find out how local people view their art, how it has been used in the recent past, and how it fits into their reality.

Rock art was first viewed by colonialists as a Western-introduced concept and art form, as the indigenous people were seen as incapable of innovation without external intervention. When it was grudgingly accepted as African, colonialists termed the art "primitive." This attitude has of course had an impact on the study and conservation of rock art in Africa.

In some cases, rock art has been used for political purposes such as land claims. For example, because rock art was perceived to have been the preserve of the Khoisan, who had been more or less wiped out, those who occupied the land considered themselves, rather than the Bantu, the rightful owners. It is no coincidence that rock art studies were dominant in South Africa in the 1970s and 1980s, during apartheid. The protection of rock art throughout this time can be attributed to the local communities who owned and used it; systematic studies and formal government protection came late in Africa.

Africa's incredible rock art paintings and engravings did not attract serious attention from archaeologists until the 1960s. Colonial governments enacted laws protecting rock art from theft and vandalism but rarely enforced them. Even today the art's uniqueness and value is not fully recognized by many independent African countries as an extremely valuable heritage that should be the responsibility of all, not just of private rock art societies. The whole issue of ownership is contested, as are the roles of various stakeholders, including conservation bodies, governments, and local communities. This has resulted in a huge challenge to the posterity of rock art in Africa.

Challenges to Rock Art Conservation

Today rock art is threatened by many factors, ranging from local to international. As the tourism industry expands, more people are visiting rock art sites. As visitorship increases, so do threats to the rock art. People pour water on the art to make it more visible and scrawl graffiti across it to add detail; visitors often touch the paintings, steal engravings on loose stones, or cut pieces of paintings from the rock face. Moreover, the large volume of visitors has an impact on the environment in which the art is found. Of even greater concern are threats from mining, the spread of agriculture, and the construction of roads and dams in environments where rock art is found. There is a need for concerted efforts to address the issue. How can this be achieved when the various stakeholders are suspicious of one another? The questions arise, Who owns the rock art? Who is best placed to conserve it? It is even argued that because most people living around the rock art sites may not have been the creators, they have no stake in it. This argument is touted even when the rock art is of spiritual significance to the people and when the surrounding communities own the land on which the sites are found.

Africa is at a disadvantage in terms of development. Many African states have no meaningful industries, and governments are confronted with numerous problems, including the lack of infrastructure, education, health facilities, roads, and clean water. Rock art conservation is not a government priority in countries requiring the provision or improvement of such services. As a result, there is little if any investment in rock art heritage. In addition, governments—apart from a few such as South Africa—are making little meaningful contribution to the development of legal and administrative frameworks within which to manage the heritage. Where they have, they have done so by imposing state control on sites without consultation or the concurrence of the local community, resulting in hostile resistance and, in some cases, destruction of the sites. In many places this heritage is not appreciated as part of a living environment that could serve as inspiration in the quest for social well-being, improved quality of life, and sustainable development—sustainable development in this case being a process that takes into account the social, cultural, economic, and environmental needs of an area and its community. Archaeologists are partly to blame for distancing rock art from the present inhabitants and for portraying it as a specialized subject that cannot be appreciated by the uninitiated.

In many African countries environmental impact assessments are rarely carried out; where they are, they are funded and controlled by developers, who are given free rein. It is not uncommon to see roads being cut across rocks containing artwork, or the quarrying of such rocks for road construction or mineral exploration. (Botswana was once a case in point; however, it now has one of the best cultural impact assessment programs in Africa.) There are constant changes

to the cultural landscape without concern for the adverse impact of these actions on local communities. This ignorance or simple lack of acceptance by government that Africa's diverse heritage remains an integral part of the continuing, living environment for many communities is a great threat to rock art.

It is not only governments that are responsible for the various challenges facing rock art sites. As noted above, problems caused by tourism are evident. Other problems result from greedy developers, lack of community participation, ignorance on the part of potential beneficiaries, illicit trafficking, and the assumption by scholars and professionals that they have a monopoly on conservation knowledge and therefore should be the sole players. In addition, the tendency of professionals to look for conservation solutions in faraway places rather than use locally accumulated knowledge has in some cases added to the problems of managing rock art sites.

While the exchange of ideas, information, experience, and techniques of rock art conservation is a healthy exercise, local and regional experience should form the basis of any management strategy. Cases are given below in which the community has not been engaged either in dialogue or in the day-to-day management of the site and, as a result, the heritage has been destroyed.

Outside Harare, Zimbabwe, on the red rock outcrops of the Domboshawa area, are some of the most spectacular rock art sites in southern Africa. Like many other spiritual sites, there is a sacred forest with the same name adjacent to the site. The Domboshawa rock art site and sacred forest, which is probably one of the most visited sites in Zimbabwe apart from the site of Great Zimbabwe, is now under the management of the National Museums and Monuments of Zimbabwe. The site has been completely fenced and secured from the local community and is a good example of state/community conflict. It is a typical example of a hotly contested heritage site where the state shows its muscle by imposing control. It appears that the site was appropriated from the local community without consultation and without considering a plan to benefit the community. Nor were its spiritual needs, based on usage of the rock shelter, considered. The resulting conflict between the state and the community led to defacement of the rock art. Today, rather than being joint custodians with the government, the local community has been pushed to the periphery, the site secured, and access controlled. Although it is rumored that the rock art could have been defaced by a disgruntled former museum staff member who had been sacked, there is no doubt that the local community of Domboshawa feels aggrieved.

In western Kenya at the Kakapel rock art site stands probably the most elaborate artwork of its time, representing different periods over a span of nearly three thousand years. This site has attracted the attention of scholars and has had intermittent visitors for some time. For years the site saw no damage; however, since interest in it has increased and dialogue with the locals has decreased, the site has been defaced by graffiti. It is said that as the site started to attract high-profile visitors, jealous neighbors of the owner on whose land the site is located, decided to destroy it so that the owner did not benefit. Until recently there had been little dialogue to explain the potential economic importance of the site to the community as a whole and to involve them in its study and conservation.

Botswana is known for its rich rock art heritage, including the site of Tsodilo, which is on the World Heritage List. The rock art is in constant danger from a rich and powerful elite, who indulge in mountaineering and helicopter rides on the rough terrain. In addition, the act of moving communities, particularly hunter-gatherers, from their natural environment into permanent settlements takes them away from their spiritual sites and renders the heritage meaningless. It only encourages conflicts and resistance and results in the state taking control of the heritage.

It was not uncommon, especially during colonial times, to find cases in which archaeologists or palaeontologists physically assaulted members of the local community just because their herds strayed into archaeological sites. Even today some researchers treat sites as their personal property divorced from the real owners, the local community. In such cases it is difficult to develop a positive relationship with the locals. The results are disastrous.

Conflict Resolution and a New Conservation Strategy

Conflicts of interest at archaeological sites are mostly the result of the competing interests of the various stakeholders, including government, local communities, and scholars and professionals. Successful site management requires dialogue and a participatory approach to the whole issue of conservation and use.

In the past, community knowledge, interest, and involvement have been placed at the periphery either by gov-

ernments, scholars or professionals, or sometimes a combination of the latter two groups. The communities feel alienated from their heritage as they see "foreign" bodies turning their sites into research and public use areas without their involvement, and the communities are seen to be and are treated as threats to heritage. To avoid this continuous conflict, management strategies should be based on a participatory approach whereby all stakeholders have a role, especially local communities. It is important to begin by acknowledging that ownership of the sites rests with the local population. Government and professionals are facilitators whose role is to ensure that there are appropriate conditions, facilities, and support for heritage management.

There is a need to establish channels of communication, roles, and responsibilities and to include the local community in management. The professional must build capacity from within the local community and, where possible and appropriate, incorporate local conservation knowledge. Site management plans should take into consideration all the stakeholders' interests and engage the local communities in building better management systems. Heritage management itself must be incorporated in the development framework of the local area or region; it must be understood and owned by the local community.

The government has the responsibility to invest in sites to attract responsible tourism that will create job opportunities and other economic benefits. If this is done the communities will appreciate, protect, and conserve the heritage. Thus archaeological sites, including rock art sites, must contribute to employment and empowerment of the people. Conservation is not simply about care of the fabric; it is also about creating the right atmosphere and marshaling community support for preventive care, including guarding against vandalism, as opposed to physical intervention once the problem has arisen.

Governments must invest seriously in conservation of national heritage through adequate financing. Communication efforts should include constant public awareness programs aimed at a variety of stakeholders rather than rock art lovers alone.

There may be negative consequences to opening sites to community participation, as raised expectations, if not met, may lead to the destruction of sites by the very same communities. These expectations may include job creation, financial gains through visitorship, and opening up of markets for local products, which, if not met, could lead to disgruntlement. However, the benefits of involving the community outweigh the potential disadvantages, especially as these people have lived with and protected the heritage all along.

As long as the study of rock art remains the preserve of a small elite, it will not attract attention from governments with an eye solely on numbers that translate into votes. It is local community involvement that will attract their attention, not a few elite groups of rock art scholars. Moreover, rock art sites are so widespread and numerous in southern Africa that they cannot be taken care of by professionals alone. This is all the more reason why local communities must be involved.

In managing rock art sites, the potential power of goodwill from the young people must not be taken for granted. In many cases, they come into contact with rock art sites only during school visits. Urbanization and lack of contact between these young people and their elders—whose storytelling used to provide the opportunity to explain the heritage and its importance—pose a threat to heritage protection. These are tomorrow's stakeholders, yet they hardly understand the importance of this heritage and are prone to destroying it by adding their own "art."

It is important, in addition to the local communities, art societies, government, scholars, and professionals, that undiscovered audiences or stakeholders be involved in rock art conservation. This may include the formation of friends-of-rock-art groups from adjacent schools, which can be involved in frequent cleanups, tree planting, and community sensitization. The youth can also take part in "research" by helping to record the art, which may produce the only records that remain when the art itself has gone.

Conclusion

Any management initiative, including the conservation of rock art, must adopt an inclusive approach that involves all stakeholders. It must be a participatory process in which the voices and needs of local communities are given as much—if not more—weight as the others. It is imperative that local people be empowered through capacity building; the day-to-day management of sites can be in their hands when it is not provided by other agencies. Rock art is a unique, nonrenewable resource that is faced with various challenges—both manmade and natural. It must be properly protected for all of humanity.

Acknowledgments

I would like to thank the Getty Conservation Institute and the World Archaeological Congress for organizing the session "Of the Past, for the Future: Integrating Archaeology and Conservation" at the conference in Washington, D.C., in which I was invited to participate. I am especially grateful to the Getty Conservation Institute for sponsoring my participation.

References

Coulson, D., and A. Campbell. 2001. *African Rock Art: Paintings and Engravings on Stone.* New York: Harry N. Abrams.

Deacon, J. 1994. *Some Views on Rock Paintage in Cederberg.* Cape Town: National Monuments Council.

Dowson, A. T. 1992. *Rock Engraving of Southern Africa.* Johannesburg: Witwatersrand University Press.

Gramly, R. M. 1975. Meat-feasting sites and cattle brands: Partners of rock-shelter utilisation in eastern Africa. *AZANIA* 10:107–21.

Leakey, M. 1983. *Africa's Vanishing Art: The Rock Paintings of Tanzania.* London: Hamish Hamilton/Rainbird.

Lewis-Williams, D., and T. Dowson. 1989. *Images of Power: Understanding Bushman Rock Art.* Johannesburg: Southern Book Publishers.

Masao, F. T. 1979. *The Late Stone Age and Rock Paintings of Central Tanzania.* Studien zur Kulturkunde 48. Wiesbaden: Franz Steiner Verlag.

Phillipson, D. W. 1976. *The Rock Paintings of Eastern Zambia: The Prehistory of Eastern Zambia.* Memoir 6. Nairobi: British Institute in Africa.

Solomon, A. 1998. *Guide to San Rock Art.* Cape Town: David Philip Publishers.

Walker, N. 1996. *The Painted Hills: Rock Art of the Matopos.* Gweru: Mambo Press.

Building the Capacity to Protect Rock Art Heritage in Rural Communities

Webber Ndoro

Abstract: This paper focuses on the need to involve local communities in managing their own rock art heritage. It emphasizes the importance of establishing a dialogue between heritage managers and local communities by involving all stakeholders from the beginning. In most of Africa, community involvement is necessary given the limited capacity of many heritage organizations to effectively manage sites in rural areas.

Rock art sites exist throughout southern Africa. In Zimbabwe alone, more than three thousand sites have been recorded, and it is estimated that this represents perhaps less than half the number that actually exist (Garlake 1995). Given the limited resources and capacities of most heritage management organizations and the way they operate currently, it is impossible to protect every site.

At most rock art sites, managers tend to concentrate on the art as the paramount resource to manage. This approach does not clearly define the important aspects of a place's cultural heritage or the context of the art. The paintings are usually treated as museum objects to be studied, curated, and separated from the larger context of the sociocultural environment. As directed by the World Heritage Convention, we need to adopt general policies that give cultural and natural heritage a function in the life of the community. Very often when we talk about the importance of a rock art site, we emphasize its attractiveness to the scientific community and to tourists. In some instances this is important; however, this suggests that only scientific values and tourist-generated income are important.

The economic situation, often with sociopolitical overtones, inevitably affects the preservation and presentation of a heritage site. The view that rock art sites are scientific specimens to be treated as though they were in a museum has meant that in most countries they are omitted from the general development plans of the area. This is compounded by the fact that there is a tendency to view rock art as a specialized field that can be handled only by the initiated few. This generally leads to management practices that do not consider the interests or attitudes of the local communities regarding the paintings or the sites in general. Thus it is academic researchers who alone are involved in the process of protecting the sites. Often, managers regard the local people as a problem. There is a tendency to think that global or international interests are more important than local and indigenous ones; thus the interests of the communities and the ways in which they have traditionally been custodians of the heritage place are ignored.

During the precolonial period, most places of cultural significance enjoyed protection in the sense that no one was allowed to go to them without the sanction of religious leaders. Any meaningful management system of rock art places has to recognize the following factors: (1) the definition of rock art as heritage does not always coincide with the concepts held by local communities, and generally one has to consider African heritage in its totality, including nonphysical elements such as spiritual and sacred values and the special notion of cultural landscapes; (2) a management system may already exist and still be in use today, and the system often has an element of sustainability for local people; (3) local communities have inalienable rights of access to heritage sites and to earn a livelihood from them; and (4) the aspirations of local communities must be taken into account. Unless the communities have been removed from the sites, generally a passive protective system is in place (explicit or implicit, institutionalized or not). The problem lies in understanding the system. Management planning should incorporate these factors as guidelines for developing an improved system.

Present-day heritage managers also need to recognize the general characteristics of the traditional and customary management systems that apply to any given site, be it a rock art site or another place of significance. These characteristics are as follows:

- The systems are unwritten and passed orally from generation to generation.
- They are prone to change.
- A series of rites and taboos generally regulate the use of resources.
- Regulation differs in application from one section to another of the same site.
- Regulation differs from group to group.
- The site is linked to life sustenance.
- The approach to nature and culture is holistic.
- There are penalties for infringement, varying from death to excommunication from the clan or tribe to occurrence of misfortune.
- Group solidarity is of primary importance.
- The intangible aspects of the heritage are of the utmost significance.

Culture and Nature Issues

Rock art sites are part of the cultural landscape. In some traditions in southern Africa, caves and rocks are the abode of ancestral spirits. It is no coincidence that places like Silozwane and Domboshawa in Zimbabwe, Chongoni in Malawi, and Kondoa in Tanzania are considered shrines by the local communities. Caves especially have important functions in the religious lives of many Bantu societies. Because in African tradition and custom rocks and caves have special roles as intermediaries with the divine, the relationship between nature and culture is also important. Traditional African heritage management, though not thought of in these terms, finds natural expression in environmental knowledge and technical and ritual practices. For example, the ritual of rainmaking requires a clear understanding of the environment as well as the technique. Heritage resource management is therefore embedded in the belief systems that have in turn contributed to the preservation and sustainable use of both cultural and natural features. Usually shrines represent a quintessential natural source of culture where the two are inseparable, so

that human society has no meaning without the rocks, the pools, the caves, and the trees; and these are given meaning only by the residence among them of human beings (Ranger 1999).

Given the controlled management applied at a number of rock art places, several observations can be made. It is normally assumed that the subsistence methods of the indigenous communities ignore the ecological carrying-capacity threshold of the area and thereby threaten the paintings. At times outright ignorance among the local population of the significance of the rock art is assumed. Authorities forget that nature and people coexisted in the area from time immemorial, and the paintings were not deliberately harmed. There is mounting evidence that many natural landscapes that have historically been considered to be deteriorating as a result of human impacts are in fact deteriorating because humans are excluded from the systems. This has been demonstrated in New Guinea (Fairhead and Leach 1996) and in Australia (Jones 1969). Research in Australia has found that the distribution and diversity of biota across the continent are artifacts of Aboriginal people's intentional management. This is also seen in Namibia in the Nyae Nyae area where the ecology is a result of careful strategic burning. The local community, the Ju/hoansi, argue that many places in the northern reaches of Nyae Nyae have degraded, claiming that this is due to the absence of a burning regime during the colonial period (Powell 1998). In addition to recognizing the relationship between nature and culture, any heritage management system in Africa needs to recognize the way in which community looks at the heritage as a resource rather than as an artifact. It can also be argued that the opening up of sites by present-day managers has led to many problems, including graffiti.

Kondoa-Irangi Rock Paintings

The example of Kondoa in Tanzania illustrates some of these issues. The majority of painted shelters in the Kondoa-Irangi area occur on the slopes or around the base of a steep eastward-facing escarpment that forms the rim of the Masai Steppe bordering the Great Rift Valley. The Kondoa-Irangi area contains an impressive concentration of rock shelters with prehistoric paintings. The rock paintings are spread out over a wide area in the Kondoa district.

Some of the sites were declared national monuments by the Department of Antiquities in 1937 in recognition of the exceptional qualities of the paintings in the area. According to the Department of Antiquities, the paintings do not seem to have any significant meaning to the local communities. However, at least some of the painted sites have spiritual significance to the local agropastoral Irangi people, who have continued to carry out ceremonies such as healing and rain-making rituals at these sites (see Leakey 1983:17; Loubser, this volume).

These activities have not been recognized by the Department of Antiquities. For example, the resulting millet spatters are considered detrimental to the preservation of the paintings. In relation to the use and function of the place, the present management system and legislation fail to recognize a number of issues. Although the inhabitants no longer paint, the most significant shelters, such as Mungume wa Kolo, have been associated with their belief systems from time immemorial. The hunter-gatherer art in the area is related to shamanistic belief systems. The later white paintings, which in many instances in Kondoa are superimposed on the hunter-gatherer art, are related to the initiation ceremonies of the farming communities. The same shelters play a role in the ritual and healing potency of the people today; thus there has been continuity in terms of use and function. The rock shelters have been used in the cosmology of the inhabitants of the place. Unless the communities' aspirations are taken into account and recognized under Tanzanian law, there will always be antagonism over the management of these heritage places.

The paintings are part of a cultural landscape that is dynamic, and they cannot be frozen within the defined boundary of a single time period. This cultural landscape is regulated by a series of customary practices that do not recognize the relevant state legislation. According to customary law and traditions, the paintings are part of a large cosmological environment and cannot be treated as single components.

Furthermore, sites like these cannot be owned by an individual. They are owned by the community, and they have traditional custodians. Their boundaries are amorphous for the simple reason that they fluctuate according to use and seasons. An adjunct to the issue of boundaries is that of ownership, which implicitly carries with it the issue of legislation. A protected site must have fixed boundaries.

Capacity Building

Management policies that seek to exclude populations from the management of their own heritage emanate in part from the training received by heritage professionals. When we talk of capacity building in heritage management, often this refers to capacity building among professionals. Hence most train-

ing initiatives target the professional heritage manager. They include a certain degree of rigidity and centralization, as well as a bias toward the traditional view of what constitutes cultural heritage, that is, monuments and sites. Generally capacity building emphasizes that communities have to be educated about and made aware of their own heritage. It is generally held that communities should have limited access because they are ignorant of what is significant and might harm the paintings.

Moreover, the protective legislation operating in most parts of Africa was enacted during the colonial period and has not been revised. Most of the laws therefore remain antagonistic to public and community interests (Mumma 1999). South Africa, however, has taken steps to rectify its heritage protection legislation so that it reflects the aspirations of the majority of its citizens.

Currently, the type of training provided to professionals gives rise to a number of problems in accommodating local values and alternative management systems. In most instances the training is highly technical in content and does not equip managers with the skills to engage the public. Given the limited resources, particularly trained personnel, and the number of heritage places to be protected, it is doubtful that such training efforts will achieve the intended goals of protecting heritage places. Training initiatives must recognize that heritage sites are situated within communities that in most cases have provided limited care of these places. It is myopic to think that the public always poses a threat to heritage sites. The development of management plans that take into consideration all the stakeholders' interests affords us a chance to involve the surrounding communities in better heritage management systems. With this approach, the creation of a meaningful dialogue is encouraged between professional heritage managers and communities by making sure that no side imposes unrealistic management regimes on the other. This also helps to incorporate heritage management in a developmental framework.

It is essential that issues relating to community participation and indigenous practices be considered and dealt with from the beginning of the process of managing heritage sites. In building capacity, an explicit process for the involvement of stakeholders and the identification of all heritage values should be established. Provision has to be made for the conservation of all the values identified, for the identification of potential conflicts in this area, and for the management system to address the economic and social issues of local communities and traditional custodians. The following steps would be useful in developing this joint cooperation to protect the sites: (1) social assessment, identification of stakeholders, and formation of an inclusive management committee, aided by social scientists trained to understand and analyze social organization at sites; (2) data gathering that fully involves the local community; (3) data analysis to determine the values of the site, which entails identification of "universal" as well as community values, analysis that requires community involvement; (4) a collectively agreed-upon action plan; and (5) a collectively agreed-upon management system. The latter is a formal agreement among all the stakeholders as to the future management and use of the site.

Conclusion

Capacity building is a never-ending process. It not only involves technical training; it involves means of developing a dialogue with communities that interact with the site on a daily basis. It should emphasize dialogue between site managers and the communities around them. It should be initiated at various levels, both technical and political. It should draw on the wisdom and human resources already existing in local communities rather than import solutions.

There is also the issue of ownership. As long as heritage organizations treat sites as scientific specimens, the local com-

munities will be alienated. This would be detrimental to the heritage, given that most heritage authorities have limited manpower and capacity to protect all sites.

References

Fairhead, J., and M. Leach. 1996. *Misreading the African Landscape: Society and Ecology in a Forest-Savanna Mosaic.* Cambridge: Cambridge University Press.

Garlake, P. 1995. *The Hunter's Vision: The Prehistoric Art of Zimbabwe.* Seattle: University of Washington Press.

Jones, R. 1969. Fire stick farming. *Australian Natural History* 16 (7):224–28.

Leakey, M. 1983. *Africa's Vanishing Art: The Rock Paintings of Tanzania.* London: Hamish Hamilton/Rainbird.

Mumma, A. 1999. Legal aspects of cultural protection in Africa. In *The World Heritage Convention and Cultural Landscapes in Africa,* ed. M. Rossler and G. Saouma-Forero, 30–34. Paris: UNESCO.

Powell, N. 1998. *Co-Management in Non-Equilibrium Systems.* Uppsala: Acta Universitatis Agriculturae Suecia.

Ranger, T. O. 1999. *Voices from the Rocks: Nature, Culture and History in the Matopos Hills of Zimbabwe.* Harare: Baobab.

Conservation of Non-Western Rock Art Sites Using a Holistic Medical Approach

Johannes Loubser

Abstract: *This paper addresses the role of specialist conservators and site managers in conserving and managing rock art sites that are still used by non-European people. Citing ethnographic examples from Tanzania and the northwestern United States, it proposes that the indigenous people in these regions view rock art sites and the human body in similar ways. And it recommends that when assessing and treating rock art sites in non-Western contexts, specialist conservators and site managers should acknowledge, consult, study, understand, and incorporate traditional concepts.*

A conventional archaeological conservation premise is that only well-trained conservators with the necessary skills are entitled to undertake treatment at rock art sites and only those versed in generally accepted site management principles should write management plans. An important reason for this position is that botched conservation and management attempts by unqualified people with insufficient skills have been expensive and time-consuming to rectify. A number of objections can be raised against such a premise. First, it wrongly assumes that qualified people never make mistakes; mistakes may in fact occur when "first world" specialists are not properly versed in local conditions and traditions. Second, the paucity and comparatively high cost of the services of trained rock art conservators suggests that it is not always practical or affordable to hire such specialists. Third, considering the various interest groups involved in a rock art site, sometimes from different cultural backgrounds with divergent worldviews, the question arises as to who identifies and prioritizes conservation problems and appropriate remedial actions. Additional questions are: Under what circumstances does it become necessary to involve a specialist conservator

and/or management planner? Where do specialists fit into the site management process?

This paper presents an analogy with medical practice as one way of thinking about these questions. As in the case of medicine, currently prevailing Eurocentric conceptions about conservation differ from the traditional conceptions held by nonindustrial societies in a variety of ways; to try to remedy problems in indigenous settings by exclusive reference to Western paradigms and practices often is bound to be futile. Although conservators tend to think in Eurocentric terms, knowledge and acknowledgment of traditional practices are vital prerequisites for any conservation action to be acceptable and workable in an underdeveloped rural setting. Whereas the autochthonous inhabitants of the "third world" realize the value of European, or Western, medicine, the use of alternative "traditional" treatments and remedies is still pervasive. Consequently, when drawing up a management plan for a rock art site and recommendations for hands-on conservation actions, it is important to investigate and incorporate established "non-Western" beliefs and patterns of site use.

Rock Art Sites as Human Bodies

That some traditional users and custodians of rock art sites view them as similar to human bodies is strongly suggested by at least two ethnographic instances, the people of the Masai Steppe in central Tanzania and the people of the Columbia Plateau in the northwestern United States. The geographic and archaeological contexts of each rock art tradition are outlined below, prior to discussing the relevant ethnographic contexts of each tradition.

In central Tanzania, the majority of painted shelters in the Kondoa-Irangi area occur on the slopes or around the base of a steep eastward-facing escarpment that forms the western rim of the Masai Steppe. Painted shelters within the escarpment are part of exposed and relatively resistant granite rim rock. The shelters occur mostly along exposed cliff lines, although a few are found underneath isolated boulders. Mary Leakey's 1983 publication of *Africa's Vanishing Art: The Rock Paintings of Tanzania* first brought to the world's attention the colorful Kondoa-Irangi paintings.

Radiocarbon dates for excavated charcoal from the Kisese 2 shelter suggest that the first pastoralists occupied the Kondoa-Irangi area approximately fifteen hundred years ago. The white and black pastoralist paintings of cattle on top of red hunter-gatherer paintings indicate that the red paintings are even older (Leakey 1983). If this minimum age estimate for the underlying red paintings is accepted, then they must have withstood millennia of natural deterioration. Archaeological evidence, collected by Ray Inskeep and Fidel Masao, has shown that in addition to hunter-gatherers and pastoralists, agropastoralist ancestors of the current Irangi inhabitants used the shelters as well (Leakey 1983). According to oral histories, the more recent white and pale red paintings of grids and other geometric patterns are the work of Irangi agropastoralists. Chipping of a few early red hunter-gatherer paintings and numerous other human activities in the painted rock shelters, such as the spattering of millet beer against the hunter-gatherer paintings, are material evidence that the Irangi people continue to interact with the painted rock surface.

According to Louis Leakey (1936), the earliest written mention of rock paintings in the Kondoa-Irangi area is in a short paper by Nash published in 1929. Even at that relatively early date of European presence in the area, Nash (1929:199) noted that "most of them [the paintings] are in a rather bad state of preservation." This remark suggests that by the early twentieth century, natural conditions and/or human actions had already damaged at least some of the rock paintings. Local Irangi agropastoralists thought that the various scholars who intermittently visited the Kondoa-Irangi paintings during the first half of the twentieth century were treasure hunters (Leakey 1983:16). One result of this mistaken perception was that Irangi people started to dig the deposits in front of some rock paintings (Amini Mturi pers. com.). Partly as an attempt to discourage this practice, which not only destroyed the archaeological deposits but also posed a dust threat to the paintings, the conservator of Tanzanian Antiquities at that

time, Hamo Sassoon, had wooden frames and wire cages erected on stone and cement walls at selected shelters between 1965 and 1968. These cages proved ineffective; Irangi people from nearby settlements soon dismantled the frames and wire mesh for alternative use as building material for human and animal shelters. Fortunately, the removal of the wooden frames and wire fence did not seem to have caused any noticeable damage, as the cages were not attached to the rock surface in any way. All that is left now of the cages are the stone and cement walls within the rock art shelters (fig. 1).

The cages also proved an obstacle to Irangi ritual practitioners who continued to visit the more prominent rock art shelters for their healing and rainmaking ceremonies. This practice has some antiquity, as evidenced by Louis Leakey's 10 July 1951 entry in his field journal: "five local elders . . . told us that before we could start work we would have to provide a goat for a sacrifice to propitiate the spirits of the painted site, which are regarded as very powerful" (Leakey 1983:17). Sacrificing goats to the ancestor spirits as part of rainmaking and healing ceremonies is an ongoing practice at one of the most prominent rock art sites on the landscape, locally known as Mungumi wa Kolo (Amini Mturi and Jasper Chalcraft pers. com.). Moreover, local Irangi people have told Mturi that diviners demonstrate their supernatural potency by staying in a cavernous hollow below the painted site for two weeks. Informants told Chalcraft that this is the same hollow into which half of the sacrificed goat bones were placed. Weathered prehistoric fragments of a goat's cranium and tooth enamel from looted archaeological deposits in the nearby Kwa Mtea rock shelter could be the remains of such a ritual sacrifice too.

As part of the healing rituals, female Irangi supplicants spatter millet beer using castor oil leaves (known as *méraa*) at the prehistoric paintings. Dried leaves of the castor oil plant seen on the floor of the Mungumi wa Kolo rock shelter in November 2001 show that this practice is ongoing (Loubser 2001). Interestingly, the ritual sprinkling of the rock art is reminiscent of simbó rituals among the neighboring Sandawe, where "a woman takes a *méraa* twig, dips it in beer and sprinkles the dancers with it" (Van de Kimmenade 1936:413). Some of the millet spatter against the rock wall at Mungumi wa Kolo is pink and resembles pigment. Similar-looking but fainter white pigment spatters, some of which are covered by silica-like skins, have been documented at both Mungumi wa Kolo and the nearby Kwa Mtea. In terms of their granular texture and overall shape and size, these white marks likely are older millet spatters. The spattering of the rock surface and the spattering of dancers with millet beer by ritual practitioners

FIGURE 1 Stone wall of dismantled cage in front of Mungumi
wa Kolo rock art panel with spatters of millet beer. Photo:
Johannes Loubser

with the leaves and branches of castor oil plants suggest that
the same underlying cognitive principles are involved.

That these ritualized activities tend to occur in secret
makes them difficult to detect in the conventional way, as
done by Gale and Jacobs (1986) when they observed tourist
behavior at rock art sites in Australia. To conduct proper
research on ritual activities at the Tanzanian rock art sites, a
necessary first step would be to gain the trust and permission
of Irangi practitioners. Without due consultation, rock art site
managers and conservators might find it necessary to remove
beer spatters that obscure "aesthetically pleasing" prehistoric
rock art. Of course, this would not stop the spattering of the
rock or the roasting of goat near the rock face. Denying ritual
practitioners access to the sites would be even a more disas-

trous management decision, as can be seen by the defiant
defacement of rock art in Zimbabwe by disgruntled local people barred from accessing rainmaking shrines near Harare
(Webber Ndoro pers. com.).

Compared to the African example, the Indians on the
Columbia Plateau of Oregon and Washington have less direct
access to most of their traditional rock art sites; mainly they
live in small reservations that are scattered across the region.
Despite this physical separation, some of the most detailed
ethnography related to rock art comes from the Columbia
Plateau Indian groups, and indications are that a significant
proportion of these people still revere rock art sites as places
with special spiritual powers (Keyser and Whitley 2000). The
vast majority of rock art sites on the Columbia Plateau are

small panels that can be found scattered along a line of basalt cliffs or in a boulder field. Rock art on the plateau dates from roughly seven thousand years ago to the early twentieth century (Keyser 1992). Primary rock art motifs on the Columbia Plateau include abstract designs such as rayed arcs, tally marks, and zigzags that are associated with stick-figure humans and block-body animal figures.

According to ethnographic information from the Columbia Plateau, rock art sites are associated with body symbolism in at least two instances: scratched motifs from the Columbia and Snake River drainages and red ocher smears from the western Montana foothills. Scratched motifs primarily comprise a variety of geometric designs, several of which are also common in pecked and painted examples on the plateau. Smears are not merely areas where paint-covered hands were cleaned; they represent application for the purposes of deliberately coloring certain areas of the rock wall, notably within and directly below natural hollows in the rock (fig. 2). On closer inspection, palm prints and finger lines are detectable in well-preserved smears (Loubser 2004).

Paintings and scratches of generally the same kind as the rock art also occur on the faces of Columbia Plateau Indians (e.g., Teit 1909). Moreover, the personal spirit helper of an individual is depicted both on the rocks and on the face. To become acceptable members of their communities, all Indian children had to acquire spirit helpers through vision quests at isolated places believed to possess supernatural powers. Frequently these quests involved "fixing" one's spirit helper or other aspects from the spirit world on the rock face by means of paint or on one's face by tattooing (e.g., Teit 1918). Later in life adults might revisit the sites where they first acquired their spirit helpers in order to receive personal help from the spirit world, such as to cure disease or to reverse bad luck in hunting or gambling (Teit 1928). Sometimes supplicants might leave at the sites painted tally marks, repainted motifs, or gifts.

Application of red smears to the rock surfaces and in natural hollows of the Big Belt Mountains in Montana might also reflect an interaction with the rock surface and the spirit world believed to reside within the rock (e.g., Cline 1938). Among the Shuswap of the Columbia Plateau, Teit (1909:616) documented that whenever a certain healer shaman "rubbed his fingers over his face to wipe away the tears, blood oozed out and he became terrible to behold." Shuswap Indians told Teit (1909:616) a similar story of another shaman who cured a patient by rubbing "his fingers four times across the man's face." "Blood came out in great quantities. This shaman had blood for one of his guardians." The comment of another informant that blood and the color red "stood for the power of healing" (Cline 1938:44) probably sums up the significance of the smeared red pigment.

FIGURE 2 Hand-applied red pigment emanating from a natural hollow, west central Montana. Photo: Johannes Loubser

Throughout the Columbia Plateau, the shaman is distinguished from other members of the community as one who has greater but not necessarily qualitatively different powers (Park 1938). The shaman's greater powers came from more vision quests, more spirit helpers, more clearly defined spirit helpers, and better skills to benefit from spiritual assistance, such as curing diseases, than the rest of the population (Ray 1939). Unlike other cultures in the world, then, such as the southern African San, entire communities partook in the production of rock art on the Columbia Plateau. Today descendants of the rock artists still visit certain sites, often leaving behind small material items, ranging from coins to ocher powder, as testimony of their visits.

Europeans might mistake the ostensibly random scratches and smears on the rock surfaces for historic period graffiti. To prevent the accidental removal of such "graffiti" at rock art sites, conservators should first conduct background research and consultations, both on and off site. Moreover, managers who try to market these rock art sites simply in terms of their aesthetic appeal not only miss the point of their significance but also might create false expectations among visitors.

Implications

Bearing in mind that the indigenous people considered here do not view or use rock art sites as art galleries, it behooves managers and conservators trained in a Western scientific tradition to acknowledge, consult, research, and understand indigenous views and wishes. If a rock art site is viewed as a patient in need of care, then it is after all the most immediate family (i.e., people with the closest connections or most vested interests) who must decide what is best for the patient. For example, relatives might not necessarily feel that the tattooing of a family member is a bad thing, or that graffiti at a rock art site is unfavorable. Accordingly, consultation with indigenous people is necessary before removing or reintegrating the graffiti.

Another ramification of the medical analogy is that preventive care is preferable to intervention; the specialist conservator and manager should at least advise people on what is bad for the longevity of rock art, such as throwing water on the pigment. Moreover, hands-on treatments by specialists should be avoided until absolutely necessary. For example, if the site has flakes that pose no threat to the rock support, then there is no need for stabilization. If treatment is necessary,

then it is prudent to keep it minimal; like back surgery, hands-on treatments and interventions at rock art sites have a way of creating subsequent complications.

Consultation with indigenous stakeholders before intervening or implementing management decisions is always necessary. It is important that custodians and other interested parties agree on whether intervention is necessary, and, if so, what kinds of treatment should be employed. Local communities should get basic training to identify problems and to be able to conduct noninvasive treatments. It is highly advisable that workshops be arranged where local custodians receive basic training in site condition assessments and regular maintenance, such as dust removal.

As in the case of current medical practice, it is best that professional assistance be sought during emergencies or difficult situations, such as reaffixing loose slabs or removing harmful graffiti on top of rock paintings. Also, specialists should convey to interested parties that there are no miracle cures at poorly preserved sites and that as a last ditch effort alternative treatments can be explored.

Different levels of care and expertise are involved in rock art conservation; specialists and the surrounding community play different but supportive roles. As is the case in current Western medical practice, the trained specialist is expected to conduct basic condition assessment checkups, archive site records, and limit intervention only to severe cases. To do an acceptable job, the rock art specialist operates not merely within a preexisting natural landscape but also in one informed by ongoing cultural notions and practices that might have considerable antiquity.

Acknowledgments

I thank the Getty Conservation Institute for affording me the opportunity to participate in the conservation theme at the Fifth World Archaeology Congress. Gratitude is also due to Janette Deacon for her organizational efforts. I thank Webber Ndoro of ICCROM and Donatius Kamamba of the Tanzanian Antiquities Department for taking me to the Kondoa-Irangi rock art. I benefited from comments by Amini Mturi and Jasper Chalcraft at the Kondoa-Irangi sites. Phillip Cash-Cash made insightful comments at rock art sites along the Columbia River between Oregon and Washington. Sara Scott, Carl Davis, and Jim Keyser arranged for assistance at rock art sites on U.S. Forest Service land.

References

Cline, W. 1938. Religion and world view. In *The Sinkaietk or Southern Okanogan of Washington,* ed. W. Cline, R. S. Commons, M. Mandelbaum, R. H. Post, and L. V. W. Walters, 133–44. Menasha, General Series in Anthropology, 6. Menasha: University of Wisconsin Anthropology Laboratory.

Fosbrooke, H. A. 1950. *Tanganyika Rock Paintings: A Guide and Record.* Tanganyika Notes and Records No. 29. Dar es Salaam.

Gale, E., and J. Jacobs. 1986. Identifying high-risk visitors at Aboriginal art sites in Australia. Rock Art Research 3 (1):3–19.

Keyser, J. D. 1992. *Indian Rock Art of the Columbia Plateau.* Seattle: University of Washington Press.

Keyser, J. D., and D. S. Whitley. 2000. A new ethnographic reference for Columbia Plateau rock art: Documenting a century of vision quest practices. *International Newsletter on Rock Art* 25:14–20.

Leakey, L. S. B. 1936. *Stone Age Africa.* London: Oxford University Press.

Leakey, M. 1983. *Africa's Vanishing Art: The Rock Paintings of Tanzania.* London: Hamish Hamilton/Rainbird.

Loubser, J. H. N. 2001. Condition and management assessment of ten selected rock art sites within the Kondoa-Irangi Conservation Area, central Tanzania. New South Associates Report submitted to ICCROM, Rome.

———. 2004. Rock art recording at 24LC27A and 24LC27B, Helena National Forest, the Gates of the Mountains, Big Belt Mountains, Montana. New South Associates Report submitted to the United States Forest Service, Helena, Mont.

Nash, T. A. M. 1929. Note on the discovery of some rock paintings near Kondoa Irange in Tanganyika Territory. *Journal of the Royal Anthropological Institute* 59:199–206.

Park, W. 1938. *Shamanism in Western North America: A Study in Cultural Relationships.* Evanston, Ill.: Northwestern University Press.

Ray, V. F. 1939. *Cultural Relations in the Plateau of Northwestern America.* Los Angeles: Publications of the Frederick Webb Hodge Anniversary Publication Fund Number 3.

Teit, J. A. 1909. The Shuswap. *Memoir of the American Museum of Natural History* 4 (7):588–789.

———. 1918. Notes on rock paintings in general. Spences Bridge. Unpublished manuscript. On file at the National Archives of Canada.

———. 1928. *The Salishan Tribes of the Western Plateau.* Annual Report No. 45. Washington D.C.: Bureau of American Ethnology.

Van de Kimmenade, M. 1936. Les Sandawe. *Anthropos* 31:395–416.

Why "Conserve"? Situating Southern African Rock Art in the Here and Now

Sven Ouzman

Abstract: The language of archaeological "conservation" is often passive, officious, and removed from conditions on the ground. The fundamental question—why conserve?—is seldom asked. Yet it is often assumed a priori that conservation is both necessary and beneficial. In the reflexive spirit of regularly questioning accepted practices, this paper situates "conservation" at three southern African rock art sites. These sites help to foreground indigenous notions of materiality and history that both embrace and eschew curatorial intervention. They also speak of imperial, colonial, and apartheid pasts that carry their burdens into the present. Finally, restoring to prominence the role of the present, along with conservation's benefits to the past and the future, offers multiple temporal, spatial, and cultural perspectives that situate conservation as a set of negotiated, evolving practices.

Why conserve? And why, "conserve"? The first question addresses a first principle. The second question asks how words shape actions. I engage with these questions by turning archaeology's gaze less on the past than on the present and consider how indigenous and nonindigenous attitudes to the past and its products intertwine—in positive and in conflictual ways. This intertwining is often burdened by recent and remembered histories in which inequality and violence were, and sometimes remain, prominent. Southern African[1] rock art is a powerful and accessible link between past and present, between malice and reconciliation. It is also an artifact that challenges conservation as a theory and a practice. Before moving to three rock art case studies, I offer some general thoughts on conservation as tempered by the material, human, and historic contexts.

Contexts—Competencies and Compromises

The stuff of archaeology and conservation—material culture—is invariably fragmented and its original context absent, destroyed, or radically displaced. Conservation attempts to piece these fragments into coherence by arresting or improving the artifact's physical state or even substituting a more complete simulacrum (see Eco 1986). Best practice? For archaeologists, conservators, and museologists—perhaps. But what of the people represented by these artifacts and the artifacts' audiences? Conserving artifacts can harden our imaginations of people of deep time, separating them from people such as ourselves who exist in shallow time (Werbart 1996). We try to overcome this separation anxiety with a continuum approach whereby the past inevitably arrives at the present, making it possible for us to work back from "our" present to "their" past. Furthermore, curators and researchers often seek out pristine artifacts that act as metonyms—microcosms of whole cultures and epochs—that conservation science is able to nudge toward a physical wholeness that substitutes for conceptual wholeness. But such conservation tends to be predicated on the principle that an artifact's "original" state can be ascertained and restored, effectively freezing the artifact synchronically rather than adopting a wider diachronic approach that stresses its biography (Hoskins 1998) so that its life—and death—is considered as important as its putative original state. Alternatively, "preservationists" try to retain the widest possible sample of artifacts and types of artifacts given the constraints of available time, skill, and resources. Both conservative and preservative approaches try to compensate for the violation of a key archaeological principle—context.

Indeed, conservation can attract as much attention to its own technical and theoretical prowess as to the artifacts conserved—leading to a fetishization of the archaeological "record" at the expense of the makers and users of that record (Hamilakis 2003).

Indigenous Notions of Materiality and History

One critically important context that is still not routinely institutionalized in the ever-growing "audit culture" (Ouzman 2003; Strathern 2000) experienced by the heritage sector is that of indigenous and descendant voices. This is simply bad science; indigenous perspectives, where they exist, are another source of information that needs to be included in any comprehensive, durable plan for the management of any given past and its products (Stocking 1985). At a social and political level, conservation is often applied to artifacts and sites without the permission or input of the original or custodial communities that generated them. Similarly, conservators and academics usually choose etically to represent those communities via archaeological artifacts and their staging in contexts such as books and museum displays (Brown 2003). Artifacts and heritage sites are the "contact zones" (Clifford 1997) at which much intercultural imagining takes place, and can be contested terrain. We need to be aware, rather than just conscious, of the political and ethical dimensions of our work (van Drommelin 1998). For example, we must question powerful words like *heritage* (a cognate of *conservation*) that imply common interest and access but often disguise sectional interests and exclusive ownership (Omland 1997; see also Hardin 1968). Self-examination of disciplinary terms and practices can be difficult, so it is useful to use Johannes Fabian's (2001) insight that anthropology is a form of "out of body" experience that allows us to step outside of our familiar frames of reference and adopt, however imperfectly, the perspectives of the people whose histories and identities we typically study and display.

Contextualizing Southern African Rock Art Sites

I had a glimpse into such an alternative perspective in June 2000 when consulting with resident Zhu[2] at Tsodilo Hills in northwesternmost Botswana prior to that site complex's UNESCO World Heritage Site nomination. At one of Tsodilo's more than six hundred rock art sites, I initially suggested—informed by standard conservation practice—installing a nonobtrusive dripline in one rock painting shelter to prevent rainwater from damaging the spiritually important rock art. But Zhu adviser Toma said this was not necessary because the rock art's authors were gone and the mountain was reclaiming its images. Toma's comment offered a way for archaeological conservation to respond to conditions on the ground rather than uncritically apply an unvarying conservation template. Furthermore, Toma's "folk" view is consonant with archaeological research that suggests that the rock artists believed in a spirit world located behind the rock and that the rock art "images" were understood as real Beings emerging from the San spirit world. Given the violence of imperial, colonial, and apartheid southern Africa, it is perhaps appropriate for these images/Beings to return to their home rather than be gazed upon by strangers. Toma's insight was informed by the understanding that artifacts have lives—and also deaths. Conservation can therefore interrupt an artifact's or site's life cycle, upsetting the balance of life and death. Tsodilo is but a single example, and we must take care that we do not apply generalizations but rather adopt a case-by-case approach. For example, the life cycle approach can veer dangerously close to neoliberal romanticizing, creating the impression that heritage specialists condone all artifact decay and site death. This approach can also create the perception that heritage specialists are not vigilant and encourage vandalism and the illicit antiquities trade (Renfrew 2001). Fortunately, the indigenous world is inclusive of numerous conservation strategies, many of which are compatible with our own such practices.

One such instance of compatibility between indigenous and academic conservation occurred while repairing fire damage to Tandjesberg rock art national monument in central South Africa (Morris, Ouzman, and Tlhapi 2001). In September 1998 a bush fire badly damaged this site, which was popular both with tourists and with sectors of the local community, especially schoolchildren. The severity of the fire damage—extensive spalling of painted rock wall, soot covering approximately 40 percent of the over 350 rock paintings, alteration of the rock shelter's sandstone's crystalline structure—meant that not repairing and closing the site to public visitation was a viable conservation strategy. After all, bush fires and sandstone spalling (and frost-freezing, earth tremors, etc.) are larger processes that create these rock shelters in the first place and that are part of their ongoing lives and eventual physical deaths. But a combination of the site's allure, personal and situational ethics, and local demands mitigated for a more active conservation intervention. None of the local communities—in their considerable diversity—had any demonstrable immediate genetic link to the site's rock art.

The San of this region were killed or assimilated into immigrant Bantu-speaking and, later, European groups by the early 1800s. Combined with the displacement of people caused by nineteenth-century British colonialism and twentieth-century apartheid, the state had the greatest binding claim on the site as a heritage resource. As I was a civil servant at the time and in the heart of the beast, this claim seemed too exclusive, such that my colleague Gabriel Tlhapi and I felt it necessary to consult with genetic and moral descendants of Tandjesberg's rock artists. To this end the Khwe and Xun San from Angola—settled in central South Africa in 1990—provided opinions on how to intervene. That these San were, at the time, not even South African citizens was a clear irony in our site management plan. Heritage sites in southern Africa are inextricably linked to contemporary identity politics. It was therefore critical to be clear that we were driving the site's rehabilitation and would take responsibility for the consequences thereof.

Nonetheless, the broad consultative process helped us to realize that directing attention to the fire-damaged rock art rather than concealing the damage better conveyed the life history of this site. For example, one painted rock fragment was too large to reaffix to the rock wall. The site's legal owner and long-term custodian, John Ligouri, wanted us to take this painted fragment to the National Museum in Bloemfontein 120 kilometers away for safekeeping. Instead, we convinced him to let us display the fragment on site in a metal cradle with interpretive notice boards that outlined the site's history, fire damage, and rehabilitation. Similarly, rather than make all of the spalled rock wall blend in with the unspalled wall, we left most spallings unaltered, except where Mike van Wieringen, a geotechnical engineer, felt this would promote structural faults. Showing visitors Tandjesberg's fire damage (fig. 1a) and our conservation interventions (fig. 1b), with their necessarily imperfect results (fig. 1c), has helped people to

(a)   (b)   (c)

FIGURE 1 Tandjesberg rock art national monument, South Africa: (a) Fire damage; (b) rehabilitation; (c) site museum. Photos: Sven Ouzman

understand that the people and products of the past are not static. Visitors also better appreciate the skills and limits of conservation professionals—information that would go unnoticed had we selected a "passive" approach by leaving the site in a seemingly pristine condition via complete restoration or by closing it to public visitation.

The "original" meanings of the Tsodilo and Tandjesberg rock art sites are by no means unimportant contexts. But because these meanings are necessarily approached via the present, the present needs must intrude into our conservation interventions. This intrusion is nowhere made clearer than in a rock art site that simultaneously exists in two geographically distinct locations and within a national consciousness.

Linton rock shelter commands a majestic view over the southern Drakensberg mountains that abut Lesotho (fig. 2a). Linton is one of hundreds of San rock art sites for which the Drakensberg was accorded UNESCO World Heritage Site status in 2000. Long before this, in 1916, the fine, detailed Linton rock paintings attracted the attention of Louis Péringuey, then director of the South African Museum (SAM) in Cape Town. Eager to bolster the museum's rock art collection and to protect what was then perceived as a fast-fading heritage,

Péringuey arranged to have two approximately 1.85-by-0.850-meter "panels" of Linton's rock art chiseled out (leaving behind two holes of about 5 square meters) and transported 1,050 kilometers to Cape Town (SAM archives and correspondence). The removal took place on and off between 1916 and 1918 and cost about £122-00 (SAM correspondence). Through this violent intervention (fig. 2b) the material life of Linton's rock art fragments extends to a museum context. This geographic extension has been followed by a conceptual extension: one of Linton's painted human figures was included in South Africa's new coat of arms (see fig. 1 in Smith, this volume), unveiled on 27 April 2000 (Barnard 2003; Smith et al. 2000), and thus impressed into a national identity. Accordingly, the 150,000-plus people who annually view the Linton fragments ensconced in a softly lit display hall generally report feeling reverence and mystery. Yet no contextual information helps visitors to imagine where the artifact came from or what it "cost" in terms of money, effort, or destruction to the site to preserve it. Understanding these costs and the intertwining of past and present reveals a critical absence—the voices of Linton's authors. The Linton San succumbed to colonial genocide after a protracted war of resistance, and their silence is

(a)

(b)

FIGURE 2 (a) Linton rock shelter; (b) South African Museum display (1918–present). Photos: Sven Ouzman

painful, eloquent, and especially acute at the South African Museum. On 20 March 2001 the (in)famous Bushman diorama, located in the hall next to Linton and intervisible, was closed for fear of public offense, though the diorama was one of the museum's oldest (ca. 1911) and most popular exhibits (Davison 2001):

> Within the changing social context of South Africa, museums have a responsibility to reconsider their roles as sites of memory, inspiration and education. . . . In this context a decision has been taken to "archive" the famous hunter-gatherer diorama while its future is reviewed. It will not be dismantled but will be closed to the public from the end of March 2001. This move shows commitment to change and encourages debate within the museum, with the public and especially with people of Khoisan descent.[3]

This officious and unilateral closure of the diorama caused controversy—especially among the majority of then self-identified KhoeSan descendants who were receptive, even insistent, on keeping the diorama open. The variables that determined that it was acceptable to display rock art but not body casts of people—both artifacts collected during a particular and unequal period in history—powerfully demonstrate the complexities of conservation as concept and practice. Hiding or ameliorating the effects of violence on artifacts through conservation and simulacra-like displays patronizes visitors. The multiple processes by which the Linton fragments came to the museum are easily accommodated into standard display techniques and would seem more true to life for most South African museum visitors, who are conversant with violence and its effects (Coombes 2002). Displays that appear politically disengaged even when the material displayed speaks explicitly of destructive histories (Lewis-Williams and Dowson 1993) contribute to accusations of the heritage sector's "irrelevance."

"Of the Past, for the Future"—And What of the Present?

The perceived disjuncture between artifacts of the past and circumstances of the present can lead to decisions not to preserve certain pasts. "Sites of hurtful memory" such as sites of genocide and humiliation are often left unmemorialized and their attendant material culture allowed and encouraged to decay (Dolf-Bonekämper 2002). But too complete an absence of material cultures that are primary evidence of human

events can lead to willful amnesia. Therefore, reembedding artifacts in their physical context—in whatever state of decay or repair these artifacts or contexts may be—in the form of site museums helps to push "conservation" into a more informed and socially responsive role. Most archaeological sites are not located in cities, though the museums, archives, and universities located there do valuable expository work. But this work is necessarily derivative, and we should always be encouraged to travel beyond our familiar surrounds and experience the intangibles and tangibles of heritage sites. Among these, rock art sites enjoy good public engagement, both because of their visual nature and because of the multiple levels at which sensory input, site, and audiences intersect. Site museums have a further human dimension in that many are run by local people who transfer knowledge visually, aurally, and kinetically by invoking the power of landscape, carefully framed by curatorial interventions such as notice boards, site flow, planned surprises, and the like. On site, storytelling is immensely important and empowering (Joyce 2002). Sites are "conversation pieces" that skilled interlocutors use to discuss ongoing site and artifact biographies. In aftermath circumstances, site visits can also help to heal dislocations of people from their places (Bender and Winer 2001) by situating the site and its audiences in a wider flow of human history.

This paper is overtly political to counter common perceptions of "conservation" as politically conservative rather than as a varied and constantly evolving set of practices. Using alternative perspectives such as indigeneity, artifact biographies, and violence more closely connects our research and curation with the tenor of the societies in which we operate and which permit us to operate. But we must be aware that this connection between past and present makes us susceptible to manipulation by vested political interests. David Lowenthal observes:

> Archaeology has long capitalised on public fascination with death and treasure, but its current popularity stems, I suggest, from three further attributes specific to the field. One is archaeology's unique focus on the remotest epochs of human existence, imbued with an allure of exotic, uncanny secrets hidden in the mists of time. A second is archaeology's concern with tangible remains, lending it an immediacy and credibility unique among the human sciences. The third is archaeology's patent attachment to pressing issues of identity and possession—of post-imperial hegemony and of ethnic cleansing, the retention or restitution of land and bones

and artifact—that embroil First and Third World states, mainstream and minority people. Devotion to priority, to tangibility, and to contemporary relevance have brought the discipline many genuine benefits. Archaeology, however, would benefit from acknowledging the harm as well as the good that such devotion has wrought. It might enable archaeologists to face up more frankly to often justified public doubts about the rectitude of the discipline. (2000:2)

Facing up to disciplinary rectitude in the face of public scrutiny places the present foresquare as a non-negotiable element of conservation. The challenge to archaeological conservation that seeks both epistemic rigor and contemporary relevance (Appadurai 2001) is how to let people marvel at artifacts while being aware of their place in a continuum of practice and existing in a continual state of always already becoming something else. This volume is titled *Of the Past, for the Future*, into which I would insert *in the Present*. It is true that the "present" is fleeting—as this fragment of Thomas de Quincey's *Savannah-la-Mar* reminds us:

Look here. Put into a Roman clepsydra one hundred drops of water; let these run out as the sands in an hour-glass, every drop measuring the hundredth part of a second, so that each shall represent but the three-hundred-and-sixty-thousandth part of an hour. Now, count the drops as they race along; and, when the fiftieth of the hundred is passing, behold! forty-nine are not, because already they have perished, and fifty are not, because they are yet to come. You see, therefore, how narrow, how incalculably narrow, is the true and actual present. (1845:n.p.)

If the present is "incalculably narrow," then so too are the specific pasts we seek to understand. Ditto the futures we hope for. But it does not mean that conservation has to be similarly narrow. Acknowledging and foregrounding the present most clearly presences our responsibility and accountability. It is also our recompense. Archaeology and conservation are solitary, laborious, and mostly unthanked activities. Our rewards should not be deferred but enjoyed now. The present lets us appreciate artifacts in this moment, in addition to imagining their past and future lives and deaths.

Acknowledgments

I thank the organizers of the Fifth World Archaeological Congress, the Getty Conservation Institute for organizing the session that led to this publication, Graham Avery for access to South African Museum archives, and Rentia Ouzman for preparing the images. The South African Department of Arts, Culture, Science and Technology and the South African Heritage Resources Agency funded the Tandjesberg rehabilitation.

Notes

1   Here "southern Africa" refers to the modern countries of Angola, Botswana, Lesotho, Moçambique, Namibia, South Africa, Swaziland, and Zimbabwe.

2   The Zhu are one of the many "San" or "Bushman" communities resident in southern Africa. These communities are descendants of the region's First People, who are responsible for making much of the region's rock art.

3   Available at www.museums.org/za/sam/resources/arch/bushdebate.htm. Accessed 8 June 2002.

References

Appadurai, A. 2001. The globalization of archaeology and heritage: A discussion with Arjun Appadurai. *Journal of Social Archaeology* 1 (3):35–49.

Barnard, A. 2003. !Ke e: /xarra //ke: Khoisan imagery in the reconstruction of South African national identity. Occasional Paper 94, 6–48. Centre for African Studies, Edinburgh.

Bender, B., and M. Winer. 2001. *Contested Landscapes: Movement, Exile and Place*. Oxford: Berg.

Brown, M. 2003. *Who Owns Native Culture?* Cambridge, Mass.: Harvard University Press.

Clifford, J. 1997. Museums as contact zones. In *Routes: Travel and Translation in the Late Twentieth Century*, 188–219. Cambridge, Mass.: Harvard University Press.

Coombes, A. E. 2002. *History after Apartheid: Visual Culture and Public Memory in a Democratic South Africa*. Durham, N.C.: Duke University Press.

Davison, P. 2001. Typecast: Representations of the Bushmen at the South African Museum. *Public Archaeology* 1:3–20.

de Quincey, T. 1845. *Savannah-la-Mar. Blackwoods Edinburgh Magazine*, n.p.

Dolf-Bonekämper, G. 2002. Sites of hurtful memory. *Conservation* 17 (2):4–10.

Eco, U. 1986. *Faith in Fakes: Travels in Hyperreality*. London: Minerva.

Fabian, J. 2001. *Anthropology with an Attitude: Critical Essays*. Stanford, Calif.: Stanford University Press.

Hamilakis, Y. 2003. Iraq, stewardship and "the record": An ethical crisis for archaeology. *Public Archaeology* 3:104–11.

Hardin, G. 1968. The tragedy of the commons. *Science* 162:1243–48.

Hoskins, J. 1998. *Biographical Objects: How Things Tell the Stories of People's Lives.* London: Routledge.

Joyce, R. 2002. *The Languages of Archaeology: Dialogue, Narrative, and Writing.* Oxford: Blackwell.

Lewis-Williams, J. D., and T. A. Dowson. 1993. Myths, museums and southern African rock art. *South African Historical Journal* 29:44–60.

Lowenthal, D. 2000. Commentary: Archaeology and history's uneasy relationship—Archaeology's perilous pleasures. *Archaeology* 53 (2):1–2.

Morris, D., S. Ouzman, and G. Tlhapi. 2001. The Tandjesberg San rock art rehabilitation project: From catastrophe to celebration. *Digging Stick* 18 (1):1–4.

Omland, A. 1997. World heritage and the relationships between the global and the local. http://folk.uio.no/atleom/master/contents.htm. Accessed 21 June 2003.

Ouzman, S. 2003. Is audit our object? Archaeology, conservation, sovereignty. *Antiquity* 77 (297). http://antiquity.ac.uk/wac5/ouzman.html..

Renfrew, C. 2001. *Loot, Legitimacy and Ownership: The Ethical Dilemma in Archaeology.* London: Duckworth.

Smith, B. J., J. D. Lewis-Williams, G. Blundell, and C. Chippindale. 2000. Archaeology and symbolism in the new South African coat of arms. *Antiquity* 74:467–68.

Stocking, G. W., ed. 1985. *Objects and Others: Essays on Museums and Material Culture.* Madison: University of Wisconsin Press.

Strathern, M., ed. 2000. *Audit Cultures: Anthropological Studies in Accountability, Ethics and the Academy.* London: Routledge.

Van Drommelin, P. 1998. Between academic doubt and political involvement. *Journal of Mediterranean Archaeology* 11:117–21.

Werbart, B. 1996. All those fantastic cultures? Concepts of archaeological cultures, identity and ethnicity. *Archaeologia Polona* 34:97–128.

The Authors

George H. O. Abungu is a Cambridge University–trained archaeologist specializing in urban archaeology and human-environment interaction in Africa. He was formerly director general of the National Museums of Kenya. Currently he is chair of the Kenya Cultural Centre, which among other things manages the Kenya National Theatre, and chief executive officer of Okello Abungu Heritage Consultants. During 2004–5, he was a visiting scholar at the Getty Conservation Institute. Abungu is widely published on subjects ranging from archaeology to heritage management and museology.

Neville Agnew is principal project specialist at the Getty Conservation Institute. Prior to joining the Getty Conservation Institute in 1988, he headed the conservation section at the Queensland Museum, Australia. Previously his career had been in academic and research chemistry. Agnew has led or participated in many of the international conservation projects of the GCI. He is a former board member and chair of the U.S. National Park Service's National Center for Preservation Technology and Training. In 2000 he received the Friendship Award from the People's Republic of China in acknowledgment of his contribution to heritage conservation.

Aysar Akrawi is executive director of the Petra National Trust in Amman, Jordan, responsible for the preparation and execution of the organization's many projects and publications. She coordinates with the Jordanian government, nongovernmental organizations, and international donor agencies. In addition, Akrawi serves on the boards of the Petra Archaeological Park, the Petra National Foundation, and the National Committee of the International Union for the Conservation of Nature.

Larry Armony is general manager of the Brimstone Hill Fortress National Park Society, which is a registered nonprofit membership organization entrusted by legislation to manage the Brimstone Hill Fortress, a World Heritage Site. He was born in St. Kitts (St. Christopher and Nevis) and educated there and at the University of the West Indies at Mona, Jamaica. Armony has written several articles on cultural, heritage, and historical matters in local magazines and presented numerous lectures on such topics at home and abroad. He is a member and past president of the St. Christopher Heritage Society, a member of ICOM, and the immediate past president of the Museums Association of the Caribbean.

Zainab Bahrani is Edith Porada Associate Professor of Ancient Near Eastern Art History and Archaeology at Columbia University. She is a specialist in the art and architecture of Mesopotamia and has written extensively on the cultural heritage of Iraq. Among her publications are *Women of Babylon: Gender and Representation* (Routledge, 2001) and *The Graven Image: Representation in Babylonia and Assyria* (Pennsylvania, 2003).

Bruce Bernstein is assistant director for cultural resources of the National Museum of the American Indian in Washington, D.C., where he oversees all aspects of the museum's collections and research programs. He was previously chief curator and director at the Indian Arts and Culture/Laboratory of Anthropology in Santa Fe, New Mexico. Bernstein has published broadly and curated numerous exhibitions on American Indian art and the history of museums.

Osmund Bopearachchi is director of research of the French National Centre for Scientific Research in Paris and professor in charge of Central Asian and Indian archaeology and numismatics of the Paris IV Sorbonne University. He is a world authority on central Asian, Indian, and Sri Lankan archaeology and history. He has published seven books, two translations, and more than one hundred research articles in international journals and has edited four volumes.

Giorgio Buccellati is professor emeritus in the Department of History and the Department of Near Eastern Languages and Cultures at the University of California, Los Angeles (UCLA). He founded the Institute of Archaeology at UCLA, of which he served as first director and where he is now director of the Mesopotamian Lab. He is currently director of the International Institute for Mesopotamian Area Studies. In addition to archaeology, his research interests include the ancient languages, literature, religion, and history of Mesopotamia. With his wife, Marilyn Kelly-Buccellati, he has worked for many years in the Near East, especially in Syria, Iraq, and Turkey. They are at present codirectors of the archaeological expedition to Tell Mozan/Urkesh in northeastern Syria.

Ángel Emilio Cabeza Monteira is executive secretary of the Chilean National Monuments Council. He is a member of various Chilean scientific and professional institutions, including ICOMOS-Chile. Cabeza has participated in the nomination of World Heritage Sites for Chile and has been adviser to the Getty Conservation Institute in heritage management and preservation projects in many countries. He is the author of a wide range of articles on archaeology, anthropology, environmental education, and preservation.

Dirk Callebaut is acting director of the Institute for the Archaeological Heritage of the Flemish Community of Belgium and executive director of the Ename Center for Public Archaeology and Heritage Presentation. Since initiating the Ename 974 Project in 1982, he has been involved in the implementation and management of cultural interpretation projects using new technologies. He serves on several international committees dealing with public interpretation and public archaeology policy.

Pisit Charoenwongsa is director of the Southeast Asian Ministers of Education Organization's Regional Centre for Archaeology and Fine Arts (SEAMEO-SPAFA), an intergovernmental organization comprising ten member countries devoted to the promotion and development of archaeological and cultural programming in Southeast Asia through collaborative research, training, and publication. Charoenwongsa is president of the Indo-Pacific Prehistory Association and of the Archaeological Society of Thailand, adviser to the Society for Conservation of National Treasures and Environment, and a member of the ICOMOS Executive Council. He is also a member of the Editorial Advisory Board of the *Journal of Conservation and Management of Archaeological Sites.*

Chen Tongbin is director of the Institute of Architectural History in the China Architecture Design and Research Academy. She is involved in, among other things, the development of master plans for large sites, including the Palace Museum in Beijing and the Mogao Grottoes of Dunhuang. Among Chen Tongbin's major publications are conservation planning for the new Niuheliang site in Liaoning province, the Dadiwan site in Gansu province, and conservation planning for her heritage sites in Turfan, Xinjiang, as well as illustrations of Chinese ancient interior design and Chinese ancient architecture. Recently, her work has also concerned the regulations for conservation planning at Chinese heritage sites.

S. Terry Childs is an archaeologist in the Archeology and Ethnography Program of the U.S. National Park Service. She has used the Internet to draw attention to archaeological collections and related management issues by developing the self-motivated Web course "Managing Archeological Collections." She is coauthor, with Lynne P. Sullivan, of *Curating Archaeological Collections: From the Field to the Repository,* and editor of the volume, *Our Collective Responsibility: The Ethics and Practice of Archaeological Collections Stewardship.* Childs is chair of the Society for American Archaeology's Committee on Curation. Her primary research interests are the Iron Age of sub-Saharan Africa and the anthropology of technology.

Douglas C. Comer is principal of Cultural Site Research and Analysis, Inc., which provides international archaeological research services and consultation in CRM, with a specialization in cultural site management. Comer has extensive experience in archaeological research, managing archaeological sites, cultural resource management, satellite and aerial remote sensing, and planning and design for site development and protection. He is a former Fulbright Scholar in CRM and has published widely on archaeology and site management.

Scott Cunliffe is a planning consultant specializing in tourism development planning, risk assessment and risk management, and sustainable approaches to cultural and natural resource conservation. He has undertaken tourism and heritage conservation projects in more than twenty-five countries, primarily in Asia. Among his recent clients are the Asian Development Bank, the World Tourism Organization, Asia Pacific Economic Cooperation, the United Nations Development Program, and the Overseas Economic Cooperation Fund (OECF-Japan).

Janette Deacon has been involved in archaeological research, teaching, and site management in South Africa for more than forty years, including eleven years as archaeologist at the National Monuments Council. She retired in 2000 but continues to undertake contract work and serve on councils and committees, mainly related to rock art and heritage management. She received her Ph.D. in archaeology from the University of Cape Town.

Martha Demas joined the Getty Conservation Institute in 1990. She is senior project specialist in Field Projects and currently manages the Mosaics Project, which addresses issues of in situ conservation of mosaics, and the *China Principles* project, which is aimed at developing and applying national guidelines for conservation and management of cultural heritage sites in China. She studied Aegean archaeology at the University of Cincinnati and historic preservation at Cornell University, where she specialized in conservation of archaeological heritage.

Brian Egloff is associate professor of cultural heritage studies at the University of Canberra and president of the International Committee for Archaeological Heritage Management, ICOMOS. He is currently writing a book on the theft and illegal export of the Ambum stone, a prehistoric carved stone artifact that is in the collection of the National Gallery of Australia.

Brian Fagan is emeritus professor of anthropology at the University of California, Santa Barbara. He spent his early career in Central and East Africa. Since arriving in the United States in 1966, he has focused on communicating archaeology to general audiences. Fagan's many books include several university texts and *The Rape of the Nile, The Little Ice Age,* and *The Long Summer,* an account of climate changes and human societies over the past fifteen thousand years.

Pilar Fatás Monforte is curator of the State Museums of Spain. Before taking this post, she participated in several archaeological projects at Palaeolithic and Mesolithic sites. As museum curator, Fátas has been responsible for the Documentation Department of the Spanish Institute of Historic Heritage, before joining the Altamira Project in 2000, first in the State Museums Directorate of the Ministry of Culture and then in the Museum of Altamira. She has published numerous articles concerning the Altamira Project as well as prehistory and museology.

António Pedro Batarda Fernandes received a degree in archaeology in 1999 from the University of Coimbra and an M.A. degree in management of archaeological sites from University College London in 2003. Since February 2000 he has been working in the Côa Valley Archaeological Park, where he coordinates the conservation program.

Abdul Wassey Feroozi is general director of the National Archaeological Institute of the Ministry of Information and Culture of the Islamic State of Afghanistan and assistant chief researcher in the Academy of Sciences of Afghanistan. He received an M.A. degree in archaeology in 1978 from the Kurukshetra University of India.

Anabel Ford, director of the ISBER/Mesoamerican Research Center at the University of California, Santa Barbara, has worked in the Maya forest since 1972. Beginning in Guatemala with surveys between Tikal and Yahxa, she continued her focus on archaeological settlement and environment in the Belize Valley. Now, in Belize and Guatemala, Ford is actively forming the foundation for El Pilar as a model that sustains the culture and nature of the Maya forest through collaboration and community participation.

Patty Gerstenblith has been professor of law at DePaul University College of Law since 1984. She served as editor in chief of the *International Journal of Cultural Property* (1995–2002) and as a public representative on the President's Cultural Property Advisory Committee (2000–2003). She is currently co-chair of the American Bar Association's International Cultural Property Committee. She is an internationally recognized expert in the field of cultural heritage law. Among her most recent articles are "Acquisition and Deacquisition of Museum Collections and the Fiduciary Obligations of Museums to the Public," 11 *Cardozo Journal of International & Comparative Law* 409 (2003), and "Cultural Significance and the Kennewick Skeleton: Some Thoughts on the Resolution of Cultural Heritage Disputes," in *Claiming the Stones/ Naming the Bones: Cultural Property and the Negotiation of National and Ethnic Identity* (2003). Before joining the DePaul faculty, she clerked for the Hon. Richard D. Cudahy of the U.S. Court of Appeals for the Seventh Circuit.

Guan Qiang has been division chief of archaeology in the Department of Protection of Monuments and Sites in China's State Administration of Cultural Heritage since 1993. His current administrative and management functions relate to archaeology and site conservation, including infrastructure projects such as the Three Gorges Dam, and other major undertakings of the government, such as the gas line from the west to the east of China. His responsibilities also include academic archaeology, liaison with foreign archaeological teams, and large-scale projects of heritage conservation and management. He is a member of the editorial board of the annual publication of the State Administration on significant archaeological discoveries in China. Guan is a graduate of the Department of Archaeology at Beijing University and holds a master's degree in archaeology from Jilin University. He has studied at Cairo University's Department of Archaeology and has worked at the Palace Museum in Beijing.

Rodney Harrison is a research fellow with the Centre for Cross-Cultural Research at the Australian National University in Canberra. The work presented here was undertaken while he was employed in the cultural heritage research unit of the Department of Environment and Conservation, New South Wales (previously the NSW National Parks and Wildlife Service) in Sydney. His research has focused on contact archaeology, the historical archaeology of the pastoral (cattle and sheep ranching) industry in Australia, collaborative and community-based archaeologies, and the role of material culture in negotiating cross-cultural encounters. He is the author of *Shared Landscapes* (UNSW Press, 2004), and editor (with Christine Williamson) of *After Captain Cook* (University of Sydney, 2002; AltaMira Press, 2004). He is currently working on a project that examines the concepts of memory and value in cultural heritage assessment in Australia. He holds a Ph.D. from the University of Western Australia.

Louise Haxthausen has worked for UNESCO since 1993. She currently serves as focal point for the Middle East in the Office of the Director-General, at UNESCO Headquarters (Paris). Previously, she spent one and a half years in Kabul, Afghanistan, on secondment from UNESCO to the Ministry of Information and Culture of the Transitional Islamic State of Afghanistan. Her tasks consisted of giving advice and assistance to the Ministry of Information and Culture and to the National Afghan Olympic Committee on foreign aid management and coordination in the field of culture, media, and sports. Haxthausen has an academic background in international public law and political science.

James Pepper Henry, a member of the Kaw Nation of Oklahoma and Muscogee Creek Nation, is assistant director for Community Services at the National Museum of the American Indian (NMAI), Washington, D.C. For the past decade, he has been active in Native American repatriation efforts for the Kaw Nation as director of the tribe's Kanza Museum and historic preservation officer and as the former repatriation program manager for NMAI. He has worked to promote Native American art, culture, and heritage as interim curator at the Institute of Alaska Native Arts in Fairbanks and the Portland Art Museum.

Kristín Huld Sigurðardóttir is director of the Archaeological Heritage Agency of Iceland and a lecturer in archaeology at the University of Iceland. Previously, she was an associate professor in objects conservation at the University of Oslo, Norway, conservator at the National Museum of Iceland, and an archaeologist at various excavations in Iceland. She received a Ph.D. in archaeology from University College London in 1999 and a diploma in business administration from the University of Iceland in 2003. She completed a teachers' training course in Oslo in 2001. She has been a member of ICOM since 1984 and was on the board of ICOM-Iceland. She has been a member of the IIC-Nordic Section since 1984 and of ICOMOS since 2003. She was a founding member of the Association of Icelandic Archaeologists in 1987. She has published various articles on conservation and archaeology.

Jessica S. Johnson is senior objects conservator for the National Museum of the American Indian. Previously, she was the conservator for the Museum Management Program of the U.S. National Park Service. For eleven years she was also the head of the Gordion Objects Conservation Program for the Gordion Project in Turkey, sponsored by the University Museum at the University of Pennsylvania. She has an M.A. in anthropology from the University of Arizona and received her conservation training at the Institute of Archaeology, University College London.

Rosemary A. Joyce is professor of anthropology at the University of California, Berkeley. Her archaeological fieldwork, since 1977 conducted in Honduras, employs ceramic analysis, household archaeology, and settlement pattern studies to understand how material culture shapes identity, especially ethnicity, sex and gender, and age. Her engagement with cultural heritage issues stems from her experiences as assistant director of the Peabody Museum, Harvard University (1986–89) and director of the Hearst Museum of Anthropology, University of California, Berkeley (1994–99).

Philip L. Kohl is professor in the Department of Anthropology at Wellesley College in Massachusetts. In 1999 he was appointed Kathryn Wasserman Davis Professor of Slavic Studies. He received an M.A. degree in 1972 and a Ph.D. in 1974, both in anthropology from Harvard University. Kohl is a corresponding member of the Deutsches Archäologisches Institut and the recipient of numerous honors and research grants from, among others, the Wenner-Gren Foundation for Anthropological Research and the National Geographic Society. He has conducted fieldwork in southern Daghestan, Russia, and Azerbaijan, and in August 2003 he visited archaeological sites in Mongolia as a Fulbright Senior Specialist. He has published more than 135 articles and book reviews and has written and edited numerous books.

Hande Kökten is associate professor and director of Başkent Vocational School, Ankara University, Turkey, where she has taught since 1991. She has a Ph.D. in classical archaeology and a certificate in conservation from the Institute of Archaeology, University College London. Her professional interests are archaeological conservation, preventive conservation, conservation training, field conservation and legal issues, and the conservation of mosaics.

José Antonio Lasheras Corruchaga is director of the National Museum and Research Center of Altamira. He is the founder and director of the museological program for the new Museum of Altamira, which was inaugurated in 2001, as well as of the facsimile reproduction of Altamira Cave, the neocave that is exhibited at the museum. Lasheras has published more than forty articles and monographs on archaeology and museology, most recently, *Rediscover Altamira*, the first research monograph on Altamira Cave, and *Altamira: Forever and Ever*, a television documentary and DVD that is available in six languages.

Johannes (Jannie) Loubser earned his Ph.D. in archaeology at the University of the Witwatersrand, Johannesburg, South Africa. He also holds a postgraduate diploma in rock art conservation and management jointly presented by the Getty Conservation Institute and the University of Canberra. Loubser established the Rock Art Department at the National Museum in Bloemfontein, South Africa. Since the end of 1993 he has been working as a CRM archaeologist and rock art specialist at New South Associates, Stone Mountain, Georgia. AltaMira Press has recently published his archaeology textbook, *Archaeology: The Comic*.

Claire L. Lyons is collections curator of the history of archaeology and ancient art at the Getty Research Institute in Los Angeles. She received her Ph.D. in classical archaeology from Bryn Mawr College in 1983. A specialist in Italian archaeology, Lyons has published on the site of Morgantina in Sicily, on ancient gender and sexuality, and on the archaeology of colonialism. She is an active contributor to issues of cultural heritage, collecting, and the illicit antiquities trade, and she has published articles in *Antichità senza provenienza II* (2000) and *Claiming the Stones/Naming the Bones: Cultural Property and the Negotiation of National and Ethnic Identity in the American and British Experience* (2003). She is the author of "Archaeology, Conservation, and the Ethics of Sustainability," in *Theory and Practice in Mediterranean Archaeology: Old and New World Perspectives* (2003). Lyons sits on the advisory boards of the *International Journal of Cultural Property*, the *Journal of the History of Collections*, and the *American Journal of Archaeology*.

Richard Mackay is managing director of Godden Mackay Logan Pty Ltd., a specialist archaeological and heritage management consulting company based in Sydney, Australia. He is an adjunct professor in the Archaeology Program at La Trobe University, Melbourne. He has served on state and national committees and councils related to archaeology and heritage management. Mackay's research interests include urban archaeology and colonial history. He is currently chair of the World Heritage–listed Jenolan Caves. He was made a Member of the Order of Australia (AM) in 2003 for services to archaeology and heritage management.

Fernando Maia Pinto is an architect who has devoted his professional activities to the management and protection of cultural heritage sites. He has been director of the Côa Valley Archaeological Park in Portugal since 1996.

Christian Manhart, art historian and archaeologist (University of Munich and Sorbonne in Paris), joined UNESCO in 1986, where he worked as program specialist in the Culture Sector and the Executive Office of the Director General. Currently, he is in charge of seventeen member states in the Europe-Asia region at the Division of Cultural Heritage, including Afghanistan. His tasks consist of direct assistance to these countries in the development of policies and strategies for the preservation of their cultural heritage, in particular through fund-raising, preparation, implementation, and evaluation of extrabudgetary projects. Within UNESCO's mandate, assigned by the Afghan government and the United

Nations for the rehabilitation of Afghanistan's cultural heritage, he is acting as secretary of the International Coordination Committee for the Safeguarding of Afghanistan's Cultural Heritage.

Omara Khan Masoodi has worked at the National Museum in Kabul, Afghanistan, since 1976. When the museum was bombed and looted in 1993, he inspired other members of the staff to assist him in safeguarding whatever was possible and assessing and recording the damage. Taking extraordinary risks to preserve the most important items, secretly removing some to safe places and disguising others, Masoodi was directly responsible for saving a large proportion of what remains of the museum's unique collections. In 2001 he was named director of the National Museum. He has continued his efforts to rehabilitate the museum building and restore its collections, as well as prevent the plunder of Afghanistan's important historical and cultural sites. He is president of the ICOM National Committee of Afghanistan and recipient of the Prince Claus award for his courage and his continuing commitment to defending and promoting culture in the most extreme circumstances.

Frank G. Matero is professor of architecture, chair of the Graduate Program in Historic Preservation at the Graduate School of Design, and director and founder of the Architectural Conservation Laboratory at the University of Pennsylvania. He is also a member of the Graduate Group in the Department of Art History and is a research associate of the University Museum of Archaeology and Anthropology. His teaching and research is focused on historic building technology and the conservation of masonry and earthen structures, surface finishes, and archaeological sites, and issues related to preservation and appropriate technology for traditional societies and places.

Webber Ndoro is working for ICCROM in the Africa 2009 Programme, which seeks to develop capacity to manage and conserve sub-Saharan Africa's immovable heritage. From 1994 to 2002 he taught heritage management at the University of Zimbabwe, and before that he was involved with the conservation program at the Great Zimbabwe World Heritage Site.

Sven Ouzman is former head of the Rock Art Department, National Museum, South Africa (1994–2002), and currently a Fulbright Scholar at the University of California, Berkeley. His research interests include contemporary visual culture, nonvisual aspects of artifacts, indigenous intellectual property rights, rock art, and origin sites. His conservation interests center on developing nonurban sites for community empowerment.

Gaetano Palumbo is director of archaeological conservation for Africa, Europe, and the Middle East at the World Monuments Fund and Honorary Lecturer at the University College London. Previously, he taught management of archaeological sites at the University College London and was a project specialist at the Getty Conservation Institute. He has consulted for UNESCO, ICOMOS, the World Bank, and the European Community on training, site management, site interpretation, and development.

Jerry Podany is head of antiquities conservation at the J. Paul Getty Museum. His archaeological conservation fieldwork has included projects in Syria, Egypt, Greece, Peru, Italy, and Tanzania. He has led collections management projects and training seminars related to protecting collections from earthquake damage for the Turkish Ministry of Culture at the Topkapi Palace and the National Archaeological Museum; conducted seismic risk assessments for museums in Taiwan and in Kobe, Japan; and has advised a number of U.S. museums on seismic mitigation for exhibitions. He currently serves on the Board of Heritage Preservation, a nonprofit organization based in Washington, D.C., dedicated to advancing the preservation of cultural heritage. In addition, he is an adjunct professor at the University of Southern California and an advisor to the Cultural Affairs Council of the City of Los Angeles.

Nelly Robles García is senior researcher with the National Institute of Anthropology and History (INAH) in Mexico and Director of the archaeological zone of Monte Albán, a World Heritage Site. She was trained as an archaeologist at the National School of Anthropology and History in Mexico City, in pre-Hispanic architectural restoration at the National School of Conservation, Restoration, and Museums in Mexico City, and as an anthropologist at the University of Georgia. Her professional interests lie in the areas of Mesoamerican archaeology, archaeological heritage conservation, management of archaeological resources, cultural tourism, and the history of Mesoamerican archaeology. She is an active member of ICOMOS and ICAHM and a member of the Society for American Archaeology Board of Directors. She is a member of the governing council of ICCROM and of INAH's Council of Archaeology.

Neil Silberman is coordinator of International Programs at the Ename Center for Public Archaeology and Heritage Presentation in Belgium. He is a historian with a special interest in the politics and policy of public heritage. He served for ten years as a contributing editor for *Archaeology* magazine in the United States and is a frequent contributor to other archaeological and general-interest periodicals.

Benjamin W. Smith is director of the Rock Art Research Institute and acting head of the Archaeology Division of the School of Geography, Archaeology, and Environmental Sciences at the University of the Witwatersrand, Johannesburg, South Africa. He is treasurer and secretary of the Association of Southern African Professional Archaeologists and the African Representative for the Society of Africanist Archaeologists. Smith was educated at the University of Newcastle-upon-Tyne (B.A. hons., 1991) and Cambridge University (Ph.D., 1995). His research interests include cognitive archaeology, theory and method in rock art studies, rock art management, and the past and present meanings of the rock arts of Africa.

Sharon Sullivan is adjunct professor in the School of Natural and Rural Systems Management, University of Queensland, and adjunct professor in the Department of Archaeology and Paleoanthropology, School of Human and Environmental Studies, University of New England. Previously, Sullivan was deputy executive director of the New South Wales National Parks and Wildlife Service and executive director of the Australian Heritage Commission. She is a Fellow of the Australian Academy of the Humanities and a member of the Australian Institute of Aboriginal and Torres Strait Islander Studies. She has worked extensively in the field of cultural heritage management.

Hedley Swain is head of Early London History and Collections at the Museum of London and has worked in London archaeology for many years. He is an honorary lecturer at the Institute of Archaeology, University College, and also teaches at Birkbeck College, University of London and Royal Holloway, University of London. He is currently chair of the British Society of Museum Archaeologists and Archaeological Archives Forum. In 1998 he published a major survey of archaeological archives in England.

Phenyo Churchill Thebe is senior curator of archaeology at the Botswana National Museum, responsible for coordinating

the Research and Rock Art Unit. Previously, he was site manager at Tsodilo, where he was responsible for the successful implementation of the Tsodilo Management Plan and the nomination of the monument as a World Heritage Site. He received a B.A. degree from the University of Botswana in October 1966. In September 2002 he was a Fulbright Scholar at the graduate school of the University of Texas at Austin. Among Thebe's research interests are lithic micro-wear studies and cultural resource management.

Wang Jingchen has been director of the Liaoning Provincial Cultural Relics and Archaeology Research Institute since 2000 and is executive chief editor of Liaoning *Provincial Cultural Relics Journal*. For some seventeen years prior to that, he worked as director, deputy director, and a staff member in the Liaoning Provincial Cultural Relics Management Office and was responsible for several national- and provincial-level protected sites. He is a graduate of the Department of History, Liaoning University, and has published on the stele of Liaoning and the restoration of Zhaoyang Pagoda and has compiled publications on Liaoning archaeology.

Willeke Wendrich is associate professor of Egyptian archaeology at the University of California, Los Angeles. She co-directed the excavations at the Greco-Roman Red Sea harbor town of Berenike for eight years (1994–2001) and at present is co-director of a large survey and excavation project in the Fayum. Wendrich received her Ph.D. in 1999 from Leiden University, the Netherlands.

Gamini Wijesuriya is project manager, Heritage Settlements, at ICCROM. Prior to November 2004 he was principal regional specialist with the Department of Conservation of the Government of New Zealand. From 1983 to 1999 he was director of conservation, Department of Archaeology, for the Government of Sri Lanka. He has worked closely with the World Heritage Centre and the two advisory bodies, ICOMOS and ICCROM, and is currently vice president of the World Archaeological Congress.

Jim Williams, art historian, anthropologist, and archaeologist (National Autonomous University of Mexico and University of Paris, Sorbonne), has worked for UNESCO since 1990, first as a consultant in culture and education and in the Executive Office of the Director-General and later as program specialist in the Culture Sector. For two years, he was UNESCO culture adviser in Afghanistan. Currently, he is head of the Africa

Unit, which includes all the sub-Saharan Africa member states and is also in charge of sixteen European member states, including the Russian Federation, in the Europe-Africa region at the Division of Cultural Heritage. His tasks consist of direct assistance to these countries in the development of policies and strategies for the preservation of their cultural heritage through fund-raising, preparation, implementation, and evaluation of extrabudgetary projects. Williams is an expert in antique oriental carpets, and in 1990, after the Soviet withdrawal from Afghanistan, he undertook a mission for UNESCO to Kabul and Mazar-i Sharif to reintroduce natural dyes and traditional designs to the Afghan carpet industry. This program was repeated in Herat in 1994 and is still ongoing and self-sufficient.

Rita Wright has conducted archaeological research in Afghanistan, Iran, and Pakistan and is currently assistant director of the Harappa Archaeological Research Project and director of the Beas Regional Survey. Her principal areas of research are urbanism and state development and the negotiation of power relations on local (gender, class, ethnicity, and age) and regional and interregional levels (technology, social boundaries, trade, and exchange). Wright is also associate professor of anthropology at New York University, where she teaches courses in cultural heritage, stewardship, and ethical issues in archaeology, and president of the New York City Society of the Archaeological Institute of America.

Wu Xiaohong is associate professor and vice director of the Department of Conservation Science and laboratory director at the School of Archaeology and Museology, Beijing University, China. She has a Ph.D. in chemistry. Wu's special field of interest is archaeological sciences. She has been involved in a variety of nationally ranked research projects and has published many academic research papers.

Wolfgang W. Wurster received a diploma in architecture from the Technical University in Munich. He later specialized in archaeological investigations, the history of architecture, and town planning. He doctoral research was on a classical Greek temple at Aegina. After field research in Greece, Italy, and Turkey with the German Archaeological Institute, he dedicated his research to the pre-Hispanic cultures of Latin America, especially Ecuador, Peru, and Guatemala. In 1980, after directing the excavation of the Dionysos theater in Athens for the Greek government, he became scientific director of KAVA,

the Commission for Extra-European Archaeology of the German Archaeological Institute. He was the first director of this institution from 1992 until his death in late 2003. He published 130 articles and 5 books, mainly on historical architecture, archaeology, and town planning.

Yang Zhijun is director of the Department of Protection of Monuments and Sites in China's State Administration of Cultural Heritage. Previously, he was deputy director of the Heilongjiang Provincial Cultural Relics Bureau and director of the Heilongjiang Provincial Museum. A graduate of Beijing University's Department of History with a major in archaeology, Yang Zhijun has expertise in archaeological survey and excavation, survey and research at the national level, museum interpretation and exhibition, and conservation administration and management. He has published widely in the field of archaeology, particularly with regard to sites in northeastern China.

Yuan Jiarong has been director of the Hunan Provincial Cultural Relics and Archaeology Research Institute since 1982. He holds bachelor's and master's degrees from the Department of Archaeology at Beijing University. From 1975 to 1982, he conducted archaeological work at the Hunan Provincial Museum. His expertise is in the Paleolithic period, specifically the environment in the Hunan area. He is also a visiting researcher at the Ancient Civilization Research Center of the Chinese Social Science Academy, the Lingnan Archaeology Center of Zhongshan University, and the Longgupo Wushan Ape-man Research Institute. Under his guidance, some two hundred Paleolithic sites were discovered, making Hunan province one of the most well documented Paleolithic regions in China. Among these, the Dao County Yuchanyan site project was selected as one of the top ten archaeology projects in 1995. He has published more than thirty works, on topics ranging from the origins of rice to Hunan Paleolithic stoneware.

Eugenio Yunis is a civil engineer and development economist who worked for many years as consultant throughout the world, advising governments, local authorities, and the tourism industry on development, marketing, organization, and the environment. From 1982 to 1989 he was in charge of the World Tourism Organization's (WTO's) activities in the Americas and Europe and was deputy director for technical cooperation. In 1990 he was appointed director general of the National Tourism Board of Chile, his home country. Yunis returned to the WTO in 1997 to head the Sustainable Development of Tourism Section. He is responsible for the organization's program on the development and management of all forms of sustainable tourism. He handles WTO relationships with UN agencies involved in sustainable development matters, including the preparation and outcomes of the World Summit on Sustainable Development. He directed WTO's activities related to the International Year of Ecotourism and the World Ecotourism Summit.